AI- Idea to Platform

By

Nihar Malali

DEDICATION

This book is dedicated to
the three goddesses in my life:
my mother, Geeta,
my wife, Sushma,
and my daughter, Araina.

TABLE OF CONTENTS

PART I

THE GENESIS OF AN AI IDEA

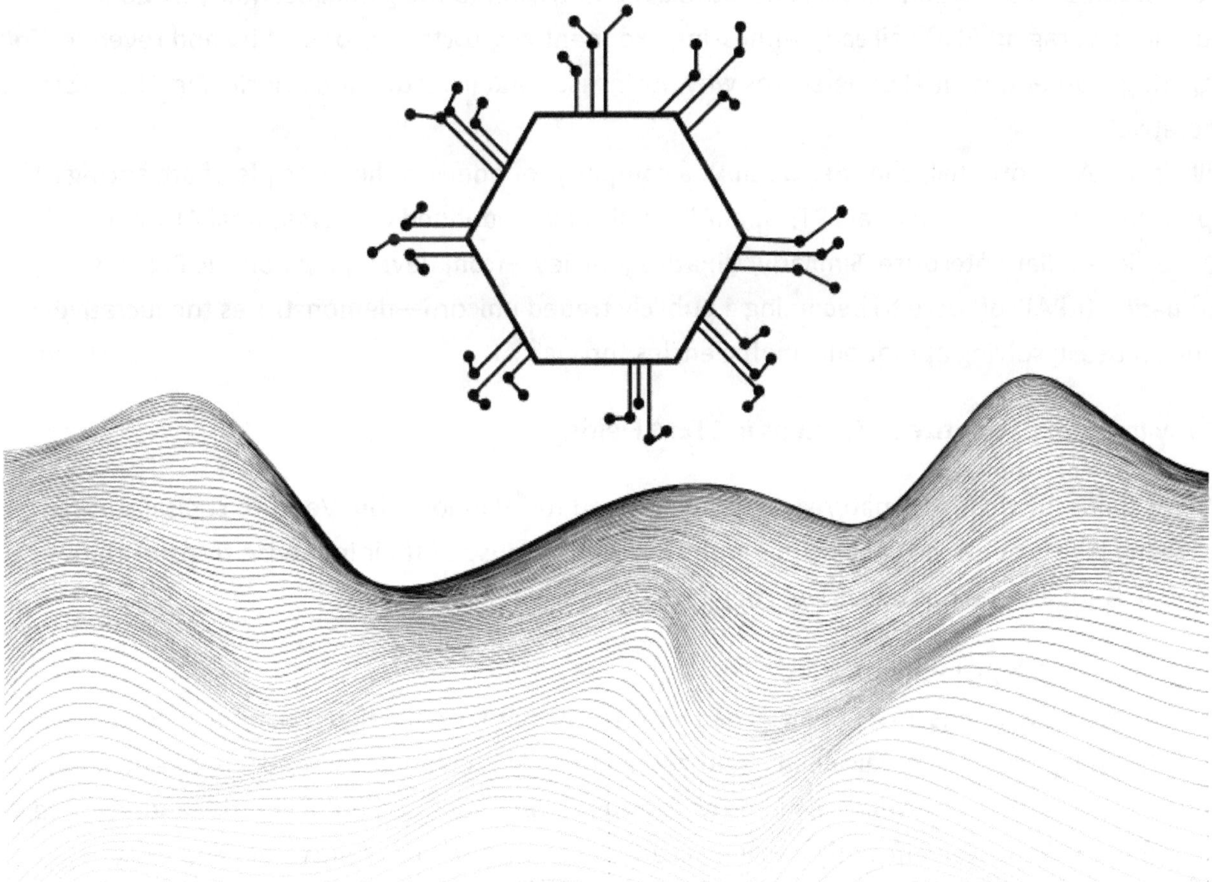

CHAPTER 1: IDENTIFYING PROBLEMS RIPE FOR AI SOLUTIONS

The Billion-Dollar Question: Why AI? Why Now?

Artificial Intelligence (AI) is no longer a concept of science fiction—it has become a transformative force reshaping industries across the globe. From automating complex processes to unlocking new possibilities in research and development, AI is fueling a new wave of innovation and growth. But why is now the pivotal moment for AI?

AI's penetration into Science, Technology, Engineering, and Mathematics (STEM) fields has been revolutionary. In healthcare, for instance, AI-powered algorithms are enabling early detection of diseases, while in engineering, predictive analytics are optimizing production lines. Such applications highlight AI's ability to solve deeply technical problems at scale.

Recent studies forecast that AI will contribute over $2 trillion to the global economy by 2030. Industries leveraging AI are already witnessing exponential growth in productivity and revenue. This staggering market potential underscores why businesses and investors are prioritizing AI as a strategic imperative.

To illustrate AI's potential, consider OpenAI, a company founded on the principle of advancing AI responsibly. From GPT-3 to ChatGPT, OpenAI's tools have redefined conversational AI while scaling into a billion-dollar enterprise. Similarly, UiPath's journey—from developing Robotic Process Automation (RPA) software to becoming a publicly traded unicorn—demonstrates the lucrative opportunities in solving operational inefficiencies through AI.

Why Investors Prioritize AI Startups in STEM Fields

STEM fields, by their very nature, are fertile ground for AI innovation. Venture capitalists are channeling investments into AI startups in these areas because of their immense transformative potential. Here are the primary drivers behind this trend:

- **High ROI Potential**
  AI-based solutions in STEM often deliver returns that far outweigh the initial investment. Consider precision medicine in healthcare, where AI is enabling tailored treatments based on individual genetic profiles. By improving patient outcomes and reducing trial-and-error costs, these solutions significantly enhance profitability for healthcare providers and drug manufacturers alike. Similarly, in renewable energy, AI-powered platforms are reducing operational costs, such as optimizing wind turbine performance, leading to long-term savings and higher returns for investors.

- **Opportunities in Niche Markets**

AI startups targeting specific STEM niches are aligning with broader global trends, such as the demand for sustainability and personalized solutions. For example:

  - **Personalized Medicine**: Startups like **Tempus** are leveraging AI to analyze clinical and molecular data, enabling doctors to personalize cancer treatment plans.

  - **Sustainable Manufacturing**: AI-powered solutions are optimizing manufacturing processes to reduce waste and improve efficiency. Companies like **Bright Machines** are automating manufacturing lines with AI, driving innovation in sustainable production.

- **First-Mover Advantage in Emerging Fields**

In nascent fields like quantum computing, AI startups are at the forefront of developing new tools and techniques, offering investors the chance to capture first-mover advantage. Companies like **Rigetti Computing** are merging AI with quantum technology to create next-generation solutions that could redefine fields ranging from cryptography to materials science.

- **Addressing Grand Challenges**

Many STEM-focused AI startups are tackling some of humanity's most pressing challenges, such as climate change, food security, and global health. For example, **Blue River Technology**, acquired by John Deere, uses AI to improve agricultural yields while minimizing environmental impact, showcasing how AI can drive sustainability in agriculture. These startups align with investors' growing focus on impact-driven innovation.

What This Chapter Offers

This chapter aims to provide readers with a strong foundation for navigating the AI startup ecosystem. It equips aspiring entrepreneurs and investors with actionable insights:

- **A Framework for Identifying High-Growth Problems**

What makes a problem worth solving? This section introduces criteria for identifying problems with high-growth potential in the AI landscape. Whether it's the scalability of the solution or its alignment with market needs, the framework ensures a systematic approach to problem discovery.

- **Tools to Validate Scalability and Business Viability**

Even the best ideas can falter without proper validation. This section highlights tools and methodologies for assessing whether an AI-based idea can scale profitably. From conducting market validation to developing business models that attract investors, the tools outlined here will help refine ideas into viable business opportunities.

1.1 UNDERSTANDING AI'S CORE STRENGTHS

1.1.1 WHAT MAKES AI A GAME-CHANGER?

AI is a revolutionary force in technology and business due to its unique ability to optimize processes, discover deep insights, and automate tasks that were traditionally time-consuming and error-prone. Unlike previous technologies that were primarily tools for human operation, AI operates as an adaptive system, learning and improving over time. This capability allows organizations to enhance productivity, reduce costs, and unlock entirely new possibilities.

1. **Optimization of Processes**: AI can fine-tune operations by analyzing real-time data and recommending or executing changes, leading to improved efficiency. For instance, AI-powered predictive maintenance systems in manufacturing reduce downtime by identifying equipment failures before they occur.

2. **Discovery of Insights**: AI models excel in processing vast amounts of structured and unstructured data to uncover patterns, trends, and correlations that might be invisible to human analysts. This capability is pivotal in fields like genomics, where AI accelerates the identification of gene-disease relationships.

3. **Automation of Tasks**: From routine administrative work to complex decision-making, AI automates tasks with precision and scalability. Examples include robotic process automation (RPA) for back-office operations and natural language processing (NLP) for customer support chatbots.

1.1.2 AI-DRIVEN MATERIALS DISCOVERY FOR FASTER R&D CYCLES

AI is transforming research and development (R&D) in STEM disciplines by accelerating discovery cycles and reducing costs. One prominent example is **AI-driven materials discovery**, where machine learning models predict the properties of new materials, allowing researchers to identify optimal compounds without the need for laborious physical experiments.

1. **Speeding Up Innovation**: Traditional materials discovery involves iterative experimentation, often taking years to develop new substances. AI, on the other hand, analyzes vast datasets of material properties and predicts potential combinations, significantly shortening this timeline.

2. **Case Study – Drug Development**: In pharmaceuticals, AI-powered platforms like Atomwise use deep learning to analyze molecular interactions, enabling the rapid identification of promising drug candidates.

3. **Application Beyond Pharma**: AI is also used in clean energy research, such as identifying new battery materials or solar panel components, helping to address global challenges like climate change.

4. **Integration with Simulation Tools**: By combining AI predictions with simulation software, scientists can test the feasibility of new materials virtually, refining options before physical prototyping.

Through AI-driven materials discovery, industries are not only cutting down the R&D cycles but also significantly reducing associated costs, enabling faster time-to-market for innovations.

1.1.3 AI IN ACTION: HIGH-VALUE USE CASES

This section focuses on practical, high-impact applications of AI across various industries, highlighting their clear return on investment (ROI). By exploring real-world examples and providing a structured overview through a matrix, readers gain insight into the transformative potential of AI in addressing critical challenges while driving tangible outcomes.

FEW EXAMPLES WITH ROI

HEALTHCARE: EARLY CANCER DETECTION

The healthcare industry faces a significant challenge with the late diagnosis of cancer, which often leads to lower survival rates and exponentially higher treatment costs. Early detection is critical, but traditional methods are limited by human error and time constraints.

AI Solution: AI-powered diagnostic tools offer a transformative approach by analyzing medical images such as mammograms, CT scans, and MRIs with greater speed and accuracy than human radiologists. These tools leverage machine learning models trained on vast datasets to identify subtle patterns and abnormalities that might be overlooked by manual examination.

Return on Investments (ROI):

- **Clinical Impact**: The implementation of AI in cancer detection significantly increases early diagnosis rates, which improves patient outcomes and survival rates. Early intervention also enables less invasive and more effective treatment options.

- **Financial Impact**: Detecting cancer early can save healthcare providers billions of dollars annually by reducing the need for expensive late-stage treatments, prolonged hospital stays, and complex procedures.

Example: Google Health's AI model for breast cancer detection has demonstrated diagnostic accuracy comparable to top radiologists. This innovation not only showcases cost efficiency but also underscores the scalability of AI solutions, enabling broader access to quality diagnostics in underserved regions.

ENERGY: PREDICTIVE ANALYTICS FOR GRID MANAGEMENT

Energy grids worldwide grapple with inefficiencies and failures that lead to power outages, increased operational costs, and heightened environmental impacts. These challenges are further exacerbated by aging infrastructure and the increasing demand for reliable energy.

AI Solution: AI-driven predictive maintenance systems monitor and analyze real-time data from sensors deployed across the grid. By detecting patterns and anomalies, these systems can forecast equipment failures, optimize energy distribution, and automate maintenance scheduling.

Return on Investments (ROI):

- **Operational Efficiency**: By proactively addressing potential issues, predictive analytics reduce equipment downtime and lower maintenance costs, ensuring a more resilient energy grid.

- **Sustainability Impact**: Optimizing energy flow and usage minimizes wastage, leading to reduced carbon emissions and a smaller environmental footprint.

Example: Siemens Energy has implemented AI models for smart grid management, resulting in a 20% reduction in operational inefficiencies in pilot regions. This demonstrates how AI can enhance the reliability and sustainability of energy infrastructure.

EDUCATION: ADAPTIVE LEARNING PLATFORMS

Traditional education systems often fall short in delivering personalized learning experiences at scale, particularly in regions with limited access to resources. These systems struggle to address the diverse needs and learning paces of individual students.

AI Solution: Adaptive learning platforms use AI algorithms to assess a learner's progress in real-time. By analyzing data on performance, engagement, and knowledge gaps, these platforms dynamically adjust lesson plans and content to cater to each student's unique needs.

Return on Investments (ROI):

- **Educational Impact**: Tailored learning experiences improve student outcomes by fostering engagement, retention, and mastery of concepts. This personalization bridges gaps in understanding and ensures students achieve their full potential.

- **Economic Impact**: Expanding access to quality education through adaptive platforms drives workforce development and economic growth, particularly in underserved areas.

Example: Khan Academy has integrated AI-driven tools into its offerings, significantly improving math proficiency by over 30% in underprivileged schools. These platforms are not only effective but also scalable, providing global access to personalized education.

AI Use Cases by Industry Matrix with Market Size Estimates

Industry	AI Use Case	Market Size Estimate (2024)	Key Benefit
Healthcare	Early disease detection	$50 billion	Improved patient outcomes and reduced treatment costs.
Energy	Predictive maintenance	$25 billion	Minimized grid outages and operational costs.
Education	Adaptive learning platforms	$15 billion	Scaled personalized learning experiences globally.
Retail	Dynamic pricing optimization	$35 billion	Enhanced profitability through real-time demand and inventory management.
Manufacturing	Predictive quality control	$20 billion	Reduced defects and waste in production lines.
Transportation	Autonomous vehicle navigation	$60 billion	Improved safety and reduced logistics costs.
Finance	Fraud detection and prevention	$40 billion	Mitigated financial losses and enhanced trust in digital transactions.

1.1.4 AI'S COMPETITIVE EDGE

In the rapidly evolving landscape of technology-driven businesses, AI-powered startups hold distinct advantages that set them apart from their competitors. These advantages often serve as the foundation for long-term differentiation and market dominance. Two critical pillars of this edge are **data as a moat** and **continuous improvement via machine learning feedback loops**.

Data as a Moat

Data is often referred to as the "new oil," and for AI startups, it is much more than just a resource—it is a defensible moat. Proprietary, high-quality, and domain-specific datasets form the backbone of any successful AI application. Startups that collect unique data through their operations, user interactions, or partnerships can develop algorithms that are difficult to replicate. For instance, a company with access to real-time user behavior data can personalize services in ways competitors cannot, creating a self-reinforcing cycle of user satisfaction and loyalty.

This competitive moat deepens over time as the startup gathers more data, enabling increasingly accurate predictions, recommendations, and decision-making capabilities. In addition, the integration of external data sources and leveraging third-party APIs can further enrich the dataset, making the startup's AI offerings robust and tailored to specific market needs.

Continuous Improvement via Machine Learning Feedback Loops

AI systems have the unique advantage of learning and improving over time, a process driven by machine learning feedback loops. Every interaction, transaction, or event provides new data that refines the model's accuracy and effectiveness. Unlike traditional software, which requires manual updates, AI models can adapt dynamically, ensuring they stay relevant and effective in changing environments.

For example, recommendation engines in platforms like Netflix or Spotify rely on feedback loops where user behavior informs future recommendations. Similarly, predictive maintenance solutions in industrial IoT improve over time as sensors gather more operational data, reducing downtime and enhancing efficiency.

Feedback loops also provide startups with an innovation edge by accelerating product development. Insights derived from user interactions can identify gaps, prioritize features, and guide the evolution of the product roadmap. Over time, these loops create a compounding advantage, where the AI system becomes smarter, faster, and more reliable, giving the startup an unassailable lead.

AI startups achieve competitive differentiation by harnessing the twin forces of data and feedback loops. Data as a moat creates defensibility and exclusivity, while machine learning feedback loops drive continual improvement. Together, they enable startups to deliver unmatched value, build customer loyalty, and maintain a significant edge in their respective markets.

1.2: THE BUSINESS AND SOCIETAL VALUE OF AI

1.2.1 DUAL IMPACT: MARKET GROWTH AND SOCIETAL BENEFITS

1.2.1.1 AI'S FINANCIAL IMPACT

AI is revolutionizing industries by driving efficiency, reducing operational costs, and enabling faster decision-making. Through automation and optimization, businesses can streamline their processes, resulting in significant financial gains. For example, in the financial technology (fintech) sector, AI platforms are reshaping lending practices. AI-powered algorithms can assess creditworthiness with greater accuracy, increasing loan approval rates by 20% while simultaneously reducing default risks. Companies like *Upstart* and *Zest AI* have successfully leveraged machine learning models to expand access to credit for underserved populations, creating a win-win scenario for both businesses and consumers.

Additionally, AI contributes to economic growth by enabling the creation of new revenue streams in emerging markets. Technologies like autonomous vehicles not only disrupt traditional industries but also generate demand for complementary products and services, such as data services, advanced IoT devices, and smart city infrastructure. With the global AI market projected to grow at a compound annual growth rate (CAGR) of 36%, sectors like healthcare, retail, and logistics are at the forefront of this transformation. AI's role as a driver of innovation underscores its potential to deliver exponential returns for businesses.

1.2.1.2 SOCIETAL BENEFITS THAT ATTRACT INVESTOR INTEREST

Beyond financial gains, AI offers profound societal benefits that capture the attention of socially conscious investors. One notable area is environmental sustainability. AI-driven solutions are helping combat climate change by improving energy efficiency, optimizing supply chains, and accelerating the adoption of renewable energy sources. For instance, Google's DeepMind utilized AI to reduce energy usage in its data centers by 40%, setting a powerful example of how technology can align profitability with environmental responsibility.

AI is also making strides in global healthcare. Predictive analytics and AI-assisted diagnostics are revolutionizing early disease detection and enabling personalized treatment plans. These advancements are particularly impactful in underserved regions, where access to traditional healthcare resources is limited. For example, AI platforms have been used to identify disease outbreaks earlier than traditional methods, significantly improving global pandemic preparedness and response.

In education, AI democratizes learning opportunities by offering personalized content tailored to individual needs. Platforms like Khan Academy's AI tutors help bridge the educational gap, particularly in regions with a shortage of teachers. Additionally, AI creates high-tech jobs, counteracting fears of widespread unemployment due to automation. New roles, such as AI ethics specialists and prompt engineers, are emerging, highlighting how AI contributes to workforce evolution while addressing societal challenges.

1.2.1.3 MARKET OPPORTUNITY

AI's ability to unlock new markets is unparalleled. Autonomous vehicles, for example, are not just transforming transportation but also creating an ecosystem of complementary services. These include tailored insurance solutions, delivery optimization, and in-vehicle entertainment systems, all of which represent new avenues for market expansion. In agriculture, AI enables precision farming techniques that improve crop yields, optimize resource usage, and connect small-scale farmers to broader markets, thereby addressing food security challenges.

A clear visual representation of these market opportunities could include a chart showing AI's potential across sectors. For instance, healthcare AI is projected to generate $150 billion in market value by 2030, while the automotive sector is expected to reach $120 billion within the same timeframe. This visualization could also illustrate the dual trajectory of AI's financial return on investment (ROI) alongside societal benefits, such as improved healthcare outcomes or reduced carbon emissions.

A compelling example is Amazon's use of AI to enhance logistics efficiency, which not only drives financial growth through faster deliveries but also aligns with sustainability goals by reducing the carbon footprint of its operations. Such cases highlight the dual impact of AI in creating business value while addressing critical societal needs.

AI's Role in Unlocking New Markets: Key Highlights

1. Sector-Specific Opportunities:

- **Autonomous Vehicles:**

- Transform transportation by enabling self-driving technology.
- Create complementary markets, such as:
  - **Tailored Insurance Solutions:** Policies customized to autonomous vehicle risks.
  - **Delivery Optimization Services:** Real-time logistics powered by AI.
  - **In-Vehicle Entertainment Systems:** Personalized and immersive experiences.

- **Agriculture:**
  - Revolutionize farming with **precision agriculture**, including:
    - Enhanced crop yields using AI-driven insights.
    - Optimized resource usage (water, fertilizers, pesticides).
    - Improved market connectivity for small-scale farmers, fostering economic growth and addressing food security.

2. Financial and Societal Impact Across Sectors:

- **Healthcare:**
  - **Market Value Projection:** $150 billion by 2030.
  - **Societal ROI:** AI-assisted diagnostics and early disease detection improve global health outcomes and accessibility.
- **Automotive:**
  - **Market Value Projection:** $120 billion by 2030.
  - **Societal ROI:** Reduced traffic accidents, enhanced mobility solutions, and decreased emissions with electric and autonomous vehicles.
- **E-commerce and Logistics:**
  - Companies like **Amazon** leverage AI for:
    - **Financial Growth:** Faster delivery times and operational efficiency.

- **Sustainability Impact:** Lower carbon footprints through optimized delivery routes.

3. Dual Trajectory of Financial ROI and Societal Benefits:

- Financial ROI:
  - Expansion into untapped markets and innovation-driven revenue growth.
- Societal Benefits:
  - AI's role in addressing global challenges such as:
    - Climate change mitigation.
    - Food security enhancement.
    - Healthcare accessibility and outcomes.

Examples of AI-Driven Market Expansion:

1. **Amazon's Logistics AI:**
   - Drives faster deliveries, resulting in higher customer satisfaction and revenue.
   - Aligns with sustainability goals by reducing emissions.
2. **AI in Precision Agriculture:**
   - Combines drones, IoT, and machine learning to optimize farming practices.
   - Connects small farmers to global markets, reducing poverty and improving productivity.

1.2.2 DE-RISKING AI INVESTMENTS

Investing in AI can be transformative, but it also involves significant risks due to the complexity of the technology, ethical concerns, and increased regulatory scrutiny. De-risking AI investments requires a proactive approach that emphasizes ethical AI principles and strategic problem-solving to mitigate risks and maximize returns.

1.2.2.1 HOW ETHICAL AI REDUCES REGULATORY RISKS AND ENHANCES TRUST

Ethical AI is not just a moral imperative—it is a critical strategy for reducing regulatory risks and building trust with stakeholders. It achieves this in several keyways:

1. **Regulatory Compliance:**
    - Governments and regulatory bodies around the world are enacting stringent AI laws to ensure fairness, transparency, and accountability, such as the EU AI Act and the U.S. Blueprint for an AI Bill of Rights. Ethical AI practices help organizations align with these frameworks, reducing the risk of penalties, sanctions, or reputational harm.
    - By proactively addressing issues such as bias, discrimination, and explainability, ethical AI minimizes compliance risks and facilitates smoother regulatory audits and reviews.
2. **Enhanced Stakeholder Trust:**
    - Ethical AI fosters transparency, enabling organizations to explain how their algorithms function and ensuring that decisions made by AI systems are interpretable and justifiable.
    - Building trust extends to customers, investors, and partners who increasingly value socially responsible and sustainable AI usage. For example, customers are more likely to engage with AI systems that respect their privacy and operate fairly.
    - Ethical practices ensure that AI aligns with societal values, helping organizations avoid potential backlash or boycotts resulting from perceived injustices or harm caused by AI-driven decisions.
3. **Reputation Management:**
    - Organizations that demonstrate a commitment to ethical AI can proactively prevent scandals related to biased outcomes, data breaches, or unfair practices.
    - Companies such as Microsoft and Google have established comprehensive ethical AI frameworks, showcasing leadership in responsible AI adoption and gaining competitive advantages by aligning their strategies with public and regulatory expectations.

1.2.2.2 STRATEGIES FOR ADDRESSING COMMON AI CHALLENGES

Effectively addressing common AI challenges such as bias, data privacy, and governance is essential for mitigating risks and ensuring successful AI deployment. The following strategies provide actionable solutions:

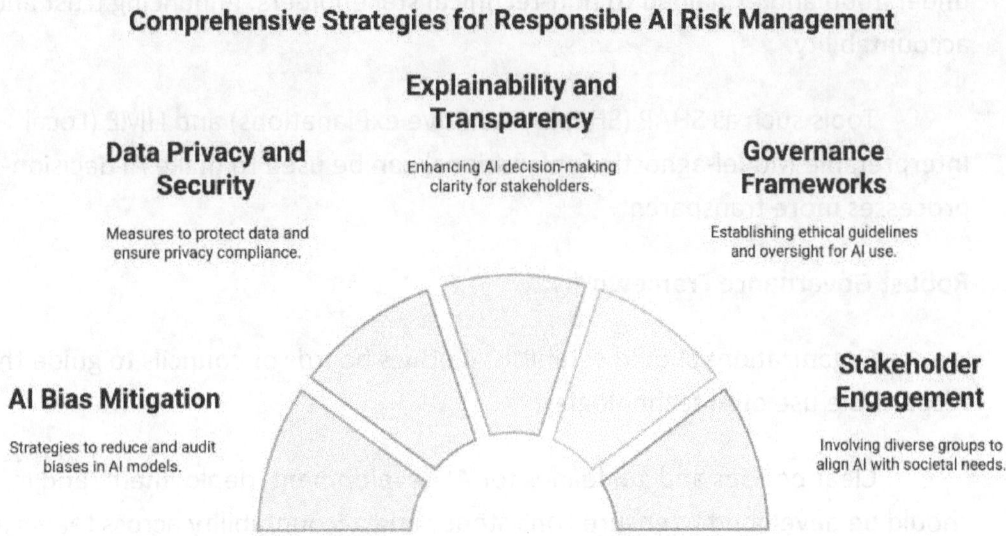

1. **Addressing AI Bias:**
   - **Diverse Training Data:** Organizations should use datasets that reflect diverse populations to reduce biases embedded in AI models.
   - **Bias Audits:** Conduct regular audits of AI models using bias-detection tools such as IBM AI Fairness 360 or Google's What-If Tool to identify and address potential disparities.
   - **Human Oversight:** Multidisciplinary teams should oversee AI development and deployment, providing critical perspectives to ensure models are scrutinized for unintended biases.
2. **Ensuring Data Privacy and Security:**
   - **Data Minimization:** Organizations should collect and process only the minimum amount of data necessary for the AI system's purpose, reducing exposure to potential data breaches and privacy violations.
   - **Secure Data Practices:** Employ robust security measures such as encryption, anonymization, and strict access controls to safeguard sensitive information.
   - **Privacy by Design:** Privacy considerations should be integrated into AI systems from the outset to ensure compliance with regulations like GDPR and CCPA.
3. **Explainability and Transparency:**

- Interpretable AI models should be implemented to ensure decisions can be understood and explained to non-technical stakeholders, enhancing trust and accountability.
- Tools such as SHAP (SHapley Additive exPlanations) and LIME (Local Interpretable Model-agnostic Explanations) can be used to make AI decision-making processes more transparent.

4. **Robust Governance Frameworks:**
   - Organizations should establish AI ethics boards or councils to guide the responsible use of AI technologies.
   - Clear policies and guidelines for AI development, deployment, and monitoring should be developed to ensure consistency and accountability across teams and projects.
5. **Scenario Planning and Stress Testing:**
   - Simulating adverse scenarios such as biased decisions or data breaches helps organizations identify vulnerabilities in their AI systems.
   - Contingency plans should be in place to address potential failures or incidents, reducing operational and reputational risks.
6. **Stakeholder Engagement:**
   - Actively involving stakeholders, including customers, regulators, and employees, throughout the AI lifecycle ensures that AI systems align with societal expectations and address real-world concerns.
   - Open communication about AI objectives, limitations, and potential impacts fosters trust and creates opportunities for collaborative problem-solving.

De-risking AI investments is a critical step in ensuring sustainable AI adoption and long-term success. By prioritizing ethical AI practices and addressing common challenges with robust strategies, organizations can navigate the complexities of AI while minimizing regulatory, operational, and reputational risks. These measures not only protect against potential harms but also position companies as leaders in responsible AI, enhancing their reputation and driving innovation.

1.2.3 KEY METRICS FOR VCS AND ENTREPRENEURS

For venture capitalists (VCs) and entrepreneurs in the AI domain, understanding and leveraging critical business metrics is essential for evaluating opportunities and scaling startups effectively. This section outlines two key areas: **market sizing (TAM and SAM)** and **performance metrics (KPIs)**, providing insights into how they influence decision-making and growth strategies.

1.2.3.1 TAM AND SAM CALCULATIONS FOR AI STARTUPS

Market sizing is foundational for assessing the growth potential of an AI startup. Investors and entrepreneurs rely on these calculations to gauge the scope of opportunity and define realistic market penetration goals.

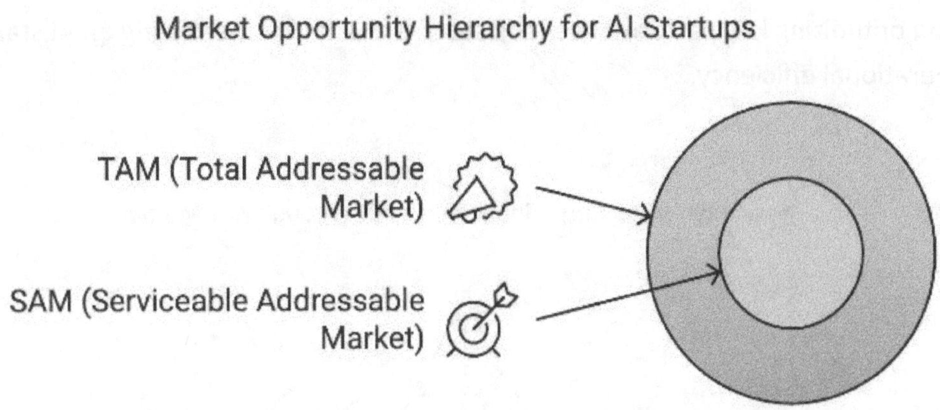

1. **TAM (Total Addressable Market):** TAM represents the total revenue opportunity available if a product or service were to capture 100% of the market. For AI startups, this involves estimating the size of the market related to their core application area, such as healthcare, finance, or logistics. The calculation often includes:

   - **Market trends**: Analyzing the growth trajectory of AI adoption in the industry.
   - **Target population or businesses**: Estimating the number of potential customers.
   - **Pricing strategy**: Multiplying the average price of the solution by the potential customer base.

Example: An AI-based predictive healthcare platform might calculate TAM by considering the global healthcare analytics market, estimated at $75 billion, and projecting revenue opportunities based on adoption rates.

2. **SAM (Serviceable Addressable Market):** SAM narrows TAM to the portion of the market that the startup can realistically target given its geographic focus, resources, and product applicability. AI startups refine SAM by considering:

   - **Market access limitations**: Geographic or regulatory constraints.
   - **Customer segments**: Focused on demographics or industries where their technology is most relevant.

- **Competitor landscape**: Adjusting for market share already captured by established players.

Example: If the healthcare platform is targeting medium-sized hospitals in North America, the SAM might be calculated at $10 billion based on the subset of potential customers.

1.2.3.2 KEY PERFORMANCE INDICATORS (KPIS)

Tracking and optimizing key performance indicators is crucial for measuring an AI startup's financial health and operational efficiency.

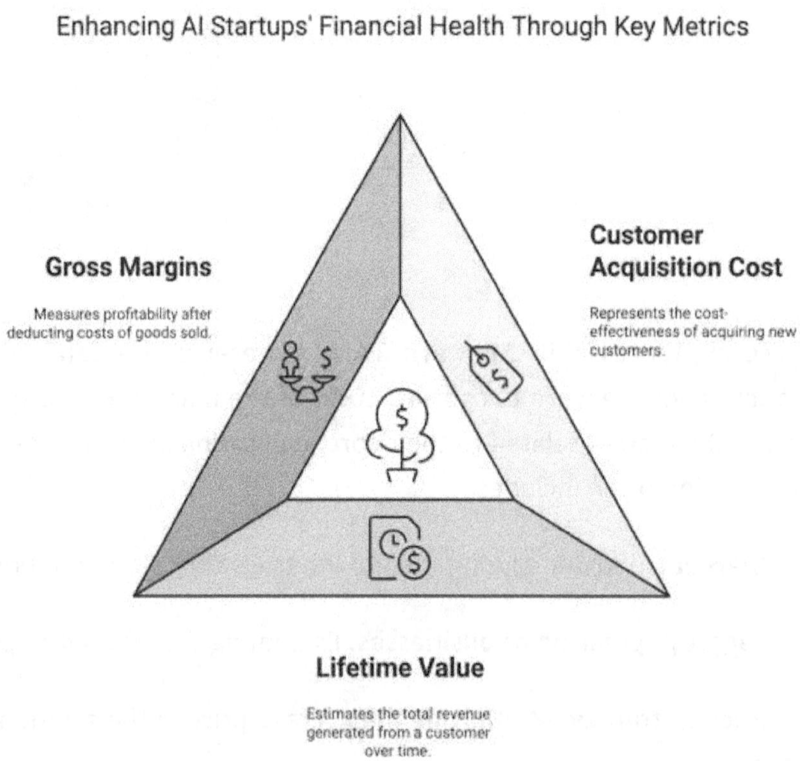

The following KPIs provide actionable insights for both VCs and entrepreneurs:

1. **Customer Acquisition Cost (CAC):** CAC represents the cost of acquiring a new customer, calculated by dividing total sales and marketing expenses by the number of new customers acquired during a specific period.
    - **Why it matters**: High CAC indicates inefficiency or limited market readiness; sustainable businesses ensure CAC is proportional to the revenue generated.
    - **Optimization**: Leverage AI-driven marketing tools and analytics to reduce acquisition costs through personalized campaigns and data-driven targeting.

Example: If an AI SaaS startup spends $50,000 on marketing and acquires 200 customers, CAC = $250/customer.

2. **Lifetime Value (LTV):** LTV estimates the total revenue a customer generates over their lifecycle with the company. This is calculated using metrics like average purchase value, purchase frequency, and customer retention rates.

    - **Why it matters**: A high LTV compared to CAC ensures long-term profitability and supports scalable growth.
    - **Optimization**: Enhance customer retention through continuous updates, personalized experiences, and superior support.

Example: If the average customer spends $1,000 annually and remains a client for 3 years, LTV = $3,000.

3. **Gross Margins:** Gross margin measures the profitability of delivering the product or service, calculated as (Revenue - Cost of Goods Sold) / Revenue. For AI startups, this includes cloud computing costs, model development, and infrastructure maintenance.

    - **Why it matters**: High gross margins indicate operational efficiency and a competitive edge.
    - **Optimization**: Streamline costs by optimizing AI models and leveraging scalable infrastructure solutions like cloud platforms.

Example: If an AI startup generates $1 million in revenue with $400,000 in operational costs, gross margin = 60%.

By integrating these metrics, VCs can better evaluate the investment potential, and entrepreneurs can ensure alignment with growth objectives and financial sustainability.

1.3: FRAMEWORK FOR IDENTIFYING AI-SUITABLE PROBLEMS

AI technology is most transformative when applied to problems with certain inherent characteristics. This section provides a structured framework for identifying problems where AI can deliver substantial value. The discussion will explore the defining features of AI-suitable problems, present STEM-focused examples, and offer practical tools, such as a decision tree, to assist innovators in assessing AI's applicability.

1.3.1 CRITERIA FOR HIGH-GROWTH PROBLEMS

Identifying high-growth problems is essential to maximize the transformative potential of AI solutions. Problems with specific characteristics often present the best opportunities for impactful AI applications. High-growth problems typically share several key features, which make them suitable candidates for AI intervention.

1.3.1.1 FEATURES OF PROBLEMS RIPE FOR AI

Identifying problems that are best suited for Artificial Intelligence (AI) is a foundational step in leveraging the technology effectively. Certain problem characteristics make them particularly amenable to AI solutions. These characteristics include the presence of large data volumes with exploitable patterns, high costs associated with errors, and the existence of repetitive, scalable workflows. Each feature represents an opportunity for AI to provide significant value, from efficiency gains to risk reduction and scalability.

1. Large Data Volumes with Patterns to Exploit

AI systems excel in environments where vast amounts of data are generated, especially when that data contains hidden patterns that may be difficult for humans to identify. Problems characterized by substantial data generation are ideal for AI because algorithms can efficiently process, analyze, and extract meaningful insights from these datasets. The ability of AI to uncover trends, correlations, and anomalies allows decision-makers to take actions that are data-driven and precise.

- **Example: Social Media Platforms**
  Social media platforms like Twitter, Instagram, and Facebook produce enormous volumes of data daily, ranging from user interactions and posts to metadata and behavioral trends. AI models can process this data to identify emerging trends, optimize content recommendations, and gauge public sentiment. For instance, sentiment analysis powered by AI can help brands understand how users feel about their products or services, enabling them to make strategic adjustments in real time.
    - **Impact**: By analyzing millions of data points quickly, AI systems provide insights that are both timely and actionable, which would be impossible to achieve manually.
- **Broader Applications**: Other fields leveraging large datasets include finance (fraud detection), retail (inventory optimization), and healthcare (genomics research). In all these cases, AI's ability to process data at scale creates a competitive advantage.

2. High Cost of Errors

In domains where errors can lead to significant financial, legal, or human consequences, minimizing mistakes is crucial. AI's ability to consistently make accurate, data-informed decisions reduces the likelihood of errors. These capabilities are particularly valuable in industries like healthcare, finance, and aviation, where the cost of errors can be catastrophic.

- **Example: Medical Diagnostics**
  In medical imaging, AI-powered tools have revolutionized diagnostics by analyzing radiology

scans with exceptional accuracy. AI algorithms trained on large datasets of X-rays, CT scans, and MRIs can detect anomalies such as tumors, fractures, or other abnormalities that might be missed by human radiologists. For example, an AI tool might identify early-stage lung cancer in a CT scan with a higher degree of accuracy than traditional methods.

  - **Impact**: By improving diagnostic accuracy, AI reduces the risk of misdiagnosis, which can save lives and prevent costly follow-up treatments.

- **Broader Applications**: AI also plays a critical role in fraud detection within the banking sector, where errors in identifying fraudulent transactions could lead to massive financial losses. Similarly, in autonomous driving, AI systems make split-second decisions to avoid accidents, reducing the risk of human error on the road.

3. Repetitive, Scalable Workflows

Tasks that are repetitive in nature, require consistent execution, and can be scaled across large operations are prime candidates for AI automation. By automating routine processes, AI enhances efficiency, reduces human error, and allows human workers to focus on more strategic or creative tasks.

- **Example: Email Sorting and Categorization**
AI-powered natural language processing (NLP) models can automate the sorting and categorization of emails for businesses, ensuring that each message reaches the appropriate department or individual. For instance, customer service emails can be automatically routed to the right team based on their content, while spam messages are filtered out.

  - **Impact**: Automating email processing saves organizations time, improves response rates, and enhances overall communication efficiency.

- **Broader Applications**: Beyond email, AI automation is widely applied in manufacturing (robotic assembly lines), customer service (chatbots), and finance (automated reporting). In all these domains, AI scales seamlessly to handle increasing workloads without compromising quality or consistency.

The features of problems ripe for AI—large data volumes with patterns to exploit, high costs of errors, and repetitive, scalable workflows—highlight the strengths of AI in addressing complex challenges. These characteristics not only underscore where AI can add the most value but also serve as criteria for decision-makers to identify opportunities for AI integration. From enabling data-driven insights to reducing risks and automating processes, AI transforms how organizations approach problem-solving, paving the way for innovation and growth.

Examples

AI has demonstrated its potential across a wide range of fields, particularly in STEM (Science, Technology, Engineering, and Mathematics). The following examples illustrate how AI can be leveraged to solve high-impact problems:

1. **AI for Genomics: Accelerating Drug Discovery with Structured Data**
The field of genomics generates vast datasets from sequencing and clinical studies, making it impossible to analyze these datasets manually. AI, particularly deep learning models, can identify patterns in genetic information to accelerate drug discovery and develop personalized medicine. By leveraging structured datasets, AI can predict protein structures, identify potential drug targets, and streamline the discovery process.

2. **Supply Chain AI: Reducing Inefficiencies through Predictive Analytics**
Supply chains involve complex systems that depend on accurate demand forecasting, inventory management, and logistics optimization. AI tools can analyze historical and real-time data to predict demand trends, optimize transportation routes, and reduce delivery times. By addressing inefficiencies, AI minimizes costs and enhances operational agility.

1.3.1.2 IDENTIFYING SCALABLE AI OPPORTUNITIES

When considering whether to apply Artificial Intelligence (AI) to a problem, decision-makers need a structured approach to assess the feasibility, scalability, and potential impact of AI solutions. A decision tree provides a step-by-step framework to evaluate these factors systematically. Each branch of the decision tree represents a critical consideration, ensuring that the right problems are targeted for AI implementation.

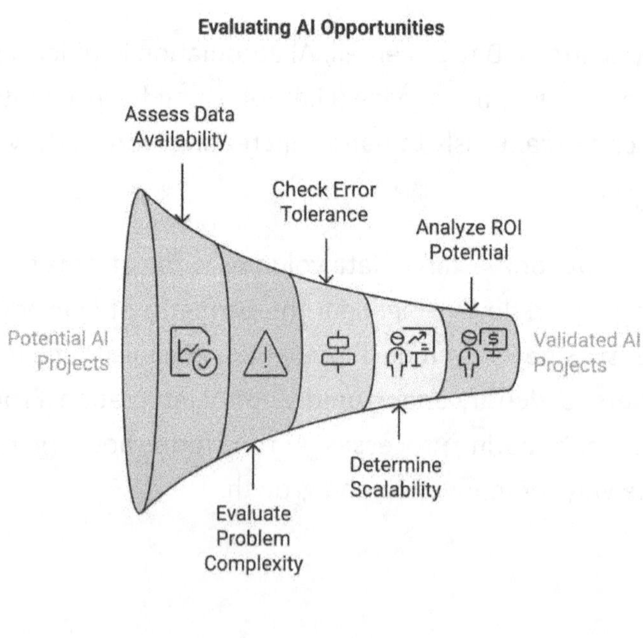

1. Data Availability and Quality

Data forms the foundation of any AI system. Without sufficient and high-quality data, AI models cannot learn effectively or deliver accurate predictions. This part of the decision tree focuses on assessing whether the necessary data is available and usable.

- **Key Questions**:
  - Are there sufficient datasets available to train an AI model?
    - Large datasets are often necessary for training AI models to recognize patterns and make predictions. If data is sparse or incomplete, the model may fail to perform effectively.
  - Is the data clean, well-structured, and labeled, or will significant preprocessing be required?
    - AI thrives on clean, labeled data. Messy, unstructured data adds complexity and costs to the project due to the preprocessing effort required. For instance, unlabeled image datasets require extensive annotation before being used for training.
- **Decision Point**: If data is unavailable or unusable without significant investment in collection or preprocessing, alternative solutions or problem redefinition might be necessary before pursuing AI.

2. Problem Complexity

The next branch of the decision tree evaluates whether the problem is complex enough to benefit from AI intervention. AI is best suited for problems requiring intricate analysis, prediction, or decision-making that surpasses traditional software capabilities.

- **Key Questions**:
  - Is the problem too simple for AI to add significant value?
    - Problems that can be solved with basic automation or simple algorithms may not justify the cost and effort of deploying AI.
  - Does the problem require advanced predictive or optimization capabilities?
    - Problems involving forecasting, pattern recognition, or optimization—such as demand prediction, fraud detection, or route optimization—are ideal candidates for AI.

- **Decision Point**: If the problem can be solved through simpler methods or does not require advanced AI features, traditional tools might be more appropriate.

3. Error Tolerance

AI applications should align with the tolerance for errors in the specific problem domain. This branch helps determine whether the acceptable level of error aligns with AI's capabilities.

- **Key Questions**:
    - What level of precision is necessary?
        - High-precision requirements, such as those in medical diagnostics or financial risk modeling, demand robust AI models with rigorous validation and testing.
    - Does the problem domain have low tolerance for errors?
        - In critical domains like healthcare or autonomous driving, even minor errors can lead to significant consequences. AI models in these areas must be designed with redundancy and accuracy safeguards.
- **Decision Point**: If the domain requires near-perfect precision and the available AI models cannot guarantee it, either alternative solutions or additional error-mitigation strategies must be considered.

4. Scalability

Scalability determines whether the AI solution can grow and adapt to new demands or be applied to other problems or domains. This factor is crucial for maximizing return on investment.

- **Key Questions**:
    - Can the AI solution be scaled across multiple processes or domains?
        - For example, an AI model developed for fraud detection in banking could potentially be adapted for detecting anomalies in supply chain operations.
    - Will the solution improve as more data becomes available?
        - AI models often become more accurate and reliable as they are exposed to larger datasets over time, creating compounding value.
- **Decision Point**: If the solution cannot be scaled or improved with additional data, its long-term ROI may be limited, making it less attractive for investment.

5. ROI Potential

The final branch of the decision tree evaluates whether the problem is worth the investment in AI development. Even if the other criteria are met, projects with low return on investment may not justify the effort.

- **Key Questions**:
  - Is the investment in AI development likely to yield measurable returns?
    - Returns can include cost savings, improved accuracy, enhanced operational efficiency, or revenue generation. For example, a recommendation engine might boost e-commerce sales by personalizing customer experiences.
  - How quickly can the benefits of AI be realized?
    - The timeline for achieving tangible results is critical. Projects with longer payback periods may face challenges in securing funding and support.
- **Decision Point**: If the expected ROI is low or uncertain, alternative projects with clearer or higher-value outcomes might take precedence.

The decision tree serves as a comprehensive framework for evaluating the suitability of AI for specific problems. By addressing key considerations—data availability, problem complexity, error tolerance, scalability, and ROI potential—this tool ensures that decision-makers can focus their resources on the most promising AI opportunities. Visualizing these criteria as a decision tree simplifies the evaluation process and enables systematic decision-making. For innovators, entrepreneurs, and organizations, this structured approach minimizes risks and maximizes the chances of successfully deploying AI to create impactful solutions.

This section provides a comprehensive approach to identifying problems where AI can deliver the most value. By understanding the features of AI-suitable problems, studying real-world examples, and using tools like the decision tree, organizations and innovators can focus their resources on impactful applications. This framework enables stakeholders to unlock the transformative potential of AI in diverse domains and maximize the return on their AI investments.

1.3.2 EVALUATING SCALABILITY AND ROI

Evaluating scalability and ROI involves analyzing an AI solution's potential for growth and its ability to deliver measurable financial returns. This includes assessing market size, cost efficiency, revenue impact, and key metrics like payback period and unit economics.

1.3.2.1 HOW TO DETERMINE IF AN AI SOLUTION IS SCALABLE

Determining if an AI solution is scalable involves assessing its ability to expand seamlessly while maintaining efficiency and delivering consistent value. This requires evaluating market potential, cost-reduction capabilities, and metrics like payback period and unit economics to ensure sustainable growth and investor appeal.

1. **Market Size and Venture Capital Interest**

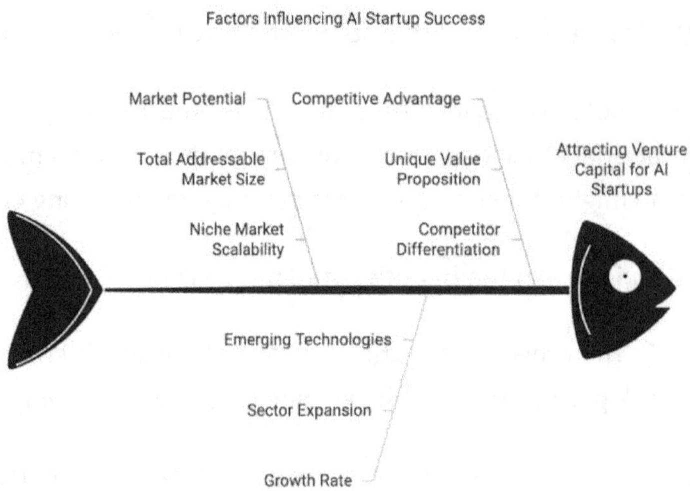

- **Addressable Market Potential**: Assess whether the total addressable market (TAM) is large enough to sustain long-term growth and attract venture capital (VC) funding. Startups targeting niche markets may succeed in the short term but may lack scalability unless the niche has potential for expansion or is part of a larger ecosystem.

- **Growth Trajectory**: Evaluate the market growth rate. Fast-growing sectors such as healthcare AI, autonomous technologies, and AI-driven sustainability solutions are more likely to attract VC interest.

- **Competitive Landscape**: A scalable AI solution should have a unique value proposition that stands out in a crowded market. Ensure the solution is not easily replicable by competitors.

2. **Cost Efficiency and Margin Improvement**

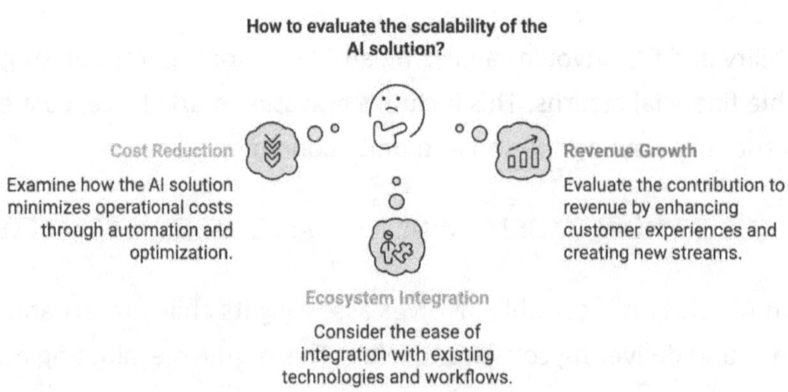

- **Cost Reduction Potential**: Examine how the AI solution minimizes operational costs by automating repetitive tasks, optimizing resource allocation, or improving decision-making. Scalable solutions tend to provide measurable cost savings across multiple business units or geographies.

- **Revenue and Margin Growth**: Evaluate how the AI solution contributes to top-line revenue by enhancing customer experiences, introducing new revenue streams, or enabling premium pricing through differentiation.

- **Ecosystem Integration**: Consider whether the AI can seamlessly integrate with existing technologies and workflows. Scalable solutions typically have a modular architecture that allows for easy adaptation to diverse environments.

EXAMPLES OF SCALABLE AI SOLUTIONS

1. **AI-Powered Sustainability Startups**

   - *From Pilot to Global Impact*: Startups that leverage AI for sustainability—such as optimizing energy consumption, predictive maintenance for industrial systems, or smart agriculture—often start with small-scale pilots. By demonstrating measurable impact (e.g., energy savings, carbon reduction), they attract funding to scale globally.

   - *Case Example*: An AI platform that predicts energy usage patterns for renewable energy grids could start with a single city pilot, proving value by reducing energy waste and operational costs. Once success is demonstrated, it can scale to regional and national levels, supported by partnerships with governments and utility companies.

2. **Healthcare AI Platforms**

   - *Scalability through Diagnostics*: AI solutions for diagnostics, such as image recognition for radiology or predictive analytics for patient outcomes, show scalability by addressing universal healthcare challenges. Pilots in specific hospitals can expand to national healthcare systems.

   - *Case Example*: An AI startup providing diabetic retinopathy screening through automated image analysis began with a few clinics and scaled to national health programs, demonstrating cost savings and improved patient outcomes.

1.3.2.2 METRICS FOR EVALUATING SCALABILITY AND ROI

Metrics for evaluating scalability and ROI focus on quantifying an AI solution's financial viability and growth potential. Key measures like payback period, unit economics, and operating margins provide insights into cost efficiency, profitability, and long-term scalability.

How to evaluate the financial viability of AI solutions?

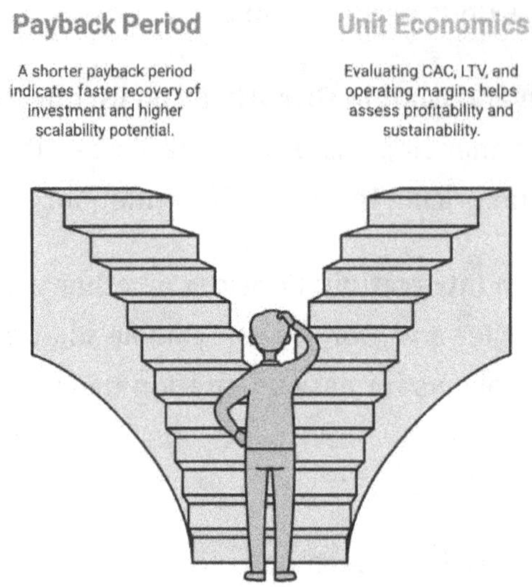

1. **Payback Period**

    - Define how quickly the investment in the AI solution is recovered through cost savings or revenue generation. Shorter payback periods (e.g., under 18 months) signal higher scalability potential and attractiveness to investors.

    - *Example Metric*: Calculate the total cost of ownership (TCO) for the AI system and compare it to the net savings or incremental revenue generated over time.

2. **Unit Economics for AI Solutions**

    - Measure the profitability of scaling the AI solution by evaluating unit-level costs and revenues. Focus on:

        - **Customer Acquisition Cost (CAC)**: Assess whether the cost to acquire new users decreases as the business scales.

        - **Lifetime Value (LTV)**: Determine if the long-term value derived from each customer justifies the upfront investment.

        - **Operating Margins**: Analyze how margins improve with increased adoption. Scalable solutions often benefit from economies of scale, where marginal costs decline as user numbers grow.

    - *Example Metric*: For an AI SaaS product, track the LTV:CAC ratio to ensure sustainable growth.

- Scalability hinges on addressing a large, growing market and demonstrating clear cost savings or revenue enhancement.

- A successful path from pilot to scalability includes measurable results, clear ROI metrics, and an adaptable architecture.

- Metrics like payback period and unit economics provide tangible evidence of scalability, aiding in securing funding and partnerships for expansion.

1.3.3 HIGH-GROWTH USE CASES

As artificial intelligence (AI) continues to mature, its transformative potential is becoming increasingly evident across industries. High-growth use cases demonstrate not only the capacity for innovation but also significant economic and societal benefits. This section explores industries poised for AI-driven disruption and highlights a compelling case study to illustrate AI's impact on the STEM field.

INDUSTRIES RIPE FOR DISRUPTION

AI is reshaping traditional industries, unlocking new opportunities for growth and innovation. Among the most promising are:

1. Healthcare
AI is revolutionizing patient care and medical research by:

- Enabling personalized treatment plans through predictive analytics.
- Enhancing diagnostic accuracy with imaging technologies.
- Optimizing clinical trials and accelerating drug discovery using generative AI models.

Growth Potential: The global AI healthcare market is projected to reach $200 billion by 2030, driven by cost-saving innovations and improved patient outcomes.

2. Agriculture
AI addresses global food security challenges by:

- Optimizing crop yield predictions with real-time environmental data.
- Automating irrigation and pest control systems using robotics.
- Reducing waste through AI-driven supply chain management.

Growth Potential: Precision agriculture powered by AI could boost global crop production by 70% by 2050, aligning with population growth.

3. Clean Energy
AI supports the clean energy transition by:

- Enhancing grid management to balance supply and demand dynamically.
- Improving renewable energy forecasting (e.g., wind, solar) to minimize losses.
- Driving innovations in battery storage and energy efficiency.

Growth Potential: The integration of AI could enable a 20% reduction in global CO_2 emissions by 2035.

4. Finance
AI reshapes financial services by:

- Automating fraud detection with machine learning.
- Personalizing investment portfolios using AI-driven insights.
- Enhancing risk assessment for loans and insurance products.

Growth Potential: AI could save financial institutions $1 trillion annually in operational costs by 2030.

CASE STUDY: AI IN RENEWABLE ENERGY OPTIMIZATION

The global push toward clean energy has elevated the importance of optimizing renewable energy systems. AI is playing a pivotal role in ensuring that clean energy sources like wind and solar are both efficient and sustainable.

AI algorithms analyze vast datasets, including weather forecasts, energy consumption patterns, and grid performance metrics, to optimize energy production and distribution in real-time. By predicting fluctuations in supply and demand, AI enables utilities to reduce energy waste and improve overall efficiency.

Application:

- **Forecasting Models:** AI models predict solar and wind energy generation with 95% accuracy, enabling better integration into the grid.
- **Energy Distribution:** AI optimizes load balancing across grids, minimizing downtime and preventing overloads.
- **Maintenance:** Predictive maintenance powered by AI reduces downtime for renewable energy equipment like turbines and solar panels.

ROI Example:

A leading utility company implemented an AI-driven energy management system and achieved the following outcomes:

- Annual savings of $100 million by reducing energy waste.
- Improved energy utilization by 25%, enabling the integration of an additional 30% renewable energy into the grid.
- Reduced carbon emissions equivalent to taking 50,000 cars off the road annually.

High-growth use cases in AI underscore its transformative potential across diverse industries. The combination of cutting-edge innovation, economic returns, and societal benefits positions AI as a cornerstone for future industrial evolution. With industries like healthcare, agriculture, clean energy, and finance leading the charge, these use cases illustrate the broader potential for AI to revolutionize both established and emerging sectors.

1.4: VALIDATING YOUR AI IDEA

Validation is a critical step in transforming an AI idea into a sustainable platform. It ensures the concept is not just innovative but also addresses real-world problems and has the potential to succeed in the market. This chapter outlines essential strategies for validating AI ideas.

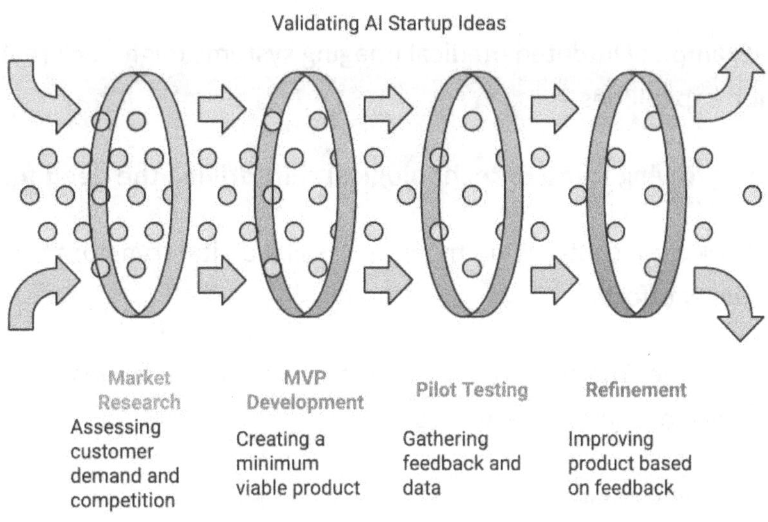

1.4.1 MARKET RESEARCH FOR AI STARTUPS

Market research is the cornerstone for validating any AI startup idea. It bridges the gap between innovation and real-world application by ensuring that the solution addresses tangible needs in the industries. This section delves into methods to assess customer demand and strategies for competitive differentiation.

Industries are rife with complex, high-impact problems that AI can uniquely address. However, solutions must be tailored to the intricate workflows and stringent requirements of these domains. Misaligned products often fail to gain traction, making it critical for startups to:

- Understand domain-specific workflows.
- Stay updated on compliance and regulatory standards.
- Align AI capabilities with measurable outcomes valued by professionals.

Key Questions to Explore

1. **What persistent problems exist in your target domain?**
    - Identify pain points that remain unresolved despite existing tools.
    - Example: In engineering, AI could optimize design workflows, reducing prototyping costs and time.
2. **How well are these problems currently being addressed?**
    - Evaluate the effectiveness of incumbent solutions. Are they too generic, outdated, or costly?
    - Example: Outdated medical imaging systems might lack real-time anomaly detection capabilities.
3. **Is there a growing trend or technological shift driving the need for your solution?**
    - Look for industry-wide movements like digital transformation, automation, or sustainability efforts.
    - Example: The rise of renewable energy opens avenues for AI in predictive maintenance of solar and wind assets.

Practical Tips for Gauging Demand

- **Conduct Surveys and Interviews with STEM Professionals**
    - Use structured interviews to understand daily challenges and existing inefficiencies.
    - Include open-ended questions to uncover hidden opportunities.
- **Review Industry Reports and Market Trends**

- Leverage resources like Gartner, McKinsey, and IEEE for insights into technological priorities.
- Identify growth areas (e.g., AI in healthcare diagnostics or robotics in manufacturing).

- **Monitor Social Media Discussions and Professional Forums**
  - Platforms like LinkedIn, GitHub, and niche forums (e.g., ResearchGate) reveal pain points and desired features.
  - Analyze trends in hashtags or discussion threads to spot emerging needs.

1.4.1.2 COMPETITIVE ANALYSIS

Identifying Gaps Where Incumbents Fail to Address Pain Points

The dominance of established players often leaves untapped opportunities for startups, especially in underserved niches.

- **Examine Existing Solutions for Inefficiencies or Unmet Needs**
  - Analyze reviews and feedback on existing products to pinpoint customer dissatisfaction.
  - Example: A scheduling tool that fails to integrate well with lab equipment could be a gap to target.
- **Explore Case Studies of Failed AI Implementations to Learn What Went Wrong**
  - Identify common pitfalls such as overpromising capabilities or lacking user-centric design.
  - Use lessons from failures to refine your approach.

Tools for Competitive Analysis

- **SWOT Analysis**
  - Identify Strengths, Weaknesses, Opportunities, and Threats to position your solution effectively.
- **Competitor Benchmarking**
  - Compare features, pricing, scalability, and support offered by competitors.
  - Tools like SimilarWeb or Crunchbase can help track competitors' performance.

1.4.1.3 DIFFERENTIATION STRATEGIES FOR STARTUPS

Focus on Niche Areas That Large Players Overlook

Startups often thrive by targeting markets that are too small or specialized for incumbents.

- Example: While major players might focus on general-purpose AI tools, a startup could specialize in AI-powered tools for rare disease diagnosis.

Leverage Speed and Agility to Adapt to Emerging Needs

Startups can iterate faster, responding quickly to new regulations or technological advancements.

- Example: Rapidly incorporating generative AI to enhance user interaction within applications.

Highlight Unique Features

1. **Ease of Integration**
    - AI solutions that seamlessly plug into existing workflows are highly attractive.
    - Example: An AI tool for engineers that integrates with CAD software.
2. **Enhanced User Experience**
    - Simplify complex AI functions into intuitive interfaces, minimizing the learning curve.
    - Example: A no-code AI tool for biologists to analyze gene expression.
3. **Cost-Effectiveness**
    - Demonstrate how your solution saves time or reduces costs compared to alternatives.
    - Example: A predictive maintenance platform that reduces machine downtime by 30%.

Effective market research ensures that AI startups build solutions that resonate with professionals. By understanding customer demand, identifying market gaps, and emphasizing differentiation, startups can position themselves as indispensable players in their chosen domains.

1.4.2 BUILDING AN MVP TO TEST SCALABILITY

A Minimum Viable Product (MVP) is a fundamental step in validating AI concepts. By focusing on creating a basic, functional version of the solution, startups can quickly test feasibility, market demand, and scalability with minimal investment.

1.4.2.1 RAPID PROTOTYPING

Importance of Quick Iteration in AI Development

- **Risk Mitigation**:
  - Prototyping allows startups to identify potential flaws in the concept or technology before investing heavily in development.
  - Example: Testing an AI model's accuracy on a smaller, controlled dataset can reveal issues early.
- **Early Feasibility Checks**:
  - Building prototypes provides a tangible way to assess whether the proposed AI technology can deliver the desired outcomes.
  - Example: A startup working on speech-to-text software can prototype using a small corpus of voice data to evaluate recognition accuracy.
- **User Feedback**:
  - Even simple prototypes enable startups to gather early feedback from potential users or customers, ensuring alignment with their needs.

1.4.2.2 USING OPEN-SOURCE TOOLS TO TEST AI CONCEPTS CHEAPLY

AI development can be resource-intensive, but open-source tools and APIs allow startups to build functional prototypes without incurring significant costs.

Examples of Tools

1. **TensorFlow or PyTorch for Basic Model Creation**:
   - Both frameworks provide extensive libraries and community support, making them ideal for creating foundational AI models.
   - Use Case: Developing a recommendation system for e-commerce platforms.
2. **Rasa for Conversational AI/Chatbot Prototypes**:

- Rasa is a robust open-source framework for building chatbots with natural language understanding (NLU).
- Use Case: Automating customer support for small businesses.

3. **OpenCV for Computer Vision Applications**:
   - OpenCV is a widely-used library for real-time image processing tasks.
   - Use Case: Creating an AI tool for object detection in warehouse inventory management.
4. **Cost-Effective Access to APIs**:
   - APIs like OpenAI's GPT for text generation or Hugging Face for pre-trained models offer ready-made functionalities.
   - Use Case: Quickly building sentiment analysis tools for social media monitoring.

Benefits of Using Open-Source Tools

- **Lower Costs**: Access high-quality tools without license fees.
- **Speed of Development**: Leverage pre-built components to focus on unique features.
- **Scalability**: Most open-source tools are designed to handle growth as the solution evolves.

Example: Building a Chatbot Prototype for Education

Target Problem: Students often struggle to create personalized study plans that align with their goals, learning pace, and schedules.

Approach:

1. Use Rasa to build a simple chatbot that interacts with students.
2. Include features for gathering information about learning preferences, goals, and available time.
3. Leverage a recommendation engine to generate tailored study schedules.

Outcome:

- Deploy the prototype to a small group of students or online forums.
- Gather feedback on usability, accuracy, and value.

- Use the results to refine the chatbot or expand features.

1.4.2.3 MVP DEVELOPMENT LIFECYCLE FOR AI STARTUPS

A well-structured lifecycle ensures that MVP development progresses smoothly from idea to scalability.

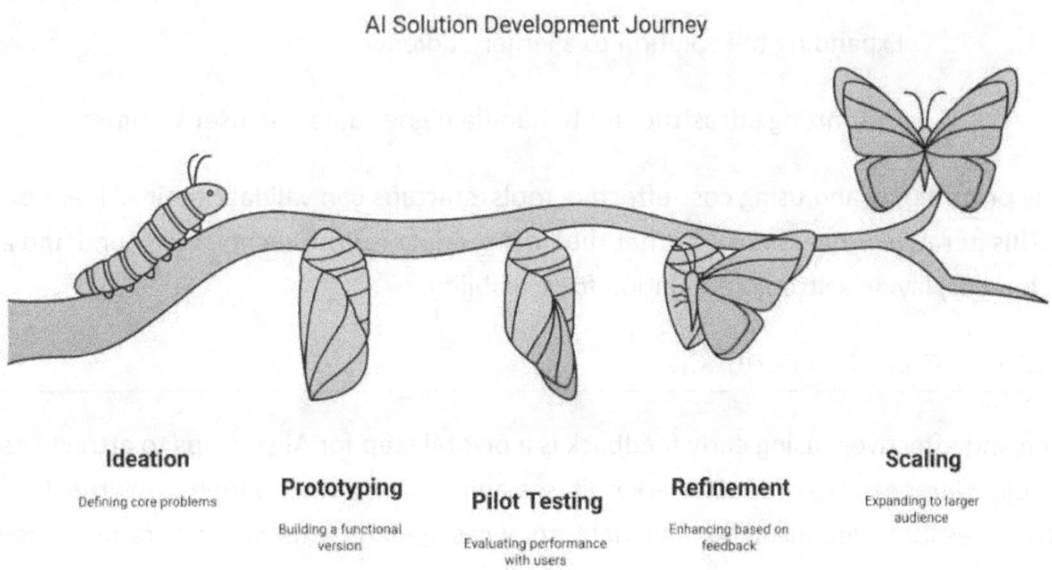

The stages include:

1. **Ideation**:
   - Brainstorming and defining the core problem your AI solution will solve.
   - Identifying the target audience and potential use cases.
2. **Prototyping**:
   - Using tools and frameworks to build a basic, functional version of the AI solution.
   - Testing technical feasibility and initial user interaction.
3. **Pilot Testing**:
   - Deploying the prototype to a small, controlled audience to evaluate performance and collect feedback.

4. **Refinement**:

    - Improving the solution based on user feedback, fixing bugs, and enhancing functionality.
    - Adding features that improve usability or address gaps.

5. **Scaling**:

    - Expanding the solution to a larger audience.
    - Optimizing infrastructure to handle higher data and user volumes.

By rapidly prototyping and using cost-effective tools, startups can validate their AI ideas quickly and efficiently. This iterative process ensures that the final product is both technically sound and aligned with market needs, laying a strong foundation for scalability.

1.4.3 LEVERAGING EARLY FEEDBACK

Gathering and effectively using early feedback is a pivotal step for AI startups to attract seed funding. It helps demonstrate product-market fit, scalability, and a clear path to growth. This section explores strategies for collecting actionable data, showcasing early traction, and crafting a compelling narrative to appeal to investors.

1.4.3.1 STRATEGIES FOR USING PILOT RESULTS TO ATTRACT SEED FUNDING

Collecting Actionable Data During Pilot Testing

Actionable data provides measurable evidence of your product's effectiveness and potential. During pilot testing, focus on both quantitative metrics and qualitative insights.

Key Metrics to Monitor:

- **User Adoption Rates**: Measure how quickly users start using your product and how often they return.
    - Example: Daily active users (DAU) vs. monthly active users (MAU) ratios.
- **Engagement Patterns**: Identify which features are most used and which are ignored.
    - Example: If an AI platform for healthcare sees most interaction with the scheduling assistant, this could guide feature prioritization.
- **Error Rates**: Track performance issues, such as incorrect AI predictions or system downtime, to showcase improvements over time.
    - Example: Error reduction from 15% to 5% after fine-tuning algorithms.

- **Satisfaction Scores**: Use Net Promoter Scores (NPS) or customer satisfaction surveys to gauge overall user sentiment.
    - Example: An NPS of 70+ can demonstrate strong user enthusiasm.

Qualitative Feedback:

- Conduct **surveys and interviews** to understand user perspectives:
    - What did users like or dislike?
    - How does the product impact their daily workflows or challenges?
- Gather anecdotes that highlight transformative user experiences.
    - Example: A teacher using your AI platform might report saving 5 hours per week on lesson planning.

1.4.3.2 SHOWCASING EARLY TRACTION WITH DATA

Investors are more likely to support startups with tangible evidence of success. Present your pilot results in a way that emphasizes the product's value and scalability.

Present Clear, Compelling Metrics

Quantify your early success with specific, impactful statistics:

- **User Growth**:
    - Example: "500 active users in three months, with a retention rate of 75%."
- **Efficiency Improvements**:
    - Example: "30% reduction in manual data entry time using our AI-powered tool."
- **Market Penetration**:
    - Example: "Achieved a 15% adoption rate among local clinics within the pilot region."

Examples of Strong Evidence

1. **Adoption Metrics**: High user retention or engagement rates indicate that your solution resonates with the target audience.
2. **Impact Metrics**: Data that proves your platform improves productivity, reduces costs, or solves critical pain points.

- Example: "Our chatbot saved users an average of 2 hours per week by automating repetitive tasks."

1.4.3.3 CRAFTING A NARRATIVE

Numbers tell a story, but an engaging narrative makes them memorable. Use the pilot results to build a compelling story that aligns with your startup's vision.

Demonstrate Market Demand and Scalability

- Link pilot results to broader market opportunities.
    - Example: "Our pilot with 50 small businesses revealed that 80% were willing to pay for an annual subscription, showing strong market potential."
- Highlight the ease of scaling:
    - "The modular design of our platform allows us to scale from small businesses to enterprise clients with minimal reconfiguration."

Use Customer Testimonials or Case Studies

- Showcase real-world use cases to build credibility and emotional appeal.
    - Example: "After implementing our AI scheduling assistant, Company X saw a 25% improvement in team productivity, enabling them to take on more clients without hiring additional staff."
- Include quotes from enthusiastic users:
    - "The AI tool transformed the way we manage our projects—what used to take hours now happens in seconds."

By collecting actionable data, highlighting early traction, and weaving it into a compelling narrative, startups can attract seed funding effectively. This approach not only proves the viability of the product but also builds investor confidence in its potential for long-term growth.

READER EXERCISES

Exercise 1: Identify 3 High-Growth AI Use Cases in Underserved Markets

1. **Objective:** Help readers discover impactful AI opportunities in niche markets.
2. **Instructions:**
    - Research emerging trends in AI applications.

- Choose three industries or demographics that are underserved by current solutions (e.g., rural healthcare, low-resource education, sustainable agriculture).
- Identify potential high-growth AI use cases. For each, describe:
    - The problem being addressed.
    - How AI can provide a solution.
    - Expected benefits and challenges.

Example Format:

- **Market:** Rural Healthcare
- **Problem:** Lack of access to diagnostic tools.
- **AI Use Case:** AI-powered remote diagnostics.
- **Expected Benefits:** Increased access, early diagnosis, cost savings.
- **Challenges:** Connectivity issues, regulatory approval.

Exercise 2: Conduct a SWOT Analysis for an AI Startup Idea

1. **Objective:** Teach readers how to critically assess AI business opportunities.
2. **Instructions:**
    - Think of an AI-based startup idea.
    - Conduct a SWOT analysis, covering:
        - **Strengths:** Unique capabilities or advantages.
        - **Weaknesses:** Internal limitations.
        - **Opportunities:** Market gaps or trends.
        - **Threats:** External risks like competition or regulations.

Template:

Strengths	Weaknesses
- What internal advantages does the AI solution offer? (e.g., innovative features, strong technical expertise, unique datasets) - How does this solution offer a competitive edge?	- What internal limitations or challenges exist? (e.g., resource constraints, technical limitations, data quality issues) - What potential bottlenecks might hinder its success?
Opportunities	**Threats**
- What external opportunities can you leverage? (e.g., market demand, partnerships, regulatory incentives) - Are there trends that could accelerate the adoption of this AI solution?	- What external risks could undermine your idea? (e.g., competition, shifting regulations, ethical concerns) - How could competitors, societal perception, or rapid technological changes create challenges?

1. Industry Use Case Matrix with Potential ROI Estimates

- **Purpose:** Help readers visualize AI use cases across industries and evaluate their potential returns.
- **Description:**
    - A grid comparing industries (e.g., Healthcare, Finance, Retail) with AI use cases (e.g., predictive analytics, chatbots, fraud detection).
    - Include an ROI estimate (Low, Medium, High) for each combination.

Example Format:

Industry/Use Case	Predictive Analytics	Chatbots	Fraud Detection
Healthcare	High	Medium	Low
Finance	High	Low	High
Retail	Medium	High	Low

2. TAM vs. SAM vs. SOM (Share of Market) Visual for AI Startups

- **Purpose:** Illustrate market segmentation and the total addressable opportunity.
- **Description:**
  - Create a layered Venn diagram or concentric circles:
    - **TAM (Total Addressable Market):** Broadest circle, all potential users.
    - **SAM (Serviceable Addressable Market):** Middle circle, users within reach.
    - **SOM (Serviceable Obtainable Market):** Smallest circle, realistic early adopters.

Key Data Points to Include:

- Dollar values or user estimates for each segment.
- Examples of how SOM can grow with scalability.

---

3. Framework for Validating Scalability and Market Readiness

- **Purpose:** Provide readers with a checklist for testing scalability and market feasibility.
- **Description:**
  - A flowchart or framework with the following steps:
    1. **Prototype Validation:** Build an MVP (minimum viable product) and gather feedback.
    2. **Market Fit Analysis:** Test in small but diverse markets.

3. **Operational Scalability:** Ensure infrastructure supports growth.
4. **Regulatory Readiness:** Meet compliance and data privacy laws.
5. **Customer Acquisition:** Test sustainable channels for acquiring users.

Flowchart with checkpoints, e.g.:

- Start → Prototype Validation → Market Fit Analysis → Regulatory Readiness → Operational Scalability → End.

CHAPTER 2: DATA AND ETHICAL FOUNDATIONS

INTRODUCTION

DATA AS THE FOUNDATION

AI systems are inherently data-driven, relying on vast data for training, validation, and continuous improvement. The quality of this data determines the accuracy, reliability, and fairness of the AI system's outcomes. Poor-quality data—incomplete, inconsistent, or irrelevant—can lead to erroneous predictions and flawed insights. For example:

- Biases in Data: Training an AI model with biased data skews its outputs, leading to systemic issues.
- Insufficient Data: A limited dataset may prevent the model from generalizing to real-world scenarios, reducing its usability.
- Noisy Data: Excessive irrelevant or erroneous information can confuse the model, reducing accuracy.

The saying "garbage in, garbage out" perfectly encapsulates the importance of data as the foundation for building robust AI systems.

REAL-WORLD IMPACTS

Neglecting data quality can lead to many problems that ripple across the entire lifecycle of an AI solution. Some notable impacts include:

- Inefficiencies: Flawed data increases the time and cost required for data cleaning and preprocessing.
- Increased Costs: Poor data can result in the development of ineffective models, necessitating costly rework or system overhauls.
- Unreliable Models: AI systems trained on low-quality data often fail in real-world applications, damaging the organization's credibility.
- Legal and Regulatory Risks: Using data that violates privacy or copyright laws can have significant legal repercussions.

Consider a retail recommendation engine trained on outdated purchase data. It would fail to reflect current customer preferences, leading to poor customer experience and lost revenue opportunities.

ETHICAL DIMENSIONS

Ethical considerations are critical in AI development. These principles ensure that AI systems are built responsibly, avoiding harm and fostering user trust. Key dimensions include:

- Fairness: AI systems should not perpetuate existing biases or discriminate against individuals or groups. For example, a hiring AI tool should evaluate candidates objectively, regardless of gender, race, or other protected attributes.

- Accountability: Developers and organizations must take responsibility for their AI systems' actions and decisions, ensure process transparency, and promptly address errors.

- Inclusivity: AI systems should be designed to serve diverse populations, reflecting varied needs and contexts.

Neglecting these dimensions can result in unethical outcomes, such as biased hiring decisions or unfair credit scoring. This not only harms individuals but also undermines trust in AI technologies.

CASE STUDY: FAILURE OF AN AI HEALTHCARE SOLUTION DUE TO BIASED DATA

A promising healthcare startup aimed to revolutionize cardiology by developing an AI model capable of diagnosing heart disease based on patient medical records and imaging data. The solution used machine learning algorithms to analyze data points such as electrocardiograms (ECGs), lab test results, and historical patient outcomes. The intended goal was to assist physicians in making faster, more accurate diagnoses, particularly in emergencies, while reducing the strain on healthcare systems.

The AI solution was trained on historical patient data from hospitals in a specific region, encompassing thousands of cases. This dataset was intended to reflect real-world scenarios and provide the AI with diverse examples for training and validation.

The Problem

Despite initial excitement, the AI system began to show significant performance disparities when deployed in different hospitals and patient populations. The core issue stemmed from the training dataset:

- **Bias in Data Representation**: The dataset disproportionately included data from middle-aged Caucasian males, with limited representation of women, older adults, and individuals from minority ethnic groups.

- **Incomplete Data**: Many records lacked key variables, such as lifestyle factors or comorbidities, critical for accurate diagnosis.

- **Skewed Outcomes**: Since the training data reflected historical biases in diagnosis (e.g., underdiagnosis in women), the AI inherited these biases, resulting in missed diagnoses for underrepresented groups.

For example, the AI was 25% less accurate in diagnosing heart disease in women compared to men, particularly for atypical symptoms, which are more common in female patients.

Consequences

The biased AI system led to a series of cascading issues:

1. **Misdiagnoses**: Patients, especially women and minorities, received incorrect or delayed diagnoses. This led to worsened health outcomes and, in some cases, severe medical complications.

2. **Patient Harm**: The lack of accurate diagnosis increases the risk of preventable heart attacks and other severe conditions, undermining the core purpose of the solution.

3. **Regulatory Penalties**: Healthcare regulators flagged the solution for failing to meet fairness and accuracy standards. The startup faced fines and restrictions on further deploying the system.

4. **Reputational Damage**: News of the AI system's failure to diagnose patients fairly spread quickly. This eroded trust among physicians, patients, and investors.

5. **Financial Fallout**: The startup lost key hospital contracts and faced lawsuits from patients harmed by the system. Investors pulled out, leading to the project's eventual shutdown.

Lessons Learned

This case underscores critical lessons for AI development in healthcare:

1. **Thorough Dataset Evaluation**: Data must be representative of all target user demographics. A diverse dataset helps mitigate biases and ensures the AI performs equitably across different populations.

2. **Inclusion of Diverse Perspectives**: Involving diverse technical and clinical teams can help identify potential blind spots in data collection and model development.

3. **Ethical Oversight**: Establishing a robust framework for ethical AI development, including fairness assessments and bias audits, can help prevent such failures.

4. **Continuous Testing and Validation**: Before deployment, models must undergo rigorous testing across varied datasets to ensure they perform well under real-world conditions.

5. **Transparency**: Communicating the limitations of the AI system to end users is essential. Clear documentation of the training process, datasets, and potential biases can help build trust and enable informed decision-making.

WHY THIS MATTERS FOR ENTREPRENEURS AND VCS

RELIABILITY AND SCALABILITY

Reliability and scalability are essential for long-term success in the competitive AI-driven marketplace. For entrepreneurs and VCs, a data-driven approach to AI development ensures the creation of robust models capable of adapting to diverse applications and user bases. Key considerations include:

- **Reliable Data Pipelines**: AI models are only as strong as the data they ingest. A reliable data pipeline ensures:
    - Consistent data quality.
    - Real-time updates for dynamic AI systems.
    - Accurate insights that build user trust.
- **Scalable Solutions**: Reliable, well-prepared data supports models that scale across geographies, industries, and applications. For example, a predictive maintenance AI solution trained on clean, diverse datasets can be adapted to different sectors such as manufacturing, transportation, and energy. This scalability attracts investors eager to back solutions with high growth potential.

Investor Impact: Reliable AI systems, backed by robust data infrastructure, signal to investors that the startup is well-prepared for market expansion, reducing risk and increasing the likelihood of funding.

RISK MITIGATION

Ethical compliance is more than a moral obligation—it's a business imperative. Entrepreneurs and VCs face substantial risks if AI systems fail to align with ethical standards and regulatory frameworks. These include:

- **Legal Issues**:
    - Non-compliance with GDPR (General Data Protection Regulation) and HIPAA (Health Insurance Portability and Accountability Act) can lead to fines, litigation, and restrictions.

- For example, an AI system using improperly anonymized healthcare data could incur significant penalties under GDPR's data privacy provisions.

- **Reputational Damage**:
  - An AI tool accused of bias or unfair practices can tarnish a company's reputation. For instance, a hiring AI system rejecting qualified candidates due to biased algorithms could lead to public backlash and erode customer trust.

- **Operational Risks**:
  - AI systems that lack ethical oversight are prone to errors, leading to inefficiencies and potential harm to users. Regulatory scrutiny compounds these issues, adding costs and delays.

Investor Impact:

Startups with strong ethical practices demonstrate foresight and responsibility, which appeals to investors. Ethical compliance reduces risks, creating a safer and more predictable investment opportunity.

COMPETITIVE ADVANTAGE

Ethics and data quality are emerging as critical differentiators for AI companies in a crowded marketplace. Investors increasingly prioritize startups that adopt responsible AI principles, recognizing their potential for sustainable growth and resilience. Key aspects include:

- **Building Trust**: Companies prioritizing fairness, transparency, and inclusivity in their AI systems foster trust among users, clients, and partners. For example:
  - A lending platform that transparently explains credit decisions builds confidence among borrowers and regulators.

- **Attracting Strategic Partnerships**: Organizations that demonstrate ethical practices are likelier to form partnerships with other forward-thinking companies, universities, and NGOs.

- **Positioning for the Future**:
  - As regulatory frameworks evolve, ethical AI practices provide a competitive edge. Companies proactively adopting responsible frameworks are better positioned to adapt to future legal and societal expectations.
  - Ethical considerations can also attract customers seeking responsible, socially aware solutions.

Investor Impact:

Startups that commit to ethics and high-quality data practices are more likely to secure funding.

Investors recognize that these companies can navigate complex regulatory environments and maintain a strong market presence.

For entrepreneurs and VCs, prioritizing data reliability and ethical compliance is no longer optional—it's a key driver of business success. By ensuring scalability, mitigating risks, and leveraging ethical AI as a competitive advantage, startups can attract investors and achieve sustainable growth.

- Data-driven AI ensures reliability and scalability.
- Ethical compliance mitigates risks (e.g., regulatory issues, reputational damage).

WHAT THIS CHAPTER OFFERS

A. PRACTICAL STRATEGIES

This chapter provides readers with actionable insights and proven methodologies to address the fundamental challenges of data and ethics in AI development. Key strategies include:

- **Sourcing High-Quality Data**:
  - Identifying reliable open datasets, such as those available on Kaggle, UCI Machine Learning Repository, and domain-specific sources like genomic or climate datasets.
  - Strategies for securing proprietary datasets through partnerships with universities, NGOs, and industry collaborators.
  - Navigating ethical and legal considerations, including user consent, licensing agreements, and avoiding data scraping violations.
- **Preparing Data for AI Training**:
  - Comprehensive preprocessing techniques to enhance data quality, such as handling missing values, outliers, and inconsistencies.
  - Feature engineering methods to extract maximum value from datasets, making models more robust and accurate.
  - Scaling and normalization processes to ensure compatibility with AI algorithms.
- **Governing Data Effectively**:
  - Implementing data governance principles, including ownership, lifecycle management, and security protocols.

- Data practices should be aligned with privacy laws like GDPR and HIPAA through techniques such as anonymization and encryption.
- Leveraging automated tools to streamline data governance, such as AI-driven data cataloging platforms.

B. FRAMEWORKS FOR SUCCESS

Readers will gain access to practical frameworks and tools designed to build ethical, scalable, and high-performance AI solutions. These include:

- **Ethical AI Development Frameworks**:
  - A step-by-step guide to identifying and mitigating biases in AI systems.
  - Introduction to ethical toolkits like IBM's AI Fairness 360 and Microsoft's Responsible AI Dashboard.
  - Techniques for fostering fairness, inclusivity, and accountability in AI projects.
- **Scalable Data Practices**:
  - Frameworks for managing large-scale datasets, including storage optimization, real-time data integration, and efficient data processing pipelines.
  - Guidance on aligning AI systems with explainable AI (XAI) principles to ensure transparency and trustworthiness.
- **Case Study Frameworks**:
  - Real-world examples demonstrate how startups successfully implement responsible data and ethical AI practices.
  - Lessons learned from companies that faced challenges due to poor data governance or ethical oversights.

C. INTERACTIVE ELEMENTS

To enhance learning and ensure practical application, this chapter includes a variety of interactive elements:

- **Exercises**:
  - Identify three potential sources of bias in a dataset and propose methods to mitigate them.

- Practice cleaning a sample dataset by handling missing values, normalizing data, and addressing outliers.
- Analyze a real-world case study and outline a data governance plan to align with ethical AI practices.

- **Visual Aids**:
  - Detailed diagrams illustrating preprocessing pipelines, bias detection workflows, and privacy compliance checklists.
  - Tables comparing different data sources, preprocessing tools, and ethical AI frameworks.
- **Case Studies**:
  - Examples of successful and failed AI projects provide a balanced perspective on the importance of data and ethics.
  - Insights into how leading companies like Google and Microsoft incorporate ethical principles into their AI solutions.

This chapter combines practical strategies, robust frameworks, and interactive elements to equip readers with the knowledge and tools necessary to excel in building responsible and scalable AI solutions. Whether you're an entrepreneur launching a startup or a VC evaluating investment opportunities, this chapter offers invaluable guidance for navigating the complex world of data and ethics in AI.

2.1: DATA SOURCES AND ACQUISITION

WHERE TO FIND DATA

Data is the cornerstone of every AI solution. The success of AI models depends not only on their design and algorithms but, more critically, on the quality and relevance of the data used for training and validation. As AI becomes integral to industries ranging from healthcare to finance and climate science, the demand for diverse and high-quality datasets has surged. However, finding the correct data for your specific AI use case can be challenging.

Data sources vary widely in terms of accessibility, quality, and structure. Open datasets, such as those on platforms like Kaggle and the UCI Machine Learning Repository, provide free and easy-to-access options for experimentation and learning. For more specialized needs, STEM-specific datasets—such as genomic databases or climate archives—offer domain-specific insights crucial for advancing AI in niche areas. Additionally, proprietary datasets acquired through partnerships with organizations or institutions can unlock highly valuable, structured, and often untapped data.

Alongside identifying data sources, ethical considerations are vital in ensuring responsible AI development. Issues like user consent, licensing compliance, and avoiding improper data scraping are fundamental to maintaining trust and adhering to legal frameworks. This chapter provides a roadmap for navigating these data sources while addressing the ethical responsibilities of data acquisition. Whether you are building AI for research, entrepreneurship, or industry innovation, this section will guide you in finding the data you need effectively and responsibly.

2.1.1 TYPES OF DATA SOURCES

A robust AI solution begins with identifying and acquiring the correct datasets. Understanding the types of data sources available and their specific use cases can help guide the selection process. Below, we explore three key categories of data sources: open datasets, STEM-specific datasets, and proprietary datasets through partnerships.

2.1.1.1 OPEN DATASETS

Open datasets are publicly available resources ideal for starting projects or experimenting with AI models. These datasets are freely accessible and offer diverse structured and unstructured data collections for multiple domains.

Examples

1. **Kaggle**: A popular platform hosting a variety of datasets across industries, Kaggle also features competitions that challenge participants to apply AI models to solve real-world problems. For instance, it offers datasets for tasks like image recognition, time series forecasting, and natural language processing.

2. **UCI Machine Learning Repository**: This historical archive provides machine learning datasets for academic research and practical applications. The datasets include those for classification, regression, and clustering tasks.

3. **Data.gov**: A government initiative that provides open access to datasets related to policy, economy, demographics, and more. These datasets help build AI models that analyze public sector trends or predict socioeconomic outcomes.

Benefits

- **Free to Use**: Open datasets eliminate the financial barrier to data access, making them ideal for startups and academic projects.

- **Diverse Data Domains**: They cover a broad spectrum of industries, including healthcare, finance, transportation, and climate science, providing flexibility for AI experimentation.

Challenges

- **Quality Variability**: Since these datasets are freely available, the quality and completeness of the data may vary significantly.

- **Limited Domain-Specific Customization**: Open datasets may not meet specific requirements for niche applications.

2.1.1.2 STEM-SPECIFIC DATASETS

STEM-specific datasets address specialized science, technology, engineering, and mathematics needs. Interpreting and applying these datasets effectively often requires domain expertise.

Examples

1. **Genomic Databases**: Platforms like NCBI GenBank offer extensive genetic and biological data, which are critical for advancing research in drug discovery, disease prevention, and personalized medicine.

2. **Climate Data**: NOAA (National Oceanic and Atmospheric Administration) datasets provide detailed records of weather patterns, ocean currents, and historical climate trends, supporting AI applications in environmental science and disaster management.

Use Cases

- **Drug Discovery**: Genomic datasets aid in identifying biomarkers and creating AI models for predicting drug efficacy.

- **Climate Change Mitigation**: AI models trained on climate data can predict natural disasters and optimize resource allocation for disaster response.

Benefits

- **High Relevance**: These datasets are tailored to specific STEM domains, ensuring their applicability to niche AI projects.

- **Depth of Information**: STEM datasets often include detailed, well-curated records, enabling precise model training.

Challenges

- **Complexity:** Interpreting and preprocessing these datasets require domain knowledge and technical expertise.

- **Restricted Access**: Some STEM datasets are proprietary or require subscriptions for access.

2.1.1.3 PROPRIETARY DATASETS THROUGH PARTNERSHIPS

Proprietary data sources involve collaborations with organizations to access unique datasets. While these datasets are often high-quality, they require legal agreements and compliance with licensing terms.

Examples

1. **Healthcare Partnerships**: Collaborating with hospitals or research institutions to access anonymized patient records can support AI applications in medical diagnostics and treatment planning.

2. **Retail Collaborations**: Partnering with e-commerce companies provides access to customer purchase behavior data, which can be used for personalization and predictive analytics.

Benefits

- **Domain-Specific Insights**: Proprietary datasets are often highly relevant to the industry or problem being addressed.

- **Structured Data**: These datasets are usually well-organized, reducing the need for extensive preprocessing.

Challenges

- **Licensing Costs**: Acquiring proprietary datasets can be expensive, making them less accessible to startups.

- **Compliance Requirements**: Strict data sharing and usage regulations must be followed, especially for sensitive information like healthcare or financial records.

2.1.2 ETHICAL CONSIDERATIONS

Ethical considerations are integral to responsible data acquisition. Ensuring that data collection practices respect user privacy and comply with legal standards is essential for maintaining trust and avoiding reputational risks.

User Consent and Licensing Agreements

1. **User Consent**: Personal information data must be collected with explicit user consent. Adhering to HIPAA guidelines, for example, ensures the ethical use of healthcare data.

2. **Licensing**: Understanding and adhering to licensing terms is crucial when using open or proprietary datasets. For instance, many datasets on Kaggle are distributed under Creative Commons licenses, which outline specific usage limitations.

Avoiding Data Scraping Violations

Data scraping from websites can lead to violations of terms of service or legal disputes.

Best Practices

- Use APIs provided by websites to access data in a structured and authorized manner.
- Seek permission before scraping non-public or sensitive information.

Example of Legal Consequences

Facebook's legal actions against companies that scraped user data highlight the risks of unauthorized data collection. Such practices can result in significant legal and financial penalties.

By understanding these data sources and adhering to ethical principles, you can ensure that your AI project is built on a solid foundation of high-quality, responsibly sourced data.

2.2 ASSESSING DATA RELEVANCE

Assessing the relevance of data is a critical step in designing and developing successful AI solutions. An AI model's effectiveness hinges on the quality and appropriateness of the data used to train it. This section outlines key considerations and a systematic approach to evaluating datasets, ensuring that the chosen data aligns with the solution's goals and represents the intended user base.

2.2.1 HOW TO EVALUATE DATASETS FOR YOUR AI SOLUTION

2.2.1.1 IS THE DATA SUFFICIENT FOR YOUR TARGET AI MODEL?

The sufficiency of data is determined by its quantity, quality, and variety. Here are the key points to consider:

- **Volume:** Ensure the dataset contains enough records or samples to train the AI model effectively. Larger datasets reduce the risk of overfitting and improve generalization.
  - *Example:* A facial recognition model requires thousands of labeled images representing diverse angles, lighting conditions, and expressions.
- **Feature Coverage:** The dataset should include all the relevant features the AI model needs to learn. Missing critical data points can lead to suboptimal performance.
  - *Example:* A customer churn prediction model must include purchase history, customer interactions, and demographic information.
- **Temporal Relevance:** Ensure the recent data reflects current trends or conditions for time-sensitive applications.

- *Example:* Predicting stock market trends requires up-to-date financial and market data.

- **Label Quality (for Supervised Learning):** Verify the accuracy of the labels or annotations in the dataset. Incorrect labels can introduce noise and degrade model performance.
  - *Example:* Mislabeled X-rays can lead to inaccurate medical diagnostic AI system predictions.

2.2.1.2. DOES THE DATA REPRESENT YOUR INTENDED USER BASE?

The dataset must reflect the diversity and characteristics of your target audience to ensure fairness, inclusivity, and usability. Consider the following factors:

- **Demographic Representation:** Ensure the dataset captures variations in age, gender, ethnicity, geography, and other relevant demographic factors.
  - *Example:* A voice assistant trained exclusively on data from American English speakers may struggle to understand accents or dialects from other regions.
- **Domain-Specific Relevance:** The data should align with the context in which the AI solution will operate.
  - *Example:* An AI model for detecting crop diseases must use data specific to the crops and diseases prevalent in the target region.
- **Bias and Fairness:** Assess the dataset for potential biases that may lead to unfair or discriminatory outcomes.
  - *Example:* Loan approval models should not disproportionately reject applications based on biased historical data.
- **Edge Cases and Anomalies:** Include rare or edge-case scenarios in the dataset to improve the model's robustness.
  - *Example:* A self-driving car's training data should include diverse weather and road conditions, such as fog, snow, and heavy traffic.

Example: Evaluating Satellite Data for an AI-Driven Agricultural Platform

Consider an AI solution designed to optimize crop yield using satellite imagery.

Data Relevance Assessment for AI in Agriculture

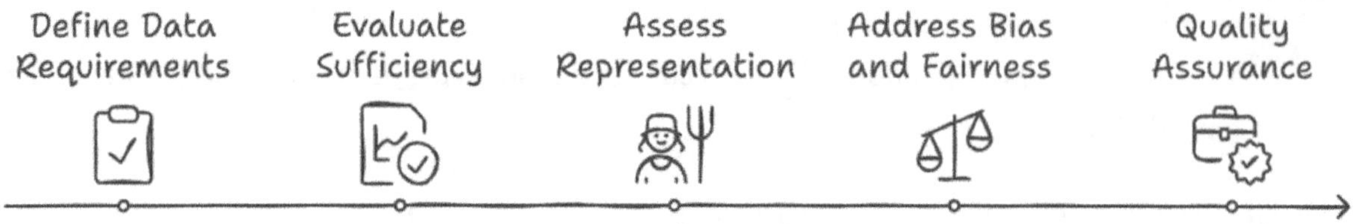

The following steps illustrate how to assess data relevance in this scenario:

1. **Define the Data Requirements:**
   - **Target AI Model:** A convolutional neural network (CNN) for image analysis.
   - **Required Features:** High-resolution satellite images, vegetation indices, soil moisture levels, and historical climate data.
2. **Evaluate Sufficiency:**
   - **Volume:** Ensure the dataset includes images for multiple growing seasons and covers the geographical regions of interest.
   - **Feature Coverage:** Verify that the dataset provides all relevant features, such as NDVI (Normalized Difference Vegetation Index) and temperature patterns.
   - **Temporal Relevance:** Confirm that the satellite data is updated regularly to reflect current agricultural conditions.
3. **Assess Representation:**
   - **Geographic Diversity:** Check that the dataset includes images from different terrains, climates, and farming practices.
   - **Crop Variability:** Ensure the dataset covers various crops and their growth stages.
   - **Anomaly Detection:** Include data capturing events like pest infestations or extreme weather conditions.

4. **Bias and Fairness:**

   - Ensure the dataset does not represent certain crops or regions disproportionately, leading to skewed model performance.

5. **Quality Assurance:**

   - Verify the resolution and clarity of satellite images to ensure they meet the technical requirements for accurate analysis.

   - Cross-validate labels or annotations (e.g., ground-truth data from local farmers).

Evaluating data relevance is a foundational step that ensures your AI model is well-prepared to deliver accurate, reliable, and equitable outcomes. Thoroughly assessing data sufficiency and repeal mitigate risks and set the stage for a successful AI solution. The example of satellite data evaluation demonstrates how these principles can be applied practically, highlighting the importance of a structured approach to data relevance.

2.1.3 DATA PARTNERSHIPS AND APIS

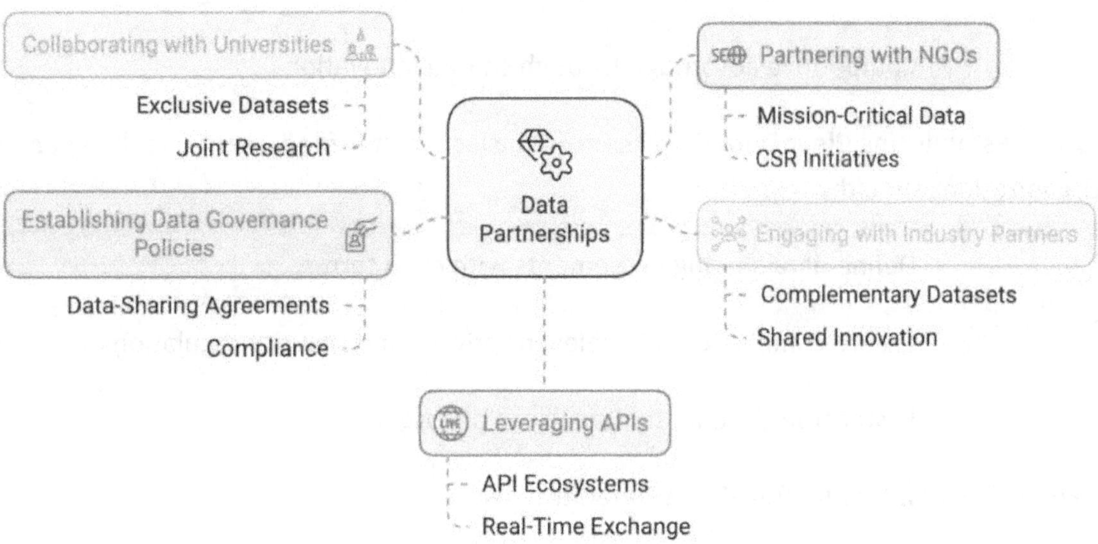

Strategies for Securing Data Partnerships

To harness the power of external data and foster innovation, organizations must adopt effective strategies for securing data partnerships. Key approaches include:

- **Collaborating with Universities**: Academic institutions are valuable partners for accessing cutting-edge research and experimental data. Establishing partnerships with universities can provide the following:

- Exclusive access to specialized datasets.
- Opportunities for joint research and innovation.
- Collaboration with thought leaders and emerging talent.

- **Partnering with NGOs**: Non-governmental organizations (NGOs) often manage data in critical domains such as public health, environment, and social sciences. Collaborating with NGOs enables organizations to:
  - Access mission-critical data for societal impact projects.
  - Strengthen corporate social responsibility (CSR) initiatives.
  - Gain insights from grassroots-level data sources.
- **Engaging with Industry Partners**: Strategic alliances with other companies can lead to mutually beneficial data sharing. This approach provides:
  - Access to complementary datasets.
  - Enhanced capabilities for joint product or service offerings.
  - Competitive advantage through shared innovation.
- **Establishing Clear Data Governance Policies**: Trust is fundamental in data partnerships. Organizations should:
  - Define data-sharing agreements with clear terms.
  - Ensure compliance with relevant privacy and security regulations.
  - Foster transparency in data usage and rights.

Leveraging APIs to Integrate Real-Time Data Streams

Application Programming Interfaces (APIs) are critical tools for effectively integrating and managing real-time data streams. Organizations can leverage APIs by:

- **Building API Ecosystems**:
  - Develop and maintain APIs that allow seamless integration with external systems.
  - Offer developers comprehensive API documentation and support.
- **Enabling Real-Time Data Exchange**:

- Use APIs to collect, process, and distribute live data streams.
- Ensure high availability and low latency in API services.

- **Enhancing Decision-Making**:
  - Incorporate real-time data from APIs into dashboards and analytics tools.
  - Enable dynamic responses to changing market or operational conditions.
- **Implementing Robust Security Measures**:
  - Authenticate API users with secure protocols (e.g., OAuth 2.0).
  - Monitor API traffic to prevent abuse or breaches.
- **Encouraging External Innovation**:
  - Provide APIs for external developers to create complementary applications.
  - Foster a developer community through hackathons and partnerships.

By strategically forming data partnerships and leveraging APIs, organizations can unlock new opportunities for innovation, enhance operational efficiency, and strengthen their competitive edge in the data-driven economy.

2.2: DATA TYPES AND FORMATS

2.2.1 TYPES OF DATA IN AI

Structured Data: Structured data is organized and stored in a defined manner, typically within tables or databases. It is easy to search, process, and analyze.

- **Examples:**
  - Spreadsheets containing financial transactions.
  - Relational databases for customer information.
  - Data warehouses are used for predictive modeling in business intelligence.

Unstructured Data: Unstructured data lacks a predefined format, making it more challenging to analyze. However, it represents a significant portion of data available today and is highly valuable in AI applications.

- **Examples:**
  - Images: Used in computer vision for object detection and recognition.
  - Text: Utilized in natural language processing (NLP) tasks like sentiment analysis and machine translation.
  - Audio: Leveraged in speech recognition systems and virtual assistants.

Semi-Structured Data: Semi-structured data is not stored in relational databases but still has some organizational properties, such as tags or markers, that make it easier to analyze than unstructured data.

- **Examples:**
  - JSON files are used in web APIs for data exchange.
  - XML formats for configuration files in software applications.
  - Logs and metadata that blend structured and unstructured elements.

Multimodal Data: Multimodal data combines multiple data types to create more comprehensive insights, particularly in complex AI systems.

- **Examples:**
  - Image and text data are used in healthcare diagnostics to improve diagnosis accuracy, such as by combining X-ray images with patient records.
  - Video data with embedded audio for video analytics in surveillance systems.
  - IoT sensor data combined with geospatial data for innovative city applications.

Industry-Standard Formats for Data Exchange: Maintaining standardized data formats is critical for interoperability and efficient processing in AI systems. Common standards include:

- **CSV (Comma-Separated Values):** Widely used for structured data.
- **JSON (JavaScript Object Notation):** A lightweight format for data exchange, especially in APIs.
- **XML (Extensible Markup Language):** Common in legacy systems and for hierarchical data.
- **Parquet and ORC:** Optimized formats for big data storage and processing.
- **HDF5:** High-performance data format for storing large, complex datasets.

Best Practices for Handling Large-Scale Datasets: Efficient handling of large datasets ensures optimal performance of AI models. Key practices include:

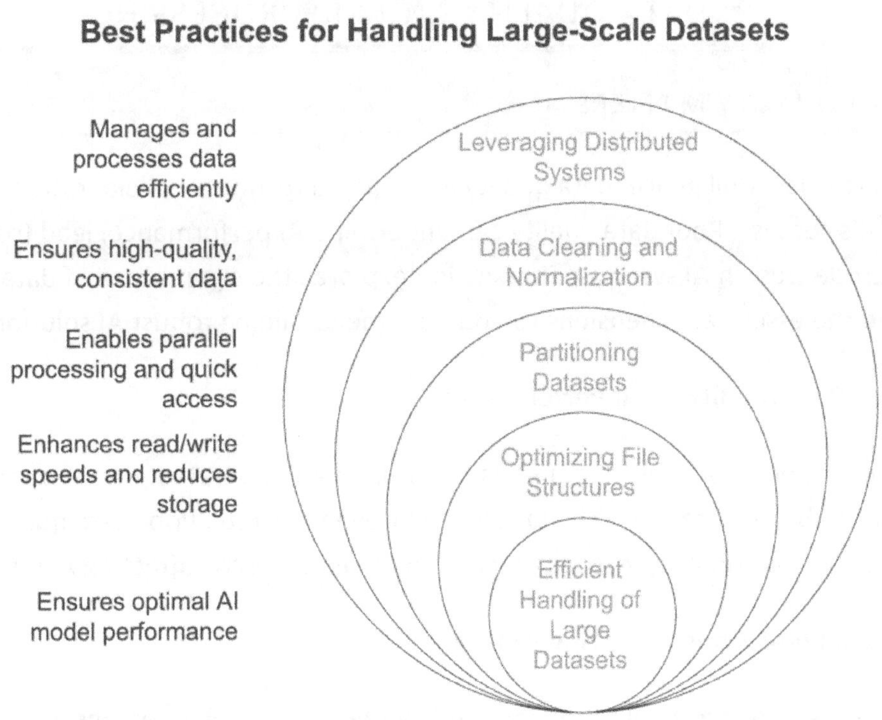

- **Optimizing File Structures:**
  - Use binary formats like Parquet or Avro for faster read/write speeds.
  - Compress files to reduce storage requirements and enhance processing speed.

- **Partitioning Datasets:**
    - Break datasets into smaller chunks for parallel processing.
    - Implement indexing to allow quicker access to specific data points.
- **Data Cleaning and Normalization:**
    - Eliminate duplicates and inconsistencies to ensure high-quality data.
    - Normalize data to a consistent format, such as standardizing date formats and units of measurement.
- **Leveraging Distributed Systems:**
    - Use distributed frameworks like Apache Hadoop or Apache Spark to efficiently manage and process large datasets.

Adhering to these best practices and standards allows AI systems to process data more effectively, resulting in better performance and scalability.

2.3: DATA QUALITY AND PREPROCESSING

2.3.1 WHY DATA QUALITY MATTERS

In the age of artificial intelligence, data quality is not just a technical consideration—it is a critical determinant of AI's success. Poor data quality can undermine AI performance, lead to biased outcomes, and erode trust in AI systems. This section explores the significance of data quality, its impact on AI, and the essential dimensions to address when building robust AI solutions.

Impact of Poor Data Quality on AI Performance

Data is the foundation upon which AI models are trained and operated. If this foundation is flawed, the results produced by AI systems can be unreliable or even harmful. Poor data quality manifests in various ways, such as inaccuracies, inconsistencies, and biases directly affecting AI performance.

Example: Biased Predictions in a Hiring AI Tool

Consider a hiring AI tool designed to recommend candidates for job openings. It could produce biased predictions if the training dataset is incomplete—omitting key variables like candidates' educational backgrounds or prior achievements. For instance:

- **Unintended Bias**: The model may favor candidates from specific demographics due to historical biases embedded in the data.

- **Missed Opportunities**: Highly qualified candidates could be overlooked due to the model's inability to recognize critical, missing data patterns.

- **Legal and Ethical Ramifications**: Biased hiring processes violate ethical standards, putting the organization at risk of legal challenges and reputational damage.

This example underscores the ripple effect of poor data quality on AI's technical performance, organizational goals, and societal impact.

Key Quality Dimensions

To mitigate the risks associated with poor data quality, organizations must prioritize the following key dimensions of data quality:

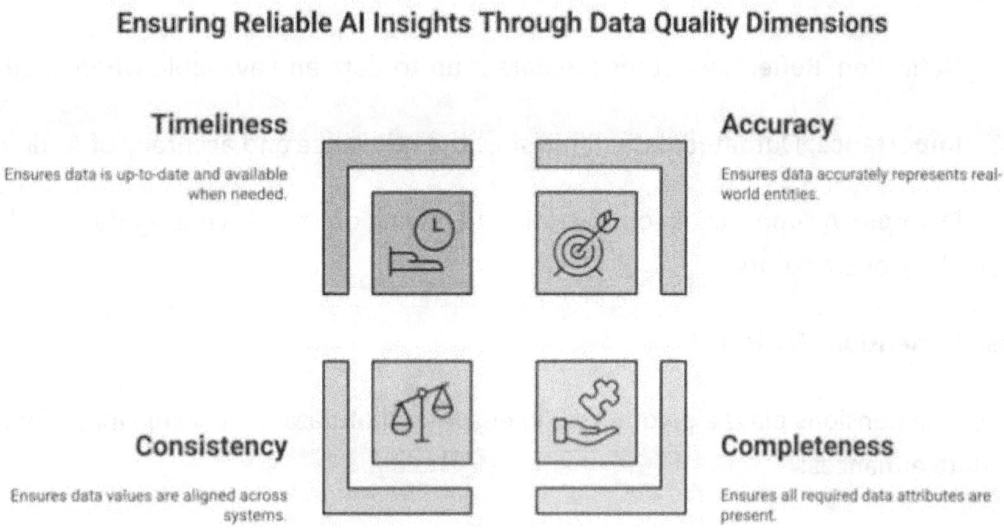

1. Accuracy

- **Definition**: Refers to how well the data represents the real-world entities it aims to describe.

- **Importance**: Accurate data ensures that AI models make correct inferences and decisions.

- **Example**: In a healthcare AI system, inaccurate patient records could lead to incorrect diagnoses and treatment plans.

2. Completeness

- **Definition**: Ensures all required data attributes are present and no critical information is missing.

- **Importance**: Incomplete data leads to gaps in model training, reducing the reliability of AI predictions.
- **Example**: A financial AI system missing transaction details might fail to detect fraudulent activities.

3. Consistency

- **Definition**: Ensures that data values are aligned across all systems and datasets.
- **Importance**: Consistent data prevents conflicts and errors in AI algorithms.
- **Example**: Inconsistent date format (e.g., MM/DD/YYYY vs. DD/MM/YYYY) can lead to errors in time-series forecasting models.

4. Timeliness

- **Definition**: Reflects whether the data is up-to-date and available when needed.
- **Importance**: Outdated data diminishes the relevance and accuracy of AI-driven insights.
- **Example**: A supply chain optimization AI relying on stale inventory data could result in overstocking or stockouts.

Why These Dimensions Matter

Each of these dimensions plays a pivotal role in ensuring that data is a reliable input for AI models. High-quality data enhances:

- **Model Performance**: Improves the precision and recall of AI predictions.
- **Scalability**: Enables AI models to adapt effectively to new data and scenarios.
- **Trustworthiness**: Builds confidence in AI outcomes among stakeholders.

In contrast, neglecting these dimensions increases the likelihood of errors, inefficiencies, and ethical breaches, ultimately limiting AI systems' potential to deliver value.

Data quality is not optional but a prerequisite for building trustworthy and high-performing AI systems. Organizations can unlock AI's true potential while mitigating risks and biases by addressing critical quality dimensions—accuracy, completeness, consistency, and timeliness. This proactive approach ensures that AI serves as a force for innovation, fairness, and success.

2.3.2 PREPROCESSING TECHNIQUES

Data preprocessing is a crucial step in any AI project, as the quality of the input data directly impacts the performance of machine learning models. This section explores key preprocessing techniques, their methodologies, and their importance in building robust AI systems.

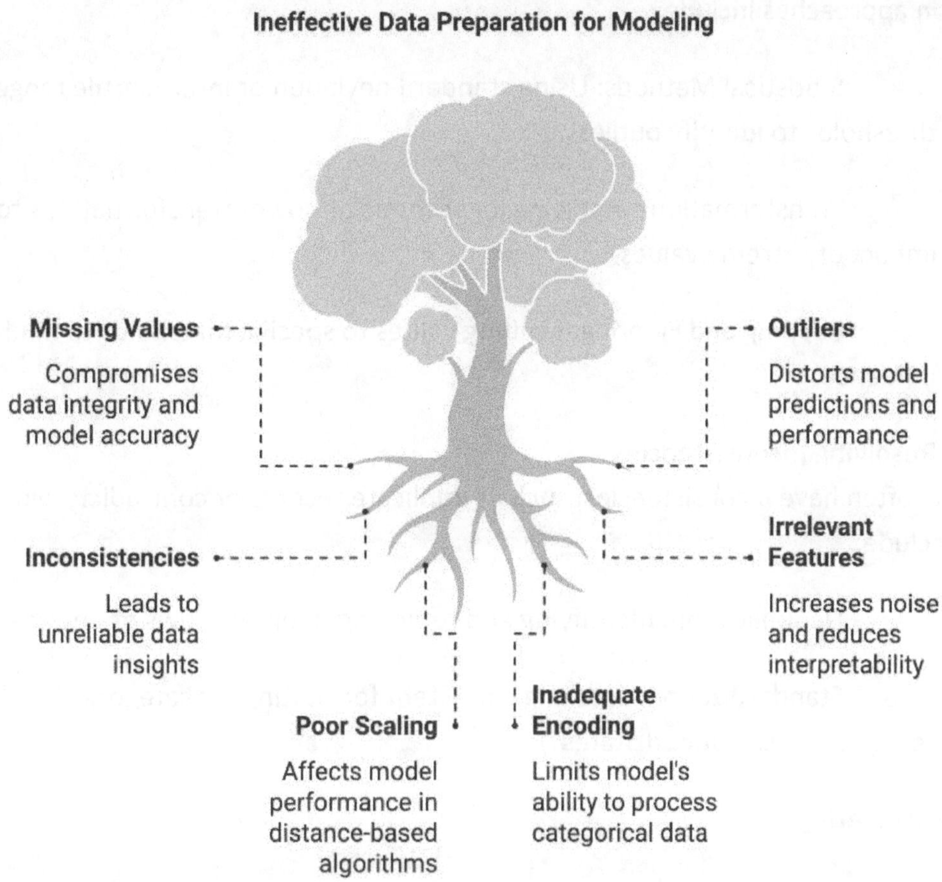

1. Data Cleaning

Data cleaning focuses on preparing raw data to ensure consistency, accuracy, and usability. The primary objectives are to handle missing values, outliers, and inconsistencies that could adversely affect model performance.

- **Handling Missing Values**

  Missing data can arise due to various reasons, such as equipment failure, data entry errors, or incomplete data collection processes. Techniques include:

  - Imputation: Filling in missing values using statistical methods (mean, median, or mode) or machine learning-based predictions.

  - Deletion is the Removal of records or features with significant missing data, significantly when it doesn’t compromise the dataset's integrity.

- Domain-Specific Handling: Leveraging business rules or domain knowledge to fill gaps.

- **Outlier Detection and Treatment**

Outliers can distort model predictions, especially in sensitive algorithms like regression. Common approaches include:

  - Statistical Methods: Using standard deviation or interquartile range (IQR) thresholds to identify outliers.
  - Transformations: Applying logarithmic or power transformations to reduce the impact of extreme values.
  - Capping and Flooring: Limiting values to specific thresholds to minimize their influence.

- **Resolving Inconsistencies**

Datasets often have inconsistencies, such as duplicate records or contradictory data entries. Steps include:

  - Deduplication: Identifying and removing duplicate rows or entities.
  - Standardization: Ensuring consistent formatting for categorical and textual data (e.g., "USA" vs. "United States").

2. Feature Engineering

Feature engineering involves creating new variables or modifying existing ones to represent the underlying patterns in the data better, thereby enhancing model performance.

- **Creating New Features**
  - **Derived Features**: Combining or transforming existing features, such as creating an "age" feature from a "birthdate."
  - **Aggregated Features**: Summarizing granular data, such as calculating average purchase frequency or total sales.
  - **Interaction Features**: Combining two or more features to capture relationships, such as multiplying "price" and "quantity" to calculate "revenue."
- **Feature Selection**
  - Removing irrelevant or redundant features to reduce noise and improve model interpretability.

- Utilizing correlation analysis, mutual information, and feature importance scores from tree-based models.

- **Dimensionality Reduction**
Techniques such as Principal Component Analysis (PCA) or t-SNE can reduce the dataset's dimensionality while retaining its informational value.

3. Data Transformation

Data transformation prepares data for machine learning algorithms by altering its scale, distribution, or encoding.

- **Scaling**
Ensures that all features contribute equally to the model, particularly for distance-based algorithms. Techniques include:
    - **Standardization**: Rescaling data with a mean of 0 and a standard deviation 1.
    - **Normalization**: Converting values to a [0, 1] range.
- **Encoding**
Converts categorical data into numerical formats. Methods include:
    - **One-Hot Encoding**: Representing categories as binary vectors.
    - **Label Encoding**: Assigning unique numerical labels to categories.
- **Normalization of Text and Time-Series Data**
    - Text: Tokenization, stemming, lemmatization, and stop-word removal.
    - Time-Series: Smoothing techniques, resampling, and trend removal.

4. Visual: Preprocessing Pipeline for AI Projects

Visualizing preprocessing steps aids in understanding the flow of data transformation and ensuring reproducibility.

- **Pipeline Design**
A preprocessing pipeline typically includes:
    1. Data Ingestion
    2. Cleaning and Validation
    3. Feature Transformation

4. Feature Selection

5. Output Preparation for Modeling

- **Visualization Tools**
Tools like Python's sklearn.pipeline, pandas profiling, and visual flowcharts in tools like Airflow or Dragster can depict these steps.

By implementing the above preprocessing techniques, AI practitioners can create cleaner, more representative datasets, ensuring better model performance and reliability.

2.3.3 AUTOMATION IN PREPROCESSING

Data preprocessing is a critical step in any AI or machine learning pipeline. It ensures that the data fed into models is clean, consistent, and in the correct format. Automation in preprocessing improves efficiency and minimizes human errors, enabling faster and more reliable model development. This section delves into the tools and libraries available for data preprocessing and explores how AI pipelines can automate repetitive tasks.

Tools and Libraries for Data Preprocessing
The availability of robust tools and libraries has revolutionized the preprocessing stage by enabling seamless handling of diverse datasets. Below are some widely used tools and their roles in preprocessing:

1. **Pandas**

    - A Python library designed for data manipulation and analysis.

    - It offers functionalities like filtering, aggregation, handling missing values, and reshaping datasets.

    - Example Use Case: Cleaning a dataset by removing null values or imputing missing values with the median or mean.

    - Automatable Feature: Chaining operations with method chaining (df.pipe()) to create reproducible workflows.

2. **NumPy**

    - The backbone of numerical computations in Python.

    - Enables efficient array operations, mathematical transformations, and statistical analysis.

    - Example Use Case: Standardizing numerical features to a standard scale using numpy.mean and numpy.std.

- Automatable Feature: Integration with loops and batch processing for large datasets.

3. **TensorFlow Data**

   - A specialized library for handling large-scale datasets for machine learning.

   - Provides functionality to create input pipelines that preprocess data on the fly during model training.

   - Example Use Case: Loading and preprocessing image datasets using tf.data—dataset for real-time augmentation.

   - Automatable Feature: Seamless integration with TensorFlow workflows, reducing manual intervention.

Automating Repetitive Tasks with AI Pipelines

Preprocessing automation primarily reduces manual effort in repetitive tasks such as cleaning, normalization, feature engineering, and augmentation. AI pipelines enable the systematic and automated execution of these tasks.

1. **Building Pipelines with Scikit-learn**

   - Scikit-learn's Pipeline module helps chain preprocessing steps such as scaling, encoding, and feature selection.

   - Example: Combining StandardScaler and OneHotEncoder for automated scaling and encoding during cross-validation.

2. **Feature Stores**

   - Tools like Databricks Feature Store and Feast allow centralized storage of preprocessed features.

   - These features can be shared across teams and reused in different models, saving preprocessing time.

3. **AI-Powered Data Cleaning Tools**

   - Emerging tools powered by AI, like Cleanlab, detect and correct mislabeled or inconsistent data.

   - They reduce human intervention by leveraging machine learning to identify anomalies.

4. **Batch Processing and Parallelization**

- Libraries like Apache Spark and Dask enable preprocessing at scale by distributing tasks across multiple nodes.
- Example: Handling terabytes of unstructured log data to extract meaningful features.

5. **End-to-End Workflow Automation**
   - Platforms like Kubeflow and Apache Airflow allow the orchestration of preprocessing steps in a reproducible manner.
   - These pipelines can trigger preprocessing automatically when new data is ingested.

Automation in preprocessing accelerates the data preparation phase while ensuring consistency and quality. By leveraging tools like Pandas, NumPy, and TensorFlow Data and adopting AI pipelines, organizations can streamline their workflows, focus on model innovation, and reduce the time to market for AI solutions.

2.4: DATA GOVERNANCE AND PRIVACY

2.4.1 THE NEED FOR GOVERNANCE

Data governance is the framework of policies, standards, practices, and tools that ensures data is managed as an asset across its lifecycle. As enterprises become increasingly data-driven, robust governance is critical for maintaining data integrity, usability, and security. Below are three core principles of data governance:

1. **Ownership:**
   - **Definition:** Ownership refers to clearly assigning accountability for data assets. Every dataset should have a designated data owner responsible for its accuracy, accessibility, and relevance.
   - **Key Aspects:**
     - Data ownership is often divided across departments or roles to ensure domain-specific expertise is applied.
     - Data stewards may assist owners in implementing policies and handling day-to-day oversight.
   - **Challenges:**

- Lack of ownership often results in inconsistent data practices and data silos.
- Overlapping responsibilities can create confusion about who is accountable for specific datasets.

2. **Security:**
   - **Definition:** Security focuses on protecting data from unauthorized access, breaches, and misuse.
   - **Key Aspects:**
     - Access Control: Implementing least-privilege principles ensures that only authorized personnel can access sensitive data.
     - Encryption: Data should be encrypted both in transit and at rest to protect it from malicious actors.
     - Monitoring and Auditing: Regular and real-time tracking is crucial to detect vulnerabilities or unauthorized activities.
   - **Challenges:**
     - Balancing robust security measures with accessibility for legitimate users can be complex.
     - Adapting to evolving cyber threats requires continuous updates and training.
3. **Lifecycle Management:**
   - **Definition:** Lifecycle management involves overseeing data from its creation to its disposal.
   - **Key Aspects:**
     - Data Creation: Ensuring data is captured accurately and in a standardized format.
     - Maintenance: Regularly updating, cleaning, and archiving data to retain its value.
     - Disposal: Securely delete data that no longer needs to be deleted, ensuring compliance with legal and regulatory requirements.
   - **Challenges:**

- Inadequate disposal practices can lead to data leaks or compliance breaches.
- Outdated data can distort analytics and decision-making.

Examples from High-Stakes Industries

The importance of data governance becomes evident in industries where data accuracy, security, and compliance directly impact lives and finances. Below are two examples:

1. **Healthcare:**
    - **Context:** In healthcare, data governs patient records, research data, and operational information. Proper governance ensures compliance with regulations such as HIPAA (Health Insurance Portability and Accountability Act).
    - **Case Study:**
        - Inaccurate patient records can lead to incorrect diagnoses or treatments, endangering lives.
        - Governance frameworks help ensure patient data is accurate, secure, and accessible to authorized healthcare providers.
    - **Challenges and Consequences:**
        - Breaches in healthcare data can result in lawsuits, regulatory penalties, and erosion of trust.
        - A lack of standardized governance can impede data sharing across hospitals and research institutions.
2. **Finance:**
    - **Context:** Data underpins decision-making, fraud prevention, and regulatory compliance in the financial sector. Governance is essential to meeting standards like GDPR, SOX (Sarbanes-Oxley Act), and Basel III.
    - **Case Study:**
        - During the 2008 financial crisis, inadequate data governance contributed to the lack of transparency in mortgage-backed securities, amplifying systemic risks.
        - Effective governance ensures transparency, auditability, and risk management in financial transactions.
    - **Challenges and Consequences:**

- Data breaches or inaccuracies can lead to significant financial losses, reputational damage, and legal repercussions.
- Poor data lifecycle management may result in outdated or redundant financial models.

Data governance is no longer a "nice-to-have" but a necessity for modern enterprises. By adhering to principles of ownership, security, and lifecycle management, organizations can mitigate risks and harness the full potential of their data assets. High-stakes industries such as healthcare and finance exemplify how governance frameworks safeguard lives and livelihoods while enabling innovation and growth. As data grows in volume and complexity, the need for robust governance will only intensify.

2.4.2 PRIVACY LAWS AND COMPLIANCE

In an era where data is the lifeblood of businesses, adhering to privacy laws and compliance standards is not just a legal obligation but a crucial component of building trust with customers and stakeholders. This section explores key regulations such as GDPR, CCPA, and HIPAA and discusses actionable strategies for aligning with these legal requirements through advanced data protection techniques

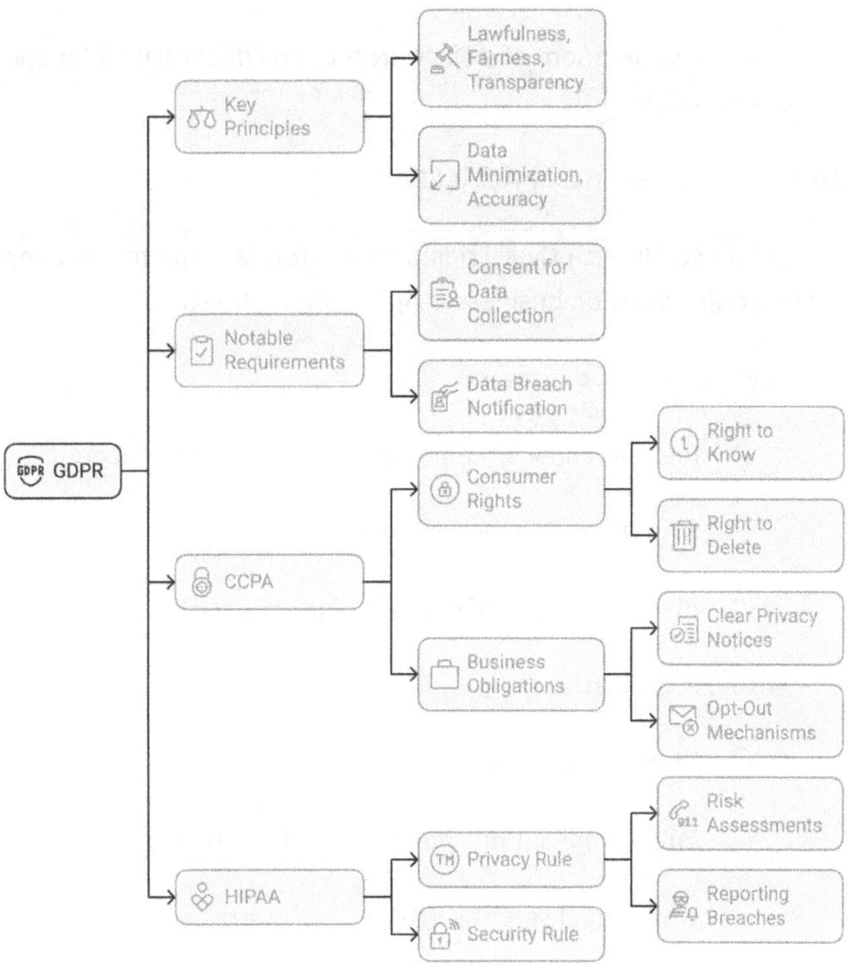

Key Regulations

1. **General Data Protection Regulation (GDPR)**
   - GDPR is a comprehensive data protection law enacted in the European Union. It has a global impact on organizations that process the personal data of EU residents.
   - **Key Principles**:
     - Lawfulness, fairness, and transparency.
     - Data minimization and accuracy.
     - Accountability and purpose limitation.
   - **Notable Requirements**:
     - Consent for data collection and usage.
     - Data breach notification within 72 hours.
     - Right to access, rectification, and data erasure ("right to be forgotten").
     - Appointment of a Data Protection Officer (DPO) for specific organizations.
2. **California Consumer Privacy Act (CCPA)**
   - CCPA establishes privacy rights for California residents and imposes data protection obligations on businesses operating in the state.
   - **Key Rights for Consumers**:
     - Right to know what personal data is being collected.
     - Right to delete personal data.
     - Right to opt out of the sale of personal data.
   - **Business Obligations**:
     - Provide clear privacy notices.
     - Enable opt-out mechanisms for data sharing.
     - Offer equal services irrespective of privacy choices.
3. **Health Insurance Portability and Accountability Act (HIPAA)**

- HIPAA governs the protection of health information in the United States.
- **Key Components**:
  - Privacy Rule: Safeguards the confidentiality of Protected Health Information (PHI).
  - Security Rule: Specifies technical safeguards for electronic PHI (ePHI).
- **Requirements for Covered Entities**:
  - Risk assessments for data security.
  - Implementation of access controls, encryption, and audit trails.
  - Reporting of breaches to affected individuals and authorities.

How to Align with Legal Requirements

Organizations can achieve compliance with privacy laws by adopting best practices in data protection and governance. Below are some of the most effective strategies:

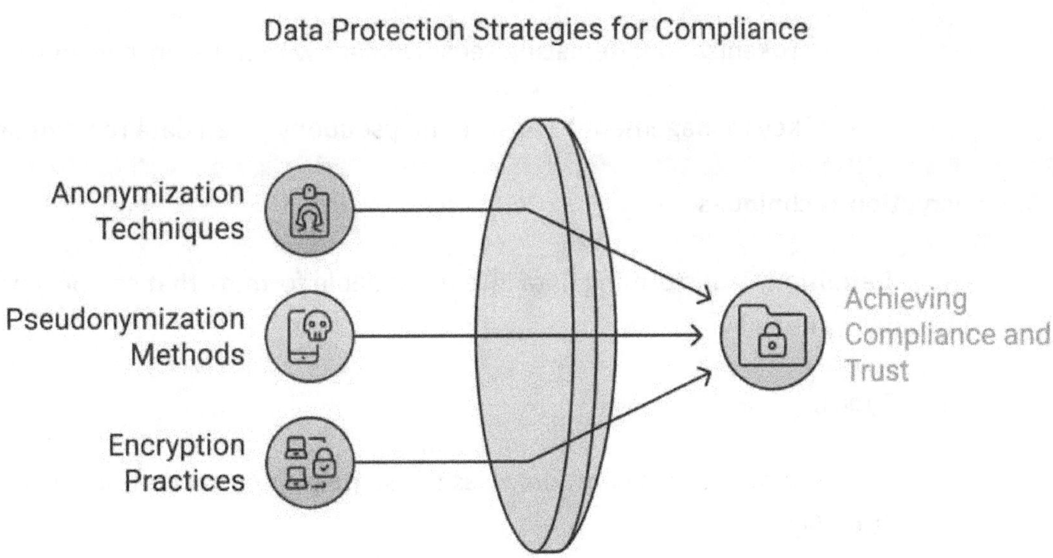

1. **Anonymization**
   - **Definition**: Irreversibly altering data to ensure it can no longer be associated with a specific individual.
   - **Techniques**:

- Generalization: Reducing data granularity, e.g., replacing exact birthdates with age ranges.
- Suppression: Removing identifiers such as names and social security numbers.

o **Applications**:

- Useful for statistical analysis and research where individual identification is unnecessary.

2. **Pseudonymization**

o **Definition**: Replacing identifiable data with pseudonyms (e.g., unique codes or tokens) while maintaining the ability to re-identify under strict controls.

o **Advantages**:

- Balances usability with privacy.
- Supports GDPR compliance by reducing data subject risks.

o **Implementation**:

- Tokenization: Replacing sensitive data with non-sensitive equivalents.
- Key management to ensure the pseudonymized data remains secure.

3. **Encryption Techniques**

o **Definition**: Transforming data into unreadable formats that can only be decoded with a decryption key.

o **Types**:

- Symmetric Encryption: Uses the same key for encryption and decryption (e.g., AES).
- Asymmetric Encryption: Uses public and private key pairs (e.g., RSA).

o **Best Practices**:

- Encrypt data at rest and in transit.
- Regularly update and rotate encryption keys.
- Use secure protocols like TLS for communication.

- **Compliance Benefits:**
    - Meets HIPAA's Security Rule for ePHI.
    - Strengthens data security for GDPR and CCPA adherence.

Compliance with privacy laws such as GDPR, CCPA, and HIPAA is a multifaceted challenge that requires technical and organizational measures. By employing advanced techniques like anonymization, pseudonymization, and encryption, businesses can safeguard personal data while maintaining compliance. Beyond legal obligations, these practices reinforce consumer trust, enhance data security, and position organizations as responsible data stewards in the digital age.

2.4.3 ENSURING SECURITY

Protecting Sensitive Data from Breaches

Data is the lifeblood of AI platforms, and ensuring its security is paramount to building trust and sustaining long-term success. Here's how to effectively protect sensitive data:

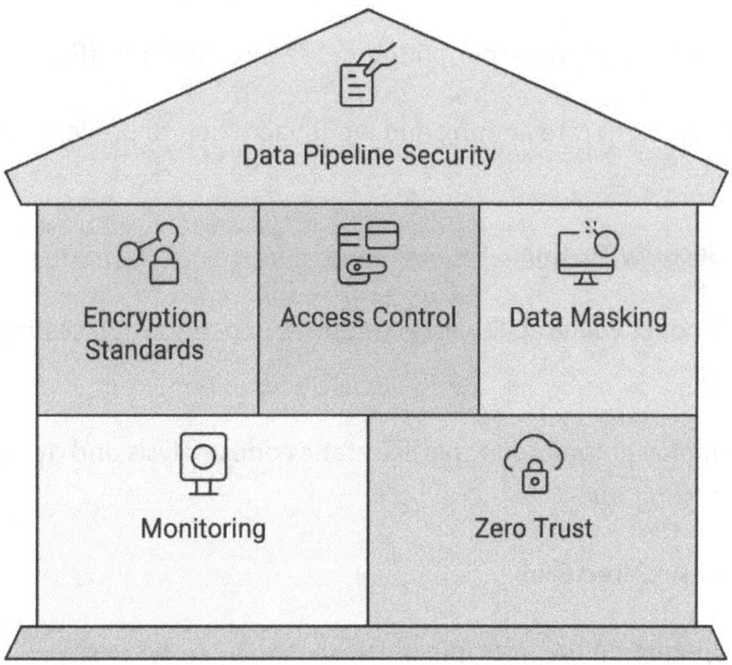

Best Practices for Securing Data Pipelines:

1. **Implement Encryption Standards**:
    - Use end-to-end encryption (e.g., AES-256) for data at rest and in transit.
    - Employ secure protocols like HTTPS, TLS, or VPNs to prevent data interception.

2. **Access Control and Authentication**:
   - Enforce role-based access control (RBAC) to ensure users only access what is necessary.
   - Implement multi-factor authentication (MFA) to add an extra layer of security.
3. **Data Masking and Anonymization**:
   - Use data masking techniques to obscure sensitive data in non-production environments.
   - Anonymize personal data to comply with regulations like GDPR and HIPAA.
4. **Monitor and Audit**:
   - Set up real-time monitoring of data pipelines to detect unusual activity.
   - Regularly audit logs for unauthorized access or anomalies.
5. **Secure API Endpoints**:
   - Use API gateways to monitor and secure all API traffic.
   - Implement rate limiting and input validation to prevent abuse or injection attacks.
6. **Regular Security Testing**:
   - Conduct vulnerability assessments and penetration testing to uncover weak points.
   - Employ automated tools like static code analysis and dynamic application security testing (DAST).
7. **Zero Trust Architecture**:
   - Operate on the principle of "never trust, always verify."
   - Continuously validate all users, devices, and applications accessing the data pipeline.

Common Security Pitfalls to Avoid:

- Weak or shared passwords among employees.
- Outdated software or unpatched vulnerabilities.

- Lack of encryption for sensitive datasets in storage.
- Failure to revoke access for terminated employees or vendors.

Case Study: AI Startup That Failed Due to a Security Breach

Overview: In 2022, an AI healthcare startup, "MediAI Solutions," faced catastrophic failure after a significant security breach exposed sensitive patient data. The breach caused irreparable harm to their reputation, leading to customer loss, regulatory fines, and eventual shutdown.

What Went Wrong:

1. **Unsecured Data Pipelines:**
   - MediAI transmitted sensitive patient data over unencrypted channels.
   - API endpoints were left exposed, making them vulnerable to malicious actors.
2. **Poor Access Control**:
   - Employees had unrestricted access to production systems.
   - Credentials for cloud services were stored in plaintext on shared documents.
3. **Lack of Monitoring**:
   - No intrusion detection system (IDS) was in place to identify unauthorized access.
   - The breach went unnoticed for months, exacerbating its impact.
4. **Non-compliance with Regulations**:
   - MediAI failed to comply with HIPAA standards, leading to hefty fines from regulatory authorities.

Impact:

- **Financial Loss**: The company faced over $5 million in fines and legal settlements.
- **Reputation Damage**: The breach eroded customer trust, leading to contract terminations and market withdrawal.
- **Business Closure**: Within six months of the breach, MediAI declared bankruptcy.

Lessons Learned:

1. Prioritize security from day one as a core component of your business strategy.

2. Regularly update and test security protocols to adapt to evolving threats.

3. Invest in a robust incident response plan to minimize damage during a breach.

By adopting best practices for securing data pipelines and learning from real-world failures like MediAI Solutions, AI startups can proactively safeguard their platforms and build trust in an increasingly competitive and security-conscious market.

2.4.4 TOOLS FOR GOVERNANCE

AI Governance Platforms and Frameworks

The success of AI governance depends heavily on the tools and platforms organizations use to manage, monitor, and enforce responsible AI practices. These tools enhance transparency and accountability and ensure alignment with ethical principles, compliance requirements, and organizational objectives. Below are some key aspects of AI governance platforms and frameworks, with an example for context.

1. Key Features of AI Governance Tools: AI governance platforms are designed to address various facets of the AI lifecycle. These tools often include:

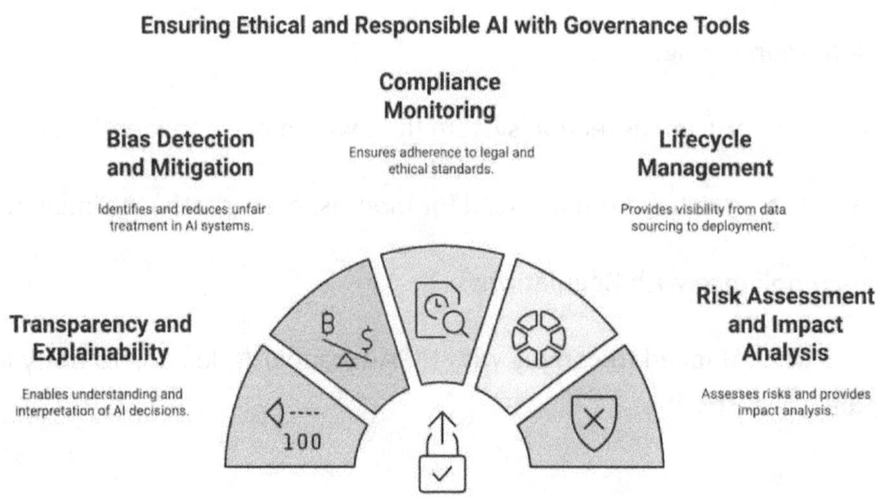

- **Transparency and Explainability:** Tools that enable organizations to understand and interpret AI model decisions. This is critical for gaining the trust of stakeholders and ensuring decisions are explainable to regulators and end-users.

- **Bias Detection and Mitigation:** Frameworks equipped with bias detection algorithms to identify and reduce unfair treatment or unintended outcomes across demographic groups.

- **Compliance Monitoring:** Features that ensure AI systems adhere to relevant legal, ethical, and regulatory standards, such as GDPR, CCPA, or industry-specific guidelines.

- **Lifecycle Management:** Tools that provide end-to-end visibility into the AI lifecycle, from data sourcing and model development to deployment and ongoing monitoring.
- **Risk Assessment and Impact Analysis:** Governance platforms often include mechanisms to assess risks associated with AI applications and provide impact analysis reports.

2. Example: Microsoft's Responsible AI Dashboard One standout tool in the AI governance landscape is Microsoft's **Responsible AI Dashboard**, which offers a robust set of features to manage AI ethics and compliance effectively. Here's how it addresses key governance needs:

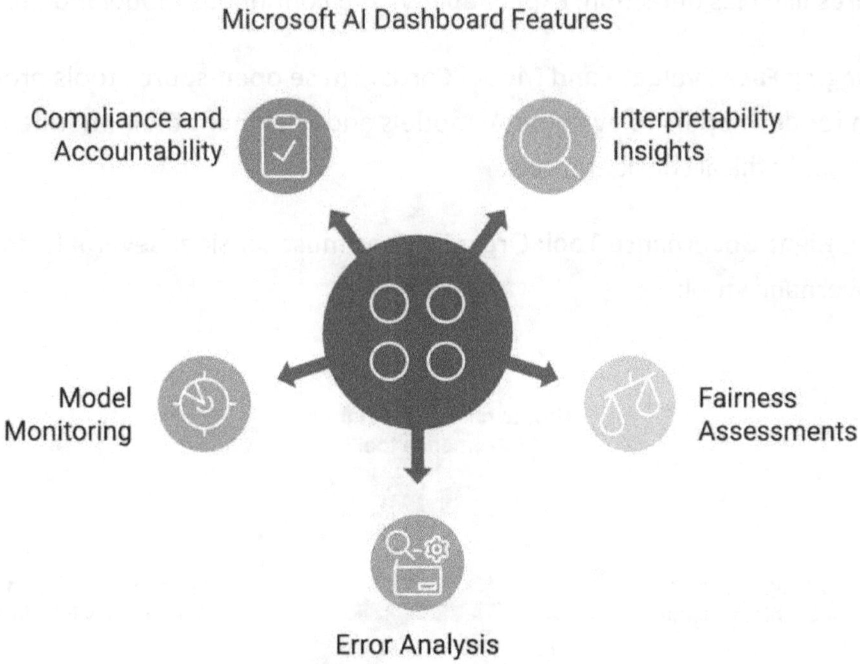

- **Interpretability Insights:** The dashboard provides interpretability tools to help developers and stakeholders understand the factors driving model predictions. This enables organizations to make informed decisions about deploying AI systems.
- **Fairness Assessments:** The Responsible AI Dashboard uses fairness metrics and visualization tools to highlight potential disparities in model performance across different demographic groups, helping organizations systematically address bias.
- **Error Analysis:** The platform includes error analysis features to identify data segments or scenarios where AI models may perform poorly, allowing targeted improvements.
- **Model Monitoring:** The dashboard integrates with tools for ongoing monitoring of AI systems post-deployment, ensuring that models remain effective and fair over time.

- **Compliance and Accountability:** By centralizing AI governance processes, the dashboard enables organizations to document decisions,.track changes, and demonstrate compliance to regulators or internal auditors.

3. Other Notable Tools and Frameworks: While Microsoft's Responsible AI Dashboard is a prominent example, other platforms also play significant roles in AI governance:

- **Google's Explainable AI:** Google offers tools for building interpretable and transparent AI systems, including What-If Tool and Explainable AI SDK.

- **IBM Watson OpenScale:** IBM's AI governance tool emphasizes trust and transparency, with features like bias detection, explainability, and continuous model monitoring.

- **Hugging Face Evaluate and Model Cards:** These open-source tools provide an ecosystem for developers to evaluate AI models and document their intended use cases, limitations, and ethical considerations.

4. Choosing the Right Governance Tool: Organizations must consider several factors when selecting an AI governance tool:

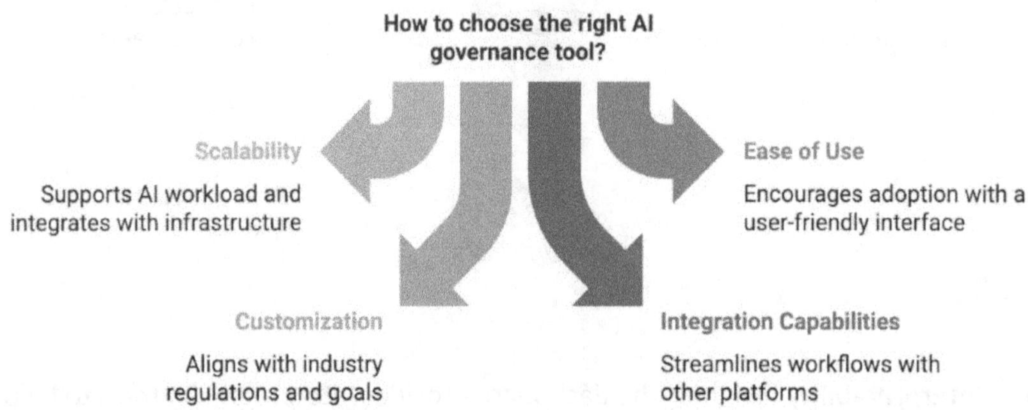

- **Scalability:** The platform should support the organization's AI workload and integrate seamlessly with existing infrastructure.

- **Ease of Use:** A user-friendly interface and clear documentation are essential for encouraging adoption across teams.

- **Customization:** Tools should allow customization to align with specific industry regulations and organizational goals.

- **Integration Capabilities:** Governance tools must integrate with other AI development and deployment platforms to streamline workflows.

In conclusion, AI governance platforms like Microsoft's Responsible AI Dashboard and similar tools provide critical support in enforcing responsible AI practices. By leveraging these tools, organizations can achieve greater transparency, fairness, and accountability, setting a strong foundation for the ethical deployment of AI systems.

2.5: ETHICAL CONSIDERATIONS IN AI

2.5.1 SOURCES OF BIAS IN AI

Artificial Intelligence systems are only as unbiased as the data they are trained on and the algorithms that define their behavior. Bias in AI can stem from various sources, ranging from the data collection process to the optimization strategies employed. Understanding these sources is critical to mitigating bias and ensuring AI fairness, accuracy, and inclusivity.

Data Bias

Data bias occurs when the dataset used to train AI models does not accurately represent the diversity of the real-world scenarios the AI will encounter. This can manifest in multiple forms, such as underrepresentation, overrepresentation, or erroneous labeling of certain groups or characteristics. Data bias is one of the primary reasons AI models fail to perform equitably across different populations.

Example: Underrepresentation in Datasets for Facial Recognition AI

Facial recognition systems have often been criticized for their inability to identify individuals from underrepresented demographics accurately. For instance:

- Many facial recognition datasets predominantly feature lighter-skinned individuals, and models perform significantly better for these groups than individuals with darker skin tones.
- A study by MIT Media Lab revealed that commercial facial recognition systems had error rates of up to 34.7% for darker-skinned women, while the error rate for lighter-skinned men was only 0.8%.

Impact: This bias can lead to disproportionate adverse effects, such as wrongful arrests or exclusion from critical systems like ID verification for financial transactions.

Solution: To address data bias, organizations should adopt practices like:

- Collecting diverse, representative datasets across all demographic and contextual variations.
- Employing data augmentation techniques to balance datasets.

- Applying fairness-aware pre-processing techniques to identify and correct biases before model training.

Algorithmic Bias

Algorithmic bias arises from how AI systems are designed, optimized, and evaluated. Even with unbiased data, the chosen optimization goals or decision rules can unintentionally prioritize one group over another, leading to unfair outcomes.

Example: Misaligned Optimization Goals Causing Fairness Issues

AI systems are often optimized for metrics like accuracy or efficiency, which may not account for fairness or equity. For example:

- Optimizing solely for past hiring trends in hiring algorithms could reinforce existing disparities by perpetuating biases against underrepresented groups in specific industries.

- In healthcare, an algorithm predicting patient risk might overestimate risk for one group while underestimating it for another, leading to unequal treatment access.

Impact: Algorithmic bias can systematically disadvantage certain groups, perpetuating inequities in access to resources, opportunities, or justice.

Solution: Effective strategies to mitigate algorithmic bias include:

- Implementing fairness constraints during model training.

- Regularly auditing algorithms for disparate impacts across demographic groups.

- Leveraging Explainable AI (XAI) techniques to understand and address bias in decision-making processes.

Case Study: Addressing Bias in an AI-Powered Lending Platform

AI-powered lending platforms are one real-world application where bias has significant consequences. These platforms use predictive models to assess creditworthiness, but biases in data and algorithms can lead to discriminatory lending practices.

Scenario:

- A lending platform uses historical data to predict loan defaults and assigns credit scores accordingly.

- Historical data reflects systemic biases, such as lower credit availability to specific demographics due to discriminatory lending practices.

Challenges:

- Data Bias: The training data underrepresents borrowers from historically marginalized communities or inaccurately associates them with higher risk.
- Algorithmic Bias: The optimization goals prioritize minimizing loan defaults without factoring in fairness, leading to discriminatory loan approval rates.

Interventions:

1. **Dataset Evaluation**:
   - Identify and rectify biases in historical data by ensuring adequate representation of all demographic groups.
   - Apply techniques like reweighting or sampling to correct historical imbalances.
2. **Fairness-Aware Modeling**:
   - Use fairness-aware algorithms that balance predictive accuracy with equitable outcomes.
   - Implement multi-objective optimization to incorporate fairness constraints.
3. **Continuous Monitoring**:
   - Regularly audit the lending decisions to detect and address new biases that emerge as societal patterns shift.
   - Engage diverse stakeholders, including regulators, consumer advocates, and technical experts, to review the platform's performance.

Outcome: By addressing data and algorithmic biases, the lending platform can improve fairness, increase user trust, and ensure compliance with anti-discrimination regulations.

Bias in AI is a multifaceted challenge that requires a proactive and holistic approach. Every stage of the AI development lifecycle offers opportunities to reduce bias, from ensuring diverse and representative datasets to designing algorithms that explicitly prioritize fairness. By adopting robust mitigation strategies and learning from case studies like lending platforms, organizations can develop AI systems that are accurate, efficient, equitable, and inclusive.

2.5.2 FAIRNESS AND TRANSPARENCY

Why Explainable AI (XAI) Matters for Trust

Incorporating fairness and transparency in AI systems is essential for fostering trust and ensuring ethical outcomes, especially in sensitive applications such as healthcare, finance, and legal systems. Explainable AI (XAI) bridges the opaque decision-making processes of complex AI models and human comprehension. XAI enables stakeholders to understand, trust, and effectively debug AI systems, aligning their functionality with ethical standards and organizational objectives.

Transparency is a regulatory requirement and a foundational element of responsible AI. Without it, users and stakeholders question the credibility and motivations behind AI-driven decisions. Fairness and transparency also help address bias-related concerns, mitigate potential risks, and increase the adoption of AI systems across diverse sectors.

Key Techniques for Achieving Explainable AI

1. **SHAP (SHapley Additive exPlanations):**

    - SHAP is a unified framework that explains the output of machine learning models by allocating contributions of each input feature toward the final prediction.
    - **How it works:** SHAP calculates feature importance based on cooperative game theory, assigning each feature a "Shapley value" that represents its contribution.
    - **Use cases:** This is ideal for high-stakes applications like credit scoring or fraud detection, where stakeholders require detailed explanations of how features influence predictions.

2. **LIME (Local Interpretable Model-Agnostic Explanations):**

    - LIME creates locally interpretable surrogate models for complex AI systems. It explains predictions by approximating the original model with a simpler, interpretable model like a linear regression or decision tree in a localized area of interest.
    - **How it works:** LIME perturbs the input data and observes changes in the model's predictions, allowing it to highlight which features influence a specific decision most.
    - **Use cases:** This is suitable for real-time scenarios, such as recommendation systems or customer service chatbots, where quick, interpretable feedback is necessary.

3. **Decision Trees:**

    - Decision trees are inherently interpretable models representing decisions as a tree structure with clear paths from the root to the leaf nodes.
    - **How it works:** Each node in the tree represents a feature split, and leaf nodes provide the prediction. The simplicity of the tree makes it easy for humans to trace and understand the decision process.

- **Use cases are** handy in domains like medical diagnostics or compliance checks, where clarity is paramount for stakeholder acceptance.

Example: Debugging Predictions for Medical Diagnostics

Imagine an AI model deployed for early cancer detection in a healthcare setting. While the model achieves high accuracy, a lack of transparency in its predictions makes it difficult for healthcare professionals to trust its results fully. Here's how XAI can address this challenge:

1. **SHAP Application:**
   - SHAP can identify which clinical features (e.g., tumor size, patient age, genetic markers) contributed most to the model's prediction for a particular patient. For instance, if the model predicts a high likelihood of cancer, SHAP can show that the presence of specific biomarkers was a primary driver of the decision.
2. **LIME in Action:**
   - LIME can simplify the local explanation of why the model flagged a specific case as positive or negative. This allows doctors to focus on key features influencing the decision and potentially identify errors or biases in the model.
3. **Decision Tree Analysis:**
   - Decision trees can serve as interpretable alternatives or supplements to complex models. For example, a tree could determine how input variables like family history or imaging results lead to a diagnostic decision. We can build trust with medical practitioners by offering an understandable rationale behind the predictions.

Benefits of Explainable AI in Trust-Building

1. **Improved Stakeholder Confidence:**
   - By providing clear explanations, XAI empowers stakeholders to trust AI predictions, especially in high-stakes environments.
2. **Bias Detection and Mitigation:**
   - Transparency allows organizations to identify and address biases in model predictions, ensuring fairness across demographics.
3. **Enhanced Debugging and Model Iteration:**
   - Explanations make it easier to debug erroneous predictions and improve model accuracy, reducing risks and increasing reliability.

4. **Regulatory Compliance:**

    - XAI supports adherence to legal and ethical requirements, such as GDPR or AI-specific governance frameworks, that mandate explainability.

Fairness and transparency, bolstered by XAI techniques, are indispensable for creating trustworthy and responsible AI systems. These approaches mitigate risks and pave the way for more widespread adoption of AI technologies in ethically sensitive and high-impact domains.

2.5.3 BUILDING RESPONSIBLE AI

Responsible AI is a foundational principle that ensures artificial intelligence systems are designed, developed, and deployed ethically and sustainably, minimizing potential harm while maximizing societal benefit. This section delves into ethical frameworks, practical tools, and guidelines for fostering responsible AI development and deployment.

Ethical Frameworks for Responsible AI

Ethical frameworks ensure that AI systems align with societal values, promote fairness, and avoid harm. They provide structured guidelines to address bias, transparency, accountability, and privacy issues.

- **IBM AI Fairness 360 Toolkit (AIF360):**
    - The IBM AI Fairness 360 toolkit is an open-source library that offers metrics to test datasets and machine learning models for bias and algorithms to mitigate bias throughout the AI lifecycle.
    - Example Use Case: A bank leveraging AIF360 to ensure their credit scoring models do not unfairly discriminate based on gender or ethnicity. The organization can improve equitable access to financial services by analyzing fairness metrics and applying mitigation techniques.
    - Advantages:
        - Accessibility: Easy-to-use tools and tutorials for developers.
        - Transparency: The open-source nature ensures it can be adapted for various use cases.
- **Other Ethical Frameworks:**
    - **Google AI Principles:** These principles emphasize safety, accountability, privacy, and avoiding creating or reinforcing unfair bias.

- **OECD Principles on AI:** These guidelines advocate for AI systems to benefit people and the planet, focusing on inclusivity, human rights, and democratic values.

These frameworks ensure that ethical considerations are embedded at every stage of the AI lifecycle, from ideation to deployment.

Guidelines for Responsible Development

Developing responsible AI requires adhering to practical guidelines addressing technical and social challenges. The following strategies are critical:

1. **Involving Diverse Teams to Reduce Bias:**
   - A diverse and multidisciplinary team brings varied perspectives, ensuring a more comprehensive approach to identifying and mitigating biases in data and algorithms.
   - **Example:** A healthcare company developing an AI diagnostic tool collaborates with doctors, data scientists, ethicists, and patient advocacy groups. This diversity ensures the tool accounts for different demographic needs and avoids biased outcomes.
   - Benefits:
     - Greater inclusivity in AI system design.
     - Enhanced understanding of societal and cultural nuances.
2. **Adopting Transparency and Explainability Practices:**
   - Transparency in AI models involves clear documentation of decision-making processes and potential limitations.
   - Explainability ensures end-users and stakeholders understand how AI systems reach their conclusions, fostering trust.
   - Example Tools:
     - **SHAP (SHapley Additive exPlanations):** A tool to interpret and explain predictions made by machine learning models.
     - **LIME (Local Interpretable Model-Agnostic Explanations):** A technique to explain model predictions by approximating them locally with simpler models.
3. **Implementing Continuous Monitoring and Auditing:**
   - AI systems must undergo regular evaluations to maintain ethical and operational integrity.

- Example: A retail company using AI for personalized recommendations implements routine bias audits to confirm the system treats customers equitably across demographic groups.

4. **Privacy-Preserving Techniques:**

    - Techniques such as differential privacy and federated learning protect sensitive data while enabling AI model training and updates.

    - Example: A healthcare AI system using federated learning allows hospitals to collaborate on model improvements without sharing patient data directly.

Building responsible AI continuously requires robust ethical frameworks, diverse development teams, and adherence to transparent and accountable practices. By leveraging tools like IBM AI Fairness 360 and following straightforward guidelines, organizations can ensure their AI systems are practical, equitable, and aligned with societal values.

2.5.4 REAL-WORLD EXAMPLES

Companies Implementing Ethical AI Successfully

Ethical AI is not just a theoretical concept but a practical necessity that organizations adopt to align technology with societal values. Leading tech companies have been at the forefront of integrating ethical AI principles into their operations. Two exemplary implementations stand out for their innovation and influence: **Google's Model Cards for transparency** and **Microsoft's Responsible AI principles**. These initiatives illustrate how ethical AI can be woven into the fabric of organizational processes, offering valuable lessons for enterprises across industries.

Google's Model Cards for Transparency

One of the most significant challenges in AI ethics is ensuring transparency in how AI models operate. Google introduced **Model Cards** as a practical solution to address this issue.

1. **Overview of Model Cards**:

    - Model Cards are structured documentation that provides detailed information about an AI model's intended use, performance, and potential limitations.

    - These cards include critical metrics such as accuracy, fairness, and robustness, broken down by demographics like age, gender, or geographic region.

2. **Ethical Impact**:

    - **Enhanced Accountability**: By openly sharing the strengths and weaknesses of models, Google fosters trust with stakeholders, from developers to end users.

- **Bias Mitigation**: The transparency provided by Model Cards helps identify and address potential biases, reducing harm to marginalized communities.
- **Industry Adoption**: The concept has inspired other organizations to adopt similar transparency practices, promoting ethical standards across the industry.

3. **Real-World Application**:
   - Google implemented Model Cards in several projects, including **Facial Recognition AI** and **Natural Language Processing tools**, to ensure users understood these technologies' limitations and ethical considerations.
   - For example, Model Cards for Google's Cloud Vision API explicitly disclose how the model performs differently across diverse demographic groups, preventing misuse.

Microsoft's Responsible AI Principles

Microsoft has taken a holistic approach to ethical AI through its **Responsible AI principles**, which guide the development and deployment of AI technologies across its ecosystem.

1. **Core Principles**:
   - **Fairness**: Ensuring AI systems treat all individuals equitably.
   - **Reliability and Safety**: Building robust AI solutions that operate reliably under various conditions.
   - **Privacy and Security**: Safeguarding user data and privacy throughout the AI lifecycle.
   - **Inclusiveness**: Designing AI systems that are accessible and inclusive for diverse populations.
   - **Transparency**: Making AI systems understandable and clearly explaining how they function.
   - **Accountability**: Assigning clear responsibility for the outcomes of AI systems.
2. **Ethical Frameworks and Tools**:
   - **AI Fairness Checklist**: Microsoft uses a comprehensive checklist to evaluate potential biases and mitigate unfair outcomes during model development.
   - **InterpretML**: A tool for understanding and interpreting machine learning models, allowing developers to improve transparency.

- **Differential Privacy**: A technique embedded in products like Azure that ensures data privacy while maintaining AI functionality.

3. **Success Stories**:

   - Microsoft's Responsible AI principles have been applied in projects like **Seeing AI**, an app that uses AI to help visually impaired individuals navigate the world. The app is designed to be inclusive and transparently inform users about its functionality.

   - In **Azure AI**, Microsoft integrates these principles to ensure that enterprise-grade AI solutions, from predictive analytics to conversational AI, comply with ethical standards.

Key Takeaways for Enterprises

- **Cultural Shift**: Both Google and Microsoft emphasize that ethical AI is not just about tools but about fostering a culture of responsibility within the organization.

- **Scalable Frameworks**: These examples demonstrate that ethical AI practices can be scaled across large enterprises and serve as blueprints for smaller organizations.

- **Leadership in Ethical AI**: By prioritizing transparency and fairness, these companies have positioned themselves as leaders in ethical AI and gained the trust of customers, partners, and regulators.

By learning from these pioneers, enterprises can adopt ethical AI practices to build trust, mitigate risks, and create AI systems that align with societal values. These case studies prove that ethical AI is a moral imperative and a competitive advantage in today's technology-driven landscape.

PART II

BUILDING AND LAUNCHING

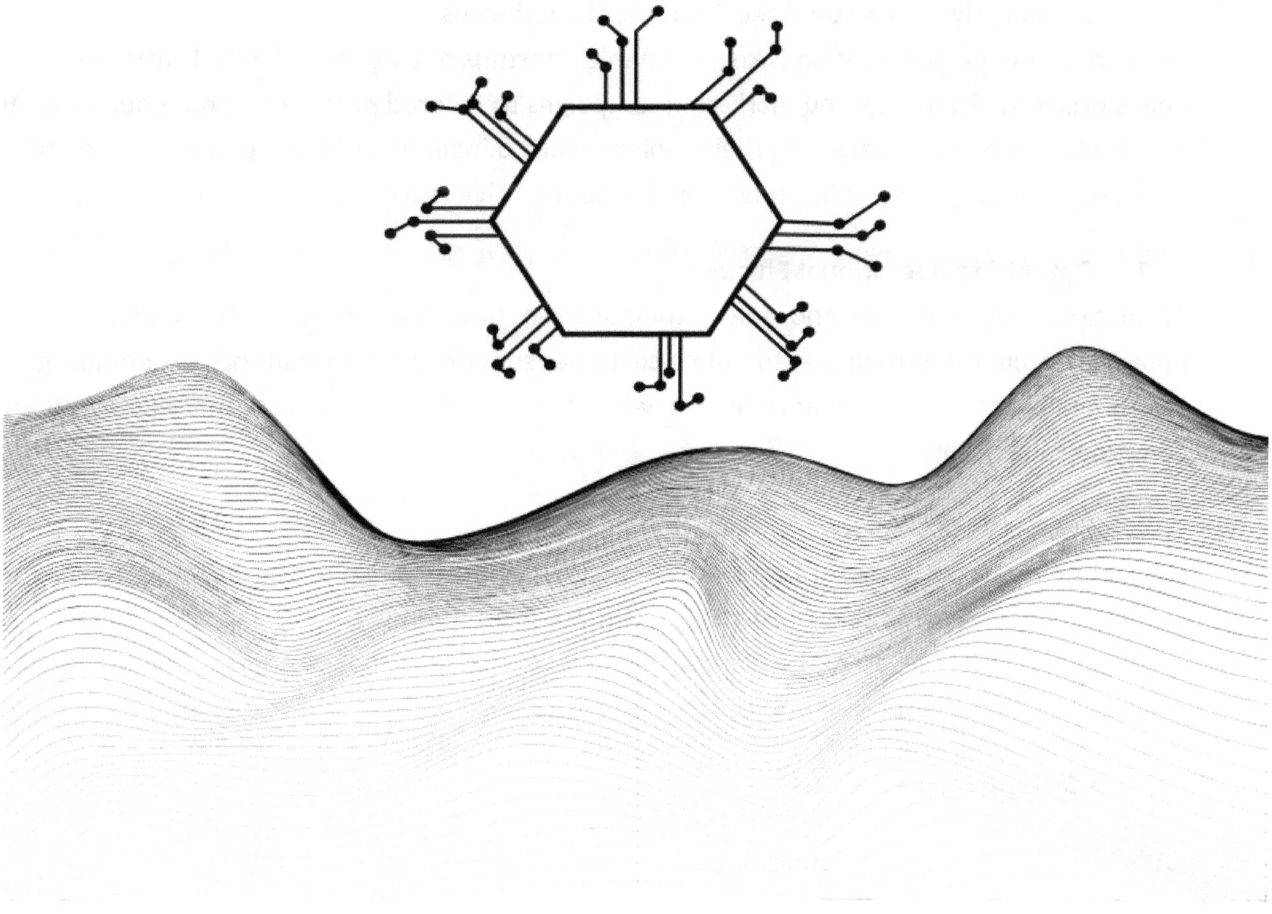

CHAPTER 3: CREATING YOUR AI SOLUTION

INTRODUCTION

AI AS THE FOUNDATION FOR DISRUPTION

The emergence of artificial intelligence (AI) has redefined the competitive landscape for startups. No longer just a tool for efficiency, AI has become a catalyst for innovation, enabling startups to challenge industry norms and unlock new opportunities. Startups that fail to leverage AI risk themselves being outpaced by competitors who harness its potential to create transformative solutions.

1. **Driving Innovation at Scale**
   AI empowers startups to solve complex problems that were previously deemed insurmountable. For example, AI systems can analyze massive datasets to identify trends, generate predictions, and provide insights that guide strategic decisions. This capability allows startups to innovate faster, entering markets with offerings that disrupt traditional practices.

2. **Creating Hyper-Personalized Customer Experiences**
   In an era where personalization is key, AI enables startups to cater to individual customer needs precisely. From targeted marketing campaigns to tailored product recommendations, AI ensures businesses resonate with their audience on a deeper level. This is particularly critical for startups looking to establish their brand in competitive markets.

3. **Optimizing Operational Efficiency**
   AI solutions streamline operations by automating repetitive tasks, reducing costs, and improving accuracy. Whether automating customer support through chatbots or optimizing supply chains with predictive analytics, AI helps startups maximize resource utilization without compromising quality.

4. **Enhancing Scalability**
   Unlike traditional solutions, AI-powered systems scale effortlessly. For startups, this means serving an increasing number of customers without proportionally increasing operational overhead. For instance, an AI-driven platform can handle thousands of queries simultaneously, providing real-time responses without additional staffing.

Examples of Disruptive AI Solutions

OpenAI's GPT Models for Text Generation

One of the most striking examples of AI-driven disruption comes from OpenAI's **Generative Pre-trained Transformers (GPT)**. These models have revolutionized the field of natural language processing (NLP), demonstrating how AI can mimic human-like understanding and text generation.

1. **Applications Across Industries**
GPT models are widely used to automate tasks like content creation, customer service, and even complex tasks such as legal document summarization or financial report generation. For example:

   - **Customer Support**: Businesses deploy GPT-powered chatbots to handle routine customer queries, offering instant and accurate responses.

   - **Content Generation**: GPT enables media companies to produce articles, social media posts, and marketing copy at unprecedented speeds, freeing creative teams to focus on strategy.

2. **Impact on Startups**
Startups leveraging GPT technology gain a competitive edge by automating traditionally time-consuming processes. This reduces operational costs and enhances user satisfaction by delivering faster, more consistent results.

Healthcare AI Startups Revolutionizing Diagnostics

The healthcare industry is undergoing a seismic transformation thanks to AI-driven diagnostic tools developed by innovative startups. These solutions address critical pain points, such as misdiagnoses, delayed treatments, and resource shortages.

1. **AI in Medical Imaging**
AI models excel at analyzing medical images, such as X-rays, MRIs, and CT scans, to detect anomalies with greater accuracy and speed than human experts. For instance:

   - **Cancer Detection**: AI systems identify early-stage tumors that radiologists might overlook, improving survival rates through timely intervention.

   - **Cardiovascular Diagnostics**: Startups use AI to predict heart-related conditions by analyzing patient data, enabling preventive care.

2. **Predictive Analytics in Patient Care**
Beyond imaging, AI revolutionizes how healthcare providers predict patient outcomes and personalize treatments. AI algorithms analyze patient history, genetic data, and lifestyle factors to recommend tailored treatment plans, ensuring better outcomes.

3. **Impact on Startups**
By adopting AI, healthcare startups are reducing diagnostic costs and improving accessibility. These advancements enhance patient care and create new business opportunities in underserved markets. For example, portable AI-powered diagnostic devices can bring advanced healthcare to remote areas.

AI is not just a tool for startups—it is the foundation for building disruptive, scalable, and impactful solutions. By embracing AI, startups can innovate rapidly, serve their customers more effectively, and challenge the status quo in their industries. Whether it's OpenAI's GPT transforming how we interact with technology or healthcare startups using AI to save lives, these examples highlight how AI is reshaping the future of business and society. For startups, the path forward is clear: those who adopt and innovate with AI will lead, while those who hesitate risk being left behind.

GOALS OF THIS CHAPTER

The primary aim of this chapter is to equip readers with practical knowledge and actionable strategies for effectively leveraging artificial intelligence (AI). As AI continues transforming industries, understanding how to build, implement, and scale AI solutions is critical for businesses and startups. This chapter focuses on two key objectives:

1. Provide a Step-by-Step Guide for Selecting, Building, and Evaluating AI Models

Navigating the complexities of AI development can be daunting, especially with the abundance of models and tools available. This chapter breaks the process into clear, manageable steps to guide readers through:

- **Selecting the Right AI Model**: Learn how to identify the best model based on your use case, whether supervised learning for prediction tasks, unsupervised learning for clustering, or generative models for creativity. To streamline this process, practical tools, frameworks, and decision-making criteria will be covered.

- **Building and Training Models**: Explore best practices for preparing data, choosing the appropriate architecture, and optimizing algorithms. Readers will gain insights into how to train models effectively, addressing real-world challenges like data imbalance and computational constraints.

- **Evaluating AI Models**: Discover how to assess model performance using industry-standard metrics. From accuracy and precision for classification tasks to BLEU and ROUGE scores for generative models, readers will learn to measure success and ensure their solutions meet business objectives.

2. Highlight Strategies to Optimize for Scalability and Efficiency

Building an AI model is just the beginning. It is essential for long-term success to scale it to meet real-world demands and ensure it operates efficiently. This chapter will explore:

- **Scalability Techniques**: Learn how to design AI systems that handle increasing data volumes and user interactions without compromising performance. Readers will understand the trade-offs between cloud-based and on-premise solutions and the benefits of hybrid architectures.

- **Efficiency Strategies**: Discover cost-effective methods for training and deploying AI models. This includes leveraging pre-trained models, optimizing resource utilization (e.g., GPU/TPU management), and employing fine-tuning techniques like Low-Rank Adaptation (LoRA) to reduce computational overhead.

By the end of this chapter, readers will have a solid understanding of how to design AI solutions that are not only innovative but also scalable, efficient, and aligned with their strategic goals. Whether you are a startup founder, a technical lead, or an AI enthusiast, these insights will empower you to build AI systems that deliver real impact.

3.1: UNDERSTANDING LLMS AND GENERATIVE AI

3.1.1 WHAT ARE LARGE LANGUAGE MODELS (LLMS)?

Large Language Models (LLMs) represent a transformative category of artificial intelligence (AI) systems designed to understand, process, and generate human language. These models are built on the foundation of neural networks trained on massive datasets, enabling them to perform a wide range of natural language processing (NLP) tasks with remarkable proficiency. LLMs, such as GPT (Generative Pre-trained Transformer), BERT (Bidirectional Encoder Representations from Transformers), and DALL-E, are pivotal in the evolution of AI technologies.

Overview of Foundational AI Models

1. **GPT (Generative Pre-trained Transformer):**
   - GPT, developed by OpenAI, is a state-of-the-art generative language model. It leverages the Transformer architecture, a mechanism that excels at processing sequential data by attending to relationships between tokens (words or subwords) in a sentence.
   - Unlike traditional models, GPT is pre-trained on a diverse range of text data from the internet and fine-tuned for specific tasks, making it highly adaptable.
   - Key strength: GPT can generate coherent and contextually relevant text, making it ideal for creative writing, drafting emails, or even coding assistance.
2. **BERT (Bidirectional Encoder Representations from Transformers):**
   - Created by Google, BERT is a bi-directional model that focuses on understanding the context of a word based on its surrounding words. This bi-directional approach significantly advances traditional left-to-right or right-to-left language models.
   - BERT excels in tasks requiring deep comprehension, such as question answering and summarization.

- Key strength: Its ability to capture nuanced meanings makes it practical for applications requiring precise understanding, like scientific document analysis.

3. **DALL-E:**

   - DALL-E, also developed by OpenAI, extends the capabilities of language models into the visual domain by generating images from textual descriptions.
   - This model demonstrates the versatility of foundational AI, as it connects language understanding with visual creativity.
   - Key strength: Enables the creation of unique visual content based on imaginative textual prompts.

Use Cases

1. **GPT for Customer Support Chatbots:**

   - GPT-based chatbots revolutionize customer service by offering human-like conversational capabilities. They can handle various queries, from answering FAQs to troubleshooting complex issues.
   - Key benefits:
     - 24/7 availability, ensuring continuous support for customers.
     - Scalability allows organizations to serve millions of users simultaneously.
     - Personalization, where the chatbot tailors responses based on user history and preferences.
   - Real-world application: Companies like e-commerce platforms and SaaS providers employ GPT-powered bots to enhance customer experience and reduce operational costs.

2. **BERT for Scientific Research Summarization:**

   - With the exponential growth of academic publications, BERT-powered summarization tools help researchers stay informed by condensing vast amounts of information into digestible summaries.
   - Key benefits:
     - Accurate extraction of key insights, preserving the context and intent of the original work.
     - Time efficiency enables researchers to focus on analysis rather than sifting through extensive literature.

▪ Multi-domain adaptability, supporting summarization across various scientific disciplines.

○ Real-world application: Platforms like Semantic Scholar and PubMed utilize BERT-based systems to assist researchers and academics.

Large Language Models like GPT, BERT, and DALL-E signify a paradigm shift in how machines understand and generate language. By leveraging vast training data and innovative architectures, these models provide immense value across domains, from customer service to academic research and creative industries. As AI continues to evolve, LLMs will undoubtedly play a critical role in shaping future applications, fostering efficiency, and enabling innovation.

3.1.2 APPLICATIONS OF GENERATIVE AI

Generative AI has revolutionized numerous industries by offering innovative solutions to complex problems. Its versatility stems from its ability to create data, designs, and content that mimic human creativity and intelligence. Below, we explore two significant real-world applications of generative AI with examples, highlighting its transformative potential in STEM research and creative industries.

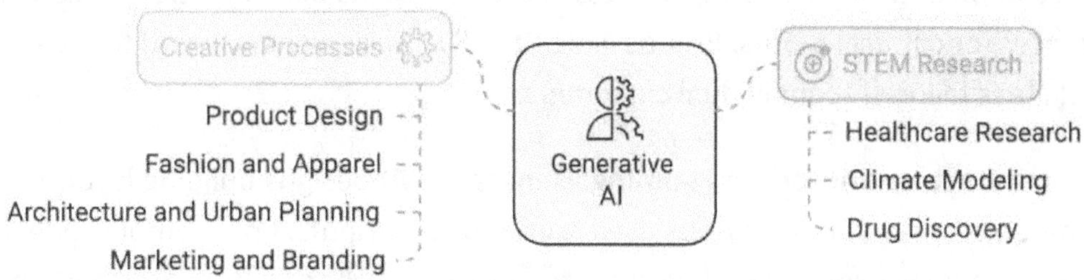

1. Generating Synthetic Data for STEM Research

Generative AI has become a game-changer in scientific and technical fields by addressing challenges related to data scarcity, privacy concerns, and experimental costs. Synthetic data generated by AI can replicate the statistical properties of real-world datasets, enabling researchers to perform studies and analyses without compromising sensitive information or waiting for expensive data collection processes.

- **Healthcare Research**: Generative AI models like GANs (Generative Adversarial Networks) create synthetic medical images, such as MRI scans, to train diagnostic algorithms. This approach accelerates research while ensuring patient privacy. For example, Nvidia's Clara platform leverages generative AI to synthesize realistic medical imaging data, facilitating the development of AI-powered diagnostic tools.

- **Climate Modeling**: Synthetic weather data is generated using AI models to simulate future climate scenarios. These datasets allow researchers to test and improve predictive algorithms, helping governments and organizations prepare for extreme weather events.

- **Drug Discovery**: In pharmaceutical research, generative AI helps create novel molecular structures that could lead to breakthrough medications. Platforms like Insilico Medicine use AI to generate potential drug candidates, significantly reducing the time and cost of traditional discovery methods.

The ability to generate diverse, high-quality datasets has transformed STEM research, enabling faster innovation and more accurate simulations.

2. Automating Creative Processes Like Design Prototyping

In creative industries, generative AI streamlines processes that once required extensive manual input, particularly in design and prototyping. Autonomously generating ideas, layouts, and visual elements allows professionals to focus on refining concepts rather than starting from scratch.

- **Product Design**: Companies like Autodesk use generative AI in tools like Fusion 360 to create design prototypes for manufacturing. Engineers can input constraints like material type, weight, and functionality, and the AI generates optimal designs, often uncovering solutions that humans might overlook.

- **Fashion and Apparel**: AI generates clothing designs based on trends, consumer preferences, or cultural motifs. Brands like Stitch Fix utilize generative AI to create unique apparel ideas tailored to individual customers.

- **Architecture and Urban Planning**: Generative AI designs building layouts or urban environments by simulating various use cases and constraints. For example, Sidewalk Labs, an Alphabet company, used generative tools to prototype urban layouts for smart cities, considering factors like energy efficiency and livability.

- **Marketing and Branding**: AI tools like Adobe Firefly and DALL-E generate creative assets for branding campaigns, including logos, social media visuals, and video content. This automation reduces costs while maintaining high-quality outputs.

Integrating generative AI in design prototyping accelerates the creative process and democratizes access to professional-grade design capabilities, empowering small businesses and independent creators.

Generative AI's applications continue to expand across domains, driven by its ability to produce high-quality, human-like outputs. From advancing scientific discoveries to democratizing creative processes, generative AI sets a new standard for innovation. Its adoption will only grow as the technology matures, unlocking previously unimaginable possibilities.

3.1.3 BENEFITS AND LIMITATIONS

Artificial Intelligence (AI) systems have transformed the technological landscape by offering numerous advantages that enable organizations to innovate and scale efficiently. However, these benefits have inherent challenges that require careful consideration to maximize effectiveness and minimize risks.

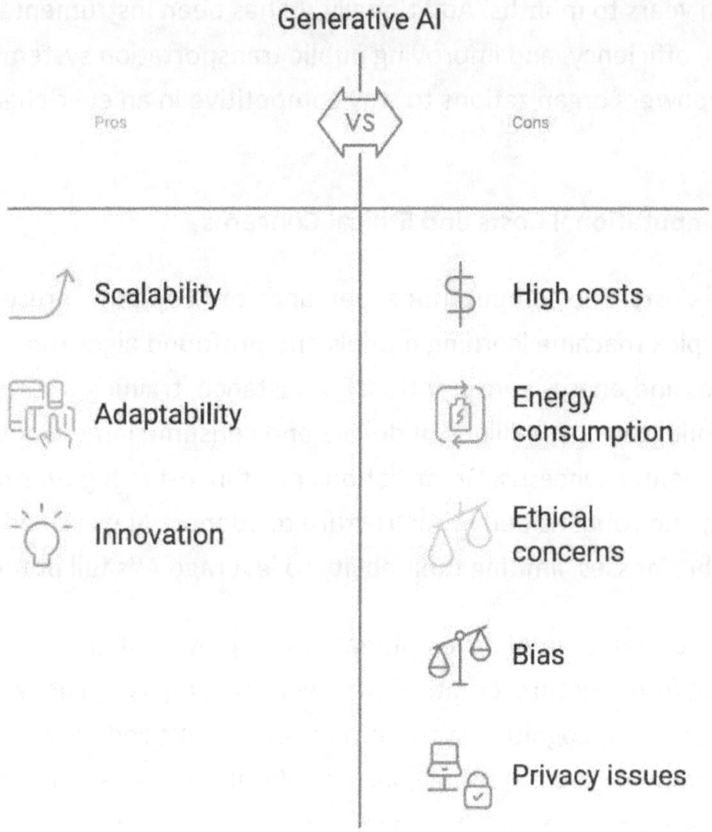

Strengths: Scalability, Adaptability, and Innovation

Scalability: AI systems excel in scalability, allowing organizations to manage massive amounts of data and execute complex tasks efficiently. Unlike traditional systems that require significant manual intervention, AI systems can handle increased workloads without proportionate increases in operational costs. For example, cloud-based AI platforms can seamlessly process terabytes of data across multiple industries, from healthcare diagnostics to financial fraud detection. This scalability ensures that businesses can expand their operations and meet growing demands without compromising speed or accuracy.

Adaptability: One of AI's most compelling strengths is its adaptability. Machine learning models, a subset of AI, are designed to learn and improve over time. This dynamic learning capability allows AI systems to adapt to new data patterns and evolving circumstances. For instance, recommendation algorithms used by e-commerce platforms continuously refine their suggestions based on user behavior, enhancing customer experience and increasing sales. Furthermore, AI's adaptability suits diverse applications across industries, such as optimizing supply chains, personalizing customer interactions, and predicting market trends.

Innovation: AI drives innovation by enabling solutions to complex problems that were previously unsolvable. The ability to process vast datasets and uncover hidden patterns fosters groundbreaking advancements in drug discovery, climate modeling, and autonomous vehicles. For example, AI-powered drug discovery platforms have accelerated the identification of potential treatments, reducing timelines from years to months. Additionally, AI has been instrumental in creating smart cities, enhancing energy efficiency, and improving public transportation systems. By enabling creative problem-solving, AI empowers organizations to stay competitive in an ever-changing market landscape.

Challenges: High Computational Costs and Ethical Concerns

High Computational Costs: The computational demands of AI systems present a significant challenge. Training complex machine learning models and profound algorithms requires substantial computational resources and energy consumption. For instance, training a state-of-the-art natural language processing model can cost millions of dollars and consume large amounts of electricity, contributing to environmental concerns. Organizations must invest in high-performance hardware, such as GPUs and TPUs, and robust cloud infrastructure to support AI workloads. These costs can be prohibitive for smaller businesses, limiting their ability to leverage AI's full potential.

Ethical Concerns: Ethical issues in AI development and deployment are another critical challenge. Bias in AI models, arising from unrepresentative or flawed training data, can lead to discriminatory outcomes. For example, facial recognition systems have been criticized for exhibiting higher error rates for specific demographic groups, raising concerns about fairness and inclusivity. Additionally, AI's use in surveillance and predictive policing has sparked debates about privacy and civil liberties. Addressing these ethical concerns requires a commitment to transparency, accountability, and inclusive practices in AI design and implementation.

While AI's strengths—scalability, adaptability, and innovation—offer unparalleled opportunities, its limitations—high computational costs and ethical concerns—demand strategic solutions. Organizations must balance these aspects by investing in sustainable AI infrastructure, fostering ethical practices, and prioritizing responsible AI development. By doing so, they can harness AI's transformative power while mitigating its challenges, ensuring a positive impact on society and business.

3.1.4 STEM-SPECIFIC USE CASES

Healthcare: Generative AI for Synthesizing Medical Data

Generative AI is revolutionizing healthcare by enabling advanced synthesis of complex medical data. With the exponential growth in patient records, diagnostic imaging, genomic data, and clinical trial results, healthcare professionals are increasingly leveraging AI models to derive meaningful insights that were previously unattainable.

- **Enhanced Diagnostics:** Generative AI can integrate and analyze disparate datasets—such as electronic health records (EHRs), imaging scans, and laboratory results—to produce a comprehensive patient profile. This holistic view aids in identifying subtle patterns that could indicate the early onset of diseases like cancer or cardiovascular conditions.

- **Drug Discovery and Development:** Generative AI accelerates drug discovery by synthesizing biological studies, chemical structures, and historical drug performance data. It enables researchers to simulate potential drug interactions and predict efficacy, reducing the time and cost of clinical trials.

- **Personalized Medicine:** AI algorithms can generate personalized treatment plans by analyzing patient-specific data, including genetic information and lifestyle factors. This tailored approach enhances the effectiveness of therapies while minimizing adverse effects.

- **Virtual Assistants and Training:** Generative AI creates realistic simulations to train professionals. Virtual patients with synthesized histories and symptoms allow practitioners to hone diagnostic and treatment skills in a risk-free environment.

- **Healthcare Accessibility:** AI-powered language models are breaking down barriers in telemedicine, providing multilingual support, and synthesizing patient notes into actionable summaries for clinicians, improving global healthcare access.

Engineering: AI-Driven Design Optimization for CAD Tools

AI-driven design optimization transforms how products, structures, and systems are conceived, analyzed, and manufactured in engineering. Generative AI embedded in CAD tools empowers engineers to achieve previously unattainable Irecision, efficiency, and creativity.

- **Automated Design Exploration:** AI models can rapidly generate multiple design iterations based on predefined parameters, such as material properties, cost constraints, and performance goals. Engineers can evaluate and refine these designs to select the optimal solution.

- **Topology Optimization:** Generative AI analyzes stress distribution, load paths, and material efficiency to propose innovative structures that minimize weight while maintaining strength. This is particularly valuable in aerospace, automotive, and civil engineering applications.

- **Rapid Prototyping:** Generative AI integrates seamlessly with 3D printing technologies, producing designs ready for prototyping. This accelerates the product development lifecycle, reducing the need for manual adjustments and iterations.

- **Energy Efficiency:** AI-powered CAD tools optimize designs for sustainability by analyzing energy consumption and environmental impact. For example, generative AI ensures optimal efficiency and minimal waste in HVAC systems or renewable energy projects.

- **Collaborative Engineering:** Generative AI facilitates interdisciplinary collaboration by integrating diverse data streams, such as fluid dynamics simulations, electrical schematics, and mechanical components. It enables a unified design environment where teams can work cohesively on complex projects.

These STEM-specific use cases highlight the transformative potential of generative AI in addressing some of the most pressing challenges in healthcare and engineering. By leveraging the power of AI, these fields are experiencing unprecedented innovation, paving the way for breakthroughs that will define the future of science and technology.

3.2: MODEL SELECTION

3.2.1 TYPES OF AI MODELS AND ALGORITHMS

Artificial Intelligence (AI) encompasses diverse models and algorithms, each tailored to solve specific problems. This section delves into the major types of AI models and algorithms and provides an overview of their practical applications in various domains.

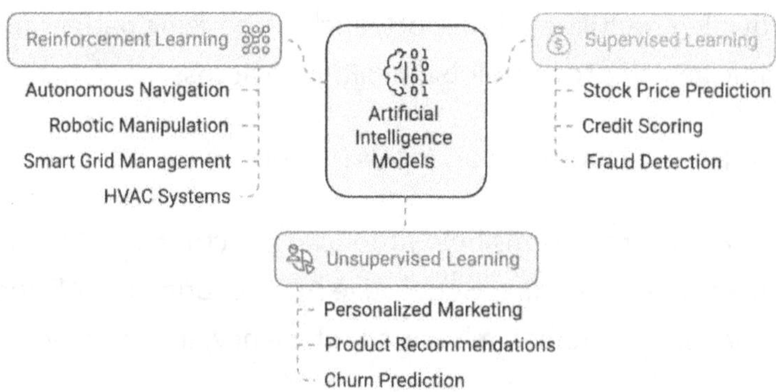

1. Supervised Learning: Prediction Tasks in Financial Modeling

Supervised learning involves training a model on labeled data, where the input-output relationship is predefined. These algorithms excel in prediction tasks where historical data can inform future outcomes.

- **Applications in Financial Modeling**:
  - **Stock Price Prediction**: Algorithms such as regression models and Long-Short-Term Memory (LSTM) networks analyze historical stock data to predict future trends.
  - **Credit Scoring**: Classification models such as logistic regression and Random Forest classify loan applicants into risk categories, aiding in credit decision-making.

- **Fraud Detection**: Supervised models are trained to recognize patterns in fraudulent transactions, ensuring real-time fraud prevention in banking systems.

- **Common Algorithms**:
  - Linear Regression for continuous variables.
  - Support Vector Machines (SVM) for classification.
  - Neural Networks for complex, non-linear prediction tasks.

Financial institutions can leverage supervised learning to achieve accurate forecasting and risk mitigation, empowering decision-making in volatile markets.

2. Unsupervised Learning: Clustering for Customer Segmentation

Unsupervised learning operates on unlabeled data to identify hidden patterns and structures. Clustering, a key method in unsupervised learning, is particularly effective for segmenting customers based on shared characteristics.

- **Applications in Customer Segmentation**:
  - **Personalized Marketing**: Clustering algorithms such as K-Means and DBSCAN group customers by behavior, enabling targeted marketing campaigns.
  - **Product Recommendations**: Identifying customer clusters helps businesses suggest products that align with user preferences.
  - **Churn Prediction**: Companies can implement retention strategies by understanding segments of high-risk customers.
- **Techniques and Tools**:
  - Dimensionality reduction techniques like Principal Component Analysis (PCA) to visualize clusters.
  - Hierarchical clustering for defining nested customer relationships.

Unsupervised learning unlocks hidden insights, driving customer-centric strategies and enhancing the overall user experience.

3. Reinforcement Learning: AI for Robotics and Energy Optimization

Reinforcement learning (RL) is a paradigm where an agent learns to make decisions by interacting with an environment, aiming to maximize cumulative rewards.

- **Applications in Robotics**:
    - **Autonomous Navigation**: RL algorithms like Q-Learning and Deep Q Networks enable robots to learn optimal paths in dynamic environments.
    - **Robotic Manipulation**: RL teaches robots to perform complex tasks such as assembly, leveraging trial-and-error methods.
- **Applications in Energy Optimization**:
    - **Smart Grid Management**: RL optimizes energy distribution in power grids, balancing supply and demand in real time.
    - **HVAC Systems**: By learning environmental dynamics, RL reduces energy consumption in heating, ventilation, and air conditioning systems.

Reinforcement learning provides a robust framework for real-time decision-making, pushing boundaries in automation and sustainable energy practices.

3.2.1.1 DECISION TREE FOR SELECTING THE RIGHT AI MODEL

Given the variety of available techniques, selecting the appropriate AI model can be complex. A decision tree provides a transparent, step-by-step approach to identifying the most suitable model based on the problem's characteristics.

- **Components of the Decision Tree**:
    - **Problem Type**: Classification, regression, clustering, or decision-making tasks.
    - **Data Availability**: Labeled vs. unlabeled data and the available data volume.
    - **Performance Requirements**: Speed, accuracy, and interpretability needs.
    - **Complexity vs. Simplicity**: Trade-offs between sophisticated models like deep learning and simpler ones like linear regression.
- **Example Path**:
    - Is the data labeled? → Yes → Is the task classification or regression? → Classification → Use Random Forest.
    - Is the data unlabeled? → Yes → Is the goal pattern recognition? → Yes → Use K-Means clustering.

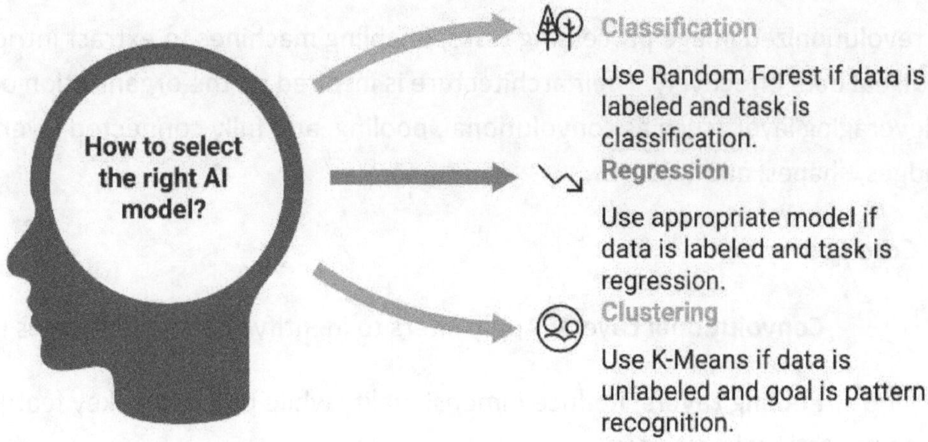

This section provides a foundational understanding of AI models and algorithms, equipping readers with the knowledge to approach AI problems systematically. Each method has unique strengths, and understanding when and how to apply them is key to unlocking their potential.

3.2.2 DEEP LEARNING ARCHITECTURES

Deep learning architectures are the backbone of modern AI systems, offering specialized approaches to processing and analyzing complex data across various domains. This section delves into the most prominent architectures—Convolutional Neural Networks (CNNs), Recurrent Neural Networks (RNNs), and Transformers—exploring their core principles, applications, and specific examples in STEM-related problems.

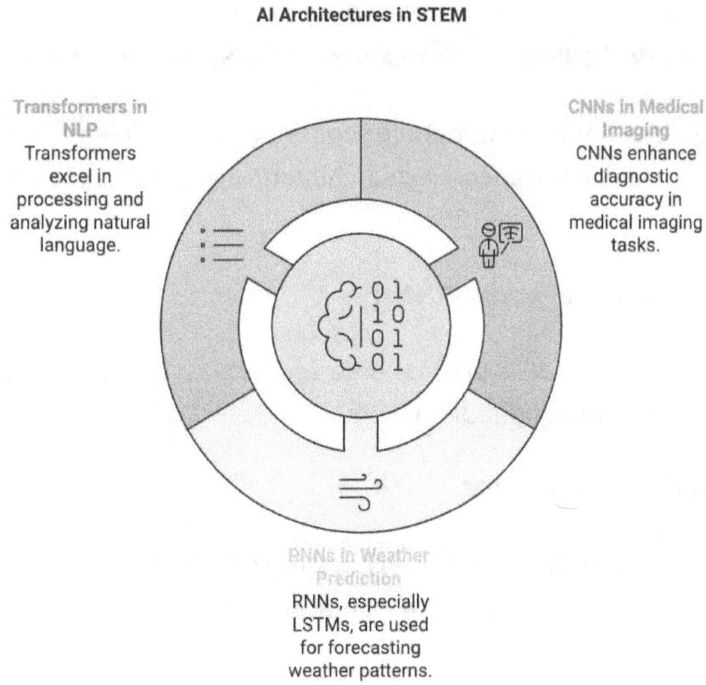

Convolutional Neural Networks (CNNs) for Image Processing

CNNs have revolutionized image processing tasks, enabling machines to extract intricate spatial features from visual data effectively. Their architecture is inspired by the organization of the animal visual cortex, leveraging layers such as convolutional, pooling, and fully connected layers to detect patterns like edges, shapes, and textures.

- **Core Concepts**:
  - **Convolutional Layers**: Apply filters to identify spatial hierarchies in data.
  - **Pooling Layers**: Reduce dimensionality while preserving key features, improving computational efficiency.
  - **Fully Connected Layers**: Aggregate extracted features for final predictions.
- **Applications in STEM**:
  - **Medical Imaging**: Using CNN-based diagnostic tools to identify anomalies like tumors in MRI scans or X-rays.
  - **Astronomy**: Analyzing celestial images to detect exoplanets or classify galaxies.
  - **Material Science**: Automated classification of microscopic structures in materials.
- **Example**: In medical imaging, a CNN trained on labeled datasets of MRI brain scans can outperform traditional methods in detecting early signs of Alzheimer's disease by focusing on subtle changes in brain structure.

Recurrent Neural Networks (RNNs) and Transformers for Sequential Data

RNNs and Transformers are designed to handle sequential data, such as time series or text, where the order of data points carries significance. Each architecture addresses the challenges of sequential modeling differently.

1. **Recurrent Neural Networks (RNNs)**:
   - **Mechanism**: RNNs process data sequentially, maintaining a "memory" of previous states through hidden layers.
   - **Applications in STEM**:
     - **Natural Language Processing (NLP)**: Sentiment analysis, language translation, and speech recognition.

- **Time-Series Analysis**: Predicting weather patterns or stock market trends.

- **Limitations**:

  - Struggles with long-term dependencies due to vanishing gradients.

- **Enhancements**: Variants like Long Short-Term Memory (LSTM) and Gated Recurrent Units (GRU) mitigate these issues by introducing mechanisms for selective memory retention.

2. **Transformers**:

   - **Mechanism**: Transformers eliminate the sequential bottleneck by processing all data points simultaneously, relying on an attention mechanism to weigh the importance of each input element.

   - **Applications in STEM**:

     - **NLP Tasks**: Text summarization, question answering, and code generation.

     - **Bioinformatics**: Protein structure prediction (e.g., AlphaFold).

   - **Advantages**:

     - Greater scalability and parallelization.

     - Superior performance on large datasets.

- **Example**: In drug discovery, a Transformer-based model can analyze molecular sequences to predict properties like solubility or binding affinity, significantly accelerating the drug design process.

Examples: Comparing Architectures for Specific STEM Problems

- **Medical Imaging (CNNs)**:

  - Task: Tumor detection in CT scans.

  - Result: CNNs excel due to their ability to focus on localized spatial features.

- **Weather Prediction (RNNs)**:

  - Task: Forecasting temperature and precipitation over time.

  - Result: LSTMs perform well on short-term dependencies but struggle with multi-year forecasts.

- **NLP in Scientific Literature (Transformers)**:
    - Task: Extracting insights from biomedical research papers.
    - Result: Transformers outperform RNNs by capturing contextual relationships across paragraphs.

These comparisons highlight the strengths and trade-offs of each architecture, emphasizing the importance of choosing the right model for specific STEM challenges.

3.2.3 PRE-TRAINED MODELS VS. CUSTOM MODELS

Choosing between leveraging pre-trained models and building custom models from scratch is critical in developing AI systems.

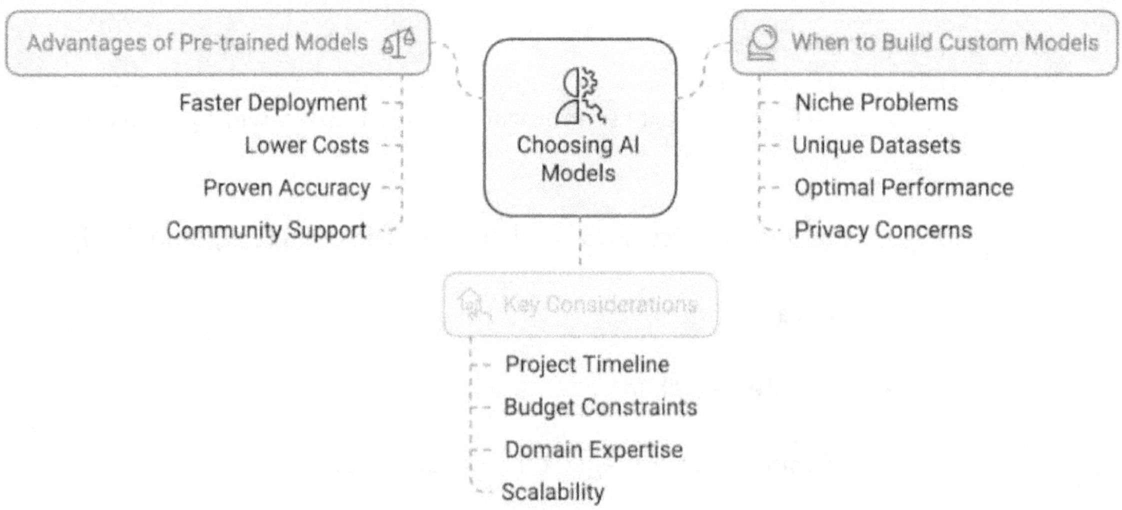

Depending on a project's specific requirements, both approaches have advantages and trade-offs. This section will delve into the pros and cons of each approach, when to use them, and how they impact various aspects of AI development.

ADVANTAGES OF USING PRE-TRAINED MODELS

Pre-trained models, such as those available from platforms like OpenAI, Hugging Face, or Google's TensorFlow Hub, come with several advantages:

1. **Faster Deployment:**
    - Pre-trained models eliminate the need to start from scratch. These models have already been trained on large datasets, reducing the time required to prepare and train a new model.

- For example, a natural language processing (NLP) task like sentiment analysis can be implemented in hours by leveraging a model like BERT or GPT, compared to weeks if a model is built from scratch.

2. **Lower Costs:**

   - Training models from scratch requires significant computational resources, such as GPUs or TPUs, which can be expensive. Pre-trained models, on the other hand, provide a cost-effective alternative. They utilize pre-trained weights developed using high-performance infrastructure.

   - Moreover, pre-trained models often include optimizations that make them suitable for deployment on resource-constrained environments, such as mobile or edge devices.

3. **Proven Accuracy and Generalization:**

   - Pre-trained models have undergone rigorous testing and optimization, ensuring they generalize well to various tasks within the domain they are trained for. For instance, vision models like ResNet or VGG have proven effective across diverse image recognition tasks.

   - Fine-tuning pre-trained models on task-specific data often achieves better results than training a model from scratch on the same data.

4. **Ease of Use and Community Support:**

   - With extensive documentation, pre-built APIs, and active community support, using pre-trained models reduces the learning curve for developers and data scientists.

   - Popular frameworks like PyTorch and TensorFlow provide pre-trained models as part of their libraries, making integration seamless.

WHEN TO BUILD CUSTOM MODELS

Despite the advantages of pre-trained models, there are scenarios where building custom models is a more suitable choice. Custom models are essential when:

1. **Solving Niche Problems:**

   - Pre-trained models are designed for general-purpose use cases and may perform poorly on highly specific or niche problems. For instance, a healthcare AI model diagnosing rare diseases may require custom training to ensure it accurately identifies domain-specific anomalies.

- Industries like finance or aerospace often require custom models tailored to unique regulatory and operational constraints.

2. **Using Unique Datasets:**

   - When the available data significantly differs from the datasets used to train pre-trained models, custom models can better adapt to the unique characteristics of the data.

   - For example, a language model trained on colloquial text may fail to process formal or domain-specific language unless retrained on the specific data.

3. **Achieving Optimal Performance:**

   - Custom models can be optimized for higher accuracy, lower latency, or better efficiency than generic pre-trained models.

   - Customization allows the incorporation of specific architectural innovations or domain-specific constraints, which may not be feasible when fine-tuning pre-trained models.

4. **Addressing Privacy and Security Concerns:**

   - Sensitive industries such as healthcare and finance often require strict control over data and model architecture. Building custom models ensures that data never leaves secure environments and complies with regulatory standards like GDPR or HIPAA.

KEY CONSIDERATIONS IN CHOOSING BETWEEN PRE-TRAINED AND CUSTOM MODELS

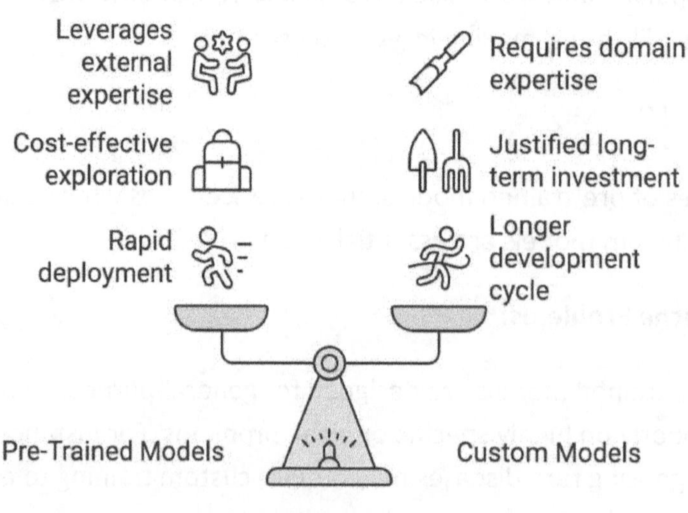

Evaluate model choices based on project needs.

The decision to use pre-trained or custom models should consider factors such as:

1. **Project Timeline:**
   - If rapid deployment is critical, pre-trained models are typically the better choice. Custom models require a longer development cycle, including data preprocessing, model design, and training.
2. **Budget Constraints:**
   - Pre-trained models are cost-effective for initial exploration and proof of concept. However, the investment in a custom model may be justified in long-term projects where performance is critical.
3. **Domain Expertise:**
   - Custom models often require more domain expertise to design and train effectively. On the other hand, pre-trained models allow developers to leverage external expertise encapsulated in the pre-trained architecture and weights.
4. **Scalability and Maintenance:**
   - Pre-trained models simplify scaling as the provider often manages updates and improvements. Custom models may require continuous retraining and optimization to maintain performance as data and requirements evolve.

Pre-trained models are generally ideal for quick, cost-effective, and general-purpose applications. They are particularly beneficial for startups, small teams, or projects with limited resources. On the other hand, custom models shine when addressing niche problems, handling unique datasets, or achieving optimal performance in specialized domains. A hybrid approach, combining pre-trained models with custom fine-tuning, often balances cost, performance, and flexibility.

3.3: TRAINING AND FINE-TUNING

3.3.1 TRAINING AI MODELS

Key Steps in Training AI Models

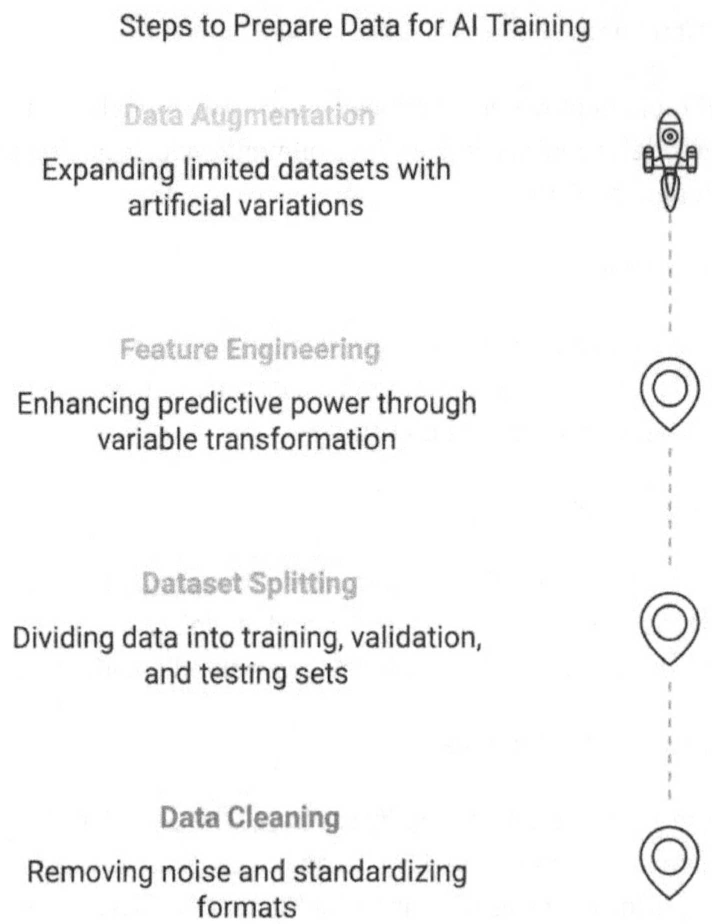

1. Data Preparation

Data preparation is a crucial step in training AI models. Without well-prepared data, even the most sophisticated algorithms can fail. Data preparation involves several substeps:

- **Cleaning and preprocessing:** Raw data often contains noise, missing values, or irrelevant information. Cleaning involves removing or imputing missing values, eliminating duplicates, and standardizing formats.
- **Splitting datasets:** For practical model training, datasets are divided into three subsets:
  - **Training set:** This subset trains the model and makes it learn patterns.
  - **Validation set:** Used during training to tune hyperparameters and prevent overfitting.
  - **Testing set:** Reserved for evaluating the model's performance on unseen data.
- **Feature engineering** involves creating, selecting, or transforming variables to enhance the model's predictive power. Techniques such as one-hot encoding, scaling, and dimensionality reduction (e.g., PCA) may be applied.

- **Data augmentation (if applicable):** In cases where data is limited (e.g., images), techniques like rotation, flipping, or color changes can artificially expand the dataset.

2. Choosing Loss Functions and Optimization Algorithms

The choice of loss functions and optimization algorithms significantly influences the training process and the model's effectiveness.

- **Loss Functions:**

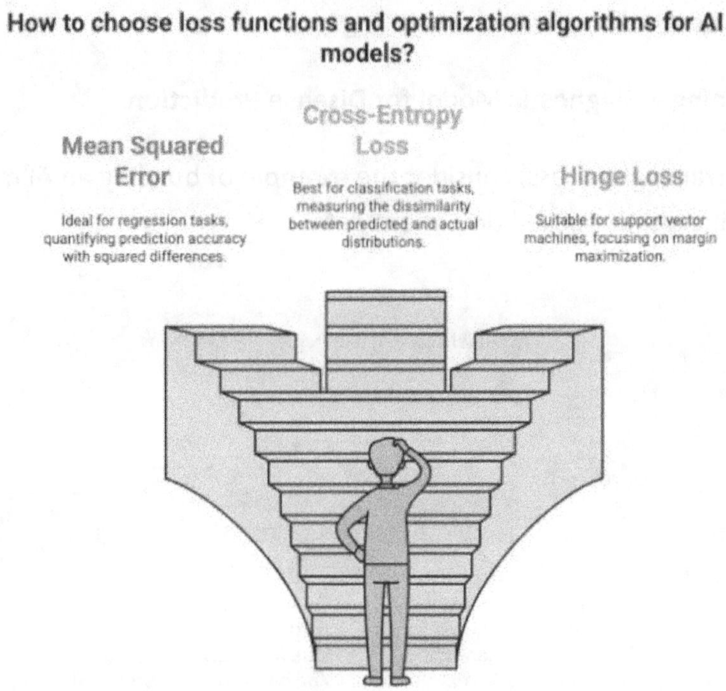

  - Loss functions quantify the difference between predicted and actual outcomes. The choice depends on the type of problem:
    - **Mean Squared Error (MSE):** Commonly used for regression tasks.
    - **Cross-Entropy Loss:** Standard for classification problems.
    - **Hinge Loss:** Suitable for support vector machines.
  - For more complex tasks, custom loss functions may be designed to address specific requirements (e.g., imbalanced datasets).

- **Optimization Algorithms:**
  - Optimization algorithms adjust the model's parameters to minimize the loss function. Popular algorithms include:

▪ **Stochastic Gradient Descent (SGD):** A simple and widely used optimization technique.

▪ **Adam Optimizer** combines the advantages of momentum and RMSProp, which are often preferred for deep learning tasks.

▪ **Adaptive Gradient Algorithm (Adagrad):** Adapts the learning rate based on parameter updates.

- Regularization techniques, such as L1 (Lasso) and L2 (Ridge), may also be incorporated to prevent overfitting.

3. Example: Training a Diagnostic Model for Disease Prediction

To illustrate the training process, consider the example of building an AI model to predict the likelihood of a specific disease based on patient data.

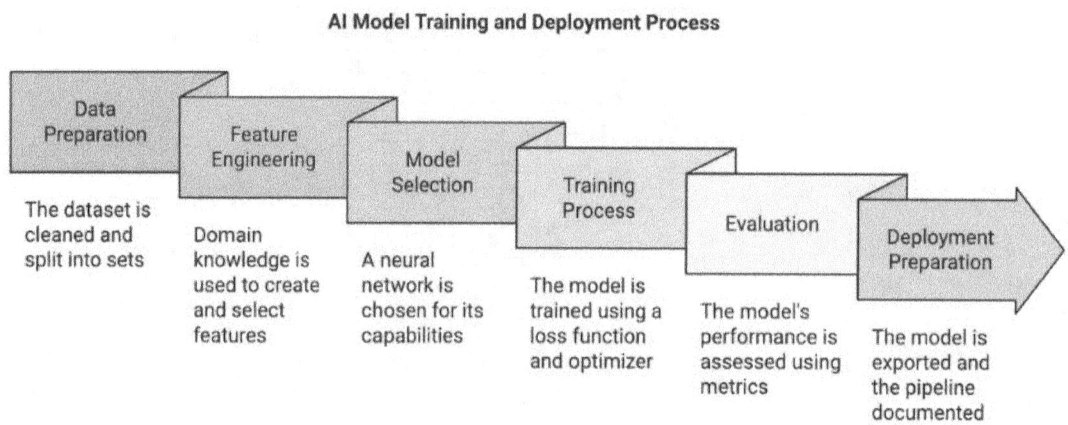

1. **Data Preparation:**

   - The dataset includes patient records, demographic information, medical history, lab results, and imaging data.

   - Data is cleaned by filling in missing values (e.g., using median imputation for continuous variables), normalizing lab results, and encoding categorical features such as gender and ethnicity.

   - The data is split into training (70%), validation (20%), and testing (10%) sets.

2. **Feature Engineering:**

   - Domain knowledge is leveraged to create derived features, such as Body Mass Index (BMI) from weight and height.

- Feature selection methods (e.g., Recursive Feature Elimination) identify the most predictive variables.

3. **Model Selection:**

   - A neural network is chosen due to its ability to capture nonlinear relationships. It consists of input layers for each feature, hidden layers with ReLU activation, and a softmax output layer for classification.

4. **Training Process:**

   - **Loss Function:** Binary Cross-Entropy measures the difference between predicted probabilities and actual outcomes.

   - **Optimization Algorithm:** The Adam optimizer adjusts weights iteratively to minimize the loss.

   - **Validation:** The validation set monitors the model's performance, ensuring hyperparameters like learning rate and batch size are optimized without overfitting.

5. **Evaluation:**

   - Once trained, the model is evaluated on the testing set. Metrics such as accuracy, precision, recall, and F1 score provide a comprehensive view of its performance.

   - In this case, an F1 score of 0.85 indicates a good balance between precision and recall, making it reliable for real-world use.

6. **Deployment Preparation:**

   - The trained model is exported as a serialized file (e.g., ONNX format).

   - The training pipeline is documented for reproducibility, ensuring consistent results when retraining with new data.

3.3.2 FINE-TUNING TECHNIQUES

Fine-tuning is critical in adapting pre-trained models to specific tasks or domains. This section explores advanced fine-tuning techniques that enable customization while balancing computational efficiency and performance.

Fine-Tuning AI Models: Balancing Efficiency and Performance

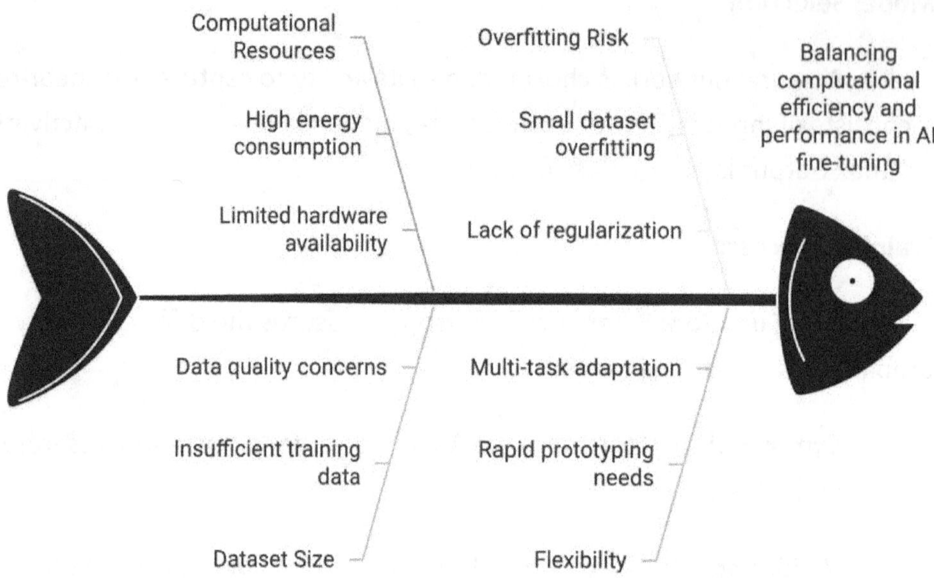

Full Fine-Tuning for Domain-Specific Applications

Full fine-tuning involves updating a pre-trained model's parameters to adapt it to a specific domain or task. This approach ensures that the model is fully aligned with the nuances of the target data, but it requires substantial computational resources and a large dataset.

Advantages:

- **Complete Adaptation:** Ensures that the model fully captures domain-specific knowledge.
- **High Performance:** Achieves state-of-the-art results when sufficient training data is available.

Challenges:

- **Resource Intensive:** Requires significant computational power and time.
- **Overfitting Risk:** Prone to overfitting on small datasets unless regularization techniques are applied.

Use Cases:

- Medical diagnosis models trained on specialized datasets.
- Legal document summarization systems.

Low-Rank Adaptation (LoRA) for Efficient Fine-Tuning

LoRA is a parameter-efficient fine-tuning technique that modifies only a subset of parameters while keeping most pre-trained weights frozen. LoRA inserts low-rank matrices into the model architecture, enabling effective adaptation without the computational cost of full fine-tuning.

Advantages:

- **Efficiency:** Significantly reduces memory and computational requirements.
- **Flexibility:** Enables rapid prototyping across multiple tasks or domains.

Implementation Steps:

1. Identify key layers (e.g., attention layers) where low-rank matrices will be inserted.
2. Train these additional parameters on the target dataset while freezing the rest of the model.
3. Integrate the fine-tuned components back into the pre-trained model.

Use Cases:

- Customer service chatbots require multiple language adaptations.
- Models for resource-constrained devices.

Prompt Tuning for Large Language Models

Prompt tuning is an innovative approach where task-specific prompts are optimized rather than the model's parameters. This technique involves crafting or training small sets of task-relevant tokens, which guide the model to produce desired outputs.

Advantages:

- **Lightweight:** Requires tuning only a small number of parameters.
- **Reusability:** Allows adaptation to new tasks without altering the core model.

Key Techniques:

- **Manual Prompt Engineering:** Designing prompts based on domain expertise.
- **Automated Prompt Optimization:** Using gradient-based methods to refine prompts.

Use Cases:

- Sentiment analysis with minimal labeled data.

- Few-shot or zero-shot learning scenarios.

Workflow for Fine-Tuning a Pre-Trained LLM

The following visual outlines a typical workflow for fine-tuning a pre-trained large language model (LLM):

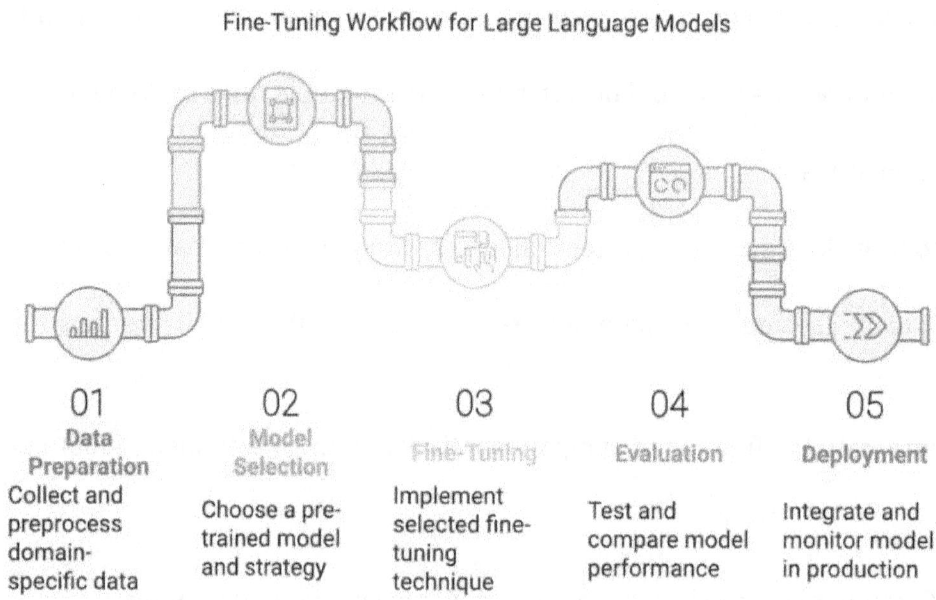

1. **Data Preparation:**
    - Collect and preprocess domain-specific data.
    - Ensure data diversity and quality to prevent bias.
2. **Model Selection:**
    - Choose a pre-trained model appropriate for the task (e.g., GPT, BERT).
    - Determine the fine-tuning strategy (full fine-tuning, LoRA, or prompt tuning).
3. **Fine-Tuning:**
    - Implement the selected fine-tuning technique:
        - For full fine-tuning, update all model weights.
        - For LoRA, train only the low-rank matrices.
        - For prompt tuning, optimize task-specific prompts.

4. **Evaluation:**
   - Test the fine-tuned model on validation datasets.
   - Compare results against benchmarks to assess performance.
5. **Deployment:**
   - Integrate the fine-tuned model into production environments.
   - Monitor model performance and update as needed.

This structured workflow ensures that fine-tuning processes are systematic and adaptable, enabling efficient customization of LLMs for diverse applications.

3.3.3 COST OPTIMIZATION IN TRAINING

Effective cost optimization in AI training is critical for maintaining budgetary constraints while ensuring robust model performance. This section explores practical strategies and provides a real-world example to illustrate cost-effective training methodologies.

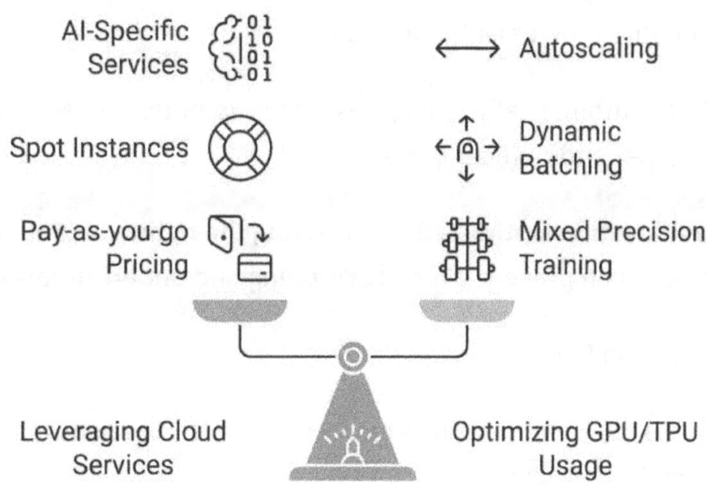

Balancing Cloud and Hardware Strategies for Cost-Effective AI Training

Strategies for Reducing Training Costs

1. Leveraging Cloud Services

Cloud platforms such as AWS, Google Cloud, and Microsoft Azure provide flexible, scalable, and cost-efficient solutions for AI training. These platforms offer:

- **Pay-as-you-go Pricing:** Organizations only pay for the resources used, avoiding upfront infrastructure costs.
- **Spot Instances and Preemptible VMs** are significantly cheaper than on-demand instances and can be used for non-critical workloads or batch training jobs.
- **AI-Specific Services:** Platforms like Google Vertex AI and AWS SageMaker provide pre-configured environments optimized for machine learning, reducing setup time and operational costs.
- **Multi-cloud Strategies:** Organizations can utilize competitive pricing and service-specific strengths by distributing workloads across multiple cloud providers.

2. Optimizing GPU/TPU Usage

Efficient utilization of hardware accelerators like GPUs and TPUs can significantly reduce training costs:

- **Mixed Precision Training:** Using lower precision (e.g., FP16) for computations reduces memory usage and accelerates training without sacrificing accuracy.
- **Dynamic Batching:** Adjusting batch sizes dynamically based on available resources ensures maximum utilization of GPUs or TPUs.
- **Autoscaling:** Automatically scaling resources up or down depending on the workload prevents idle resources and reduces costs.
- **Resource Allocation Optimization:** Selecting the right type and number of GPUs/TPUs for specific workloads can prevent over-provisioning and underutilization.

3. Decentralized Training on Edge Devices

In scenarios like IoT systems, where multiple devices are distributed geographically, decentralized training can be a cost-effective approach:

- **Federated Learning:** This method involves training models locally on edge devices and aggregating results centrally, reducing the need for large-scale centralized infrastructure.
- **On-device Training:** Lightweight models can be trained directly on edge devices using their computational capabilities, minimizing reliance on cloud infrastructure.
- **Bandwidth and Latency Savings:** Decentralized approaches reduce data transfer costs and latency when sending data to centralized servers for training.

Example: Using Edge Devices for Decentralized Training in IoT Systems

Devices such as thermostats, cameras, and smart plugs generate massive amounts of data in an IoT-enabled smart home system in an IoT-enabled smart home system. Centralized training for predictive models might incur substantial cloud computing and data transfer costs.

Instead, by leveraging edge devices:

- Each device trains a small part of the model using its local data and computational power.
- Results are periodically aggregated at a central server, combining insights without transferring raw data.
- This approach reduces training costs, enhances data privacy, and reduces network load.

For instance, Google's federated learning system on Android devices exemplifies decentralized training. Predictive text models are trained locally on user devices, improving the keyboard's performance while preserving user data privacy and significantly cutting cloud infrastructure costs.

These strategies can help organizations achieve significant cost savings in AI training while maintaining model accuracy and efficiency. These methods align with evolving trends in AI development, ensuring that projects remain scalable and economically sustainable.

3.3.4 TOOLS AND FRAMEWORKS

In AI development, the choice of tools and frameworks plays a pivotal role in building, training, and deploying robust AI models. These tools streamline development workflows, abstract complex processes, and enable scalability. This section introduces popular AI frameworks and guides you in selecting the most suitable one for your problem.

Introduction to Popular AI Tools and Frameworks

1. **TensorFlow**
   TensorFlow, developed by Google, is one of the most widely used frameworks in AI development. Known for its flexibility and scalability, it supports small-scale research experiments and large-scale industrial applications. TensorFlow excels in:

   - **Ease of Use**: High-level APIs like Keras make it beginner-friendly while retaining low-level operations for advanced users.
   - **Distributed Training**: Built-in support for training on multiple GPUs and TPUs.
   - **Versatility**: Suitable for computer vision, natural language processing (NLP), time-series analysis, and more.
   - **Deployment Options**: TensorFlow Lite and TensorFlow.js enable deployment on mobile devices, edge devices, and web platforms.

2. **PyTorch**
PyTorch, developed by Facebook, is a highly popular choice among researchers due to its dynamic computation graph and intuitive Pythonic design. Key features include:

   - **Dynamic Graphing**: Enables flexible experimentation, making it easier to debug and prototype.
   - **Community and Research Support**: Frequently adopted in academic research, resulting in cutting-edge AI advancements.
   - **Integration with Other Tools**: Seamlessly integrates with libraries like NumPy and Pandas.
   - **TorchServe**: Facilitates model serving for production environments.

3. **Hugging Face**
Hugging Face is revolutionizing NLP by offering pre-trained models and tools that reduce development time significantly. Features include:

   - **Transformers Library**: Contains state-of-the-art models for tasks like sentiment analysis, text summarization, and machine translation.
   - **Ease of Customization**: Allows fine-tuning models for specific tasks with minimal coding.
   - **Model Hub**: A vast repository of pre-trained models that can be deployed directly or fine-tuned for bespoke solutions.
   - **Focus on Usability**: Accessible APIs with a strong emphasis on developer experience.

How to Choose the Right Framework for Your Problem

Selecting the proper framework is critical to project success. The decision depends on the problem domain, team expertise, scalability requirements, and deployment needs.

Here's a step-by-step guide to making an informed choice:

1. **Define Your Problem Domain**
   - Hugging Face is the go-to choice for working on NLP due to its specialized pre-trained models.
   - TensorFlow and PyTorch are excellent options for **deep learning tasks** like computer vision or custom model development.
2. **Evaluate Team Expertise**
   - Teams familiar with Python often prefer PyTorch for its intuitive syntax and debugging ease.
   - With its extensive documentation and community support, TensorFlow is ideal for teams needing a production-ready solution.
3. **Consider Development Stage**

- **Prototyping and Research**: PyTorch's dynamic graphing is better suited for rapid experimentation.
- **Production Deployment**: TensorFlow's mature deployment tools make it suitable for scaling to production environments.

4. **Performance and Scalability Needs**
   - For distributed training on large datasets, TensorFlow's support for TPUs and multi-GPU setups outshines others.
   - PyTorch's DataParallel module simplifies distributed training for smaller-scale applications.
5. **Deployment Platform**
   - For deploying on edge devices, TensorFlow Lite provides optimized performance.
   - For cloud-based APIs or RESTful services, frameworks like TorchServe and Hugging Face Transformers are practical.
6. **Community and Ecosystem**
   - A strong community ensures access to resources, tutorials, and troubleshooting help. TensorFlow has a broader ecosystem, while PyTorch excels in research-focused communities.

By understanding the strengths and limitations of these tools and frameworks, developers can align their choices with project goals and ensure efficient and effective AI model development.

3.4: MODEL TRAINING AND EVALUATION

3.4.1 STEPS FOR EFFECTIVE MODEL TRAINING

Practical model training is a critical aspect of machine learning that determines the success and accuracy of your AI systems. This section details a systematic approach to model training, focusing on hyperparameter tuning, optimization algorithms, and a practical example of optimizing a recommendation engine for e-commerce.

Techniques for Hyperparameter Tuning

Hyperparameters are crucial settings that control the training process of a machine learning model. Unlike parameters learned during training, hyperparameters are defined before the training begins. Here are key techniques for practical hyperparameter tuning:

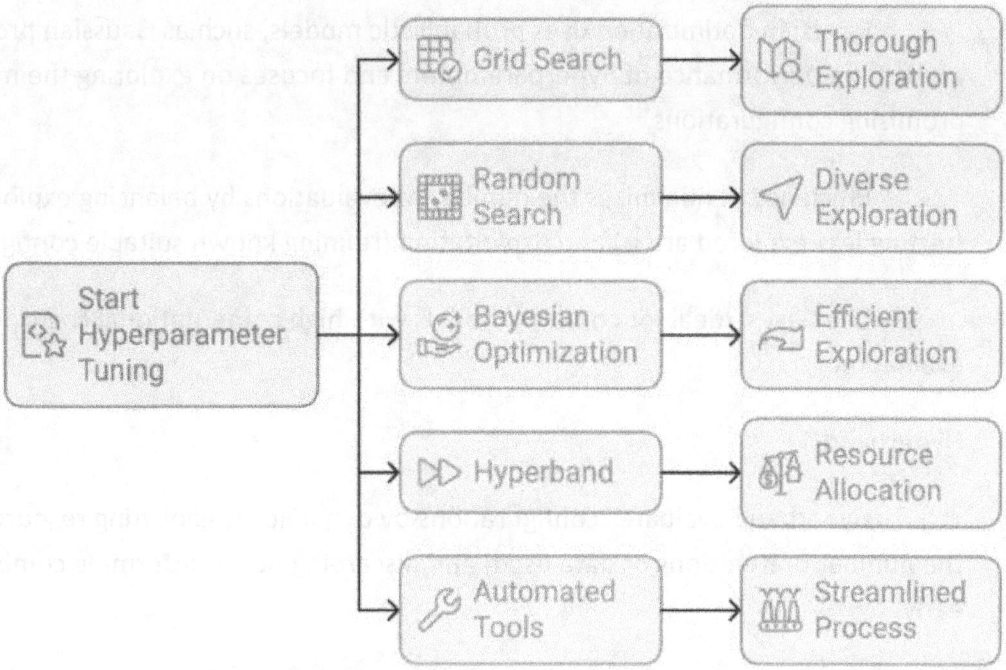

1. **Grid Search**

   ○ This involves specifying a set of hyperparameter values and exhaustively searching through all possible combinations to find the best configuration.

   ○ While computationally intensive, grid search ensures a thorough exploration of the hyperparameter space, which can be advantageous for small-scale problems or when prior knowledge about the parameter ranges is limited.

   ○ Applications: These are typically used for simpler models or when computing resources are ample.

2. **Random Search**

   ○ Instead of testing every combination, random search samples hyperparameters randomly within defined ranges.

   ○ This approach is less computationally expensive than grid search and often yields results comparable to grid search by focusing on broader exploration rather than exhaustive evaluation.

   ○ Benefits: Particularly effective when some hyperparameters are more critical than others, as random sampling allows for a diverse exploration.

3. **Bayesian Optimization**

   - Bayesian optimization uses probabilistic models, such as Gaussian processes, to predict the performance of hyperparameters and focuses on exploring the most promising configurations.

   - Efficiency: It minimizes the number of evaluations by balancing exploration (testing less-explored areas) and exploitation (refining known suitable configurations).

   - Use Cases: Ideal for complex models with high computational costs per evaluation.

4. **Hyperband**

   - Hyperband evaluates configurations by dynamically allocating resources (e.g., the number of iterations or data used) and discarding poor-performing combinations early.

   - Advantages: It reduces wasted computation by focusing resources on promising candidates, making it suitable for models requiring long training, such as deep neural networks.

   - Methodology: Combines random sampling with early stopping rules to identify high-potential configurations efficiently.

5. **Automated Tools**

   - Tools like Optuna, Hyperopt, and Google's AutoML streamline hyperparameter tuning by implementing advanced algorithms like Bayesian optimization and Hyperband.

   - Features: These tools often include visualization dashboards, multi-objective optimization, and parallelization, making them accessible even for non-experts.

   - Recommendations: Use automated tools when handling large-scale problems or aiming for reproducibility and efficiency in tuning workflows.

Optimization Algorithms: Adam, SGD, and Beyond

Optimization algorithms play a pivotal role in model training by adjusting weights and biases to minimize loss functions. Here's an overview of some widely used algorithms:

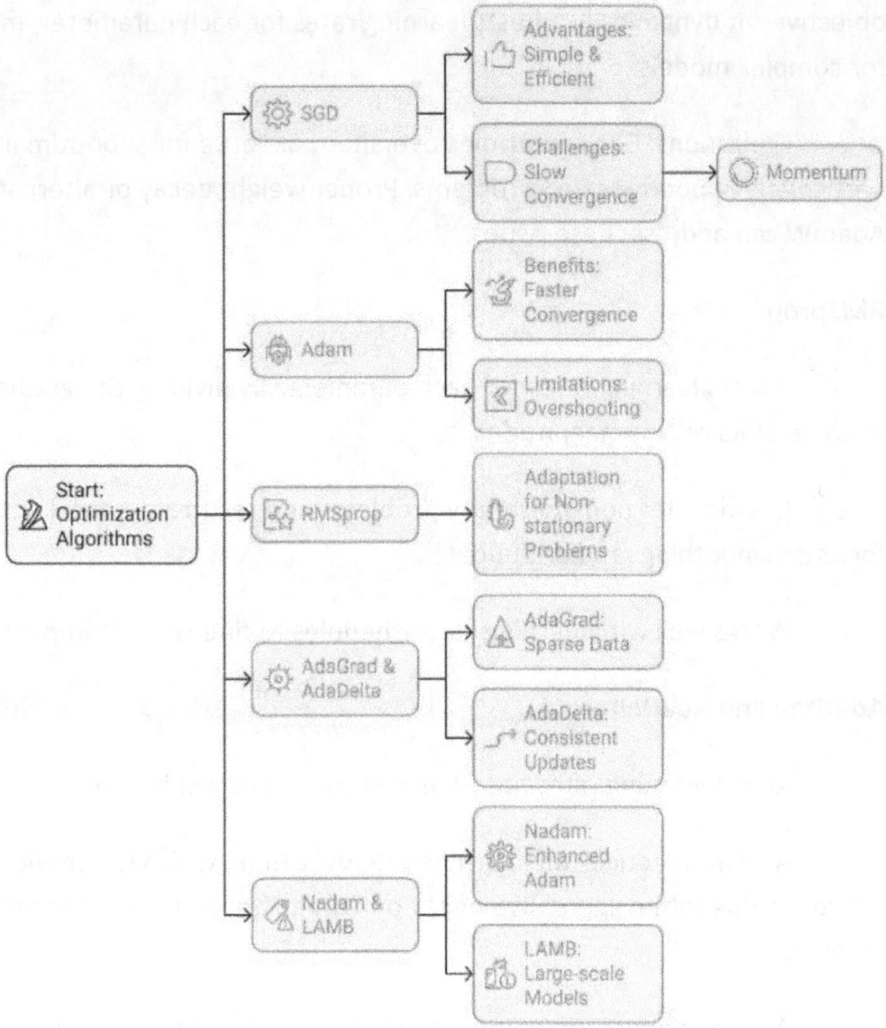

1. **Stochastic Gradient Descent (SGD)**
   - SGD updates model parameters iteratively for each data point or mini-batch.
   - Advantages: Simple and efficient for large datasets.
   - Challenges: It may converge slowly and get stuck in local minima due to its reliance on the gradient's direction without accounting for past updates. Techniques like momentum can help mitigate this by adding a fraction of the previous update to the current one, improving convergence speed, and helping escape local minima.
2. **Adam (Adaptive Moment Estimation)**
   - Combines the benefits of SGD with momentum and adaptive learning rates by maintaining an exponentially decaying average of past gradients and their squares.

- Advantages: Faster convergence and robust performance for non-stationary objectives. It dynamically adjusts learning rates for each parameter, making it practical for complex models.

- Limitations: Can sometimes overshoot or settle for suboptimal solutions, particularly in poorly scaled problems. Proper weight decay or alternate variants like AdamW can address these issues.

3. **RMSprop**

   - Adapts learning rates for each parameter by dividing the gradient by a moving average of its recent magnitudes.

   - It is ideal for non-stationary problems and recurrent neural networks due to its focus on smoothing gradient updates.

   - Works well with learning rate schedules to fine-tune its impact on convergence.

4. **AdaGrad and AdaDelta**

   - Adjust learning rates based on historical gradient information.

   - AdaGrad reduces the learning rate over time, which is beneficial for sparse data. However, due to the aggressive decay of learning rates, it may struggle with long-term learning.

   - AdaDelta addresses this limitation by introducing a fixed window of historical gradients, ensuring consistent updates without diminishing learning rates too much.

5. **Nadam and LAMB**

   - Nadam (Nesterov-accelerated Adaptive Moment Estimation) enhances Adam by incorporating Nesterov momentum, providing more precise updates and improved convergence.

   - LAMB (Layer-wise Adaptive Moments for Batch Size) is tailored for large-scale models and adapts learning rates layer-wise, enabling efficient training for massive datasets while maintaining stable gradients.

EXAMPLE: OPTIMIZING A RECOMMENDATION ENGINE FOR E-COMMERCE

E-commerce platforms rely heavily on recommendation engines to personalize user experiences. Below is a step-by-step illustration of optimizing such a system:

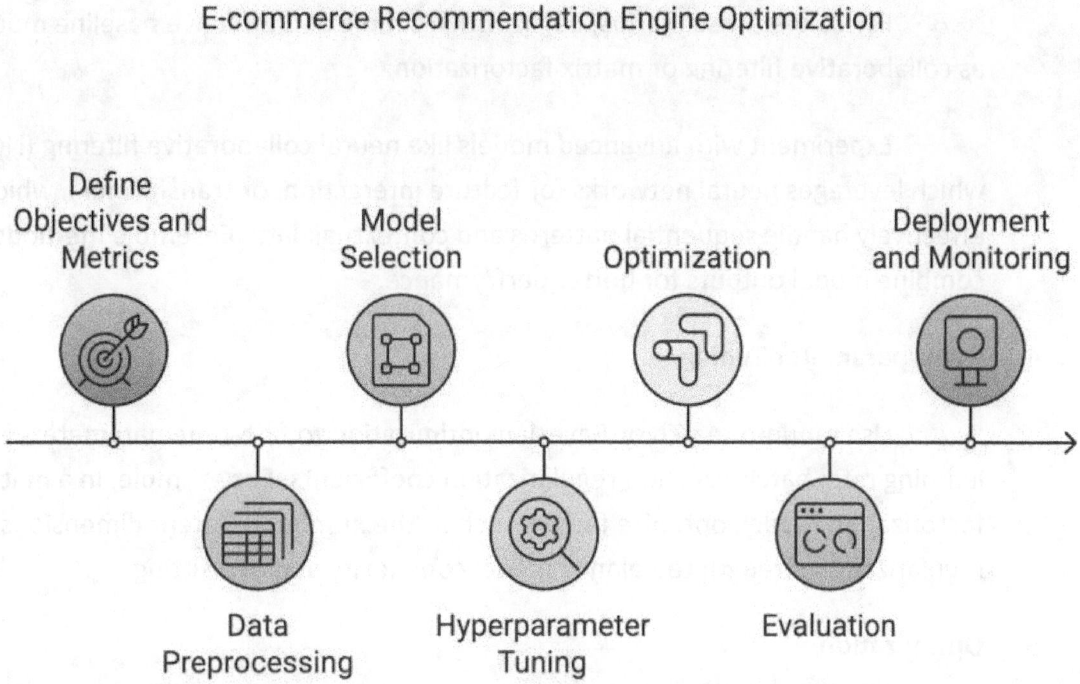

1. **Define Objectives and Metrics**

   ○ Objective: Maximize click-through rate (CTR) or conversion rate. In an e-commerce platform, CTR can indicate how often users engage with recommended items. At the same time, the conversion rate measures the percentage of users who complete purchases based on recommendations.

   ○ Metrics: Precision (the percentage of relevant recommendations among the total), recall (the ability to retrieve all relevant items), F1-score (the harmonic mean of precision and recall), or normalized discounted cumulative gain (DCG, which accounts for the ranking quality of recommendations). The selection of metrics depends on the specific business goals and user behaviors.

2. **Data Preprocessing**

   ○ Collect user interactions, product metadata, and contextual information. For example, include data such as past purchases, browsing history, user demographics, and seasonality trends.

   ○ Clean data to handle missing values (e.g., imputing with means or medians), remove duplicates (to avoid redundant training), and standardize formats (e.g., consistent date-time formats or categorical encoding). Employ feature engineering to extract meaningful variables, such as frequency of user visits or product popularity.

3. **Model Selection**

   o For cold-start scenarios, begin with a simple and effective baseline model, such as collaborative filtering or matrix factorization.

   o Experiment with advanced models like neural collaborative filtering (NCF), which leverages neural networks for feature interaction, or transformers, which effectively handle sequential patterns and contextual data. Ensemble methods can also combine model outputs for better performance.

4. **Hyperparameter Tuning**

   o Use random search or Bayesian optimization to fine-tune parameters like learning rate, batch size, and regularization coefficients. For example, in a matrix factorization model, optimize factors such as the number of latent dimensions or regularization strength to balance model complexity and overfitting.

5. **Optimization**

   o Start with Adam for faster convergence and switch to SGD for fine-tuning near the global minimum. This hybrid approach ensures both efficiency and precision in reaching the optimal weights.

   o Experiment with different learning rate schedules, such as cosine annealing (for gradual reduction) or cyclical learning rates (for periodic resets), which can improve convergence and avoid local minima.

6. **Evaluation**

   o Data were split into training, validation, and test sets using stratified sampling to ensure all user groups are represented.

   o Use cross-validation to ensure robust performance evaluation and test various data slices, such as new users versus returning users, to validate model generalization across scenarios.

7. **Deployment and Monitoring**

   o Deploy the optimized model to a production environment with minimal latency. For seamless integration, use frameworks like TensorFlow Serving or PyTorch Serve.

   o Monitor performance through live A/B testing or multi-armed bandit approaches to test variations. Periodically, retrain the model with updated data to adapt to changing user behaviors and preferences.

Leveraging advanced hyperparameter tuning techniques and selecting appropriate optimization algorithms ensures that the recommendation engine delivers highly personalized and efficient suggestions, improving user satisfaction and business outcomes.

3.4.2 EVALUATION METRICS

Evaluation metrics play a pivotal role in assessing the effectiveness of AI models. Selecting the right metrics is crucial to ensure the models meet the task's objectives while adhering to the domain's constraints. This section delves into specific metrics for classification and generative tasks, supplemented with STEM examples highlighting their practical applications.

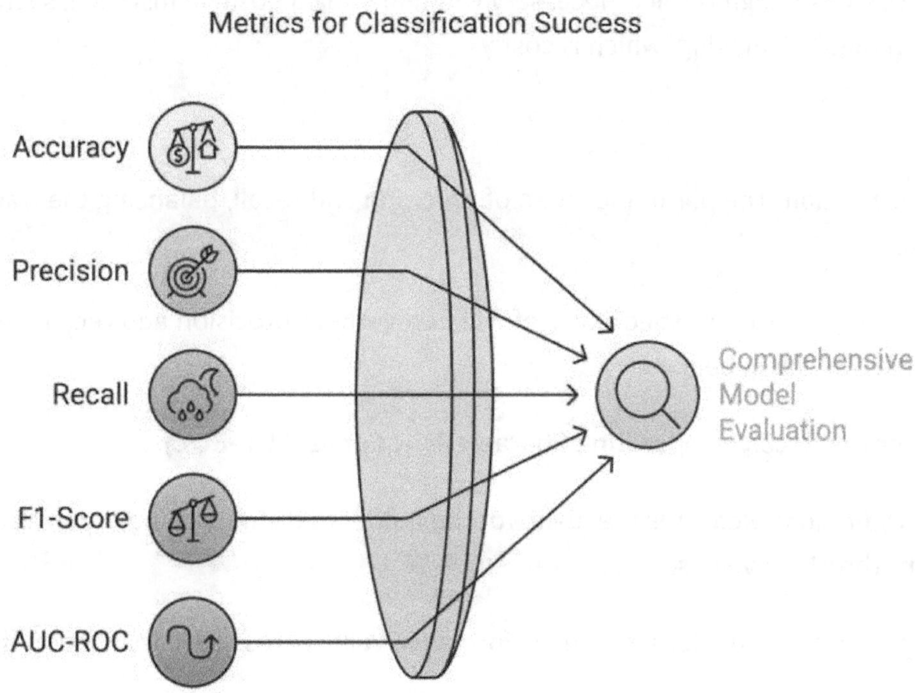

METRICS FOR CLASSIFICATION TASKS

Classification tasks involve categorizing inputs into predefined classes, making accurate performance measurement essential for their success. The following metrics are widely used:

1. Accuracy

- Definition: The ratio of correctly predicted instances to the total cases.
- Strengths: Useful when the dataset is balanced, and all classes are equally important.
- Weaknesses: Can be misleading in imbalanced datasets. For example, in a medical test where 99% of the samples are negative, a model predicting all samples as unfavorable will have 99% accuracy but fail to detect true positives.

2. Precision

- Definition: The ratio of true positives to the total predicted positives.
- Use Case: Precision is critical when false positives are costly. For instance, flagging an essential email as spam (false positive) can cause inconvenience in email spam detection.

3. Recall

- Definition: The ratio of true positives to the total actual positives.
- Use Case: High recall is necessary when missing a positive instance, such as detecting cancer in medical imaging, which is costly.

4. F1-Score

- Definition: The harmonic mean of precision and recall, balancing the trade-off between the two.
- Use Case: This is especially useful in cases where precision and recall are essential, such as fraud detection in banking.

5. Area Under the Receiver Operating Characteristic Curve (AUC-ROC)

- Definition: Measures the ability of the model to distinguish between classes across different threshold values.
- Strengths: Provides a single performance value across all classification thresholds.
- Use Case: Often used in binary classification tasks like predicting customer churn.

METRICS FOR GENERATIVE TASKS

Generative models produce outputs such as text, images, or designs. Their evaluation requires specific metrics, often complemented by human judgment:

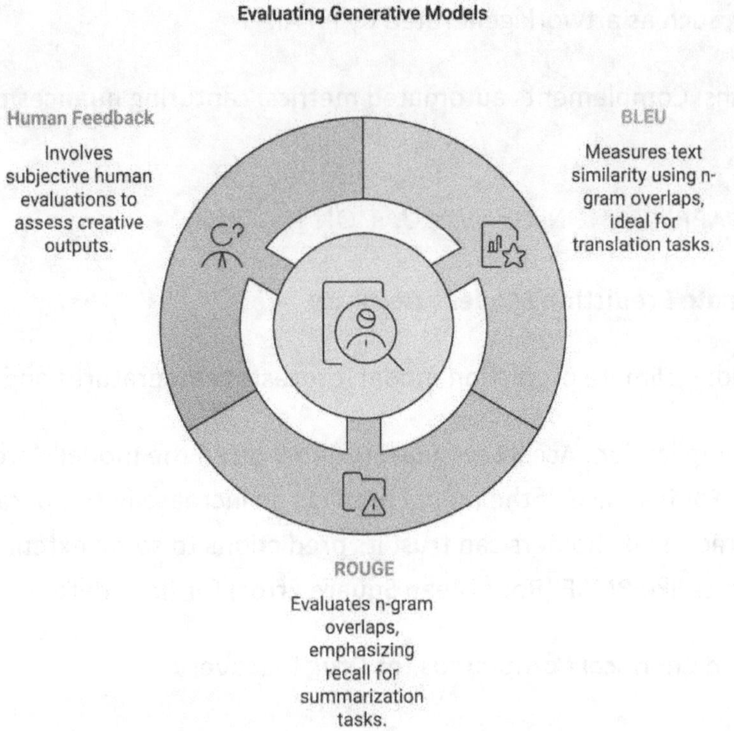

1. BLEU (Bilingual Evaluation Understudy)

- Definition: Measures the similarity between the generated text and reference text, focusing on n-gram overlaps.
- Use Case: Commonly used in machine translation tasks. For example, assessing the quality of English-to-Spanish translations.
- Limitations: It may fail to capture semantic meaning, as it only considers exact matches.

2. ROUGE (Recall-Oriented Understudy for Gisting Evaluation)

- Definition: Evaluate the n-grams, word sequences, or word pairs overlap between generated and reference text.
- Use Case: Popular in summarization tasks. For instance, scoring the quality of automated news summaries.
- Strengths: Places more emphasis on recall, critical for generating comprehensive summaries.

3. Human-in-the-Loop Feedback

- Definition: Involves subjective evaluations by human experts or users to assess the quality of outputs.

- Use Case: This is essential for evaluating outputs that require creativity or contextual understanding, such as artwork generated by an AI.
- Strengths: Complements automated metrics, capturing nuances that algorithms might miss.

STEM EXAMPLES: APPLICATION OF EVALUATION METRICS

1. Evaluating a Climate Prediction Model's Accuracy

- Scenario: A climate prediction model forecasts temperatures and precipitation levels.
- Metric Application: Accuracy measures how often the model's predictions match observed data. For instance, if the model predicts an increase in temperature and precipitation with 80% accuracy, stakeholders can trust its predictions to some extent. Still, they may need additional metrics like RMSE (Root Mean Square Error) for finer details.

2. Scoring Generated Chemical Compounds for Drug Discovery

- Scenario: A generative model creates chemical compounds to target specific diseases.
- Metric Application:
    - BLEU or a domain-specific equivalent can assess the structural similarity of generated compounds to known effective drugs.
    - Human-in-the-loop feedback from chemists can validate the viability and novelty of these compounds. For instance, a compound scoring high on BLEU but deemed toxic by experts would be discarded.

The evaluation of AI models is multifaceted and depends on the problem domain and the stakeholders' objectives. Classification tasks often demand precision and recall in critical scenarios, whereas generative tasks benefit from automated metrics like BLEU and ROUGE, complemented by human evaluations. STEM examples underscore the real-world implications of these metrics, highlighting their relevance in advancing science and technology.

3.4.3 DEBUGGING AND ITERATIVE IMPROVEMENT

Building effective AI systems often requires continuous debugging and iterative refinement. This involves systematically identifying, understanding, and resolving issues that arise during model training and deployment. To streamline this process, practitioners rely on various interpretability tools, visualization techniques, and diagnostic workflows. Below, we explore key strategies for debugging and improving AI models, focusing on interpretability tools and visualization methods to enhance model performance.

Using Interpretability Tools (e.g., SHAP, LIME)

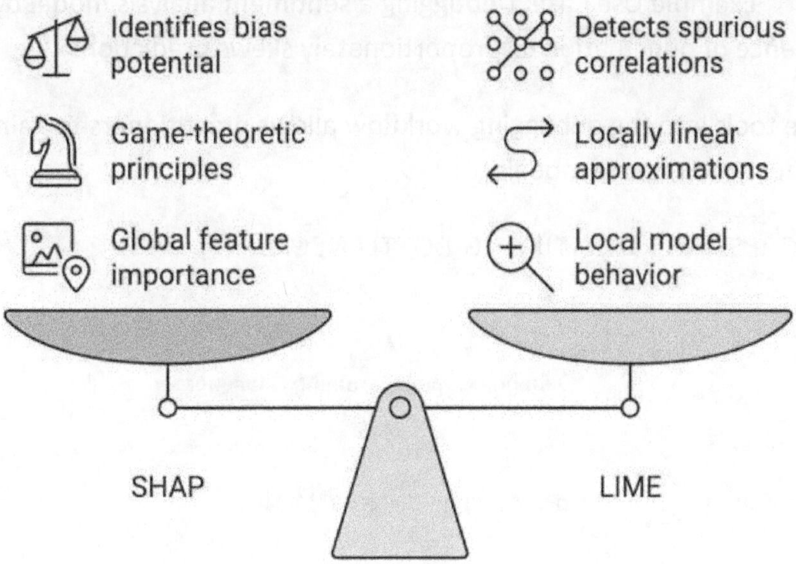

Comparing SHAP and LIME for model interpretability.

Interpretability tools such as SHAP (SHapley Additive exPlanations) and LIME (Local Interpretable Model-Agnostic Explanations) play a critical role in debugging AI models by providing insights into model behavior. These tools help identify potential areas of improvement, assess feature importance, and understand decision-making processes:

- **SHAP (SHapley Additive exPlanations):**
  - SHAP explains individual predictions by attributing them to input features using game-theoretic principles.
  - It provides a global view of feature importance and a local perspective on how specific features influence individual predictions.
  - For debugging, SHAP can identify features that contribute disproportionately to errors or anomalies, guiding targeted adjustments in feature engineering or model tuning.
  - Example Use Case: Diagnosing bias in a credit scoring model by revealing that specific demographic features influence predictions contrary to ethical guidelines.
- **LIME (Local Interpretable Model-Agnostic Explanations):**
  - LIME generates locally linear approximations of model behavior around individual data points.

- It helps detect issues like spurious correlations by showing how small perturbations in input data affect predictions.
- Example Use Case: Debugging a sentiment analysis model by identifying that the presence of punctuation disproportionately skews predictions.

Integrating these tools into the debugging workflow allows practitioners to gain actionable insights, leading to more robust and reliable models.

TRAINING PROGRESS AND IDENTIFYING BOTTLENECKS

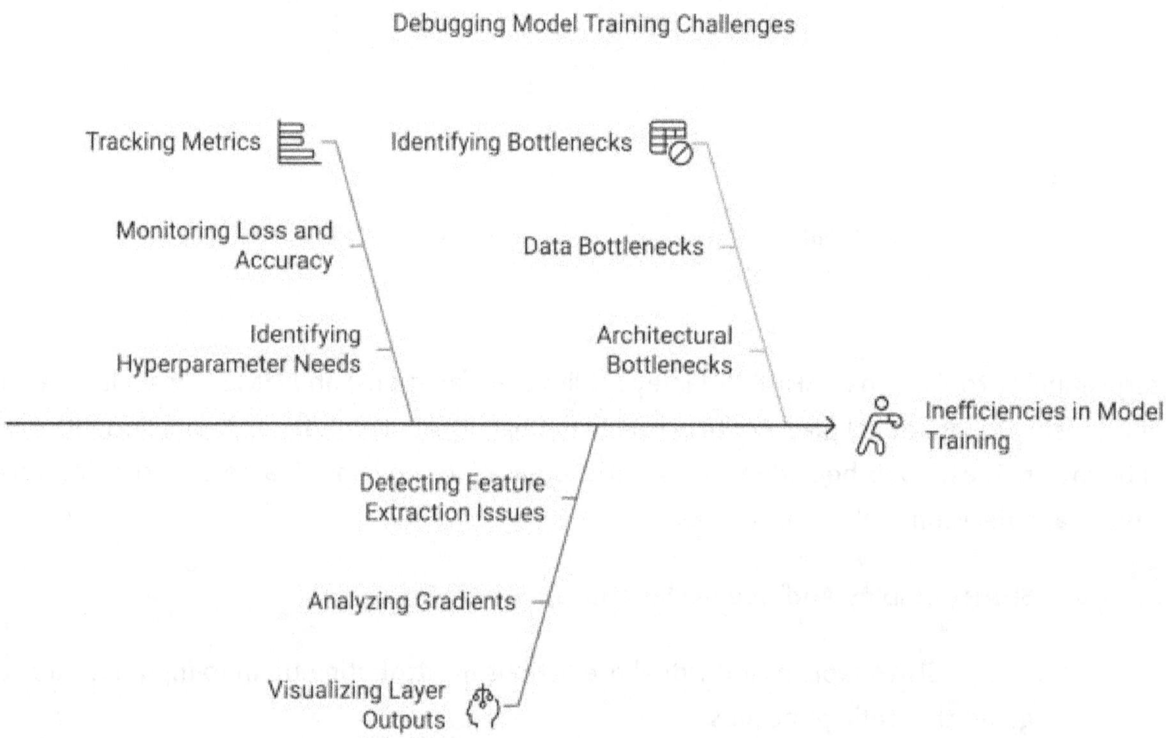

Effective debugging also involves monitoring and visualizing the training process. Visualization tools and techniques provide a window into the model's learning dynamics, helping identify inefficiencies, overfitting, underfitting, and other training-related challenges:

- **Tracking Metrics Over Time:**
  - Monitoring loss, accuracy, and other relevant metrics during training help identify when the model converges, diverges, or plateaus.
  - Example Tools: TensorBoard, Weights & Biases.
  - Common Issues: Sudden spikes in loss may indicate numerical instability, while stagnant metrics suggest the need for hyperparameter tuning.

- **Visualizing Layer Outputs and Gradients:**
    - Layer activations and gradients provide insight into how data flows through the network.
    - Gradient analysis can reveal issues like vanishing or exploding gradients, prompting adjustments to network architecture or learning rate schedules.
    - Example Use Case: Analyzing convolutional layer outputs to detect poor feature extraction in image classification tasks.
- **Identifying Bottlenecks in Data or Architecture:**
    - Data Bottlenecks: Visualizing dataset distributions and input-output correlations can highlight class imbalances, noisy data, or insufficient feature diversity.
    - Architectural Bottlenecks: Visualizing neuron activations can reveal underutilized or overly complex layers, suggesting simplifications or enhancements.
    - Example Use Case: Debugging a recommendation system by visualizing user-item embeddings to uncover sparsity issues in collaborative filtering.

Iterative Debugging Workflows

Debugging is rarely a one-time process; it requires iterative refinement based on insights gained during each evaluation cycle. Key steps in an iterative debugging workflow include:

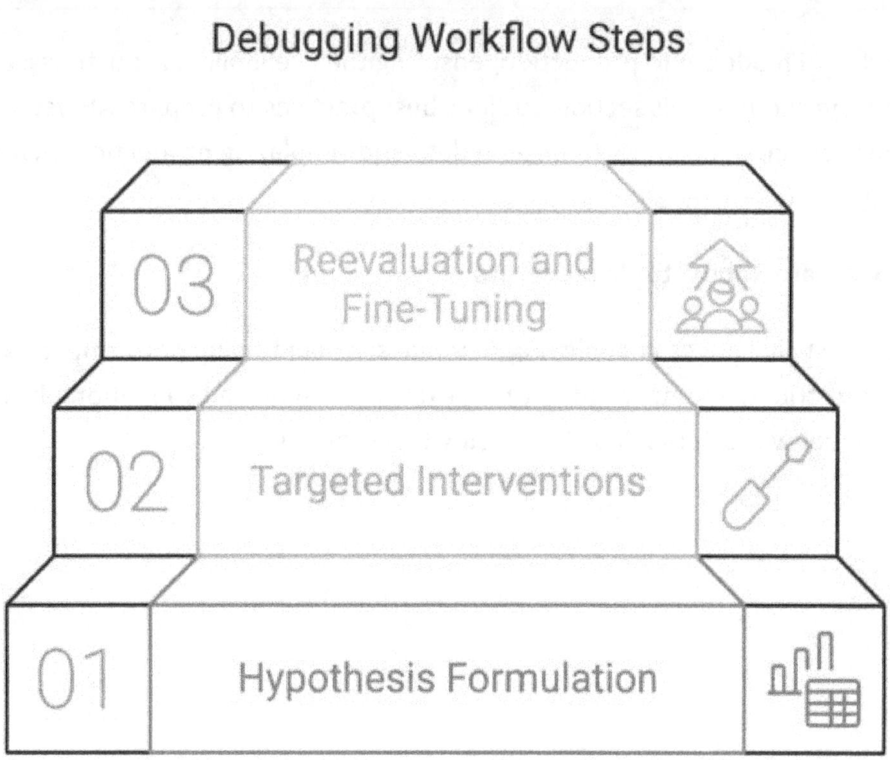

1. **Hypothesis Formulation:**
   - Use visualizations and interpretability insights to hypothesize potential root causes of observed issues.
   - Example: Hypothesizing that high variance in model predictions stems from noisy input features.
2. **Targeted Interventions:**
   - Implement changes such as feature selection, architecture adjustments, or hyperparameter tuning based on hypotheses.
   - Example: Removing or refining noisy features identified as problematic by SHAP.
3. **Reevaluation and Fine-Tuning:**
   - Reevaluate the model after interventions, using updated metrics and visualizations to assess improvements.
   - Example: Comparing pre- and post-intervention training curves to confirm reduced overfitting.

By leveraging interpretability tools and visualization techniques, practitioners can efficiently diagnose and resolve complex issues, ensuring that the final AI model is accurate, fair, and reliable.

3.4.4 BEST PRACTICES FOR DEPLOYMENT READINESS

When deploying AI models into production, ensuring their reliability, robustness, and adaptability is critical for long-term success. This section outlines best practices to prepare AI systems for real-world applications, emphasizing robustness to unseen data and simulating production environments for thorough testing.

Ensuring Models are Robust to Unseen Data

One of the biggest challenges in deploying AI models is maintaining performance when faced with unseen or out-of-distribution data. Models often excel in training and validation phases but falter when exposed to real-world variability. Addressing this requires:

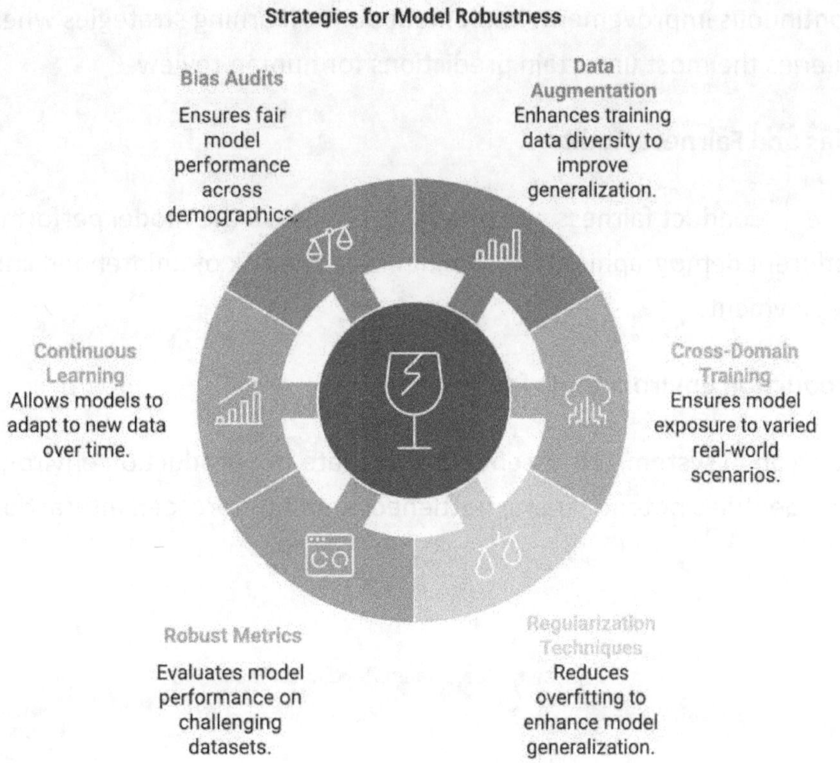

1. **Data Augmentation**
   - Employing data augmentation techniques such as noise addition, cropping, rotation, or synthetic data generation can enhance the diversity of training data. This helps models generalize better to unforeseen variations.
2. **Cross-Domain Training**
   - Include data from different distributions, domains, or sources that reflect potential variability in the production environment. This practice ensures the model is trained on a representative sample of real-world scenarios.
3. **Regularization Techniques**
   - Incorporate dropout, weight decay, and batch normalization methods to improve the model's generalization ability and reduce overfitting.
4. **Robust Metrics and Evaluation**
   - Evaluate models using robust metrics like F1 score, precision-recall curves, and domain-specific KPIs. Assess performance on adversarial datasets or edge cases to identify vulnerabilities.
5. **Continuous Learning Frameworks**

- Design mechanisms to retrain and adapt models to new data, allowing continuous improvement. Implement active learning strategies where the system queries the most uncertain predictions for human review.

6. **Bias and Fairness Audits**

   - Conduct fairness and bias tests to ensure the model performs equitably across different demographic groups, minimizing the risk of unintended consequences in deployment.

Simulating Production Environments for Testing

Before deploying an AI system, it is essential to simulate the production environment as closely as possible. This step identifies potential risks, bottlenecks, and unforeseen interactions within the system.

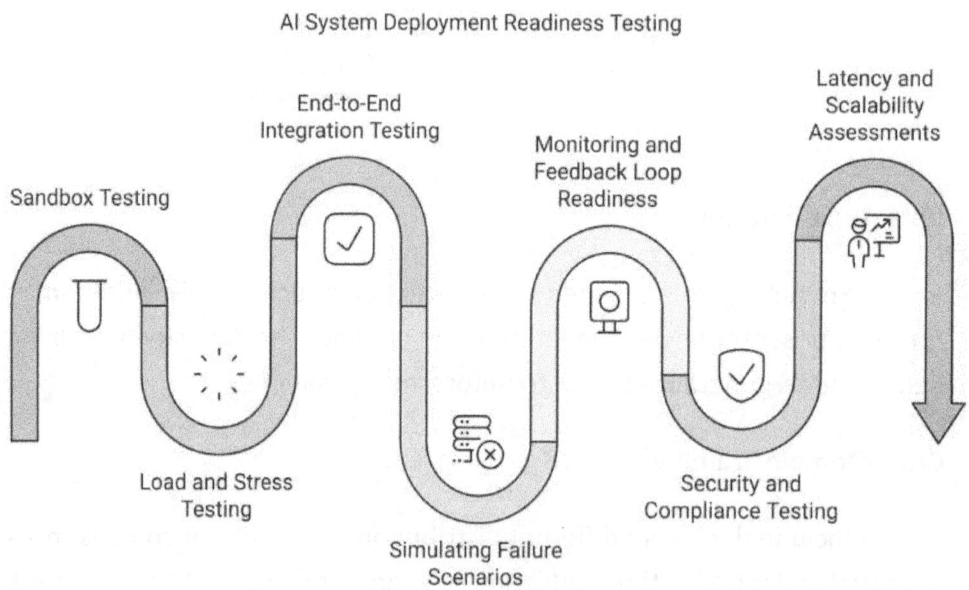

1. **Sandbox Testing**

   - Use sandbox environments to replicate production systems without impacting live operations. To mimic real-world workflows, include mock APIs, synthetic databases, and representative user interactions.

2. **Load and Stress Testing**

   - Assess the system's ability to handle various demand levels, including peak traffic scenarios. Monitor latency, throughput, and resource utilization to identify performance bottlenecks.

3. **End-to-End Integration Testing**

   - Test the entire pipeline, including data ingestion, preprocessing, model inference, and downstream applications. Ensure seamless integration with existing systems and workflows.

4. **Simulating Failure Scenarios**

   - Introduce controlled disruptions, such as network failures or corrupted data inputs, to evaluate the system's resilience and fallback mechanisms.

5. **Monitoring and Feedback Loop Readiness**

   - Ensure monitoring tools, such as logging systems, error tracking, and real-time alerts, are in place for production deployments. Design feedback loops to capture user interactions and iteratively improve system performance.

6. **Security and Compliance Testing**

   - Validate that the model and deployment architecture adhere to security standards and regulatory requirements. Conduct penetration tests to safeguard against vulnerabilities.

7. **Latency and Scalability Assessments**

   - Measure latency at various pipeline stages and assess the model's scalability to accommodate future growth. This includes evaluating inference times and optimizing for real-time or near-real-time decision-making.

Organizations can mitigate risks, enhance system reliability, and build trust in AI deployments by ensuring robustness to unseen data and rigorously simulating production environments. These practices prepare models for real-world challenges and provide a framework for continuous improvement post-deployment.

3.5: PLATFORM ARCHITECTURE

3.5.1 CLOUD VS. ON-PREMISE DEPLOYMENT

Comparing Scalability, Cost, and Control

Analyzing Deployment Models for AI Applications

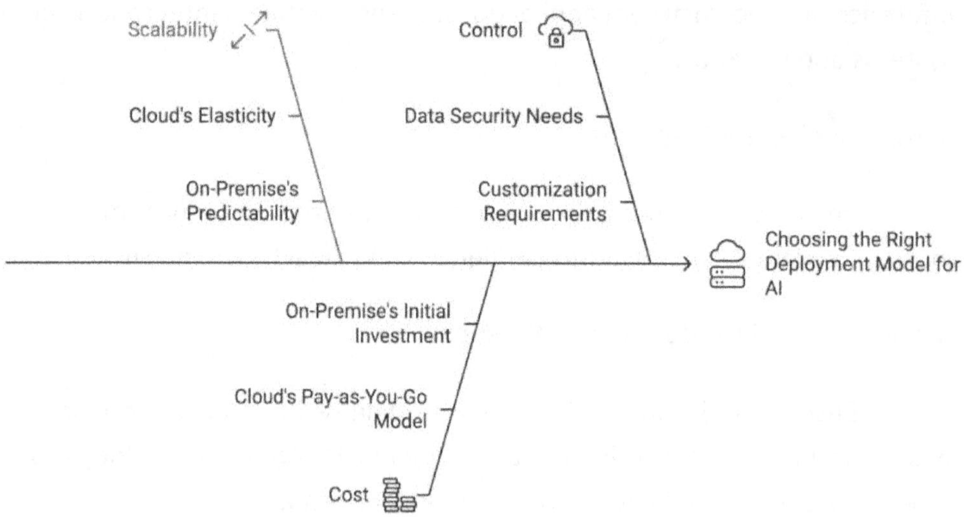

Scalability Cloud deployment offers unparalleled scalability, enabling enterprises to adjust resources dynamically based on workload demands. The cloud provides elastic scalability for AI applications, which often experience fluctuating resource needs during the training and inference phases. Public cloud providers, such as AWS, Azure, and Google Cloud, allow organizations to scale compute power, storage, and networking up or down without additional hardware. Conversely, on-premise deployments require significant upfront investment in infrastructure to accommodate peak loads, often leaving resources underutilized during low-demand periods.

In contrast, on-premise systems provide predictable performance, as the organization dedicates and controls the resources. However, scaling on-premise resources is slower and more expensive, involving procurement, installation, and hardware configuration. This is particularly challenging for real-time AI applications that require rapid response to changing demands.

Cost Cloud deployments often follow a pay-as-you-go pricing model, making them attractive for organizations looking to minimize initial capital expenditures. This model particularly benefits AI startups or small enterprises, as they can access advanced computational resources without significant upfront investments. However, operational expenses can grow significantly, especially if AI workloads run continuously or require high-end GPUs and TPUs for extended periods.

While requiring a substantial initial investment, on-premise deployments can be more cost-effective in the long run for organizations with consistent and predictable workloads. The absence of recurring subscription fees for cloud services can lead to significant savings over time. Additionally, organizations can optimize hardware usage and avoid the variable costs associated with cloud egress and data transfer.

Control On-premise deployments provide complete control over hardware, software, and data. This level of control is critical for organizations with stringent data security and compliance requirements. Industries such as healthcare, finance, and government often favor on-premise solutions to maintain full ownership of sensitive data and meet regulatory standards. Moreover, organizations can customize their infrastructure to align with specific performance and security needs.

While offering flexibility and convenience, cloud deployments often involve relinquishing some control over data and infrastructure. Security concerns, such as data breaches or vendor lock-in, can be significant barriers to cloud adoption. Despite these concerns, cloud providers have introduced robust security measures and compliance certifications to address these issues.

CASE STUDY: HYBRID CLOUD SOLUTIONS FOR REAL-TIME AI APPLICATIONS

Background A financial services company specializing in fraud detection faced significant challenges in managing transactional data's increasing volume and complexity. While secure, the company's existing on-premise infrastructure struggled to accommodate real-time processing demands during peak periods such as holiday shopping or sudden spikes in fraudulent activities. This limitation delayed responses to potential fraud, reduced customer trust, and elevated operational costs. Additionally, the organization had to comply with stringent data security and privacy regulations, including GDPR and PCI DSS, further complicating its operational strategy.

Hybrid Solution To overcome these challenges, the company implemented a hybrid cloud solution that combined the reliability of on-premise systems with the flexibility of cloud-based resources. On-premise infrastructure remained the backbone for processing and storing sensitive customer data, ensuring compliance with regulatory mandates and safeguarding against data breaches. High-performance servers with specialized GPUs handled computationally intensive tasks like training fraud detection models and executing real-time inference processes.

The company leveraged a public cloud platform for less critical operations, such as exploratory data analysis, batch processing, and training experimental AI models. This strategic division of workloads reduced the computational strain on on-premise systems and enabled cost-effective scaling. The cloud's elasticity was particularly advantageous during peak transaction periods, allowing the company to temporarily allocate additional resources without investing in permanent infrastructure upgrades.

The hybrid deployment utilized advanced orchestration and integration tools to ensure seamless communication and workflow synchronization between the on-premise and cloud environments. Automated monitoring systems were implemented to manage resource allocation, detect potential bottlenecks, and maintain low-latency data transfer. These tools ensured that sensitive data never left the secure on-premise environment, mitigating risks associated with data breaches or unauthorized access.

Enhanced Features and Benefits

- **Real-Time Fraud Detection:** By combining the scalability of the cloud with the reliability of on-premise resources, the company achieved near-instantaneous fraud detection, even during peak periods.

- **Cost Optimization:** Offloading non-critical workloads to the cloud reduced the need for extensive on-premise hardware investments, leading to significant cost savings.

- **Regulatory Compliance:** Sensitive customer data remained entirely within the on-premise infrastructure, ensuring adherence to GDPR, PCI DSS, and other data protection standards.

- **Operational Flexibility:** The hybrid setup provided the flexibility to experiment with new AI models and algorithms without disrupting the primary fraud detection operations.

- **Scalability on Demand:** The cloud's on-demand resources ensured the infrastructure could handle sudden surges in transaction volumes without compromising performance.

Challenges and Lessons Learned

- **Integration Complexity:** Combining on-premise and cloud resources required robust integration tools and expertise, particularly to manage data synchronization and workflow orchestration.

- **Latency Management:** Ensuring low-latency communication between the two environments was crucial for maintaining real-time performance, necessitating investments in advanced networking solutions.

- **Cost Monitoring:** While the cloud reduced initial capital expenditures, ongoing operational expenses required careful monitoring to prevent budget overruns.

The hybrid cloud solution enabled the financial services company to balance the competing scalability, cost-efficiency, and regulatory compliance demands. By leveraging the strengths of both deployment strategies, the organization enhanced its fraud detection capabilities and positioned itself as a leader in leveraging cutting-edge AI technologies for real-time applications. This case highlights the potential of hybrid solutions for enterprises seeking to navigate the complexities of modern AI workloads while addressing critical business and regulatory requirements.

3.5.2 BUILDING SCALABLE AI PLATFORMS

Building scalable AI platforms is a cornerstone of delivering reliable, efficient, and adaptable AI solutions that can evolve with user demands and technological advancements. This section explores the essential components, provides practical examples, and outlines visual representations of scalable architectures, emphasizing their importance in modern AI applications.

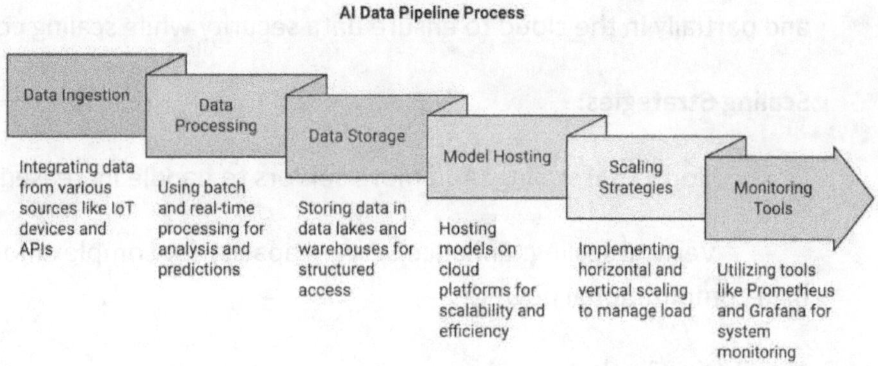

Key Components:

1. **Data Pipelines:**
   - **Ingestion Frameworks:**
     - Integrate data from diverse sources like IoT devices, transactional systems, web crawlers, and external APIs.
     - Example: A retail AI platform may collect point-of-sale data in real time while integrating historical purchase trends from data warehouses.
   - **Processing Layers:**
     - Batch processing for bulk historical data analysis and real-time streaming for on-the-fly predictions.
     - Utilize frameworks like Apache Kafka for data streaming or Apache Spark for distributed processing.
   - **Data Storage:**
     - **Data Lakes:** Store raw, unstructured data that can be cleaned and processed later.
     - **Data Warehouses:** Store structured data for quick querying and analysis using tools like Snowflake or BigQuery.
2. **Model Hosting:**
   - **Infrastructure Considerations:**
     - Host models on cloud platforms (AWS SageMaker, Azure ML, or GCP AI Platform) to leverage scalability and reduce operational overhead.

- Enable hybrid solutions where models are hosted partially on-premises and partially in the cloud to ensure data security while scaling compute power.

- **Scaling Strategies:**
  - Horizontal scaling: Add more servers to handle increased load.
  - Vertical scaling: Enhance server capacity for complex models requiring high computational power.
- **Monitoring Tools:**
  - Platforms like Prometheus and Grafana for real-time insights into system health and performance bottlenecks.

3. **APIs:**
   - **Integration Frameworks:**
     - Develop lightweight RESTful or GraphQL APIs to interface between AI models and business applications.
     - Use microservices architecture to modularize functionalities, ensuring easy scalability.
   - **Advanced Capabilities:**
     - Rate limiting to prevent overloading APIs during peak usage.
     - Built-in error handling and fallback mechanisms to ensure system resilience.

Example: Designing an AI Platform for STEM Researchers

STEM researchers often require specialized tools to analyze large datasets, derive insights, and collaborate on experimental models. A scalable AI platform for this audience could include:

- **Data Handling:**
  - Automated ingestion pipelines for collecting data from lab sensors, external databases, and published research papers.
  - Preprocessing layers to normalize and clean data for consistency across datasets.
- **Collaboration Tools:**

- Real-time dashboards to visualize model training results and experiment tracking using platforms like TensorBoard.
- Role-based access controls to ensure data security in collaborative projects.

- **Specialized Models:**
  - Pre-trained models for specific research areas, such as protein structure prediction for biologists or seismic data analysis for geologists.

- **APIs for Research Integration:**
  - APIs that interface with existing research tools like MATLAB, Python-based Jupyter Notebooks, or RStudio, providing seamless access to platform functionalities.

Implementation Best Practices: To ensure the scalability of AI platforms, consider the following best practices:

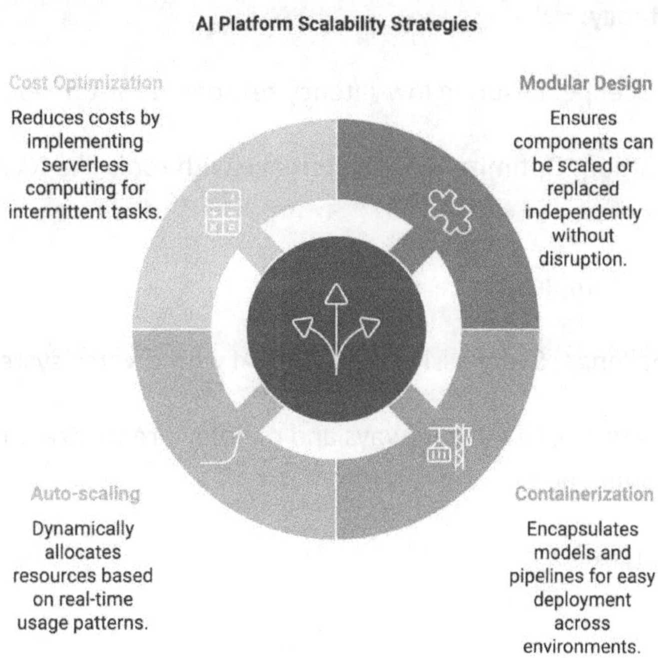

1. **Modular Design:**
   - Build components as independent modules to ensure they can be scaled or replaced without disrupting the system.

2. **Containerization:**
   - Use tools like Docker to encapsulate models and pipelines into lightweight, portable containers for easy deployment across environments.

3. **Auto-scaling:**

    ○ Leverage cloud services' auto-scaling features to allocate resources based on real-time usage patterns dynamically.

4. **Cost Optimization:**

    ○ Implement serverless computing for intermittent tasks, reducing costs while maintaining scalability.

Challenges and Solutions:

1. **Data Scalability:**

    ○ Challenge: Handling large-scale data ingestion and real-time processing.

    ○ Solution: Employ distributed systems like Apache Kafka for streaming and Delta Lake for storage.

2. **Model Latency:**

    ○ Challenge: Ensuring low-latency responses for time-sensitive applications.

    ○ Solution: Optimize model inference with tools like NVIDIA Triton Inference Server.

3. **Integration Complexity:**

    ○ Challenge: Seamlessly integrating AI with diverse systems and applications.

    ○ Solution: Use API gateways and middleware to streamline communication and reduce redundancy.

SCALABLE ARCHITECTURE

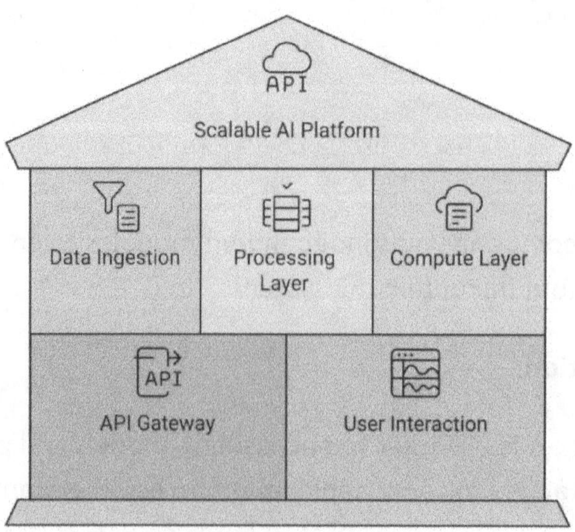

A well-designed scalable AI platform addresses current demands and anticipates future growth, enabling businesses and researchers to extract value from AI technologies without bottlenecks. By focusing on robust data pipelines, flexible model hosting, and seamless API integration, organizations can create platforms that serve as foundational pillars for AI-driven innovation.

3.5.3 SECURITY AND PRIVACY CONSIDERATIONS

Protecting sensitive data during training and inference is a critical aspect of deploying AI systems, particularly in domains like healthcare, finance, and government applications where data sensitivity is paramount. This section provides an in-depth look into safeguarding mechanisms, compliance with legal frameworks, and practical implementation of security and privacy best practices in AI systems.

Protecting Sensitive Data During Training and Inference

AI systems often require large volumes of data for training and inference, much of which may include personally identifiable information (PII) or sensitive proprietary data. To ensure robust security and privacy, organizations should consider the following strategies:

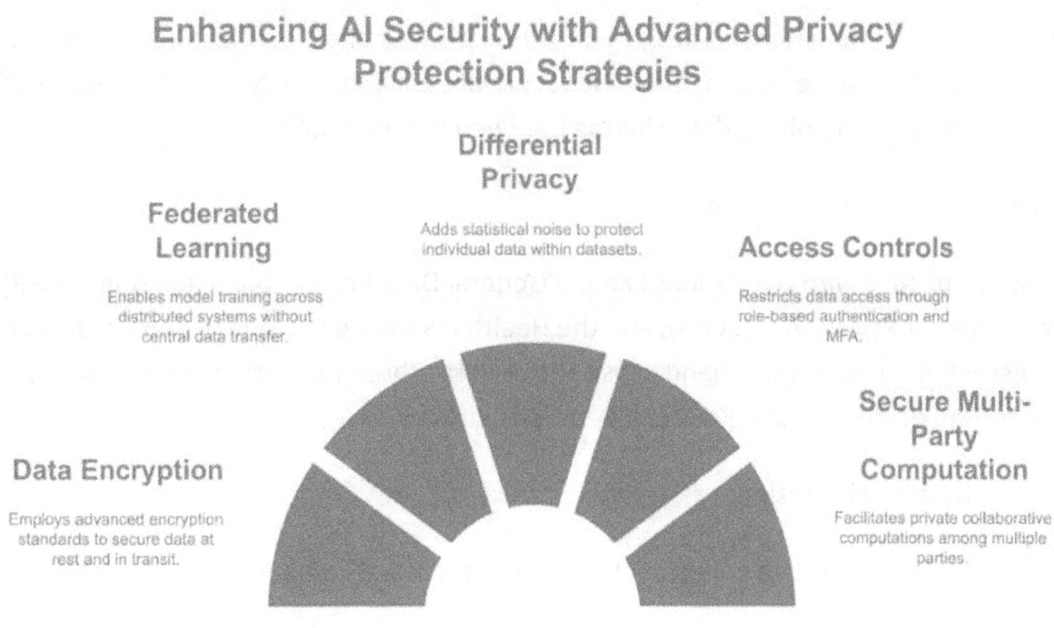

1. **Data Encryption:**
   - Employ encryption mechanisms both at rest and in transit. Advanced encryption standards (e.g., AES-256) ensure that data remains secure even if intercepted.
   - Secure inference pipelines with Transport Layer Security (TLS) to safeguard data communication between AI services and end-users.

2. **Federated Learning:**

    o Federated learning allows model training to occur across distributed devices or servers without transferring sensitive data to a central location. This approach reduces the risk of data breaches and enhances privacy.

3. **Differential Privacy:**

    o Introduce statistical noise into datasets during training to prevent the extraction of specific details about individuals. Differential privacy ensures that AI models retain utility without compromising individual data privacy.

4. **Access Controls and Role-Based Authentication:**

    o Restrict access to data and model systems based on user roles. To minimize unauthorized access risks, use robust authentication mechanisms such as multi-factor authentication (MFA) and identity management systems.

5. **Secure Multi-Party Computation (SMPC):**

    o Implement cryptographic protocols that allow multiple parties to compute a function while keeping their inputs private collaboratively. SMPC is particularly useful in scenarios involving data-sharing between organizations.

Compliance with Legal Frameworks

Ensuring compliance with regulations like the General Data Protection Regulation (GDPR), the California Consumer Privacy Act (CCPA), and the Health Insurance Portability and Accountability Act (HIPAA) is essential for AI systems handling sensitive data. These regulations emphasize user rights, transparency, and accountability. Key considerations include:

1. **Data Minimization:**

    o Limit data collection to only what is strictly necessary for the intended AI application.

    o Regularly audit datasets to ensure they meet privacy requirements.

2. **Consent Management:**

    o Obtain explicit consent from users for data collection and processing. Ensure users can access clear and detailed information about their data use.

3. **Data Anonymization and Pseudonymization:**

- Anonymize data to remove identifiable elements, making it impossible to link data back to individuals.
- Alternatively, pseudonymization techniques can replace identifiable information with reversible tokens, ensuring privacy while allowing authorized re-identification.

4. **Auditing and Documentation:**
    - Maintain thorough records of data handling practices, including how and where data is stored, processed, and shared.
    - Conduct regular audits to ensure compliance with evolving regulatory requirements.

Example: GDPR-Compliant Data Handling in AI Healthcare Platforms

AI healthcare platforms must balance the need for accurate diagnoses and predictions with stringent privacy and security measures. A GDPR-compliant AI healthcare solution might implement the following measures:

- **Data Collection and Consent:**
    - Explicitly inform patients about the data collection type (e.g., medical history, imaging data) and obtain their consent.
    - Provide options for patients to withdraw consent at any time.
- **Data Security and Encryption:**
    - Encrypt patient data using state-of-the-art encryption protocols before transferring it to cloud servers or AI models.
- **Model Training with Privacy Enhancements:**
    - Use federated learning to train AI models on patient data stored at local hospitals, ensuring data never leaves the premises.
- **Transparency and Accountability:**
    - Maintain an auditable trail of data usage and processing activities.
    - Implement explainable AI (XAI) techniques to allow patients and regulators to understand how predictions are generated.
- **Automated Data Deletion:**

- Implement automated workflows to delete patient data after a predefined retention period in compliance with GDPR's "right to be forgotten."

Employing these strategies, organizations can mitigate risks, foster trust, and comply with legal frameworks while leveraging AI systems' full potential.

CHAPTER 4: USER-CENTRIC DESIGN AND DEPLOYMENT

INTRODUCTION

Introduction

User-centric design and seamless deployment are cornerstones of successful AI solutions. As AI becomes deeply integrated into industries like healthcare, education, and finance, ensuring that these systems are user-friendly and deployable at scale is more crucial than ever. This chapter delves into the critical role of user-centric design and deployment readiness, providing readers with practical tools and strategies to achieve impactful and scalable AI applications.

1. Why User-Centric Design Matters

User-friendly AI solutions are the foundation of widespread adoption and trust. Intuitive designs allow users to quickly understand and interact with AI tools, fostering confidence and satisfaction. Consider the success of tools like Grammarly, which democratizes writing improvement by offering real-time, accessible suggestions, or Tesla's Autopilot, which builds trust by seamlessly integrating AI into daily driving tasks. These examples highlight the value of intuitive, human-centered design in driving user engagement.

Moreover, user-centric design directly impacts ROI by minimizing friction points that might deter adoption. When AI tools anticipate and meet user needs, they reduce the learning curve and promote sustained use. This approach ensures a positive feedback loop in which usability drives engagement, which in turn drives business value.

2. Why Deployment Readiness Is Critical

Deployment readiness connects a well-designed AI solution with its real-world impact. A seamless deployment process accelerates time to market and ensures scalability and reliability. Poor deployment planning can lead to critical failures, such as prolonged downtimes or compatibility issues, undermining user trust and causing reputational harm.

Take, for instance, the case of a promising AI-powered retail assistant that failed due to deployment bottlenecks. Despite having robust features, the tool's poor integration with existing e-commerce platforms rendered it unusable. Similarly, suboptimal user experiences—such as unintuitive workflows or frequent errors during deployment—can erode confidence and prevent the solution from achieving its potential.

By addressing deployment readiness early, organizations can avoid these pitfalls and ensure their solutions are scalable, secure, and aligned with user expectations.

3. Goals of This Chapter

This chapter aims to:

- Equip readers with proven frameworks and methodologies for user-centric design, helping them create solutions that resonate with diverse user groups.
- Provide actionable strategies for scalable, secure, and efficient deployment processes, ensuring AI solutions perform reliably in real-world environments.
- Illustrate principles and solutions through real-world case studies, emphasizing the transformative potential of well-executed design and deployment practices.

By the end of this chapter, readers will have the insights needed to design and deploy AI systems that meet technical requirements and prioritize user satisfaction and operational excellence.

4.1: UX PRINCIPLES FOR AI SOLUTIONS

4.1.1 DESIGNING FOR TRUST AND TRANSPARENCY

In an era where Artificial Intelligence (AI) permeates numerous aspects of human life, trust and transparency in AI systems are desirable and imperative. The design of AI systems must prioritize these principles, especially in high-stakes applications where decisions significantly impact lives. This section explores the importance of explainability and outlines UX best practices to foster trust and transparency.

Importance of Explainability in High-Stakes Applications

Explainability is the ability of AI systems to articulate their reasoning, processes, and outcomes in ways that are understandable to humans. It is pivotal in high-stakes applications such as healthcare diagnostics, autonomous driving, and financial decision-making. Without explainability, users and stakeholders may find it difficult to trust the AI system, potentially leading to resistance, misuse, or unintended consequences.

Consider the example of AI in healthcare diagnostics. When an AI model suggests a diagnosis for a patient, clinicians need to understand the reasoning behind the recommendation. Is the AI basing its decision on a pattern in the patient's medical history? Is it leveraging data from similar cases? Explainability ensures that medical professionals can verify the AI's conclusions, cross-check them with their expertise, and ultimately make informed decisions. This collaborative interaction between AI and human experts reduces the likelihood of errors and enhances trust in the system.

Moreover, regulatory compliance often necessitates explainability. For instance, the European Union's General Data Protection Regulation (GDPR) includes a "right to explanation" for individuals affected by automated decision-making. AI systems deployed in high-stakes domains must function correctly and provide clear and understandable explanations of their behavior to meet these legal requirements.

Lack of explainability can have dire consequences. In 2020, a widely reported instance involved an AI system used in the UK to predict student grades during the COVID-19 pandemic. The algorithm's lack of transparency and perceived biases led to public outcry and eventual system abandonment. This example underscores the importance of explainability as a cornerstone for maintaining trust in AI systems.

UX BEST PRACTICES FOR AI

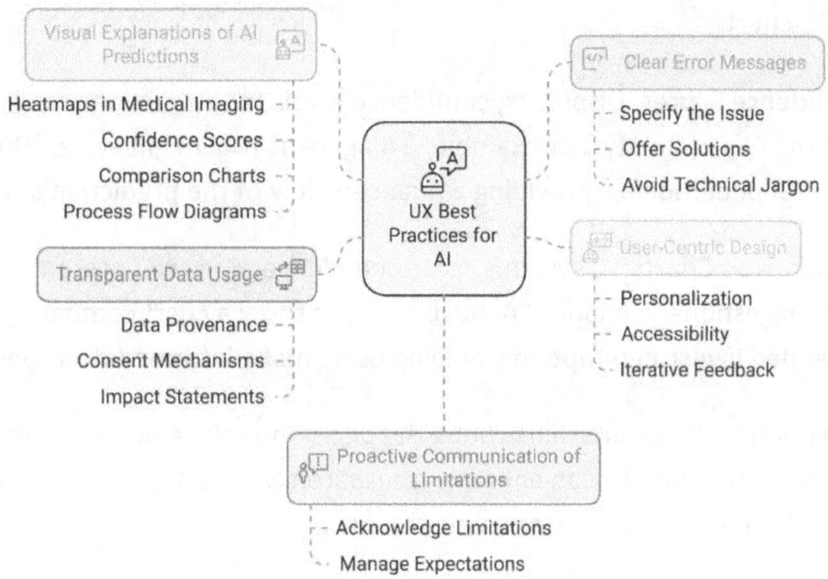

AI systems' user experience (UX) significantly influences trust and transparency. Effective UX design ensures that users understand and interact with the AI system intuitively, fostering confidence and reducing ambiguity. Below are key UX best practices for designing AI systems:

1. **Clear Error Messages**

AI systems, like all software, are prone to errors. When errors occur, providing clear and actionable error messages is crucial. Ambiguous messages such as "Something went wrong" can frustrate users and erode trust. Instead, error messages should:

- Specify the issue: "Unable to process the image due to low resolution" provides clarity.
- Offer solutions: Suggesting steps like "Try uploading a higher-resolution image" empowers users to resolve the problem.
- Avoid technical jargon: Use plain language accessible to all users, not just technical experts.

Transparent error communication reassures users that the system acknowledges issues and actively supports resolution.

2. **Visual Explanations of AI Predictions**

Visual explanations play a critical role in demystifying AI predictions. Presenting information visually allows users to grasp complex data and decision-making processes more efficiently. Some effective strategies for visual explanations include:

- **Heatmaps in Medical Imaging**: In healthcare diagnostics, AI models analyzing medical images can use heatmaps to highlight areas of concern. For instance, a heatmap on an X-ray can indicate regions where the AI detects abnormalities, enabling radiologists to focus their attention effectively.

- **Confidence Scores**: Displaying confidence levels for predictions can help users understand the AI's certainty. For example, a diagnostic tool might state, "90% confidence in the diagnosis of pneumonia," providing a nuanced view of the prediction's reliability.

- **Comparison Charts**: AI systems recommending actions can present comparative data to justify their suggestions. A financial AI advisor might show a chart comparing the performance of recommended investment options, helping users make informed decisions.

- **Process Flow Diagrams**: Illustrating the decision-making process through flow diagrams or step-by-step visualizations can enhance transparency. This approach is advantageous in applications like loan approval or risk assessment.

Visual explanations build trust and empower users by enhancing their understanding of AI systems.

3. **User-Centric Design**

Designing AI systems with a user-centric approach ensures that users' needs, preferences, and expectations are at the forefront. User-centric design incorporates:

- **Personalization** involves tailoring the system's interface and responses to individual user contexts. For instance, an AI tutor can adjust its teaching style based on a student's learning preferences.

- **Accessibility**: Ensuring that the system is usable by individuals with diverse abilities. This includes features like screen reader compatibility and alternative input methods.

- **Iterative Feedback**: Incorporating user feedback during development to refine the system and address potential concerns early.

4. **Transparent Data Usage**

Users are more likely to trust AI systems when they understand how their data is used. Transparency in data usage involves:

- **Data Provenance**: Communicating where the data originates and how it has been processed.

- **Consent Mechanisms**: Giving users options to control their data and make informed decisions about sharing it.

- **Impact Statements**: Informing users about the implications of their data on system outcomes, such as "Your recent activity is influencing these recommendations."

5. **Proactive Communication of Limitations**

AI systems should proactively communicate their limitations to manage user expectations. Acknowledging scenarios where the system might perform suboptimally fosters trust. For example, a language translation AI might notify users, "Complex idiomatic expressions may not translate accurately."

The Path Forward

As AI integrates into critical domains, designing for trust and transparency becomes non-negotiable. By prioritizing explainability and adhering to UX best practices, designers and developers can create systems that perform effectively and inspire confidence and trust among users. Ultimately, the goal is to establish a collaborative relationship between humans and AI, where each complements the other to achieve better outcomes.

4.1.2 BALANCING AUTOMATION AND USER CONTROL (2 PAGES)

- Allowing users to override AI decisions in critical scenarios:
    - Example: Human-in-the-loop systems in fraud detection.

4.1.3 ACCESSIBILITY AND INCLUSION

The balance between automation and user control is one of the most critical aspects of designing and implementing AI systems. While automation offers efficiency, scalability, and precision, it is not infallible. Human oversight remains essential, especially in critical scenarios where decisions carry significant consequences. Allowing users to override AI decisions ensures that the system is both flexible and trustworthy, fostering user confidence and ensuring better outcomes in complex environments.

Allowing Users to Override AI Decisions in Critical Scenarios

One of the foundational principles in designing AI systems is the inclusion of mechanisms that allow human intervention. This principle is particularly vital in domains where the cost of incorrect decisions is high, such as healthcare, finance, transportation, and legal systems. In such scenarios, relying solely on AI systems can be risky, as even state-of-the-art models may produce errors due to biases in the training data, unforeseen edge cases, or limitations in generalizing to novel situations. Human expertise acts as a safety net, enabling better decision-making and mitigating potential risks.

Human-in-the-Loop Systems in Fraud Detection

Fraud detection serves as an excellent example of balancing automation with user control. AI systems have transformed fraud detection by identifying patterns and anomalies that would be difficult, if not impossible, for humans to detect at scale. Machine learning models, for instance, can analyze millions of transactions in real time, flagging those that exhibit unusual behavior. However, not every flagged transaction represents fraud. False positives are common and can have serious repercussions, such as blocking legitimate transactions and frustrating customers.

In human-in-the-loop fraud detection systems, flagged transactions are reviewed by human analysts before final decisions are made. The AI system acts as the first layer of defense, identifying potentially fraudulent activities, while the human analyst provides the second layer of scrutiny, evaluating the flagged cases using contextual knowledge and judgment. This approach combines the speed and scalability of AI with the nuanced understanding of human analysts, ensuring a more accurate and fairer outcome.

For example, consider a scenario where an AI system flags a high-value transaction from an international location as potentially fraudulent. While the transaction might deviate from the user's typical behavior, it could be legitimate, such as a business expense during international travel. A human analyst can review the flagged transaction, cross-referencing it with additional data points—such as travel records, prior customer communications, or other behavioral indicators—to make a well-informed decision. This process not only minimizes the risk of false positives but also enhances the user experience by reducing unnecessary disruptions.

BENEFITS OF ALLOWING USER OVERRIDES

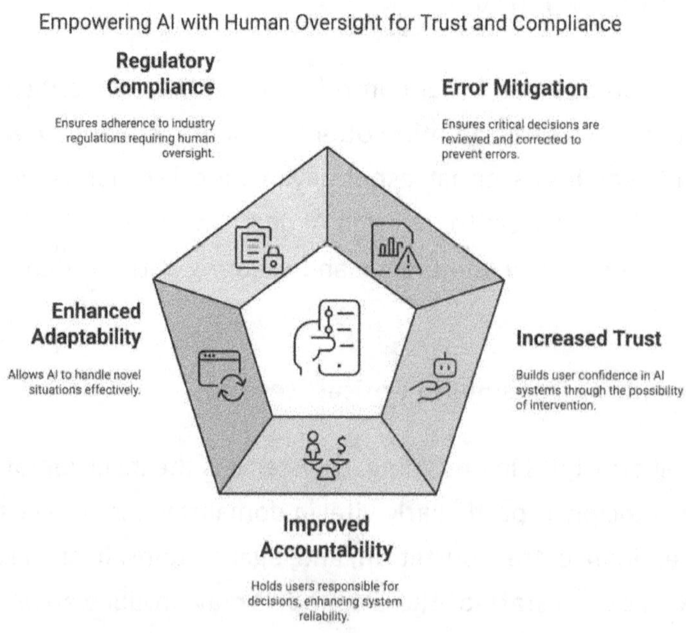

1. **Error Mitigation**: AI systems are not immune to errors, particularly in high-stakes scenarios. Allowing human intervention ensures that critical decisions are reviewed and corrected if necessary, reducing the likelihood of adverse outcomes.

2. **Increased Trust**: Users are more likely to trust AI systems when they know they can intervene and override decisions. This trust is essential for the widespread adoption of AI technologies.

3. **Improved Accountability**: Human oversight ensures accountability, as users or analysts can take responsibility for decisions rather than attributing errors solely to the AI system.

4. **Enhanced Adaptability**: Human intervention allows systems to handle novel or complex situations that fall outside the AI's training data, ensuring more robust performance in dynamic environments.

5. **Regulatory Compliance**: In many industries, such as finance and healthcare, regulations mandate human oversight of automated systems. Allowing user overrides ensures compliance with these requirements.

DESIGNING EFFECTIVE OVERRIDE MECHANISMS

To ensure that override mechanisms are effective and practical, organizations must address several key considerations:

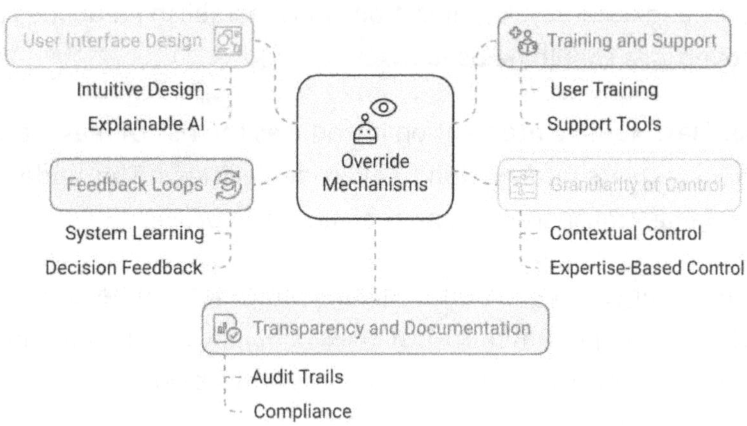

1. **User Interface Design**: Override mechanisms should be intuitive and easily accessible. Users must be able to understand why a decision was made and how to intervene if necessary. This requires clear explanations of AI decisions, often referred to as explainable AI (XAI).

2. **Training and Support**: Users need adequate training to understand the AI system's capabilities and limitations. They should also be equipped with the tools and knowledge to make informed decisions when overriding AI outputs.

3. **Granularity of Control**: Override mechanisms should offer varying levels of control, depending on the context and user expertise. For example, in fraud detection, analysts might have the ability to flag transactions for further review, approve or deny flagged transactions, or adjust the sensitivity of the AI system.

4. **Feedback Loops**: Overrides should feed back into the AI system, enabling it to learn from human decisions and improve over time. This iterative process enhances the system's accuracy and adaptability.

5. **Transparency and Documentation**: Every override decision should be documented, providing a clear audit trail. This transparency is essential for accountability, compliance, and continuous improvement.

CHALLENGES AND CONSIDERATIONS

While allowing user overrides offers numerous benefits, it also introduces challenges that must be carefully managed:

1. **Cognitive Load**: Requiring users to review and override AI decisions can increase their cognitive load, particularly if the system generates a high volume of alerts. To address this, organizations must optimize the balance between automation and manual intervention, ensuring that human involvement is limited to genuinely critical scenarios.

2. **Overreliance on Human Judgment**: In some cases, users may rely too heavily on their judgment, overriding AI decisions without sufficient justification. This can undermine the system's efficiency and accuracy. Organizations must establish guidelines and best practices for when and how overrides should be used.

3. **Potential Bias**: Human intervention introduces the risk of bias, particularly if users rely on subjective or incomplete information to override decisions. This underscores the importance of training, transparency, and robust review processes.

4. **Scalability**: In large-scale systems, manual overrides can become a bottleneck, limiting the system's scalability. Organizations must strike a balance, using human intervention selectively and augmenting it with AI improvements where possible.

Balancing automation and user control is a dynamic and ongoing process. By allowing users to override AI decisions in critical scenarios, organizations can harness the strengths of both human expertise and machine intelligence. Human-in-the-loop systems, such as those used in fraud detection, exemplify this balance, combining the efficiency and scalability of AI with the contextual understanding and judgment of human analysts. While challenges remain, careful design, training, and continuous improvement can ensure that override mechanisms enhance the overall effectiveness and reliability of AI systems. This balanced approach not only mitigates risks but also fosters trust, accountability, and long-term success in the deployment of AI technologies.

4.1.4 GOOD VS. BAD AI INTERFACES

The efficacy of artificial intelligence (AI) systems frequently depends on the quality and sophistication of their user interfaces (UIs). An optimally designed UI is a conduit between intricate AI functionalities and the end-user, promoting accessibility and ease of use. Conversely, poorly conceived interfaces can engender user dissatisfaction and ultimately undermine the adoption of AI technologies. This section delineates the hallmarks of intuitive versus suboptimal AI interfaces, bolstered by examples and a comparative analysis of effective and ineffective UX paradigms.

HALLMARKS OF EXEMPLARY AI INTERFACES

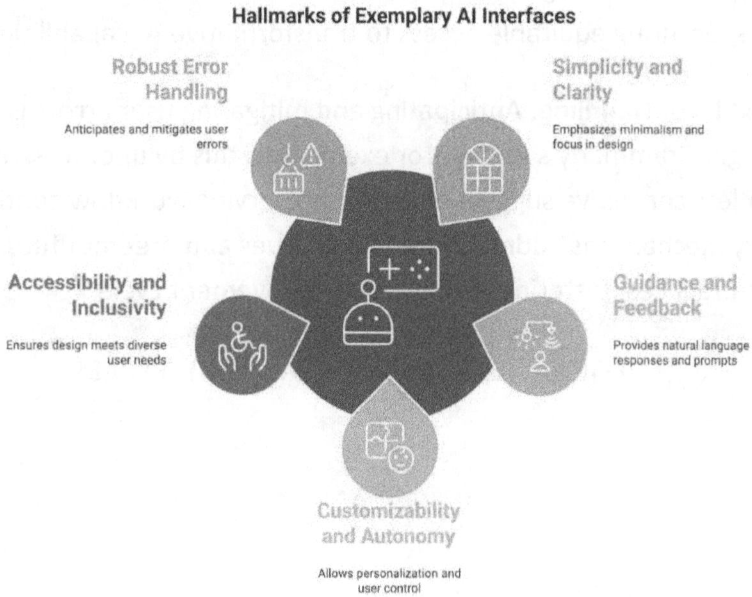

1. **Simplicity and Clarity**: Exemplary AI interfaces adhere to principles of minimalism, prioritizing clarity by minimizing visual and cognitive clutter. For instance, Google Search epitomizes this principle through its singular, unadorned search bar, which invites exploration while maintaining user focus. Simplicity ensures that users are not overwhelmed, enabling swift task execution and enhancing overall satisfaction. This principle extends beyond aesthetics to functionality, fostering a seamless alignment between user intentions and system responses.

2. **Guidance and Feedback**: Superior interfaces actively guide users through interactions and provide comprehensive, actionable feedback. Digital assistants like Google Assistant and Siri exemplify this by delivering natural language responses and actionable prompts, enhancing engagement and utility. Practical guidance minimizes ambiguity, while feedback fosters trust and reinforces user confidence in the AI's capabilities. By facilitating an ongoing dialog, these systems accommodate iterative refinement of user inputs and outputs.

3. **Customizability and User Autonomy**: A hallmark of advanced AI interfaces is their capacity for personalization, empowering users to tailor features to their preferences. For

instance, Spotify's AI-driven recommendation system complements algorithmic suggestions with tools that enable users to refine or expand their musical explorations. This empowerment extends beyond functional adjustments to include aesthetic and operational preferences, aligning the interface with diverse user-profiles and contexts.

4. **Accessibility and Inclusivity**: Inclusive design ensures that AI systems accommodate diverse user needs, including those of individuals with disabilities. Microsoft's Seeing AI application is a paradigmatic example, leveraging AI to narrate the visual environment for visually impaired users and exemplifying the integration of accessibility into interface design. By embedding universal design principles, accessible interfaces enhance usability across demographics, ensuring equitable access to transformative AI capabilities.

5. **Robust Error Handling**: Anticipating and mitigating user errors is critical to proficient interface design. Grammarly's text editor exemplifies this by unobtrusively flagging errors and offering seamless corrective suggestions, thus preserving workflow continuity. Sophisticated error recovery mechanisms address immediate issues and preempt future errors by educating users on best practices, fostering an iterative improvement cycle.

DEFICIENCIES IN SUBOPTIMAL AI INTERFACES

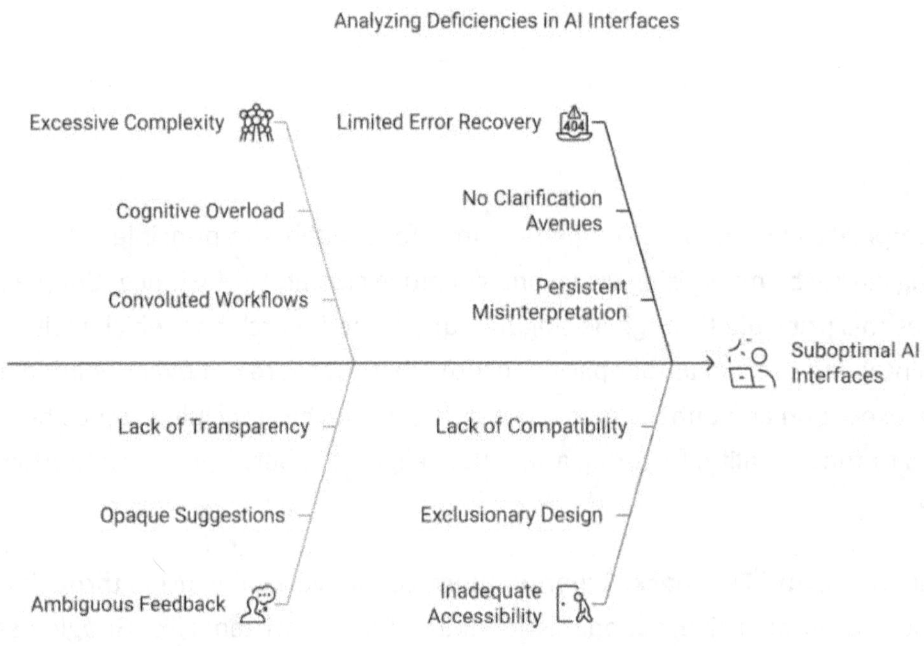

1. **Excessive Complexity**: Inferior interfaces often overwhelm users with an overabundance of information or convoluted workflows. Certain data analytics platforms, for example, inundate users with unstructured visualizations and control elements, resulting in diminished usability. Overly complex systems detract from productivity and deter user engagement, as cognitive overload impedes intuitive navigation and comprehension.

2. **Ambiguous Feedback**: Interfaces that fail to elucidate system actions or decisions foster confusion and erode user trust. A recommendation engine that provides opaque suggestions without contextual explanations exemplifies this deficiency. Without transparency, users are left to infer intent and relevance, undermining confidence in the system's outputs and reducing long-term adoption.

3. **Limited Error Recovery Mechanisms**: Deficient interfaces penalize user errors by offering no avenues for clarification or rectification. A chatbot that persistently misinterprets user queries without accommodating rephrased inputs typifies this shortcoming. Systems that lack adaptive error management diminish user satisfaction and perpetuate frustration, often leading to the abandonment of the interface altogether.

4. **Inadequate Accessibility**: Neglecting accessibility considerations renders interfaces exclusionary. For example, a predictive text application lacking screen reader compatibility disenfranchises visually impaired users. Accessibility shortcomings are not merely ethical lapses but also pragmatic failures, as they preclude engagement with significant portions of the user base, limiting the system's reach and impact.

5. **Counterintuitive Navigation**: Poorly organized interfaces with convoluted navigation schemes leave users disoriented. Some enterprise AI platforms obscure critical functionalities within labyrinthine menus, impeding user efficiency and satisfaction. Counterintuitive navigation disrupts the user's workflow, exacerbating cognitive load and undermining the perceived utility of the system.

COMPARATIVE ANALYSIS: EFFECTIVE VERSUS INEFFECTIVE UX DESIGNS

- **Exemplary Design**: Consider a healthcare application leveraging AI to track fitness objectives. A well-designed interface presents a streamlined dashboard that concisely summarizes key metrics—such as step count and heart rate—while providing actionable insights (e.g., "Increase your weekly step count by 10%"). Supplemented by responsive design, intuitive iconography, and informative tooltips, such an interface fosters user engagement and comprehension. Additionally, a robust notification system ensures timely feedback, while customizable visualizations enable users to align the interface with their unique fitness goals.

- **Deficient Design**: Contrastingly, a similar application plagued by a cluttered and poorly structured dashboard exemplifies ineffective design. Overabundant graphs devoid of explanatory context and metrics buried within nested submenus culminate in a disjointed user experience that impedes utility. Furthermore, the lack of error recovery mechanisms and inaccessible design elements compounds user frustration, reducing the system's practical value and overall adoption.

By embracing principles of intuitive navigation, transparent feedback, and inclusive design, AI interfaces can transcend usability barriers, unlocking artificial intelligence's transformative potential. As AI continues to permeate diverse domains, the onus is on designers to craft interfaces that meet functional requirements and elevate user experiences. Through iterative refinement and adherence to best practices, AI interfaces can exemplify technological innovation and user-centric design.

4.2: PROMPT ENGINEERING FOR LLMS

4.2.1 WHAT IS PROMPT ENGINEERING?

Prompt engineering is the art and science of crafting effective prompts to achieve desired outputs from AI tools. As AI systems, especially language models like GPT, become increasingly sophisticated, the ability to guide these systems through precise, well-structured prompts has emerged as a critical skill. Prompt engineering determines how effectively an AI system can perform tasks such as content generation, problem-solving, or data analysis. By mastering prompt engineering, users can interact more effectively with AI tools, maximizing their value and minimizing time spent refining outputs.

KEY ELEMENTS OF PROMPT ENGINEERING

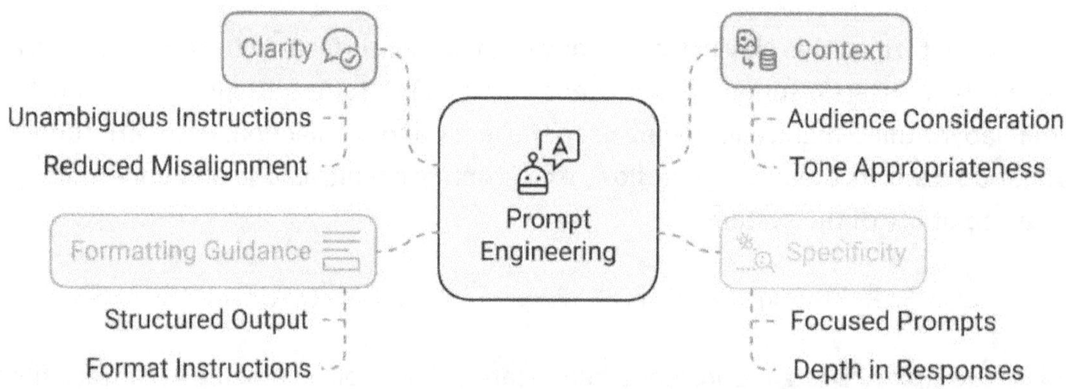

1. **Clarity**: A well-designed prompt is unambiguous. It ensures the AI understands the task without confusion. For instance, instead of saying, "Write about AI," a more effective prompt would be, "Write a 500-word article about the ethical considerations of using AI in healthcare." Clarity reduces the chances of generating irrelevant or misaligned responses and sets the foundation for a productive AI interaction.

2. **Context**: Providing context helps the AI frame its response. Context can include the target audience, the desired tone, or specific background details. For example, "Explain the importance of sustainability to a high school audience" sets expectations for the tone and complexity of the answer, ensuring the output is appropriate for younger learners.

3. **Specificity**: Specific prompts lead to more accurate results. Broad or vague prompts often result in generic outputs that lack depth. For example, asking, "List five benefits of renewable energy in bullet points," provides clear instructions and ensures the response is concise and focused, whereas the vague, "Discuss renewable energy," may lead to lengthy or unfocused text.

4. **Formatting Guidance**: The prompt should include formatting instructions if the output requires a specific structure. For instance, "Write a professional email introducing our new AI product" ensures the AI generates content in email format. Similarly, asking for numbered lists, tables, or bullet points helps the AI deliver results in the desired format.

Examples: Including examples within the prompt can guide the AI by illustrating the expected outcome. For instance, "Create a customer support response like: 'Thank you for reaching out. We're sorry to hear about your issue. Here's how we can assist...'" helps the AI better understand the tone and structure required.

APPLICATIONS OF PROMPT ENGINEERING

Prompt engineering is instrumental across a variety of domains, each with unique requirements and challenges:

1. **Chatbots**: For customer service or interactive AI systems, prompts must simulate natural and helpful conversation. Example:

    - Ineffective Prompt: "Help the customer."
    - Effective Prompt: "You are a virtual assistant for a tech company. Greet the customer and provide step-by-step troubleshooting for internet connectivity issues." Chatbots rely heavily on prompts to create seamless user experiences and ensure intuitive and efficient interactions.

2. **Content Generation**: Writers, marketers, and educators use prompts to generate tailored content. Example:

    - Ineffective Prompt: "Write a blog."
    - Effective Prompt: "Write a 700-word blog post about the top five AI trends in 2025, including real-world examples and statistics." Users can generate content that aligns with their needs by specifying word count, topic, and details, whether for blogs, social media posts, or academic articles.

3. **Data Analysis**: Analysts leverage prompts to extract insights from datasets or analyze trends. Example:

    - Ineffective Prompt: "Analyze the sales data."
    - Effective Prompt: "Analyze the sales data for Q3 2023, focusing on trends in the Midwest region, and identify the top-performing products." With clear instructions, the AI can provide actionable insights tailored to specific business requirements.

4. **Creative Tasks**: Artists and innovators use prompts to spark creativity. For example, "Generate five unique ideas for a science fiction novel set in a post-apocalyptic world" can help authors overcome creative blocks.

5. **Educational Tools**: Educators employ prompts to create quizzes, lesson plans, and explanatory content. A prompt like "Explain photosynthesis in simple terms for a fifth-grade science class" ensures the AI delivers age-appropriate and pedagogically sound material.

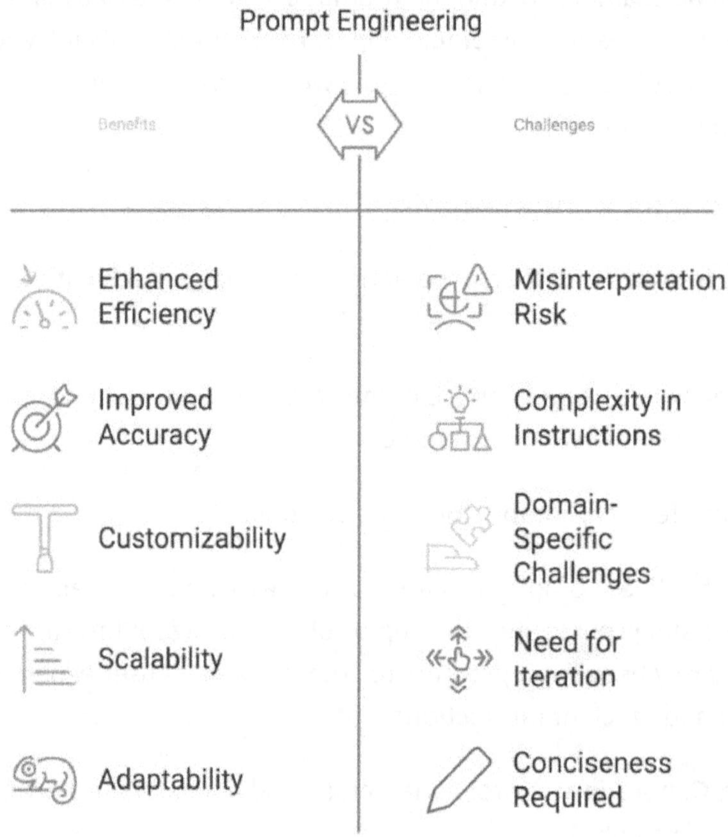

BENEFITS OF EFFECTIVE PROMPT ENGINEERING

- **Enhanced Efficiency**: Well-crafted prompts reduce the need for iterative queries and corrections, saving users significant time and effort.
- **Improved Accuracy**: Clear instructions result in precise and relevant outputs, minimizing the need for extensive editing.
- **Customizability**: Prompt engineering allows users to tailor AI responses to specific needs, audiences, or contexts, ensuring that outputs align with user goals.
- **Scalability**: It enables the reuse of optimized prompts across similar tasks, enhancing productivity by providing a framework for repeated use.
- **Adaptability**: With the correct prompts, AI tools can be adapted for various applications, from technical writing to storytelling.

CHALLENGES AND BEST PRACTICES

While prompt engineering offers significant advantages, it is not without challenges. AI may still misinterpret prompts, mainly if the instructions are overly complex or ambiguous. Users may also encounter difficulty when working with advanced or domain-specific tasks. To overcome these challenges:

- **Iterate and Refine**: Test and tweak prompts based on the AI's responses. Iteration helps identify what works best for a given application.
- **Leverage Examples**: Providing examples within the prompt often clarifies expectations and minimizes the risk of misinterpretation.
- **Consider Limitations**: Understand the AI's constraints and tailor prompts accordingly. For instance, avoid overly technical jargon if the AI model lacks domain-specific training.
- **Be Concise**: While providing context is essential, overly lengthy prompts can lead to confusion. Balance detail with brevity for optimal results.

Future of Prompt Engineering

As AI technologies evolve, prompt engineering will likely become more important. New tools and interfaces may incorporate more intuitive ways to craft prompts, such as visual cues or guided templates. Additionally, as models become more sophisticated, they may require less explicit prompting, instead relying on nuanced contextual understanding. However, clarity, context, and specificity will remain cornerstones of effective AI interaction.

In conclusion, prompt engineering bridges the gap between human intent and AI capabilities. By mastering this skill, users can unlock the full potential of AI tools for diverse applications, from automating routine tasks to generating creative content. This transformative practice is not only a technical skill but also a creative art, empowering individuals and organizations to harness the power of AI effectively and efficiently.

4.2.2 TECHNIQUES FOR EFFECTIVE PROMPTING (3 PAGES)

As large language models (LLMs) become increasingly sophisticated, developing effective prompting techniques is essential to maximizing their utility across diverse applications. This section delves into three key strategies: chain-of-thought prompting, self-reflection prompting, and crafting actionable examples for specific use cases. Each technique provides a framework to guide AI systems, ensuring outputs are accurate, meaningful, and tailored to user needs.

Chain-of-thought prompting involves guiding LLMs to explain their reasoning step by step. This method is particularly beneficial in tasks requiring logical reasoning or multi-step problem-solving. By explicitly requesting the model to articulate its thought process, users can:

- **Enhance Transparency:** Understanding how the model arrives at its conclusions makes its operations more interpretable, building trust in its outputs.
- **Boost Accuracy:** Breaking down problems into smaller components reduces the likelihood of errors by tackling challenges incrementally.
- **Facilitate Learning:** For applications in education or training, models can provide insights into their reasoning, making them valuable teaching aids and fostering user comprehension.
- **Improve Debugging:** When LLMs make mistakes, chain-of-thought prompting provides a clear path to identify where the reasoning went wrong.

PRACTICAL APPLICATION:

To employ chain-of-thought prompting effectively, consider scenarios such as:

1. **Mathematical Problem Solving:**
    - Prompt: "Solve the equation 2x + 3 = 7. Explain each step of your solution."
    - Output: "First, subtract 3 from both sides to isolate the term with x. This gives 2x = 4. Next, divide both sides by 2 to solve for x. The solution is x = 2."
2. **Legal Analysis:**
    - Prompt: "Analyze the legal implications of a breach of contract based on the following case. Outline the reasoning process step by step."
    - Output: "First, assess the contract terms to identify specific clauses that may have been violated. Next, evaluate the actions taken by each party and correlate them with these clauses. Finally, determine the potential legal outcomes based on applicable laws."
3. **Scientific Analysis:**
    - Prompt: "Explain the process of photosynthesis step by step, including its importance to ecosystems."

By encouraging detailed responses, chain-of-thought prompting enhances the depth, clarity, and utility of outputs across a wide range of disciplines.

SELF-REFLECTION PROMPTING

Self-reflection prompting encourages LLMs to review and refine their outputs iteratively. This approach is convenient for improving the accuracy and reliability of responses, especially in complex or ambiguous tasks. Iteration allows the model to correct errors, refine reasoning, and improve alignment with user expectations.

Key Benefits:

- **Error Reduction:** Models are prompted to evaluate their initial outputs, leading to more refined and precise answers.
- **Enhanced Robustness:** By iterating on their outputs, LLMs can address inconsistencies or gaps in reasoning, improving the overall coherence of their responses.
- **Contextual Adaptability:** This technique allows models to better respond to nuanced user requirements and specific feedback.
- **Iterative Learning:** Models simulate human-like review processes, aligning more closely with expert-level critical thinking.

Practical Application:

Self-reflection prompting can be employed in tasks such as:

1. **Fact Verification:**
    - Initial Prompt: "Summarize the key findings of this scientific study."
    - Reflection Prompt: "Review your summary. Are there any inaccuracies or points that need clarification? If so, revise your response."
2. **Creative Writing:**
    - Initial Prompt: "Draft a compelling opening paragraph for a marketing email."
    - Reflection Prompt: "Evaluate your draft. Does it effectively capture the reader's attention? How could it be improved?"
    - Iteration Example: "The initial draft focuses on the product features, but it could benefit from a stronger emotional appeal. Revise to include a relatable customer scenario."

3. **Academic Summaries:**

   - Initial Prompt: "Provide a detailed summary of the causes and consequences of the American Revolution."

   - Reflection Prompt: "Analyze your response for completeness. Are all significant causes and consequences addressed? Expand if needed."

Through iterative refinement, self-reflection prompting enables users to co-create outputs that are thorough, insightful, and aligned with their needs.

Examples of Crafting Effective Prompts

Effective prompts tailored to specific tasks ensure that LLMs deliver actionable and relevant outputs. Below are two illustrative examples:

1. **Summarizing Research Papers:**

   - Prompt: "Provide a concise summary of this research paper focusing on its objectives, methods, and key findings."

   - Enhanced Prompt: "Summarize this research paper in 150 words, highlighting its objectives, methodology, key results, and implications for future studies."

2. **Generating Marketing Copy:**

   - Prompt: "Create a promotional tagline for a new eco-friendly cleaning product."

   - Enhanced Prompt: "Write a promotional tagline for an eco-friendly cleaning product targeting environmentally conscious consumers. Emphasize its effectiveness and sustainability."

3. **Educational Prompts:**

   - Prompt: "Explain Newton's three laws of motion in simple terms for a high school audience."

   - Enhanced Prompt: "Describe Newton's three laws of motion in everyday language, providing one practical example for each law to help high school students understand their applications."

Considerations for Effective Prompt Design:

- **Clarity:** Be explicit about the desired outcome to minimize ambiguity and ensure precision.

- **Context:** Provide sufficient background information or relevant details to guide the model.
- **Constraints:** Specify word limits, tone, style, or format requirements to tailor the output effectively.
- **Feedback Loops:** Encourage revisions and refinements to align the response more closely with the intended purpose.

Effective prompting is a cornerstone of fully leveraging LLM capabilities. Techniques such as chain-of-thought prompting, self-reflection prompting, and crafting tailored examples empower users to extract maximum value from AI systems. By understanding and applying these methods, practitioners can optimize performance across domains, from research to marketing, education, and beyond. These strategies also open avenues for collaboration between human users and AI systems, fostering innovation and ensuring that technology continues to serve human goals with precision and adaptability.

4.2.3 COMMON MISTAKES IN PROMPT DESIGN

Prompt design is a critical aspect of effectively leveraging AI systems, particularly large language models. However, it's easy to fall into pitfalls that reduce the quality, clarity, and relevance of AI-generated outputs. Below are two common mistakes in prompt design and illustrative examples to help distinguish poorly designed prompts from optimized ones.

1. Overloading Prompts with Irrelevant Details

Including unnecessary or unrelated details in a prompt can confuse the AI, leading to vague, off-topic, or overly verbose responses. Overloaded prompts dilute the focus of the task, reducing the precision of the output.

Example of a Poorly Designed Prompt: *"As a marketing manager who oversees teams working on both digital advertising and product launches, I want you to write a blog post about how effective SEO strategies can improve our overall web traffic and customer acquisition metrics, while also considering how social media integration helps in campaign success."*

This prompt is cluttered with extraneous roles and objectives, making it difficult for the AI to discern the primary request.

Optimized Prompt: *"Write a blog post about effective SEO strategies for improving web traffic and customer acquisition."*

By removing irrelevant details, the focus shifts entirely to SEO strategies, leading to a more concise and actionable response.

2. Poorly Designed vs. Optimized Prompts

Poorly designed prompts often lack specificity, are overly vague, or ask too many things simultaneously. Optimized prompts, on the other hand, are clear, concise, and focus on a single task or question.

Example of a Poorly Designed Prompt: *"Tell me everything about marketing strategies, including digital, traditional, and social media, and how they compare with modern trends like influencer marketing."*

This prompt is overly broad and combines multiple topics without clear boundaries, likely resulting in a disorganized response.

Example of an Optimized Prompt: *"Compare digital marketing strategies with influencer marketing in the context of modern trends."*

By narrowing the scope, the AI can generate a focused and detailed comparison.

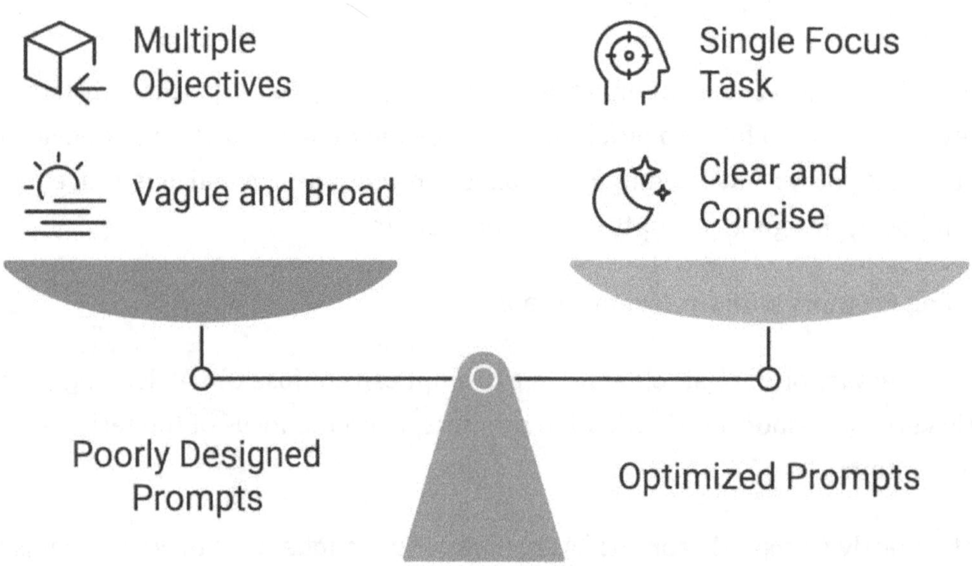

Optimize prompts for clearer AI responses.

Pro Tips for Avoiding Mistakes in Prompt Design

1. **Define the objective clearly**: Always clarify what you want the AI to achieve.

2. **Focus on one task at a time**: Avoid asking multiple unrelated questions in a single prompt.

3. **Be concise but specific**: Provide enough context without overloading the prompt.

4. **Test and refine**: Experiment with variations of your prompt to find what produces the best results.

By understanding and avoiding these common mistakes, you can design prompts that harness the full potential of AI while maintaining relevance and clarity in the generated outputs.

4.2.4 TOOLS FOR EXPERIMENTATION

Experimentation is a cornerstone of effective AI development. Whether testing hypotheses, fine-tuning models, or crafting optimal prompts, the right tools streamline the process and empower developers to achieve better results efficiently. This section focuses on tools specifically designed for experimenting with prompts—one of the foundational elements of AI interaction design. These tools provide intuitive interfaces and powerful features to test, iterate, and refine prompts for various applications.

Tools for Testing Prompts

Prompt experimentation tools allow users to input text, evaluate outputs, and iteratively improve prompts for clarity, specificity, and relevance. Among the most popular tools in this space are:

1. OpenAI Playground

- **Overview**: OpenAI Playground is an intuitive web-based interface designed to experiment with OpenAI's language models. It allows users to test prompts in real-time with various configuration options such as model selection, temperature settings, and response length.
- **Key Features**:
    - **Customizability**: Users can adjust parameters like temperature, top-p, frequency penalty, and presence penalty to shape the model's behavior.
    - **Real-time Feedback**: Instantaneous results for input prompts enable rapid iterations.
    - **API Integration**: Prompts tested in the Playground can be easily adapted for API-based applications, ensuring consistency across testing and deployment.
    - **History Tracking**: Users can save and revisit previous prompts, making it easier to refine ideas over time.
- **Best Use Cases**:
    - Crafting conversational AI responses.

- Testing instructions for specific use cases like summarization, translation, or code generation.

2. Hugging Face Inference API

- **Overview**: The Hugging Face Inference API provides an extensive platform to experiment with a wide variety of open-source models from their Model Hub. It supports diverse tasks, including text generation, question answering, sentiment analysis, and more.
- **Key Features**:
  - **Model Diversity**: Access to thousands of models, including GPT-based models, BERT variants, and domain-specific models.
  - **Task-Specific Pipelines**: Pre-configured pipelines simplify experimentation for tasks like summarization, translation, or text classification.
  - **Ease of Use**: The web interface and Python SDK allow for both hands-on and programmatic experimentation.
  - **Community Contributions**: Users can test community-contributed models, which may offer unique capabilities not found in proprietary tools.
- **Best Use Cases**:
  - Comparing model performance across different architectures.
  - Testing domain-specific prompts using fine-tuned models.
  - Exploring alternative solutions for specific tasks, such as multilingual text generation or industry-specific applications.

Practical Considerations

- **Choosing the Right Tool**: OpenAI Playground excels when working exclusively with OpenAI's models and offers robust parameter customization. Hugging Face, on the other hand, is ideal for exploring a broader range of models and tasks.
- **Iterative Process**: Both tools encourage iterative testing, enabling users to refine their prompts based on immediate feedback.
- **Scaling to Deployment**: Experimentation results from these tools can often be directly transitioned to production environments, ensuring the continuity of insights gained during testing.

By leveraging tools like OpenAI Playground and Hugging Face Inference API, AI practitioners can enhance the quality of their prompts, optimize model outputs, and create more effective and reliable AI applications.

4.3: EXPLAINABLE AI (XAI)

4.3.1 WHY EXPLAINABILITY MATTERS

In the evolving landscape of artificial intelligence (AI), explainability has emerged as a cornerstone of responsible AI deployment. Explainability refers to the ability of AI systems to provide clear, human-understandable justifications for their outputs and decisions. This concept is particularly critical in high-stakes domains such as healthcare, finance, and law, where opaque AI decisions can have significant consequences. This section delves into two primary reasons why explainability matters: building user trust and meeting regulatory requirements. We also explore a practical example of explainable AI (XAI) in financial credit scoring to highlight the importance of avoiding bias accusations.

BUILDING USER TRUST

AI systems are becoming increasingly pervasive, influencing decisions directly impacting people's lives. However, these systems often operate as "black boxes," with complex algorithms producing difficult outputs for users to interpret. This lack of transparency can erode user trust, as people are less likely to rely on systems they do not understand or perceive as fair. Explainability bridges this gap by demystifying the inner workings of AI, enabling users to grasp the rationale behind decisions.

For instance, in healthcare, an AI system used to diagnose diseases must explain its recommendations in a way clinicians and patients can understand. If the system suggests a lung cancer diagnosis, it should provide supporting evidence, such as specific patterns in a patient's CT scan. This transparency fosters trust and empowers medical professionals to validate and, if necessary, challenge the AI's conclusions. Without explainability, users may hesitate to adopt AI systems, regardless of their accuracy or efficiency.

Moreover, explainability is crucial for mitigating the risk of misinformation and fostering accountability. When users can comprehend how an AI system reaches its conclusions, they are better equipped to detect potential errors or biases. For example, an AI tool used for hiring might reject a candidate based on patterns in their resume. If the tool provides an explainable rationale—such as a mismatch between the candidate's skills and job requirements—it enables HR professionals to scrutinize the decision and ensure it aligns with organizational values. This level of transparency is essential for cultivating trust in AI-driven processes.

MEETING REGULATORY REQUIREMENTS

Regulatory compliance is another critical driver of explainability. Governments and regulatory bodies worldwide are introducing frameworks to ensure AI systems operate ethically and transparently. These frameworks often mandate that organizations explain AI-driven decisions, particularly in sectors where decisions can significantly impact individuals.

For example, the General Data Protection Regulation (GDPR) in the European Union includes provisions for the "right to explanation." This regulation grants individuals the right to understand how automated systems make decisions that affect them, such as credit approvals or job application outcomes. Similarly, the United States has enacted laws like the Equal Credit Opportunity Act (ECOA), which requires lenders to provide reasons for denying credit applications. Non-compliance with such regulations can result in hefty fines and reputational damage, making explainability a non-negotiable requirement for organizations leveraging AI.

Beyond compliance, explainability helps organizations demonstrate their commitment to ethical practices. Companies can show stakeholders that their systems prioritize fairness and accountability by providing clear justifications for AI decisions. This proactive approach minimizes the risk of legal disputes and enhances an organization's reputation as a responsible AI adopter.

Example: XAI in Financial Credit Scoring

The financial sector provides a compelling example of why explainability matters. Consider using AI in credit scoring, where algorithms evaluate a borrower's creditworthiness based on various data points, such as income, credit history, and spending patterns. These decisions have far-reaching consequences, determining whether individuals can secure loans, mortgages, or credit cards.

Credit scoring models like FICO were traditionally relatively straightforward, relying on linear relationships between input variables and outputs. However, modern AI-based credit scoring systems often leverage complex machine learning models, such as neural networks, which are less transparent. While these models can improve predictive accuracy, their opacity raises concerns about fairness and accountability.

For instance, an opaque AI model might inadvertently incorporate biases in its decision-making process. If historical data reflects systemic biases—such as lower loan approval rates for specific demographic groups—the AI model may perpetuate these biases, leading to discriminatory outcomes. Without explainability, identifying and addressing such issues would be challenging, leaving organizations vulnerable to accusations of bias and unfair practices.

Explainable AI offers a solution by making the decision-making process transparent. For example, an explainable credit scoring model might reveal that a borrower's application was declined due to a high debt-to-income ratio or insufficient credit history. By providing specific, understandable reasons, the model allows both the applicant and the lender to assess the fairness of the decision. Furthermore, explainability enables lenders to audit their models for potential biases and make necessary adjustments to ensure compliance with anti-discrimination laws.

The benefits of explainable AI in credit scoring extend beyond regulatory compliance. Transparent models can improve customer satisfaction by fostering a sense of fairness and accountability. When borrowers understand why their applications were rejected, they are more likely to accept the outcome and take steps to improve their creditworthiness. Additionally, explainability enhances operational efficiency by reducing the likelihood of disputes and appeals, which can be time-consuming and costly for financial institutions.

The Broader Implications of Explainability

The importance of explainability extends beyond individual applications, shaping public perception of AI. In recent years, high-profile incidents of AI failures have fueled skepticism and fear, highlighting the need for greater transparency. For example, controversies surrounding biased facial recognition systems and flawed predictive policing algorithms have underscored the risks of deploying opaque AI models without adequate safeguards.

Explainability addresses these concerns by promoting accountability and ethical decision-making. By making AI systems more transparent, organizations can mitigate the risk of unintended consequences and build public confidence in AI technologies. This, in turn, paves the way for broader adoption of AI across industries, unlocking its full potential to drive innovation and improve lives.

Explainability is not just a technical challenge but a fundamental requirement for responsible AI deployment. By building user trust and ensuring compliance with regulatory frameworks, explainability lays the foundation for ethical and practical AI systems. The example of explainable AI in financial credit scoring illustrates how transparency can mitigate bias, enhance fairness, and improve user satisfaction. As AI continues to permeate every aspect of society, the demand for explainability will only grow, making it a critical focus for researchers, developers, and policymakers alike.

4.3.2 TECHNIQUES FOR EXPLAINABILITY

In the rapidly evolving field of artificial intelligence (AI), explainability has become critical to developing trustworthy and ethical models. This section focuses on various techniques employed to ensure AI systems are interpretable and transparent. Specifically, we will discuss SHAP and LIME for interpretability, saliency maps for visualizing decisions in image-based models, and conclude with a case study on debugging an AI recommendation engine using SHAP.

SHAP and LIME for Interpretability

SHAP (SHapley Additive exPlanations)

SHAP is a game-theoretic approach that explains individual predictions in AI models. It assigns each feature an importance value for a specific prediction. SHAP is rooted in Shapley's values from cooperative game theory, ensuring a mathematically sound attribution of contributions.

Key Features of SHAP:

1. **Consistency:** Adding a feature that positively contributes to the prediction will not decrease its SHAP value.

2. **Accuracy:** SHAP values sum up the difference between the model and average predictions across all data points.

3. **Global Interpretability:** While the SHAP values are designed for local interpretability, aggregating them across samples provides insights into global model behavior.

Applications:

- Healthcare: Explaining why a patient is classified as high-risk for a disease.
- Finance: Understanding factors leading to loan approvals or rejections.
- E-commerce: Unveiling drivers of personalized product recommendations.

Limitations: Despite its robust mathematical foundation, SHAP can be computationally expensive, especially for large datasets and complex models. Approximation methods, such as Kernel SHAP, are often used but may compromise exactness.

LIME (Local Interpretable Model-agnostic Explanations)

LIME provides insights into model predictions by locally approximating the model with a simpler interpretable model, such as a linear regression or decision tree.

Key Features of LIME:

1. **Model-agnostic:** Works with any model type, whether a neural network, random forest, or SVM.

2. **Local Focus:** Explains individual predictions by perturbing the input data and observing the impact on forecasts.

3. **Visualization:** Offers intuitive visualizations like bar charts to showcase feature importance.

Applications:

- Natural Language Processing (NLP): Explaining sentiment analysis outcomes by identifying influential words.
- Image Classification: Highlighting parts of an image that led to a specific prediction.
- Tabular Data: Interpreting predictions in fraud detection systems.

Limitations: LIME is sensitive to the sampling method used for perturbation and may provide inconsistent explanations for similar inputs. Furthermore, its reliance on approximating models means it may not capture all nuances of the original model.

Saliency Maps for Visualizing Decisions in Image-Based Models

Saliency maps are widely used to understand and visualize decisions made by image-based models, particularly convolutional neural networks (CNNs). These maps highlight regions in an image that significantly influence the model's prediction.

Key Techniques:

1. **Gradient-based Methods:** Compute the gradient of the model output concerning the input image to identify regions with the highest impact.
   - Example: Visualizing why a model classifies an image as containing a cat by highlighting its whiskers or ears.
2. **Class Activation Mapping (CAM):** Identifies the spatial regions in an image that contribute to a specific class prediction. Extensions like Grad-CAM enhance this method by incorporating gradient information.
3. **Integrated Gradients:** This method addresses the problem of noisy saliency maps by aggregating gradients from a baseline to the input image.

Applications:

- Healthcare: Identifying tumors in medical imaging (e.g., MRI or CT scans).
- Autonomous Vehicles: Understanding object detection models for road safety.
- Security: Analyzing facial recognition systems for bias or inaccuracies.

Limitations: Saliency maps can be noisy and are sensitive to input perturbations. Moreover, they may not always align with human intuition, requiring further validation and refinement.

CASE STUDY: DEBUGGING AN AI RECOMMENDATION ENGINE USING SHAP

Background: An e-commerce company implemented an AI-powered recommendation engine to enhance user engagement. Despite its high accuracy, the model occasionally produced irrelevant recommendations, leading to user dissatisfaction.

Problem Statement: The primary objective was to identify why the recommendation engine failed for specific users and how to improve its performance without compromising global accuracy.

Methodology: The debugging process involved the following steps:

1. **Model Overview:**

- The recommendation engine was a collaborative filtering model enhanced with user demographics and behavioral data.

2. **Dataset and Features:**

   - User Features: Age, location, purchase history.
   - Item Features: Category, price, popularity.
   - Interaction Data: Click-through rates, browsing patterns.

3. **Applying SHAP:**

   - SHAP values were calculated for specific predictions where users received irrelevant recommendations.
   - Visualizations, such as waterfall plots and feature importance summaries, were generated to identify influential factors.

Findings:

1. **User Mismatch:**

   - In some cases, age and location contributed disproportionately to recommendations, overriding behavioral patterns.
   - For example, a user from a high-income area was shown luxury products despite browsing budget-friendly options.

2. **Data Bias:**

   - The training data was skewed toward popular items, leading the model to over-recommend trending products.

3. **Feature Interaction:**

   - Certain feature combinations, such as low browsing activity and high purchase frequency, confused the model, resulting in irrelevant outputs.

Solutions Implemented:

1. **Feature Reweighting:**

   - Adjusted features are essential for balancing demographic and behavioral data.

2. **Bias Mitigation:**

- o Augmented the training data with samples emphasizing less popular items.

3. **Custom Filters:**

   - o Introduced post-prediction filtering to ensure recommendations aligned with recent user activity.

Outcome: Post-implementation, user engagement metrics improved significantly, with a 20% increase in click-through rates and a 15% decrease in negative feedback. SHAP visualizations also facilitated transparent communication of changes to stakeholders.

Explainability techniques like SHAP, LIME, and saliency maps are pivotal in interpreting and debugging AI models. SHAP's game-theoretic foundation ensures precise feature attribution, while LIME's model-agnostic approach provides flexibility. Saliency maps cater specifically to visual models, offering insights into spatial decision-making. The case study on debugging a recommendation engine underscores the practical importance of these tools in refining AI systems and enhancing their trustworthiness.

4.3.3 INTEGRATING EXPLAINABILITY INTO UX

Integrating explainability into user experiences (UX) is a cornerstone of building trust and transparency in AI-powered systems. Users need to understand the outcomes delivered by an AI system and the reasoning behind these outcomes. By embedding explainability into the design process, developers can enhance user confidence, foster ethical AI practices, and improve the overall adoption of AI solutions. This section delves into the importance of explainability in UX. It offers practical strategies for its implementation, focusing on visual representations of AI predictions, such as confidence scores in medical AI tools.

Importance of Explainability in UX

Explainability in UX is essential for several reasons. First, it helps users trust the system by clarifying how decisions are made. Trust is especially critical in high-stakes domains such as healthcare, finance, and legal systems, where AI decisions can significantly impact lives. Second, explainability enables users to validate the system's decisions against their knowledge or intuition. Third, it facilitates accountability by allowing stakeholders to trace the rationale behind AI predictions or decisions.

Users may feel alienated or skeptical about the system's accuracy and fairness without explainability. A lack of transparency can lead to legal and ethical challenges, mainly when AI operates in regulated industries. By integrating explainability into UX, organizations can mitigate these risks and create functional, user-centric, trustworthy systems.

Visual Representations of AI Predictions

Visual representations are one of the most effective ways to communicate AI predictions and their underlying rationale. Humans are naturally adept at processing visual information, making graphical explanations more intuitive and accessible than textual or numerical descriptions alone. In this section, we explore how visual representations can enhance the explainability of AI systems, specifically focusing on confidence scores in medical AI tools.

Example: Confidence Scores in Medical AI Tools

Medical AI tools often make predictions or recommendations that assist clinicians in diagnosis and treatment planning. However, clinicians must understand the reliability of these predictions to make informed decisions. Confidence scores—visual indicators representing the likelihood of a prediction being correct—are a powerful tool for conveying this reliability.

Design Considerations for Confidence Scores

1. **Clarity and Simplicity**: Confidence scores should be presented in an easy way to interpret. For example, a bar graph or a circular gauge can visually represent the confidence level of an AI prediction. To ensure clarity, these visual elements should be accompanied by textual explanations.

2. **Color Coding**: Colors can indicate different levels of confidence. For instance, green might represent high confidence, yellow moderate confidence, and red low confidence. This intuitive coding allows users to quickly assess the reliability of a prediction.

3. **Interactive Elements**: Interactive features like tooltips or sliders can provide additional details about the confidence score. For example, hovering over a confidence score might reveal information about the dataset used to train the model or the factors influencing the prediction.

Benefits of Visualizing Confidence Scores

1. **Improved Decision-Making**: Visual representations help clinicians assess the reliability of AI predictions at a glance. For example, suppose a medical AI tool predicts a 90% likelihood of a malignant tumor. The clinician can combine this information with their expertise to decide on further diagnostic tests or treatment plans.

2. **Enhanced Transparency**: Confidence scores demystify the AI decision-making process by revealing the degree of certainty behind each prediction. This transparency builds trust and reduces the likelihood of over-reliance or under-reliance on the AI system.

3. **Support for Collaborative Decision-Making**: Decisions often involve multiple stakeholders in healthcare settings. Visual representations of confidence scores enable effective communication among clinicians, patients, and other stakeholders, fostering collaborative decision-making.

Case Study: Confidence Scores in Radiology

Consider a radiology AI tool designed to detect anomalies in medical images. The tool analyzes X-rays and highlights areas that may indicate diseases such as pneumonia or fractures. Alongside each highlighted area, the tool displays a confidence score (e.g., 85%).

The confidence scores are visualized using a heatmap overlaid on the medical image. Areas with higher confidence are highlighted in bright colors, while areas with lower confidence appear faded. This approach provides an intuitive understanding of where the AI is most particular about its predictions.

In addition to the heatmap, the tool includes a summary dashboard that aggregates confidence scores for all detected anomalies. The dashboard uses bar graphs and pie charts to represent the overall distribution of confidence levels across the image. Clinicians can interact with these visualizations to explore individual predictions in detail.

Outcomes

- **Increased Trust**: Radiologists reported greater trust in the AI tool because they could see the confidence levels associated with each prediction.

- **Better Workflow Integration**: The visualizations were seamlessly integrated into the existing radiology software, minimizing clinician workflow disruption.

- **Improved Diagnostic Accuracy**: By focusing on areas with high confidence scores, radiologists could prioritize their attention and reduce the likelihood of missing critical anomalies.

Challenges and Best Practices

While integrating explainability into UX offers numerous benefits, it also presents challenges. Overly complex visualizations can overwhelm users, defeating the purpose of explainability. Additionally, designers must balance the need for transparency with the risk of exposing proprietary algorithms or sensitive data.

To address these challenges, consider the following best practices:

1. **User-Centric Design**: Involve end-users in the design process to ensure that visualizations meet their needs and preferences. Conduct usability testing to identify and address potential issues.

2. **Contextual Explanations**: Provide explanations tailored to the user's expertise and use case. For example, a clinician might require detailed information about the factors influencing a prediction, while a patient might prefer a more straightforward explanation.

3. **Consistency**: Use consistent visual elements and terminology throughout the interface. This consistency reduces cognitive load and helps users navigate the system more efficiently.

4. **Ethical Considerations**: Visualizations should not mislead users or create false confidence in the AI system. The predictions should clearly indicate their limitations, and guidance on how to interpret confidence scores responsibly should be provided.

Integrating explainability into UX is a technical challenge and a human-centered design imperative. Designers can bridge the gap between complex AI models and end-users using visual representations such as confidence scores. These visual tools empower users to understand, trust, and effectively interact with AI systems, particularly in critical domains like healthcare. As AI continues to evolve, integrating explainability into UX will play a pivotal role in ensuring that these systems are practical but also ethical, and user-friendly.

4.4: DEPLOYMENT STRATEGIES

4.4.1 DEPLOYMENT MODELS

AI systems can be deployed in various models tailored to specific operational and functional needs. These models primarily support real-time interactivity and batch processing for offline or non-urgent computations. The deployment model selected significantly influences system architecture, infrastructure requirements, and performance outcomes.

Real-Time APIs for Interactive Applications

Real-time application programming interfaces (APIs) enable AI to respond instantly to user inputs or system triggers. These APIs are designed to process requests, execute the necessary computations, and deliver results within milliseconds to a few seconds. Their primary advantage is their ability to enhance user experiences through immediacy and responsiveness.

Example: AI Chatbots in Customer Service

One of the most widespread applications of real-time APIs is in AI-powered chatbots, particularly in customer service domains. These chatbots leverage natural language processing (NLP) to understand user queries and generate relevant responses in real time. For instance, a customer reaching out to a telecom service provider with an issue related to billing can receive instant guidance or resolutions through a chatbot.

Key Features of Real-Time APIs in AI Chatbots:

1. **Instant Query Handling:** Chatbots equipped with real-time APIs can instantly process natural language inputs. This capability minimizes customer waiting times and significantly enhances satisfaction.

2. **Context Awareness:** Advanced AI systems utilize real-time APIs to maintain context across multiple interactions, ensuring that users receive coherent and contextually relevant answers.

3. **Scalability:** AI systems employing real-time APIs are often deployed on scalable cloud platforms capable of handling thousands of simultaneous requests. Technologies like Kubernetes and serverless frameworks enable dynamic resource allocation to meet varying demand levels.

Implementation Considerations:

- **Latency:** Latency must be minimized for interactive applications like chatbots. API design optimization, such as efficient serialization protocols (e.g., gRPC), and edge computing, is crucial.

- **Reliability:** High uptime and consistent performance are essential for ensuring positive user experiences. Distributed architectures and fallback mechanisms can enhance system reliability.

- **Security:** Real-time APIs often handle sensitive customer data. Measures such as encryption, token-based authentication, and compliance with regulations like GDPR ensure secure data handling.

Case Study: E-commerce Customer Support

An online retailer implemented an AI chatbot to manage customer inquiries about product availability, delivery timelines, and returns. The chatbot's real-time API was integrated with the company's inventory and order management systems. As a result, customers could instantly check stock levels, retrieve their order status, or initiate returns without human intervention, significantly reducing operational costs and improving customer satisfaction.

Batch Processing for Non-Time-Sensitive Tasks

Batch processing is another prevalent deployment model for AI systems. It is particularly suited for tasks that do not require immediate feedback or action. In this model, data is collected over time and processed in bulk. Batch processing is often chosen for its efficiency in handling large datasets and executing complex computations.

Example: AI-Driven Financial Risk Analysis

In financial services, AI-driven risk analysis is a critical batch-processing application. Institutions like banks and investment firms rely on AI algorithms to assess risk profiles, identify potential fraud, and optimize portfolios. These tasks are computationally intensive and require processing vast amounts of historical data, making batch processing the ideal deployment model.

Key Features of Batch Processing in AI:

1. **Efficiency in Data Handling:** Batch processing is optimized for processing large datasets. For instance, financial institutions analyze several-year transaction histories to identify trends and anomalies.

2. **Resource Optimization:** Unlike real-time systems that require constant availability, batch processing systems operate on a scheduled basis, allowing for efficient resource allocation and cost management.

3. **Accuracy and Depth:** Since batch processes are not time-constrained, they can involve detailed computations and complex model evaluations to ensure high accuracy.

Implementation Considerations:

- **Data Preparation:** Preprocessing steps such as cleaning, normalization, and feature extraction are crucial for effective batch processing. Automated pipelines using tools like Apache Spark or Hadoop streamline these tasks.

- **Infrastructure Requirements:** Batch processing often involves distributed computing systems to handle the computational load. Cloud platforms offering elastic resources, such as AWS EMR or Google Cloud Dataproc, are commonly used.

- **Scheduling:** Tools like Apache Airflow enable organizations to schedule and monitor batch jobs, ensuring timely execution and troubleshooting.

Case Study: Credit Risk Assessment

A major bank implemented an AI-based credit risk assessment system to evaluate loan applications. Historical transaction data, credit scores, and demographic information were processed weekly. This model identified high-risk customers with 20% greater accuracy than traditional methods, enabling the bank to minimize defaults while offering competitive rates to low-risk customers.

Comparative Analysis: Real-Time APIs vs. Batch Processing

Aspect	Real-Time APIs	Batch Processing
Use Cases	Chatbots, recommendation engines, fraud alerts	Risk analysis, predictive maintenance, ETL
Response Time	Milliseconds to seconds	Minutes to hours
Data Volume	Slight to moderate per request	Large datasets processed in bulk

Resource Usage	Continuous	Periodic
Infrastructure	Low-latency, high-availability systems	Distributed computing clusters
Examples	E-commerce customer support	Financial risk modeling, batch forecasting

Hybrid Models

Many organizations adopt a hybrid approach, combining real-time APIs and batch processing to meet diverse requirements. For example, a retail company might use real-time APIs to provide personalized recommendations during shopping sessions and batch processing to optimize inventory and forecast sales.

Case Study: Integrated Retail AI System

A global retail chain deployed a hybrid AI solution where:

1. Real-time APIs provide customers with dynamic product recommendations based on browsing history.
2. Batch processing analyzed weekly sales data to optimize inventory levels and reduce stockouts.

This integrated approach improved customer engagement and operational efficiency, leading to a 15% increase in revenue.

The deployment model is a cornerstone of any AI system, determining its operational scope, efficiency, and user experience. Real-time APIs, such as customer-facing chatbots, excel in interactive scenarios requiring instant feedback. Conversely, batch processing is ideal for tasks involving large-scale data analysis and long-term insights, like financial risk assessment. By understanding these models' unique strengths and limitations, organizations can design AI systems that align with their strategic objectives and deliver maximum value.

4.4.2 CONTAINERIZATION AND ORCHESTRATION (3 PAGES)

Containerization and orchestration have revolutionized modern software application development, deployment, and maintenance, including AI systems. These technologies provide isolated, consistent, and scalable environments indispensable for AI development and deployment. This section delves into the role of Docker for isolated environments and Kubernetes for seamlessly scaling AI applications. It is supported by a visual representation of a containerization and orchestration deployment pipeline.

Using Docker for Isolated Environments

Docker is a powerful containerization platform that enables developers to package applications and their dependencies into lightweight, portable containers. These containers ensure consistency across different development, testing, and deployment stages by providing isolated environments that run seamlessly regardless of the underlying infrastructure.

Advantages of Docker in AI Development

1. **Environment Consistency:** AI applications often rely on a complex stack of libraries, frameworks, and dependencies. Docker ensures that the same environment is replicated across local development, staging, and production environments, eliminating the notorious "works on my machine" problem.

2. **Resource Efficiency:** Unlike virtual machines (VMs), which require a separate OS instance, Docker containers share the host OS's kernel. This design minimizes overhead and allows for better utilization of system resources, which is particularly beneficial for AI workloads that demand significant computational power.

3. **Rapid Prototyping:** Developers can quickly spin up containers with pre-configured environments using Docker images. Data scientists can use pre-installed pictures with TensorFlow, PyTorch, or other machine learning frameworks, accelerating experimentation and prototyping.

4. **Modularization:** Docker allows teams to build and deploy AI components independently by breaking down applications into microservices and containerizing each service. For example, the data preprocessing pipeline, model training engine, and prediction API can each reside in separate containers.

5. **Version Control:** Docker images can be tagged and versioned, enabling teams to track changes and roll back to previous versions if necessary. This capability is crucial for managing AI experiments, where minor modifications can lead to significantly different outcomes.

Real-World Example

Consider an AI application for image recognition. The development environment might include Python 3.9, TensorFlow 2.12, and OpenCV. By creating a Dockerfile that specifies these dependencies, developers can ensure that all collaborators and deployment environments use the same stack. Once the model is trained, the inference API can be containerized, ensuring that the production environment matches the testing environment.

Kubernetes for Scaling AI Applications Seamlessly

While Docker simplifies container creation and management, Kubernetes (K8s) provides the orchestration layer necessary for managing containerized applications at scale. Kubernetes automates deployment, scaling, and operations, making it ideal for AI applications that require high availability and performance.

Core Features of Kubernetes in AI Orchestration

1. **Automated Scaling:** Kubernetes can automatically scale AI applications based on workload demand. For example, during peak traffic hours, Kubernetes can scale up the number of pods running an AI inference service and scale them down during off-peak hours, optimizing resource usage.

2. **Load Balancing:** With built-in load balancing, Kubernetes ensures that incoming requests are evenly distributed across available containers. This feature is critical for AI applications serving real-time predictions to avoid bottlenecks and provide low latency.

3. **Self-Healing:** Kubernetes monitors the health of containers and automatically restarts or replaces them if they fail. For instance, if a container running a data preprocessing service crashes due to a memory leak, Kubernetes will detect the failure and spin up a new instance.

4. **Declarative Configuration:** Kubernetes uses YAML or JSON files to define the desired state of the application, including the number of replicas, resource limits, and networking configurations. This approach simplifies the management of complex AI deployments.

5. **Resource Management:** Kubernetes allows developers to set resource requests and limits for each container, ensuring that AI workloads do not consume excessive CPU or memory and affect other applications running on the same cluster.

Kubernetes in AI Workflows

An AI pipeline typically consists of data ingestion, preprocessing, model training, and inference. Kubernetes can orchestrate each stage by:

- Deploying a data ingestion service that pulls data from external sources.
- Running preprocessing jobs as batch tasks, leveraging Kubernetes's Job and CronJob resources.
- Scaling model training tasks across multiple GPUs using Kubernetes's support for specialized hardware accelerators.
- Managing a scalable inference API that serves predictions to end-users or downstream applications.

Real-World Example

A retail company uses Kubernetes to deploy an AI recommendation system. The system has multiple services, including data preprocessing, model training, and a recommendation API. During

Black Friday sales, Kubernetes automatically scales the recommendation API to handle the surge in traffic while maintaining consistent performance. The cluster scales down once the sales period ends, reducing operational costs.

Deployment Pipeline Using Containerization and Orchestration

To illustrate the synergy between Docker and Kubernetes, consider a typical deployment pipeline for an AI application:

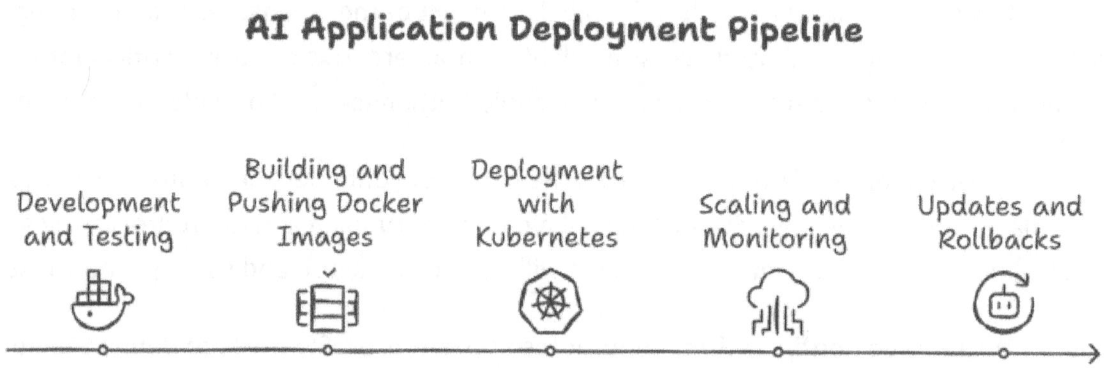

1. **Development and Testing:**
    - Developers write code and create a Dockerfile specifying the application's dependencies.
    - The code is tested locally within a Docker container to ensure compatibility.
2. **Building and Pushing Docker Images:**
    - A CI/CD pipeline builds a Docker image from the Dockerfile.
    - The image is tagged with a version number and pushed to a container registry like Docker Hub or a private repository.
3. **Deployment with Kubernetes:**
    - A Kubernetes manifest file specifies the application's desired state, including the Docker image version, number of replicas, and resource limits.
    - The CI/CD pipeline triggers a deployment to a Kubernetes cluster.
4. **Scaling and Monitoring:**
    - Kubernetes automatically scales the application based on metrics like CPU usage or the number of incoming requests.

- Monitoring tools like Prometheus and Grafana provide insights into the application's performance and health.

5. **Updates and Rollbacks:**
    - Updates are deployed using Kubernetes's rolling update strategy, ensuring zero downtime.
    - Kubernetes can roll back to a previous version if an issue is detected.

Containerization and orchestration are essential tools for modern AI workflows. Docker ensures consistency and isolation, while Kubernetes provides the scalability and resilience necessary for production-grade AI systems. Together, they empower organizations to deploy AI applications efficiently and reliably, meeting the demands of dynamic and complex environments.

4.4.3 SERVERLESS DEPLOYMENT

Serverless deployment is a cloud computing execution model where the cloud provider dynamically manages the allocation of machine resources. Unlike traditional deployment models, where developers have to worry about provisioning, scaling, and maintaining the underlying infrastructure, serverless architectures abstract these complexities, allowing developers to focus purely on their code and application logic. Serverless platforms are event-driven, meaning they execute code in response to specific events such as HTTP requests, database changes, or scheduled tasks. Popular examples of serverless platforms include AWS Lambda, Google Cloud Functions, and Microsoft Azure Functions.

Benefits of Serverless Architectures

Reduced Costs

One of the most significant advantages of serverless architectures is the potential for cost savings. Traditional infrastructure often requires provisioning resources based on anticipated peak usage, leading to periods of underutilization and wasted costs. In contrast, serverless models follow a "pay-as-you-go" billing structure, where you are only charged for the actual execution time and resource consumption of your functions. This eliminates the need to pay for idle resources, making serverless an attractive option for startups, small businesses, and enterprises seeking to optimize their IT budgets.

For example, a traditional application running on virtual machines might incur fixed costs for instances that run 24/7, even during off-peak hours. Serverless architectures eliminate this overhead. Developers can deploy lightweight functions that run only when triggered, ensuring that costs scale precisely with usage.

Faster Scaling

Serverless architectures inherently support automatic and granular scaling. When demand spikes, the serverless platform automatically provisions the necessary resources to handle the load, ensuring consistent performance. This scalability happens at the function level, meaning each function can scale independently based on its workload. This eliminates the bottlenecks in monolithic applications where scaling one part of the system requires scaling the entire application.

For instance, during an e-commerce sale or a marketing campaign, traffic to your application might surge unexpectedly. A serverless platform like AWS Lambda will seamlessly scale up the number of function instances to accommodate the increased demand. Once the traffic subsides, the platform scales down to zero, ensuring cost-efficiency without compromising user experience.

Reduced Operational Complexity

Serverless architectures abstract away infrastructure management tasks such as server provisioning, patching, and capacity planning. This allows developers to focus on writing and deploying code without worrying about the underlying hardware or software stack. Cloud providers handle the operational overhead, ensuring high availability and fault tolerance. Developers can also avoid the complexities of managing auto-scaling groups, load balancers, or container orchestration platforms like Kubernetes.

For example, Google Cloud Functions allows developers to deploy code snippets in response to specific events, such as uploading a file to Google Cloud Storage. The platform automatically deploys, runs, and scales the function, enabling rapid development and deployment cycles.

Improved Development Agility

Serverless platforms promote agile development practices by enabling rapid experimentation and iteration. Developers can deploy and test individual functions without affecting the rest of the application. This modular approach to development makes it easier to isolate and debug issues, implement new features, and iterate quickly based on user feedback.

Moreover, serverless architectures integrate seamlessly with DevOps practices, supporting Continuous Integration/Continuous Deployment (CI/CD) pipelines. Developers can automate the deployment of functions, ensuring that updates are rolled out consistently and reliably.

High Availability and Fault Tolerance

Serverless platforms are designed to provide high availability and fault tolerance out of the box. Cloud providers replicate functions across multiple availability zones, ensuring applications remain resilient to hardware failures or network outages. Developers do not need to worry about implementing complex failover mechanisms or disaster recovery strategies—these capabilities are built into the platform.

For example, AWS Lambda replicates function invocations across multiple data centers within a region, ensuring that a failure in one data center does not disrupt the application's availability. This makes serverless architectures an excellent choice for mission-critical applications where downtime is not an option.

Examples of Serverless Platforms

AWS Lambda

AWS Lambda is one of the most popular serverless platforms. It enables developers to run code without provisioning or managing servers. Lambda supports various programming languages, including Python, Node.js, Java, and Go. Various AWS services, such as Amazon S3, DynamoDB, and API Gateway, trigger Functions in AWS Lambda, making it a versatile solution for building event-driven applications.

For example, an e-commerce company can use AWS Lambda to process orders. When a customer places an order, an event triggers a Lambda function to validate the order details, update the inventory database, and send a confirmation email—all without requiring a dedicated server.

Google Cloud Functions

Google Cloud Functions is a serverless computing service provided by Google Cloud. It allows developers to run event-driven code in Python, JavaScript, or Go. Cloud Functions integrate seamlessly with other Google Cloud services, such as Cloud Storage, Pub/Sub, and Firestore, enabling developers to build scalable and responsive applications.

For instance, a media company can use Google Cloud Functions to generate image thumbnails. When a user uploads an image to Google Cloud Storage, an event triggers a Cloud Function to resize the image and save the thumbnail to storage. This workflow eliminates the need for a dedicated image processing server, reducing costs and operational overhead.

Use Cases for Serverless Architectures

1. **Web Applications**: Serverless architectures are ideal for building scalable and cost-effective web applications. Using API Gateway and serverless functions, developers can create RESTful APIs and backend services without managing servers.

2. **Data Processing**: Serverless platforms are well-suited for processing large volumes of data in real time. For example, a serverless function can analyze streaming data from IoT devices or process logs from a cloud storage bucket.

3. **Scheduled Tasks**: Developers can use serverless functions to automate scheduled tasks, such as database backups, report generation, or email notifications. These tasks can be triggered at specific intervals using AWS EventBridge or Google Cloud Scheduler services.

4. **Chatbots and Voice Assistants**: Serverless architectures power chatbots and voice assistants. Functions can handle natural language processing (NLP) requests and integrate with messaging platforms like Slack or virtual assistants like Google Assistant.

5. **Third-Party Integrations**: Serverless functions can act as glue code to integrate third-party APIs and services. For instance, a function can fetch data from an external API, process it, update a database or trigger another workflow.

Challenges and Considerations

While serverless architectures offer numerous benefits, they also come with some challenges:

1. **Cold Start Latency**: When a serverless function is invoked after a period of inactivity, it may experience a delay due to the initialization of the runtime environment. This cold start latency can impact applications requiring low-latency responses.

2. **Vendor Lock-In**: Serverless platforms are tightly integrated with their respective cloud providers, which can lead to vendor lock-in. Migrating functions to another provider may require significant effort and code changes.

3. **Debugging and Monitoring**: Serverless applications can be challenging due to their distributed and event-driven nature. Developers must rely on cloud provider tools for monitoring and troubleshooting.

4. **Resource Limits**: Serverless platforms limit execution time, memory, and concurrency. Developers must design their functions to operate within these constraints.

In conclusion, serverless deployment represents a paradigm shift in how applications are built, deployed, and managed. By abstracting away infrastructure concerns, serverless architectures enable developers to focus on delivering value to users, reducing costs, and achieving faster time to market. Whether building scalable web applications, processing data in real-time, or automating tasks, serverless platforms like AWS Lambda and Google Cloud Functions provide a flexible and cost-effective solution for modern software development.

4.4.4 DEPLOYMENT CHALLENGES AND SOLUTIONS

Several challenges can hinder the effectiveness and longevity of AI models deployed in production environments. This section explores two significant challenges—model drift and latency issues—and proposes solutions to mitigate them using continuous integration and delivery (CI/CD) pipelines for AI models.

Common Challenges

Model Drift

Model drift occurs when the statistical properties of the input data change over time, causing the AI model's predictions to become less accurate. This is a common issue in dynamic environments where data evolves due to changes in user behavior, market trends, or external factors like seasonality. For example, a recommendation system trained on historical user preferences may underperform if the preferences shift due to new trends or events.

Model drift can result in degraded model performance, reduced user trust, and missed business opportunities. Detecting and addressing model drift in real-time is crucial to ensuring the model's relevance and accuracy.

Latency Issues

Latency refers to the time it takes for a model to generate predictions after receiving input data. High latency can significantly impact user experience and the feasibility of AI applications, especially in real-time systems like fraud detection, autonomous vehicles, or conversational AI.

Latency issues can arise due to:

- **Complexity of Models:** Larger and more complex models require substantial computational resources, leading to slower inference times.
- **Inefficient Infrastructure:** Suboptimal hardware, network bottlenecks, or poorly optimized software can exacerbate latency problems.
- **Scaling Challenges:** Handling a high volume of requests simultaneously without compromising response times is another common issue.

Solutions

To address these challenges, organizations can implement continuous integration and delivery (CI/CD) pipelines tailored for AI models. These pipelines enable automated, efficient, scalable deployment processes, ensuring models remain accurate and responsive.

CI/CD Pipelines for AI Models

CI/CD pipelines for AI extend traditional software engineering practices to account for the unique requirements of machine learning workflows. They involve automating the steps of model training, validation, deployment, and monitoring. Here's how CI/CD pipelines can help tackle model drift and latency issues:

Mitigating Model Drift

1. **Automated Data Monitoring:** CI/CD pipelines can include tools to continuously monitor the input data for shifts in distribution. For example, statistical tests and drift detection algorithms can compare current and historical data to identify anomalies or trends.

2. **Frequent Model Retraining:** Automated pipelines can trigger retraining processes when drift is detected, ensuring that models stay updated with the latest data. For instance, if an e-commerce recommendation model observes a spike in demand for a new product category, the pipeline can initiate a retraining process using updated user behavior data.

3. **Version Control:** CI/CD pipelines maintain version histories for data, models, and code. This facilitates rollback to previous versions if a newly retrained model performs worse than expected.

4. **A/B Testing and Shadow Deployment:** Before entirely replacing an existing model, CI/CD pipelines can deploy the updated model in parallel (shadow deployment) or to a subset of users (A/B testing). This allows teams to evaluate their performance under real-world conditions and minimize risks.

5. **Feedback Loops:** Integrating user feedback into the pipeline ensures continuous improvement. For example, user interaction data from a recommendation system can be fed back into the training pipeline to enhance future predictions.

REDUCING LATENCY ISSUES

1. **Model Optimization:** CI/CD pipelines can incorporate optimization steps such as quantization, pruning, and distillation to reduce model size and complexity without significantly compromising accuracy. These techniques streamline inference processes and enhance computational efficiency.

2. **Scalable Infrastructure:** Pipelines can automatically provision and manage scalable infrastructure, such as cloud-based GPU clusters or edge computing devices, to handle varying workloads. Autoscaling mechanisms ensure optimal resource allocation based on demand.

3. **Efficient Model Serving:** Lightweight model-serving frameworks, such as TensorFlow Serving or TorchServe, within the CI/CD pipeline ensure fast and reliable deployment. These frameworks are designed to minimize latency while handling high-throughput scenarios.

4. **Caching and Preprocessing:** CI/CD pipelines can implement caching mechanisms for frequently used inputs or preprocessed data, reducing the computational burden during inference. For instance, a recommendation engine might cache embeddings for popular items to accelerate similarity calculations.

5. **Real-Time Monitoring and Alerts:** Latency metrics can be continuously monitored, with alerts triggered when thresholds are breached. This enables prompt investigation and resolution of performance bottlenecks.

A comprehensive CI/CD pipeline for AI typically includes the following stages:

1. **Data Ingestion and Validation:** Raw data is ingested, validated for quality, and preprocessed. Automated scripts detect anomalies, missing values, or inconsistencies.

2. **Model Training and Validation:** Training scripts leverage the latest data to retrain models. Validation steps ensure that the updated models meet predefined performance criteria.

3. **Deployment Automation:** Models passing validation are automatically deployed to production environments. Deployment strategies such as canary releases ensure minimal disruption.

4. **Monitoring and Feedback:** Post-deployment models are monitored for performance, drift, and latency. Feedback loops enable continuous improvement.

5. **Rollback Mechanisms:** In case of failure, automated rollback mechanisms restore the previous model version to maintain service continuity.

Case Study: Real-Time Fraud Detection

Consider a financial institution deploying an AI-based fraud detection system. The CI/CD pipeline monitors transaction data for changes in patterns, such as new types of fraudulent behavior. When drift is detected, the pipeline triggers retraining using recent transaction data, ensuring the model stays effective against evolving threats. Optimized models and scalable cloud infrastructure minimize latency, enabling real-time fraud detection without compromising user experience.

Benefits of CI/CD for AI Deployment

- **Resilience to Data Changes:** CI/CD pipelines ensure models adapt to changing data distributions, mitigating the effects of model drift.

- **Enhanced Performance:** Optimized models and infrastructure reduce latency, improving user experience.

- **Scalability and Automation:** Automated workflows handle large-scale deployments efficiently, reducing manual intervention and associated risks.

- **Faster Innovation:** Rapid iteration cycles enable quicker experimentation and deployment of new features or improvements.

Model drift and latency issues are critical challenges in AI deployment that can compromise AI applications' effectiveness and user acceptance. Organizations can proactively address these challenges by implementing robust CI/CD pipelines, ensuring models remain accurate, responsive, and aligned with business objectives. Investing in CI/CD practices will be essential for sustainable and successful deployments as AI systems continue to grow in complexity and scale.

4.5: MONITORING AND OPTIMIZATION (5 PAGES)

4.5.1 WHY MONITORING MATTERS (2 PAGES)

In the era of artificial intelligence (AI) and machine learning (ML), deploying a model is merely the beginning of its lifecycle. The post-deployment phase is critical, as any AI initiative's success hinges on the deployed models' continuous performance, reliability, and relevance. Monitoring is not an ancillary task; it is a fundamental process ensuring AI systems' long-term success. This section delves into the importance of monitoring, focusing on its role in maintaining model performance and reliability while highlighting key metrics to track.

Ensuring Model Performance and Reliability Post-Deployment

Once an AI model is deployed, it enters a dynamic environment that differs significantly from the controlled development and testing conditions. The data it encounters in production may evolve over time due to changes in user behavior, market conditions, or external factors like regulatory shifts. These changes can lead to model degradation without robust monitoring, rendering the AI system less effective or even harmful.

1. **Detecting Data Drift:** Data drift occurs when the statistical properties of the input data change over time. This can result from seasonal trends, new user demographics, or shifts in market dynamics. For instance, a recommendation system trained on past purchase data may become less effective as consumer preferences evolve. Monitoring enables the early detection of data drift, prompting timely retraining or adjustments to the model.

2. **Maintaining Prediction Accuracy:** AI's core value lies in its ability to make accurate predictions or classifications. Monitoring ensures that the model's performance metrics, such as precision, recall, and F1 score, remain within acceptable thresholds. A decline in these metrics can signal overfitting, underfitting, or data quality problems.

3. **Ensuring Reliability in Real-Time Systems:** Reliability is non-negotiable for real-time applications such as fraud detection or autonomous driving. Monitoring helps identify anomalies, latency spikes, or failures that could compromise system integrity. For example, delayed predictions could lead to significant losses or security breaches in a financial transaction system.

4. **Compliance and Ethical Considerations:** Many industries, such as healthcare and finance, have stringent regulatory requirements. Monitoring ensures the model operates within ethical and legal boundaries, avoiding biased outcomes or discriminatory practices. This is particularly important for models that impact human lives or sensitive business areas.

5. **Operational Efficiency:** Beyond accuracy and reliability, monitoring contributes to operational efficiency by identifying resource bottlenecks, optimizing throughput, and managing system load. This ensures that the AI system remains cost-effective and scalable.

Metrics to Track

Effective monitoring involves the continuous measurement of key performance indicators (KPIs). These metrics provide actionable insights into the model's behavior and overall system health. Below are the primary metrics to consider:

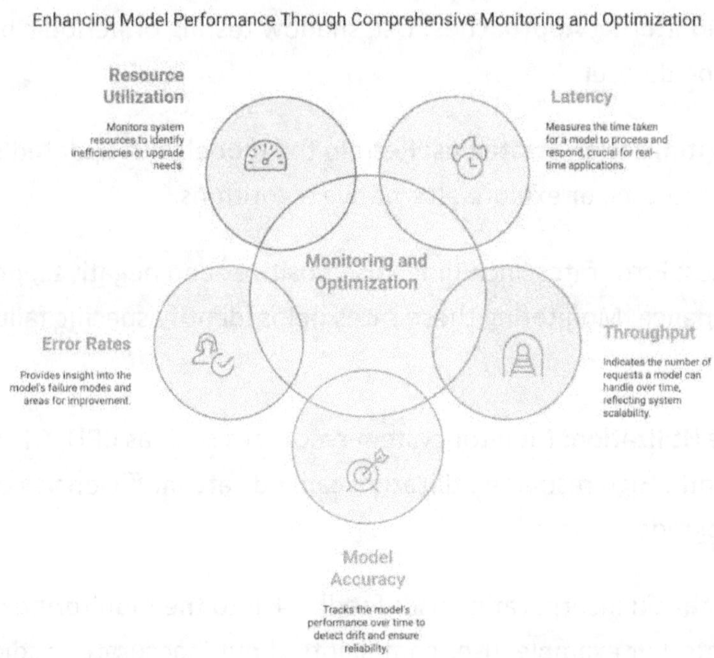

1. **Latency:** Latency measures a model's time to process input data and generate an output. This is particularly critical for applications that demand real-time or near-real-time responses, such as virtual assistants, recommendation engines, or automated trading systems. High latency can degrade user experience or lead to missed opportunities in time-sensitive scenarios.

    - **Monitoring Approaches:** Track latency at different stages, such as data preprocessing, inference, and post-processing. Identify and address bottlenecks in the pipeline.

    - **Optimization Strategies:** Use techniques like model pruning, quantization, or caching to reduce latency.

2. **Throughput:** Throughput measures the number of requests or transactions a model can handle within a given time frame. It reflects the system's capacity to scale under varying workloads.

- **Monitoring Approaches:** Evaluate throughput during peak usage periods and under stress-testing conditions.
- **Optimization Strategies:** Implement load balancing, horizontal scaling, or distributed computing to enhance throughput.

3. **Model Accuracy Over Time:** Accuracy encompasses various metrics depending on the task, such as classification accuracy, mean squared error (MSE), or area under the curve (AUC). Monitoring accuracy over time is essential to detect model drift, performance degradation, or data anomalies.

   - **Monitoring Approaches:** Use shadow testing or periodic benchmarking against a validation dataset.
   - **Optimization Strategies:** Retrain the model with updated data, fine-tune hyperparameters, or explore alternative algorithms.

4. **Error Rates:** Error rates, including false positives and negatives, provide a granular view of model performance. Monitoring these rates helps identify specific failure modes and areas for improvement.

5. **Resource Utilization:** Monitor system resources such as CPU, GPU, memory, and network bandwidth. High resource utilization can indicate inefficiencies or the need for infrastructure upgrades.

6. **User Feedback:** Incorporating user feedback into the monitoring process can provide qualitative insights. For example, user complaints about inaccurate predictions can guide debugging and optimization efforts.

Practical Implementation

Implementing effective monitoring requires a combination of tools, processes, and expertise. Modern monitoring frameworks offer features like real-time dashboards, automated alerts, and anomaly detection. Key steps include:

1. **Define Monitoring Objectives:** Identify the specific goals and KPIs relevant to the application. For instance, a customer support chatbot may prioritize low latency and high accuracy in sentiment analysis.

2. **Establish Baselines:** Use pre-deployment testing results to establish baseline performance metrics. Compare real-time data against these baselines to identify deviations.

3. **Leverage Automation:** Automated monitoring systems can proactively detect anomalies and trigger alerts. Tools like Prometheus, Grafana, or proprietary solutions offered by cloud providers streamline this process.

4. **Enable Continuous Learning:** Integrate monitoring with continuous integration/continuous deployment (CI/CD) pipelines to facilitate regular updates and improvements. This ensures the model remains relevant in dynamic environments.

5. **Foster Cross-Functional Collaboration:** Monitoring is a shared responsibility involving data scientists, DevOps teams, and business stakeholders. Collaboration ensures that monitoring efforts align with organizational goals.

Monitoring is the backbone of sustainable AI deployment. It safeguards models' performance and reliability and enhances their adaptability and alignment with organizational objectives. By tracking key metrics like latency, throughput, and accuracy, organizations can ensure that their AI systems deliver consistent value while remaining efficient and compliant. In an ever-evolving landscape, robust monitoring transforms AI from a one-time achievement into a long-term asset, driving innovation and success.

4.5.2 TECHNIQUES FOR OPTIMIZATION

Fine-tuning AI models involves the process of adapting pre-trained models to specific tasks or datasets by making small adjustments to their parameters. This approach leverages the general knowledge encoded in a pre-trained model while specializing it for a particular use case, ensuring accuracy, efficiency, and relevance in real-world scenarios. Fine-tuning is critical in scenarios where a pre-trained model might not capture domain-specific nuances or where data distribution differs significantly from the model's original training set.

Importance of Fine-Tuning:

1. **Adaptation to Specific Use Cases:** Pre-trained models are usually trained on general datasets. For example, a language model trained on large corpora might excel at understanding general language structures but falter in technical or domain-specific contexts like healthcare or law. Fine-tuning allows the model to adapt to these specialized contexts by exposing it to relevant data.

2. **Improving Performance Metrics:** Models may not achieve optimal performance in new environments due to differences in data quality, variety, or domain. Fine-tuning enables them to achieve better accuracy, precision, recall, and F1 scores tailored to the new dataset.

3. **Cost Efficiency:** Training a model from scratch requires significant computational resources and time. Fine-tuning pre-trained models is a cost-effective alternative, as it builds upon the existing knowledge encoded in the base model.

4. **Continuous Learning:** In real-world scenarios, data distributions change over time. Models fine-tuned on real-world data are better equipped to adapt to these changes, ensuring their continued relevance and utility.

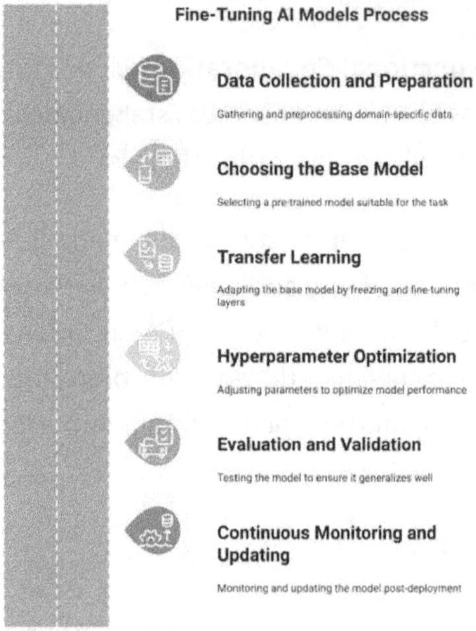

1. **Data Collection and Preparation:** Collect a domain-specific dataset that reflects the real-world environment where the model will be deployed. Clean, annotate, and preprocess the data to ensure its quality.

2. **Choosing the Base Model:** Select a pre-trained model that aligns closely with the target task. For instance, BERT for natural language processing or ResNet for image recognition tasks.

3. **Transfer Learning:** Use the base model as a starting point. Freeze the earlier layers, which capture general features, and fine-tune the later layers that deal with task-specific features.

4. **Hyperparameter Optimization:** Adjust learning rates, batch sizes, and regularization parameters to find the optimal settings for the fine-tuning process.

5. **Evaluation and Validation:** Test the fine-tuned model on a validation dataset to ensure it generalizes well to unseen data.

6. **Continuous Monitoring and Updating:** Once deployed, monitor the model's performance and periodically fine-tune it using fresh data to address changes in the real-world environment.

Applications of Fine-Tuning:

- **Customer Support Chatbots:** Fine-tuning language models to understand specific terminology or FAQs in industries like banking or retail.

- **Medical Diagnosis:** Adapting computer vision models for detecting anomalies in medical imaging datasets.
- **Recommendation Systems:** Personalizing product recommendations by fine-tuning based on user preferences and behavior.

4.5.2 OPTIMIZING RESOURCE UTILIZATION

As AI systems scale and become more complex, resource utilization optimization emerges as a critical factor. Efficient resource utilization ensures that AI systems can deliver high performance without incurring unnecessary costs or environmental impacts. Techniques like dynamic scaling for cloud-based AI illustrate how systems can adapt resource allocation to meet fluctuating demands efficiently.

Why Resource Optimization Matters:

1. **Cost Reduction:** Cloud-based AI services can incur significant operational costs, especially when resources are over-provisioned. Optimizing resource usage minimizes these expenses.

2. **Improved Performance:** Efficient allocation of computational resources ensures that models run faster and deliver results with minimal latency, which is crucial for real-time applications.

3. **Scalability:** Resource optimization enables systems to handle increasing workloads seamlessly by scaling resources up or down as needed.

4. **Environmental Impact:** Reducing unnecessary resource consumption aligns with sustainable computing practices, lowering the carbon footprint of AI deployments.

Techniques for Optimizing Resource Utilization:

1. **Dynamic Scaling for Cloud-Based AI:** Dynamic scaling is a resource management technique that automatically adjusts computational resources based on workload demands. In cloud environments, this involves provisioning or de-provisioning virtual machines, storage, and other resources to match the current needs of the AI system.

Example Scenario:

- A real-time recommendation system for an e-commerce platform experiences variable traffic throughout the day. During peak hours, the system dynamically scales up resources to handle increased traffic and maintain performance. At night, when traffic decreases, resources scale down, reducing costs without compromising service availability.

Implementation Steps:

- **Monitoring:** Continuously monitor system metrics such as CPU usage, memory consumption, and request rates.
- **Threshold-Based Rules:** Define thresholds for resource utilization. For instance, if CPU usage exceeds 80%, scale up resources; if it drops below 30%, scale down.
- **Load Balancers:** Use load balancers to distribute workloads evenly across available resources, ensuring optimal utilization.
- **Automation Tools:** Leverage tools like Kubernetes for containerized applications or cloud provider services like AWS Auto Scaling or Azure Virtual Machine Scale Sets.

2. **Efficient Model Deployment:** Deploy models in lightweight formats such as ONNX or TensorFlow Lite for edge devices, reducing memory and compute requirements without compromising accuracy.

3. **Pruning and Quantization:**

   - **Model Pruning:** Remove redundant weights or neurons in a neural network to reduce its size and computational requirements.
   - **Quantization:** Convert model weights from high-precision formats (e.g., 32-bit) to lower-precision formats (e.g., 8-bit) to save memory and speed up inference.

4. **Batch Processing:** Aggregate multiple requests into a single batch for processing. This technique improves throughput and reduces the overhead associated with processing individual requests.

5. **Caching:** Cache frequently accessed data or model predictions to reduce the need for redundant computations.

6. **Energy-Aware Scheduling:** Schedule resource-intensive tasks during periods of low energy costs or when renewable energy sources are more available.

Challenges in Resource Optimization:

1. **Balancing Trade-offs:** Optimization often involves trade-offs between cost, performance, and resource usage. Striking the right balance requires careful planning and experimentation.

2. **Dynamic Workloads:** Predicting resource requirements accurately for highly dynamic workloads can be challenging.

3. **Tool Complexity:** Implementing advanced optimization techniques like dynamic scaling or pruning requires familiarity with specialized tools and frameworks.

Case Study: Cloud-Based AI Optimization An AI-driven video analytics platform analyzes live surveillance feeds to detect anomalies. The platform operates in a cloud environment and uses dynamic scaling to optimize resource usage. During high-traffic periods, such as public events, the system scales up to handle increased video streams. At other times, it scales down, significantly reducing operational costs. By implementing batch processing and caching, the platform further minimizes redundant computations, ensuring high performance and cost efficiency.

Optimizing resource utilization is essential for scaling AI systems sustainably. Techniques like dynamic scaling, model pruning, and energy-aware scheduling provide practical solutions for achieving efficiency without compromising performance. Fine-tuning and resource optimization together ensure that AI systems remain effective, cost-efficient, and environmentally responsible in real-world applications.

4.5.3 TOOLS FOR MONITORING (1 PAGE)

Monitoring is a critical component in the lifecycle of AI and machine learning (ML) projects. It ensures models are performing as intended, metrics are tracked effectively, and systems are operating within acceptable parameters. This section explores some of the most widely used tools for monitoring in the field: MLflow, TensorBoard, and Prometheus.

MLflow

MLflow is an open-source platform designed for managing the end-to-end ML lifecycle. It is widely recognized for its robust tracking capabilities that allow data scientists and engineers to monitor experiments and their results effectively. With MLflow, users can log various parameters, metrics, and artifacts, making it easier to compare different experiment runs.

For monitoring purposes, MLflow enables:

1. **Parameter Logging:** Users can track hyperparameters used in different models, such as learning rates or the number of layers in a neural network.

2. **Metric Tracking:** Key metrics like accuracy, precision, recall, and loss functions can be logged and visualized.

3. **Artifact Storage:** It allows saving artifacts such as model files, data visualizations, or any other relevant output generated during experiments.

One of MLflow's unique features is its ability to integrate seamlessly with various ML libraries and frameworks, including TensorFlow, PyTorch, and Scikit-learn. It also supports multi-user collaboration, making it ideal for teams working on complex AI projects. With MLflow Tracking Server, metrics from different projects can be aggregated and monitored, enabling comprehensive oversight of performance trends over time.

TensorBoard

TensorBoard, an open-source visualization toolkit for TensorFlow, is another powerful tool for monitoring ML models. It offers a comprehensive suite of features that help visualize metrics, understand model behavior, and debug training processes.

TensorBoard provides:

1. **Scalars Dashboard:** Tracks scalar metrics like loss, accuracy, and learning rate over training epochs. These graphs allow users to monitor trends and identify anomalies.

2. **Histograms and Distributions:** Visualizes the distribution of weights and biases in the neural network, enabling deeper insights into how the model is learning.

3. **Graph Visualization:** Displays the computational graph of the model, which is particularly useful for debugging complex architectures.

4. **Embedding Projector:** Offers a way to explore high-dimensional data by reducing it to 2D or 3D embeddings, often used to visualize word embeddings or other feature representations.

TensorBoard's real-time updates make it especially useful for monitoring ongoing training processes. By plugging TensorBoard into a training pipeline, developers can spot overfitting, identify performance bottlenecks, and adjust hyperparameters dynamically.

Prometheus

Prometheus, an open-source monitoring system and time-series database, is widely adopted in DevOps and AI operations for its scalability and flexibility. Unlike MLflow and TensorBoard, which are tailored for ML-specific metrics, Prometheus is a general-purpose monitoring tool that can be configured for various system-level and application-level metrics.

Prometheus excels at:

1. **Time-Series Data Collection:** It gathers metrics over time, making it ideal for monitoring the performance and health of deployed AI systems.

2. **Alerting:** Prometheus can trigger alerts based on pre-defined thresholds, such as a spike in latency or a drop in throughput.

3. **Visualization:** With integrated visualization tools like Grafana, Prometheus provides intuitive dashboards that combine system-level metrics (CPU, memory, etc.) with application-specific ones (e.g., API response times or prediction rates).

For ML use cases, Prometheus can monitor the infrastructure that supports models, such as Kubernetes clusters or virtual machines, ensuring that compute resources are utilized efficiently, and potential issues are addressed proactively.

Each tool—MLflow, TensorBoard, and Prometheus—serves distinct but complementary roles in the monitoring ecosystem of AI and ML projects. MLflow focuses on experiment tracking and reproducibility, TensorBoard offers in-depth visual insights into model training and behavior, and Prometheus ensures the reliability of deployed systems. By integrating these tools into the AI development pipeline, organizations can achieve robust monitoring, improve model performance, and mitigate risks effectively.

CHAPTER 5: NAVIGATING THE STARTUP JOURNEY

INTRODUCTION

THE CHALLENGES AND OPPORTUNITIES OF AI STARTUPS

Artificial Intelligence (AI) represents one of the most transformative technological advancements of the 21st century. From revolutionizing industries to reshaping how we live and work, AI has become a cornerstone of innovation and progress. However, building an AI startup is no easy feat. Entrepreneurs in this domain face a unique landscape characterized by immense potential for disruption and formidable challenges in execution.

The allure of AI lies in its ability to solve complex problems, automate tasks, and create entirely new markets. From healthcare and finance to retail and transportation, AI-powered solutions have demonstrated their capability to drive efficiency, improve decision-making, and unlock previously unattainable insights. This means a chance to be at the forefront of industry transformation for startups. However, this opportunity comes with significant hurdles. AI startups must navigate a complex technology, talent, regulation, and market dynamics ecosystem. Success often hinges on balancing innovation and practicality, vision, and execution.

In this chapter, we explore the unique characteristics of AI startups, examine a case study of a successful AI startup—DeepMind—and outline a comprehensive framework to help entrepreneurs avoid common pitfalls, optimize resources, and scale effectively. By understanding the challenges and opportunities inherent in this space, founders can better position themselves to create sustainable, impactful AI-driven ventures.

The Unique Landscape of AI Startups

AI startups occupy a distinctive position in the entrepreneurial ecosystem. Unlike traditional startups, they operate at the intersection of cutting-edge research and practical application. This dual focus presents unique opportunities and challenges for the field.

High Potential for Disruption

AI startups can remarkably disrupt existing industries and create new ones. For example:

1. **Healthcare**: AI-driven diagnostic tools can analyze medical data with unprecedented accuracy, reducing errors and improving patient outcomes.
2. **Finance**: Predictive analytics and algorithmic trading models powered by AI are revolutionizing investment strategies and risk management.

3. **Transportation**: Autonomous vehicles are redefining mobility and logistics, with profound implications for urban planning and environmental sustainability.

The potential for AI startups to create value and drive change is immense. However, this potential is matched by significant obstacles that can impede progress.

Challenges in Execution

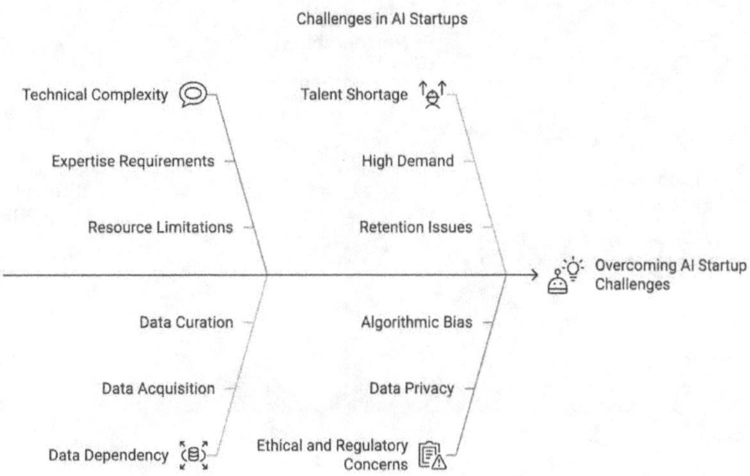

The journey of an AI startup is fraught with challenges:

1. **Technical Complexity**: Developing AI solutions requires expertise in data science, machine learning, and software engineering. The technical demands can be daunting, particularly for startups with limited resources.

2. **Data Dependency**: AI models function effectively using high-quality, diverse datasets. Acquiring and curating such data can be time-consuming and expensive.

3. **Talent Shortage**: The demand for AI talent far exceeds the supply, making it difficult for startups to attract and retain skilled professionals.

4. **Ethical and Regulatory Concerns**: Data privacy, algorithmic bias, and compliance with emerging AI regulations complicate product development and deployment.

5. **Market Acceptance**: Convincing customers to adopt AI solutions often requires overcoming skepticism and demonstrating clear value propositions.

Despite these challenges, many AI startups have successfully navigated this landscape, offering valuable lessons for aspiring entrepreneurs.

Case Study: DeepMind—Lessons from a Successful AI Startup

DeepMind, founded in 2010 and acquired by Google in 2014, is a beacon of success in the AI startup ecosystem. The company's journey offers several insights into what it takes to build a thriving AI enterprise.

1. **Vision and Focus**: DeepMind's mission—"to solve intelligence and use it to make the world a better place"—provided a clear and ambitious direction. This vision attracted top talent and aligned stakeholders around a common purpose.

2. **Technical Excellence**: DeepMind's emphasis on cutting-edge research resulted in groundbreaking achievements, such as the development of AlphaGo, the first AI program to defeat a human world champion in the game of Go.

3. **Strategic Partnerships**: By collaborating with academic institutions, industry partners, and eventually Google, DeepMind leveraged external resources to accelerate its progress.

4. **Ethical Considerations**: DeepMind's commitment to ethical AI development helped build trust with stakeholders and set a standard for responsible innovation.

5. **Scalability**: Google's acquisition provided DeepMind with the resources and infrastructure needed to scale its operations and tackle even more ambitious projects.

Key lessons from DeepMind's journey include the importance of a clear vision, investment in talent and research, and strategic partnership use to amplify impact.

WHAT THIS CHAPTER OFFERS

This chapter will equip entrepreneurs with the tools and strategies to succeed in the AI startup ecosystem. It empowers founders to navigate the complexities of building and scaling AI-driven ventures by addressing common pitfalls and providing actionable insights. Here's what you can expect:

Frameworks to Avoid Common Pitfalls

AI startups often fall prey to predictable mistakes, such as:

- **Overpromising and Underdelivering**: Setting unrealistic expectations can erode trust and damage credibility.
- **Neglecting Customer Needs**: Focusing solely on technology without understanding the market can lead to misaligned solutions.
- **Scaling Prematurely**: Expanding too quickly without a solid foundation can strain resources and jeopardize sustainability.

This chapter provides frameworks to help founders:

1. **Validate Their Ideas**: By aligning technological capabilities with market demand, startups can ensure that their solutions address real-world problems.
2. **Prioritize Resources**: Effective resource management is critical for startups operating under constraints. This paper discusses strategies for optimizing time, talent, and funding.
3. **Iterate and Improve**: Continuous feedback and iteration are essential for refining AI solutions and achieving product-market fit.

STRATEGIES TO SECURE FUNDING, BUILD A TEAM, AND GAIN TRACTION

1. **Securing Funding**: Raising capital is one of the biggest challenges for AI startups. This chapter explores:

- **Funding Sources**: Startups have multiple funding sources to explore, from venture capital and angel investors to government grants and corporate partnerships.
- **Pitching AI Solutions**: Crafting a compelling narrative highlighting the startup's vision, technology, and market potential is key to attracting investors.

2. **Building a Team**: The success of an AI startup hinges on its people. Strategies for:
   - **Attracting Talent**: Offering competitive compensation, equity, and a compelling mission can help startups attract top-tier professionals.
   - **Fostering a Collaborative Culture**: Creating an environment encouraging innovation and collaboration is critical for long-term success.
3. **Gaining Traction**: Achieving market traction requires a combination of the following:
   - **Product-Market Fit**: Ensuring that the startup's solution meets the needs of its target audience.
   - **Customer Engagement**: Building trust and loyalty through effective communication and value delivery.
   - **Strategic Marketing**: Leveraging digital channels, thought leadership, and partnerships to raise awareness and drive adoption.

By the end of this chapter, readers will have a clear understanding of the challenges and opportunities in the AI startup ecosystem, along with practical tools to build, fund, and scale their ventures. The frameworks and strategies outlined here are designed to help founders turn their ideas into impactful, sustainable AI platforms that shape the future of technology and society.

5.1: COMMON STARTUP PITFALLS

5.1.1 MISJUDGING MARKET NEEDS

Understanding market needs is pivotal in the rapidly evolving artificial intelligence (AI) world. Many AI projects fail not because of technological inadequacy but because they misjudge market demands and user needs. This section delves into the importance of problem-solution fit, examines a real-world example of a failed AI product that misunderstood its users, and outlines strategies for validating ideas early to prevent such failures.

Importance of Problem-Solution Fit

Problem-solution fit is the cornerstone of any successful AI product or platform. It ensures the product addresses users' genuine problems and meets their expectations. Without this alignment, even the most advanced AI solutions can falter.

At the heart of problem-solution fit lies an in-depth understanding of the target market. This involves identifying not just the technical feasibility of an idea but also its relevance and utility to the end users. It requires empathy, curiosity, and a systematic approach to uncovering what users truly need rather than what creators think they need.

Example: A Failed AI Product That Misunderstood User Needs

Consider the case of Jibo, the social robot. Jibo was marketed as an AI-powered social assistant designed to bring emotional warmth to human interactions. It was equipped with facial and voice recognition features and could perform simple tasks such as telling jokes or providing weather updates. While the concept initially generated significant excitement and secured substantial funding, Jibo failed to gain market traction and was discontinued.

The primary reason for Jibo's failure was its misjudgment of market needs. Although the idea of a social robot seemed innovative, it did not address a pressing problem for users. Customers did not see enough value in having a robot that could perform basic tasks already handled by smartphones or smart speakers like Amazon Alexa and Google Assistant. Additionally, Jibo's high price point further alienated potential buyers who perceived it as a novelty rather than a necessity.

Jibo's creators underestimated the importance of problem-solution fit. They focused on technological sophistication without ensuring the product addressed a significant pain point or offered unique advantages over existing solutions. This misalignment ultimately led to its downfall, serving as a cautionary tale for AI innovators.

Strategies to Validate Ideas Early

Validating ideas early in the product development cycle is essential to avoid the pitfalls of misjudging market needs. This process involves gathering real-world feedback to ensure the proposed solution meets user needs and expectations. Two critical strategies for early validation are conducting customer interviews and testing a Minimum Viable Product (MVP).

Conducting Customer Interviews

Customer interviews are powerful tools for uncovering insights into market needs and preferences. They provide direct access to potential users' thoughts, challenges, and expectations, enabling developers to refine their ideas based on real-world input.

Best Practices for Customer Interviews:

1. **Define Your Target Audience:** Identify your ideal users' demographic, professional, or behavioral characteristics. This will help you select participants who can provide relevant and actionable feedback.

2. **Prepare Open-Ended Questions:** Focus on questions encouraging users to share their experiences, challenges, and desires. For example:

    - "What are your biggest challenges in [specific context]?"
    - "How do you currently address these challenges?"
    - "What would an ideal solution look like for you?"

3. **Listen Actively:** Pay attention to both verbal and non-verbal cues. Take detailed notes and look for recurring themes or pain points.

4. **Avoid Bias:** Frame questions neutrally to avoid leading the participant toward a particular answer. For instance, instead of asking, "Would you like an AI tool to help with this?" ask, "What kind of tools or solutions would you find helpful?"

Engaging in meaningful conversations with potential users allows AI creators to gain valuable insights that inform their product design and development decisions.

MVP Testing

An MVP is a simplified product version that includes only its core functionalities. An MVP aims to test the product's viability with minimal investment and risk. MVP testing allows developers to gather feedback, measure interest, and identify areas for improvement before committing to a full-scale launch.

STEPS TO DEVELOP AND TEST AN MVP:

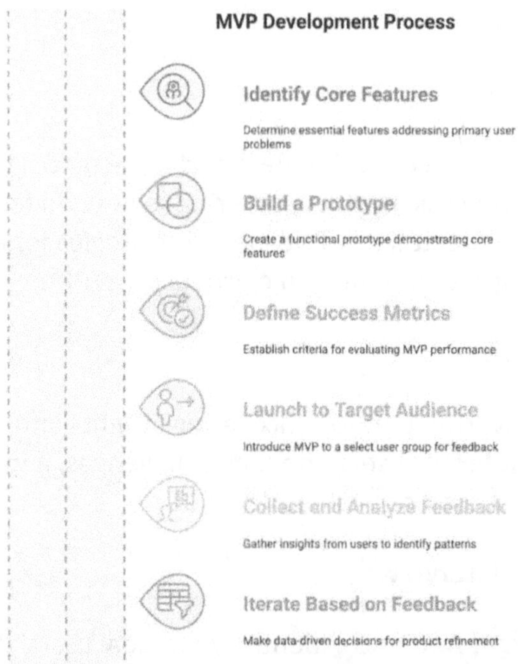

1. **Identify Core Features:** Determine the essential features that address the primary user problem. At this stage, avoid including secondary or "nice-to-have" features.

2. **Build a Prototype:** Create a functional prototype that demonstrates the core features. Depending on the complexity of the solution, this can range from a simple landing page to a working application.

3. **Define Success Metrics:** Establish clear criteria for evaluating the MVP's performance. Metrics may include user engagement, conversion rates, or qualitative feedback.

4. **Launch to a Target Audience:** Introduce the MVP to a select user group representing your target market. This allows for focused and relevant feedback.

5. **Collect and Analyze Feedback:** Use surveys, interviews, and usage analytics to gather insights from MVP users. Identify patterns in their responses to refine the product.

6. **Iterate Based on Feedback:** Use the insights gained to make data-driven decisions about which features to enhance, modify, or remove. This iterative process ensures continuous improvement and alignment with user needs.

Example of Successful MVP Testing: Dropbox, the cloud storage platform, began as a simple explainer video that showcased its core functionality. The video generated significant interest and allowed the creators to gauge demand before investing in full-scale development. By validating the idea through an MVP, Dropbox avoided the risk of misjudging market needs and successfully launched a product that resonated with users.

Misjudging market needs is a common pitfall that can derail even the most promising AI projects. Developers can mitigate this risk by prioritizing problem-solution fit, employing customer interviews and MVP testing strategies, and creating solutions that genuinely address user needs. The case of Jibo underscores the importance of aligning technological innovation with real-world demand, while the success of companies like Dropbox highlights the value of early validation. For AI innovators, the key to success lies in staying attuned to the voices of their users and embracing a culture of iterative learning.

5.1.2 DATA QUALITY AND AVAILABILITY

The success of AI systems hinges on the availability and quality of data used for training, validation, and deployment. However, the journey to secure clean, relevant, and actionable data is fraught with challenges. These challenges can have far-reaching implications, influencing AI systems' performance, reliability, and trustworthiness. In this section, we will explore the issues surrounding data quality and availability, emphasizing the critical need for robust data practices and illustrating these challenges through a real-world example of a failed predictive AI tool.

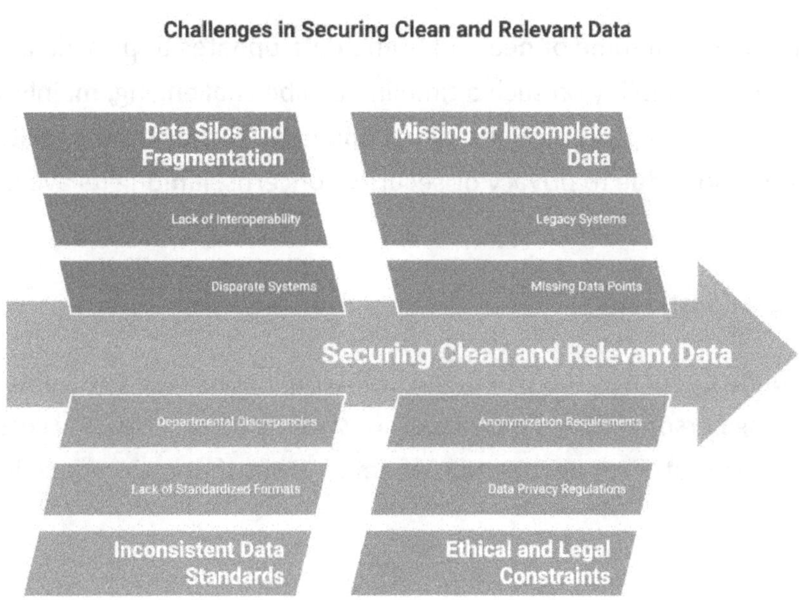

Challenges in Securing Clean and Relevant Data

1. Data Silos and Fragmentation

Data is stored in disparate systems designed for specific purposes in many organizations. These systems often lack interoperability, creating data silos that hinder seamless access. When AI projects require integrated data from multiple sources, teams may face significant difficulties extracting, cleaning, and harmonizing this fragmented information.

2. Inconsistent Data Standards

Data inconsistency arises when organizations lack standardized formats or schemas across data sources. For instance, two departments may record customer names differently, one using uppercase letters and the other following title case. Such discrepancies lead to additional preprocessing steps, increasing project complexity and time to deployment.

3. Missing or Incomplete Data

Incomplete datasets are pervasive, especially in legacy systems where fields were not consistently populated. Missing data points reduce the accuracy of AI models, as these gaps either need to be imputed—introducing potential biases—or ignored, which could lead to incomplete analyses.

4. Data Quality and Noise

Data quality directly affects the reliability of AI predictions. Noisy data, including outliers, erroneous entries, or irrelevant attributes, can skew results, leading to flawed conclusions. For instance, in a retail dataset, erroneous entries for product prices, such as a pair of shoes listed at $0.00, can significantly distort revenue forecasting models.

5. Data Availability and Timeliness

AI models often require real-time or near-real-time data updates to provide actionable insights. However, ensuring data availability on such a timeline can be challenging, mainly when dealing with systems that operate on batch processes or manual updates. Furthermore, sensitive data may be subject to access restrictions due to privacy or security concerns, limiting its availability for AI applications.

6. Ethical and Legal Constraints

Data privacy regulations such as the GDPR and CCPA impose stringent requirements on collecting, processing, and sharing personal data. These legal constraints often restrict access to rich datasets, necessitating the anonymization or aggregation of data—steps that may reduce its utility for AI purposes.

Real-World Example: A Failed Predictive AI Tool

To illustrate the challenges of data quality and availability, consider the case of a predictive AI tool designed to forecast patient admissions in a healthcare network. The tool aimed to help hospitals optimize staffing levels, ensuring sufficient resources were available during peak times. However, the project failed due to inconsistent data sources and poor quality.

The Project's Objective

The goal was to create a predictive model that leveraged historical patient admission data from multiple hospitals within the network. By analyzing patterns in admissions, such as seasonal trends or the impact of local events, the AI tool was expected to forecast daily admission rates accurately.

Challenges Encountered

1. **Data Silos**: Each hospital in the network maintained its patient records in separate systems, ranging from modern electronic health records (EHR) to outdated paper-based systems that were manually digitized. This fragmentation made it challenging to consolidate the data into a unified dataset.

2. **Inconsistent Formats**: Hospitals used different coding standards for diagnoses and treatments. For example, one hospital utilized ICD-10 codes, while another relied on older ICD-9 codes. Additionally, timestamps were recorded in varying formats, some including time zones and others omitting them entirely.

3. **Missing Data**: Many records lacked critical information, such as the reason for admission or discharge status. In some cases, fields like patient age or gender were left blank, further complicating the analysis.

4. **Noisy Data**: Erroneous entries were standard, such as duplicate records for the same patient, incorrect dates (e.g., discharge dates preceding admission dates), and implausible values (e.g., a recorded age of 150 years).

5. **Privacy Constraints**: Access to specific fields was restricted due to patient privacy concerns. The anonymization process removed identifiers that could have been useful for tracking patient histories across multiple visits, limiting the model's ability to detect recurring patterns.

The Consequences

Despite extensive efforts to clean and preprocess the data, the resulting dataset lacked the consistency and reliability required for robust AI training. The predictive model produced inaccurate forecasts, often overestimating or underestimating patient admissions by wide margins. For example, during a major flu outbreak, the model failed to account for the sudden surge in admissions, leading to severe understaffing and operational inefficiencies.

Lessons Learned

This failure highlights several critical lessons for future AI projects:

1. **Invest in Data Infrastructure**: Organizations must prioritize the development of centralized data repositories and enforce standardized data formats across all systems.

2. **Conduct Comprehensive Data Audits**: Before embarking on AI initiatives, it is essential to assess the quality, completeness, and consistency of available data. Identifying gaps early can prevent costly rework later.

3. **Foster Cross-Departmental Collaboration**: Overcoming data silos requires cooperation between departments to share and integrate data effectively.

4. **Implement Advanced Data Cleaning Techniques**: Leveraging tools and techniques, such as automated error detection algorithms and data imputation methods, can enhance data quality and reduce preprocessing time.

5. **Address Ethical and Legal Considerations Proactively**: Compliance with data privacy regulations should be a priority from the outset. Techniques like federated learning, which allows models to be trained on decentralized data without sharing sensitive information, can mitigate privacy concerns.

Data quality and availability are foundational to the success of AI systems. Poor-quality or unavailable data can undermine even the most sophisticated algorithms, resulting in unreliable predictions and failed projects. By understanding and addressing these challenges, organizations can maximize the value of their data assets and build AI solutions that deliver meaningful, actionable insights. The example of the failed predictive AI tool underscores the importance of a robust data strategy, emphasizing that clean, relevant, and accessible data is not just a technical requirement but a cornerstone of AI success.

5.1.3 UNDERFUNDING AND RESOURCE MISMANAGEMENT

Underfunding and resource mismanagement can significantly hinder an organization's ability to achieve its objectives, especially in research and development (R&D), data acquisition, and scaling operations. These issues often arise due to limited financial resources, misaligned priorities, or inefficient allocation of available resources. Addressing these challenges is crucial for ensuring sustainable growth and maintaining competitive advantages.

Impact of Limited Funds on R&D, Data Acquisition, and Scaling

Research and Development (R&D)

R&D is often the driving force behind innovation and competitive differentiation. However, when funding is limited, organizations may struggle to allocate sufficient resources to critical R&D initiatives. This can have several repercussions:

1. **Delayed Innovation**: Inadequate funding often leads to slower development cycles, delaying the introduction of new products or services. Competitors with better-funded R&D programs can seize the opportunity to capture market share by launching superior solutions earlier.

2. **Compromised Quality**: Underfunded R&D teams may cut corners or adopt suboptimal approaches to meet financial constraints, resulting in products that fail to meet market expectations or regulatory requirements.

3. **Talent Drain**: A lack of funding can discourage top-tier talent from joining or remaining with the organization, as they may seek better-funded environments with more robust opportunities for innovation.

4. **Inability to Explore New Opportunities**: Limited R&D budgets restrict the organization's ability to diversify or pursue exploratory projects, which could be pivotal in addressing emerging trends or disruptions.

Data Acquisition

Data is the lifeblood of modern decision-making and AI-driven strategies. However, acquiring high-quality data often comes at a significant cost. Underfunding in this area can lead to:

1. **Incomplete Data Sets**: Insufficient funding may prevent organizations from acquiring comprehensive and representative data, leading to biased or inaccurate insights.

2. **Dependency on Free or Low-Cost Data**: While cost-effective, free or low-cost data sources may lack accuracy, timeliness, or relevance, diminishing the quality of analysis and decision-making.

3. **Inadequate Data Infrastructure**: Limited resources can also mean underinvestment in storage, processing, and analytics infrastructure, further impeding the effective use of acquired data.

4. **Missed Opportunities**: Without sufficient data, organizations may miss critical insights that could drive innovation, customer engagement, or market expansion.

Scaling Operations

Scaling is critical for growth, particularly for startups and rapidly growing enterprises. However, underfunding can create significant obstacles:

1. **Inability to Meet Demand**: Insufficient funding may result in operational bottlenecks, preventing the organization from scaling production or services to meet growing demand.

2. **Suboptimal Technology Investments**: Underfunding may force the organization to adopt stop-gap solutions rather than invest in scalable, long-term technologies.

3. **Reputation Risk**: Scaling challenges due to underfunding can lead to delayed deliveries, poor customer experiences, or operational failures, harming the organization's reputation and customer trust.

4. **Competitive Disadvantage**: Well-funded competitors can scale faster, capture larger market shares, and establish more substantial brand recognition, leaving underfunded organizations struggling to keep up.

How to Prioritize Spending for Long-Term Growth

Given the constraints posed by underfunding, strategic prioritization is essential for maximizing the impact of available resources. Below are strategies for effective prioritization:

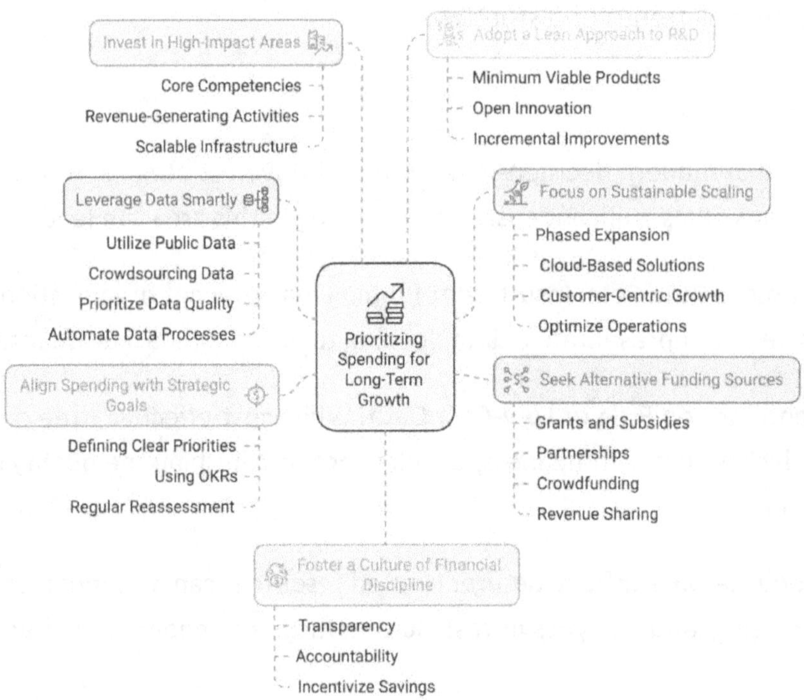

1. Align Spending with Strategic Goals

Organizations must ensure that every dollar spent contributes directly to achieving strategic objectives. This involves:

- **Defining Clear Priorities**: Establishing a hierarchy of goals, such as market penetration, product innovation, or operational efficiency, helps focus resources on the most critical areas.

- **Using OKRs (Objectives and Key Results)**: Implementing frameworks like OKRs can help ensure resource allocation aligns with measurable outcomes.
- **Regular Reassessment**: Periodically revisiting priorities ensures that spending remains aligned with evolving business needs and market dynamics.

2. Invest in High-Impact Areas

Organizations should concentrate resources on areas that yield the highest returns:

- **Core Competencies**: Focus on strengthening areas where the organization excels and can achieve a competitive edge.
- **Revenue-Generating Activities**: Prioritize initiatives directly contributing to revenue growth, such as customer acquisition or product launches.
- **Scalable Infrastructure**: Invest in technologies and processes that enable future scalability, even if they require higher upfront costs.

3. Adopt a Lean Approach to R&D

Lean R&D practices can help maximize innovation within constrained budgets:

- **Minimum Viable Products (MVPs)**: Developing MVPs allows organizations to test concepts with minimal investment and refine them based on market feedback.
- **Open Innovation**: Collaborating with external partners, such as universities or startups, can provide access to resources and expertise without significant internal investment.
- **Incremental Improvements**: Focusing on iterative enhancements rather than groundbreaking innovations can deliver value while minimizing risk.

4. Leverage Data Smartly

To overcome funding constraints in data acquisition, organizations can adopt cost-effective strategies:

- **Utilize Public Data**: Open datasets provided by governments or research institutions can serve as valuable resources.
- **Crowdsourcing Data**: Engaging customers or stakeholders to contribute data can reduce acquisition costs while fostering engagement.
- **Prioritize Data Quality Over Quantity**: Using smaller, high-quality datasets often yields better results than relying on large, low-quality datasets.

- **Automate Data Processes**: Investing in automation for data collection, cleansing, and analysis can reduce long-term costs while improving efficiency.

5. Focus on Sustainable Scaling

Scaling should be approached with a long-term perspective, even under financial constraints:

- **Phased Expansion**: Scaling in stages allows organizations to build capabilities incrementally and avoid overextension.

- **Cloud-Based Solutions**: Leveraging cloud technologies enables scalable operations with minimal upfront investment.

- **Customer-Centric Growth**: Focusing on retaining existing customers and expanding their lifetime value can be a cost-effective way to scale.

- **Optimize Operations**: Streamlining processes and eliminating inefficiencies can free up resources for scaling without additional funding.

6. Foster a Culture of Financial Discipline

Creating a culture where every team member understands the importance of financial discipline can help maximize resource efficiency:

- **Transparency**: Sharing budget constraints and priorities with teams ensures alignment and reduces unnecessary expenditures.

- **Accountability**: Establishing clear accountability for spending decisions encourages careful consideration of costs.

- **Incentivize Savings**: Rewarding teams or individuals who identify cost-saving opportunities can foster a proactive approach to resource management.

7. Seek Alternative Funding Sources

Exploring additional funding avenues can help mitigate underfunding challenges:

- **Grants and Subsidies**: Many governments and organizations offer grants or subsidies for R&D and innovation projects.

- **Partnerships**: Collaborating with larger organizations or investors can provide access to resources and funding.

- **Crowdfunding**: Engaging the public through crowdfunding platforms can raise funds while validating market demand.

- **Revenue Sharing**: Establishing revenue-sharing agreements with partners or stakeholders can reduce upfront costs.

Underfunding and resource mismanagement pose significant challenges, particularly in critical areas like R&D, data acquisition, and scaling. However, by prioritizing spending, adopting innovative approaches, and fostering a culture of financial discipline, organizations can overcome these constraints and position themselves for long-term growth. Proactively addressing these challenges ensures survival in the short term and the ability to thrive and innovate in an increasingly competitive landscape.

5.2: BUILDING AN AGILE TEAM

5.2.1 BALANCING TECHNICAL AND BUSINESS EXPERTISE

Building a thriving AI startup requires harmoniously integrating technical and business expertise. This balance ensures that groundbreaking technology aligns with market needs, scalability, and profitability. Achieving this balance involves structuring the organization to facilitate collaboration between technical and business teams, fostering interdisciplinary expertise, and leveraging the strengths of a diverse workforce. Here, we explore essential roles within AI startups and examine how interdisciplinary teams drive innovation and success.

Essential Roles for AI Startups

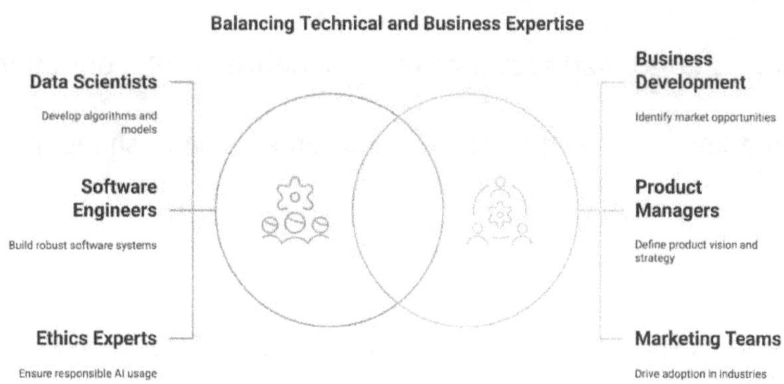

AI startups thrive on their ability to innovate while addressing market demands. To achieve this, they require a combination of technical prowess and business acumen. Key roles include:

1. Data Scientists and Machine Learning Engineers

Data scientists and machine learning engineers form the technical backbone of AI startups. These professionals:

- Develop algorithms and models that solve complex problems.
- Analyze and process vast amounts of data to extract meaningful insights.

- Ensure models are accurate, efficient, and scalable.

For example, a data scientist might design a predictive model for customer behavior, while a machine learning engineer implements it into a scalable system that integrates with the startup's product.

2. Software Engineers and DevOps Specialists

Beyond algorithm development, software engineers and DevOps specialists play crucial roles in ensuring the operational success of AI solutions. Their responsibilities include:

- Building robust software systems that host AI models.
- Deploying AI models into production environments.
- Ensuring system reliability, scalability, and performance through continuous integration and deployment practices.

3. Business Development Professionals

Business development experts bridge the gap between technology and market needs. Their responsibilities include:

- Identifying market opportunities and customer pain points.
- Building partnerships and securing clients.
- Developing go-to-market strategies to monetize AI solutions effectively.

Their insight into market trends and customer requirements helps shape the startup's product roadmap.

4. Product Managers

Product managers are at the intersection of technical and business teams. They:

- Define product vision and strategy.
- Collaborate with technical teams to ensure the product aligns with business goals.
- Prioritize features based on market demand, technical feasibility, and customer feedback.

Product managers ensure that innovations meet market expectations by mediating between business and technical teams.

5. Ethics and Compliance Experts

In the age of AI, ethical considerations are paramount. Ethics and compliance professionals:

- Establish frameworks for responsible AI usage.
- Ensure compliance with regulatory requirements.
- Mitigate risks related to bias, privacy, and transparency.

This role ensures that the startup's innovations align with societal values and legal standards, fostering trust among customers and stakeholders.

Examples of Successful Interdisciplinary Teams

Several successful AI startups exemplify the power of interdisciplinary teams. These teams demonstrate how technical and business expertise can coalesce to drive innovation and market success.

Example 1: DeepMind (Acquired by Google)

DeepMind, a pioneer in AI research, achieved breakthroughs like AlphaGo by combining technical excellence with strategic business acumen. The interdisciplinary team included:

- World-class researchers and engineers who developed cutting-edge AI models.
- Business strategists who secured partnerships with healthcare organizations and other industries to apply AI solutions.

The collaboration between these groups ensured that DeepMind's innovations had technical depth and practical applications, eventually leading to its acquisition by Google.

Example 2: OpenAI

OpenAI's mission to ensure artificial general intelligence benefits humanity showcases the value of diverse expertise. Key contributors include:

- Researchers and engineers are developing state-of-the-art AI models like GPT.
- Policy experts and ethicists addressing societal and regulatory implications.
- Business leaders securing funding and partnerships to sustain operations.

This interdisciplinary approach has allowed OpenAI to maintain its leadership in the AI space while fostering trust and transparency.

Example 3: UiPath

UiPath, a leader in robotic process automation (RPA), leveraged a balanced team to scale its business globally. Their team composition featured the following:

- Engineers and developers building user-friendly automation solutions.
- Business professionals identify enterprise needs and craft tailored solutions.
- Marketing and sales teams driving adoption in diverse industries.

This synergy between technical innovation and market understanding enabled UiPath to achieve a billion-dollar valuation.

Strategies for Balancing Expertise

Achieving the right balance of technical and business expertise requires deliberate strategies:

1. **Fostering a Collaborative Culture** Encouraging open communication and collaboration between technical and business teams minimizes silos. For example:

- Joint workshops can align product goals with market needs.
- Cross-functional meetings ensure all perspectives are considered during decision-making.

2. **Hiring Interdisciplinary Talent** Employees with experience in both technical and business domains can bridge gaps. For instance:

- Data scientists with an MBA understand both algorithm design and market positioning.
- Product managers with coding experience can better communicate with engineering teams.

3. **Continuous Learning and Development** Providing opportunities for employees to upskill fosters mutual understanding:

- Business teams can attend technical boot camps to understand AI basics.
- Technical teams can participate in business strategy workshops.

4. **Leveraging AI Tools for Communication** AI tools can facilitate collaboration by translating technical data into actionable business insights. For example:

- Visualization tools make complex model outputs accessible to non-technical stakeholders.
- Natural language processing applications can automate reporting for business teams.

Challenges and Solutions

Balancing expertise comes with challenges, but proactive measures can address them:

- **Challenge:** The priorities of technical and business teams are misaligned. **Solution:** Establish shared goals and metrics that reflect technical and business success.
- **Challenge:** Communication barriers due to differing terminologies and perspectives. **Solution:** Implement training programs to bridge knowledge gaps and encourage team empathy.
- **Challenge:** Limited resources in early-stage startups. **Solution:** Leverage external advisors and consultants to fill gaps temporarily while scaling internal teams strategically.

Balancing technical and business expertise is not just a strategic advantage—it is essential for the success of AI startups. Startups can sustain growth and impact by assembling interdisciplinary teams, fostering collaboration, and aligning innovation with market needs. Learning from examples like DeepMind, OpenAI, and UiPath, emerging AI companies can emulate strategies that integrate technical brilliance with business savviness, ensuring their solutions effectively address technological and societal challenges.

5.2.2 FOSTERING CROSS-FUNCTIONAL COLLABORATION

Cross-functional collaboration is a critical pillar for success in any organization, particularly in AI-driven initiatives where diverse expertise is required. When technical and non-technical teams work in synergy, they enhance productivity, foster innovation, streamline processes, and drive better decision-making. This section delves into strategies to effectively align technical and non-technical teams, supported by a real-world case study of an AI startup that achieved rapid scaling through team alignment.

Strategies to Align Technical and Non-Technical Teams

Organizations must implement structured strategies that bridge understanding, communication, and objectives gaps to foster seamless collaboration between technical and non-technical teams. Below are some effective methods:

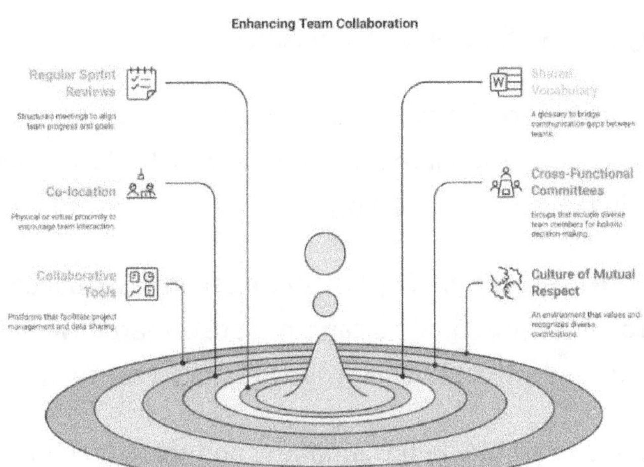

1. **Regular Sprint Reviews and Shared KPIs**

    - **Purpose and Implementation**: Regular sprint reviews provide a structured platform for discussing progress, challenges, and upcoming goals. Technical teams should give concise presentations on their achievements, followed by discussions with non-technical stakeholders to align priorities and address questions.

    - **Shared KPIs**: Establishing shared Key Performance Indicators (KPIs) ensures that all teams are aligned toward common objectives. For example, while the technical team's KPIs might focus on system uptime or model accuracy, non-technical teams could align their goals around customer adoption rates or revenue impact. By having overlapping KPIs, both groups have a vested interest in each other's success.

    - **Benefits**: Regular sprints and shared KPIs create transparency and foster a culture of accountability. They ensure that all teams understand their role in the larger picture and feel motivated to contribute to overarching goals.

2. **Creating a Shared Vocabulary**

    - **Bridging the Communication Gap**: Jargon is one of the primary barriers to collaboration between technical and non-technical teams. Technical teams often use domain-specific language, while non-technical teams may rely on market—or customer-focused terminology. Creating a shared glossary of terms can help demystify technical concepts and reduce misunderstandings.

    - **Training and Workshops**: It can be highly effective to host periodic workshops where technical teams explain key AI concepts to non-technical members and vice versa. These sessions should focus on practical applications rather than abstract theories, ensuring everyone gains a functional understanding.

    - **Outcome**: A shared vocabulary minimizes miscommunication and enhances collaboration, enabling faster decision-making.

3. **Co-locating teams (Physically or Virtually)**

    - **Promoting Proximity**: When feasible, co-locating technical and non-technical teams can encourage spontaneous interactions, brainstorming sessions, and a better understanding of each other's work.

    - **Virtual Co-Location**: For distributed teams, virtual co-location tools such as Slack, Microsoft Teams, or Miro can simulate a shared workspace. Encouraging informal conversations and virtual brainstorming fosters a sense of camaraderie.

    - **Impact**: Proximity builds empathy and trust, leading to smoother collaboration and a deeper appreciation of diverse contributions.

4. **Aligning Goals Through Cross-Functional Committees**

    - **Establishing Cross-Functional Groups**: Setting up committees or working groups that include members from technical and non-technical teams helps ensure that perspectives from all stakeholders are considered. For instance, a product steering committee might consist of software engineers, data scientists, marketers, and sales representatives.

    - **Rotating Membership**: Rotating membership in these committees ensures fresh perspectives and broader organizational involvement over time.

    - **Outcome**: Such committees foster holistic decision-making and help resolve conflicts early by balancing technical feasibility with business needs.

5. **Investing in Collaborative Tools and Platforms**

    - **Centralized Project Management**: Tools like Jira, Trello, or Asana can help centralize workflows, making it easier for all teams to stay updated on project milestones, blockers, and deliverables.

    - **Data Sharing and Visualization**: Platforms like Tableau, Power BI, or custom dashboards allow non-technical teams to access and interpret data insights without relying entirely on technical teams. Conversely, tools like Figma can enable non-technical stakeholders to contribute effectively to UI/UX discussions.

    - **Benefits**: Collaborative tools reduce friction, empower teams to work autonomously, and ensure consistent progress tracking.

6. **Fostering a Culture of Mutual Respect**

    - **Recognizing Contributions**: Organizations should celebrate technical achievements (e.g., deploying a high-performing AI model) and non-technical successes (e.g., closing a high-value client deal).

    - **Cultural Training**: Encourage teams to participate in cultural exchange programs to learn about their counterparts' challenges and workflows.

    - **Impact**: Mutual respect builds a foundation of trust, making it easier for teams to work through conflicts and align on priorities.

Case Study: An AI Startup That Scaled Rapidly Through Team Alignment

Background: XYZ.ai, an AI startup specializing in predictive analytics for retail, faced significant challenges during its early scaling phase. The technical team, composed of data scientists and software engineers, prioritized model optimization, while the non-technical team, comprising marketers and sales professionals, focused on acquiring customers and securing partnerships. The misalignment in priorities led to product launch delays and team friction.

Challenges:

- **Communication Barriers**: Non-technical teams struggled to understand the complexities of AI models, while technical teams felt their efforts were undervalued.
- **Conflicting Goals**: The technical team's focus on perfection delayed deliverables, frustrating the sales team, which needed rapid iterations to meet customer demands.
- **Lack of a Unified Vision**: Teams operated in silos, with limited understanding of how their work contributed to the company's overall mission.

Intervention: To address these challenges, XYZ.ai's leadership implemented the following changes:

1. **Instituting Regular Sprint Reviews**:
   - Bi-weekly sprint reviews were introduced, bringing both teams together to discuss progress and roadblocks. Technical teams presented simplified updates on model development while sales and marketing shared customer feedback and market trends.
   - These meetings created a feedback loop, allowing technical teams to prioritize features aligned with customer needs.
2. **Defining Shared KPIs**:
   - The leadership established shared KPIs, such as the number of successful customer deployments and the time it takes to resolve client issues. This encouraged both teams to work collaboratively to improve customer satisfaction.
3. **Conducting Cross-Training Sessions**:
   - Data scientists hosted workshops on AI basics, demystifying concepts like algorithm selection and model accuracy. Similarly, sales and marketing teams conducted sessions on customer personas and market dynamics.
   - These sessions improved mutual understanding and helped teams appreciate each other's challenges.
4. **Adopting Collaborative Tools**:
   - The company implemented a centralized project management tool (Jira) to track tasks and milestones. Additionally, a shared dashboard provided real-time product performance and customer metrics updates.

5. **Establishing a Cross-Functional Product Committee:**
    - A product committee, including members from both technical and non-technical teams, was formed to oversee major decisions. This ensured that product features balanced technical feasibility with market demands.

Results:

- **Improved Time-to-Market**: By aligning priorities, XYZ.ai reduced its product development cycles by 30%, enabling faster launches.
- **Enhanced Customer Satisfaction**: Shared KPIs encouraged teams to collaborate on customer success, leading to a 25% improvement in client retention.
- **Increased Revenue**: The streamlined collaboration helped XYZ.ai secure five major clients within six months, doubling their revenue.
- **Stronger Team Cohesion**: Surveys revealed a 40% improvement in team satisfaction scores, with employees citing better communication and mutual respect as key factors.

The XYZ.ai case underscores the transformative impact of cross-functional collaboration. Organizations can accelerate innovation, improve operational efficiency, and achieve sustainable growth by fostering a culture of alignment and shared goals. The strategies outlined in this section provide a robust framework for bridging the gap between technical and non-technical teams, ensuring that all stakeholders contribute effectively to organizational success.

5.2.3 REMOTE VS. ON-SITE TEAMS

Benefits and Challenges of Remote Work in AI Startups

The shift toward remote work has transformed how AI startups operate, offering significant advantages and notable challenges. For these innovative organizations, which rely heavily on knowledge work, agility, and cross-disciplinary collaboration, the decision between remote and on-site models carries unique implications.

Benefits of Remote Work in AI Startups

1. **Access to Global Talent**: Remote work enables AI startups to tap into a global talent pool unrestricted by geographical boundaries. This is particularly beneficial in the AI sector, where niche skills such as natural language processing, computer vision, and advanced machine learning are often in short supply locally. Startups can hire top talent from diverse locations, bringing varied perspectives and expertise.

2. **Cost Efficiency**: Operating remotely reduces overhead costs such as office space, utilities, and supplies. For startups working on tight budgets, this financial relief can be reallocated to research and development or scaling efforts.

3. **Flexibility and Work-Life Balance**: Remote work allows employees to manage their schedules, increasing job satisfaction and retention. In a competitive field like AI, where burnout can be high, fostering a work environment that supports well-being can be a strategic advantage.

4. **Diverse Perspectives and Innovation**: A globally distributed team often brings a variety of cultural and professional perspectives. Such diversity can fuel innovation, a key driver for AI startups that aim to solve complex, real-world problems.

Challenges of Remote Work in AI Startups

1. **Collaboration and Communication**: AI projects typically require intensive cooperation between developers, data scientists, and domain experts. Remote setups can create barriers to spontaneous brainstorming sessions and quick problem-solving, which are often more manageable on-site.

2. **Time Zone Differences**: While global talent is a boon, managing a team across multiple time zones can hinder synchronous communication and slow decision-making.

3. **Cultural and Organizational Cohesion**: Building a unified company culture can be challenging in a remote environment. Employees may feel disconnected, which can impact motivation and engagement.

4. **Infrastructure and Security**: AI startups often handle sensitive data, requiring robust security protocols. Ensuring secure access to systems and safeguarding intellectual property can be more complex with a distributed team.

5. **Onboarding and Training**: Remote work can complicate onboarding new employees and upskilling existing ones. Without in-person interactions, it may take longer for new hires to assimilate into the team and for knowledge transfer to occur efficiently.

Tips for Maintaining Productivity in Distributed Teams

To harness the benefits of remote work while mitigating its challenges, AI startups must adopt deliberate strategies for maintaining productivity and fostering collaboration. Below are actionable tips for leaders and teams:

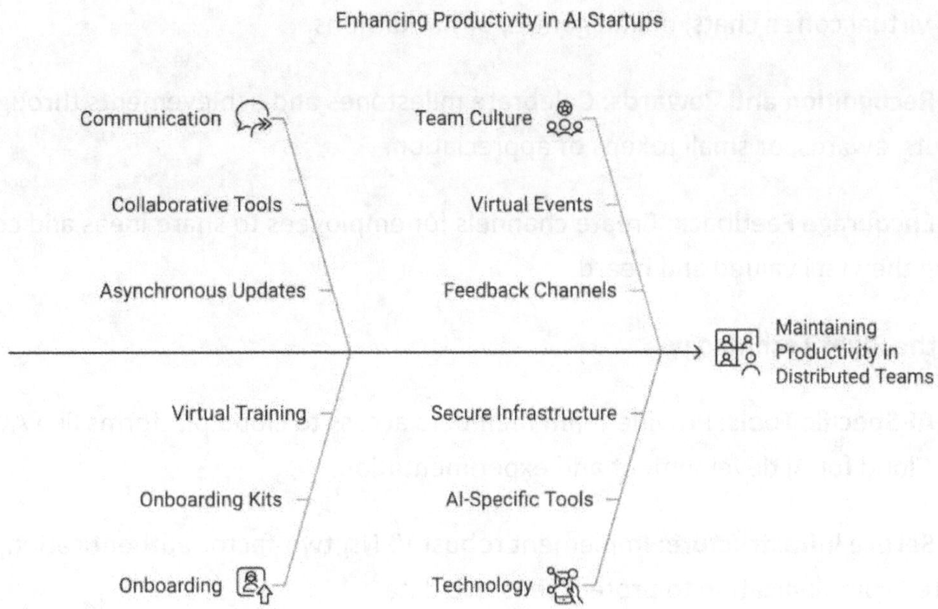

1. Establish Clear Communication Protocols

- **Use Collaborative Tools**: Leverage platforms like Slack, Microsoft Teams, or Asana to facilitate real-time communication and project management. Tools like GitHub and Jupyter Notebooks enable seamless code sharing and collaboration for AI projects.

- **Define Communication Norms**: Set expectations for response times, meeting etiquette, and modes of communication. For instance, specify when to use email versus instant messaging.

- **Asynchronous Communication**: To accommodate time zone differences, encourage asynchronous updates through recorded video briefs, detailed documentation, or shared dashboards.

2. Create a Robust Onboarding Process

- **Standardized Onboarding Kits**: Provide new hires with comprehensive onboarding materials, including project overviews, key contacts, and access to necessary software.

- **Buddy Systems**: Pair new employees with mentors to accelerate their integration and provide a point of contact for questions.

- **Virtual Training Programs**: Use interactive, online training sessions to ensure team members understand tools, workflows, and security protocols.

3. Build a Strong Team Culture

- **Regular Virtual Events**: To foster a sense of camaraderie, host team-building activities such as virtual coffee chats, online games, or hackathons.
- **Recognition and Rewards**: Celebrate milestones and achievements through virtual shoutouts, awards, or small tokens of appreciation.
- **Encourage Feedback**: Create channels for employees to share ideas and concerns, ensuring they feel valued and heard.

4. Invest in the Right Technology

- **AI-Specific Tools**: Provide team members access to cloud platforms like AWS, Azure, or Google Cloud for AI development and experimentation.
- **Secure Infrastructure**: Implement robust VPNs, two-factor authentication, and encrypted communication to protect sensitive data.
- **High-Quality Hardware**: Ensure team members have reliable laptops, monitors, and ergonomic setups to support productivity.

5. Focus on Deliverables and Outcomes

- **OKRs and KPIs**: To align team efforts, define clear Objectives and Key Results (OKRs) or Key Performance Indicators (KPIs) for projects.
- **Regular Check-Ins**: Use weekly or biweekly one-on-one meetings to track progress and address roadblocks.
- **Agile Methodologies**: Adopt agile frameworks like Scrum or Kanban to manage workflows and maintain transparency in tasks and responsibilities.

6. Encourage Work-Life Balance

- **Flexible Schedules**: Employees should be allowed to set working hours that suit their time zones and personal obligations, as long as core collaboration periods are respected.
- **Monitor Workloads**: Use tools like Clockify or RescueTime to help employees track their hours and avoid burnout.
- **Mental Health Support**: Offer resources such as counseling, meditation apps, or wellness stipends to promote well-being.

7. Conduct Regular Performance Evaluations

- **Feedback Loops**: Schedule quarterly or biannual reviews to assess individual and team performance.

- **Data-Driven Insights**: Use analytics tools to monitor productivity metrics and identify areas for improvement.
- **Skill Development Plans**: Invest in ongoing learning opportunities, such as courses or certifications, to keep the team's skills sharp and aligned with industry trends.

8. Align Remote and On-Site Strategies

- **Hybrid Models**: Consider a hybrid approach where employees can choose between remote and on-site work, depending on their roles and preferences.
- **Periodic On-Site Gatherings**: Organize in-person retreats or workshops to strengthen relationships and collaboration.
- **Localized Hubs**: Create small coworking hubs in major cities to provide optional shared spaces for team members.

By embracing these strategies, AI startups can unlock the full potential of their distributed teams while minimizing the friction that comes with remote work. With thoughtful implementation, remote and on-site teams can coexist and thrive, driving innovation and success in the highly competitive AI landscape.

5.3: COST OPTIMIZATION

5.3.1 EFFICIENT USE OF CLOUD RESOURCES

Cloud computing has revolutionized business operations, enabling unprecedented scalability, flexibility, and innovation. However, the costs associated with cloud services can quickly escalate if not managed efficiently. For organizations, especially startups and small—to medium-sized enterprises, optimizing cloud resources is essential to maintaining financial health while leveraging the power of the cloud. This section delves into strategies for reducing cloud computing costs, with practical examples highlighting their effectiveness.

Strategies for Reducing Cloud Computing Costs

Optimizing Cloud Costs for Startups

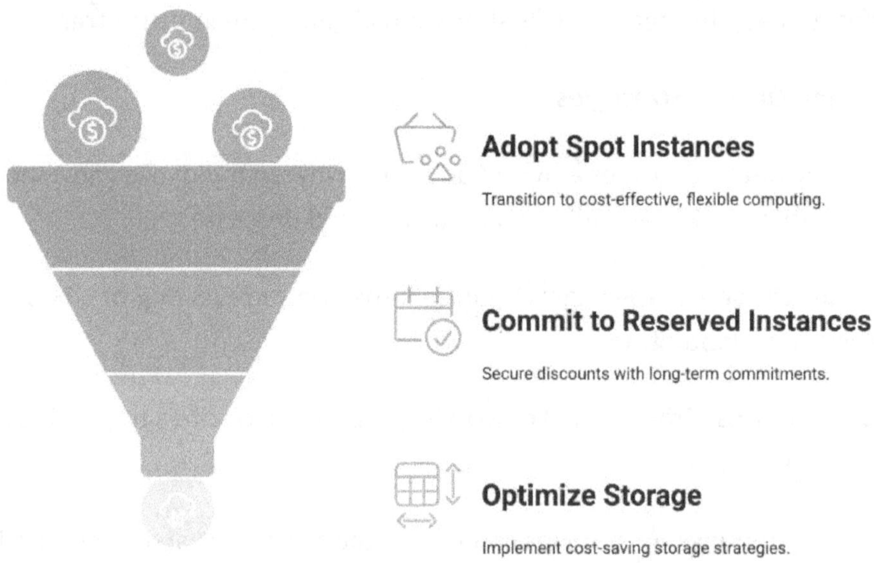

1. Leveraging Spot Instances

Spot instances offer cloud users access to unused computing capacity at significantly reduced prices. Platforms like AWS, Google Cloud, and Azure provide spot or preemptible instances, allowing users to perform tasks that can tolerate interruptions. While spot instances may not be suitable for high availability workloads, they are ideal for batch processing, big data analysis, and machine learning model training.

Key Benefits:

- **Cost Reduction:** Spot instances can reduce computing costs by up to 90% compared to on-demand instances.
- **Scalability:** Organizations can scale resources dynamically during non-peak hours.
- **Flexibility:** Spot instances can be integrated into hybrid workloads, utilizing on-demand resources for critical tasks and spot instances for less time-sensitive operations.

Practical Example:

An AI startup specializing in natural language processing (NLP) leveraged spot instances for training large-scale transformer models. By scheduling model training during low-demand periods and using spot instances, the startup reduced its training costs by 75%, allowing it to allocate more resources to research and development.

2. Committing to Reserved Capacity

Reserved instances or savings plans allow businesses to commit to a specific cloud usage over one to three years in exchange for significant discounts. These commitments are beneficial for predictable workloads and can complement dynamic scaling strategies.

Key Benefits:

- **Predictable Savings:** Discounts of up to 75% compared to on-demand pricing.
- **Budget Planning:** Fixed pricing enables better financial forecasting.
- **Consistency:** Reserved capacity ensures resource availability even during peak times.

Practical Example:

A fintech company operating a critical payments platform identified a consistent baseline workload that did not fluctuate significantly. By committing to a three-year reserved instance plan, the company reduced its annual cloud expenditure by 40%, freeing up funds for customer acquisition and platform innovation.

3. Optimizing Storage Costs

Cloud storage costs can accumulate rapidly, especially with the proliferation of unstructured data. Implementing efficient storage practices can significantly reduce expenses without compromising accessibility or performance.

Strategies for Optimization:

- **Data Tiering:** Use lifecycle policies to move less frequently accessed data to cheaper storage tiers such as AWS Glacier or Azure Cool Blob Storage.
- **Compression and Deduplication:** Compressing data and eliminating duplicate files can reduce storage requirements.
- **Rightsizing Volumes:** Monitor and adjust storage allocations to prevent over-provisioning.
- **Object Storage for Cold Data:** Object storage solutions offer cost-effective archiving and long-term data retention options.

Practical Example:

An AI startup providing predictive analytics services noticed that historical data consumed over 60% of its storage budget. The startup reduced its storage costs by implementing a data lifecycle policy to archive cold data into Amazon S3 Glacier and leveraging compression algorithms by 50% while maintaining data accessibility for compliance.

Combining Strategies for Maximum Efficiency

Using these cost-saving measures in isolation provides benefits but combining them yields even greater efficiencies. For instance, businesses can:

- Use spot instances for non-critical workloads and reserved instances for baseline capacity.
- Implement automated storage tiering while rightsizing storage volumes.
- Monitor and optimize cloud usage with tools like AWS Cost Explorer, Azure Cost Management, or Google Cloud Billing reports.

Example: AI Startup Saves 30% by Optimizing Cloud Usage

Consider an AI startup focusing on personalized recommendation systems for e-commerce platforms. Initially, the startup relied heavily on on-demand instances and default storage options, leading to spiraling costs. By conducting a thorough cloud usage audit, the startup identified inefficiencies and implemented the following changes:

1. **Adopted Spot Instances:** Migrated machine learning model training jobs to spot instances, reducing compute costs by 70% for these tasks.
2. **Committed to Reserved Instances:** Reserved baseline capacity for their recommendation engine API, which operated 24/7, saving 40% on compute costs for these workloads.
3. **Optimized Storage:** Archived old training datasets and logs to lower-cost storage tiers while rightsizing active storage volumes, cutting storage costs by 50%.

Through these measures, the startup reduced monthly cloud expenses by 30%. The cost savings were reinvested in customer acquisition campaigns, accelerating the company's growth trajectory.

Additional Considerations for Efficient Cloud Usage

Automation and Monitoring

- **Automated Scaling:** Use tools like AWS Auto Scaling or Google Cloud's Compute Engine autoscaler to adjust resources dynamically based on real-time demand.
- **Monitoring Tools:** Employ services like AWS CloudWatch, Azure Monitor, or Google Cloud's Operations Suite to gain insights into cloud usage and identify cost-saving opportunities.

Cost Allocation and Tagging

Tagging resources appropriately enables organizations to track spending across teams, projects, or departments. This visibility helps identify inefficiencies and promotes accountability.

Educating Teams

Organizations should foster a cost-conscious culture by training employees on efficient cloud usage practices. Cloud providers often offer training programs and certifications to help teams build expertise.

Conclusion

The efficient use of cloud resources is not merely a technical exercise but a strategic imperative. Organizations can significantly reduce their cloud computing costs by leveraging spot instances, committing to reserved capacity, and optimizing storage while maintaining performance and scalability. An AI startup's 30% cost reduction underscores the tangible benefits of these strategies. Optimizing usage is the key to unlocking long-term sustainability and innovation in an era where cloud computing is indispensable.

5.3.2 LEVERAGING OPEN-SOURCE TOOLS

Open-source tools have become a cornerstone for artificial intelligence (AI) innovation. These frameworks provide developers and organizations with powerful, community-supported resources that accelerate development and significantly reduce costs. The ability to tap into a global community of contributors fosters rapid innovation, robust documentation, and a wealth of examples that can be leveraged across industries.

Key Open-Source Frameworks

The landscape of open-source AI tools is vast, but specific frameworks have become the gold standard for AI development:

TensorFlow: Developed by Google, TensorFlow is a versatile open-source library widely used for machine learning (ML) and deep learning. Its modular architecture allows developers to build, train, and deploy models across various platforms, from mobile devices to cloud environments. TensorFlow's pre-built models, such as BERT for natural language processing (NLP) and EfficientNet for image classification, enable rapid prototyping and deployment. The TensorFlow ecosystem also includes tools like TensorBoard for visualization and TFX (TensorFlow Extended) for production pipelines, making it an end-to-end solution for AI development.

PyTorch: Created by Facebook, PyTorch is renowned for its ease of use and dynamic computation graph. This flexibility makes it a favorite among researchers and practitioners experimenting with novel architectures. PyTorch supports a Pythonic interface, enabling seamless integration with Python-based workflows. Its popularity in academia ensures a steady flow of state-of-the-art research models and methodologies. Libraries like Hugging Face Transformers, built on PyTorch, have revolutionized NLP by offering pre-trained models for tasks like translation, summarization, and question-answering.

Scikit-learn: This lightweight yet powerful library for traditional ML tasks is built on NumPy, SciPy, and Matplotlib. It simplifies the implementation of classification, regression, clustering, and dimensionality reduction algorithms. Its intuitive API and extensive documentation make it ideal for beginners and professionals. Scikit-learn is particularly effective for data preprocessing and exploratory data analysis, providing a strong foundation for model development and evaluation.

Other Noteworthy Tools: Frameworks like Keras, an abstraction layer for TensorFlow, simplify the design of neural networks with a user-friendly interface. ONNX (Open Neural Network Exchange) enables interoperability between frameworks, allowing models trained in PyTorch to be deployed in TensorFlow environments and vice versa. Tools like Apache MXNet and OpenCV also cater to specialized needs like scalable training and computer vision.

Advantages of Open-Source Tools

Organizations and developers alike benefit from leveraging open-source tools:

1. **Cost Savings:** Open-source frameworks eliminate licensing fees, making them accessible to startups and enterprises with limited budgets.

2. **Rapid Prototyping:** The development lifecycle is accelerated by pre-built models, extensive documentation, and active community support.

3. **Customization:** The open nature of these tools allows developers to modify code to meet specific project requirements, fostering innovation.

4. **Interoperability:** Standards like ONNX and support for multiple programming languages enable seamless integration into existing workflows.

5. **Scalability:** Many open-source frameworks, such as TensorFlow and PyTorch, are optimized for scalability, supporting distributed training and deployment in production environments.

Case Study: A Startup Reduces Development Costs with Open-Source Solutions

Background: A healthcare analytics startup aimed to develop a predictive model for early diagnosis of chronic diseases using patient data. Operating on a limited budget, the startup faced challenges in acquiring proprietary software and hiring a large team of data scientists.

Solution: The team adopted open-source frameworks to build its AI pipeline. They used TensorFlow to develop deep learning models, Scikit-learn for preprocessing and feature selection, and Jupyter Notebooks for collaborative development and visualization. Additionally, they leveraged pre-trained models from PyTorch's ecosystem to fine-tune tasks like medical image classification.

Implementation:

- **Data Collection and Preprocessing:** The team cleaned and preprocessed patient records using open-source tools like Pandas and Scikit-learn. Scikit-learn's robust feature selection algorithms helped identify the most relevant predictors of chronic diseases.

- **Model Development:** Using TensorFlow, the team built a convolutional neural network (CNN) for analyzing medical images. For textual patient records, they fine-tuned a BERT model using the Hugging Face library, enabling the extraction of actionable insights from clinical notes.

- **Deployment:** The startup deployed its models using TensorFlow Serving, an open-source tool that simplifies model serving in production. They also utilized Kubernetes for container orchestration, ensuring scalability and reliability.

Results:

1. **Cost Reduction:** The startup saved an estimated $150,000 in software licensing fees over two years by relying on open-source tools.

2. **Accelerated Development:** Pre-trained models and community support reduced development time by approximately 40%.

3. **Improved Accuracy:** The models achieved a 92% accuracy rate in early diagnosis, outperforming industry benchmarks.

4. **Scalability:** Kubernetes and TensorFlow Serving enabled seamless scaling as the startup's user base grew.

Challenges and Considerations

While open-source tools offer numerous advantages, organizations should be mindful of potential challenges:

1. **Steep Learning Curve:** Advanced frameworks like TensorFlow and PyTorch require expertise, which can be a barrier for small teams.

2. **Support:** Unlike proprietary solutions, open-source tools rely on community support, which may not always be timely or comprehensive.

3. **Security:** Organizations must ensure open-source tools comply with regulatory standards and not introduce vulnerabilities.

4. **Integration:** Compatibility with legacy systems and third-party tools can pose integration challenges.

Leveraging open-source tools is a strategic decision that empowers organizations to innovate while optimizing resources. Frameworks like TensorFlow, PyTorch, and Scikit-learn provide unparalleled flexibility and community-driven enhancements. As the healthcare analytics startup demonstrated, these tools can drive significant cost savings, improve efficiency, and deliver high-quality outcomes. However, organizations must balance these benefits with considerations around expertise, support, and security to maximize the value of open-source solutions.

5.3.3 SCALING SMARTLY

Scaling operations is a critical phase for any AI startup. It signifies that the organization is moving beyond its initial proof-of-concept and entering a broader adoption and impact stage. However, scaling requires meticulous planning and execution to ensure that resources are utilized efficiently and minimize waste. This section delves into strategies and tools for cost-effective scaling, focusing on serverless computing, edge AI, and a cost optimization roadmap for AI startups.

SCALING OPERATIONS WHILE MINIMIZING WASTE

Minimizing waste during scaling involves optimizing resource usage and ensuring that every dollar spent contributes directly to value creation. The following strategies highlight how startups can achieve this:

1. **Adopting Serverless Computing**:
   - Serverless computing eliminates the need for provisioning and managing infrastructure. By leveraging serverless platforms such as AWS Lambda, Google Cloud Functions, or Azure Functions, startups can run code without worrying about server maintenance. The billing model for serverless computing is based on actual usage, ensuring startups only pay for the computing power they use.
   - Benefits include:
     - **Dynamic Scaling**: Automatically adjusts to varying workloads.
     - **Cost Efficiency**: Eliminates the cost of idle resources.
     - **Reduced Complexity**: Frees teams from managing servers, enabling focus on development and innovation.

For example, an AI startup providing on-demand inference services can use serverless computing to allocate resources dynamically based on user demand. This approach ensures performance and minimizes over-provisioning.

2. **Utilizing Edge AI**:

- Edge AI refers to deploying machine learning models directly on edge devices such as smartphones, IoT devices, or other hardware at the network's edge. This reduces the need for continuous data transfer to and from centralized cloud servers.
- Benefits include:
    - **Reduced Latency**: Processing data closer to the source ensures faster responses.
    - **Cost Savings**: Reduces bandwidth and cloud processing costs.
    - **Scalability**: Expands reach without overburdening centralized systems.

For instance, an AI-powered smart home device manufacturer can embed models within devices to provide real-time responses without depending on cloud infrastructure. This approach reduces operational costs and improves user experience.

3. **Leveraging Cloud-Native Architectures**:
    - Cloud-native architectures such as Kubernetes enable startups to manage workloads efficiently while scaling. Kubernetes orchestrates containers, ensuring optimal resource allocation across distributed environments.
    - Best practices include:
        - **Auto-Scaling**: Use Kubernetes' auto-scaling features to adjust resources based on real-time demands.
        - **Cost Monitoring**: Utilize tools like Kubernetes Cost Analyzer to track and optimize expenditures.
4. **Implementing FinOps (Financial Operations)**:
    - FinOps integrates financial accountability into cloud operations. By fostering collaboration between engineering, finance, and operations teams, startups can optimize cloud spend and maximize ROI.
    - Key practices:
        - **Setting Budgets**: Define and monitor spending limits.
        - **Tagging Resources**: Use tags to track resource utilization and identify inefficiencies.
        - **Continuous Optimization**: Regularly analyze spending patterns to uncover saving opportunities.

A cost optimization roadmap is essential for guiding AI startups through scaling while maintaining financial discipline. Below is an outline of a potential roadmap:

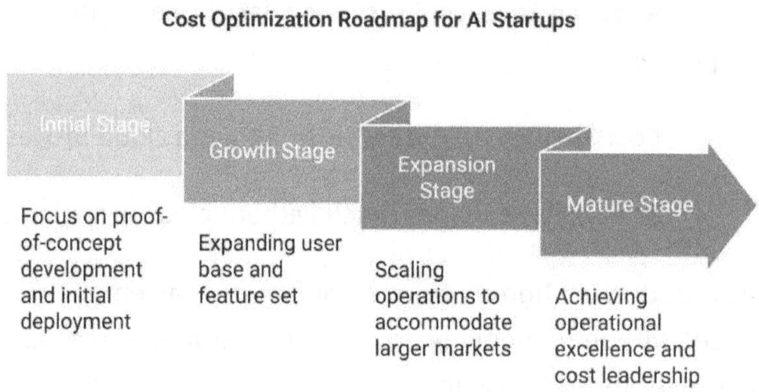

1. **Initial Stage (0–6 Months)**:
   - Focus: Proof-of-concept development and initial deployment.
   - Actions:
     - Use free-tier cloud services for early experimentation.
     - Optimize code for efficiency to reduce computational overhead.
     - Monitor costs using essential tools like AWS Cost Explorer or Google Cloud Billing Reports.
2. **Growth Stage (6–12 Months)**:
   - Focus: Expanding user base and feature set.
   - Actions:
     - Transition to serverless architectures for elastic scaling.
     - Implement auto-scaling policies for cloud resources.
     - Begin tracking costs with more sophisticated tools like CloudHealth or Spot.io.
3. **Expansion Stage (1–2 Years)**:
   - Focus: Scaling operations to accommodate larger markets.

- Actions:
    - Deploy edge AI solutions to offload processing from centralized servers.
    - Migrate to containerized environments with Kubernetes for resource efficiency.
    - Conduct cost audits quarterly to identify and rectify inefficiencies.

4. **Mature Stage (2+ Years)**:
    - Focus: Achieving operational excellence and cost leadership.
    - Actions:
        - Integrate FinOps into the organizational culture.
        - Use predictive analytics to forecast demand and optimize resource allocation.
        - Establish a dedicated cost management team to oversee scaling expenses.

Case Study: Scaling Smartly in an AI Startup

Consider an AI startup specializing in image recognition for e-commerce platforms. Initially, the startup deployed its model using virtual machines in the cloud. As user demand increased, scaling became challenging due to rising costs and inefficiencies. By transitioning to serverless computing, the startup achieved elastic scaling, significantly reducing idle resource costs. Further, by deploying lightweight versions of their models on edge devices, they minimized bandwidth expenses and improved end-user response times. Over a year, these strategies led to a 30% reduction in operational costs while doubling user adoption.

Tools and Platforms for Smart Scaling

1. **Serverless Platforms**:
    - AWS Lambda
    - Google Cloud Functions
    - Azure Functions
2. **Edge AI Tools**:
    - TensorFlow Lite

- AWS IoT Greengrass
- NVIDIA Jetson

3. **Cost Management Tools**:
    - AWS Cost Explorer
    - Google Cloud Billing
    - Kubernetes Cost Analyzer
4. **Monitoring and Optimization**:
    - Prometheus for resource monitoring.
    - Spot.io for cloud cost optimization.
    - CloudHealth for multi-cloud cost management.

By integrating these tools into their workflows, AI startups can enhance operational efficiency, minimize waste, and scale effectively.

Scaling smartly is not just about expanding capabilities; it's about doing so sustainably and efficiently. Serverless computing, edge AI, and cloud-native architectures provide the technological foundation for cost-effective scaling. With strategic financial operations and a well-defined cost optimization roadmap, AI startups can achieve growth without compromising resource efficiency or fiscal responsibility.

5.4: FUNDING YOUR AI VENTURE

5.4.1 EXPLORING FUNDING SOURCES

Securing adequate funding is one of the most critical steps for AI startups aiming to scale their operations, develop innovative technologies, and achieve market penetration. AI startup funding options are diverse, ranging from venture capital to crowdfunding. Each has advantages, challenges, and suitability depending on the startup's stage, focus, and vision. Below, we delve into these funding sources and provide an example to illustrate how they can be strategically leveraged.

Options for AI Startups

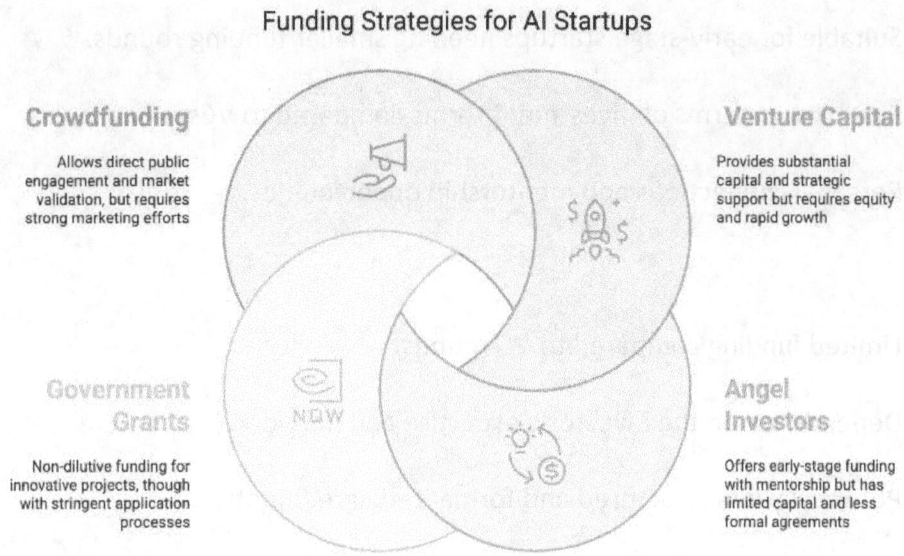

1. Venture Capital (VC)

Venture capital is a primary funding source for many AI startups, especially those with high growth potential. VCs typically provide significant financial resources in exchange for equity and often bring industry expertise, networks, and strategic guidance.

Advantages:

- Access to substantial capital, enabling startups to scale quickly.
- Strategic support from experienced investors.
- Enhanced credibility and visibility in the market.

Challenges:

- VCs often require a considerable stake in the company, leading to a dilution of ownership.
- High expectations for rapid growth and returns may lead to pressure.
- The selection process is highly competitive, and only startups with strong business models and market potential are considered.

2. Angel Investors

Angel investors are individuals who provide capital for startups in their early stages. Unlike VCs, angel investors often invest smaller amounts but may also offer mentorship and industry connections.

Advantages:

- Suitable for early-stage startups needing smaller funding rounds.
- Flexibility in terms of investment terms compared to VCs.
- Personal connections and mentorship opportunities.

Challenges:

- Limited funding compared to VC rounds.
- Dependence on the investor's expertise and network.
- Potentially less structured and formalized agreements.

3. Government Grants

Government grants are an excellent funding source for AI startups focused on innovation, research, and social impact. These grants are often non-dilutive, meaning startups do not have to give up equity.

Advantages:

- Non-dilutive funding helps retain ownership.
- Encourages projects with long-term societal benefits.
- Often tailored for specific industries, fostering niche innovation.

Challenges:

- Stringent application processes with detailed documentation.
- Limited funding amounts may not suffice for larger-scale operations.
- Specific project alignment with grant requirements is necessary.

4. Crowdfunding

Crowdfunding platforms, such as Kickstarter and Indiegogo, allow startups to raise funds directly from the public. This method is increasingly popular for startups with innovative products that resonate with a broad audience.

Advantages:

- Direct engagement with potential customers and supporters.
- Opportunity to validate market interest early on.

- Retention of equity, as most platforms, does not require ownership stakes.

Challenges:

- Requires a compelling campaign and marketing efforts to stand out.
- Uncertainty in meeting funding goals.
- Funds raised might not suffice for extensive development.

Example: AI Startups Funded Through Grants for Social Impact Projects

One prominent example of an AI startup leveraging government grants for social impact projects is [Startup Name], a company dedicated to using AI for sustainable agriculture. The startup aims to optimize crop yields and reduce waste through advanced machine-learning algorithms.

Case Study:

- **Funding Source:** [Startup Name] applied for a government grant under a program to foster technological innovation in sustainable development. The program specifically targeted startups that contribute to environmental and societal benefits.
- **Grant Objectives:** The grant focused on solutions to mitigate climate change and enhance food security. [Startup Name] proposed using AI-powered drones to analyze soil conditions, predict optimal planting schedules, and identify pest infestations.
- **Process:** The startup prepared a detailed application outlining its technology, expected outcomes, and alignment with the grant's goals. This included technical feasibility studies, projected social impacts, and a roadmap for implementation.
- **Outcome:** The grant provided $500,000 in funding, enabling the company to:
    - Develop and test its prototype.
    - Collaborate with local farmers to gather data.
    - Demonstrate measurable improvements in crop yields and resource efficiency.

Key Takeaways:

- Grants can be pivotal for startups addressing societal challenges, particularly in areas where commercial investment might be limited.
- Successful grant applications require precise alignment with program objectives and detailed documentation.

- The non-dilutive nature of grants allows startups to maintain control while advancing their projects.

Integrating Funding Sources for Growth

Many AI startups adopt a hybrid approach, combining different funding sources to achieve financial sustainability and strategic flexibility. For example:

- An AI startup might begin with angel investments to build a minimum viable product (MVP) and gain initial traction.
- It could then apply for government grants to fund research and innovation, particularly for projects with societal impacts.
- As it scales, the startup may seek venture capital for large-scale funding and market expansion.
- Crowdfunding could be a supplementary source, especially for product launches requiring public engagement.

By strategically leveraging these diverse funding options, AI startups can navigate the financial challenges of the innovation ecosystem while aligning their resources with long-term goals.

5.4.2 CRAFTING A COMPELLING PITCH

A successful pitch is your gateway to winning the trust and interest of potential investors, partners, or stakeholders. Whether you pitch to secure funding, gain strategic partnerships, or expand your market presence, crafting a compelling pitch is an art and science combined. It should deliver clarity, excitement, and a vision for the future grounded in practicality and data. This section delves into the key elements of a successful pitch and provides an example of an annotated pitch deck from a thriving AI startup to illustrate best practices.

Key Elements of a Successful Pitch

1. **Problem Statement**: Every great pitch begins with clearly articulating the problem. Investors and stakeholders are drawn to opportunities that address significant and urgent pain points. A compelling problem statement should:
    - Be specific and relatable.
    - Highlight the gravity of the issue (e.g., financial loss, inefficiencies, or unmet needs).
    - Use data or anecdotes to illustrate the problem's impact.

Example: "Small and medium-sized businesses lose over $150 billion annually due to inefficiencies in manual inventory management. These losses often result in shrinking profit margins and decreased competitiveness."

2. **Solution**: After highlighting the problem, the natural segue is to present your solution. This is your opportunity to showcase your innovation and value proposition. A strong solution presentation includes:

   - A concise explanation of your product or service.
   - A demonstration of how it addresses the stated problem effectively.
   - Differentiators that set your solution apart from existing alternatives.

Example: "Our AI-powered inventory management platform automates tracking, predicts stock needs with 95% accuracy, and reduces manual errors by 80%. This enables businesses to optimize inventory costs and improve operational efficiency."

3. **Market Size**: Investors are keen on understanding the scale of the opportunity. Addressing market size convincingly demonstrates the potential return on investment (ROI). Include:

   - Total Addressable Market (TAM) is the overall revenue opportunity if your solution captures 100% of the market.
   - Serviceable Available Market (SAM): The segment of the TAM your business can realistically serve.
   - Serviceable Obtainable Market (SOM): The portion of SAM you can capture within the next 3-5 years.

Use visuals like graphs or charts to make the data digestible.

Example: "The global AI software market is valued at $387 billion and is expected to grow at a CAGR of 20%. Our focus on inventory management targets a $25 billion niche, with a projected SOM of $1 billion by 2028."

4. **Traction**: Demonstrating traction proves that your solution works and has market validation. Highlight:

   - Key milestones achieved (e.g., customer acquisition, partnerships, or revenue).
   - Metrics include Monthly Recurring Revenue (MRR), user growth rates, and product adoption statistics.
   - Testimonials or endorsements from credible sources.

Example: "Since launching six months ago, we have onboarded 50 paying clients, generated $200,000 in ARR, and secured partnerships with two leading supply chain firms."

5. **Financial Projections**: Financial projections offer your business's future performance roadmap. This section should:
   - Provide realistic revenue and expense forecasts for the next 3-5 years.
   - Highlight key assumptions driving these projections.
   - Address anticipated profitability or breakeven points.

Use tables or graphs for clarity.

Example: "We project a 3x growth in revenue year-over-year, reaching $5 million in ARR by Year 3, driven by a scalable SaaS model and expanding enterprise partnerships."

Example: Annotated Pitch Deck of a Successful AI Startup

To solidify the above principles, let's examine an annotated pitch deck from an AI startup that successfully raised $5 million in seed funding.

Slide 1: Title Slide

- **Content**: The company name, tagline, and a captivating visual.
- **Example**: "AIventory: Revolutionizing Inventory Management for SMEs."
- **Annotation**: The tagline succinctly captures the mission, while the visual (a dashboard screenshot) hints at the product's interface and functionality.

Slide 2: Problem Statement

- **Content**: A bold statement of the problem and supporting data.
- **Example**: "Manual inventory management costs SMEs billions in preventable losses annually."
- **Annotation**: Statistics are cited with sources for credibility. Using a customer quote adds relatability: "Before AIventory, managing inventory was a nightmare."

Slide 3: Solution

- **Content**: Description of the product and how it solves the problem.
- **Example**: "AIventory uses predictive algorithms and real-time analytics to optimize stock levels."

- **Annotation**: Include a visual representation of the product (e.g., a dashboard screenshot or workflow diagram).

Slide 4: Market Opportunity

- **Content**: TAM, SAM, and SOM figures.
- **Example**: "TAM: $387B, SAM: $25B, SOM: $1B (2028)."
- **Annotation**: A pie chart illustrates the breakdown, making the data visually compelling.

Slide 5: Traction

- **Content**: Key metrics and milestones.
- **Example**: "50 paying clients, $200k ARR, 95% customer retention."
- **Annotation**: A graph showing month-over-month growth highlights momentum.

Slide 6: Competitive Landscape

- **Content**: Comparison table showing differentiation.
- **Example**: Features like "AI-driven forecasts" and "Integration with ERP systems" are highlighted.
- **Annotation**: Positioning against competitors clarifies your unique advantages.

Slide 7: Business Model

- **Content**: Explanation of revenue streams.
- **Example**: "SaaS subscription: $500/month per client."
- **Annotation**: Include lifetime value (LTV) and customer acquisition cost (CAC) metrics.

Slide 8: Financial Projections

- **Content**: Revenue and expense forecasts.
- **Example**: "Year 1: $200k; Year 3: $5M ARR."
- **Annotation**: Graphs show upward trends, making the projections visually appealing.

Slide 9: Team

- **Content**: Brief bios of key team members.
- **Example**: "Jane Doe, CEO: 10+ years in supply chain management."
- **Annotation**: Photos and notable achievements build credibility.

Slide 10: Ask

- **Content**: Specific funding request and usage.
- **Example**: "$5M to scale operations, enhance R&D, and expand marketing."
- **Annotation**: A breakdown of fund allocation reassures investors about strategic planning.

Slide 11: Closing

- **Content**: Call to action and contact information.
- **Example**: "Join us in transforming inventory management. Contact: info@ainventory.com."
- **Annotation**: A bold closing statement reinforces confidence.

Tips for Delivering the Pitch

1. **Know Your Audience**: Tailor your pitch to resonate with your audience's interests. For instance, a venture capitalist may focus on ROI, while a strategic partner may care more about product synergies.
2. **Engage Visually and Verbally**: Use visuals like infographics and animations to complement your verbal delivery. Practice storytelling to make your pitch memorable.
3. **Anticipate Questions**: Be prepared to address potential concerns about competition, scalability, or financial assumptions.
4. **Practice and Refine**: Rehearse your pitch multiple times, incorporating feedback from peers or mentors.
5. **End with Impact**: Conclude with a powerful call to action that leaves a lasting impression.

By mastering these elements and learning from successful examples, you can craft a pitch that captivates and convinces stakeholders to invest in your vision.

5.4.3 NEGOTIATING WITH INVESTORS

Entrepreneurs often negotiate with investors at the intersection of valuation and control. This delicate balancing act is critical to securing investment without sacrificing the business's vision or direction. The following explores strategies for achieving this balance, focusing on understanding term sheets and equity distribution.

Tips for Balancing Valuation and Control

Negotiating with investors requires both preparation and strategy. Entrepreneurs must be well-versed in the nuances of investment agreements and adept at articulating their business while safeguarding their long-term influence. Here are key considerations:

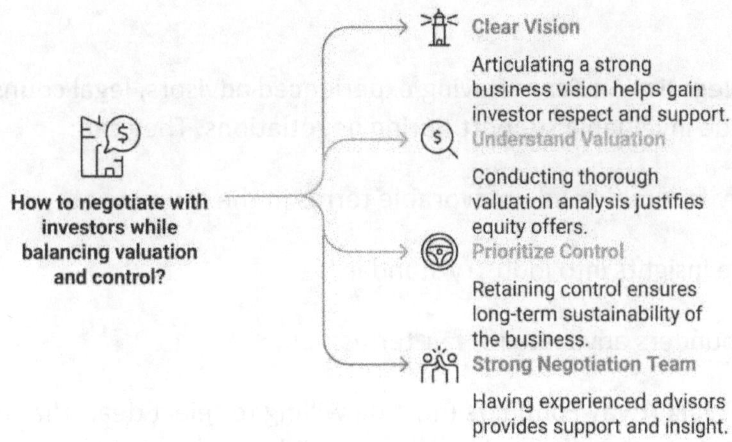

1. Start with a Clear Vision A well-defined business vision forms the foundation of negotiations. Entrepreneurs need to:

- Articulate the purpose, mission, and goals of the company.
- Highlight the unique value proposition of their product or service.
- Present a roadmap that outlines how the investment will drive growth.

Investors are more likely to respect the founder's desire for control if they perceive a strong, coherent vision.

2. Understand Your Valuation Valuation is often the focal point of negotiation. Entrepreneurs should:

- Conduct a thorough analysis of the company's finances, market potential, and growth prospects.
- Use industry benchmarks and comparables to justify their valuation.
- Be prepared to explain the rationale behind their valuation regarding the value created for the investor and the business.

A reasonable valuation attracts investors while allowing room for negotiation on equity.

3. Prioritize Long-term Control While securing funds is essential, retaining control over the company's direction is crucial for its sustainability. Founders can:

- Limit the percentage of equity offered in exchange for funding.
- Implement dual-class share structures to retain voting control.
- Set clear boundaries in the term sheet regarding board composition and decision-making authority.

Balancing valuation with control ensures that founders can execute their vision without undue interference.

4. Build a Strong Negotiation Team Having experienced advisors, legal counsel, or financial consultants can provide invaluable support during negotiations. They can:

- Identify favorable and unfavorable terms in the term sheet.
- Provide insights into industry standards.
- Help founders advocate for fair terms.

5. Be Prepared to Walk Away Founders must be willing to reject deals that excessively compromise their vision or control. A strategic fallback position provides leverage during negotiations. This mindset signals confidence to investors and often results in more favorable terms.

UNDERSTANDING TERM SHEETS

A term sheet outlines the basic terms and conditions of an investment. Understanding its components is essential for navigating negotiations effectively.

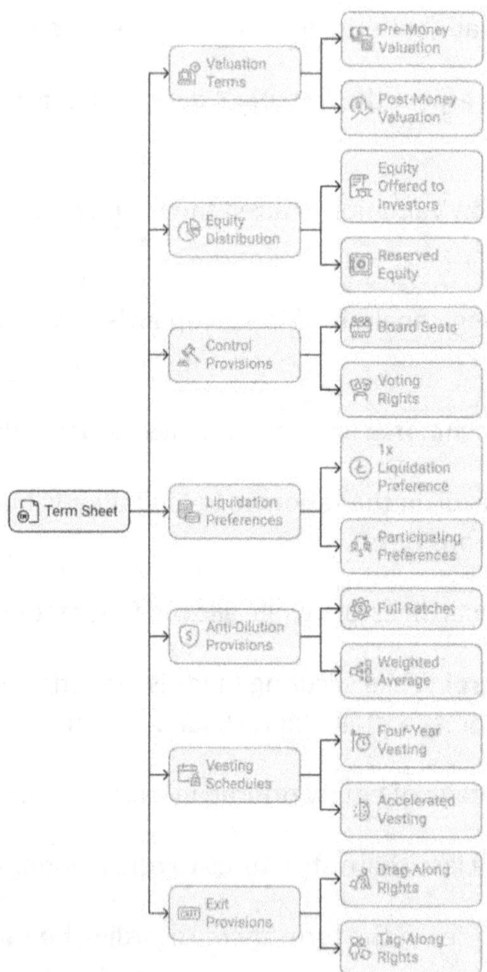

Key sections of a term sheet include:

1. Valuation Terms

- *Pre-Money Valuation:* The company's evaluation before the investment.
- *Post-Money Valuation:* The valuation after the investment is made.

Understanding these metrics helps founders gauge the impact of the investment on their ownership stake.

2. Equity Distribution Equity allocation dictates the proportion of ownership retained by founders, employees, and investors. Key considerations include:

- The percentage of equity being offered to investors.
- Reserved equity for future fundraising or employee stock options.
- Dilution impacts and strategies to minimize them.

3. Control Provisions Investors often seek a degree of control to protect their interests. Founders should pay close attention to the following:

- *Board Seats:* The number of board seats allocated to investors versus founders.
- *Voting Rights:* Rights tied to decision-making on critical issues such as mergers, acquisitions, or leadership changes.
- *Protective Provisions:* Special rights that allow investors to veto certain decisions.

4. Liquidation Preferences Liquidation preferences determine the order in which proceeds are distributed in the event of a sale or liquidation. Common structures include:

- *1x Liquidation Preference:* Investors return their money before others share the remaining proceeds.
- *Participating Preferences:* Investors receive their preferred amount and then share the remaining proceeds, often called a "double dip."

Founders should negotiate preferences that align with fair outcomes for all parties.

5. Anti-Dilution Provisions Anti-dilution clauses protect investors from dilution during future fundraising rounds. Types include:

- *Full Ratchet:* Adjusts the share price of previous rounds to match the new lower price.

- *Weighted Average:* Adjusts the share price based on the weighted average of the old and new prices.

Entrepreneurs must understand the implications of these clauses on their ownership and valuation.

6. Vesting Schedules For founders and employees, vesting schedules ensure long-term commitment to the company. Common terms include:

- A standard four-year vesting schedule with a one-year cliff.
- Accelerated vesting in cases of acquisition or change in control.

7. Exit Provisions Term sheets often include clauses that address exit scenarios, such as:

- *Drag-Along Rights:* Requiring minority shareholders to agree to a sale if the majority approves.
- *Tag-Along Rights:* Allowing minority shareholders to participate in a sale under the same terms as majority shareholders.

EQUITY DISTRIBUTION STRATEGIES

Balancing equity distribution is integral to maintaining control while attracting investors.

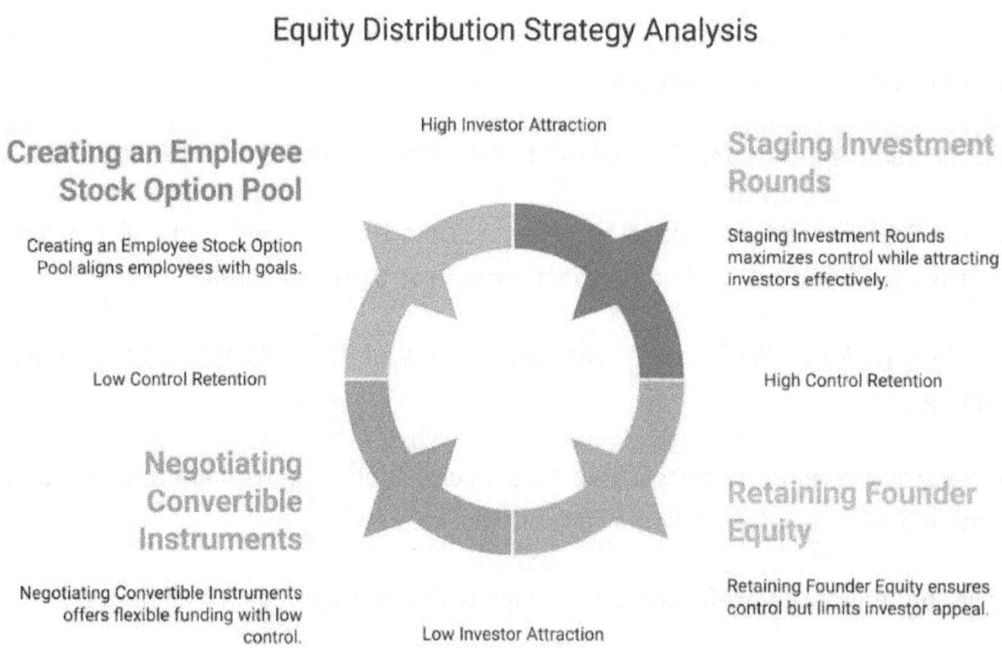

Founders can employ strategies such as:

1. Retaining Founder Equity Founders should aim to retain a significant portion of equity to influence strategic decisions. Offering too much equity in early rounds can:

- Limit future fundraising flexibility.
- Reduce the founder's ability to guide the company's direction.

2. Creating an Employee Stock Option Pool (ESOP) An ESOP ensures that employees are incentivized and aligned with the company's goals. It also:

- Reduces the percentage of equity allocated to external investors.
- Strengthens the company's acquisition and retention capabilities.

3. Staging Investment Rounds Raising funds in multiple rounds allows founders to:

- Secure higher valuations in later rounds based on proven milestones.
- Minimize equity dilution in earlier stages.

4. Negotiating Convertible Instruments Convertible notes or SAFE (Simple Agreement for Future Equity) agreements offer flexible funding options that defer valuation discussions to a later stage. These instruments:

- Allow founders to raise funds without immediate equity dilution.
- Provide investors with equity conversion at a discount during the next funding round.

Negotiating with investors is a critical phase in an entrepreneur's journey. Success lies in balancing valuation and control through thorough preparation, strategic equity distribution, and a deep understanding of term sheets. Founders who prioritize their vision and advocate for fair terms can secure the resources needed to grow their business while retaining the influence required to steer it toward long-term success.

5.4.4 FUNDING LIFECYCLE

Overview of Funding Stages

Navigating the funding lifecycle is one of the most critical aspects of building and scaling an AI startup. Each stage of funding reflects the maturity of the business and corresponds to specific milestones and requirements. Below, we explore the various stages: Pre-seed, Seed, Series A, and beyond, providing an in-depth understanding of each phase, its objectives, and strategies for securing investment.

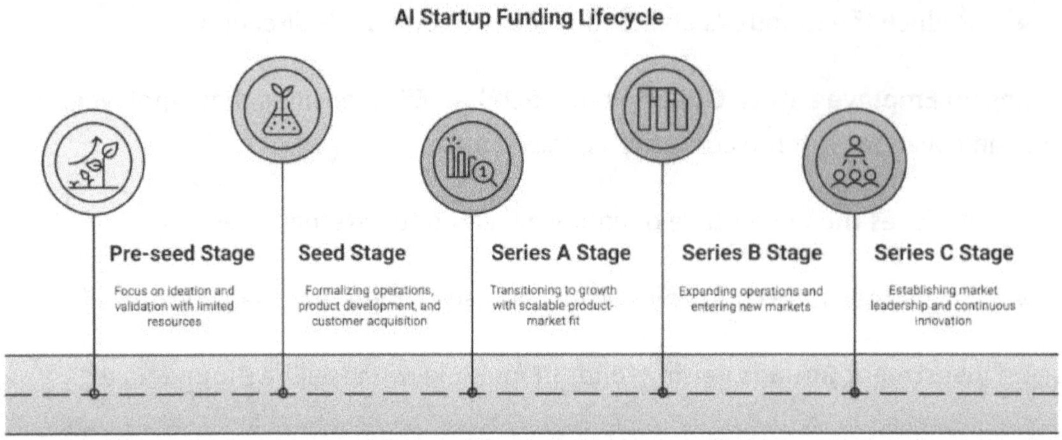

Pre-seed Stage

The pre-seed stage marks the very beginning of the funding lifecycle. At this stage, startups are primarily focused on ideation and validation. Founders typically work to refine their AI-based product concept, identify a target market, and validate the problem-solution fit. This stage is often characterized by limited resources and heavy reliance on personal savings, friends, family, or early angel investors.

Key objectives:

- Define the core AI problem the startup aims to solve.
- Build a minimum viable product (MVP) to demonstrate the feasibility of the concept.
- Validate the market demand through customer interviews, surveys, or pilot studies.

Funding sources:

- Personal savings or bootstrapping.
- Friends and family.
- Angel investors or small grants.

Challenges:

- Convincing early investors of the potential of an AI concept without substantial proof of market traction.
- Balancing technical development with early business operations.

Seed Stage

In the seed stage, startups begin to formalize their operations and lay the groundwork for scaling. At this stage, the focus shifts to product development, market research, and initial customer acquisition. AI startups often use seed funding to build and improve their AI models, hire a small team, and test their go-to-market strategy.

Key objectives:

- Enhance the MVP based on early feedback.
- Acquire initial paying customers or generate strong user engagement.
- Develop a detailed go-to-market strategy and business plan.

Funding sources:

- Seed funds or venture capital firms specializing in early-stage investments.
- Crowdfunding platforms.
- Government or private grants focused on AI innovation.

Challenges:

- Demonstrating clear differentiation in a competitive AI landscape.
- Aligning technical development with market demands and investor expectations.

Series A Stage

The Series A stage marks the transition from early operations to growth. Startups at this phase aim to scale their product, expand their team, and grow their customer base. For AI startups, this often involves fine-tuning AI algorithms, integrating advanced machine learning features, and optimizing data pipelines to handle increased demand.

Key objectives:

- Achieve scalable product-market fit.
- Build operational infrastructure to support growth.
- Implement strategies for customer retention and revenue generation.

Funding sources:

- Institutional venture capital firms.

- Corporate venture arms of tech companies.
- Strategic partnerships with industry players.

Challenges:

- Scaling AI models and ensuring their reliability in production environments.
- Managing operational and financial complexities during rapid growth.

Series B and Beyond

Series B and subsequent funding rounds are focused on scaling operations, entering new markets, and establishing the startup as a market leader. Substantial investments in marketing, research, development, and global expansion typically mark these stages.

Key objectives:

- Expand into new geographical markets or verticals.
- Build a strong brand presence and enhance customer loyalty.
- Continuously innovate to stay ahead in the rapidly evolving AI sector.

Funding sources:

- Late-stage venture capital firms.
- Private equity firms.
- Corporate investments or strategic mergers and acquisitions.

Challenges:

- Maintaining growth momentum while controlling operational costs.
- Navigating regulatory and ethical challenges, particularly in AI-driven industries.

By understanding and effectively navigating these stages, AI startups can secure the financial resources needed to transform innovative ideas into impactful, scalable solutions.

5.5: SCALING YOUR STARTUP

5.5.1 LEVERAGING STRATEGIC PARTNERSHIPS

Strategic partnerships are pivotal enablers in the evolving landscape of enterprise AI governance. They allow organizations to access expertise, share risks, and accelerate innovation. By collaborating with academia, government agencies, and corporations, enterprises can build a robust ecosystem that fosters mutual growth and delivers sustainable competitive advantages. In this section, we will explore the mechanisms for creating such partnerships, delve into the risks and rewards of joint ventures, and illustrate these concepts with practical examples.

Building Partnerships with Academia, Government, and Corporations

Strategic partnerships with academia, government, and corporations enable enterprises to access diverse knowledge pools, specialized resources, and complex regulatory landscapes. Each partnership brings unique opportunities and challenges that must be carefully managed.

COLLABORATING WITH ACADEMIA

Academia has long been a breeding ground for cutting-edge research, innovation, and talent development.

By partnering with universities and research institutions, enterprises can:

1. **Access Cutting-Edge Research**: Collaborating with academic researchers provides enterprises with early insights into emerging technologies, theories, and methodologies. For instance, companies like Google and IBM regularly partner with universities to advance AI research, exploring machine learning algorithms, natural language processing, and ethical AI frameworks.

2. **Develop Talent Pipelines**: Academic partnerships often include initiatives such as internships, co-op programs, and collaborative research projects. These efforts help enterprises attract top talent and nurture skills aligned with their strategic objectives. For example, Microsoft's AI residency program allows participants to work alongside top researchers and engineers, blending academic theory with industry application.

3. **Enhance Credibility**: Joint research publications and participation in academic conferences bolster an enterprise's reputation as a thought leader in AI governance. This credibility can be instrumental in attracting customers, investors, and other partners.

Collaborating with Government Agencies

Partnerships with government agencies allow enterprises to influence policy, secure funding, and address societal challenges. Governments are increasingly interested in ensuring AI's ethical and equitable deployment, making them valuable allies for enterprises focused on responsible AI governance.

1. **Navigating Regulatory Frameworks**: Collaborative efforts with government agencies can help enterprises align their AI initiatives with evolving regulations and standards. For example, the European Union's AI Act has prompted several corporations to engage with policymakers to shape compliant and ethical practices.

2. **Securing Grants and Funding**: Governments often provide AI research and development funding through grants and public-private partnerships. Initiatives such as the U.S. National AI Initiative Act encourage corporations to collaborate with federal agencies and research institutions to advance AI innovation.

3. **Addressing Societal Challenges**: Government partnerships enable enterprises to contribute to public welfare through projects such as AI-driven healthcare solutions, innovative city initiatives, and disaster response systems. These collaborations enhance societal impact and strengthen an enterprise's brand equity.

Collaborating with Corporations

Corporate partnerships—whether through alliances, joint ventures, or consortiums—enable enterprises to pool resources, share risks, and scale their AI governance frameworks.

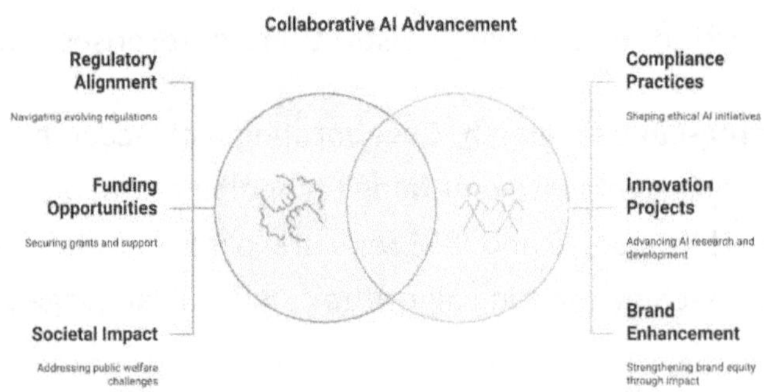

1. **Driving Innovation**: Cross-industry collaborations allow enterprises to explore synergies and co-develop innovative solutions. For instance, the partnership between NVIDIA and Mercedes-Benz leverages NVIDIA's AI expertise and Mercedes-Benz's automotive prowess to develop next-generation autonomous vehicles.

2. **Expanding Market Reach**: Partnerships with corporations in complementary sectors help enterprises penetrate new markets and customer segments. For example, a fintech

company might partner with a telecommunications firm to offer AI-driven financial services to underserved communities.

3. **Enhancing Operational Efficiency**: Shared infrastructure, tools, and expertise can reduce costs and improve efficiency. Collaborative platforms like the AI Ethics Consortium enable corporations to address bias, fairness, and transparency challenges jointly.

Example: Collaborating with Universities for Cutting-Edge Research

A notable example of academia-industry collaboration is the partnership between Stanford University and Google's AI division. This collaboration has yielded significant breakthroughs in natural language processing, including developing transformer models that underpin technologies like ChatGPT and BERT. By leveraging Stanford's academic rigor and Google's computational resources, the partnership has accelerated the pace of AI innovation while addressing complex ethical and technical challenges.

Another example is the Massachusetts Institute of Technology (MIT) and IBM's joint AI Lab. This initiative focuses on advancing AI research in healthcare, cybersecurity, and ethics. The partnership has resulted in practical applications, including AI systems that assist in diagnosing medical conditions and detecting cybersecurity threats, showcasing the tangible benefits of academia-industry collaboration.

RISKS AND REWARDS OF JOINT VENTURES

While strategic partnerships offer numerous advantages, they also have risks. Enterprises must carefully evaluate potential pitfalls and implement robust governance mechanisms to maximize the rewards.

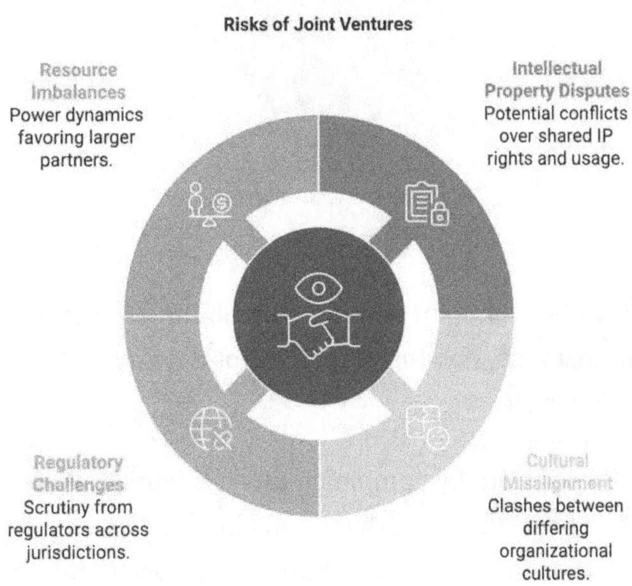

Risks of Joint Ventures

1. **Intellectual Property Disputes**: Collaborative projects often involve shared intellectual property (IP), leading to disputes over ownership and usage rights. Enterprises must establish clear IP agreements to prevent conflicts.

2. **Cultural Misalignment**: Differences in organizational culture, priorities, and operating models can hinder collaboration. For example, academia's emphasis on openness and long-term exploration may clash with a corporation's focus on confidentiality and short-term results.

3. **Regulatory and Compliance Challenges**: Regulators may scrutinize joint ventures, mainly when operating across multiple jurisdictions. Enterprises must ensure compliance with all relevant laws and standards.

4. **Resource Imbalances**: Partnerships between entities of unequal size or influence can result in power imbalances, with the more significant partner dominating decision-making. This dynamic may limit the minor partner's ability to contribute meaningfully.

REWARDS OF JOINT VENTURES

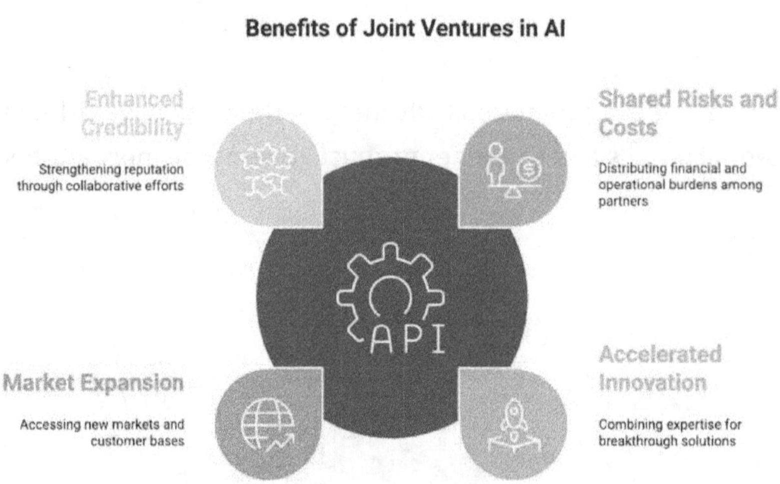

1. **Shared Risks and Costs**: Joint ventures distribute large-scale AI initiatives' financial and operational risks. For instance, pooling resources for data collection and infrastructure reduces the burden on individual partners.

2. **Accelerated Innovation**: By combining diverse expertise and perspectives, joint ventures often achieve breakthroughs that would be difficult for a single entity to accomplish. For example, collaboration in AI ethics and fairness has led to more robust solutions for mitigating bias in machine learning models.

3. **Market Expansion**: Joint ventures enable partners to access new markets, customer bases, and geographies. For example, partnerships between AI startups and established corporations often facilitate rapid scaling and market entry.

4. **Enhanced Credibility and Visibility**: Collaborative efforts signal a commitment to innovation and responsibility, strengthening an enterprise's reputation among stakeholders. Joint ventures in AI governance demonstrate a proactive approach to addressing ethical and societal concerns.

BALANCING RISKS AND REWARDS

To maximize the benefits of strategic partnerships while mitigating risks, enterprises should:

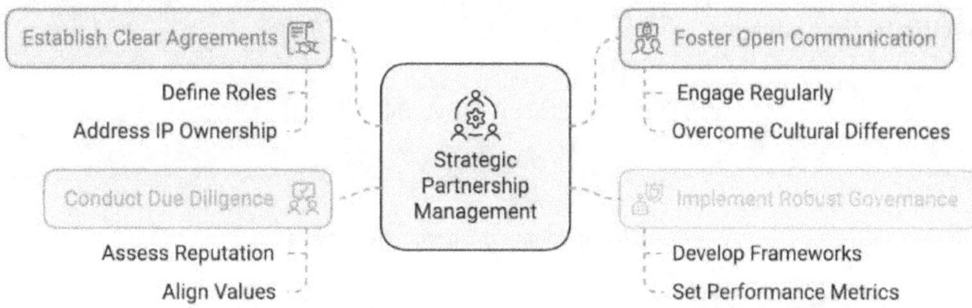

1. **Establish Clear Agreements**: Define partnership agreements' roles, responsibilities, and expectations. Address key issues such as IP ownership, data sharing, and conflict resolution.

2. **Foster Open Communication**: Regularly engage partners through transparent communication channels. Building trust is essential for overcoming cultural and operational differences.

3. **Implement Robust Governance**: Develop governance frameworks that ensure accountability, compliance, and alignment with strategic objectives. This includes setting up joint steering committees and performance metrics.

4. **Conduct Due Diligence**: Carefully assess potential partners' capabilities, reputation, and alignment with enterprise values. Due diligence reduces the likelihood of unexpected challenges.

Strategic partnerships are indispensable for enterprises navigating the complexities of AI governance. Organizations can access unparalleled expertise, share risks, and drive innovation by collaborating with academia, government, and corporations. However, these partnerships require careful planning, robust governance, and a balanced approach to managing risks and rewards. When executed effectively, strategic partnerships advance an enterprise's objectives and contribute to the broader goal of responsible and impactful AI development.

5.5.2 MARKET EXPANSION STRATEGIES

Market expansion is a critical phase for businesses seeking sustainable growth. By entering new industries or geographic regions, organizations can unlock new revenue streams, diversify their operations, and build resilience against market fluctuations. Expanding strategically involves identifying opportunities, mitigating risks, and leveraging core competencies to ensure long-term success.

Entering New Industries

Expanding into new industries allows businesses to diversify their portfolios, reducing dependence on a single market or product. This strategy is essential in rapidly evolving sectors like artificial intelligence (AI), where technological advancements open possibilities across multiple industries. For AI-driven businesses, entering a new industry can also mean adapting their solutions to solve problems specific to that sector.

STEPS TO ENTER NEW INDUSTRIES:

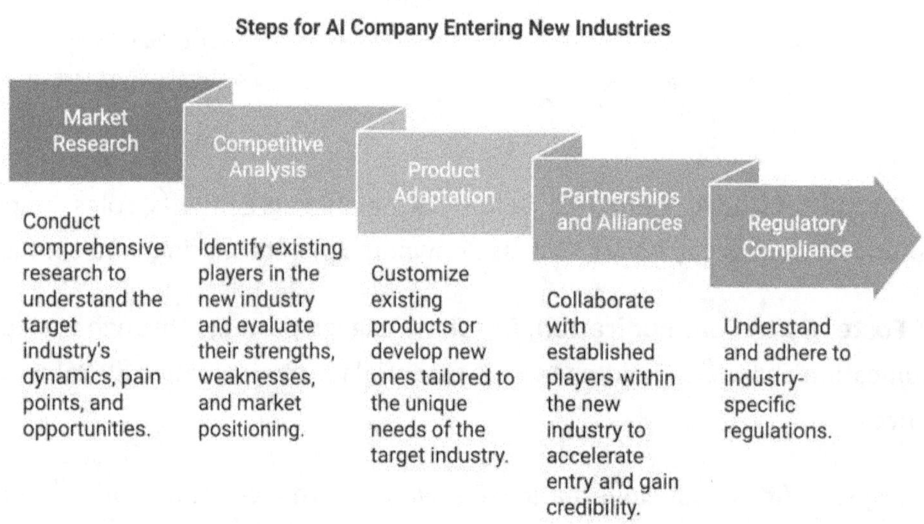

1. **Market Research:** Conduct comprehensive research to understand the target industry's dynamics, pain points, and opportunities. For example, an AI company specializing in healthcare might explore how its technology can address challenges in the logistics or education sectors.

2. **Competitive Analysis:** Identify existing players in the new industry and evaluate their strengths, weaknesses, and market positioning. This analysis helps pinpoint gaps that the company's AI solution could fill.

3. **Product Adaptation:** Customize existing products or develop new ones tailored to the unique needs of the target industry. For example, an AI analytics platform initially designed for e-commerce might require significant retooling to serve the energy sector.

4. **Partnerships and Alliances:** Collaborate with established players within the new industry to accelerate entry and gain credibility. Strategic alliances can provide insights into the industry's nuances and open doors to potential customers.

5. **Regulatory Compliance:** Understand and adhere to industry-specific regulations. For instance, an AI company entering the financial sector must ensure compliance with strict data privacy and security standards.

Example:

An AI startup that began in the retail industry with predictive analytics tools could identify opportunities in the real estate sector. The company could gain a foothold in a lucrative and relatively untapped market by adapting its algorithms to forecast housing market trends and property values.

Entering New Geographic Regions

Geographic expansion can provide access to untapped markets, larger customer bases, and diverse revenue streams. However, it also presents challenges such as cultural differences, varying regulatory environments, and logistical complexities.

Strategies for Geographic Expansion:

1. **Market Selection:** Select target regions based on demand potential, competitive landscape, and company value proposition compatibility. Emerging markets often provide fertile ground for expansion due to less competition and higher growth rates.

2. **Localized Solutions:** Tailor products and services to meet the specific needs and preferences of the new region. Localization might involve adapting languages, interfaces, or cultural elements.

3. **Building Local Expertise:** Employ local talent or collaborate with regional experts to better understand the market. Local teams can more effectively navigate cultural and regulatory challenges.

4. **Regulatory Adherence:** Follow local laws governing data usage and intellectual property. For instance, the General Data Protection Regulation (GDPR) must be followed when entering the European market.

5. **Infrastructure Development:** Establish a robust distribution and support network. Companies may need to invest in local infrastructure to ensure seamless delivery of their products and services.

Example:

An AI company specializing in precision agriculture could expand to developing markets in Asia or Africa. These regions often face low agricultural yields, making them ideal candidates for AI-powered solutions like crop monitoring and predictive weather analytics. By partnering with local governments and non-profits, the company can contribute to cultural development.

Case Study: An AI Tool for Agriculture Expanding to Developing Markets

To illustrate the potential of market expansion, consider an AI tool designed for precision agriculture. Initially developed in North America, the tool helps farmers optimize crop yields by providing insights into soil quality, irrigation needs, and pest control. After achieving significant domestic success, the company expanded into developing markets in Africa and South Asia.

Challenges:

1. **Infrastructure Limitations:** Many developing regions lack the technological infrastructure to support advanced AI tools, such as reliable internet access or high-tech farming equipment.

2. **Affordability:** Farmers in these markets may have limited financial resources, necessitating innovative pricing models like subscription-based or pay-per-use systems.

3. **Cultural Differences:** Farming practices in these regions often differ significantly from those in developed markets. The company must adapt its tools to align with local practices and traditions.

4. **Regulatory Barriers:** Navigating agricultural policies and import/export regulations in multiple countries can be complex.

Strategies:

1. **Partnerships:** To introduce the technology and collaborate with local agricultural cooperatives, non-governmental organizations (NGOs), and government bodies. These partnerships can provide funding, training, and distribution channels.

2. **Adaptation:** The AI tool can be modified to function on low-tech devices like smartphones, and its interface can be translated into local languages. Simplifying the user experience can significantly enhance adoption rates.

3. **Pricing Models:** To subsidize small-scale farmers' costs, introduce tiered pricing models or leverage funding from international development agencies.

4. **Capacity Building:** Offer training programs to help farmers understand and use the AI tool effectively. This approach boosts adoption and builds trust in the technology.

Results:

By implementing these strategies, the company successfully penetrates new markets. The AI tool helps farmers increase yields by 30%, leading to higher incomes and improved regional food security. Simultaneously, the company significantly boosts revenue and strengthens its global brand presence.

Market expansion into new industries or geographic regions is a transformative growth strategy that requires careful planning and execution. By leveraging market research, localized solutions, strategic partnerships, and regulatory compliance, businesses can navigate the complexities of expansion and unlock new opportunities. The example of an AI tool for agriculture expanding to developing markets highlights the potential rewards of a well-executed market expansion strategy—not only for the company but also for the communities it serves.

5.5.3 DEVELOPING A CUSTOMER RETENTION STRATEGY

In today's competitive business landscape, customer retention is just as necessary—if not more critical—than customer acquisition. Retaining customers ensures a steady revenue stream and creates brand advocates who amplify your business through word-of-mouth and social proof. Developing a robust customer retention strategy is essential for building long-term loyalty, and one key pillar of such a strategy involves offering **value-added services** and driving **continuous improvements** in your offerings.

Offering Value-Added Services

Value-added services are enhancements beyond the core product or service. They give customers additional reasons to remain loyal to your brand. These services can differentiate a company in the eyes of its customers and foster deeper engagement.

For example, a SaaS (Software as a Service) company might provide free training webinars, advanced analytics dashboards, or priority support to premium customers. Similarly, a retail brand can implement personalized shopping experiences through loyalty programs, exclusive offers, or early access to new products. These added benefits demonstrate a commitment to meeting customer needs beyond transactional relationships.

Providing value-added services is also about anticipating customer needs and solving problems before they arise. For instance, a business in the healthcare industry might offer telehealth consultations or access to educational content that empowers patients to make informed decisions. These thoughtful gestures enhance the customer experience and position the brand as a trusted partner in the customer's journey.

Driving Continuous Improvements

Continuous improvement is another cornerstone of a successful retention strategy. Customers today expect businesses to evolve alongside their needs and preferences, and stagnation can lead to disengagement. Continuous improvement involves soliciting feedback, monitoring trends, and proactively refining products, services, and processes.

A practical way to achieve this is through feedback loops, such as customer surveys, interviews, and focus groups. By actively listening to customers, businesses can identify pain points and areas for enhancement. For example, an e-commerce platform might use customer feedback to improve website navigation or reduce delivery times. Acting on such insights demonstrates to customers that their voices are valued, building trust and loyalty.

Another approach is leveraging technology to stay agile and adaptable. Artificial intelligence (AI) and data analytics can help businesses understand customer behaviors, predict trends, and personalize interactions at scale. For instance, a streaming service might use AI-driven algorithms to recommend content tailored to individual preferences, creating a seamless and enjoyable user experience.

The Synergy Between Value and Improvement

Value-added services and continuous improvements are most effective when they work in synergy. While value-added services enhance the customer experience in the short term, continuous improvements ensure sustained engagement over the long term. Together, they create a virtuous cycle that reinforces loyalty.

For instance, a fitness app that provides personalized workout plans (value-added service) and regularly updates its interface and features based on user feedback (continuous improvement) keeps customers engaged while addressing evolving expectations. Over time, such strategies retain customers and turn them into ambassadors who advocate for the brand.

The Importance of Authenticity

Finally, building loyalty through retention strategies requires authenticity. Customers are savvy and can discern whether a business is genuinely interested in their well-being or merely pursuing short-term gains. Companies can cultivate long-lasting relationships built on mutual trust and respect by consistently delivering on promises, demonstrating empathy, and acting in the customer's best interest.

In conclusion, developing a customer retention strategy focused on value-added services and continuous improvements is essential for fostering long-term loyalty. Businesses can build lasting connections that drive sustained success by exceeding expectations and evolving alongside customers.

CHAPTER 6: BUILDING STRATEGIC PARTNERSHIPS

INTRODUCTION

THE POWER OF PARTNERSHIPS

In the fast-paced artificial intelligence (AI) world, startups face unique opportunities and challenges. The rapid evolution of technology, fierce competition, and the immense demand for innovation create an environment where collaboration is beneficial and essential. Partnerships have become a cornerstone for success in the AI ecosystem, offering startups the tools, knowledge, and networks they need to thrive. This chapter delves into why partnerships are critical for AI startups, explores a case study of successful collaboration, and provides actionable insights for building effective partnerships.

The Power of Partnerships

Why Partnerships Are Critical for AI Startups

AI startups often operate with constrained resources, including limited access to data, expertise, infrastructure, and market reach. Partnerships offer a pathway to overcome these constraints and accelerate growth.

1. **Access to Data**

Data is the lifeblood of AI. Startups need large, diverse, high-quality datasets to train their models effectively. However, data acquisition can be a significant hurdle due to privacy concerns, proprietary restrictions, or financial costs. Partnerships with organizations that possess extensive data repositories—whether corporations, governments, or academic institutions—can bridge this gap. For instance, a healthcare AI startup might collaborate with a hospital network to gain access to anonymized patient data for developing diagnostic tools.

2. **Expertise**

The AI landscape is vast and complex, requiring a blend of technical, domain-specific, and business expertise. Partnerships can provide startups access to seasoned professionals and researchers who can guide their development. Universities, in particular, are fertile grounds for such collaborations, as they house experts at the forefront of AI research.

3. **Infrastructure**

Building and scaling AI solutions requires robust computational resources, including cloud services, GPUs, and storage. However, these resources are often prohibitively expensive for startups. Partnering with tech giants that offer infrastructure as a service—like Google, AWS, or Microsoft—can significantly reduce operational costs and enable startups to focus on innovation rather than logistics.

4. **Market Reach**

Another challenge for AI startups is breaking into competitive markets. Strategic partnerships with established companies can open doors to new customer bases, distribution channels, and branding opportunities. For instance, a startup developing AI-powered retail analytics might partner with a major retailer to pilot its solution and gain visibility.

Case Study: A Successful Partnership Between an AI Startup and a University

Consider the case of DeepMind, a pioneering AI company, and its collaboration with University College London (UCL). This partnership focused on advancing research in reinforcement learning, a subfield of AI that trains algorithms to make decisions by interacting with their environment. UCL provided DeepMind access to world-class researchers and a collaborative environment for exploring cutting-edge theories. DeepMind funded scholarships, research projects, and infrastructure at UCL, creating a mutually beneficial relationship.

The outcomes of this partnership were profound. It resulted in groundbreaking research and contributed to the development of real-world applications such as AlphaGo, the AI that famously defeated a human champion in the board game Go. This case underscores the transformative potential of partnerships in driving innovation and scaling AI technologies.

WHAT THIS CHAPTER OFFERS

In the following sections, this chapter equips readers with actionable strategies and tools to identify, evaluate, and build successful partnerships. It also addresses the potential risks involved in partnerships and how to mitigate them to ensure mutual benefits.

Strategies to Identify, Evaluate, and Build Partnerships

1. **Identifying Potential Partners**

Startups must identify organizations that align with their goals, values, and needs. This involves researching companies, universities, and institutions active in their domain. Networking events, industry conferences, and online platforms like LinkedIn can be valuable channels for discovering potential partners.

2. **Evaluating Suitability**

Not all partnerships are created equal. Startups need to assess potential partners based on factors such as:

- Complementary strengths: Does the partner provide what the startup lacks?
- Shared vision: Are the goals of both parties aligned?
- Track record: Does the partner have a history of successful collaborations?

3. **Building Relationships**

Building a partnership involves cultivating trust and mutual understanding. This can be achieved through clear communication, setting realistic expectations, and establishing a shared roadmap for collaboration. Formal agreements, such as Memorandums of Understanding (MoUs) or contracts, can solidify the terms of the partnership.

Tools to Mitigate Risks and Ensure Mutual Benefits

Partnerships, while beneficial, come with their own set of risks, including misaligned expectations, data security concerns, and unequal power dynamics. Startups can use the following tools to address these challenges:

1. **Risk Mitigation Frameworks**

Implementing a risk mitigation framework helps identify and address potential issues early. For example, startups can conduct a SWOT analysis (Strengths, Weaknesses, Opportunities, Threats) for the partnership and develop contingency plans for identified risks.

2. **Data Security Protocols**

Ensuring data privacy and security is critical, especially when handling sensitive information. Startups should establish robust data governance policies and leverage encryption, anonymization, and access controls to protect shared data.

3. **Performance Metrics and KPIs**

Defining clear metrics and Key Performance Indicators (KPIs) allows both parties to track progress and measure the partnership's success. Regular reviews and feedback loops ensure the partnership remains on track and delivers value to both sides.

4. **Conflict Resolution Mechanisms**

Disagreements are inevitable in any collaboration. A predefined conflict resolution mechanism, such as mediation or arbitration, ensures that disputes are addressed constructively and do not derail the partnership.

6.1: TYPES OF STRATEGIC PARTNERSHIPS

6.1.1 ACADEMIC PARTNERSHIPS

Academic partnerships are pivotal strategies for AI organizations leveraging universities and research institutions' vast intellectual, technological, and human resources. These collaborations bridge the gap between theoretical research and practical implementation, offering many benefits to startups, established enterprises, and academic institutions.

BENEFITS OF ACADEMIC PARTNERSHIPS

1. **Access to Cutting-Edge Research**

    - Academic institutions are often at the forefront of groundbreaking research in artificial intelligence and related fields. Partnering with universities allows organizations to stay ahead of the curve by gaining early access to innovations in AI, machine learning, natural language processing, and robotics. This can significantly accelerate the R&D process for AI startups and enterprises.

    - For instance, research labs like MIT, Stanford, and Carnegie Mellon are globally recognized for their contributions to AI advancements. Partnering with such institutions can provide companies with insights into next-generation technologies that may not be commercially available.

2. **Skilled Talent Pool**

    - Universities are home to some of the brightest minds in the world. Partnering with them provides organizations access to highly skilled students, postdoctoral researchers, and faculty members. Companies can collaborate with these individuals through internships, joint research projects, or consulting arrangements, allowing them to build a strong talent pipeline.

    - Moreover, engaging with academic talent enables organizations to nurture long-term relationships. For instance, students who work on industry-sponsored research projects during their studies are more likely to join the sponsoring company after graduation, ensuring a steady influx of talent.

3. **Credibility and Reputation**

    - Collaborating with prestigious academic institutions lends credibility to an organization. Being associated with renowned universities like Stanford or MIT can enhance a company's reputation in the market and attract attention from investors, customers, and other stakeholders.

- This credibility can be a critical differentiator for startups, helping them stand out in a crowded, competitive AI landscape. For established enterprises, it reinforces their commitment to innovation and thought leadership.

4. **Cost-Effective Innovation**

   - Academic partnerships often represent a cost-effective way to conduct high-quality research. Instead of building in-house research facilities or hiring full-time staff, organizations can collaborate with universities to leverage existing resources, including labs, data, and computing infrastructure.

   - Universities often receive funding for their research from government grants or private foundations. Companies can co-sponsor these projects, benefiting from the outcomes without shouldering the entire financial burden.

5. **Real-World Problem Solving**

   - Many universities are keen to engage in applied research that addresses real-world challenges. Organizations can bring their industry-specific problems to academic partners, who, in turn, can use their expertise to develop innovative solutions.

   - This collaboration often results in a win-win scenario: companies gain actionable insights and solutions, while universities get to validate their research in practical settings.

EXAMPLES OF ACADEMIC PARTNERSHIPS IN AI

---

1. **Collaborating with Universities to Test AI Models in Real-World Scenarios**

   - AI models often require extensive testing and validation before being deployed in the real world. Academic partnerships enable companies to test these models in controlled environments provided by universities.

   - For example, an AI startup developing a predictive maintenance algorithm for manufacturing equipment might partner with a university's engineering department to test the model on simulated factory data.

2. **Co-developing AI Algorithms and Frameworks**

   - Companies can work with academic researchers to co-develop advanced AI algorithms tailored to specific industries. For instance, financial institutions might collaborate with university researchers to design machine learning models for fraud detection or credit risk analysis.

3. **Accessing Specialized Research Labs**

- Many universities host specialized labs dedicated to AI research, such as MIT's Computer Science and Artificial Intelligence Laboratory (CSAIL) or Stanford's Human-Centered Artificial Intelligence (HAI) Institute. Collaborating with these labs provides companies with unique facilities, datasets, and domain expertise.

4. **Industry-Sponsored Research Projects**

   - Organizations often fund research projects at universities in exchange for insights, intellectual property rights, or early access to the findings. For example, an automotive company might sponsor a project on autonomous vehicle navigation algorithms.

5. **Workforce Development Programs**

   - Some partnerships focus on workforce development, where universities design curricula and training programs tailored to the needs of industry partners. This ensures a steady supply of job-ready graduates with skills in AI, data science, and related fields.

CASE STUDY: AI STARTUPS COLLABORATING WITH MIT AND STANFORD

Overview: AI startups have increasingly turned to institutions like MIT and Stanford to accelerate their growth and development. These universities, renowned for their AI research, offer unparalleled resources, expertise, and networking opportunities.

MIT's CSAIL (Computer Science and Artificial Intelligence Laboratory):

- Several AI startups have collaborated with MIT's CSAIL to refine their algorithms and validate their models. For instance, a startup working on natural language processing (NLP) might collaborate with CSAIL researchers to improve the accuracy of its language models.
- CSAIL hosts programs like the MIT Startup Exchange, facilitating connections between startups and academic researchers. This program has helped numerous AI startups access cutting-edge research and mentorship.

Stanford's AI Ecosystem:

- Stanford University's AI programs are deeply integrated with Silicon Valley, making it a natural partner for AI startups. Companies like OpenAI and DeepMind have historically engaged with Stanford researchers to advance their projects.
- For example, an AI startup developing healthcare diagnostics tools might partner with Stanford's School of Medicine to validate its algorithms using real-world medical data. This collaboration enhances the credibility of the startup's product and ensures that the solution is robust and reliable.

Outcomes:

- Such collaborations have led to deep learning, computer vision, and robotics breakthroughs. Startups that partner with academic institutions often gain a competitive edge by being at the forefront of innovation.
- Furthermore, these partnerships often result in co-authored research papers, which bolster the startups' academic credentials and help attract additional funding.

CHALLENGES AND BEST PRACTICES

While the benefits of academic partnerships are numerous, there are challenges that organizations must navigate to maximize the value of these collaborations:

1. **Intellectual Property (IP) Agreements:**
   - One of the most common challenges in academic partnerships is negotiating intellectual property rights. Organizations must ensure that the agreement's terms align with their business goals while respecting the educational institution's mandate for open research.
2. **Alignment of Objectives:**
   - Universities often prioritize fundamental research, while companies focus on applied outcomes. Establishing clear objectives and expectations at the outset is crucial to ensuring a successful collaboration.
3. **Timeline Management:**
   - Academic research typically operates on longer timelines than industry, which is fast-paced. Organizations must account for this and plan their projects accordingly.
4. **Best Practices:**
   - Establish a dedicated liaison team to manage the partnership and ensure smooth communication.
   - Clearly define the project's scope, including deliverables, timelines, and funding arrangements.
   - Foster a culture of mutual respect and collaboration, recognizing the unique strengths that each partner brings to the table.

Academic partnerships are a powerful mechanism for driving innovation in the AI landscape. By collaborating with universities, organizations can access cutting-edge research, build a robust talent pipeline, and enhance their credibility in the market. From testing AI models in real-world scenarios to co-developing advanced algorithms, these partnerships offer many opportunities for mutual growth and success.

Case studies involving AI startups and institutions like MIT and Stanford highlight the transformative potential of these collaborations. By addressing challenges and adopting best practices, organizations can unlock the full potential of academic partnerships, ensuring long-term impact and competitive advantage in the dynamic world of AI.

6.1.2 CORPORATE PARTNERSHIPS

Corporate partnerships are a cornerstone in developing and deploying AI solutions, offering a symbiotic relationship that benefits both parties. These transactional and strategic alliances drive innovation, scale, and market impact. Let us delve deeper into the benefits, examples, and visual representation of how such collaborations can accelerate the time to market for AI initiatives.

BENEFITS OF CORPORATE PARTNERSHIPS

1. Access to Proprietary Data

One of the most significant advantages of corporate partnerships is access to proprietary data. Data is the lifeblood of AI systems, and having rich, diverse datasets can drastically enhance model training and accuracy. For instance:

- Retail companies can share customer purchasing patterns, enabling AI algorithms to predict demand and optimize inventory.
- Financial institutions can provide historical transaction data, paving the way for more robust fraud detection systems.

With proprietary data, AI developers can create more accurate models tailored to specific industries and use cases, giving them a competitive edge in the market.

2. Expanded Market Reach

Corporate partners often possess an established customer base and extensive distribution networks. Leveraging these assets allows AI startups or smaller firms to introduce their solutions to a broader audience. This expanded reach accelerates adoption and provides invaluable feedback for iterative improvement.

For example, a partnership between an AI healthcare startup and a hospital network enables the startup to test its diagnostic tools in real-world settings. Hospitals benefit from cutting-edge technology that improves patient outcomes.

3. Financial Resources and Stability

Many AI initiatives require significant investment in infrastructure, talent, and research. Corporate partnerships can alleviate financial constraints by providing funding, shared resources, or co-development arrangements. This financial support ensures the following:

- Faster R&D cycles
- Scalability of AI solutions
- Ability to attract top talent

A well-funded project backed by corporate resources is more likely to succeed in a competitive marketplace.

4. Brand Credibility and Industry Expertise

Partnering with established corporations lends credibility to emerging AI ventures. The association with a reputable brand assures potential customers and investors of the technology's reliability and value. Additionally, corporate partners bring decades of industry expertise, which can be instrumental in fine-tuning AI solutions to align with market demands.

Examples of Successful Corporate Partnerships

AI-Powered Logistics Optimization for a Retail Giant

A notable example of a successful corporate partnership is between an AI solutions provider and a leading retail corporation. In this collaboration:

- The AI provider used the retailer's historical sales data and warehouse inventory records to develop predictive algorithms for logistics.
- The system optimized delivery routes, reduced fuel consumption, and ensured on-time delivery to customers.
- The retailer, in turn, gained a more efficient supply chain and improved customer satisfaction.

This partnership highlights how corporate resources (data and market access) and AI innovation can create mutually beneficial outcomes.

Predictive Maintenance in Manufacturing

Another compelling example is the partnership between a manufacturing company and an AI-driven predictive maintenance firm. Here:

- The AI firm developed models to predict equipment failures based on sensor data from manufacturing plants.

- The manufacturing company provided the necessary operational data and infrastructure for testing.
- The result was significantly reduced downtime and maintenance costs for the manufacturer, while the AI firm gained insights to enhance its product offerings.

How Corporate Partnerships Accelerate Time-to-Market

The relationship between corporate partnerships and time-to-market can be visualized as a flywheel, where each element feeds into the next to generate momentum. This acceleration is achieved through:

1. **Shared Resources:**
   - Access to corporate data, infrastructure, and expertise reduces the time needed for AI model development and testing.
   - Example: A telecom company shares network data to train an AI system for predictive analytics, cutting the typical development timeline in half.
2. **Market Validation:**
   - Corporate partnerships enable early validation of AI solutions in real-world environments, leading to quicker iterations and refinements.
   - Example: A partnership with a pharmaceutical company allows an AI drug discovery platform to test compounds faster, ensuring regulatory approval within shorter timeframes.
3. **Scaling Infrastructure:**

- With corporate backing, startups can scale their infrastructure to meet market demands without delays.
- Example: Cloud computing credits provided by a tech giant to an AI startup accelerate deployment capabilities.

4. **Distribution Channels:**

   - Established corporate distribution networks ensure that AI solutions reach end-users rapidly.
   - Example: A collaboration with an e-commerce giant enables the integration of an AI-based recommendation engine across millions of product pages within weeks.

Corporate partnerships are potent catalysts for AI innovation. By combining the agility of AI startups with the resources and expertise of established corporations, these collaborations unlock unprecedented opportunities for growth, efficiency, and market impact. As AI continues to reshape industries, the importance of strategic corporate partnerships will only grow, making them a critical component of successful AI strategies.

6.1.3 GOVERNMENT AND NGO COLLABORATIONS

Governments and Non-Governmental Organizations (NGOs) often form partnerships to address complex societal challenges, leveraging each sector's unique strengths. In the context of Artificial Intelligence (AI), such collaborations can yield transformative benefits, mainly when applied to areas like urban planning, healthcare, education, and environmental sustainability. These partnerships combine resources and expertise and ensure AI technologies are deployed ethically and inclusively.

BENEFITS OF GOVERNMENT AND NGO COLLABORATIONS

1. Funding Opportunities: Governments typically have access to substantial financial resources, which can be allocated to AI initiatives through grants, subsidies, or direct investments. Collaborating with NGOs enables these funds to be directed toward projects aligned with societal needs. NGOs often deeply understand their communities, allowing them to advocate for impactful and efficient initiatives. For example, a government might fund an NGO to develop AI tools for monitoring deforestation, combining public-sector funding with on-the-ground expertise.

2. Regulatory Support: Navigating the complex landscape of AI regulations can be daunting for NGOs or private entities working alone. NGOs can benefit from regulatory insights and support by collaborating with governments, ensuring their AI projects comply with national and international laws. Moreover, such partnerships can help shape pragmatic regulations and promote innovation. For instance, an NGO working on AI-driven healthcare solutions can collaborate with health ministries to ensure compliance with patient privacy laws while advocating for adaptive regulations that facilitate innovation.

3. Access to Public-Sector Data: Governments are custodians of vast amounts of data across various domains, such as census records, geographic information, and public health statistics. Access to this data is invaluable for developing robust AI models. NGOs often bring expertise in leveraging such data to create actionable insights. For instance, an NGO working on urban planning might use government data to train AI models that optimize traffic flow, reduce pollution, and improve public transportation systems. These collaborations ensure the data is utilized responsibly and for the greater public good.

EXAMPLES OF COLLABORATIONS

1. AI-Driven Urban Planning: Urban areas face challenges such as overpopulation, traffic congestion, pollution, and inadequate housing. Governments and NGOs can collaborate to develop AI solutions that address these issues. For instance, an NGO focused on sustainable cities could partner with local governments to implement AI algorithms that analyze traffic patterns and suggest real-time solutions for congestion. Similarly, AI can identify areas prone to flooding or other environmental risks, enabling proactive urban planning and disaster preparedness.

A notable example is the partnership between the Indian government and the World Resources Institute (WRI) to improve urban mobility. Using AI tools to analyze traffic data, they have developed solutions that enhance public transportation systems, reduce travel times, and lower greenhouse gas emissions.

2. AI in Healthcare Solutions: Government-NGO collaborations can profoundly impact the healthcare sector. AI-driven tools can assist in disease diagnosis, treatment planning, and patient monitoring, particularly in underserved areas. For example, African governments have collaborated with NGOs like PATH to use AI to diagnose malaria and other infectious diseases. These tools analyze medical images or patient data to provide accurate diagnoses, even in remote regions with limited access to medical professionals.

Another example is the collaboration between the UK's National Health Service (NHS) and the NGO DeepMind, which developed AI tools to predict acute kidney injuries. This partnership has improved patient outcomes by leveraging NHS data and DeepMind's AI expertise while setting standards for data governance and ethical AI use.

3. Education and Skill Development: Governments and NGOs can also collaborate to use AI to improve education systems and bridge the digital divide. For instance, AI tools can personalize learning experiences, identify at-risk students, and recommend interventions. An example is the collaboration between UNESCO and NGOs in developing AI platforms that provide digital learning resources to marginalized communities. These platforms analyze student performance data to tailor educational content, ensuring that learning is accessible and practical.

4. Environmental Conservation: AI can significantly address environmental challenges such as deforestation, wildlife conservation, and climate change. Governments and NGOs can combine their efforts to develop AI tools that monitor environmental changes and recommend sustainable practices.

For instance, the Norwegian government's partnership with Global Forest Watch has resulted in AI-driven systems that use satellite data to track deforestation in real-time. These tools enable rapid responses to illegal logging and support reforestation initiatives.

5. Crisis Response and Humanitarian Aid: AI can enhance the effectiveness of humanitarian aid during crises, such as natural disasters or pandemics. Governments and NGOs can collaborate to deploy AI-driven systems for disaster prediction, resource allocation, and relief coordination. For example, during the COVID-19 pandemic, several governments partnered with NGOs to use AI to track virus spread, manage healthcare resources, and disseminate accurate information. Such collaborations ensure a faster and more coordinated response, minimizing the impact on vulnerable populations.

CHALLENGES AND SOLUTIONS

While the benefits of government-NGO collaborations are substantial, these partnerships are not without challenges. Differences in organizational goals, bureaucratic hurdles, and data privacy concerns can hinder progress. However, these challenges can be mitigated through:

- **Clear Communication:** Establishing open lines of communication to align objectives and expectations.
- **Defined Roles and Responsibilities:** Delineate the roles of each partner to avoid overlaps and conflicts.
- **Ethical Frameworks:** Developing robust frameworks to ensure data privacy and ethical AI use.
- **Capacity Building:** Providing training and resources to government and NGO staff to maximize the effectiveness of AI tools.

Government and NGO collaborations hold immense potential to harness the power of AI for societal benefit. By combining public-sector resources with NGO expertise, these partnerships can drive innovation, address pressing challenges, and ensure that AI technologies are used responsibly and inclusively. The examples of AI-driven urban planning and healthcare solutions illustrate the transformative impact of such collaborations, paving the way for a future where AI serves as a force for good.

6.2: EVALUATING POTENTIAL PARTNERSHIPS

6.2.1 CRITERIA FOR A GOOD PARTNERSHIP

Forming a successful partnership is a cornerstone of driving growth, fostering innovation, and achieving long-term success in any industry. Whether the partnership involves businesses, non-profits, or public entities, specific criteria must be evaluated to ensure the collaboration is mutually beneficial and strategically aligned. Below are the primary criteria for establishing a good partnership:

One fundamental aspect of a successful partnership is alignment with the organization's mission and goals. Partnerships are most effective when both parties share a common vision and are committed to similar objectives. This alignment creates a foundation of trust and ensures that the partnership's efforts contribute meaningfully to the overarching goals of both entities.

For instance, consider a technology company focused on developing AI-driven solutions for climate change mitigation partnering with an environmental organization. Both parties are committed to sustainability and climate resilience in such a partnership. This common ground enables them to work seamlessly towards innovative solutions while ensuring their values and missions reinforce each other. Conversely, a misalignment in mission or priorities can lead to conflicts, inefficiencies, and, ultimately, the failure of the collaboration.

To evaluate alignment, organizations must:

- Clearly articulate their mission, vision, and strategic goals.
- Assess the partner's stated mission and goals to ensure congruence.
- Engage in open dialogue to identify shared values and objectives.
- Avoid partnerships that could compromise their core values or dilute their focus.

Assessing Complementary Strengths

A good partnership leverages the complementary strengths of the organizations involved. No single entity possesses all the expertise, resources, or market reach required to achieve its goals. By identifying and combining their unique capabilities, partners can amplify their collective impact and achieve outcomes that would be unattainable individually.

Expertise is a critical area of complementarity. Each partner should bring specialized knowledge or skills that enhance the partnership's ability to address challenges and seize opportunities. For example, an AI startup specializing in predictive analytics might collaborate with a manufacturing company to improve supply chain efficiency. The startup provides cutting-edge technology and technical expertise, while the manufacturer contributes deep industry knowledge and operational insights.

Resources Resources are another vital dimension of complementary strengths. These include financial resources, infrastructure, technology, and human capital. A partnership in which one party provides funding while the other offers technical capabilities can be highly effective. For example, a nonprofit organization focused on education might partner with a technology company to develop and deploy online learning platforms. The nonprofit contributes domain expertise and access to underserved communities, while the tech company provides the technological tools and financial investment needed to scale the initiative.

Market Presence Market presence and access are equally important. Partnerships often succeed when one partner has a strong foothold in a specific market or demographic the other wishes to target. For example, a healthcare AI startup aiming to validate its diagnostic tools might partner with a hospital with access to large patient data volumes. Hospitals benefit from innovative technology that improves patient outcomes, while startups gain the clinical validation and data necessary to refine and market their products.

To assess complementary strengths, organizations should:

- Conduct a strengths and weaknesses analysis for both parties.
- Clearly define the roles and contributions of each partner.
- Ensure that the partnership creates more significant value than the sum of its parts.

Example: A Healthcare AI Startup Partnering with a Hospital for Testing Diagnostic Tools

To illustrate these principles, consider a healthcare AI startup specializing in developing diagnostic tools based on machine learning. The startup seeks to partner with a hospital to test and validate its solutions in a clinical setting.

Alignment with Mission and Goals The startup aims to revolutionize healthcare through AI, improving diagnostic accuracy and efficiency. The hospital's mission is to provide high-quality patient care while staying at the forefront of medical innovation. Both organizations are aligned in their commitment to enhancing patient outcomes through cutting-edge technology. This shared vision ensures that the partnership's goals are mutually reinforcing.

Assessing Complementary Strengths

- **Expertise:** The AI startup brings technical expertise in developing and deploying machine learning algorithms, while the hospital provides clinical expertise and access to healthcare professionals who can evaluate the tools' efficacy.
- **Resources:** The hospital offers access to a large, diverse patient population and the necessary infrastructure for clinical testing. Meanwhile, the startup contributes its innovative technology and funding for the pilot program.
- **Market Presence:** The hospital's reputation as a leading healthcare institution lends credibility to the startup's technology, facilitating adoption by other hospitals and healthcare providers. Conversely, the startup's innovation enhances the hospital's leadership in medical technology adoption.

The startup and hospital create a partnership that drives value for both parties by aligning their missions and leveraging complementary strengths. The hospital benefits from access to state-of-the-art diagnostic tools that improve patient care while the startup gains critical validation and feedback, accelerating its path to commercialization.

Additional Considerations for a Good Partnership

While alignment with mission and complementary strengths are foundational, other considerations can further enhance a partnership's success:

- **Clear Communication:** Open and transparent communication is essential for setting expectations, resolving conflicts, and adapting to changing circumstances.

- **Defined Metrics for Success:** Establishing measurable outcomes and KPIs ensures that progress can be tracked and adjustments made as needed.

- **Cultural Compatibility:** Beyond strategic alignment, organizations should assess whether their cultures and working styles are compatible. Misaligned cultures can lead to friction and inefficiencies.

- **Long-term Commitment:** A good partnership should be built on trust and a shared commitment to achieving long-term goals. Short-term opportunism can undermine the potential for lasting success.

The criteria for a good partnership—alignment with mission and goals and leveraging complementary strengths—are essential for mutual benefit and long-term success. Organizations can amplify their impact and achieve outcomes that exceed individual capabilities by fostering partnerships rooted in shared values and strategic complementarity. The example of a healthcare AI startup partnering with a hospital underscore how these principles can be applied in practice, creating a collaboration that drives innovation and enhances patient care. As industries continue to evolve, the ability to form and nurture effective partnerships will remain a critical determinant of organizational success.

6.2.3 RISK ASSESSMENT

Organizations that develop, deploy, and manage AI-driven solutions or platforms inevitably face a range of risks that, if unaddressed, can jeopardize the success and sustainability of their initiatives. This section examines common risks and explores practical mitigation strategies for managing these challenges effectively.

Common Risks

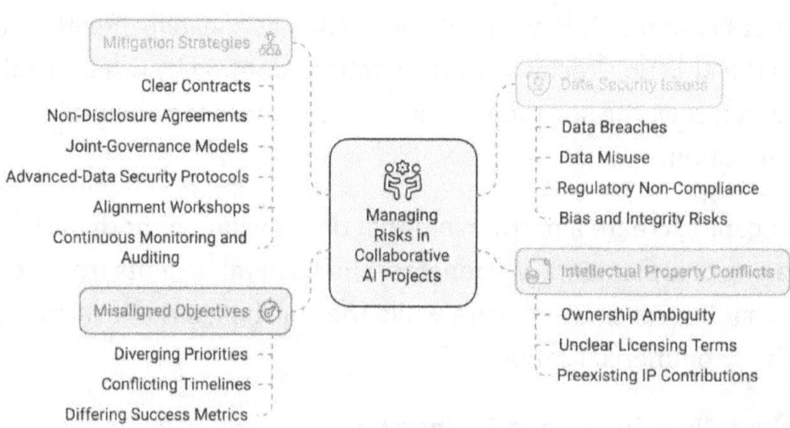

Intellectual Property (IP) Conflicts

One of the most significant risks in collaborative AI projects, especially partnerships between multiple entities, is the potential for intellectual property (IP) conflicts. These conflicts often arise when:

- **Ownership Ambiguity:** It is unclear which party owns the intellectual property generated during the collaboration. Disputes may arise over the rights to algorithms, datasets, or resulting products.

- **Unclear Licensing Terms:** Disagreements on licensing arrangements, including who can commercialize the outcomes and under what terms, can lead to friction.

- **Preexisting IP Contributions:** When preexisting IP from one party is integrated into a joint project, challenges may emerge, potentially leading to disputes about how it can be used or modified.

Misaligned Objectives

Collaborative efforts can be hindered by misaligned objectives between stakeholders. This risk manifests in several ways:

- **Diverging Priorities:** Partners may have differing goals for the project. One party might prioritize innovation and experimentation, while another focuses on immediate commercial viability.

- **Conflicting Timelines:** Mismatches in timelines can disrupt progress, with one party needing faster results while another is willing to take a more measured approach.

- **Differing Success Metrics:** What constitutes a "success" might vary, leading to disagreements on resource allocation, performance benchmarks, or final deliverables.

Data Security Issues

Given the critical role of data in AI systems, ensuring its security is paramount. Common risks in this domain include:

- **Data Breaches:** Unauthorized access to sensitive datasets can result in financial losses, reputational damage, and legal repercussions.

- **Data Misuse:** Partners or third parties may misuse shared data intentionally or due to inadequate safeguards.

- **Regulatory Non-Compliance:** Failure to adhere to data protection regulations such as GDPR, CCPA, or HIPAA can lead to significant fines and operational disruptions.

- **Bias and Integrity Risks:** Using low-quality or biased datasets can compromise the fairness and accuracy of AI models, undermining trust in the resulting platform or application.

Mitigation Strategies

Clear Contracts

Establishing comprehensive, well-defined contracts at the outset of a collaboration is one of the most effective ways to mitigate risks. Key elements to include are:

- **IP Ownership Clauses:** Delineate ownership rights for any IP developed during the partnership and specify joint ownership, licensing, and commercialization rights terms.

- **Performance Expectations:** Define milestones, deliverables, and success metrics to align stakeholder objectives.

- **Dispute Resolution Mechanisms:** Incorporate procedures for addressing disputes, such as mediation or arbitration, to avoid prolonged legal battles.

Non-Disclosure Agreements (NDAs)

NDAs play a critical role in safeguarding sensitive information. Their implementation should ensure:

- **Comprehensive Coverage:** Protect all proprietary information, including datasets, algorithms, and strategic plans.

- **Tailored Terms:** Customize NDAs for specific collaborations, detailing what constitutes confidential information and the permissible use of shared data.

- **Enforcement Measures:** Include provisions for penalties in breach cases to deter misuse and ensure accountability.

JOINT-GOVERNANCE MODELS

A joint governance model fosters shared accountability and decision-making, minimizing the risk of misaligned objectives. Components of effective governance include:

- **Steering Committees:** Form committees comprising representatives from all stakeholders to oversee progress, address issues, and make strategic decisions collaboratively.

- **Defined Roles and Responsibilities:** Assign roles and responsibilities to avoid duplication of effort and ensure that all aspects of the project are managed effectively.

- **Regular Communication:** Establish consistent communication channels, such as monthly review meetings, to maintain transparency and adapt to evolving needs.

Given the critical nature of data in AI projects, robust security protocols are essential. Recommendations include:

- **Encryption and Access Controls:** Strong encryption standards should be employed for data storage and transfer, and access should be limited to authorized personnel only.

- **Third-Party Audits:** Engage independent auditors to assess compliance with data protection regulations and identify vulnerabilities.

- **Data Anonymization involves** Removing personally identifiable information (PII) from datasets to reduce privacy risks while preserving data utility.

- **Incident Response Plans:** Develop and regularly update plans to address data breaches or security lapses quickly.

Alignment Workshops

To address the risk of misaligned objectives, conducting alignment workshops at the beginning and during key phases of the collaboration can be invaluable. These workshops should:

- **Clarify Objectives:** Establish shared goals and priorities to ensure all parties work towards a shared vision.

- **Set Expectations:** Align on resource commitments, timelines, and success metrics to prevent misunderstandings.

- **Foster Trust:** Build mutual understanding and respect, strengthening relationships and improving collaboration outcomes.

Continuous Monitoring and Auditing

Regular monitoring and auditing technical and strategic elements are crucial for maintaining alignment and security. Best practices include:

- **Performance Reviews:** Conduct periodic evaluations to ensure milestones are met and adjust plans as necessary.

- **Security Assessments:** Continuously monitor systems for vulnerabilities and update protocols in response to emerging threats.

- **Feedback Loops:** Incorporate mechanisms for stakeholders to provide feedback, enabling proactive identification and resolution of issues.

By recognizing and addressing these common risks through proactive and collaborative strategies, organizations can more effectively navigate the complexities of AI projects. Such measures mitigate potential disruptions and foster trust and long-term partnerships among stakeholders, ultimately contributing to the successful realization of AI-driven initiatives.

6.2.3 CASE STUDY: SUCCESSFUL AND FAILED PARTNERSHIPS

Partnerships can catalyze growth, innovation, and market expansion in the business world. However, not all partnerships succeed, and understanding the dynamics of successful and failed collaborations is crucial for crafting robust strategies. This section explores one exemplary successful partnership and a failed one, drawing actionable lessons from each.

Successful Partnership: Apple and Nike (Nike iPod)

The collaboration between Apple and Nike, launched in 2006, is a quintessential example of a successful partnership. This partnership combined Nike's expertise in sports and fitness with Apple's technological prowess, resulting in the Nike iPod Sports Kit. The device allowed runners to sync their Nike running shoes with their iPods to track performance metrics such as distance, speed, and calories burned.

The success of this partnership can be attributed to several factors:

1. **Complementary Strengths**: Both companies leveraged their unique strengths. Nike's dominance in athletic wear and Apple's reputation for user-friendly technology created a product that appealed to fitness enthusiasts and tech-savvy consumers.

2. **Shared Vision**: Both organizations shared a clear vision of promoting health and fitness through innovative technology. This alignment ensured seamless collaboration and effective product integration.

3. **Market Synergy**: Both companies' target markets overlapped significantly. The product appealed to athletes and fitness enthusiasts, creating a natural customer base for the collaboration.

4. **Effective Marketing**: The partnership was supported by a strong marketing campaign that capitalized on both companies' iconic branding. The combined branding added credibility and attracted a broad audience.

Key Lessons:

- **Alignment of Vision and Values**: Successful partnerships thrive when both parties have a shared vision.

- **Leveraging Complementary Strengths**: Collaborations that combine each partner's unique capabilities are more likely to deliver innovative products.

- **Effective Communication**: Clear communication and joint strategic planning are crucial to success.

Failed Partnership: DaimlerChrysler Merger

In stark contrast, the 1998 merger of Daimler-Benz and Chrysler Corporation, intended to create a global automotive powerhouse, is often cited as a cautionary tale of a failed partnership. The $36 billion "merger of equals" was plagued by cultural clashes, misaligned expectations, and operational challenges, ultimately leading to its dissolution in 2007.

Key reasons for the failure include:

1. **Cultural Differences**: Daimler-Benz, a German company known for luxury and precision, struggled to integrate with Chrysler, an American company with a more cost-driven and mass-market focus. This cultural divide created friction at all organizational levels.

2. **Lack of Synergy**: The anticipated synergies between the two companies failed to materialize. The differences in product lines, customer bases, and operational approaches proved too challenging to bridge.

3. **Misaligned Expectations**: While Daimler viewed the merger as an acquisition, Chrysler saw it as an equal partnership. This disparity in perspectives created confusion and resentment.

4. **Poor Execution**: Insufficient planning and execution exacerbated the challenges, leading to operational inefficiencies and financial losses.

Key Lessons:

- **Cultural Compatibility**: Cultural differences must be thoroughly understood and addressed before entering a partnership.

- **Realistic Synergy Expectations**: Overestimating synergies can lead to disappointment and failure.

- **Clear Roles and Governance**: Clearly defining roles, responsibilities, and decision-making processes is essential for operational harmony.

Comparative Analysis and Conclusion

Examining the Apple-Nike partnership and the DaimlerChrysler merger highlights the critical importance of alignment, cultural compatibility, and strategic planning. Successful partnerships require a shared vision, leveraging complementary strengths, and effective communication. Conversely, failed collaborations often stem from misaligned expectations, cultural clashes, and inadequate planning. By studying these examples, organizations can better navigate the complexities of partnerships, minimizing risks and maximizing potential benefits.

6.3: STRUCTURING AND NEGOTIATING PARTNERSHIPS

6.3.1 SETTING CLEAR OBJECTIVES

The foundation of any successful partnership is setting clear, well-defined objectives. This clarity ensures that all stakeholders are aligned, resources are allocated efficiently, and outcomes are measurable. Determining these objectives begins with identifying success metrics that accurately capture the partnership's impact and can guide its trajectory over time.

DEFINING SUCCESS METRICS FOR PARTNERSHIPS

Success metrics, or Key Performance Indicators (KPIs), serve as the benchmarks against which the performance of a partnership is evaluated. They offer a quantifiable way to measure the success and alignment of the collaboration with the overarching goals. In the context of alliances, KPIs can vary widely depending on the industry, the nature of the partnership, and the specific objectives in question. Below are some critical success metrics commonly employed:

1. **Market Penetration:**
   - This metric gauges the partnership's ability to expand into new or existing markets. For example, a collaboration between a health tech company and a hospital chain might measure market penetration by the number of hospitals adopting their joint solutions.
   - A successful partnership might aim for a 30% increase in market share within the first year, showcasing the effectiveness of their combined efforts in capturing demand.

2. **User Adoption:**

   - User adoption metrics assess how effectively the partnership attracts and retains users for its products or services. For instance, a software-as-a-service (SaaS) platform partnering with a major distributor might focus on the number of new user sign-ups or active monthly users gained through the collaboration.

   - A goal could be to achieve 50,000 active users within six months of the partnership launch.

3. **Cost Savings:**

   - Partnerships often aim to reduce operational or production costs through resource sharing or economies of scale. For example, a manufacturing AI solution partnering with a logistics company might measure cost savings through reduced delivery times or fuel costs.

   - For example, a 15% decrease in supply chain costs within the first quarter could indicate a successful partnership.

4. **Revenue Growth:**

   - Revenue growth is a critical indicator of a partnership's financial success. This metric evaluates how the collaboration contributes to increased sales, higher profit margins, or expanded product lines.

   - For instance, a 25% increase in quarterly revenue could be a target for a retail company partnering with an AI-driven customer analytics provider.

5. **Innovation Metrics:**

   - These metrics measure the extent to which the partnership fosters new ideas, technologies, or business models. The number of patents filed, prototypes developed, or innovative features launched can indicate success.

   - An innovation-driven partnership might aim to release three new product features within the first year.

6. **Customer Satisfaction and Retention:**

   - Customer-centric partnerships often evaluate success through metrics such as Net Promoter Scores (NPS), customer satisfaction ratings, or retention rates.

   - To measure partnership effectiveness, a joint venture between a telecom company and a smart device manufacturer could aim for a 90% customer satisfaction rate.

Examples of Clear Partnership Goals

Moving beyond abstract aspirations and establishing tangible, actionable goals is vital when setting objectives. Let's explore examples of clear partnership goals to illustrate how well-defined objectives can drive successful collaborations.

1. A Fintech AI Startup Aiming for Improved Fraud Detection Accuracy

Objective: A 20% increase in fraud detection accuracy through collaboration with a leading bank.

- **Context:**
    - A fintech startup specializes in AI-driven fraud detection. By partnering with a well-established bank, the startup aims to enhance its algorithms by accessing its extensive transaction datasets.
- **Defined Metrics:**
    - Fraud detection accuracy will increase from 80% to 96% within one year.
    - Reduction in false favorable rates by 15%.
- **Implementation Strategy:**
    - Integration of the bank's data streams into the AI model to improve training and validation processes.
    - Conducting bi-monthly model performance reviews to track improvements.
    - Collaborating on pilot projects to test real-world applicability and refine the system based on feedback.
- **Expected Outcomes:**
    - Enhanced security for the bank's customers, leading to higher trust and retention rates.
    - Greater credibility and market positioning for the fintech startup, enabling it to attract additional clients and partnerships.

2. A Health Tech Partnership Focused on Patient Outcomes

Objective: Reduce hospital readmission rates by 25% using predictive analytics.

- **Context:**

- A health tech company develops AI models that predict patient health risks. Partnering with a hospital network, the company seeks to improve post-discharge patient outcomes by providing actionable insights to healthcare providers.

- **Defined Metrics:**
    - Readmission rates will decrease from 20% to 15% within 12 months.
    - Increase in follow-up appointment adherence by 30%.

- **Implementation Strategy:**
    - Deploying AI-powered tools within the hospital's electronic health record (EHR) system.
    - Training medical staff on the interpretation and application of AI-driven insights.
    - Monitoring patient outcomes and conducting quarterly reviews to identify areas for improvement.

- **Expected Outcomes:**
    - Improved quality of care for patients and reduced strain on hospital resources.
    - Enhanced reputation for the hospital network as a leader in innovative healthcare solutions.

3. A Retail Collaboration to Boost E-commerce Sales

Objective: Increase online sales by 40% within six months by partnering with an AI recommendation engine provider.

- **Context:**
    - An online retailer is partnering with an AI company to enhance the shopping experience by offering personalized product recommendations. The retailer aims to boost customer engagement and conversion rates.

- **Defined Metrics:**
    - E-commerce sales to grow by 40% within the specified timeline.
    - Increase in average order value (AOV) by 20%.
    - The customer retention rate should improve by 15%.

- **Implementation Strategy:**

- Integrating the AI recommendation engine into the retailer's website and mobile app.
- Running A/B tests to optimize the recommendation algorithms.
- Collecting customer feedback to refine the system and address pain points.

- **Expected Outcomes:**
    - Higher sales revenue and stronger customer loyalty for the retailer.
    - Expanded use case portfolio and improved algorithms for the AI provider.

4. An Educational Partnership to Drive Enrollment

Objective: Achieve a 50% increase in enrollments for online courses through collaboration between a university and an AI-based education platform.

- **Context:**
    - A university seeks to expand its online course offerings. Partnering with an AI platform, the institution aims to provide personalized learning experiences that attract more students.
- **Defined Metrics:**
    - Enrollment numbers to rise from 1,000 to 1,500 students per semester.
    - Completion rates for online courses will improve by 25%.
- **Implementation Strategy:**
    - Leveraging AI to offer customized learning paths based on student profiles and preferences.
    - Utilizing predictive analytics to identify at-risk students and provide timely support.
    - Conducting marketing campaigns highlighting the benefits of the AI-enhanced learning platform.
- **Expected Outcomes:**
    - Broader reach and higher revenue streams for the university.
    - Enhanced reputation for the AI platform as a pioneer in personalized education solutions.

Setting clear objectives is a cornerstone of successful partnerships. By defining success metrics that align with the collaboration's goals, organizations can ensure that all efforts are directed toward achieving meaningful outcomes. The examples demonstrate how tangible, actionable goals can drive progress and deliver value for all stakeholders. Whether the focus is improving fraud detection, enhancing patient outcomes, boosting e-commerce sales, or driving educational enrollment, clear objectives pave the way for impactful and sustainable partnerships.

6.3.2 NEGOTIATION TIPS FOR WIN-WIN AGREEMENTS

Negotiating effective agreements is critical for building strong partnerships, especially in a fast-paced and competitive landscape like the startup ecosystem. A successful negotiation goes beyond securing favorable terms—it establishes a foundation of trust, collaboration, and shared success. This section focuses on negotiation tips for startups aiming for win-win agreements that ensure long-term sustainability and mutual benefit.

KEY ELEMENTS OF PARTNERSHIP AGREEMENTS

The foundation of any strong partnership is a well-crafted agreement. For startups, these agreements not only define the terms of collaboration but also protect their interests and ensure clarity. Below are the three critical elements to consider:

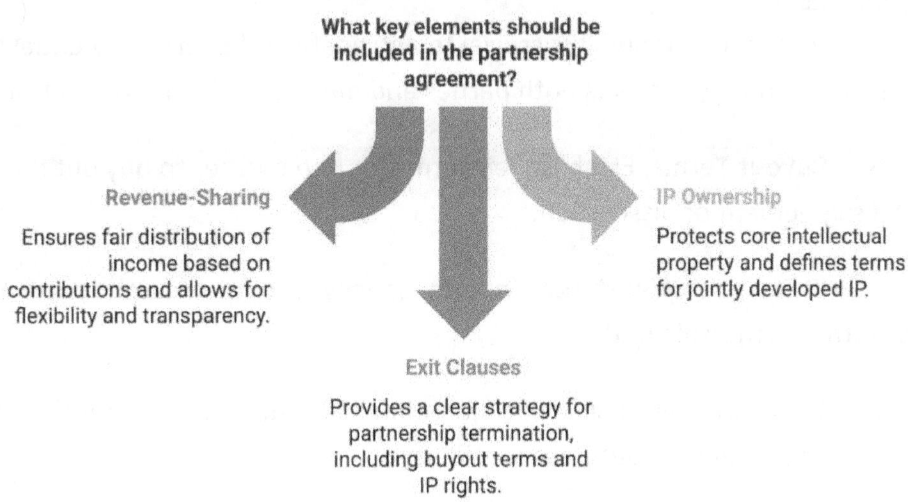

1. **Revenue-Sharing**
One of the primary aspects of partnership agreements is how revenue will be shared between the parties involved. Startups must negotiate revenue-sharing terms that are fair and aligned with the contributions of each partner. Key considerations include:

    - **Proportional Contribution:** Ensure the revenue-sharing model reflects each partner's resources, expertise, and risks.

- **Flexibility:** Include provisions for revisiting revenue-sharing terms as the partnership evolves. For instance, a startup's initial contribution might be undervalued if they grow rapidly.

- **Transparency:** Build mechanisms for regular audits and transparent reporting to avoid disputes over revenue calculations.

2. **Ownership of Intellectual Property (IP)**

Intellectual property often represents the core value of a startup. Negotiating IP ownership and usage rights is critical to maintaining a startup's competitive edge. Key points to address include:

- **Retention of Core IP:** Startups should aim to retain ownership of their foundational IP, ensuring they are not overly reliant on the partnership for future growth.

- **Joint Development:** For IP developed collaboratively during the partnership, specify clear ownership terms and how licensing or profit-sharing will be handled.

- **Protection of Trade Secrets:** Include robust confidentiality clauses to safeguard sensitive information shared during the partnership.

3. **Exit Clauses**

No partnership lasts forever, and it is crucial to anticipate and plan for potential termination. A well-defined exit strategy protects both parties and minimizes disruption. Consider:

- **Buyout Terms:** Establish fair terms for one partner to buy out the other in case of disagreement or dissolution.

- **IP Ownership Post-Termination:** Specify who retains rights to jointly created IP after the partnership ends.

- **Transition Periods:** Define clear timelines and processes for winding down the partnership to ensure business continuity.

TIPS FOR STARTUPS TO MAINTAIN LEVERAGE

Startups often enter negotiations with limited resources, making it crucial to play to their strengths. Here are some strategies to help startups maintain leverage during negotiations:

1. **Highlighting Unique Value Propositions**

Startups can differentiate themselves and strengthen their bargaining position by emphasizing their unique value. Key tactics include:

- **Showcase Innovation:** Clearly articulate what sets your product, service, or technology apart. For example, if your startup has developed a cutting-edge AI algorithm, provide compelling evidence of its superiority, such as case studies or performance metrics.

- **Quantify Impact:** Demonstrate how your solution delivers measurable value to the partner, whether in terms of cost savings, increased efficiency, or market expansion. For instance, if your product can reduce operational costs by 30%, make this a central part of your pitch.

- **Leverage Scarcity:** If your startup offers a rare or highly sought-after capability, emphasize its exclusivity to increase its perceived value during negotiations.

2. **Establish Credibility**

Trust and credibility are essential for successful negotiations. Startups can build credibility by:

- **Presenting Data-Driven Arguments:** Support your claims with solid data and evidence, such as customer testimonials, market research, or financial projections.

- **Highlighting Team Expertise:** Showcase the experience and qualifications of your team to build confidence in your ability to deliver on promises.

- **Demonstrating Traction:** If your startup has achieved significant milestones, such as securing funding or acquiring key clients, use these accomplishments to strengthen your position.

3. **Avoid Overcommitting**

Startups should be cautious about making overly ambitious commitments that could strain their resources or hinder future growth. To avoid this:

- **Negotiate Phased Commitments:** Start with smaller, manageable commitments and scale up as the partnership proves successful.

- **Retain Flexibility:** Avoid agreeing to terms that lock you into rigid obligations, such as fixed revenue percentages that cannot be adjusted.

- **Prioritize Core Objectives:** Focus on negotiating terms that align with your startup's long-term goals rather than short-term gains.

4. **Leverage Third-Party Validation**

External endorsements can enhance your credibility and strengthen your negotiating position. Strategies include:

- **Partner with Trusted Advisors:** Engage industry experts or mentors to advocate for your startup during negotiations.

- **Highlight Strategic Investors:** Mention support from prominent investors or partners who can vouch for your capabilities.
- **Use Case Studies:** Present examples of successful collaborations with other organizations to demonstrate your reliability.

5. **Create a Competitive Environment**

Generating interest from multiple potential partners can significantly increase your leverage. To achieve this:

- **Network Effectively:** Actively engage with potential partners at industry events, conferences, or through professional networks.
- **Showcase Optionality:** Make it clear that you are exploring multiple opportunities, which can encourage partners to offer more favorable terms.
- **Set Deadlines:** Introduce reasonable deadlines for decision-making to create urgency and prevent prolonged negotiations.

6. **Focus on Mutual Benefits**

A win-win agreement requires aligning the interests of both parties. Tactics to ensure mutual benefit include:

- **Understand Partner Goals:** Research the partner's priorities and challenges to propose solutions addressing their needs.
- **Offer Creative Solutions:** Open to unconventional terms, such as performance-based incentives or co-marketing agreements, that create value for both sides.
- **Emphasize Long-Term Value:** Highlight how the partnership can evolve to deliver sustained benefits, such as expanding into new markets or launching innovative products together.

Practical Scenarios and Examples

To illustrate these strategies, consider the following scenarios:

- A startup specializing in renewable energy technology is negotiating with a large utility company. By highlighting their patented solar panel technology's higher efficiency than competitors and presenting data on reduced energy costs, the startup secures a revenue-sharing agreement that increases as adoption grows.
- A healthcare AI startup partners with a hospital chain. To retain leverage, the startup negotiates to maintain ownership of its core algorithms while granting the hospital chain a

license to use the AI system. Additionally, the startup includes an exit clause ensuring the hospital continues to pay for ongoing support if the partnership ends.

Negotiating win-win agreements is an art that requires preparation, strategy, and a clear understanding of your value proposition. For startups, protecting their interests while fostering collaboration with partners is key to long-term success. By focusing on the critical elements of partnership agreements—revenue-sharing, IP ownership, and exit clauses—and employing strategies to maintain leverage, startups can build strong, sustainable partnerships that drive growth and innovation.

6.3.4 GOVERNANCE MODELS

Structuring Decision-Making Processes for Partnerships

Effective governance models are critical for the success of any partnership, particularly in complex environments such as large organizations, multi-stakeholder projects, or collaborative ventures involving public and private entities. Structuring decision-making processes ensures that all stakeholders have clear roles, responsibilities, and channels for communication and conflict resolution. The goal is to foster transparency, accountability, and alignment with shared objectives.

Joint Steering Committees

Joint steering committees (JSCs) serve as the central governing body for partnerships. These committees bring together representatives from all key stakeholders to oversee the partnership's strategic direction, monitor progress, and address challenges. Here are the core elements to consider when establishing a JSC:

1. **Composition:**
    - The JSC should include senior representatives with decision-making authority from each partner organization. Members should bring diverse perspectives, such as operational, technical, and strategic insights, to ensure well-rounded decision-making.
    - A balance between executive-level stakeholders and operational leaders can enhance strategic alignment and practical implementation.

2. **Roles and Responsibilities:**

   - **Strategic Oversight:** The JSC defines the partnerships' overarching goals with each partner's objectives and ensures adherence to agreed-upon principles and policies.

   - **Monitoring and Evaluation:** The committee tracks performance metrics, ensures compliance with governance frameworks, and assesses the partnership's overall health.

   - **Resource Allocation:** The JSC identifies and allocates resources, including budget, personnel, and technology, to efficiently achieve partnership objectives.

3. **Frequency of Meetings:**

   - Regularly scheduled meetings, such as monthly or quarterly, ensure continuous engagement and responsiveness to emerging issues. Ad hoc meetings may also be required to address urgent matters.

4. **Decision-Making Processes:**

   - Decisions should be guided by pre-defined protocols, such as majority voting or consensus-building, depending on the nature and stakes of the issue. Documenting these processes avoids ambiguity and disputes.

   - Decisions on critical matters, such as financial investments or strategic pivots, may require unanimous agreement, while operational issues require only a majority vote.

5. **Documentation and Transparency:**

- Minutes of meetings, decisions, and action plans should be documented and shared with all stakeholders. Transparency fosters trust and reduces the risk of miscommunication.

ESCALATION PROTOCOLS

Despite the best intentions, disagreements and challenges are inevitable in any partnership. Escalation protocols provide a structured mechanism to address these issues before they escalate into significant conflicts. Effective escalation protocols should be designed with the following considerations:

1. **Defined Escalation Tiers:**
   - The project teams should first address issues at the operational level. Only unresolved or critical issues should escalate to higher tiers like the JSC or an executive oversight committee.
   - Tiers may include:
     - **Operational Level:** Project managers and team lead.
     - **Mid-Level:** Functional managers or departmental heads.
     - **Strategic Level:** JSC or executive stakeholders.
2. **Criteria for Escalation:**
   - Clearly define what types of issues warrant escalation, such as deviations from budget, missed milestones, or conflicting strategic priorities.
   - Establish thresholds for escalation, such as financial thresholds or the impact on timelines.
3. **Communication Protocols:**
   - Documented processes for escalation, including how and when issues should be communicated, ensure consistency, and prevent misunderstandings.
   - Use structured templates for issue reporting, including a problem summary, impact, attempted resolutions, and proposed actions.
4. **Timeframes for Resolution:**
   - Escalation protocols should include timelines for addressing issues at each level to avoid prolonged delays. For example, operational-level matters must be resolved within 48 hours, while strategic-level topics might have a two-week window.
5. **Conflict Mediation:**

- Consider involving neutral mediators or facilitators for particularly contentious issues. This can help depersonalize conflicts and focus on constructive solutions.

6. **Feedback Loops:**

   - Once an issue is resolved, ensure feedback loops are in place to prevent recurrence. This may involve updating governance frameworks, processes, or agreements.

Governance Structure for a Partnership

Below is a proposed governance structure for a partnership. This visualization captures the key components and their interactions:

1. **Joint Steering Committee (JSC):** The apex governing body responsible for strategic decisions and overall partnership alignment.

2. **Executive Oversight Committee:** A higher-level body that provides additional oversight and resolves critical escalations from the JSC.

3. **Operational Teams:** Functional teams that handle day-to-day implementation and report to the JSC.

4. **Escalation Pathways:** Defined routes for raising issues from operational teams to the JSC or executive committee.

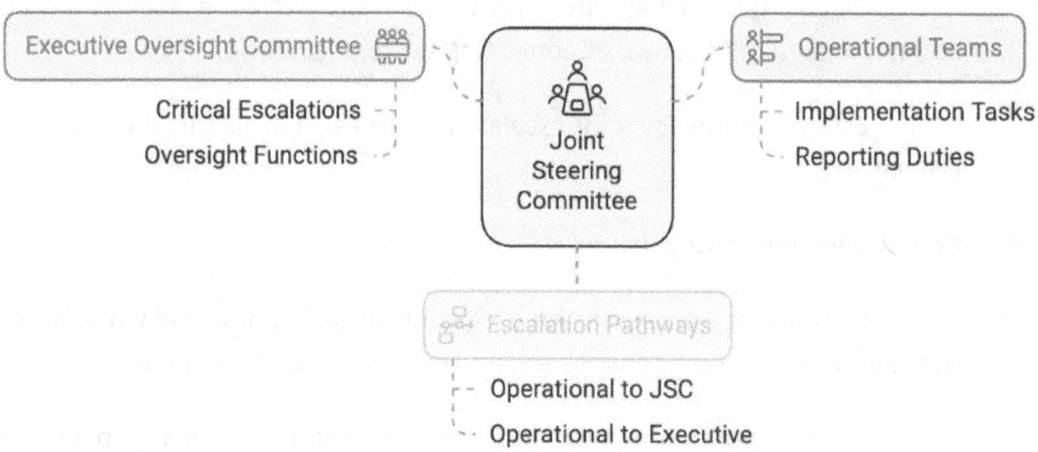

The governance structure ensures a clear hierarchy, well-defined roles, and seamless communication channels across all levels of the partnership.

By adopting these governance models, partnerships can mitigate risks, enhance collaboration, and achieve their shared objectives effectively.

6.4: MAINTAINING AND SCALING PARTNERSHIPS

6.4.1 ENSURING LONG-TERM SUCCESS

Ensuring long-term success in partnerships, particularly in the dynamic world of startups, requires careful planning, continuous monitoring, and adaptive management. Startups, by nature, are fast-moving entities that often evolve their goals and strategies in response to market conditions, growth phases, and technological advancements. Maintaining alignment and momentum in partnerships demands proactive strategies and tools. This section explores how regular check-ins, progress evaluations, and adaptability can contribute to the enduring success of startup partnerships.

REGULAR CHECK-INS AND PROGRESS EVALUATIONS

Regular check-ins and progress evaluations are the backbone of any successful partnership. These practices ensure transparency, foster mutual understanding and allow timely identification of challenges or misalignments. Establishing structured mechanisms to review a partnership's health and outcomes is crucial.

Tools for Tracking Partnership Performance

The success of regular check-ins and progress evaluations hinges on the tools and frameworks employed to monitor performance effectively. Some essential tools and approaches include:

1. **Key Performance Indicators (KPIs):**
   - Setting clear KPIs is fundamental to tracking partnership progress. KPIs should be aligned with the partnership's objectives, whether they pertain to revenue growth, customer acquisition, product development, or other strategic goals. Examples of KPIs include customer retention rates, joint marketing ROI, and the number of co-developed products.
2. **Collaboration Platforms:**
   - Tools like Asana, Trello, or Monday.com provide a centralized space for tracking tasks, deliverables, and timelines. These platforms enhance visibility and accountability, ensuring all stakeholders remain aligned.
3. **Customer Relationship Management (CRM) Systems:**
   - CRM platforms like Salesforce or HubSpot can track customer interactions, shared leads, and joint sales efforts. By integrating these systems, startups and their partners gain insights into shared successes and areas needing improvement.
4. **Data Analytics Dashboards:**

- Advanced analytics tools, such as Tableau or Power BI, enable real-time tracking of partnership metrics. Visualizing data through dashboards helps stakeholders quickly grasp trends and make informed decisions.

5. **Regular Reporting Templates:**
   - Establishing standardized reporting formats ensures consistency and comparability over time. Templates can include sections for KPI updates, qualitative feedback, and action plans for the next period.

Best Practices for Regular Check-ins

To maximize the value of check-ins, consider these best practices:

1. **Frequency:**
   - Based on the partnership's dynamics, determine an appropriate frequency for check-ins. Frequent reviews (e.g., bi-weekly or monthly) may be necessary for early-stage startups, while mature collaborations may benefit from quarterly evaluations.
2. **Agenda Setting:**
   - Ensure every meeting has a clear agenda shared in advance. Agendas should focus on key metrics, progress updates, challenges, and next steps.
3. **Action-Oriented Discussions:**
   - Check-ins should result in actionable outcomes. Assigning tasks and deadlines ensures follow-through on decisions made during the meeting.
4. **Open Communication:**
   - Create an environment where stakeholders feel comfortable sharing concerns, insights, and constructive criticism. Transparent communication fosters trust and collaboration.

Managing Evolving Goals as Startups Grow

Startups are inherently fluid, often pivoting their strategies or expanding their objectives as they grow. Managing these evolving goals within the context of a partnership requires flexibility, foresight, and shared commitment.

Understanding the Nature of Startup Growth

1. **Phases of Growth:**

o Startups typically go through distinct phases, from ideation and product development to scaling and market expansion. Each phase brings new priorities and challenges impacting the partnership's focus.

2. **Triggers for Change:**

o Changes in funding, market conditions, competition, or customer needs often drive shifts in startup goals. Partnerships must anticipate and adapt to these shifts to remain relevant and practical.

STRATEGIES FOR MANAGING EVOLVING GOALS

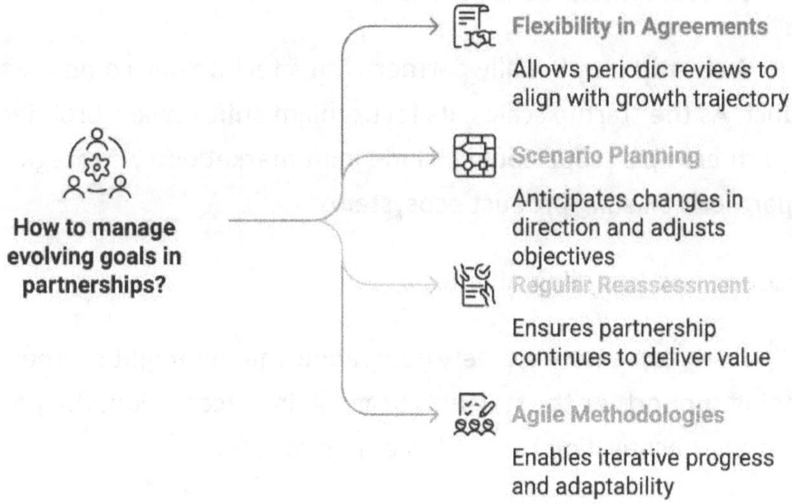

1. **Flexibility in Agreements:**

o Craft partnership agreements that allow for periodic reviews and renegotiations. This flexibility ensures the terms align with the startup's growth trajectory and emerging priorities.

2. **Scenario Planning:**

o Engage in scenario planning to anticipate potential changes in the startup's direction. For example, if a startup pivots from B2C to B2B, how might the partnership's objectives and deliverables change?

3. **Regular Reassessment of Objectives:**

o Schedule strategic reviews to reassess the partnership's objectives and alignment. These reviews should examine whether the partnership continues to deliver value and meet the evolving needs of both parties.

4. **Building Agility into Processes:**

    - Adopt agile methodologies for managing partnership projects. Agile frameworks like Scrum or Kanban allow for iterative progress and adaptability to changing priorities.

5. **Investing in Relationship Building:**

    - Strong personal relationships between key stakeholders can help navigate periods of change. Regular informal interactions complement formal check-ins, building trust and fostering mutual understanding.

Examples of Adaptation in Partnerships

1. **Product Development Collaboration:**

    - A startup may initially partner with a technology company to co-develop a niche product. As the startup scales, its focus might shift toward broader market applications. The partnership's scope could include joint market entry strategies or integration with the partner's existing product ecosystem.

2. **Marketing and Branding Alliances:**

    - A startup entering a new geographic market might partner with a local firm for branding support. As the startup's brand gains recognition, the partnership might shift to customer acquisition campaigns or joint events.

3. **Investment Partnerships:**

    - An investor-partner may initially provide seed funding and mentorship. As the startup progresses, the partnership could evolve to include strategic advisory roles, introductions to additional investors, or participation in later funding rounds.

Ensuring the long-term success of startup partnerships requires a dual focus on consistent performance tracking and adaptability to changing circumstances. Regular check-ins and progress evaluations, supported by robust tools and best practices, provide a foundation for transparency and accountability. Simultaneously, managing evolving goals through flexibility, scenario planning, and relationship building ensures the partnership remains relevant and mutually beneficial as the startup grows. By embracing these strategies, startups and their partners can forge enduring collaborations that drive sustained success in an ever-changing business landscape.

6.4.2 SCALING PARTNERSHIPS FOR BROADER IMPACT

Scaling partnerships to achieve broader impact is a critical strategy for AI startups aiming to expand their influence, grow market share, and solidify their reputation. This section delves into how AI startups can leverage existing partnerships to expand into new markets or industries, focusing on the mechanics, benefits, challenges, and a real-world example.

EXPANDING INTO NEW MARKETS OR INDUSTRIES WITH EXISTING PARTNERS

AI startups often rely on strategic partnerships to bridge resource, capability, and network gaps. Existing partners already familiar with the startup's offerings and value proposition can play a pivotal role in enabling seamless expansion. Whether entering a new geographical market or diversifying into an unfamiliar industry, these partnerships provide a tested framework for scaling operations efficiently.

Key Strategies for Scaling Partnerships

1. **Leverage the Partner's Existing Infrastructure**
   - Partners with established operations in target markets provide startups with immediate access to physical infrastructure, distribution networks, and local expertise. This eliminates the need to build from scratch, reducing initial investments and risks.
2. **Mutual Alignment on Growth Objectives**
   - Aligning on shared goals ensures that both parties are equally motivated to expand into new markets. For instance, a corporate partner interested in AI innovation might co-invest in market entry strategies.
3. **Co-branding and Shared Market Presence**
   - Joint marketing campaigns can introduce the startup's solutions to a broader audience under the partner's credibility and brand equity.
4. **Regulatory and Cultural Navigation**
   - Expanding internationally often requires understanding local regulations, cultural nuances, and business practices. Established partners can guide startups through these complexities, ensuring compliance and resonance with local audiences.

Example: Scaling Internationally with a Corporate Partner

Scenario Overview: Imagine an AI startup, *VisionAI*, specializing in computer vision technology for retail analytics. The startup has partnered with RetailMax, a global retail conglomerate, *RetailMax*, which has a robust presence in over 30 countries. Together, they decided to scale *VisionAI*'s solution into international markets where *RetailMax* operates.

Step-by-Step Strategy:

1. **Market Selection**
    - Using data insights, *RetailMax* identifies five high-priority markets in Europe and Asia with significant potential for AI-driven retail transformation—the selection process factors in variables such as retail density, growth projections, and technology adoption rates.
2. **Resource Alignment**
    - *RetailMax* offers local warehouses, marketing channels, and on-ground staff to support *VisionAI* in these new markets. Simultaneously, *VisionAI* customizes its product offerings to align with region-specific requirements, such as language support and GDPR compliance in Europe.
3. **Joint Launch Campaigns**
    - The two entities co-create marketing campaigns tailored to each market. For example, in Germany, the focus might be on data security and precision, while in India, campaigns emphasize affordability and operational scalability.
4. **Knowledge Sharing**
    - *RetailMax* provides critical insights into customer preferences, competitor activity, and market dynamics. This partnership allows *VisionAI* to localize its product and appeal to regional demands efficiently.

5. **Continuous Iteration and Feedback**

   - *RetailMax*'s local teams regularly collect feedback from retail clients using *VisionAI*'s solutions. This real-time input enables rapid iteration, ensuring the AI solution remains competitive and relevant.

Impact of the Partnership: Within a year, *VisionAI*'s technology will be adopted by over 1,000 retail stores across the five new markets. The partnership will enhance *VisionAI*'s revenue streams and strengthen *RetailMax*'s position as a technology leader in the retail space.

Benefits of Scaling Partnerships

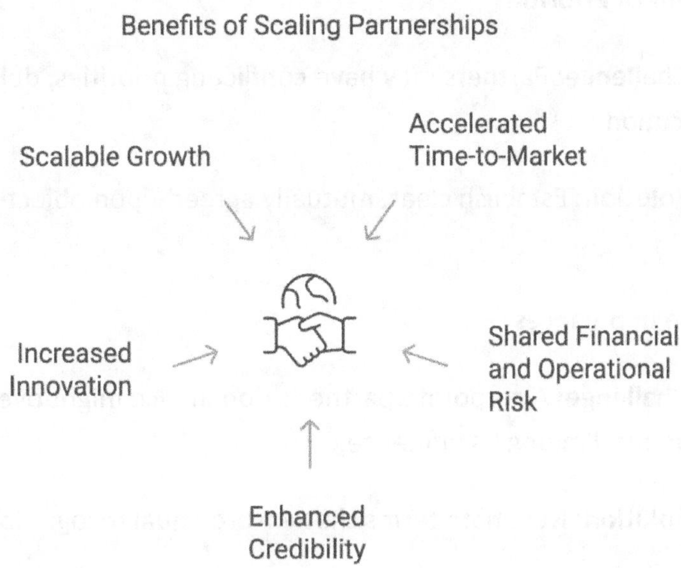

1. **Accelerated Time-to-Market**

   - Partnerships with established entities enable faster entry into new markets by leveraging the partner's operational infrastructure and market presence.

2. **Shared Financial and Operational Risk**

   - The costs and risks of expansion, such as compliance, logistics, and customer acquisition, are distributed between the startup and its partner.

3. **Enhanced Credibility**

   - Association with a reputable partner enhances the startup's credibility, fostering trust among new customers and stakeholders.

4. **Increased Innovation**

- Collaboration often sparks innovation as the startup accesses the partner's resources, insights, and customer base.

5. **Scalable Growth**
   - Partnerships provide a repeatable framework for expansion, allowing startups to replicate success across multiple markets or industries.

CHALLENGES AND MITIGATION STRATEGIES

While scaling partnerships offers significant advantages, it also comes with challenges that require careful navigation.

1. **Alignment of Priorities**
   - **Challenge:** Partners may have conflicting priorities, delaying decision-making and execution.
   - **Solution:** Establish clear, mutually agreed-upon objectives and KPIs at the outset.
2. **Resource Imbalances**
   - **Challenge:** A corporate partner's dominance might overshadow the startup's contributions, limiting its influence.
   - **Solution:** Negotiate terms that ensure equal recognition and shared decision-making.
3. **Cultural Differences**
   - **Challenge:** Misaligned corporate cultures can lead to misunderstandings and inefficiencies.
   - **Solution:** Invest in joint training sessions and regular communication to foster a shared understanding.
4. **Dependency Risk**
   - **Challenge:** Over-reliance on a single partner can create vulnerabilities.
   - **Solution:** Diversify partnerships and develop internal capabilities to maintain independence.
5. **Regulatory Hurdles**

- **Challenge:** Navigating complex regulatory landscapes in new markets can be daunting.
- **Solution:** Leverage the partner's legal and compliance teams to ensure adherence to local regulations.

Scaling partnerships for broader impact is not just a growth strategy—it's a competitive necessity in the AI-driven world. AI startups can overcome market entry barriers by aligning with established partners, tapping into vast resources, and accelerating their journey toward global influence. However, achieving this requires a balance of collaboration, strategic planning, and adaptability.

The journey to scale for AI startups begins with choosing the right partners. It thrives on nurturing mutual trust and delivering shared value. And it culminates in creating a lasting impact, one market or industry at a time.

PART III

GROWTH AND BEYOND

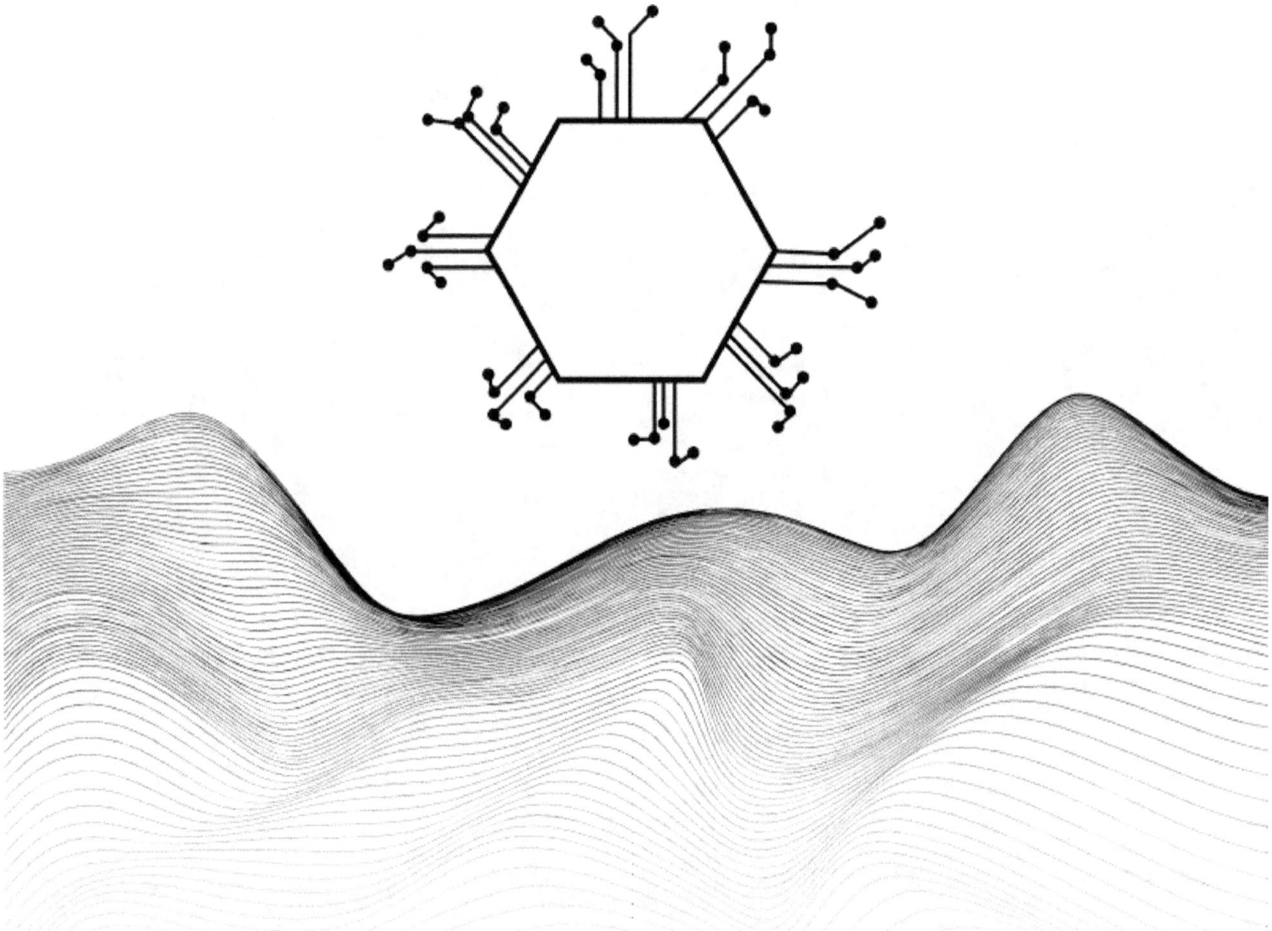

CHAPTER 7: BUILDING A VISION AND ROADMAP

INTRODUCTION

WHY VISION AND ROADMAP MATTER

Creating a vision and roadmap is crucial for any organization aiming to navigate the competitive landscape of modern business. Whether you're building an AI platform, launching a startup, or leading a product team in an established company, a well-defined vision and actionable roadmap provide the foundation for sustained success. This chapter explores the importance of crafting a compelling vision and a structured roadmap, offering actionable frameworks and tools to help you achieve your goals.

Why Vision Matters

Inspiring Teams

A strong vision is the emotional and intellectual core of any organization. It provides a sense of purpose that inspires and aligns teams, fostering a culture of motivation and collaboration. Without a compelling vision, teams may lack direction, leading to inefficiencies and reduced morale.

For example, consider the story of OpenAI. When the company was founded in 2015, its vision was clear: to ensure that artificial general intelligence (AGI) benefits all of humanity. This ambitious vision inspired its founding team and attracted world-class researchers and engineers passionate about making a meaningful impact. Over time, as OpenAI transitioned from a purely research-focused organization to a commercially viable enterprise with the launch of GPT models, its vision continued to evolve, maintaining its relevance and appeal. By clearly articulating its purpose, OpenAI fostered a sense of shared commitment among its team members, driving groundbreaking advancements in AI.

Attracting Investors

A clear, compelling vision can help startups and organizations seeking funding secure investor support. Investors are drawn to companies that articulate a bold yet achievable vision, demonstrating a deep understanding of market needs and the potential for significant returns. A well-crafted vision tells a story that resonates with investors, showcasing the organization's long-term potential and differentiation in the market.

Returning to OpenAI's example, the organization's vision was pivotal in attracting substantial investments from major stakeholders, including Microsoft. By emphasizing its mission to democratize

AI and create safe, beneficial technologies, OpenAI positioned itself as a leader in the field, appealing to investors who valued innovation and societal impact.

Guiding Growth

Vision acts as a strategic compass, guiding growth and decision-making. In the fast-paced world of technology and AI, where market demands and opportunities evolve rapidly, a strong vision helps organizations stay focused. It enables leaders to make consistent decisions that align with their overarching goals and values.

Take Tesla as another example. The company's vision of accelerating the world's transition to sustainable energy has driven its growth. This clear focus allowed Tesla to prioritize investments in electric vehicle technology, energy storage solutions, and renewable energy products, ensuring that every step it took contributed to its long-term mission.

Why Roadmaps Matter

While vision provides the destination, a roadmap outlines the journey. Even the most inspiring vision can falter without a detailed and actionable roadmap. A roadmap bridges the gap between ambition and execution, breaking down complex goals into manageable steps and ensuring alignment with market demands.

Turning Vision into Action

An actionable roadmap translates a lofty vision into specific, measurable, achievable milestones. It clarifies priorities, timelines, and resource allocation, enabling teams to work cohesively toward shared objectives. For instance, a company developing an AI-powered healthcare platform might envision revolutionizing patient diagnostics. The roadmap would detail the phases required to achieve this goal, such as building a prototype, conducting clinical trials, and scaling hospital deployment.

Adapting to Market Dynamics

A well-structured roadmap is not a static document. It evolves in response to market dynamics, technological advancements, and customer feedback. Organizations can remain agile and competitive by continuously revisiting and refining the roadmap. This adaptability is particularly crucial in the AI industry, where rapid innovation demands constant strategy recalibration.

Communicating with Stakeholders

A roadmap is a communication tool that aligns stakeholders, including team members, investors, and partners. Clearly outlining goals, timelines, and responsibilities ensures transparency and accountability. Stakeholders gain confidence in the organization's ability to execute its vision, fostering trust and collaboration.

Example: OpenAI's Journey from Research to Commercial Success

OpenAI's evolution exemplifies the importance of vision and roadmap in achieving organizational success. Initially, OpenAI's vision centered on conducting cutting-edge AI research to benefit humanity. However, as the organization identified opportunities to commercialize its technology, such as with GPT models, it developed a roadmap to achieve these new objectives.

1. **Vision:** OpenAI maintained its overarching mission of ensuring AGI benefits all of humanity but refined its focus to include practical applications of AI.

2. **Roadmap:**

    - **Phase 1:** Build foundational models (e.g., GPT-2) and release them for research.

    - **Phase 2:** Develop GPT-3, a more advanced language model, and launch it commercially via an API.

    - **Phase 3:** Form strategic partnerships (e.g., with Microsoft) to scale and integrate the technology into real-world applications.

By aligning its vision with a detailed roadmap, OpenAI successfully transitioned from a nonprofit research lab to a leader in the AI industry, demonstrating the power of strategic planning.

WHAT THIS CHAPTER OFFERS

Frameworks for Defining Vision

This chapter introduces frameworks to help you define an inspiring and actionable vision. Whether you are launching a new venture or reimagining an existing business, these frameworks will guide you in crafting a vision that resonates with your audience and aligns with your goals. Key components include:

- Characteristics of a strong vision: Ambitious yet realistic, user-focused, and forward-looking.

- Steps to articulate a vision that captures your unique value proposition.

- Examples of effective vision statements from leading organizations.

Setting Goals and Creating Actionable Roadmaps

Defining a vision is only the beginning. This chapter delves into setting goals and developing roadmaps that bring your vision to life. You will learn:

- Set SMART goals (Specific, Measurable, Achievable, Relevant, Time-bound).
- Techniques for breaking down long-term goals into actionable milestones.
- Tools for tracking progress and adapting to changes.

Aligning Roadmaps with Business Objectives

A roadmap is most effective when it aligns with your business objectives and market demands. This chapter provides practical tools and insights to ensure your roadmap supports key priorities such as revenue generation, user acquisition, and scalability. Topics include:

- Identifying target audiences and understanding their needs.
- Crafting a unique value proposition that differentiates your product or service.
- Prioritizing features and initiatives based on user feedback and market research.

What You Will Gain

By the end of this chapter, you will have the knowledge and tools to:

- Craft a vision statement that inspires and guides your organization.
- Set clear, actionable goals that align with your vision.
- Develop a phased roadmap to achieve your objectives.
- Adapt your strategy to changing market conditions and stakeholder expectations.

Whether you are an entrepreneur seeking to secure funding, a product manager driving innovation, or a leader aiming to inspire your team, this chapter will equip you with the skills to build a vision and roadmap that drives success.

7.1: DEFINING YOUR VISION

7.1.1 CRAFTING AN INSPIRING VISION

Crafting an inspiring vision is a cornerstone of successful leadership, strategic planning, and innovation. A well-defined vision sets the tone for organizational purpose, aligns stakeholders, and provides a roadmap for the future. This section delves into the characteristics of a strong vision and provides an illustrative example to contextualize its application.

CHARACTERISTICS OF A STRONG VISION

A compelling vision is not just a statement of aspirations—it's a beacon that guides decisions, motivates teams, and inspires stakeholder confidence.

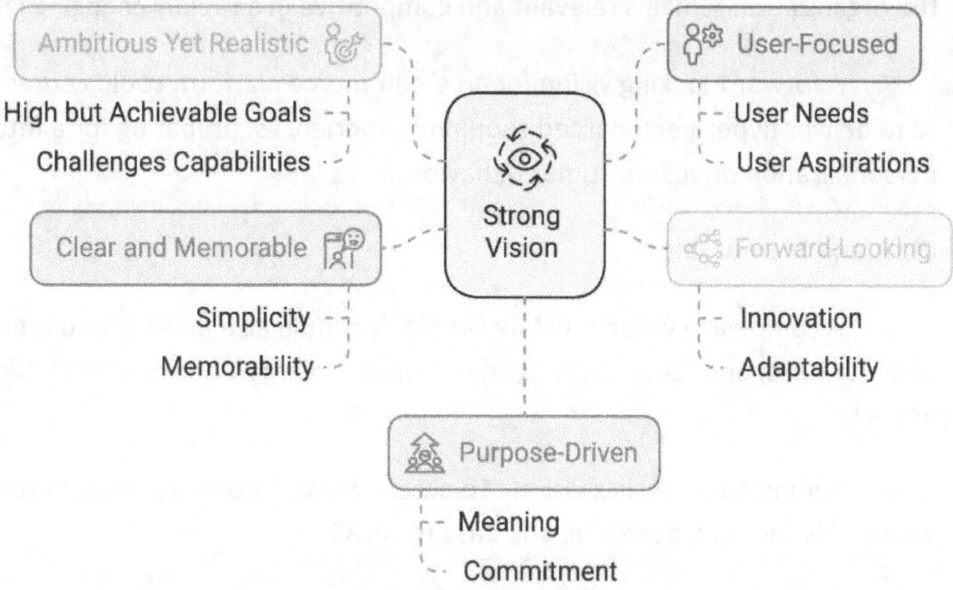

The following characteristics define a strong vision:

1. **Ambitious Yet Realistic**

    - An inspiring vision sets high but achievable goals. It should challenge the organization to stretch its capabilities while remaining grounded in reality. Overly ambitious visions risk being dismissed as unattainable, while overly cautious visions fail to ignite excitement or drive innovation.

    - For instance, a vision for a healthcare AI platform is to reduce global diagnostic errors by 50% within a decade. While ambitious, this goal is plausible with the right combination of technology, talent, and strategy.

2. **User-Focused**

    - A vision must prioritize the needs and aspirations of its target users. Understanding user pain points, desires, and challenges ensures the vision resonates with those it serves. This user-centricity not only builds trust but also drives product adoption and loyalty.

    - For example, a vision for an educational platform might focus on democratizing access to personalized learning for underserved communities. This directly addresses the user's core needs, fostering a sense of purpose and connection.

3. **Forward-Looking**

    - A vision must anticipate and embrace future trends, challenges, and opportunities. It should signal a commitment to innovation and adaptability, ensuring the organization remains relevant and competitive in a rapidly changing landscape.

    - A forward-looking vision for an e-commerce platform could center on leveraging AI to deliver hyper-personalized shopping experiences, preparing for a future where personalization drives consumer behavior.

4. **Clear and Memorable**

    - A compelling vision must be simple. It should also be easy to understand, communicate, and remember. Overly complex or jargon-heavy visions risk losing their impact.

    - For instance, Tesla's vision "To accelerate the world's transition to sustainable energy," is succinct, powerful, and easy to recall.

5. **Purpose-Driven**

    - A strong vision ties the organization's efforts to a larger purpose, evoking a sense of meaning and commitment. This connection to a higher purpose fosters motivation, alignment, and resilience.

    - For example, a fintech startup might envision "Empowering financial inclusion for the unbanked through AI-driven solutions," aligning its mission with a broader societal impact.

EXAMPLE VISION STATEMENT

To illustrate these principles, consider the following example vision for an AI platform:
"Empowering renewable energy optimization through AI-driven predictive analytics."

This vision embodies the characteristics of a strong vision:

1. **Ambitious Yet Realistic**

    - It aspires to significantly impact the renewable energy sector by enhancing optimization—a critical need in the era of climate change. At the same time, leveraging AI-driven predictive analytics is an achievable goal with current and emerging technologies.

2. **User-Focused**

- The vision addresses the needs of renewable energy stakeholders, such as operators, utilities, and policymakers. These stakeholders require innovative solutions to maximize efficiency, reduce costs, and meet sustainability goals.

3. **Forward-Looking**

   - By integrating AI and predictive analytics, the vision aligns with future trends in which data and technology play pivotal roles in transforming energy systems. It anticipates the growing importance of renewable energy and the need for scalable optimization solutions.

4. **Clear and Memorable**

   - The statement is concise, specific, and free of jargon. It communicates the essence of the platform's purpose without unnecessary complexity, making it easy for stakeholders to understand and support.

5. **Purpose-Driven**

   - The vision connects the platform's mission to the global imperative of transitioning to sustainable energy. This sense of purpose inspires commitment among team members, partners, and investors who share a passion for combating climate change.

HOW TO CRAFT AN INSPIRING VISION

Creating a vision that embodies these characteristics requires a structured approach:

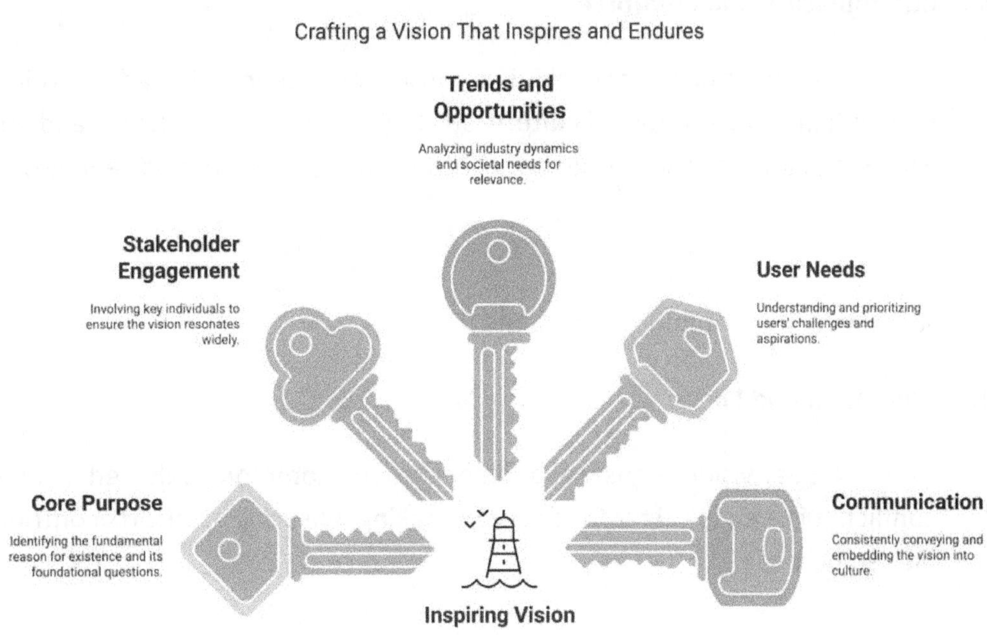

1. **Understand the Core Purpose**

    - Begin by identifying your organization or project's fundamental purpose. Why does it exist? Whom does it serve? What problems does it aim to solve? Clarity about these foundational questions provides the groundwork for a meaningful vision.

2. **Engage Stakeholders**

    - In the visioning process, involve key stakeholders—employees, users, partners, and investors. Their insights and perspectives ensure the vision resonates widely and reflects shared aspirations.

3. **Analyze Trends and Opportunities**

    - Conduct a thorough analysis of industry trends, emerging technologies, and societal needs. A vision that aligns with these dynamics will likely remain relevant and inspire action.

4. **Prioritize User Needs**

    - Use qualitative and quantitative methods to understand your users' challenges, expectations, and aspirations. A user-centered vision is more impactful and actionable.

5. **Refine and Simplify**

    - Craft an initial draft of the vision statement and refine it iteratively. Strive for simplicity, clarity, and focus. Avoid vague or overly broad language that dilutes the vision's power.

6. **Communicate and Reinforce**

    - A vision is only practical if it is consistently communicated and reinforced. Embed it into organizational culture, strategies, and actions. Revisit and update the vision regularly to ensure alignment with evolving priorities and realities.

BENEFITS OF AN INSPIRING VISION

A well-crafted vision delivers numerous benefits:

1. **Alignment and Focus**

    - A clear vision aligns stakeholders around common goals, reducing confusion and conflict. It is a guiding star for decision-making, ensuring all efforts contribute to a unified purpose.

2. **Motivation and Engagement**
   - An inspiring vision ignites passion and commitment among team members. It fosters a sense of belonging and purpose, boosting morale and productivity.
3. **Strategic Direction**
   - A vision provides a long-term perspective that informs strategies, investments, and priorities. It helps organizations navigate uncertainty and adapt to change without losing sight of their ultimate goals.
4. **Attracting Support**
   - A compelling vision attracts talent, investors, and partners who share the organization's aspirations. It builds credibility and trust, enhancing the organization's ability to secure resources and collaboration.
5. **Driving Innovation**
   - By setting ambitious goals, a strong vision encourages innovation and creativity. It challenges teams to think beyond current limitations and explore new possibilities.

Crafting an inspiring vision is both an art and a science. It requires a deep understanding of purpose, a clear focus on user needs, and a forward-looking perspective. When done effectively, a vision becomes a powerful tool for uniting stakeholders, driving innovation, and achieving lasting impact. The example vision for an AI platform, "Empowering renewable energy optimization through AI-driven predictive analytics," demonstrates how these principles can be applied to create a statement that resonates and inspires. By adhering to the characteristics outlined in this section, organizations can craft visions that articulate their aspirations, galvanize action, and transform possibilities into reality.

7.1.2 VISION AS A STRATEGIC COMPASS

A well-defined vision is an organization's strategic compass, providing clarity, purpose, and direction. It acts as a guiding force, aligning teams toward common objectives while attracting investors who share the organization's ambitions and values. Vision-driven companies often demonstrate exceptional resilience and innovation, creating value for stakeholders and achieving long-term success. This section explores how a clear vision unites teams and appeals to investors, using Tesla's commitment to autonomous driving as a real-world example of vision-driven leadership.

Aligning Teams through a Clear Vision

A clear vision creates a unified sense of purpose across an organization. It articulates the organization's long-term goals and defines the path to achieving them. This clarity empowers teams to focus their efforts and energies in the same direction, reducing inefficiencies caused by misaligned priorities. Employees who understand and connect with their organization's vision are more motivated and committed, leading to higher engagement and productivity.

Key mechanisms through which a clear vision aligns teams include:

1. **Unified Goals:** When an organization's vision is communicated, it provides a shared framework for decision-making. Teams understand how their roles contribute to broader objectives, fostering a sense of accountability and collaboration.

2. **Cultural Cohesion:** A compelling vision strengthens organizational culture by embedding shared values and beliefs. It creates a sense of belonging and inspires employees to work collectively toward a common purpose.

3. **Empowerment and Innovation:** A strong vision encourages employees to take initiative and contribute innovative ideas that align with the organization's goals. By understanding the bigger picture, team members feel empowered to solve problems and seize opportunities that advance the vision.

4. **Conflict Resolution:** Misalignments and conflicts are often mitigated when a shared vision guides teams. It provides a reference point for resolving disagreements, ensuring that decisions are consistent with organizational priorities.

Organizations with a clear and compelling vision achieve better team alignment and foster a sense of pride and inspiration among employees. This emotional connection drives sustained commitment and effort, enabling the organization to overcome challenges and maintain focus on its strategic objectives.

ATTRACTING INVESTORS WITH VISION

Investors are often drawn to organizations with bold, transformative visions. A clear vision signals ambition, long-term potential, and a commitment to creating value, making the organization an attractive investment opportunity. Vision-driven companies tend to differentiate themselves in competitive markets, gaining the attention and confidence of investors seeking impactful and innovative ventures.

Ways in which a clear vision attracts investors include:

1. **Clarity of Purpose:** A well-articulated vision communicates the organization's mission, goals, and strategies. This clarity helps investors understand the company's potential and the markets it aims to disrupt or dominate.

2. **Long-Term Perspective:** Vision-driven organizations demonstrate a focus on sustainable growth and innovation. Investors are more likely to support companies with a forward-looking perspective, as these organizations are better positioned to adapt to changing market conditions and emerging trends.

3. **Differentiation:** Companies with a strong vision often stand out from competitors by defining unique value propositions and ambitious goals. This distinctiveness makes them more appealing to investors who seek high-impact opportunities.

4. **Trust and Confidence:** A clear vision reflects strong leadership and strategic thinking, building trust and confidence among investors. Visionary leaders inspire belief in the organization's ability to execute its plans and achieve its objectives.

5. **Attracting Talent and Partnerships:** Visionary companies often attract top talent and strategic partnerships, further strengthening their value proposition. Investors recognize the synergy created by a motivated workforce and collaborative ecosystem, enhancing the organization's growth potential.

For investors, a compelling vision is more than an aspirational statement—it's a testament to the organization's commitment to innovation, resilience, and long-term value creation. Companies that articulate and execute their vision effectively are more likely to secure investment and achieve sustainable success.

VISION-DRIVEN LEADERSHIP AT TESLA

Under Elon Musk's leadership, Tesla exemplifies the power of vision as a strategic compass. The company's bold vision of advancing sustainable energy and achieving autonomous driving has revolutionized the automotive industry and inspired global innovation and investment.

The Vision: Sustainable Energy and Autonomy

Tesla's vision is rooted in the mission to "accelerate the world's transition to sustainable energy." This goal encompasses ambitious objectives, including developing electric vehicles (EVs), renewable energy solutions, and autonomous driving technology. By committing to these transformative goals, Tesla has positioned itself as a leader in the future of transportation and energy.

The vision of achieving fully autonomous driving exemplifies Tesla's commitment to innovation and disruption. Autonomous vehicles promise to redefine mobility by improving safety, reducing emissions, and enhancing efficiency. Tesla's vision-driven approach has galvanized its teams and captivated investors, fueling its growth and market leadership.

ALIGNING TEAMS AT TESLA

Tesla's vision has created an organization's culture of innovation and determination. Employees are driven by the belief that their work contributes to a sustainable future. The clarity and ambition of Tesla's vision have fostered the following:

1. **Cross-functional collaboration:** Engineering, software development, and manufacturing teams collaborate to achieve the vision of autonomy and sustainability. This collaboration has resulted in groundbreaking advancements, such as the development of Tesla's Autopilot and Full Self-Driving (FSD) features.

2. **Problem-Solving Mindset:** Pursuing ambitious goals has instilled in Tesla employees a mindset of resilience and ingenuity. Challenges are seen as opportunities to innovate and contribute to the vision.

3. **Employee Engagement:** Tesla's clear vision inspires employees to take pride in their work and its impact. This engagement has translated into higher productivity and a strong commitment to achieving organizational goals.

ATTRACTING INVESTORS TO TESLA

Tesla's vision has been instrumental in attracting investors who believe in its mission and growth potential. Key factors that have drawn investors include:

1. **Market Leadership:** Tesla's vision of sustainable energy and autonomous driving has positioned it as a pioneer in the EV market. Investors recognize the company's potential to dominate emerging industries and create significant value.

2. **Innovation and Differentiation:** Tesla's relentless focus on innovation has set it apart from competitors. Its vision-driven initiatives, from introducing advanced battery technology to rolling out autonomous driving features, have captured investor interest and confidence.

3. **Visionary Leadership:** Elon Musk's ability to articulate and execute Tesla's vision has been a critical factor in attracting investment. His leadership inspires trust and belief in Tesla's potential to achieve its ambitious goals.

4. **Long-Term Value Creation:** Investors are drawn to Tesla's commitment to sustainability and technological progress, which align with global trends and future market demands. Tesla's vision-driven strategy emphasizes long-term value creation, appealing to forward-thinking investors.

A clear and compelling vision is a powerful tool for organizations, serving as a strategic compass that aligns teams and attracts investors. By defining ambitious goals and fostering a shared sense of purpose, a strong vision empowers organizations to innovate, differentiate, and achieve sustainable success. Tesla's journey exemplifies the transformative impact of vision-driven leadership, demonstrating how a commitment to bold objectives can unite teams, inspire investors, and revolutionize industries. As organizations navigate an increasingly complex and competitive landscape, a clear vision remains essential to resilience, innovation, and growth.

7.1.3 COMMON MISTAKES IN VISION STATEMENTS

Vision statements serve as a guiding star for organizations, encapsulating their aspirations and the future they strive to create. However, crafting an effective vision statement is not without challenges. Common mistakes can undermine the purpose and clarity of the vision, rendering it ineffective. Below, we explore key pitfalls such as overpromising, lack of focus, and failing to address market needs. Additionally, we compare poorly crafted vision statements with impactful ones to illustrate these points.

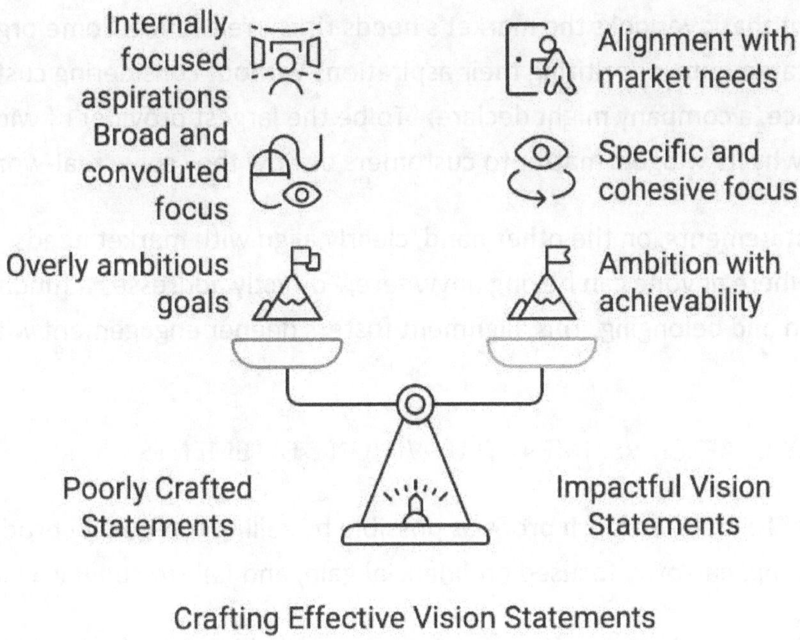

Overpromising

One of the most frequent mistakes in vision statements is overpromising. In an attempt to inspire and captivate stakeholders, organizations sometimes set unrealistic or overly ambitious goals. For instance, a startup in the renewable energy sector might declare, “We will eliminate all global reliance on fossil fuels within five years.” While noble, such a statement is impractical given technological, financial, and political constraints. Overpromising can damage credibility and lead to disillusionment when goals are not met.

Conversely, an impactful vision statement balances ambition with achievability. Consider Tesla’s vision: “To create the most compelling car company of the 21st century by driving the world’s transition to electric vehicles.” This statement is aspirational yet grounded, aligning with the company’s capabilities and long-term objectives.

Lack of Focus

Another common issue is a lack of focus. Vision statements that attempt to address too many ideas simultaneously become convoluted and fail to convey a clear purpose. For example, a company might state, “We aim to revolutionize technology, provide unmatched customer service, lead in sustainability, and create a better future for all.” While well-intentioned, this vision is overly broad and lacks a cohesive direction.

In contrast, focused vision statements resonate more strongly. Microsoft’s vision, “To empower every person and every organization on the planet to achieve more,” is a prime example. It captures a broad yet specific ambition that guides the company’s strategy and actions.

Failing to Address Market Needs

A vision statement that overlooks the market's needs risks irrelevance. Some organizations create internally focused statements, prioritizing their aspirations without considering customer or societal demands. For instance, a company might declare, "To be the largest provider of widgets globally," without addressing why its widgets matter to customers or how they solve real-world problems.

Impactful vision statements, on the other hand, clearly align with market needs. Airbnb's vision, "To create a world where anyone can belong anywhere," directly addresses a fundamental human desire for connection and belonging. This alignment fosters deeper engagement with customers and stakeholders.

EXAMPLES: POORLY CRAFTED VS. IMPACTFUL VISION STATEMENTS

Poorly Crafted: • "To make as much profit as possible by selling top-quality products." This statement is uninspiring, narrowly focused on financial gain, and fails to convey a larger purpose.

Impactful: • "To bring inspiration and innovation to every athlete* in the world." (Nike) Nike's vision is broad yet specific, emphasizing inspiration and innovation while subtly including everyone ("If you have a body, you are an athlete").

By avoiding overpromising, maintaining focus, and addressing market needs, organizations can craft vision statements that are both aspirational and actionable. Such statements inspire internal teams and resonate with customers, investors, and other stakeholders, laying a solid foundation for long-term success.

7.2: SETTING GOALS AND OBJECTIVES

7.2.1 THE IMPORTANCE OF SMART GOALS

Characteristics of SMART Goals

SMART goals stand out because they transform abstract ideas into actionable plans. Let's examine each characteristic in detail:

1. **Specific**
   A goal must clearly define what is to be achieved. Ambiguity can lead to confusion, misaligned efforts, and failure to reach the intended outcome. A specific goal answers questions such as:

   - What exactly needs to be accomplished?
   - Who is involved?
   - Where will this take place?

- Why is this goal important?

Example: Instead of setting a vague goal like "improve customer satisfaction," a specific goal would be to "achieve a 10% increase in customer satisfaction scores for our AI platform by addressing support ticket response times."

2. **Measurable**

Quantifiable metrics must be used to track progress and determine when a goal has been achieved. Measurement provides clarity and motivation and ensures accountability.

Key Questions:

- How will progress be measured?
- What are the benchmarks for success?

Example: For a goal to "expand AI platform user engagement," measurable criteria could include increasing the average daily active users (DAUs) by 20% within six months.

3. **Achievable**

Given available resources, skills, and constraints, goals should challenge individuals or teams but remain realistic. Setting unattainable goals can lead to frustration and disengagement, while overly easy goals may fail to inspire growth.

Key Questions:

- Is this goal realistic, given the current resources?
- Does it align with team capabilities?

Example: Instead of aiming to "double AI platform revenue in one month," a more achievable target might be to "increase monthly subscription revenue by 15% within three months through targeted marketing campaigns."

4. **Relevant**

A goal should align with broader objectives, contributing to the overarching mission or vision. Relevance ensures that time and resources are directed toward meaningful endeavors.

Key Questions:

- Does this goal align with organizational priorities?
- Will achieving this goal make a significant impact?

Example: A relevant goal for an AI platform might be to "launch a new feature that improves user productivity by 20%" rather than unrelated initiatives like redesigning the logo.

5. **Time-bound**

Goals need deadlines to create a sense of urgency and drive action. Without a timeline, the endpoint is unclear, leading to procrastination and a lack of focus.

Key Questions:

- What is the deadline for achieving the goal?
- Are there milestones along the way?

Example: A time-bound goal could be to "reduce AI platform churn rate by 10% within the next six months through personalized user onboarding."

THE POWER OF SMART GOALS IN ACTION

The beauty of the SMART framework lies in its versatility. It can be applied to personal aspirations, team initiatives, and organizational strategies. This approach allows individuals and organizations to translate abstract ambitions into well-defined action plans.

Example: "Increase AI Platform User Retention by 25% Within 12 Months"

Let's analyze this example through the SMART framework:

1. **Specific**: The goal specifies what needs to be achieved—"increase user retention"—and identifies the subject (AI platform users).

2. **Measurable**: The objective quantifies the desired outcome, with a 25% increase as a clear benchmark.

3. **Achievable**: A 25% increase within 12 months is an ambitious yet realistic target, assuming strategies like user experience improvements or customer loyalty programs are implemented.

4. **Relevant**: Retention is a critical metric for SaaS platforms, impacting revenue and customer lifetime value.

5. **Time-bound**: The 12-month deadline ensures a focused timeline for achieving this goal.

Benefits of SMART Goals

1. **Clarity and Focus**

SMART goals eliminate ambiguity, providing a clear roadmap for success. This clarity helps individuals and teams prioritize tasks and align efforts with strategic objectives.

2. **Motivation and Accountability**

By defining measurable and time-bound outcomes, SMART goals create a sense of urgency and purpose. Regular progress tracking fosters accountability, keeping individuals and teams on track.

3. **Improved Decision-Making**

A well-defined goal allows for better decision-making, as actions can be evaluated against their contribution to the desired outcome. Resources are allocated more effectively, reducing waste and inefficiency.

4. **Enhanced Performance**

SMART goals encourage individuals to stretch their capabilities while maintaining realism. The structured approach promotes focus, discipline, and productivity.

5. **Alignment and Collaboration**

In organizational settings, SMART goals foster alignment by ensuring everyone works toward shared objectives. This alignment enhances collaboration and reduces conflicts arising from unclear priorities.

PRACTICAL STEPS TO IMPLEMENT SMART GOALS

1. **Define the Goal**

Start with a broad objective and refine it using the SMART framework. Ensure it is specific, measurable, achievable, relevant, and time-bound.

2. **Engage Stakeholders**

Involve key stakeholders to ensure buy-in and alignment. Collaboration during goal-setting increases commitment and provides diverse perspectives are considered.

3. **Break Down the Goal**

Divide the goal into smaller milestones or tasks. These incremental steps make the goal less overwhelming and enable steady progress.

4. **Track Progress**

Use metrics, dashboards, or periodic reviews to monitor progress. Celebrate milestones to maintain momentum and motivation.

5. **Adjust as Needed**

Flexibility is essential. If circumstances change or unexpected challenges arise, revisit and adjust the goal without compromising its SMART integrity.

THE RISKS OF NOT SETTING SMART GOALS

Failing to use the SMART framework can lead to several challenges:

- **Lack of Direction**: Ambiguous goals result in scattered efforts and reduced productivity.
- **Inconsistent Progress**: Without measurable criteria, tracking success becomes impossible.
- **Wasted Resources**: Time, money, and energy may be misallocated to irrelevant or unrealistic pursuits.
- **Low Morale**: Unclear or unattainable goals can demotivate teams, leading to disengagement and burnout.

For example, a vague goal like "make the AI platform better" lacks specificity, measurement, and a timeline. Without these elements, it's unclear what success looks like or how to achieve it. In contrast, a SMART goal provides a clear path forward.

7.2.2 BREAKING DOWN LONG-TERM GOALS INTO MILESTONES

Long-term goals, often spanning several years, provide a sense of direction and purpose. However, their broad and abstract nature can make them intimidating and difficult to act upon. Individuals and organizations can create a structured path toward success by breaking these goals into smaller, actionable milestones. This approach allows for better tracking progress, adjusting strategies as needed, and maintaining motivation throughout the journey. This section explores how to effectively split a five-year vision into phased objectives and ensure consistent progress toward achieving ambitious goals.

THE IMPORTANCE OF MILESTONES

Milestones act as measurable checkpoints that break a long-term goal into manageable pieces. They provide clarity by defining specific achievements required to reach the ultimate objective. Additionally, milestones:

- **Encourage Focus:** By concentrating on one phase at a time, milestones prevent overwhelming feelings and help maintain clarity.
- **Enable Measurement:** Milestones offer tangible results to assess progress, identify potential issues, and celebrate achievements.
- **Facilitate Adaptability:** Regular evaluation of milestones allows adjustments to align with shifting circumstances or priorities.

- **Boost Motivation:** Celebrating small successes keeps morale high and sustains momentum.

HOW TO SPLIT A 5-YEAR VISION INTO ACTIONABLE, PHASED OBJECTIVES

Dividing a five-year goal into actionable steps requires a structured framework considering the end goal, resource availability, and potential challenges. Here are key steps to break down a long-term vision into phased milestones:

1. Define the End Goal

Start by articulating the long-term vision with precision. The more specific the goal, the easier it is to break it into smaller components. For example, instead of stating, "Build a successful AI platform," specify, "Develop an AI-driven platform that captures 20% market share in the retail analytics space by 2029."

2. Identify Key Phases

Divide the goal into broad phases or stages representing logical progress toward the final objective. Each phase should address a specific aspect of the goal—such as ideation, development, marketing, or scaling. These phases should build upon one another and align with the ultimate vision.

3. Establish SMART Milestones

Each phase should have milestones that are Specific, Measurable, Achievable, Relevant, and Time-bound (SMART). For instance, a milestone like "Launch a beta version by Q2 2026" is more actionable than "Work on product development."

4. Assign Timelines

Allocate realistic timelines to each phase. Consider dependencies between phases and factor in buffers for unexpected delays. While timelines provide structure, they should remain flexible to accommodate unforeseen changes.

5. Align Resources

Ensure that the necessary resources—such as funding, personnel, technology, and partnerships—are available for each phase. Adjust milestones to reflect resource availability.

6. Create Feedback Loops

Establish mechanisms to review progress at the end of each milestone. Use these reviews to evaluate outcomes, gather insights, and refine subsequent phases. Feedback loops ensure that the journey remains aligned with the ultimate goal.

7. Celebrate Achievements

Recognizing and celebrating milestone completions boosts morale and reinforces commitment to the long-term goal.

EXAMPLE: BREAKING DOWN A FIVE-YEAR VISION

Goal: Build a successful AI-driven platform that transforms retail analytics and captures 20% market share by 2029.

1. **Phase 1: Ideation and Research (Year 1)**
   - **Milestone 1:** Conduct market research to identify pain points and opportunities in retail analytics (Q1).
   - **Milestone 2:** Define the platform's value proposition and unique differentiators (Q2).
   - **Milestone 3:** Create a technical feasibility study and outline the technology stack (Q3).
   - **Milestone 4:** Secure seed funding of $500,000 to develop the Minimum Viable Product (MVP) (Q4).
2. **Phase 2: Build the MVP (Year 2)**
   - **Milestone 1:** Assemble a cross-functional development team (Q1).
   - **Milestone 2:** Develop core features of the platform, including predictive analytics and user dashboards (Q2).
   - **Milestone 3:** Launch a closed beta version and gather user feedback (Q3).
   - **Milestone 4:** Refine the MVP based on beta feedback and prepare for public launch (Q4).

3. **Phase 3: Launch in a Target Market (Years 3–4)**
   - **Milestone 1:** Develop a go-to-market strategy targeting mid-sized retailers (Q1, Year 3).
   - **Milestone 2:** Launch the platform in the target market and onboard 10 pilot clients (Q2, Year 3).
   - **Milestone 3:** Gather and analyze client data to demonstrate ROI and refine the offering (Q3, Year 3).
   - **Milestone 4:** Expand marketing efforts to acquire 50 paying clients (Q4, Year 3).
   - **Milestone 5:** Achieve $1M in annual recurring revenue (ARR) (Q4, Year 4).
4. **Phase 4: Expansion into Adjacent Industries (Years 4–5)**
   - **Milestone 1:** Conduct market research to identify high-potential adjacent industries (Q1, Year 4).
   - **Milestone 2:** Adapt the platform for new industry use cases (Q2, Year 4).
   - **Milestone 3:** Partner with key players in the new industry to accelerate adoption (Q3, Year 4).
   - **Milestone 4:** Achieve 20% market share in retail analytics and 10% in the new industry (Q4, Year 5).

BENEFITS OF BREAKING DOWN LONG-TERM GOALS

- **Improved Focus and Organization:** Clear phases and milestones streamline efforts, reducing distractions.
- **Risk Mitigation:** Milestones help identify risks early, allowing for timely intervention.
- **Enhanced Collaboration:** Defined objectives improve communication and coordination among team members.
- **Sustained Momentum:** Achieving short-term goals keeps motivation high and builds confidence.

CHALLENGES AND SOLUTIONS

While breaking down goals into milestones is practical, specific challenges may arise:

1. **Overly Ambitious Milestones:** Setting unrealistic milestones can lead to frustration and burnout.

- **Solution:** Use the SMART criteria to ensure goals are achievable.

2. **Lack of Flexibility:** Rigid plans may not account for unforeseen circumstances.
   - **Solution:** Build flexibility into timelines and periodically review progress.
3. **Insufficient Resources:** Resource constraints can hinder progress.
   - **Solution:** Plan resources meticulously and seek external support, such as partnerships or funding, when needed.
4. **Poorly Defined Milestones:** Vague or ambiguous milestones can confuse.
   - **Solution:** Use clear, measurable criteria for each milestone.

Breaking down long-term goals into actionable milestones transforms ambitious visions into achievable realities. By following a structured approach—defining clear phases, setting SMART objectives, and ensuring adaptability—individuals and organizations can maintain focus, track progress, and sustain momentum. Milestones simplify complex goals and empower teams to celebrate small wins, fostering a culture of continuous achievement and progress.

7.2.3 TRACKING PROGRESS AND ADJUSTING GOALS

Effective goal management relies on consistent tracking and timely adjustments to meet objectives, particularly in complex or rapidly changing environments. Tracking progress provides insight into current performance and informs the necessary adjustments to stay aligned with organizational priorities. This section explores practical tools for monitoring goal achievement, including OKRs (Objectives and Key Results) and Gantt charts or road mapping software.

TOOLS FOR MONITORING GOAL ACHIEVEMENT

OKRs (Objectives and Key Results)

OKRs are a framework that enables teams and organizations to define measurable goals (objectives) and track their achievement through specific, quantifiable outcomes (key results). The framework offers several advantages:

1. **Clarity and Alignment**: OKRs ensure that everyone within the organization understands the priorities and how their work contributes to broader objectives. By aligning individual and team goals with organizational strategies, OKRs create a unified direction.
2. **Measurability**: Each key result is designed to be measurable, making it easy to assess progress. For example, an objective might be to "Improve customer satisfaction," with key results such as "Increase Net Promoter Score (NPS) from 70 to 85" or "Reduce average response time for customer inquiries from 12 hours to 4 hours."

3. **Focus and Agility**: OKRs encourage ambitious yet achievable goals while allowing adaptability. Quarterly reviews help teams reassess priorities, making pivoting or adjusting key results easier based on new developments.

4. **Accountability**: Regular check-ins and progress reviews foster a culture of accountability. Transparency across teams ensures everyone knows who is responsible for what, minimizing overlap or confusion.

Tools like **Asana**, **Google Workspace**, and specialized OKR software such as **Ally.io** or **Weekdone** streamline the OKR process, enabling real-time tracking, collaboration, and reporting.

GANTT CHARTS OR ROADMAPPING SOFTWARE

Gantt charts and road mapping software are visual tools that provide a clear timeline for goal-related tasks and milestones. Thus, they are invaluable for tracking progress in complex projects.

1. **Gantt Charts**:

    - Gantt charts visually represent tasks, timelines, and dependencies, making it easy to see how individual activities contribute to overarching goals.

    - Tools like **Microsoft Project**, **Smartsheet**, or **Trello** allow for dynamic adjustments, where changes in one task automatically update the dependent timelines, ensuring accuracy.

    - They are handy for tracking project progress, determining deadlines, and identifying bottlenecks.

2. **Roadmapping Software**:

    - Unlike Gantt charts, road mapping software focuses on strategic timelines rather than granular task management. This makes it ideal for setting long-term goals and tracking progress at a higher level.

    - Tools such as **Aha!**, **ProductPlan**, and **Roadmunk** offer real-time features for creating, sharing, and updating in real-time, ensuring all stakeholders can access the latest version.

    - Roadmaps can include milestones, deliverables, and dependencies, providing a holistic view of the project lifecycle.

THE ROLE OF TRACKING IN GOAL ADJUSTMENT

While monitoring tools like OKRs and Gantt charts provide insights into progress, they also highlight areas where goals may need to be adjusted. Adjustments may occur for several reasons:

- **Shift in Priorities**: Market conditions or organizational strategy changes may require reallocating resources or redefining objectives.
- **Unforeseen Challenges**: Delays, resource shortages, or external disruptions might necessitate revising timelines or scaling down goals.
- **Opportunities for Innovation**: Progress tracking may uncover opportunities to improve or expand on initial goals, prompting adjustments to capitalize on new insights.

Regular progress reviews and stakeholder check-ins are crucial to ensure that adjustments are made thoughtfully and aligned with overarching strategies.

Conclusion

Tracking progress and adjusting goals is a dynamic process essential for sustained success. By leveraging OKRs for alignment and clarity and using Gantt charts or road mapping software for detailed planning and tracking, organizations can remain agile and responsive to opportunities and challenges.

7.3: DEVELOPING A STRATEGY

7.3.1 IDENTIFYING TARGET AUDIENCES

Identifying target audiences is a fundamental step in ensuring the success of any product, service, or platform. It involves understanding who your users are, their needs, preferences, and behaviors, as well as how they interact with your offerings. This process is especially critical in markets where user needs vary widely, such as in industries driven by technology, education, or healthcare.

UNDERSTANDING USER NEEDS IN SPECIFIC MARKETS

A clear grasp of user needs is the cornerstone of identifying and effectively targeting an audience. Each market segment has unique requirements shaped by its users' goals, challenges, and contexts. Understanding these nuances enables businesses to tailor their solutions and messages to resonate with their intended audience.

For example, consider STEM (Science, Technology, Engineering, and Mathematics) researchers. These professionals often grapple with vast datasets, requiring efficient analysis, visualization, and collaboration tools. AI tools designed for data analysis are highly relevant for this group. However, simply offering generic AI tools may not suffice. To meet their needs effectively, the tools must be:

1. **Specialized:** Equipped with domain-specific algorithms and features, such as bioinformatics modules for life sciences or simulation tools for engineering.
2. **Accessible:** Easy to integrate into their existing workflows, such as compatibility with programming languages like Python or R.

3. **Collaborative:** Supporting multi-user environments for teams to share data and insights.

4. **Scalable:** Capable of handling datasets of varying sizes and complexities.

By recognizing these specific needs, a provider can create AI tools that address these pain points and foster loyalty and advocacy among STEM researchers. This principle of aligning product features with user needs applies across industries, whether targeting creative professionals, educators, or healthcare providers.

TOOLS FOR AUDIENCE SEGMENTATION

Audience segmentation divides a broad market into smaller, more manageable groups based on shared characteristics. This process helps businesses focus on the most relevant groups, maximizing efficiency and impact. Personas and user journey mapping are widely used tools for effective audience segmentation.

Personas

Personas are fictional yet data-driven representations of key audience segments. They encapsulate users' attributes, behaviors, and goals, providing a humanized lens to view target audiences. When creating personas, the following elements are typically included:

1. **Demographics:** Age, gender, education, occupation, and other socio-economic indicators.

2. **Psychographics:** Interests, values, attitudes, and lifestyle choices.

3. **Behavioral Traits:** Buying habits, technology usage, and interaction preferences.

4. **Pain Points and Goals:** Challenges the user faces and what they aim to achieve with your solution.

For example, a persona for a STEM researcher might be described as follows:

- **Name:** Dr. Emily Carter

- **Occupation:** Data Scientist in Environmental Research

- **Demographics:** 35 years old, PhD in Applied Mathematics, based in San Francisco

- **Behaviors:** Regularly uses Python for data modeling, attends AI conferences, and reads scientific journals.

- **Pain Points:** Time-consuming data cleaning and lack of accessible tools for visualizing multi-dimensional datasets.

- **Goals:** Increase research efficiency, publish findings faster, and collaborate with interdisciplinary teams.

Businesses can better anticipate user needs, preferences, and expectations by creating detailed personas like Dr. Carter, ensuring their offerings are relevant and appealing.

User Journey Mapping

User journey mapping visualizes the end-to-end experience of a user interacting with a product or service. It highlights key touchpoints, emotions, and potential friction points. This tool is invaluable for identifying opportunities to enhance the user experience.

To create a user journey map, consider the following steps:

1. **Define the Stages:** Identify the key stages in the user's journey, such as awareness, consideration, decision, onboarding, and retention.

2. **Map User Actions:** Document the actions users take at each stage, such as researching a product, signing up, or seeking customer support.

3. **Capture Emotions:** Note how users feel at each stage—excited, confused, frustrated, or satisfied.

4. **Identify Pain Points:** Pinpoint areas where users encounter obstacles or dissatisfaction.

5. **Recommend Improvements:** Suggest ways to streamline processes, address challenges, and enhance positive experiences.

For example, a user journey map for STEM researchers using an AI data analysis platform might include the following stages:

- **Awareness:** Dr. Carter learns about the platform through an AI conference.
    - *Emotion:* Curious but cautious.
    - *Pain Point:* Lack of detailed information on capabilities.
- **Consideration:** Dr. Carter visits the website and watches demo videos.
    - *Emotion:* Growing interest.
    - *Pain Point:* Difficulty finding information on pricing and integrations.
- **Decision:** Dr. Carter signs up for a free trial.
    - *Emotion:* Hopeful.

- *Pain Point:* Complex registration process.

- **Onboarding:** Dr. Carter explores the platform and uploads a sample dataset.
  - *Emotion:* Initial satisfaction but slightly overwhelmed by the interface.
  - *Pain Point:* Limited guidance on advanced features.

- **Retention:** Dr. Carter integrates the platform into her workflow and subscribes to a premium plan.
  - *Emotion:* Loyal and confident.
  - *Pain Point:* Occasional delays in customer support.

Addressing the pain points identified in the journey map can help the platform provider refine its marketing, onboarding, and support processes, improving user satisfaction and retention.

INTEGRATING TOOLS AND INSIGHTS

Combining personas and user journey mapping offers a powerful approach to audience segmentation. While personas provide a deep understanding of who your users are, journey maps reveal how they interact with your offerings. Together, these tools inform decisions about product design, marketing strategies, and customer engagement initiatives.

For instance, insights from Dr. Carter's persona and journey map might lead to the following actions:

1. **Content Creation:** Developing blog posts and webinars on using AI for environmental data analysis.

2. **Product Enhancements:** Simplify the interface and offer templates for typical data analysis tasks.

3. **Customer Support:** Introducing a live chat feature for faster assistance.

4. **Marketing Campaigns:** Running targeted ads at AI conferences and in scientific journals.

Conclusion

Identifying target audiences requires market research, empathy, and analytical tools. By understanding user needs and employing tools like personas and user journey mapping, businesses can create offerings that resonate deeply with their intended audiences. This approach improves user satisfaction and loyalty and drives business success by ensuring that resources are focused where they yield the highest impact.

In today's competitive landscape, crafting a compelling and unique value proposition (UVP) is essential for businesses to differentiate themselves, address customer pain points, and establish a strong market presence. A well-crafted UVP succinctly communicates the unique benefits and value a product or service offers, convincing potential customers why they should choose it over competitors.

Highlighting Differentiation and Addressing Pain Points

The foundation of an effective UVP lies in understanding and articulating differentiation. This involves identifying what sets a product or service apart from competitors and emphasizing those unique attributes in a way that resonates with the target audience. Beyond differentiation, a UVP must directly address customer pain points, demonstrating how the offering solves a critical problem or satisfies a significant need.

Consider the example of a UVP in the genomics industry: "Faster and more accurate genomic analysis using AI." This proposition highlights a clear benefit—speed and accuracy—while addressing a pain point for researchers and healthcare professionals who struggle with traditional genomic analysis methods' time-consuming and error-prone nature. The product offers a transformative, innovative, and practical solution leveraging AI.

Another example is e-commerce: "Personalized shopping experiences with AI-driven recommendations." This UVP showcases differentiation through advanced technology while addressing the pain point of irrelevant product suggestions that frustrate shoppers. The proposition appeals to consumers seeking convenience and a tailored experience by emphasizing personalization and AI integration.

To craft a UVP that effectively highlights differentiation and addresses pain points, businesses must:

1. **Understand Their Audience:** Gain deep insights into the target market's needs, preferences, and pain points.

2. **Analyze Competitors:** Identify gaps or opportunities in the market where the business can excel.

3. **Leverage Strengths:** Focus on unique capabilities, features, or technologies that provide a competitive edge.

4. **Communicate Benefits Clearly:** Use simple, concise language to articulate how the offering solves a specific problem or meets a particular need.

5. **Evoke Emotion:** Appeal to the audience's desires, aspirations, or frustrations to create a stronger connection.

Real-World Examples of Effective UVPs

Several businesses have demonstrated the power of a strong UVP through real-world success stories. These examples illustrate how clear and compelling messaging can drive customer engagement and loyalty.

1. **Slack: "Be More Productive at Work with Less Effort"** Slack's UVP emphasizes improved productivity and ease of use, addressing the common workplace pain point of inefficient communication. The proposition highlights Slack's ability to streamline collaboration through intuitive tools, reducing the need for lengthy email chains and enabling faster decision-making. Slack successfully differentiates itself in the crowded team communication space by focusing on the tangible benefit of productivity.

2. **Zoom: "The #1 Video Conferencing Solution That Just Works"** Zoom's UVP underscores reliability and simplicity, tackling the frustration of technical glitches and complex user interfaces in traditional video conferencing solutions. "just works" conveys ease and dependability, appealing to professionals and organizations seeking hassle-free virtual communication. This straightforward messaging helped Zoom dominate the market during the COVID-19 pandemic.

3. **Dollar Shave Club: "A Great Shave for a Few Bucks a Month"** Dollar Shave Club's UVP disrupts the shaving industry by offering high-quality razors at an affordable price. It addresses the pain point of overpriced grooming products. The proposition appeals to cost-conscious consumers while emphasizing convenience through a subscription model. Its witty and relatable marketing further reinforces the brand's differentiation.

4. **Apple iPhone: "The Ultimate Device for Everything"** Apple's UVP for the iPhone positions it as an all-in-one device that seamlessly integrates cutting-edge technology, design, and functionality. This messaging highlights differentiation through innovation and addresses the pain point of fragmented device ecosystems. By consistently delivering on its promise, Apple has built a loyal customer base and maintained its market leadership.

5. **Spotify: "Music for Everyone"** Spotify's UVP emphasizes accessibility and inclusivity, resonating with a diverse audience seeking personalized music experiences. By addressing the pain point of limited choices in traditional radio or physical media, Spotify differentiates itself through on-demand streaming, curated playlists, and a vast library of content. The simplicity of the phrase "Music for Everyone" reinforces its universal appeal.

6. **Tesla: "Accelerating the World's Transition to Sustainable Energy"** Tesla's UVP reflects its mission-driven approach, highlighting its role in promoting sustainability through innovative electric vehicles and energy solutions. This proposition addresses environmental concerns and positions Tesla as a pioneer in the clean energy space, appealing to eco-conscious consumers and investors. The focus on sustainability and innovation sets Tesla apart from traditional automakers.

Creating a UVP that resonates with the audience requires a strategic and iterative process.

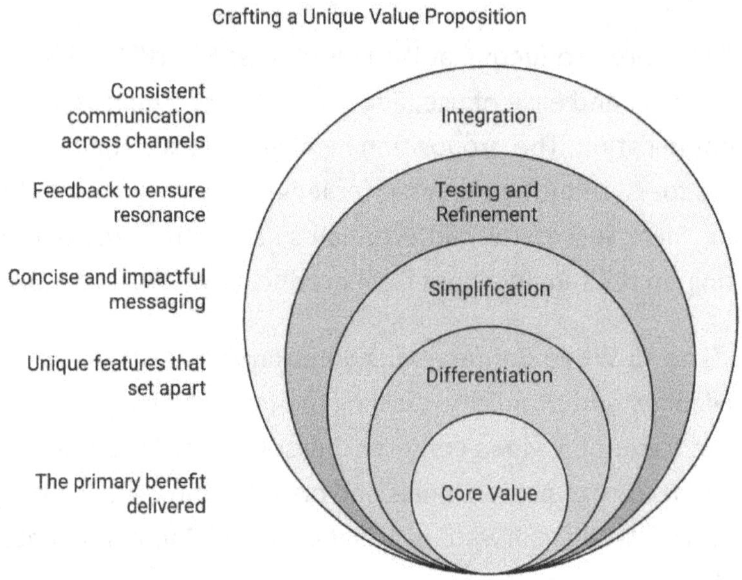

Here are actionable steps to develop a compelling proposition:

1. **Define the Core Value:** Identify the primary benefit or outcome the product or service delivers.

2. **Differentiate Clearly:** Highlight unique features, capabilities, or approaches that competitors do not offer.

3. **Simplify the Message:** Use concise and impactful language to communicate the value.

4. **Test and Refine:** Gather feedback from stakeholders and potential customers to ensure the UVP resonates and addresses key pain points.

5. **Integrate Across Channels:** Ensure the UVP is consistently communicated in marketing materials, sales pitches, and customer interactions.

A strong UVP is a cornerstone of business success, enabling companies to stand out in competitive markets, address customer pain points effectively, and build lasting relationships with their audience. Businesses can create UVPs that resonate profoundly and drive meaningful engagement by focusing on differentiation, clarity, and relevance. Real-world examples from industry leaders like Slack, Zoom, and Tesla demonstrate the transformative impact of well-crafted propositions. Ultimately, a compelling UVP is not just a statement but a promise that aligns with the company's vision and delivers tangible value to its customers.

7.3.3 DEFINING COMPETITIVE ADVANTAGES

In the highly competitive landscape of modern business, identifying and leveraging competitive advantages is essential for success. Competitive advantages are the unique strengths or assets that distinguish an organization from its competitors, enabling it to deliver superior value to its customers. These advantages must be significant and challenging to replicate and align with the organization's strategic objectives and market demands.

LEVERAGING UNIQUE STRENGTHS

Organizations derive competitive advantages from a variety of unique strengths. These strengths often fall into three primary categories: proprietary data, advanced algorithms, and exceptional customer service.

Proprietary Data

Proprietary data refers to unique datasets that an organization exclusively owns or has access to, providing a critical edge in decision-making and strategy formulation. Companies with proprietary data can:

- Develop highly personalized customer experiences.
- Create more accurate predictive models.
- Establish barriers to entry for competitors who lack equivalent data access.

For example, streaming platforms like Netflix leverage proprietary viewing data to recommend content tailored to individual user preferences, creating a distinctive customer experience that competitors struggle to replicate.

Advanced Algorithms

Advanced algorithms are another cornerstone of competitive advantage, particularly in industries driven by artificial intelligence and machine learning. Algorithms enable organizations to:

- Automate complex processes efficiently.
- Analyze large volumes of data for actionable insights.
- Optimize operations for cost-effectiveness and performance.

Consider Google's search algorithm, which processes billions of queries daily while delivering highly relevant results. This algorithm, continuously refined through proprietary data and machine learning, sets Google apart as a leader in the search engine market.

Exceptional Customer Service

While technology often takes center stage, exceptional customer service remains a powerful differentiator. Businesses that prioritize customer-centric approaches can:

- Foster long-term customer loyalty.
- Generate positive word-of-mouth referrals.
- Command premium pricing through perceived value.

Companies like Zappos have demonstrated the power of exceptional customer service by ensuring that every customer interaction exceeds expectations. This commitment to service has bolstered Zappos' brand reputation and created a strong emotional connection with its customer base.

Framework for Identifying and Communicating Competitive Advantages

A clear framework for identifying and communicating competitive advantages is crucial for ensuring these strengths translate into tangible business outcomes. Below is a visual representation of this framework, followed by an explanation of its components.

Visual Framework

Stage	Key Actions
Discovery	Assess internal resources, market trends, and customer needs to identify potential advantages.
Validation	Test the identified strengths through market research, customer feedback, and competitor analysis.
Articulation	Clearly define the value proposition and craft messaging that resonates with stakeholders.
Implementation	Integrate the advantages into core business strategies and operational workflows.
Sustainability	Continuously monitor, adapt, and innovate to maintain the relevance of competitive advantages.

Stage 1: Discovery

The first step involves identifying unique strengths that align with the organization's mission and market demands. This requires:

- **Resource assessment** involves analyzing the organization's assets, such as intellectual property, workforce expertise, and technological capabilities.
- **Market analysis:** Understanding industry trends and gaps where the organization can position itself.
- **Customer insights:** Gathering data on customer preferences and pain points to identify unmet needs.

Stage 2: Validation

Not all identified strengths are viable competitive advantages. Validation ensures that these strengths are:

- **Valuable:** Do they solve a significant problem or fulfill a critical need?
- **Rare:** Are they unique within the competitive landscape?
- **Imitable:** Can competitors easily replicate them?
- **Sustainable:** Can the organization maintain these strengths over time?

Tools such as SWOT analysis (Strengths, Weaknesses, Opportunities, Threats) and Porter's Five Forces framework can be employed to validate potential advantages.

Stage 3: Articulation

Articulating competitive advantages is critical for ensuring customers and stakeholders recognize their value. This involves:

- Crafting a compelling value proposition that highlights the benefits of the unique strengths.
- Using consistent and clear messaging across marketing and communication channels.
- Demonstrating advantages through case studies, testimonials, or tangible outcomes.

For instance, Tesla articulates its competitive advantage by emphasizing its innovation in electric vehicles, long-range battery technology, and commitment to sustainability.

Stage 4: Implementation

Once competitive advantages are defined and communicated, they must be integrated into the organization's operations and strategy. Key steps include:

- Embedding advantages in product development, service delivery, and customer engagement strategies.
- Training employees to leverage these strengths effectively.

- Aligning organizational goals and KPIs with the identified advantages.

Stage 5: Sustainability

Maintaining a competitive advantage requires staying ahead of competitors and adapting to changing market conditions. Organizations can sustain their advantages by:

- Investing in research and development to innovate continuously.
- Monitoring competitor activity to anticipate market shifts.
- Gathering feedback to refine and enhance offerings.

Defining and leveraging competitive advantages is a dynamic process that requires deep self-awareness, market insight, and strategic execution. Organizations can build robust competitive positions by focusing on proprietary data, advanced algorithms, and exceptional customer service. Through the discovery, validation, articulation, implementation, and sustainability stages, businesses can ensure their unique strengths translate into long-term success. This approach helps organizations outperform competitors and creates lasting value for customers and stakeholders.

7.3.4 CREATING A GO-TO-MARKET STRATEGY

A well-crafted Go-to-Market (GTM) strategy ensures a successful product launch. It aligns marketing, sales, and customer engagement efforts to deliver a straightforward, impactful market entry. This section outlines the key components of a GTM strategy, including the channels for product launch and the timeline for rollout phases.

Channels for Product Launch

The choice of channels plays a critical role in how effectively a product reaches its target audience. The following channels will be utilized to ensure maximum visibility and adoption:

1. **Online Marketing:** Online marketing is a cornerstone of the GTM strategy due to its scalability and ability to target specific demographics precisely.
    - **Digital Advertising:** Paid campaigns on platforms like Google Ads, Facebook, LinkedIn, and Instagram will drive traffic and awareness. Retargeting will ensure sustained engagement.
    - **Content Marketing:** Blog posts, whitepapers, case studies, and SEO-optimized articles will establish thought leadership and educate the audience on the product's value proposition.
    - **Email Campaigns:** Personalized emails will nurture and guide leads through the buyer journey.

- **Social Media:** Active engagement on social media platforms will create buzz and foster a community around the product.

2. **Partnerships:** Strategic alliances with industry influencers, complementary brands, and value-added resellers will amplify reach.

    - **Influencer Collaborations:** Industry experts and influencers will provide credibility and reach niche audiences effectively.
    - **Co-marketing Campaigns:** Joint marketing efforts with aligned partners will pool resources and share audiences for mutual benefit.
    - **Channel Partnerships:** Leveraging the distribution networks of partners will ensure broader market coverage.

3. **Direct Sales:** A direct sales approach will address enterprise clients and high-value prospects.

    - **Dedicated Sales Team:** Trained representatives will conduct one-on-one consultations to tailor solutions for specific customer needs.
    - **Live Demonstrations and Demos:** Interactive sessions will showcase product capabilities and build trust with prospective clients.
    - **Account-Based Marketing (ABM):** Custom campaigns targeted at key accounts will increase conversion rates in the B2B segment.

Timeline for Rollout Phases

A phased rollout ensures a controlled and adaptive approach to market entry. The following timeline outlines key phases:

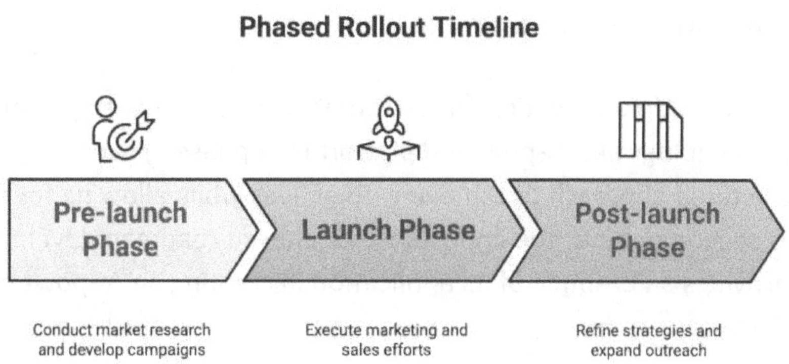

1. **Pre-launch (Month 1–2):**
   - Conducted market research and finalized target audience segments.
   - Develop marketing collateral and establish digital advertising campaigns.
   - Onboard and train sales teams and partners.
   - Engage with influencers and finalize partnership agreements.
2. **Launch (Month 3–4):**
   - Execute online marketing campaigns across platforms.
   - Activate partnerships for joint promotions and outreach.
   - Initiate direct sales efforts with targeted outreach to key accounts.
   - Monitor performance metrics and gather initial customer feedback.
3. **Post-launch (Month 5–6):**
   - Refine marketing strategies based on performance data.
   - Expand direct sales outreach and increase demo availability.
   - Deepen engagement with the existing customer base through loyalty programs and community building.
   - Assess long-term scalability and plan for broader market penetration.

This GTM strategy leverages diverse channels and adheres to a structured rollout timeline, ensuring that the product enters the market with momentum and achieves sustainable growth.

7.4: CREATING A ROADMAP

7.4.1 PHASED ROADMAP DEVELOPMENT

Developing a phased roadmap is critical for systematically implementing complex projects, especially involving technology like AI-powered platforms. A phased roadmap provides a straightforward, structured approach to achieving objectives while allowing for flexibility and iterative improvements. This section outlines the importance of phased roadmap development, highlights its components, and provides an example of its application in creating an AI-powered educational platform.

A phased roadmap divides a project's lifecycle into manageable stages, enabling focused effort and better resource allocation. Each phase builds upon the previous one, ensuring consistent progress and alignment with strategic goals. This structured approach minimizes risks and enhances project success rates.

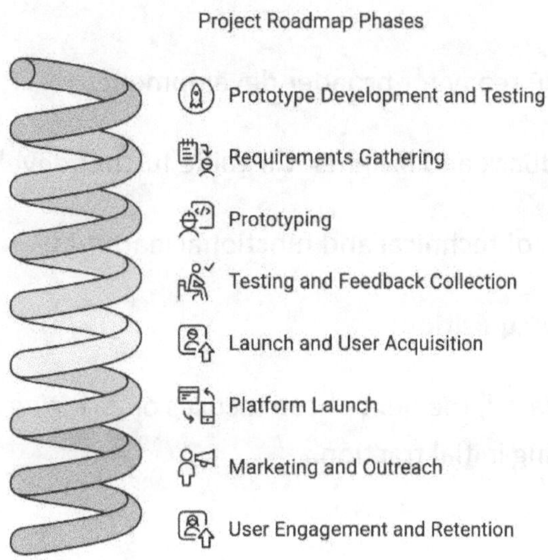

Below is an outline of the three key phases in a roadmap:

Phase 1: Prototype Development and Testing

This phase focuses on the foundational elements of the project, including idea validation, prototype creation, and testing. The goal is to establish the feasibility of the concept and address potential challenges early.

Key Activities

1. **Requirements Gathering**: Define clear objectives, target audience, and technical requirements.
    - Identify the core problem the platform aims to solve.
    - Collect input from key stakeholders like educators, students, and technical teams.
2. **Prototyping**: Develop a minimum viable product (MVP) that showcases the platform's core functionalities.
    - For an AI-powered educational platform, this might include features like adaptive learning pathways, real-time feedback, or a recommendation engine.

- Use low-code tools or frameworks to accelerate development.

3. **Testing and Feedback Collection**: Conduct usability testing with a select group of users.
   - Deploy A/B testing to evaluate different designs or algorithms.
   - Gather qualitative and quantitative feedback to refine the prototype.

Outcomes of Phase 1

- A validated MVP ready for broader development.
- Initial user feedback and insights will guide further development.
- Documentation of technical and functional learnings.

Phase 2: Launch and User Acquisition

Once the prototype is validated, the next phase focuses on bringing the platform to market, acquiring users, and establishing initial traction.

Key Activities

1. **Platform Launch**: Deploy the platform on a scalable infrastructure.
   - Ensure a seamless onboarding process for users.
   - Provide basic tutorials or support to help users navigate the platform.
2. **Marketing and Outreach**: Build awareness and attract early adopters.
   - Leverage social media, email campaigns, and partnerships with educational institutions.
   - Offer incentives like free trials or exclusive content for early users.
3. **User Engagement and Retention**: Implement strategies to keep users engaged.
   - Introduce gamification features, such as badges or leaderboards.
   - Provide responsive customer support to address issues promptly.
4. **Data Collection and Analysis**: Gather usage data to understand user behavior.
   - Track metrics like active users, session duration, and feature usage.
   - Use AI tools to analyze trends and identify areas for improvement.

Outcomes of Phase 2

- A growing user base and initial traction.
- Insights into user preferences and pain points.
- A refined platform based on real-world usage data.

Phase 3: Scaling and Feature Expansion

The final phase focuses on scaling the platform to accommodate a larger audience while introducing new features to enhance user experience and maintain competitiveness.

Key Activities

1. **Infrastructure Scaling**: Upgrade the platform to handle increased user traffic.
   - Use cloud-based solutions for elasticity and cost-efficiency.
   - Ensure robust data security measures to protect user information.
2. **Feature Expansion**: Introduce advanced functionalities based on user feedback and market trends.
   - Consider features like multi-language support, integration with third-party tools, or AI-driven predictive analytics for an AI-powered educational platform.
3. **Monetization Strategies**: Implement revenue-generating models.
   - Examples include subscription plans, pay-per-use modules, or premium content offerings.
   - Ensure monetization strategies align with user needs and platform value.
4. **Community Building**: Foster a sense of community among users.
   - Launch forums, discussion groups, or webinars to encourage collaboration.
   - Highlight success stories or case studies to build trust and credibility.
5. **Continuous Improvement**: Establish a feedback loop to improve platform design and functionality.
   - Use AI-driven insights to anticipate user needs and improve personalization.
   - Conduct regular updates to ensure the platform remains cutting-edge.

Outcomes of Phase 3

- A scalable platform capable of serving a diverse user base.
- Increased revenue streams and financial sustainability.
- A robust user community that drives organic growth and innovation.

Example Roadmap: AI-Powered Educational Platform

To illustrate the phased roadmap approach, consider an AI-powered educational platform designed to provide personalized learning experiences for students.

Phase 1: Prototype Development and Testing

- **Objective**: Build a basic version of the platform with adaptive learning capabilities.
- **Activities**:
    - Develop an MVP with a few core courses and an AI algorithm that adapts content to the learner's pace.
    - Test the platform with a small group of students and teachers.
    - Collect feedback to refine the recommendation engine and user interface.
- **Deliverables**:
    - An MVP that includes core adaptive learning functionality.
    - Feedback reports detailing user preferences and issues.

Phase 2: Launch and User Acquisition

- **Objective**: Introduce the platform to a broader audience and gain initial traction.
- **Activities**:
    - Launch the platform publicly focusing on high-demand subjects like math and science.
    - Partner with schools and educational organizations for pilot programs.
    - Roll out targeted marketing campaigns emphasizing personalized learning benefits.

Deliverables:

- A functioning platform with an active user base.
- Metrics on user engagement and retention.

Phase 3: Scaling and Feature Expansion

- **Objective:** Expand the platform's reach and capabilities.
- **Activities:**
  - Add features like live tutoring, progress dashboards, and integration with external tools (e.g., Google Classroom).
  - Scale the infrastructure to handle increased traffic and support multi-language functionality.
  - Launch premium content subscriptions for advanced courses or certifications.
- **Deliverables:**
  - A fully scalable platform with advanced features and monetization models.
  - A loyal user community contributes to organic growth.

Benefits of Phased Roadmap Development

- **Clarity and Focus**: CDefinedphases help prioritize tasks and allocate resources efficiently.
- **Risk Mitigation**: Testing and feedback loops in early phases reduce the likelihood of costly errors.
- **Adaptability**: Phased approaches allow teams to pivot based on user feedback or market changes.
- **Sustainability**: Gradual scaling ensures long-term viability and prevents overextension.

Organizations can systematically develop and launch AI-powered platforms by following a phased roadmap, ensuring alignment with strategic goals and user expectations. This structured approach enhances project success rates and provides a blueprint for continuous growth and innovation.

7.4.2 PRIORITIZING FEATURES BASED ON USER NEEDS

Delivering user-centric solutions is critical to success in today's competitive and rapidly evolving market. One of the cornerstones of achieving this is effectively prioritizing features and ensuring development resources are aligned with user needs and business objectives. This section delves into strategies for prioritizing features, leveraging user feedback, and market research to provide a robust framework for decision-making.

Leveraging User Feedback

User feedback is the most direct and authentic representation of what customers want and need from a product. By systematically collecting and analyzing this feedback, organizations can identify pain points, desired functionalities, and areas of improvement.

1. Methods of Collecting User Feedback:

- **Surveys and Questionnaires:** Targeted questions can provide insights into user satisfaction and preferences.
- **Interviews and Focus Groups:** In-depth conversations reveal nuanced user expectations and motivations.
- **Support Tickets and Reviews:** Analyzing customer complaints and reviews highlights recurring issues.
- **Behavioral Analytics:** Tracking how users interact with the product can uncover implicit feedback.

2. Categorizing Feedback: Once feedback is collected, it should be categorized based on relevance, urgency, and frequency. Tools like sentiment analysis and Natural Language Processing (NLP) can help identify patterns and prioritize actionable insights.

3. Creating Feedback Loops: Building mechanisms to regularly collect and act on user feedback ensures that the product remains aligned with evolving needs. Transparency about how user input is being addressed also fosters trust and engagement.

Conducting Market Research

Market research complements user feedback by providing a broader perspective on industry trends, competitor offerings, and emerging technologies. This ensures that prioritization decisions are not just reactive but also proactive.

1. Identifying Industry Trends: Market reports, thought leadership articles, and analyst insights could help predict user preferences and expectations changes.

2. Benchmarking Against Competitors: Competitive analysis allows organizations to identify feature gaps and opportunities to differentiate their products.

3. Understanding Market Segmentation: Different user segments often have varying needs. Segment-specific research ensures that features are tailored to high-value customer groups.

The Role of a Feature Prioritization Matrix

A feature prioritization matrix is invaluable for translating user feedback and market insights into actionable development plans. Organizations can allocate resources effectively by categorizing features based on their impact and effort.

1. Key Components of the Matrix:

- **Impact:** The potential value a feature brings to users and the business.
  - High-impact features address critical user needs or open new market opportunities.
  - Low-impact features provide incremental improvements or niche benefits.
- **Effort:** The resources required to implement the feature.
  - High-effort features demand significant development time, budget, or technical complexity.
  - Low-effort features can be implemented quickly and with minimal resources.

2. Quadrants of the Matrix: The matrix divides features into four quadrants:

- **Quick Wins (High Impact, Low Effort):** Prioritize these features for immediate implementation.
- **Major Projects (High Impact, High Effort):** Schedule these features in the roadmap with adequate resources.
- **Fill-ins (Low Impact, Low Effort):** Address these features when resources allow.
- **Low Priority (Low Impact, High Effort):** Defer or reconsider these features.

Practical Application of Prioritization Strategies

1. Collaborative Decision-Making: Feature prioritization is most effective when it involves cross-functional teams, including product managers, developers, marketers, and customer support representatives. This ensures that all perspectives are considered, balancing technical feasibility with user value.

2. Aligning with Business Goals: Features should not only meet user needs but also align with broader business objectives, such as revenue growth, market expansion, or brand differentiation. A strategic framework like OKRs (Objectives and Key Results) can help align feature prioritization with organizational goals.

3. Iterative Review and Adjustment: The prioritization process should be dynamic, with regular reviews to accommodate new data, market shifts, and user feedback. Agile methodologies are particularly effective in maintaining this flexibility.

Case Study: Prioritization in Action

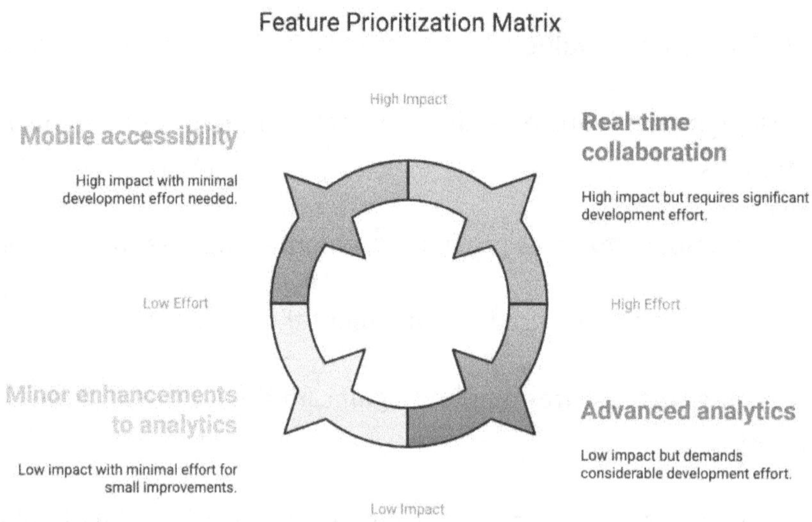

Consider a SaaS company developing a project management tool. The company identifies three frequently requested features through user feedback: real-time collaboration, advanced analytics, and mobile accessibility. Simultaneously, market research reveals a growing demand for AI-driven project recommendations.

Using a feature prioritization matrix:

- **Quick Wins:** Mobile accessibility (high impact, low effort).
- **Significant Projects:** Real-time collaboration and AI-driven recommendations (high impact, high effort).
- **Fill-ins:** Minor enhancements to existing analytics (low impact, low effort).
- **Low Priority:** Advanced analytics (low impact, high effort).

This prioritization ensures that the company addresses immediate user needs while investing strategically in long-term growth opportunities.

Prioritizing features based on user needs requires a balance of qualitative and quantitative inputs, strategic foresight, and cross-functional collaboration. By systematically leveraging user feedback, conducting market research, and utilizing tools like the feature prioritization matrix, organizations can ensure that their development efforts deliver maximum value to users and the business.

7.4.3 ALIGNING ROADMAP WITH BUSINESS GOALS

A well-aligned roadmap is a critical bridge between an organization's strategic vision and tactical execution. In technology, product development, or service delivery, aligning a roadmap with business goals ensures that every initiative supports key metrics such as revenue generation, scalability, and user retention. This alignment transforms a roadmap from a mere schedule of tasks into a strategic tool that drives organizational success.

SUPPORTING REVENUE GENERATION

One of the foremost priorities for any business is revenue generation. A roadmap aligned with this objective emphasizes features and initiatives designed to create or enhance revenue streams.

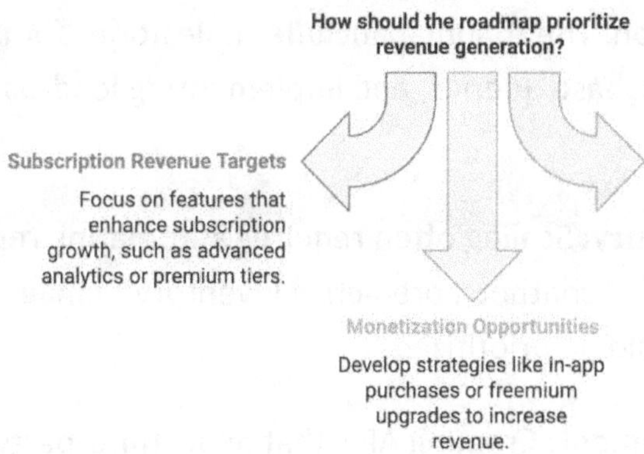

These could include:

1. **Subscription Revenue Targets:** For companies operating on subscription-based models, the roadmap might prioritize feature milestones tied to subscription revenue growth. For example, developing advanced analytics capabilities or introducing premium service tiers could attract higher-paying customers.

   Example: A SaaS company targets increasing annual recurring revenue (ARR) by 20%. The roadmap includes milestones like implementing real-time dashboards for enterprise clients, launching integrations with third-party tools like Slack or Microsoft Teams, and offering tailored onboarding experiences to reduce churn. These initiatives directly tie product evolution to revenue targets.

2. **Market Expansion:** The roadmap might include localization features such as multi-language support or compliance with regional regulations to tap into new markets. Addressing barriers to entry in international markets can generate new revenue streams for the business.

3. **Monetization Opportunities:** For platforms with an extensive user base, introducing monetization strategies like in-app purchases, advertising, or freemium-to-premium upgrades

might take precedence. The roadmap should schedule the development of these features in alignment with projected revenue impacts.

DRIVING SCALABILITY

Scalability ensures that a business can grow sustainably while maintaining performance and cost efficiency. A roadmap aligned with scalability goals incorporates technical and operational enhancements to support growth:

1. **Infrastructure Optimization:** To handle increased demand, the roadmap might include migrating to cloud-native architectures or introducing microservices to decouple and scale specific application components.

   Example: A growing e-commerce platform anticipates a 50% increase in user traffic during the holiday season. The roadmap includes milestones for upgrading server capacity, optimizing database queries, and implementing load-balancing solutions to prevent downtime.

2. **Automation and Efficiency:** Scaling often requires automating repetitive tasks. Features like automated customer support chatbots, predictive inventory management, or self-service account management tools could be prioritized.

3. **API Ecosystem Development:** Creating APIs that allow third-party developers to build on the platform enhances scalability by enabling external innovation. The roadmap should schedule API enhancements, documentation, and developer support initiatives to grow the ecosystem.

ENHANCING USER RETENTION

User retention is a key metric for long-term business sustainability. A roadmap aligned with this goal prioritizes features and enhancements that deepen user engagement and loyalty:

1. **Personalization:** Tailored experiences can significantly improve retention. The roadmap might include developing AI-driven recommendation engines, user-specific dashboards, or personalized notifications based on user behavior.

2. **Improved User Experience (UX):** Reducing friction in user journeys, such as simplifying onboarding or optimizing mobile app performance, helps retain users. The roadmap should consistently include iterative updates based on user feedback.

   Example: A fitness app observes a drop-off in user engagement after the first month. The roadmap addresses this by introducing guided workout plans, gamification features, and weekly progress reports to motivate users.

3. **Proactive Customer Support:** Investing in features that predict and address user concerns, such as in-app troubleshooting or proactive issue resolution alerts, increases satisfaction.

INTEGRATING BUSINESS GOALS INTO THE ROADMAP

Achieving alignment between a roadmap and business goals requires an iterative and collaborative process:

1. **Stakeholder Involvement:** Engaging cross-functional teams—such as sales, marketing, and operations—ensures the roadmap reflects diverse perspectives and addresses critical business needs. For instance, sales might highlight features that close deals, while marketing may focus on differentiators that enhance branding.

2. **Prioritization Frameworks:** Tools like RICE (Reach, Impact, Confidence, Effort) or MoSCoW (Must Have, Should Have, Could Have, Won't Have) help evaluate which initiatives have the most significant impact on business goals. Prioritizing high-impact features ensures efficient resource allocation.

3. **Metrics-Driven Planning:** Establishing clear metrics for success—such as ARR growth, customer lifetime value (CLV), or net promoter score (NPS)—provides a quantitative foundation for roadmap decisions. Each milestone should be tied to specific KPIs to measure its contribution to overarching goals.

4. **Feedback Loops:** Regularly reviewing progress against business goals ensures the roadmap remains relevant. For instance, if user retention lags despite new feature releases, the roadmap may need to be adjusted to prioritize engagement initiatives.

5. **Scenario Planning:** Anticipating potential challenges and opportunities allows businesses to adapt their roadmap proactively. For example, preparing for economic downturns might involve deprioritizing experimental features in favor of cost-saving optimizations.

EXAMPLE: ROADMAP ALIGNMENT IN ACTION

A streaming platform aiming to dominate the international market could align its roadmap as follows:

1. **Revenue Generation:** Launch ad-supported subscription tiers to attract price-sensitive users while expanding premium content offerings to increase ARPU (Average Revenue Per User).

2. **Scalability:** Introduce a content delivery network (CDN) to enhance streaming quality globally, even in regions with lower bandwidth.

3. **User Retention:** To boost engagement and loyalty, develop features like personalized watchlists, community-driven content ratings, and offline download options.

Each initiative is tied to specific metrics such as subscriber growth, streaming uptime, and daily active users (DAU), ensuring the roadmap supports business goals holistically.

Aligning a roadmap with business goals is a dynamic and collaborative effort that requires a deep understanding of the organization's objectives. Businesses can ensure their roadmaps drive meaningful outcomes by focusing on revenue generation, scalability, and user retention. Through stakeholder engagement, prioritization, and metrics-driven planning, the roadmap becomes a powerful tool for achieving strategic vision while maintaining operational excellence.

7.4.4 COMMON ROADMAP PITFALLS AND HOW TO AVOID THEM

Developing and managing a roadmap is critical to strategic planning, especially in AI and technology-driven projects. While a well-designed roadmap serves as a guide to achieving organizational objectives, common pitfalls can derail its effectiveness. Below, we explore two significant challenges—overloading roadmaps or failing to meet deadlines—and strategies to overcome them, emphasizing the importance of iterative updates and transparency.

RISKS OF OVERLOADING ROADMAPS OR FAILING TO MEET DEADLINES

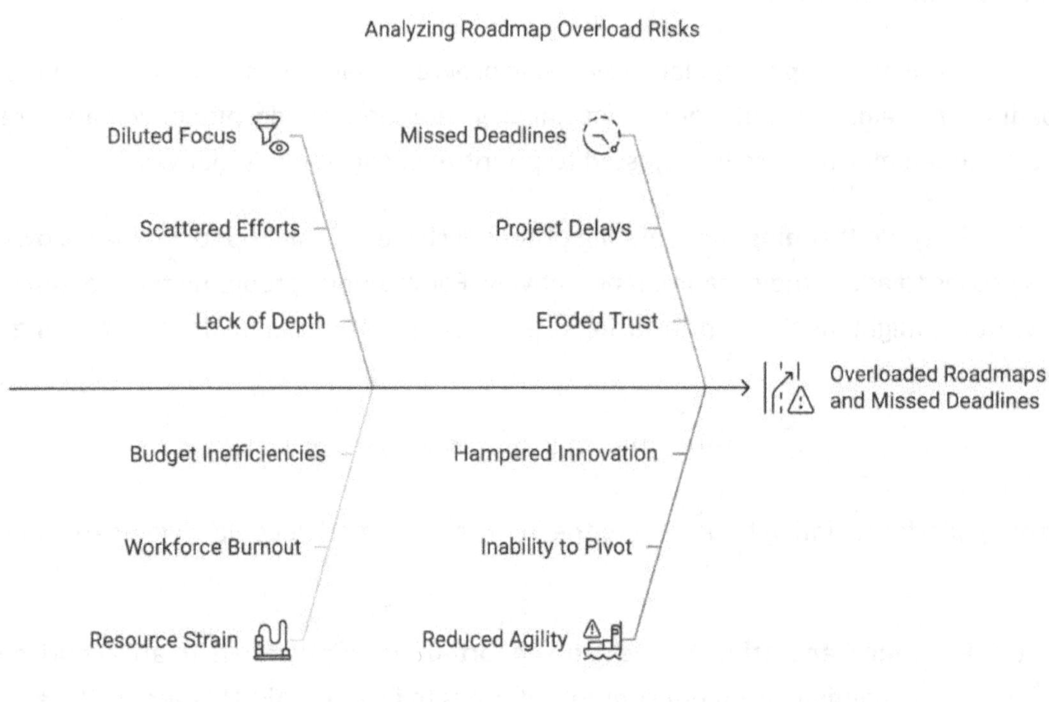

A frequent pitfall in roadmap planning is overloading it with too many initiatives, milestones, or ambitious deadlines. While it may appear proactive to tackle numerous objectives simultaneously, this approach can lead to several issues:

1. **Diluted Focus**: When a roadmap is overburdened with tasks, teams may struggle to prioritize effectively. This results in scattered efforts and a lack of depth in execution, undermining the quality of outcomes.

2. **Resource Strain**: Overambitious roadmaps often fail to consider the finite nature of organizational resources such as workforce, budget, and time. Stretching these resources thin can lead to burnout, inefficiencies, and missed targets.

3. **Missed Deadlines**: Overloading a roadmap increases the likelihood of delays. Missed deadlines impact project timelines and erode stakeholder trust and confidence.

4. **Reduced Agility**: In dynamic environments, rigid and overpacked roadmaps leave little room to pivot or respond to emerging challenges and opportunities, hampering innovation and adaptability.

Organizations must adopt a balanced approach to mitigate these risks, aligning roadmap goals with realistic timelines and available resources.

STRATEGIES FOR ITERATIVE UPDATES AND TRANSPARENCY

Iterative updates and transparency are foundational to effective roadmap management. They help organizations stay aligned with changing circumstances and maintain stakeholder confidence. Here's how:

1. **Adopt an Iterative Planning Approach**:

   - **Break Down Phases**: Divide the roadmap into more minor, manageable phases or sprints. This ensures that each milestone builds on the last, allowing incremental progress and quick course corrections.

   - **Regular Reviews**: Schedule periodic reviews to assess progress and recalibrate priorities. This enables teams to respond proactively to deviations and incorporate lessons learned.

   - **Feedback Loops**: To refine the roadmap, incorporate feedback from stakeholders, end-users, and team members. This collaborative approach fosters ownership and ensures alignment with evolving needs.

2. **Ensure Transparency Across Stakeholders**:

   - **Clear Communication**: Use tools like visual dashboards and shared repositories to give all stakeholders real-time access to roadmap updates. Clarity on timelines, priorities, and responsibilities enhances accountability.

- **Risk Disclosure**: Transparently communicate potential risks, delays, or resource constraints. This builds trust and encourages collaborative problem-solving rather than reactive blame.
- **Progress Metrics**: Share measurable progress indicators, such as key performance indicators (KPIs) or milestone achievements. This fosters a sense of accomplishment and motivates teams to stay on track.

3. **Prioritize and Sequence Effectively**:
    - **Focus on Impact**: Rank initiatives based on their strategic importance and feasibility. Addressing high-impact tasks first ensures that critical objectives are achieved even if adjustments are needed later.
    - **Limit Scope**: Avoid including "nice-to-have" features or projects. Keep the roadmap lean, focusing on the essentials.
4. **Cultivate a Culture of Flexibility**:
    - **Embrace Change**: Recognize that roadmaps are not static documents. Treat them as living guides that evolve in response to internal and external dynamics.
    - **Empower Teams**: Provide teams the autonomy to adapt tasks while ensuring alignment with overarching goals.

By addressing these pitfalls and integrating iterative updates and transparency, organizations can transform their roadmaps from static plans into dynamic tools for achieving sustained success.

CHAPTER 8: FOSTERING A THRIVING COMMUNITY

INTRODUCTION

THE ROLE OF COMMUNITY IN AI SUCCESS

Artificial Intelligence (AI) is a technological phenomenon and a transformative force reshaping industries, economies, and everyday life. While advanced algorithms, robust datasets, and powerful computational resources lay the foundation for AI, its success increasingly hinges on an often-overlooked factor: the community that supports interacts with, and contributes to it. Communities catalyze AI innovation, driving adoption, enhancing brand loyalty, and propelling cutting-edge advancements. This chapter explores the pivotal role of engaged communities in AI success, with practical insights into building, nurturing, and leveraging such communities.

The Power of Community in AI

AI platforms and solutions thrive in ecosystems where people—data scientists, developers, businesses, and end-users—collaborate and contribute to a shared vision. Communities can transform an AI project from a standalone initiative to a movement. They amplify reach, foster innovation, and create a feedback loop that ensures solutions evolve in alignment with user needs.

Engaged communities are instrumental in the following:

- **Driving Adoption:** When a community advocates for an AI tool or platform, it validates its utility and encourages broader adoption. For instance, user testimonials, tutorials, and peer support can lower the entry barrier for newcomers and help them integrate AI into their workflows.

- **Fostering Innovation:** Communities are breeding grounds for ideas. Collaborative problem-solving, shared datasets, and open-source contributions often lead to breakthroughs. These interactions spark creativity and accelerate innovation by leveraging collective intelligence.

- **Building Brand Loyalty:** Companies that invest in communities around their AI platforms build trust and a loyal user base. Community members often become brand ambassadors, helping to sustain growth and long-term success.

Examples of Thriving AI-RelateLet'smunities

Let's examine two examples, Kaggle and GitHub, to illustrate the transformative power of communities in the AI ecosystem.

Kaggle: A Hub for Data Science Enthusiasts

Kaggle, a platform renowned for its data science competitions, exemplifies how communities drive AI innovation. It's a space where data scientists and machine learning practitioners come together to solve real-world problems, often competing for prizes and recognition. Beyond competition, Kaggle fosters collaboration. Participants share code, insights, and strategies, enabling collective learning and skill enhancement.

Kaggle's community impact includes:

- **Skill Development:** By participating in Kaggle challenges, users refine their AI and data science skills, from feature engineering to model tuning.
- **Real-World Kaggle's Question:** Kaggle's datasets and competitions address industry-relevant problems, bridging the gap between academic knowledge and practical application.
- **Knowledge Sharing:** Public kernels (code notebooks) and forums on Kaggle democratize access to advanced techniques, allowing beginners to learn from experts.

GitHub: The Nexus of Developer Contributions

GitHub has redefined how developers collaborate on software projects, which has impacted AIGitHub's sound. GitHub's community accelerates AI development worldwide, from hosting repositories for popular AI frameworks like TensorFlow and PyTorch to supporting individual open-source contributions.

GitHub's AI ecosystem includes:

- **Collaboration:** Developers from diverse backgrounds contribute to AI projects, enhancing quality and innovation through peer reviews and collective brainstorming.
- **Transparency:** Open-source repositories on GitHub promote transparency, enabling users to understand, adapt, and trust AI systems.
- **Scalability:** The community-driven nature of GitHub projects ensures that they scale quickly, with rapid iterations driven by user feedback and contributions.

These examples underscore how vibrant communities drive growth and innovation in AI. They offer a model for organizations and developers aiming to harness the full potential of collective engagement.

WHAT THIS CHAPTER OFFERS

This chapter delves into actionable strategies for building, engaging, and growing a vibrant community around AI platforms. Organizations and individuals can unlock the immense value communities bring to AI initiatives by understanding and applying these strategies. The key areas of focus include:

Strategies to Build, Engage, and Grow AI Communities

1. **Define a Clear Purpose and Vision:** Every thriving community begins with a strong sense of purpose. This chapter outlines how to articulate a vision that resonates with potential members, creating a unifying goal that inspires participation.

2. **Provide Value to Members:** To attract and retain members, a community must offer tangible benefits, whether through educational content, networking opportunities, or exclusive resources. Learn how to identify and deliver the value that your audience needs.

3. **Facilitate Collaboration and Contribution:** Building a community isn't just about gathering people and empowering them to contribute. Discover tools and techniques for fostering collaboration, from hosting hackathons to enabling open-source contributions.

4. **Leverage Social Media and Online Today:** In today's digital-first world, platforms like Discord, Reddit, and LinkedIn are invaluable for community building. This chapter explores using these tools effectively to reach and engage your target audience.

5. **Recognize and Reward Contributions:** Acknowledging members'rding members' efforts is crucial for sustaining engagement. This session will cover practical tips on recognition, from gamification to public shout-outs.

Practical Tools for Leveraging Community-Driven Insights

Communities contribute to AI development and serve as a rich source of insights. This chapter guides on:

- **Listening to Your Community:** Learn how to improve your AI products by gathering feedback through surveys, forums, and social media interactions.

- **Harnessing User-Generated Content:** Community-generated content can enrich your platform and reduce development costs from tutorials to datasets.

- **Tracking Engagement Metrics:** Use analytics to measure the health of your community, identifying areas for improvement and growth.

By the end of this chapter, readers will have a comprehensive understanding of how to cultivate and harness the power of communities to drive AI success. The strategies and tools presented will empower you to create ecosystems that support your AI initiatives and propel them to new heights.

Through this exploration of community dynamics in AI, this chapter sets the stage for a deeper understanding of their transformative potential. The insights shared here aim to inspire organizations, developers, and enthusiasts to recognize and leverage the pivotal role of the community in shaping the future of AI.

8.1: ENGAGING EARLY ADOPTERS AND EVANGELISTS

8.1.1 IDENTIFYING KEY INFLUENCERS AND EARLY ADOPTERS

Introduction

The success of any emerging technology, including artificial intelligence (AI), depends significantly on its initial reception. Identifying and engaging key influencers and early adopters can set the stage for widespread adoption by establishing credibility, generating feedback, and creating momentum. This section explores the traits of effective early adopters, real-world examples of early adoption, and strategies for identifying and recruiting these pivotal users.

TRAITS OF EFFECTIVE EARLY ADOPTERS

Effective early adopters are individuals or groups with specific characteristics that enable them to champion and disseminate new technologies. Understanding these traits can help businesses and innovators target the right audience to maximize the impact of their solutions.

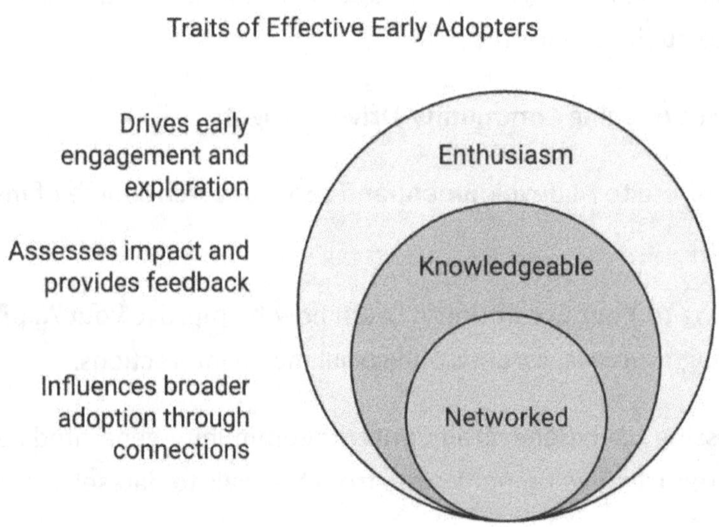

Key traits include:

1. **Enthusiasm:**
   - Early adopters are genuinely interested in new technologies and are eager to explore innovations before they become mainstream. This enthusiasm often translates into a willingness to invest time and resources in understanding and using the technology.

- They view their participation as an opportunity to stay ahead in their respective fields and derive personal or professional benefits from being at the forefront of innovation.

2. **Knowledgeable:**
   - These individuals have a strong foundational understanding of the domain to which the technology applies. Their expertise allows them to grasp the nuances of new tools and effectively assess their potential impact.
   - They often possess the technical skills to navigate complex interfaces or functionalities, making them ideal candidates for providing insightful feedback during the early stages of adoption.

3. **Networked:**
   - Effective early adopters are well-connected within their communities or industries. Their recommendations carry weight, and their influence can extend to peers, followers, or professional networks.
   - This trait is particularly critical for creating a ripple effect, as their endorsement can attract additional users and spark broader interest in the technology.

By focusing on these traits, organizations can identify individuals or groups likely to adopt their technology and act as vocal advocates.

EXAMPLES OF EARLY ADOPTION

To illustrate the role of early adopters in driving technological adoption, consider the following example:

STEM Educators Using AI Tools for Teaching

- STEM (Science, Technology, Engineering, and Mathematics) educators have emerged as early adopters of AI tools in teaching environments. Their enthusiasm for enhancing educational outcomes and their technical expertise position make them ideal users of such technologies.
- Examples include:
  - Using AI-driven platforms like ChatGPT to assist in answering student queries and generating lesson plans.
  - Adopting adaptive learning technologies to personalize the learning experience for students based on their individual needs.

- Implementing AI-powered assessment tools to grade assignments and provide tailored feedback, saving time and improving accuracy.

By leveraging AI, these educators enhance their teaching methodologies and serve as ambassadors for the technology within the broader educational community. Their success stories and experiences inspire other educators to explore similar tools, creating a cascading effect of adoption.

STRATEGIES FOR IDENTIFYING AND RECRUITING EARLY USERS

Recruiting early adopters is a strategic process that involves identifying suitable candidates and incentivizing their participation. The following strategies can help organizations effectively engage these individuals:

1. **Offering Exclusive Access or Beta Programs:**
    - Early adopters should be provided access to beta versions of the technology to create a sense of exclusivity. This approach appeals to their curiosity and fosters a sense of privilege and involvement.
    - Example: AI startups often launch beta testing programs where participants gain early access to tools, features, and updates. In return, testers provide valuable feedback to improve the product.

2. **Leveraging Industry Events and Conferences:**

    - Attend or sponsor industry-specific events, conferences, and meetups to connect with potential early adopters. These venues attract professionals who are actively seeking innovative solutions.

    - Example: Hosting a workshop at an AI summit to showcase a new AI platform and inviting attendees to become part of the pilot program.

3. **Engaging Online Communities:**

    - Online forums, social media groups, and professional networks are rich sources of potential early adopters. Participating in discussions and sharing insights can help establish credibility and attract interest.

    - Example: Engaging with members of a LinkedIn group focused on data science to introduce an AI analytics tool.

4. **Collaborating with Influencers:**

    - Partner with thought leaders and influencers within the relevant domain. Their endorsements can significantly boost credibility and attract early adopters.

    - Example: A health tech company collaborating with a prominent physician to showcase the benefits of an AI diagnostic tool.

5. **Providing Incentives:**

    - Offering tangible benefits to early adopters, such as discounts, extended trial periods, or exclusive content, can motivate individuals to adopt the technology.

    - Example: Offering a free one-year subscription to educators who adopt an AI-powered classroom management system.

6. **Conducting Targeted Outreach:**

    - Use data analytics and market research to identify potential early adopters based on their professional roles, interests, and online behaviors. Personalized outreach campaigns can then be designed to engage these individuals.

    - Example: An AI company targeting small business owners active on platforms like Twitter and showcasing how their tool can streamline operations.

7. **Establishing User Communities:**

- Create dedicated spaces for early adopters to interact, share experiences, and provide feedback. These communities foster a sense of belonging and encourage continued engagement.
- Example: Launching a user forum for an AI platform's beta testers to discuss features, report bugs, and suggest improvements.

8. **Publishing Case Studies and Success Stories:**
   - Highlight the experiences of existing early adopters through case studies, testimonials, or videos. These stories can inspire others to explore the technology and build trust in its value.
   - Example: A case study featuring a STEM educator who used AI tools to improve student engagement and performance.

Identifying and engaging key influencers and early adopters is a crucial step in the adoption curve of any technology. By understanding the traits that make these individuals effective, learning from real-world examples, and employing strategic recruitment techniques, organizations can position themselves for successful market penetration. Early adopters do not validate the technology as catalysts for broader acceptance, making their role indispensable in the innovation journey.

8.1.2 CREATING FEEDBACK LOOPS

Feedback loops are a cornerstone of building robust, user-centric AI platforms. By establishing mechanisms for continuous improvement through real-world user input, enterprises can ensure their AI systems evolve to meet user needs effectively. This section explores methods for gathering actionable insights through early feedback, supplemented with a practical example to illustrate the impact of this approach.

GATHERING ACTIONABLE INSIGHTS THROUGH EARLY FEEDBACK

Gathering feedback in the early stages of AI development is essential to validating assumptions, identifying usability challenges, and refining functionalities. This process involves collecting data from users and stakeholders through various methods, each designed to uncover specific insights. Three effective strategies for early feedback collection include surveys, usability tests, and in-app analytics.

SURVEYS

Surveys are one of the most straightforward yet powerful tools for collecting structured feedback. They allow developers to gauge user expectations, satisfaction, and pain points directly from the target audience. For instance:

- **Pre-launch surveys** can help identify user needs and preferences, guiding initial design choices.

- **Post-interaction surveys** collect data on user satisfaction and usability challenges, highlighting improvement areas.
- **Open-ended questions** in surveys provide qualitative insights that may uncover unexpected user requirements or issues.

When designing surveys, asking concise, relevant, and actionable questions is critical. For example, a study for an AI-powered content recommendation engine might include questions like:

- "How relevant were the recommendations to your interests?"
- "What types of content do you wish were recommended more often?"
- "How easy was it to find the content you were looking for?"

These responses provide a foundational understanding of user perceptions, enabling teams to align development with user expectations.

USABILITY TESTS

Usability testing involves observing real users interact with the AI system in a controlled environment. This method provides direct insights into how users navigate the platform and reveals usability strengths and bottlenecks.

- **Task-based tests:** Users are asked to perform specific tasks, such as finding a piece of content or customizing their preferences. Observing their actions highlights pain points and areas requiring refinement.
- **Think-aloud protocols:** Users verbalize their thoughts while interacting with the system, offering a deeper understanding of their decision-making processes and frustrations.
- **A/B testing involves** presenting users with different versions of the interface or algorithm to determine which performs better in engagement and satisfaction.

Usability tests often uncover unexpected challenges that may not surface in surveys, such as confusing navigation structures or unclear labeling. Addressing these issues early ensures the AI platform is intuitive and user-friendly upon launch.

IN-APP ANALYTICS

In-app analytics provide a continuous, data-driven feedback mechanism. By tracking user behavior and system performance, developers can identify trends, detect anomalies, and measure the impact of changes in real time. Key metrics to monitor include:

- **Engagement rates:** How often users interact with the AI system and its features.

- **Conversion rates:** The percentage of users who complete desired actions, such as subscribing to content or purchasing.
- **Error rates:** Frequency of system errors or user drop-offs during critical interactions.
- **Heatmaps:** Visual representations of user interaction patterns, highlighting frequently accessed features or neglected areas.

Analytics tools like Google Analytics, Mixpanel, or proprietary dashboards can be integrated into the platform to automate data collection. This approach complements qualitative feedback methods, offering a comprehensive view of user behavior and preferences.

EXAMPLE: REFINING AN AI-POWERED CONTENT RECOMMENDATION ENGINE

To illustrate the value of early feedback, consider the development of an AI-powered content recommendation engine.

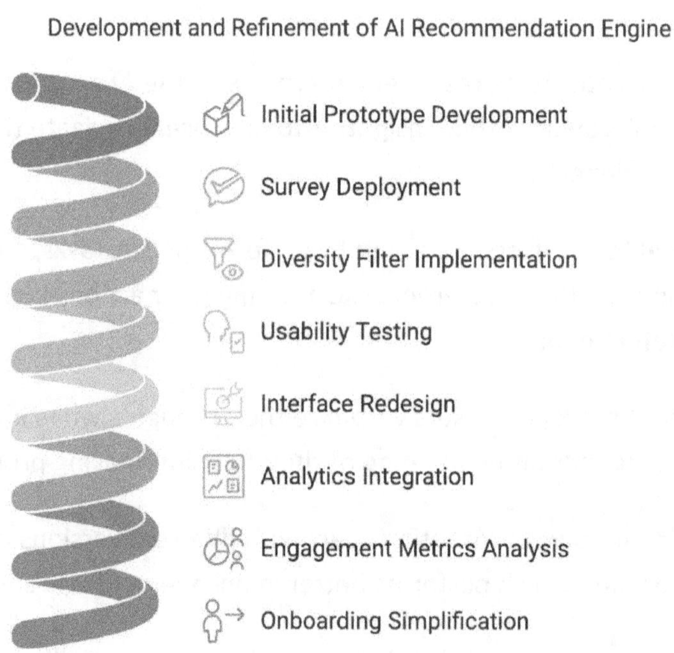

This system aims to provide users with personalized content suggestions based on their preferences and behavior.

Phase 1: Initial Prototype and Survey Deployment

The development team begins by building a basic recommendation engine prototype. Before launching the prototype to a larger audience, they distribute a pre-launch survey to a small group of target users. The survey includes questions about preferred content types, frequency of recommendations, and frustrations with existing solutions.

Survey responses reveal that users value diversity in recommendations but often find them repetitive on other platforms. Based on this feedback, the team introduces a "diversity filter" to the recommendation algorithm, ensuring that suggestions include both familiar and novel content.

Phase 2: Usability Testing

Next, the team conducts usability tests with the updated prototype. Participants are asked to:

1. Explore a set of recommended articles.
2. Mark content as "liked" or "disliked."
3. Search for a specific topic using the platform's search functionality.

During these tests, developers observe several issues:

- Users struggle to locate the "dislike" button, suggesting its placement is not intuitive.
- The search functionality occasionally returns irrelevant results, frustrating participants.

To address these findings, the team redesigned the interface to make the "dislike" button more prominent and refined the search algorithm to prioritize relevancy.

Phase 3: In-App Analytics Integration

After addressing usability issues, the platform is launched to a beta audience with in-app analytics enabled. Metrics reveal:

- A high engagement rate with recommended content but a low usage rate for the "save for later" feature.
- Frequent drop-offs during onboarding, indicating users find the initial setup process cumbersome.

The team responds by simplifying the onboarding process and reducing the steps required to set preferences. They also redesigned the "save for later" feature to make it more visible and added a tooltip explaining its benefits.

Results and Iterative Refinement

These feedback mechanisms significantly improve the recommendation engine over time. The diversity filter reduces content fatigue, the redesigned interface enhances usability, and the simplified onboarding process increases user retention. In-app analytics provide insights for ongoing refinement, ensuring the system adapts to evolving user needs.

Creating feedback loops is an essential practice for building successful AI platforms. By leveraging surveys, usability tests, and in-app analytics, enterprises can gather actionable insights that guide development and ensure their systems deliver value to users. The example of the AI-powered content recommendation engine demonstrates how early feedback can drive iterative improvements, resulting in a user-centric product that meets real-world needs. Through continuous engagement with users and stakeholders, AI platforms can remain relevant, effective, and aligned with the dynamic expectations of their audience.

8.1.3 TURNING EARLY ADOPTERS INTO EVANGELISTS

Early adopters are crucial to the success of any product or platform. They are the first users to embrace innovation, providing valuable feedback and creating initial momentum. However, a strategic approach is essential to sustain this momentum and transform early adopters into loyal evangelists. Evangelists go beyond simply using the product—they advocate for it, recruit new users, and contribute to its broader adoption. This section explores two key strategies: rewarding active contributors and building loyalty by incorporating user feedback.

Rewarding Active Contributors

Active contributors among early adopters deserve recognition for their role in shaping the product's early journey. Their enthusiasm, insights, and support can influence the product's trajectory and reputation. Rewarding these contributors fosters community and belonging while motivating them to continue advocating for the product.

1. **Public Recognition**: Acknowledging early adopters publicly is one of the simplest yet most impactful ways to show appreciation. This can include:
    - Featuring them on the company's website or social media.
    - Highlighting user success stories in newsletters or blogs.
    - Public shout-outs during webinars or product launches.

Public recognition strengthens the bond with early users and encourages others to engage more actively, knowing their efforts might also be acknowledged.

2. **Exclusive Swag**: Offering branded merchandise like t-shirts, mugs, or stickers can be a tangible way to reward contributors. Such items serve a dual purpose—they are tokens of appreciation and marketing tools when users display them publicly. For more exclusive rewards, limited-edition swag can make contributors feel like part of an elite group.

3. **Free Subscriptions**: Another effective reward is providing complimentary or extended access to premium features. This approach works particularly well for SaaS products, where free subscriptions allow users to explore advanced capabilities and become long-term advocates.

4. **Gamification and Leaderboards**: Implementing gamified elements such as points, badges, or leaderboards encourages healthy competition among early adopters. Rewarding top contributors with exclusive perks further incentivizes active participation.

Building a loyal community of evangelists hinges on making users feel heard and valued. Early adopters often provide some of the most candid and actionable feedback. By incorporating their insights into product development, companies can foster a more profound sense of trust and engagement.

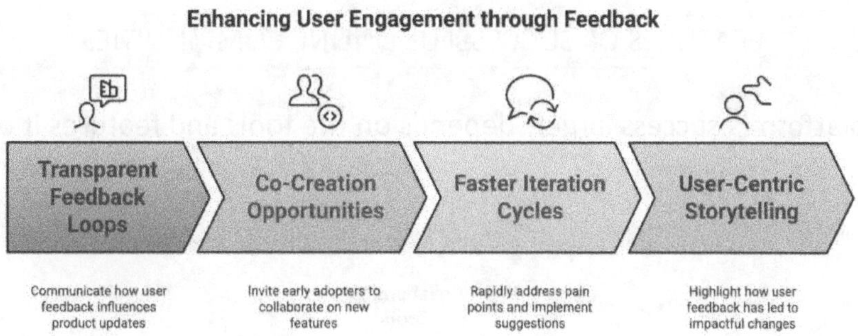

1. **Transparent Feedback Loops**: Communicate how user feedback influences product updates. For instance:
   - Share release notes that mention specific user suggestions.
   - Host "behind-the-scenes" sessions to showcase how feedback shapes the roadmap.
   - Use personalized communications to thank contributors for particular ideas.
2. **Co-Creation Opportunities**: Invite early adopters to collaborate on new features or beta testing programs. This hands-on involvement strengthens their connection to the product and makes them feel like co-creators rather than passive users.
3. **Faster Iteration Cycles**: Rapidly addressing pain points and implementing suggestions demonstrates that user feedback is taken seriously. When users see their input reflected in product improvements, they are more likely to champion the product to others.
4. **User-Centric Storytelling**: Highlight how user feedback has led to impactful changes. By turning feedback into a narrative, companies can show prospective users the value of their community-centric approach.

Companies can transform early adopters into enthusiastic evangelists by rewarding active contributors and consistently incorporating feedback. These strategies build trust and loyalty and create a network of passionate advocates who amplify the product's reach and credibility.

8.2: BUILDING A COMMUNITY

8.2.1 DESIGNING INTERACTIVE PLATFORMS FOR COLLABORATION

Interactive platforms designed for collaboration have transformed how individuals and organizations engage, share knowledge, and solve problems. These platforms serve as digital environments where communities can connect, exchange ideas, and collectively work toward shared goals. The success of such platforms hinges on the features they provide, the value they deliver, and the experiences they create for their users.

FEATURES OF SUCCESSFUL ONLINE COMMUNITIES

A collaborative platform's success largely depends on the tools and features it offers.

Below are some key features that contribute to the efficacy of online communities:

1. Forums: Forums are foundational to most online communities, offering users a structured space to discuss topics, share insights, and seek help. Features that enhance forums include:

- **Threaded Discussions:** Allow users to engage in detailed conversations while maintaining context.
- **Moderation Tools:** Ensure discussions remain constructive and adhere to community guidelines.
- **Search Functionality:** Help users quickly locate relevant threads and answers.
- **User Profiles:** Provide context about contributors, fostering trust and encouraging meaningful engagement.

2. Q&A Platforms Question-and-answer platforms are designed for direct knowledge sharing. Key characteristics of successful Q&A systems include:

- **Reputation Systems:** Encourage high-quality contributions by rewarding users through upvotes, badges, or rankings.
- **Categorization:** Organize questions by topics or tags, improving accessibility and discoverability.
- **Expert Identification:** Highlight knowledgeable users or domain experts, guiding newcomers to credible sources of information.
- **Commenting and Feedback:** Allow further clarification or enhancement of answers.

3. Collaborative Tools Platforms that prioritize real-time collaboration stand out in fostering active engagement. Essential collaborative tools include:

- **Document Sharing and Editing:** Enable users to co-create and update files within the platform.
- **Task Management:** Assign and track progress on tasks to enhance productivity.
- **Version Control:** Track changes to shared documents, preventing data loss and maintaining accountability.
- **Integrations:** Support seamless connectivity with third-party tools, such as calendars, cloud storage, and project management software.

4. Personalization and User Experience (UX)

- **Customizable Dashboards:** Allow users to personalize their interface according to their preferences.
- **Notifications and Alerts:** Keep users informed about updates or activities relevant to them.
- **Accessibility Features:** Ensure inclusivity by supporting assistive technologies and responsive design for mobile and desktop users.

5. Community-Building Features To foster a sense of belonging, platforms often integrate:

- **Discussion Groups:** Create niche communities within the broader platform.
- **Events and Webinars:** Host virtual gatherings for education or networking.
- **Gamification:** Use game-like elements such as leaderboards and achievements to motivate participation.

6. Security and Privacy: Ensuring user trust is paramount. Features supporting this include:

- **Data Encryption:** Protect sensitive information.

- **Role-Based Access Control:** Limit access to resources based on user roles.
- **Anonymous Posting Options:** Encourage participation without compromising privacy.

Examples: An AI Platform for Researchers to Share Workflows and Datasets

Consider an AI-driven collaborative platform explicitly designed for researchers. Such a platform can serve as a model for fostering effective collaboration:

Purpose and Audience: The platform caters to AI researchers, data scientists, and academicians seeking to share workflows, datasets, and methodologies. It bridges the gap between academia and industry by promoting open science and reproducible research.

Key Features:

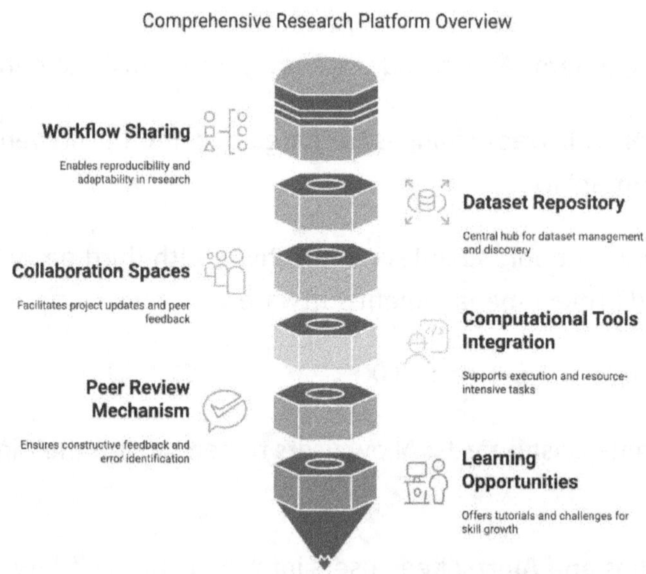

1. **Workflow Sharing:** Researchers can share detailed workflows, including algorithms, preprocessing techniques, and training strategies. This feature allows others to:
   - Reproduce results, enhancing transparency.
   - Adapt workflows to solve similar problems in different domains.
2. **Dataset Repository:** A centralized repository allows users to upload, download, and review datasets. Features include:
   - **Metadata Standards:** Ensure datasets are well-documented and easily understandable.
   - **Search and Filtering:** Help users find datasets based on criteria such as size, format, or domain.

- **Usage Metrics:** Provide insights into dataset popularity and applications.

3. **Collaboration Spaces:** Dedicated spaces for project collaboration enable researchers to:
   - Share progress updates through blogs or posts.
   - Discuss challenges and solicit feedback from peers.
   - Maintain project repositories with version control.

4. **Integration with Computational Tools:** The platform integrates with popular computational environments such as Jupyter Notebooks, TensorFlow, and PyTorch. Users can:
   - Execute shared code snippets directly within the platform.
   - Access cloud-based GPUs for resource-intensive tasks.

5. **Peer Review and Feedback Mechanism:** Researchers can solicit feedback on their workflows or datasets through a structured review process. This ensures:
   - Constructive critique to refine contributions.
   - Identification of errors or biases in data and methodologies.

6. **Learning and Skill Development:** The platform can also host:
   - Tutorials and webinars by domain experts.
   - Collaborative challenges or hackathons to solve real-world problems.

Benefits of Such a Platform:

1. **Accelerated Research:** The platform reduces redundancy and accelerates innovation by facilitating knowledge sharing.

2. **Enhanced Collaboration:** Researchers from diverse backgrounds can come together to tackle complex problems, fostering interdisciplinary approaches.

3. **Global Reach:** The platform's online nature ensures accessibility to researchers worldwide, democratizing access to resources and expertise.

4. **Reproducibility:** Shared workflows and datasets promote reproducibility, a critical aspect of scientific integrity.

5. **Recognition and Networking:** Contributors gain visibility for their work, opening opportunities for collaboration, funding, or career advancement.

Designing interactive platforms for collaboration involves balancing functionality, user experience, and community engagement. Organizations can create environments that foster innovation, enhance productivity, and build lasting networks by understanding the features that drive thriving online communities and leveraging real-world examples, such as an AI platform for researchers. The rapid evolution of technology and the growing need for interdisciplinary solutions underscore the importance of these platforms in shaping the future of work and collaboration.

8.2.2 HOSTING COMMUNITY EVENTS

Community events are a powerful tool for fostering engagement, building trust, and creating a vibrant ecosystem around an AI platform. These events provide collaboration, learning, and innovation opportunities by bringing together diverse stakeholders, including developers, users, and industry leaders. This section explores how to effectively organize impactful events and their tangible benefits strategies for maximizing community participation.

EXAMPLES OF IMPACTFUL EVENTS

1. **Hackathons**

Hackathons are structured, time-bound events that bring together participants to solve specific problems or build new features for a platform. These events are ideal for fostering creativity and showcasing the versatility of the AI platform. For instance:

- **Objective**: Participants could be challenged to develop AI solutions for real-world problems, such as healthcare diagnostics or customer service automation.
- **Structure**: A typical hackathon lasts 24 to 48 hours and includes brainstorming sessions, coding marathons, and presentations.
- **Outcomes**: Hackathons often produce innovative prototypes, new use cases, and enhanced community collaboration. They also provide a platform for identifying and nurturing talented developers.

2. **Webinars**

Webinars are virtual events that allow experts to share knowledge, demonstrate product capabilities, and engage with a global audience. They are cost-effective and accessible, making them valuable tools for scaling community engagement.

- **Topics**: Popular themes could include AI ethics, platform-specific tutorials, and industry trends.
- **Speakers:** Featuring industry leaders, internal experts, and enthusiastic community members lends credibility and attracts a broader audience.

- **Engagement**: Interactive Q&A sessions, live demonstrations, and polls can keep the audience engaged.

3. **User Conferences**

User conferences are large-scale events to showcase the latest advancements, celebrate user achievements, and strengthen community ties. Depending on the audience's preferences and logistical considerations, they can be in-person or hybrid.

- **Agenda**: Keynotes, panel discussions, and breakout sessions tailored to various user personas.
- **Networking**: Dedicated spaces for networking and collaboration, such as breakout rooms or roundtable discussions.
- **Showcase**: Offering users a platform to present their success stories fosters community pride and demonstrates the platform's impact.

BENEFITS OF HOSTING COMMUNITY EVENTS

1. **Showcasing Use Cases**

Events provide an opportunity to highlight how the AI platform is being used across industries. Use cases presented at these events serve multiple purposes:

- **Inspiration**: They inspire other users to explore similar applications or build on existing ideas.
- **Credibility**: Real-world examples build trust and validate the platform's capabilities.
- **Marketing**: Use cases serve as compelling content for promotional campaigns.

2. **Fostering Innovation**

By creating an environment where ideas are exchanged freely, community events act as a catalyst for innovation:

- **Collaborative Spaces**: Events like hackathons encourage participants to think outside the box and collaborate on groundbreaking solutions.
- **Cross-Pollination**: Bringing together people from diverse industries and backgrounds leads to unique perspectives and unexpected breakthroughs.
- **Resource Sharing**: Events provide a platform for participants to share tools, frameworks, and best practices, accelerating innovation across the community.

3. **Gathering Feedback**

Events also serve as a direct channel for collecting valuable insights from the community:

- **Feature Requests**: Interactive sessions often surface user requests and highlight pain points.
- **User Experience**: Demonstrations and hands-on activities help organizers observe how users interact with the platform, revealing usability challenges.
- **Iterative Improvement**: Feedback gathered during events can be immediately incorporated into the product roadmap.

EVENT CALENDAR FOR COMMUNITY ENGAGEMENT

Organizations should adopt a structured approach to event planning to maintain consistent engagement. An event calendar serves as a strategic tool for scheduling and promoting community events:

1. **Annual Planning**

Start by outlining key events for the year. Consider including a mix of hackathons, webinars, and user conferences to cater to different audience segments. Assign tentative dates and designate owners for each event.

- **Example Calendar**:
  - January: New Year Kickoff Webinar – Discuss the roadmap and new features.
  - April: Spring Hackathon – Develop creative solutions using the platform.
  - August: Summer Webinar Series – Address technical challenges and solutions.
  - November: Annual User Conference – Celebrate milestones and showcase user stories.

2. **Promotion Strategy**

Successful events depend on effective promotion:

- **Channels**: Use email campaigns, social media, and community forums to announce events.
- **Timelines**: Start promoting events at least one month in advance to maximize attendance.

- **Incentives**: Offer early bird discounts, exclusive content, or participation certificates to encourage registrations.

3. **Integration with Other Initiatives**

Align the event calendar with broader community-building initiatives. For example, follow up a webinar with a blog series summarizing key insights or launch a competition after a hackathon to sustain engagement.

Best Practices for Hosting Community Events

1. **Inclusive Design**

Ensure that events are accessible to all community members, regardless of location, technical expertise, or professional background. Offer virtual participation options and provide resources like recordings and transcripts.

2. **Measuring Impact**

Establish key performance indicators (KPIs) to evaluate the success of each event:

- **Attendance**: Track the number of participants and their demographics.
- **Engagement**: Monitor metrics like session participation, questions asked, and feedback provided.
- **Outcomes**: Assess tangible outcomes, such as new projects initiated or features adopted.

3. **Community Involvement**

Involve the community in planning and executing events:

- **Co-Creation**: Invite users to propose topics, lead sessions, or serve as judges for hackathons.
- **Recognition**: Highlight the contributions of community members through awards, shout-outs, or case studies.

4. **Continuous Improvement**

Feedback collected during events will be used to refine future initiatives. The event calendar will be regularly updated to reflect evolving community needs and preferences.

Event Calendar for Community Engagement

Month	Event Type	Objective	Key Highlights
January	Kickoff Webinar	Introduce roadmap and features	Q&A with product team
March	Industry Webinar	Explore AI applications in healthcare	Guest speakers from top firms
April	Hackathon	Develop creative AI solutions	Awards for best prototypes
June	Training Webinar	Hands-on session on platform tools	Live coding demonstration
August	Webinar Series	Address technical challenges and solutions	Interactive sessions with developers
November	User Conference	Showcase user success stories and milestones	Keynotes, networking, and user awards

By implementing a structured approach to community events, organizations can nurture a thriving ecosystem that drives innovation, enhances user satisfaction, and amplifies the platform's impact.

8.2.3 ENCOURAGING KNOWLEDGE SHARING

In today's interconnected world, fostering a culture of knowledge sharing is paramount for organizations and communities, especially those operating in rapidly evolving sectors like artificial intelligence (AI). Platforms prioritizing knowledge sharing enhance user engagement, drive innovation, and establish themselves as thought leaders. This section explores the role of user-generated content, such as tutorials, blogs, and case studies, in encouraging knowledge sharing and provides a concrete example to illustrate its impact.

USER-GENERATED CONTENT

User-generated content (UGC) is a powerful tool for promoting knowledge sharing. When users actively contribute to the ecosystem through their insights, experiences, and creative applications of the platform, it creates a virtuous cycle of learning and collaboration. The following forms of UGC are particularly effective in this regard:

Tutorials

Tutorials are step-by-step guides that break down complex processes into manageable tasks. They are invaluable for onboarding new users and helping existing users deepen their expertise. A well-crafted tutorial can:

- Simplify technical concepts and make them accessible to a broader audience.
- Highlight the platform's capabilities and potential applications.
- Serve as a repository of best practices, reducing the learning curve for users.

For instance, a tutorial on integrating an AI platform with popular development tools can empower software engineers to quickly and easily incorporate AI into their workflows. Tutorials can also address specific use cases, such as deploying AI models for customer sentiment analysis, enabling users to platform direct value in their domains.

BLOGS

Blogs allow users to share their experiences, insights, and innovative approaches narratively. They provide a platform for thought leadership and community engagement. Key benefits of user-generated blogs include:

- Highlighting real-world applications of the platform.
- Offering unique perspectives and creative solutions.
- Building a sense of community by showcasing the diversity of user experiences.

A blog by a data scientist describing their journey in using the platform to automate a complex task, for instance, can inspire others and generate valuable discussions. Additionally, blogs can address common challenges and their resolutions, serving as a resource for troubleshooting and continuous learning.

CASE STUDIES

Case studies offer detailed analyses of how users have successfully applied the platform to solve specific problems. They combine storytelling with technical depth, making them highly effective for knowledge sharing. Benefits of user-generated case studies include:

- Demonsplatform'se platform's versatility and real-world impact.
- Providing actionable insights and replicable strategies.
- Establishing credibility and trust within the community.

For example, a case study on using an AI platform for predictive maintenance in manufacturing can guide other users in applying similar techniques to optimize their operations. Such case studies educate and motivate users to experiment and innovate.

MEMBER'S GUIDE ON USING AN AI API FOR CLIMATE MODELING

To illustrate the power of user-generated content, consider the example of a community member publishing a guide on leveraging an AI API for climate modeling. Climate modeling is a complex and computationally intensive task that requires the integration of vast datasets and sophisticated algorithms. By sharing their knowledge, the community member contributes to the ecosystem in the following ways:

Simplifying Complex Concepts

The guide breaks down the process of using the AI API into clear, actionable steps. It might include instructions on:

- Accessing and authenticating the API.
- Preparing and integrating climate data.
- Selecting and fine-tuning machine learning models.
- Visualizing the outputs to draw actionable insights.

This simplification helps novice users and inspires confidence in tackling challenging projects.

Showcasing Practical Applications

The guide highlights the tangible benefits of the AI API by focusing on a real-world problem like climate modeling. It demonstrates how the platform can be critical in addressing global challenges and elevating its perceived value and relevance.

Encouraging Innovation

The guide serves as a starting point for others to build upon. It might inspire users to explore additional applications, such as optimizing renewable energy deployment or analyzing the impact of climate policies. This innovation has a ripple effect, strengthening the community and the platform.

Strengthening the Community

When users see their peers sharing insights and achieving remarkable results, it fosters a sense of belonging, and collaboration's guide's author becomes a role model, encouraging others to contribute their knowledge and experiences.

BEST PRACTICES FOR ENCOURAGING KNOWLEDGE SHARING

To maximize the impact of user-generated content, platforms should actively encourage and support knowledge sharing. Here are some best practices:

Provide Incentives

Recognizing and rewarding contributors can motivate users to share their expertise. Incentives might include:

- Featuring contributorsplatform'satform's homepage or social media channels.
- Offering discounts, credits, or exclusive access to advanced features.
- Organizing competitions with prizes for the best tutorials, blogs, or case studies.

Facilitate Collaboration

Creating user collaboration opportunities can lead to more prosperous and diverse content. Platforms can:

- Host webinars or hackathons that bring users together.
- Set up forums or discussion boards for knowledge exchange.
- Encourage users to co-author content with complementary skills.

Ensure Accessibility

Making it easy for users to contribute is crucial. Platforms should provide:

- Intuitive content creation tools with templates and guidelines.
- Transparent submission processes and responsive support.
- Multilingual support to reach a global audience.

Promote Content

To amplify the reach and impact of user-generated content, platforms should:

- Highlight content through newsletters, blogs, and social media campaigns.
- Create a dedicated section on the platform to showcase UGC.
- Use analytics to recommend relevant content to users based on their interests and activities.

Encouraging knowledge sharing through user-generated content is a cornerstone of building a thriving, innovative community. Tutorials, blogs, and case studies empower users to learn from each other, explore new possibilities, and tackle complex challenges. The example of a guide on using an AI API for climate modeling underscores the transformative potential of UGC. By fostering an environment that values and supports knowledge sharing, platforms can unlock the collective intelligence of their communities, driving progress and creating lasting value.

8.3: SOCIAL MEDIA AND CONTENT MARKETING

8.3.1 LEVERAGING GENAI FOR PERSONALIZED CAMPAIGNS

Generative AI (GenAI) represents a transformative force in personalized marketing campaigns, enabling organizations to deliver highly tailored content to their target audience. By leveraging advanced algorithms and models like GPT-4, businesses can create compelling, context-aware content that resonates deeply with their customers. This capability has revolutionized how marketers approach personalization, moving beyond static templates to dynamic, AI-driven interactions.

AI-GENERATED CONTENT FOR TARGETED MARKETING

AI-generated content serves as the cornerstone of modern personalized campaigns. Unlike traditional methods, where marketers manually craft messages, AI models analyze vast datasets to create content that aligns with audience preferences, behaviors, and needs. Here are a few notable examples:

1. Personalized Emails: AI enables the creation of emails tailored to individual recipients. For instance, an e-commerce platform can use GenAI to craft emails featuring products a customer recently viewed or related items they might find appealing. AI algorithms can optimize subject lines for higher open rates, adjust tones to suit customer preferences, and ensure email content remains fresh and engaging. The result is a significant increase in click-through rates and conversions.

2. Social Media Posts: Social media is a powerful channel for connecting with audiences, and GenAI excels at generating posts that captivate attention. Businesses can input key details about their campaign objectives, target demographics, and brand voice, and the AI will produce posts tailored to each platform. For instance, a fitness brand might generate Instagram posts promoting a new workout program with hashtags and visually appealing captions. AI ensures these posts are optimized for engagement and align with current trends.

3. Educational Videos: Videos have become a dominant medium for engaging audiences, and AI-generated scripts make it easier to produce educational or promotional content. For example, a software company launching a new product could use GenAI to script explainer videos. The AI can generate narratives that simplify complex topics, ensuring they resonate with the intended audience. With AI-driven video editing tools, businesses can create high-quality content with minimal effort.

These examples underscore GenAI's versatility in generating content that attracts attention and fosters meaningful customer connections.

TOOLS FOR AUTOMATION

To harness the full potential of GenAI, marketers rely on specialized tools that streamline content creation and delivery. These tools integrate AI capabilities, making it easy for users to generate personalized content at scale. Below are some of the most popular tools used for automation:

1. ChatGPT: OpenAI's ChatGPT is a powerful tool for generating conversational content. Its versatility makes it suitable for crafting everything from blog posts to customer support scripts. Marketers can use ChatGPT to ideate campaign concepts, create tailored messages, or even simulate customer interactions. With fine-tuning options, businesses can align ChatGPT's output with their brand voice and messaging guidelines.

2. Jasper: Jasper is another prominent AI tool for creating content. Known for its user-friendly interface, Jasper allows marketers to generate blog posts, social media updates, ad copies, and more. The platform includes templates optimized for different content types, ensuring users can quickly produce high-quality output. Jasper's advanced features, such as tone adjustment and keyword optimization, make it a go-to choice for creating SEO-friendly content.

3. Email Marketing Platforms with AI Integration: Mailchimp and HubSpot have integrated AI capabilities that enhance email marketing efforts. These tools analyze user behavior to recommend optimal sending times, segment audiences based on preferences, and dynamize email content. AI-generated recommendations help marketers design campaigns that are more likely to resonate with their audience.

4. Social Media Management Tools: Tools like Buffer and Hootsuite now offer AI-driven features that automate post creation and scheduling. Marketers can input campaign parameters, and the AI suggests content tailored to the target audience. These platforms also provide insights into audience engagement, enabling continuous optimization.

5. Video Creation Software: AI-powered video creation platforms such as Synthesia and Pictory allow marketers to produce videos without requiring extensive technical skills. Users can input text scripts, and the AI generates videos with voiceovers and visuals. These tools are ideal for creating tutorials, promotional videos, and product demos at scale.

The integration of GenAI into marketing workflows offers several distinct advantages:

1. Enhanced Personalization: GenAI enables hyper-personalization by analyzing customer data to identify preferences and behaviors. This ensures that every content is relevant, increasing the likelihood of engagement.

2. Scalability: Manually creating personalized content is time-consuming and resource-intensive. With GenAI, businesses can simultaneously generate thousands of unique messages, catering to diverse audience segments.

3. Cost Efficiency: AI-driven automation reduces the need for extensive marketing teams dedicated to content creation. This allows businesses to allocate resources to other strategic areas while maintaining high-quality output.

4. Improved Customer Engagement: GenAI fosters deeper connections and brand loyalty by delivering content that resonates with customers personally. This translates into higher engagement rates across all marketing channels.

5. Data-Driven Insights: GenAI tools often include analytics features that provide insights into campaign performance. These insights help marketers refine their strategies and optimize content for better results.

CHALLENGES AND CONSIDERATIONS

While GenAI offers immense potential, marketers must address specific challenges to maximize its effectiveness:

1. Ethical Concerns: The use of AI for content creation raises ethical questions, particularly around data privacy and authenticity. Businesses must ensure that their AI-generated content complies with regulations and respects customer trust.

2. Maintaining Brand Voice: AI-generated content sometimes deviates from a brand's established voice. Marketers should review and fine-tune AI outputs to ensure consistency.

3. Dependence on Data: The quality of AI-generated content depends on the quality of input data. Businesses must invest in robust data collection and management practices for accurate and effective personalization.

Leveraging GenAI for personalized campaigns represents a paradigm shift in marketing, enabling businesses to create meaningful and engaging content at scale. Tools like ChatGPT and Jasper empower marketers to craft emails, social media posts, and videos that resonate with their audience while automation platforms streamline campaign execution. By addressing challenges and adhering to ethical guidelines, organizations can harness the full potential of GenAI to drive customer engagement and achieve their marketing goals.

8.3.2 EXPANDING REACH THROUGH CONTENT MARKETING

Content marketing is a powerful strategy for organizations aiming to expand their reach, especially in a competitive and technology-driven environment. Companies can engage with various audiences by leveraging diverse content forms such as blogs, videos, and case studies. This section explores the importance of tailoring content to meet the needs of STEM researchers, educators, and students' needs and illustrates such strategies' effectiveness through a real-world example.

DEVELOPING BLOGS, VIDEOS, AND CASE STUDIES FOR DIVERSE AUDIENCES

Tailoring Content for STEM Researchers

STEM researchers represent a highly analytical and detail-oriented audience. Content must emphasize depth, accuracy, and relevance to engage this group effectively. Blogs can discuss cutting-edge scientific, technological, engineering, and mathematics developments and link these advancements to the organization's offerings. For example, a blog post about how a new machine-learning algorithm is revolutionizing drug discovery would appeal to researchers in the pharmaceutical industry.

Conversely, videos can showcase demonstrations, tutorials, or detailed walkthroughs of complex technologies. For instance, a video illustrating the real-world application of AI in astrophysics could resonate deeply with researchers in the field. Infographics and visual storytelling can enhance videos' effectiveness by simplifying complex concepts.

When targeted at researchers, case studies should include robust data, metrics, and insights highlighting a solution's practical applications. For example, a case study focusing on how an AI-powered tool reduced research timelines for a prominent lab would validate the technology and establish credibility.

ENGAGING EDUCATORS

Educators often seek informative, practical, and adaptable content in classrooms or training programs. Blogs tailored for educators might focus on pedagogical approaches, explaining how cutting-edge technologies can be integrated into curricula. For instance, a blog on "Teaching AI Concepts to High School Students" could outline lesson plans and provide downloadable resources.

Videos for educators should be instructional, offering tips, strategies, and demonstrations that can be used in teaching. Tutorials explaining how to use data visualization tools for classroom projects or videos detailing STEM experiments could be highly valuable.

Case studies for educators focus on success stories where schools or universities successfully implemented innovative technologies to enhance learning outcomes. For example, a case study describing how an AI-driven platform improved student engagement in STEM subjects would inspire educators to explore similar solutions.

Students in STEM fields are typically curious and eager to learn, but they may lack the foundational knowledge of their professional counterparts. Therefore, blogs targeting students should be engaging, beginner-friendly, and focused on building their interest in STEM topics. Titles like "5 Easy Projects to Get Started with Machine Learning" or "A Beginner's Guide to Robotics" can attract student readership.

Videos for students should be dynamic and visually appealing, incorporating elements like animations and real-life examples to explain complex concepts. For instance, a series of videos titled "AI in Everyday Life" could demonstrate how artificial intelligence impacts gaming, healthcare, and transportation, making the topic relatable.

Case studies for students could highlight young innovators who achieved breakthroughs using STEM tools. Narratives like "How a Student Built an AI Chatbot to Help Their Community" can inspire and educate students to pursue their projects.

REAL-WORLD EXAMPLE: AI STARTUP USING YOUTUBE TUTORIALS TO GAIN TRACTION

A notable example of expanding reach through content marketing is an AI startup that leveraged YouTube tutorials to establish itself as a trusted name in the tech industry. The startup, specializing in natural language processing (NLP) tools, faced the challenge of building awareness and credibility in a crowded market. Recognizing the potential of video content, the company created a YouTube channel dedicated to simplifying complex AI concepts for diverse audiences.

Engaging STEM Researchers

The startup produced in-depth tutorials on NLP algorithms to engage researchers. These videos focused on advanced topics like transformer architectures and sentiment analysis. They included detailed code walkthroughs, practical use cases, and links to research papers, making them highly valuable to academic and industry researchers. By sharing knowledge freely, the startup positioned itself as an authority in the field, attracting attention from leading research institutions and fostering collaborations.

Capturing the Attention of Educators

For educators, the startup developed a series of videos tailored to classroom use. These tutorials broke down AI concepts into easily digestible lessons with examples and exercises. One popular video, "Understanding AI Ethics: A Classroom Discussion Guide," provided educators with a framework to introduce critical topics to students. By addressing educators' needs, the startup expanded its audience and built goodwill within the educational community.

Inspiring STEM Students

The startup's videos for students focused on beginner-friendly projects, such as "Building Your First Chatbot in Python." These tutorials were designed to be accessible, requiring minimal prior knowledge while delivering tangible outcomes. By encouraging students to experiment with AI tools, the company nurtured a new generation of users and cultivated brand loyalty early on.

Results of the Content Marketing Strategy

The YouTube channel's success was evident in its rapid growth, amassing tens of thousands of subscribers within a year. The startup's tutorials were widely shared on social media, driving traffic to its website and increasing downloads of its NLP tools. Additionally, the content's educational value led to invitations for the company to speak at conferences, publish guest blogs on reputable platforms, and collaborate with universities on research projects.

By creating tailored content for researchers, educators, and students, the startup demonstrated how a well-executed content marketing strategy could transcend traditional advertising. The free educational resources expanded the company's reach and built trust and credibility, ultimately driving business growth.

Expanding reach through content marketing requires a nuanced approach that considers diverse audiences' unique needs and preferences. Organizations can effectively engage STEM researchers, educators, and students by developing tailored blogs, videos, and case studies. The real-world example of an AI startup using YouTube tutorials underscores the potential of this strategy to build awareness, foster engagement, and drive growth. As content marketing evolves, leveraging platforms and formats that resonate with target audiences will remain a cornerstone of successful outreach efforts.

8.3.3 ANALYZING ENGAGEMENT METRICS

Analyzing engagement metrics is a cornerstone of understanding the performance of digital campaigns. In today's data-driven marketing landscape, success is no longer measured by intuition or anecdotal evidence but by concrete data points that provide insights into user behavior and campaign impact. This section delves into tracking campaign success using key engagement metrics like reach, click-through rates (CTR), and user acquisition.

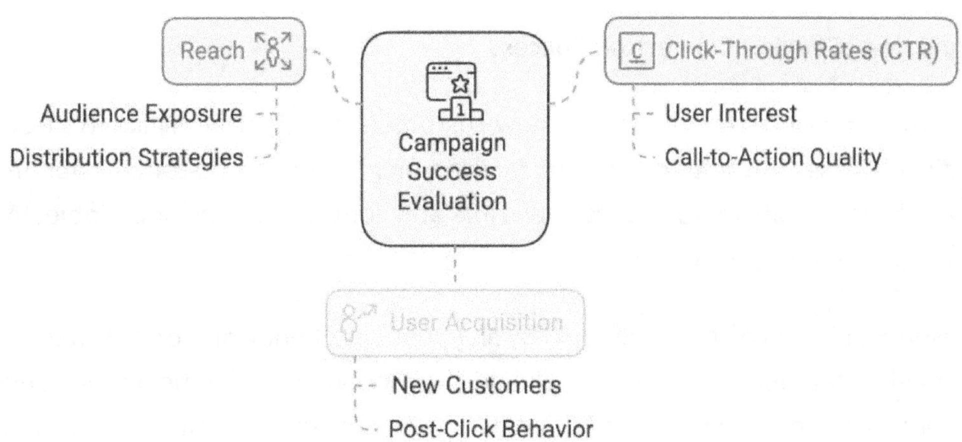

Understanding how users interact with content and platforms can help evaluate campaign success. This process involves identifying key performance indicators (KPIs) that align with campaign goals, monitoring these indicators over time, and interpreting the data to derive actionable insights. Reach, click-through rates, and user acquisition are among the most critical metrics, which together paint a comprehensive picture of a campaign's performance.

Reach: Understanding Audience Exposure

Reach measures the total number of unique users who see a campaign's content. It is a fundamental metric that indicates the breadth of an audience exposed to a brand or message. A high reach suggests effective distribution strategies and the potential for widespread awareness. For example, a social media ad targeting a broad demographic may reach hundreds of thousands, demonstrating its ability to place the content in front of many eyeballs.

However, reach alone does not guarantee engagement. While ensuring the campaign's visibility is essential, measuring how users interact with the content is equally crucial. This is where metrics like click-through rates come into play.

Click-Through Rates (CTR): Measuring Engagement Effectiveness

Click-through rates (CTR) represent the percentage of users who click on a link within a campaign compared to the total number of users who viewed the content. CTR is a vital indicator of the campaign's effectiveness in driving user interest and engagement. A high CTR signifies that the content resonates with the audience, compelling them to take action.

For instance, if an email marketing campaign is sent to 10,000 recipients and 500 of them click on the embedded link, the CTR would be 5%. This metric helps marketers assess the quality of their call-to-action (CTA), the relevance of the content to the target audience, and the appeal of the overall messaging. Consistently low CTRs might indicate a need to refine the campaign's creative elements or better align the message with audience interests.

User Acquisition: Gauging Conversion Success

User acquisition measures the number of new customers or subscribers gained through a campaign. This metric is critical for campaigns focused on growth and customer onboarding. It evaluates the campaign's ability to attract new users and contribute to business objectives such as revenue generation or audience expansion.

Tracking user acquisition often involves analyzing post-click behavior. For example, if a user clicks on a link in a paid ad but does not complete the desired action—like signing up for a service or purchasing a product—there may be friction points in the user journey. Optimizing landing pages, simplifying sign-up processes, or offering incentives can help improve conversion rates.

While reach, CTR, and user acquisition are distinct metrics, they are interconnected. A campaign with a broad reach but low CTR may indicate that the content needs better targeting. Conversely, a campaign with a high CTR but low user acquisition might suggest challenges in converting interest into action. By examining these metrics in tandem, marketers can identify strengths and weaknesses in their strategies and make data-driven adjustments.

Moreover, these metrics can be segmented by various factors, such as demographics, geography, or device type, to uncover deeper insights. Advanced analytics tools and dashboards enable marketers to track these metrics in real time, providing the agility to tweak campaigns mid-flight for optimal results.

In conclusion, analyzing engagement metrics like reach, click-through rates, and user acquisition is essential for evaluating the success of digital campaigns. By closely monitoring these KPIs, marketers can ensure their strategies are aligned with their goals, optimize performance, and achieve meaningful engagement with their target audience.

8.4: GAMIFICATION AND INCENTIVES

8.4.1 INTEGRATING GAMIFICATION INTO PLATFORMS

In today's competitive digital landscape, user engagement is a cornerstone of platform success. Gamification—applying game-design elements in non-game contexts—has emerged as a powerful strategy for fostering user participation, motivation, and loyalty. By incorporating elements such as leaderboards, badges, and achievement milestones, platforms can create compelling experiences that attract users and sustain their involvement over time. This section explores the integration of gamification into platforms, highlighting key elements and illustrating its impact through a real-world case study.

Examples of Gamification Elements

Gamification relies on various design elements that leverage human psychology, particularly intrinsic and extrinsic motivators. Below are some key examples:

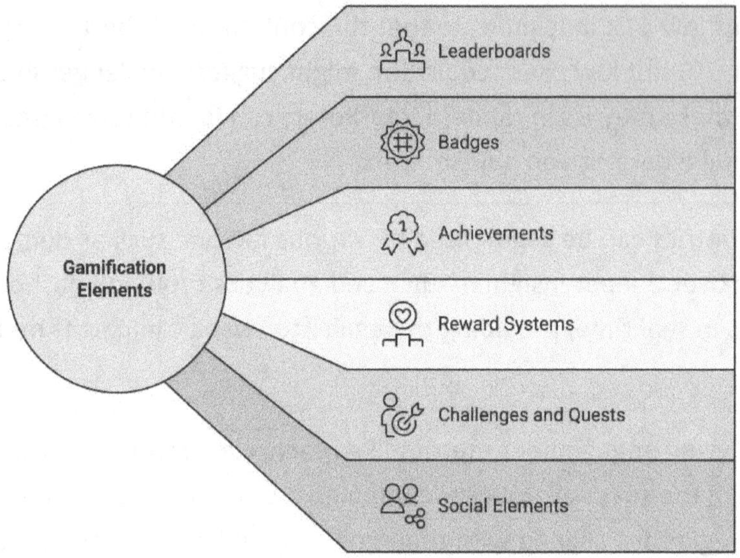

1. **Leaderboards:** Leaderboards rank users based on specific metrics, such as points, contributions, or performance. They tap into the natural desire for competition and social recognition. Users are motivated to climb the ranks and maintain their positions, fostering a sense of achievement and visibility within the community. For instance, platforms like Duolingo use leaderboards to encourage language learners to practice consistently and outperform their peers.

2. **Badges:** Badges are visual representations of achievements. They serve as status symbols that users can display on their profiles, providing tangible evidence of their skills, contributions, or milestones. By appealing to users' desire for acknowledgment and self-expression, badges create a sense of accomplishment and encourage others to strive for similar recognition.

3. **Achievements**: Milestones mark significant progress or accomplishments, such as completing a certain number of tasks, reaching a predefined goal, or surpassing a benchmark. Breaking long-term objectives into smaller, achievable steps and milestones helps maintain user motivation and reduce the likelihood of disengagement. For example, fitness apps like Strava reward users with milestones for completing a specific number of workouts or achieving a personal best.

4. **Reward Systems:** Rewards, such as points, virtual currency, or tangible incentives, reinforce positive behavior and give users a sense of value for their contributions. These systems encourage sustained engagement by creating a loop where effort leads to rewards, and rewards drive further attempts. Amazon's Mechanical Turk, for example, incentivizes users with monetary compensation for completing tasks, supplemented by badges and performance scores.

5. **Challenges and Quests:** Platforms can gamify goal-setting and problem-solving by introducing challenges or quests. Users are tasked with specific objectives requiring collaboration, creativity, or persistence. These activities foster a sense of adventure and purpose, enhancing overall user satisfaction.

6. **Social Elements** Gamification elements incorporating social interaction—such as collaborative challenges, peer recognition, or team competitions—tap into users' need for connection and community. Platforms like Reddit employ karma points and upvotes, rewarding individual contributions and building a sense of collective achievement.

CASE STUDY: A COMMUNITY PLATFORM DRIVING USER CONTRIBUTIONS THROUGH REWARD SYSTEMS

To understand the practical implications of gamification, consider the example of Stack Overflow, a leading online platform for developers to share knowledge and solve coding problems. The platform's success hinges on encouraging user-generated Content, maintaining high-quality interactions, and building a thriving Community. Gamification plays a pivotal role in achieving these objectives.

PLATFORM OVERVIEW

Stack Overflow is designed as a Q&A platform where developers can post questions, answer queries, and upvote or downvote contributions based on relevance and accuracy. The platform's gamification elements create an ecosystem that rewards expertise, collaboration, and constructive participation.

Gamification Strategies

1. **Reputation Points** Stack Overflow's reputation system assigns points to users based on their activity. For example:

    - Asking a well-received question earns points.
    - Providing an upvoted answer garners additional points.
    - Receiving an accepted answer contributes significantly to a user's score.

    Reputation points are a quantifiable measure of a user's credibility and expertise, motivating contributors to provide high-quality, accurate information.

2. **Badges** The platform awards badges for various achievements, such as providing a certain number of answers, editing posts, or earning a specific number of upvotes in a single day. These badges are categorized into bronze, silver, and gold tiers, representing different levels of accomplishment. This tiered system incentivizes ongoing participation and recognizes diverse contributions.

3. **Leaderboards** Stack Overflow's leaderboards highlight top contributors within specific tags (e.g., Python, JavaScript) and across the platform. By fostering competition and visibility, leaderboards encourage users to participate and actively become recognized experts in their chosen domains.

4. **Privileges and Access Levels** As users accumulate reputation points, they unlock privileges such as editing posts, voting to close questions, or moderating Content. These privileges gamify progression, creating a sense of contentment and responsibility. Users are motivated to contribute constructively to gain more significant influence within the community.

5. **Collaborative Challenges** During specific events or campaigns, Stack Overflow introduces collaborative challenges that encourage users to work together to achieve a collective goal, such as answering a high volume of questions in a particular programming language. These challenges promote teamwork and a shared sense of purpose.

IMPACT OF GAMIFICATION

1. **Increased User Engagement** Gamification has significantly enhanced user engagement on Stack Overflow. The reputation system, in particular, incentivizes frequent contributions, while badges and leaderboards sustain long-term involvement. As a result, the platform consistently ranks among the top destinations for developers seeking peer-to-peer learning.

2. **High-Quality Content** Stack Overflow's content elements ensure the platform maintains a high content standard by rewarding accuracy and relevance. Users are motivated to provide thoughtful answers to earn points and recognition, which benefits the broader community.

3. **Community Building** Gamification fosters a sense of belonging and collaboration among Stack Overflow's users. By highlighting individual achievements while promoting collective goals, the platform has built a loyal and active user base that supports its mission.

4. **Sustained Growth** Over the years, Stack Overflow's gamification strategies have contributed to its sustained growth and success. The platform's ability to attract and retain contributors has been instrumental in its evolution into a premier resource for developers worldwide.

KEY CONSIDERATIONS FOR INTEGRATING GAMIFICATION

While gamification offers numerous benefits, its implementation requires careful planning and execution. Below are some best practices for integrating gamification into platforms:

1. **Understand User Motivations** Tailor gamification elements to align with your target audience's needs and motivations. While competitive leaderboards may appeal to some users, others might prioritize collaborative challenges or personal milestones.

2. **Balance Intrinsic and Extrinsic Rewards** Strive to balance extrinsic rewards (e.g., points, badges) with intrinsic motivators (e.g., learning, mastery, purpose). This approach ensures that users remain engaged even when external incentives diminish.

3. **Ensure Fairness and Transparency.** Design gamification systems that are fair, transparent, and resistant to manipulation. For example, clearly define the criteria for earning points or badges and implement measures to prevent gaming the system.

4. **Avoid Over-Gamification** Excessive or poorly designed gamification can lead to user fatigue, disengagement, or a perception of triviality. Focus on meaningful elements that enhance the user experience without overwhelming it.

5. **Monitor and Iterate** Continuously monitor the impact of gamification on user behavior and platform metrics. Use feedback and data insights to refine and optimize your strategies.

Integrating gamification into platforms is a powerful strategy for driving user engagement, enhancing experiences, and building thriving communities. By leveraging elements such as leaderboards, badges, and achievement milestones, platforms can tap into fundamental human motivations and create environments that reward participation and collaboration. Stack Overflow's success illustrates that gamification enhances user satisfaction and contributes to long-term platform growth. However, effective implementation requires a thoughtful approach that prioritizes user needs, ensures fairness, and embraces continuous improvement.

8.4.2 INCENTIVIZING USER PARTICIPATION

Incentivizing user participation is crucial in fostering an engaged, active, and innovative community, especially when building platforms in domains like AI. A well-thought-out strategy to encourage user contributions adds value to the platform and drives its continuous improvement and relevance. This section explores various mechanisms to incentivize user participation, emphasizing tangible and intangible rewards and highlighting practical examples such as monetary rewards for innovative contributions.

TANGIBLE AND INTANGIBLE REWARDS

Incentives can be broadly categorized into **tangible rewards**, which have a direct financial or material value, and **intangible rewards**, which focus on recognition, access, and community engagement. Both rewards play complementary roles in creating a balanced ecosystem that encourages participation and fosters a sense of belonging.

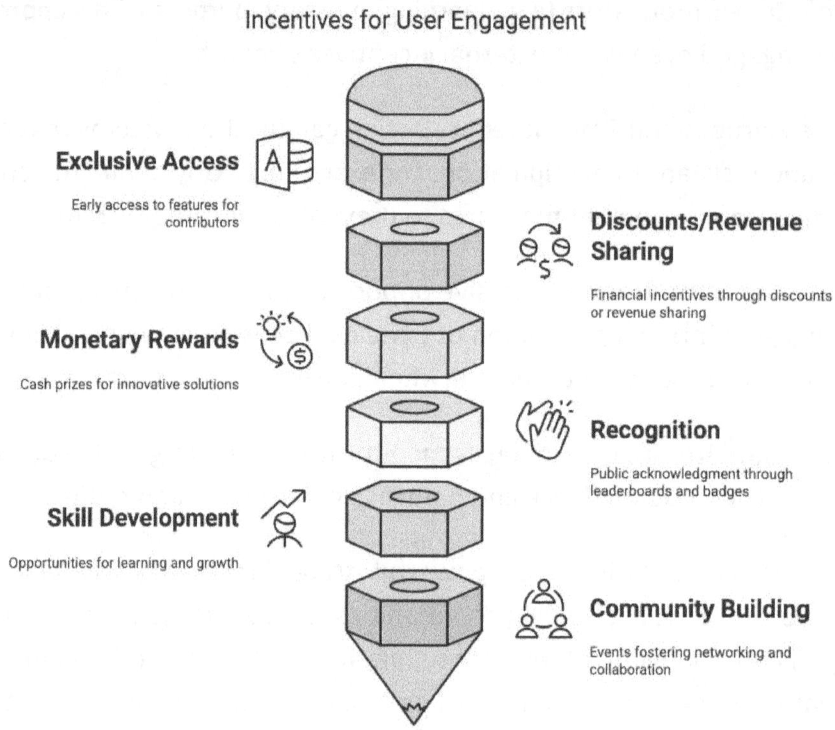

TANGIBLE REWARDS

Tangible rewards provide users with a measurable benefit for their contributions. They are particularly effective in attracting new users, encouraging repeat contributions, and rewarding innovative thinking. Key examples include:

1. **Exclusive Access to Features**

Providing contributors with early or exclusive access to new platform features is a powerful incentive. For instance, a platform might grant contributors beta access to AI tools, enabling them to test and influence the development of cutting-edge technologies before the general public.

- **Impact:** Early access creates privilege and fosters contributors' loyalty. It also allows the platform to receive real-world feedback, improving the final product.

2. **Discounts or Revenue-Sharing Models**

Another tangible incentive is offering financial rewards or sharing revenue generated from user contributions. Platforms can set up monetization options, such as:

- Providing discounts on subscription plans for users who create popular AI workflows or datasets.

- Sharing a percentage of revenue generated from user-developed tools or solutions.

- **Impact**: Revenue-sharing models incentivize high-quality contributions and align user goals with platform success, creating a mutually beneficial ecosystem.

3. **Monetary Rewards**

Monetary rewards can motivate users to create innovative solutions or participate in challenges. For example, a platform could host competitions where users submit their most creative AI workflows or models, and cash prizes could be awarded to the winners.

- **Impact**: Monetary rewards appeal to professionals and students who see opportunities to gain financial benefits while showcasing their skills.

INTANGIBLE REWARDS

While tangible rewards appeal to material motivations, intangible rewards tap into intrinsic motivators such as recognition, learning opportunities, and community building. Examples include:

1. **Recognition and Leaderboards**

Platforms can recognize top contributors through leaderboards, badges, or hall-of-fame sections. Public recognition boosts the credibility and reputation of contributors within the community.

- **Example**: A platform might rank contributors based on their activity level or the popularity of their tools and workflows, displaying their profiles prominently on the homepage.

- **Impact**: Recognition encourages healthy competition among users and fosters a culture of achievement.

2. **Skill Development Opportunities**

Many users are motivated by the opportunity to learn and grow. Platforms can incentivize participation by offering:

- Access to advanced tutorials or resources for active contributors.

- Mentorship programs connect experts with novice users.

- **Impact**: These opportunities attract users eager to upskill and remain actively engaged with the platform.

3. **Community Building**

Building a sense of belonging and community among users is a powerful intangible incentive. Platforms can organize events, virtual meetups, or forums where contributors can network, exchange ideas, and collaborate on projects.

- **Impact**: A strong community fosters long-term engagement and transforms users into advocates for the platform.

EXAMPLE: OFFERING MONETARY REWARDS FOR INNOVATIVE AI WORKFLOWS

One practical way to encourage user participation is to offer monetary rewards for creating innovative AI workflows. Such initiatives can be structured as challenges or contests, providing a competitive yet rewarding environment.

Implementation:

- The platform could announce a bi-annual contest inviting users to submit AI workflows addressing specific themes or real-world problems, such as sustainability, healthcare, or automation.
- Submissions would be evaluated based on originality, impact, and feasibility criteria.
- Winners will receive cash prizes ranging from $5,000 to $50,000 and will be recognized on the platform's homepage and promotional channels.

Benefits:

1. **Encourages Creativity**: Monetary rewards attract creative minds with diverse perspectives and innovative ideas.
2. **Increases Engagement**: Contests generate buzz, attracting existing users and new participants who might later become long-term contributors.
3. **Builds Brand Value**: The platform enhances its credibility and appeal within the AI community by promoting user success stories.

CHALLENGES AND BEST PRACTICES

While incentivizing user participation is highly effective, there are challenges and nuances to consider:

1. **Avoiding Short-Term Engagement**
   - **Challenge**: Overemphasis on tangible rewards may attract users interested in short-term gains.
   - **Solution**: To foster long-term commitment, combine tangible rewards with intangible benefits, such as recognition and skill development.
2. **Ensuring Fairness and Transparency**
   - **Challenge**: Unclear or biased evaluation criteria can lead to dissatisfaction among users.

- **Solution**: Communicate evaluation standards and involve impartial judges to ensure credibility.

3. **Balancing Cost and Return on Investment (ROI)**

   - **Challenge**: Tangible rewards can be costly, particularly for small or growing platforms.

   - **Solution**: Start with lower-cost intangible rewards and gradually introduce tangible incentives as the platform grows.

Incentivizing user participation requires tangible and intangible rewards tailored to the target audience's motivations. Platforms can create a vibrant and engaged user community by offering exclusive access to features, discounts, revenue-sharing opportunities, and recognition. Practical initiatives, such as contests with monetary rewards for innovative AI workflows, serve as compelling examples of motivating users effectively.

A thoughtful approach to incentives drives user participation and builds a thriving ecosystem where users feel valued and empowered to contribute. Ultimately, this creates a virtuous innovation cycle, engagement, and platform growth.

- Tangible and intangible rewards:
  - Exclusive access to features, discounts, or revenue-sharing for user-generated tools.
- Example:
  - Offering monetary rewards for the most innovative AI workflows.

CHAPTER 9: USER-DRIVEN INNOVATION

INTRODUCTION

THE VALUE OF USER-DRIVEN INNOVATION

Innovation has always been the heartbeat of technological progress, shaping the platforms, tools, and solutions that define modern enterprises. While organizational creativity and strategic foresight play pivotal roles, a new paradigm has emerged that magnifies innovation's potential: user-driven innovation. This concept is built on a simple yet powerful idea: users of a product, platform, or service are uniquely positioned to identify gaps, suggest improvements, and imagine entirely new use cases.

In today's hyper-competitive market landscape, where platforms vie for user engagement and loyalty, ignoring users' creative potential is a missed opportunity and a critical oversight. User-driven innovation harnesses users' ingenuity and insights, enabling platforms to evolve, adapt, and remain relevant in constantly shifting demands. Whether a developer contributes a game-changing plugin, a data scientist solves a complex problem, or a consumer suggests a new feature that transforms usability, the value of user contributions is undeniable.

This chapter explores the transformative power of user-driven innovation. By leveraging the creativity of an engaged user base, platforms can foster a virtuous cycle of growth, adaptability, and relevance. Through compelling examples and actionable strategies, this chapter outlines how enterprises can tap into this wellspring of innovation to stay competitive and lead their industries.

THE VALUE OF USER-DRIVEN INNOVATION

How Involving Users Drives Platform Growth and Adaptability

Users directly involved in the innovation process bring diverse perspectives and real-world experiences. This diversity is critical for platform growth because it reveals unmet needs and inspires solutions that might not emerge within the confines of internal development teams. Moreover, user-driven innovation creates a sense of ownership and loyalty among users, turning them into advocates and contributors rather than passive consumers.

One key advantage of involving users is the agility it imparts to platforms. By listening to users and integrating their feedback, platforms can pivot quickly in response to emerging trends and challenges. This adaptability is essential in an era of rapid technological advancements and market dynamics.

Another critical dimension is scalability. Platforms that empower users to innovate can expand their ecosystem without proportionally increasing their resource investments. User-created content, plugins, or solutions add value to the platform, creating a self-sustaining growth cycle.

Finally, involving users enhances a platform's relevance and longevity. Users are often the first to identify new opportunities or pain points that developers or managers might overlook. By integrating these insights, platforms remain aligned with user needs and preferences, ensuring their solutions are both timely and impactful.

Examples of User-Driven Innovation

GitHub's Ecosystem of User-Created Plugins

GitHub exemplifies the transformative power of user-driven innovation. As one of the world's largest code-hosting platforms, GitHub thrives on contributions from its user community. While GitHub provides foundational tools for version control and collaboration, its ecosystem has grown exponentially through user-created plugins and extensions.

For example, developers have built tools to automate code reviews, manage CI/CD pipelines, and enhance project management workflows without requiring GitHub's direct involvement. This ecosystem adds immense value to GitHub's broader user base and keeps the platform relevant to evolving developer needs. By empowering users to extend its capabilities, GitHub has positioned itself as a dynamic and indispensable part of the software development process.

Kaggle Competitions Inspiring Groundbreaking AI Models

Kaggle, a platform for data science competitions, illustrates another dimension of user-driven innovation. The platform invites data scientists worldwide to tackle complex problems, from optimizing supply chains to advancing healthcare diagnostics. Participants bring diverse skills, perspectives, and creativity, often achieving breakthroughs that traditional teams might struggle to deliver.

One notable example is the development of AI models for diabetic retinopathy detection. Kaggle organized a competition to create algorithms to identify this condition from retinal images. The winning models, developed by participants outside the organizing institution, achieved unprecedented accuracy and later informed real-world applications in healthcare. By engaging its user base, Kaggle solved specific challenges and pushed the boundaries of AI innovation.

WHAT THIS CHAPTER OFFERS

Strategies for Empowering Users to Contribute, Collaborate, and Innovate

This chapter provides a comprehensive guide to enabling and encouraging user-driven innovation. It offers actionable strategies for fostering a collaborative environment where users feel empowered to contribute their ideas, skills, and expertise. Some of these strategies include:

- **Creating Open and Accessible Platforms:** Ensuring users have the tools and frameworks needed to contribute. This involves APIs, SDKs, and documentation, making building, integrating, and innovating easy.

- **Building a Feedback-Driven Culture:** Actively soliciting, processing, and implementing user feedback. Regular communication and acknowledgment of user contributions foster a sense of partnership.

- **Offering Incentives and Recognition:** Rewarding users for their contributions through tangible incentives like monetary prizes and certifications or intangible benefits like public recognition or enhanced status within the community.

- **Nurturing Communities of Practice:** Establishing forums, discussion groups, and events where users can connect, share ideas, and collaborate. These communities often become incubators for innovative ideas.

Tools and Techniques to Turn User-Driven Ideas into Impactful Features

Empowering users to innovate is only part of the equation. The real challenge lies in transforming their ideas into impactful features that enhance the platform. This chapter explores several tools and techniques to bridge this gap:

- **Crowdsourcing Platforms:** Leveraging tools like Ideascale or UserVoice to collect, prioritize, and refine user-generated ideas.

- **Hackathons and Innovation Sprints:** Organizing events where users can collaboratively prototype solutions, often resulting in rapid, creative outcomes.

- **Data-Driven Prioritization:** Using analytics to identify the most promising user-driven ideas, ensuring that development resources are allocated effectively.

- **Prototyping and Iterative Testing:** Collaborating with users during development to test and refine features, ensuring they meet real-world needs.

- **Co-Creation Partnerships:** Establishing formal partnerships with power users or user groups to co-develop key features. These partnerships leverage engaged users' unique insights and skills while maintaining alignment with platform goals.

User-driven innovation is not a fleeting trend but a cornerstone of modern platform success. By involving users in innovation, platforms unlock new avenues for growth, adaptability, and differentiation. This chapter equips you with the knowledge and tools to harness this power, offering strategies to empower your users, foster collaboration, and turn their ideas into transformative features. The examples of GitHub and Kaggle are just the beginning—your platform could be the next to demonstrate the immense value of user-driven innovation.

9.1: EMPOWERING USER CONTRIBUTIONS

9.1.1 PROVIDING TOOLS FOR USER INNOVATION

Enabling user innovation has become a cornerstone for thriving platform ecosystems in the rapidly evolving digital landscape. Platforms enhance their value proposition and foster a vibrant community of creators and problem-solvers by equipping users with tools that empower them to innovate. This section delves into the features that enable user innovation and illustrates these concepts with a pertinent example.

FEATURES THAT ENABLE USERS TO BUILD AND INNOVATE

Workflow Builders

Workflow builders serve as intuitive interfaces that allow users to design and automate processes without requiring extensive technical expertise. These tools often include visual drag-and-drop functionalities, pre-built templates, and integrations with various systems. By abstracting the complexity of underlying technical operations, workflow builders enable users to:

- **Customize Processes:** Tailor workflows to their unique requirements without relying on professional developers.
- **Automate Tasks**: Streamline repetitive tasks to enhance efficiency and focus on higher-value activities.
- **Scale Operations**: Adapt workflows as organizational needs grow, ensuring scalability without reengineering processes from scratch.

For instance, a marketing professional can use a workflow builder to automate lead nurturing by connecting email campaigns, customer relationship management (CRM) software, and analytics tools. Such customization enables businesses to respond quickly to changing market demands.

Low-Code/No-Code Platforms

Low-code and no-code platforms have revolutionized how users interact with technology by democratizing application development. These platforms provide an accessible environment for individuals with minimal programming knowledge to create sophisticated solutions. Key benefits include:

- **Rapid Prototyping**: Users can quickly transform ideas into functional prototypes, significantly reducing time-to-market.
- **Cost Efficiency**: Businesses save on development costs as non-technical users can build applications in-house.

- **Increased Agility**: Teams can iterate on solutions faster, adapting to feedback and evolving requirements.

Such platforms often include:

- Pre-designed components and templates.
- Intuitive drag-and-drop interfaces.
- Built-in integrations with databases, APIs, and third-party services.

For example, a small business owner can use a no-code platform to develop a custom inventory management system that tracks stock levels, generates alerts for low inventory, and integrates with e-commerce platforms.

APIs (Application Programming Interfaces)

APIs enable user innovation by acting as the bridge between different software systems. By providing access to a platform's functionalities and data, APIs empower developers to:

- **Extend Functionality**: Build custom features or integrate third-party tools to enhance the platform's capabilities.
- **Access Data**: Leverage data for insights, analytics, and informed decision-making.
- **Create Ecosystems**: Foster innovation by enabling developers to create complementary applications and services.

Well-documented APIs and developer support, such as tutorials, forums, and sample code, significantly enhance usability. For example, a logistics company might use an API to integrate a mapping service with its fleet management software, optimizing delivery routes and reducing fuel consumption.

EXAMPLE: AN AI PLATFORM PROVIDING DRAG-AND-DROP TOOLS FOR CREATING PREDICTIVE MODELS

Consider an AI platform designed to democratize access to machine learning by providing drag-and-drop tools for creating predictive models. This platform exemplifies how user innovation can be facilitated through intuitive design and robust functionality.

- **Accessible Interface**: The platform's drag-and-drop interface allows users to build machine learning workflows without writing a single line of code. Users can select datasets, choose algorithms, and configure parameters through a visual canvas.
- **Pre-Built Components**: The platform includes pre-built components, such as data preprocessing modules, feature engineering tools, and evaluation metrics, to simplify the modeling process.

- **Integration Capabilities**: APIs enable users to operationalize insights by connecting their predictive models with external applications, such as CRM systems or business intelligence tools.
- **Collaboration Features**: Teams can collaborate on model development, share workflows, and iterate on designs in real time.
- **Educational Resources**: Tutorials, documentation, and community forums help users navigate the platform and maximize its potential.

For instance, a retail company can leverage this platform to create a predictive model for demand forecasting. The company's data analyst, with minimal coding experience, can upload historical sales data, select a time-series forecasting algorithm, and configure the model parameters using drag-and-drop tools. Once the model is trained and validated, it can automatically be deployed via an API to adjust inventory levels based on predicted demand.

This approach empowers retail companies to innovate, reduces dependency on external technical resources, accelerates decision-making, and improves operational efficiency.

Providing tools for user innovation is not merely a strategic choice but necessary in today's competitive landscape. Features such as workflow builders, low-code/no-code platforms, and APIs democratize access to technology, enabling users to tailor solutions to their unique needs and challenges. Platforms can drive engagement, unlock new revenue streams, and maintain a competitive edge by fostering an ecosystem where users can innovate. The example of an AI platform offering drag-and-drop tools for predictive modeling underscores the transformative impact such tools can have on users across industries, illustrating the profound value of enabling user-driven innovation.

9.1.2 CREATING CUSTOMIZATION OPTIONS

Customization is critical to ensuring the usability and adaptability of AI platforms across diverse user bases. Businesses can significantly enhance user engagement, satisfaction, and retention by allowing users to tailor the platform to their specific needs. This section explores the key elements of customization and provides a practical example to demonstrate its impact.

ALLOWING USERS TO TAILOR THE PLATFORM FOR THEIR NEEDS

Customization in an AI platform empowers users by giving them flexibility and control over how they interact with the system. This approach acknowledges that every user or organization operates uniquely and requires solutions that can adapt to their workflows, goals, and challenges.

1. **Plugins and Add-Ons**
Offering plugins or add-ons allows users to extend the platform's functionality without altering

its core. Plugins are especially beneficial in modular AI systems where specific tools can be added or removed based on user preferences. For example:

- A marketing team might need plugins for customer segmentation and campaign analysis.
- An educator could require tools for real-time feedback and grading systems.

Platforms like WordPress have mastered this concept, providing an extensive library of plugins that enable users to create bespoke experiences. Similarly, AI platforms can adopt this approach, offering a marketplace for AI-driven plugins tailored to industries such as healthcare, education, and finance.

2. **Templates for Rapid Deployment**
   Pre-designed templates tailored to specific use cases can significantly reduce the learning curve for new users. For instance:

   - An AI analytics platform could provide templates for financial forecasting, inventory optimization, or customer behavior analysis.
   - Templates can be industry-specific, such as a template for healthcare providers to track patient data or for educators to manage lesson plans.

These templates act as starting points, allowing users to customize them further to meet their requirements. By integrating ready-to-use solutions, platforms can accommodate novice users and experts seeking efficiency.

3. **Personalized Workflows**
   Allowing users to design workflows ensures the platform fits seamlessly into their daily operations. This involves:

   - **Drag-and-Drop Workflow Designers**: Providing a visual interface for users to map out their processes. For example, a user can automate repetitive tasks such as data entry, analysis, and reporting.
   - **Conditional Logic**: Enabling users to set rules and triggers that modify platform behavior based on specific inputs or events.
   - **Role-Based Customization**: Different organizational roles may require unique interfaces or access levels. Custom workflows can ensure that each role receives the necessary information and tools without unnecessary distractions.

EXAMPLE: AI PLATFORM FOR EDUCATORS ENABLING CUSTOMIZATION OF LEARNING MODULES

Imagine an AI-powered education platform designed to enhance teaching and learning experiences. Such a platform can allow educators to customize learning modules according to their curriculum requirements, student needs, and teaching preferences. Here's how this customization could be implemented:

1. **Custom Learning Modules**
Educators can create or modify lesson plans using drag-and-drop tools. They can integrate multimedia resources, quizzes, and interactive activities tailored to different learning styles.

2. **Adaptive Learning Pathways**
Using AI, the platform can suggest personalized learning pathways for students based on their performance and interests. Educators can tweak these pathways to align with specific learning objectives.

3. **Templates for Various Educational Scenarios**
The platform could provide templates for diverse classroom scenarios, such as:
    - A flipped classroom module where students review materials at home and engage in interactive activities in class.
    - A remedial education template focusing on foundational skills for struggling learners.
    - A project-based learning template emphasizing collaborative and hands-on activities.

4. **Data Dashboards for Individual Educators**
Teachers can customize dashboards to track student progress, attendance, and engagement metrics. This personalized view helps them identify trends and make data-driven decisions to improve learning outcomes.

Integrating these customization features makes the AI platform a powerful tool for enhancing educators' ability to deliver personalized and practical instruction.

BENEFITS OF CUSTOMIZATION

1. **Enhanced User Engagement**
Users are likelier to engage with a platform that adapts to their needs and preferences. Customization fosters a sense of ownership, making users feel the platform was designed specifically for them.

2. **Increased Productivity**
By aligning the platform with existing workflows and goals, users can accomplish tasks more efficiently, saving time and resources.

3. **Scalability Across Industries**
A customizable AI platform can cater to a wide range of users, from small businesses to large enterprises, making it a scalable solution that grows with the user.

4. **Competitive Advantage**
Customization options can differentiate an AI platform in a crowded marketplace, attracting users looking for tailored solutions that meet their needs.

In conclusion, offering robust customization options, such as plugins, templates, and personalized workflows, transforms an AI platform from a generic tool into a dynamic and user-centric solution. This approach enhances usability and solidifies the platform's position as an indispensable asset in its users' operations.

9.1.3 ENABLING MONETIZATION FOR USER CREATIONS

User-generated content (UGC) has become a cornerstone of the digital economy. Platforms like YouTube, TikTok, and Patreon have demonstrated the power of enabling creators to monetize their work. However, in AI, user-generated content extends beyond videos and music to include AI workflows, datasets, pre-trained models, and custom integrations. Enabling monetization for these creations fosters innovation, attracts a broader user base, and establishes a thriving ecosystem of contributors and consumers. A robust monetization strategy can elevate the platform's value, creating a win-win for both the creators and the platform itself. This section explores the mechanisms and opportunities for monetizing user-generated content within AI platforms, focusing on revenue-sharing and the development of marketplaces.

REVENUE-SHARING FOR USER-GENERATED CONTENT

Revenue-sharing models are a pivotal incentive for creators, ensuring they are rewarded for their contributions. These models allow platforms to align their success with the success of their creators, fostering a symbiotic relationship. In the AI ecosystem, revenue-sharing can be particularly impactful in the following areas:

AI Workflows

AI workflows are sequences of pre-configured tasks that automate complex processes, such as data preprocessing, feature extraction, model training, and evaluation. For instance, a creator could develop a workflow to automate customer sentiment analysis for e-commerce platforms. Platforms can attract experts who offer valuable, ready-to-use solutions by enabling creators to monetize these workflows. A revenue-sharing model could involve splitting the subscription fees or one-time purchase costs between the platform and the creator, incentivizing high-quality contributions.

Datasets

Datasets are the backbone of AI development, and curating high-quality datasets is labor-intensive. Platforms can enable users to monetize datasets they have cleaned, annotated, or compiled. For example, a creator could upload a dataset of annotated medical images for disease detection. The revenue-sharing model could include licensing fees for each usage or download, contributing to the creator's earnings. Additionally, platforms could provide tiered pricing models, allowing creators to offer different licensing terms, such as academic use versus commercial use.

Pre-trained Models

Pre-trained models significantly reduce the time and effort required to deploy AI solutions. For example, a creator could train and offer a neural network for supply chain optimization on the platform. Users could purchase the model outright or pay for access based on usage metrics like API calls. Revenue-sharing ensures that the creator benefits proportionally to the value their model generates.

Integrations

Integrations refer to plug-ins or add-ons that enhance platform functionality. For instance, a user might create an integration that connects the platform's AI capabilities to popular customer relationship management (CRM) tools. Such integrations expand the platform, making it indispensable for users. A revenue-sharing model could involve a percentage of the subscription fee for users who adopt the integration.

MARKETPLACE FOR AI WORKFLOWS, DATASETS, AND INTEGRATIONS

A marketplace is a vital infrastructure for monetizing user-generated content in the AI domain. It is a central hub where creators can showcase their work, and users can discover and acquire valuable resources. A well-designed marketplace ensures transparency, accessibility, and scalability, driving adoption and engagement.

KEY FEATURES OF THE MARKETPLACE

Search and Discovery

The marketplace should offer advanced search and filtering capabilities, allowing users to find the needed resources quickly. Tags, categories, and recommendations can help users navigate through extensive catalogs of AI workflows, datasets, and integrations. For instance, a user looking for supply chain optimization models can search by industry, application, or performance metrics.

Rating and Reviews

User feedback is critical for building trust and ensuring quality. The marketplace should include a rating and review system where buyers can share their experiences. This system incentivizes creators to maintain high standards while guiding potential buyers toward the most effective solutions.

Licensing and Pricing Models

Creators should have the flexibility to choose pricing models that suit their offerings. Options could include:

- **Pay-per-use:** Ideal for API-based models or workflows.
- **Subscription-based:** Suitable for ongoing access to updates and support.
- **One-time purchase:** For standalone datasets or integrations.

The marketplace should also support various licensing terms, such as single-use, multi-use, and unlimited-use licenses, catering to different buyer needs.

Analytics and Insights

Creators benefit from understanding how their offerings perform in the marketplace. Analytics tools can provide insights into sales, user engagement, and performance metrics, enabling creators to refine their offerings and maximize revenue.

Secure Transactions

The marketplace must prioritize secure payment processing, protecting both creators and buyers. Blockchain technology could be leveraged to ensure transparency in transactions and revenue-sharing.

Collaboration and Community

Encouraging collaboration among creators can lead to the development of more comprehensive solutions. The marketplace could include forums or communities where creators can exchange ideas, seek feedback, and form partnerships.

EXAMPLE: A USER SELLING A PRE-BUILT AI MODEL FOR SUPPLY CHAIN OPTIMIZATION

Imagine a user, Alex, who specializes in supply chain analytics. Alex develops a pre-built AI model that optimizes inventory levels, predicts demand fluctuations, and identifies potential real-time bottlenecks.

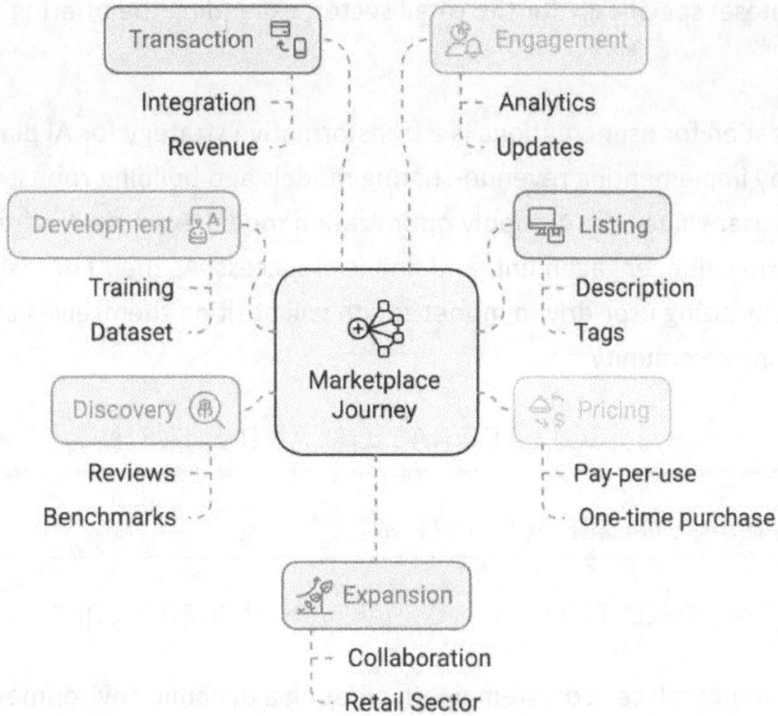

1. **Development:** Alex uses the platform and train the AI model, incorporating years of expertise in supply chain management. The model is fine-tuned with a proprietary dataset.

2. **Listing:** Alex uploads the model to the marketplace, providing a detailed description, performance metrics, and use-case examples. The model is tagged under "Supply Chain," "Optimization," and "Demand."

3. **Pricing:** AI chooses a pay-per-use pricing model, charging $0.10 per API call, and offers a one-time purchase option for $5,000. Licensing terms are outlined, with options for commercial and academic use.

4. **Discovery:** A logistics company searching for supply chain optimization solutions discovers the AI model's marketplace engine. They are impressed by the reviews and the detailed performance benchmarks provided.

5. **Transaction:** The company integrates the API-based model into its existing systems. They pay a monthly fee based on usage, and Alex earns a percentage of this revenue through the platform's re-platforming model.

6. **Engagement:** AI monitors the model's performance over time using the platform's analytics. Feedback from users helps Alex release updates and improve the model, further boosting its popularity and revenue potential.

7. **Expansion:** Encouraged by the success, Alex collaborates with another creator to develop a dataset specifically for the retail sector, expanding the offering's offerings and audience.

Enabling monetization for user creations is a transformative strategy for AI platforms. Platforms can empower creators by implementing revenue-sharing models and building robust marketplaces while delivering immense user value. The AI supply optimization model example illustrates ecosystems' potential to drive innovation, engagement, and financial success. As the AI domain continues to evolve, platforms prioritizing user-driven monetization will position themselves as leaders in fostering a dynamic and thriving community.

9.2: COLLABORATION AND SHARING

9.2.1 BUILDING A MARKETPLACE ECOSYSTEM

CREATING SPACES FOR USERS TO SHARE AND MONETIZE CONTRIBUTIONS

The essence of a marketplace ecosystem lies in creating a dynamic environment where contributors and consumers can interact seamlessly. This involves developing an infrastructure that supports the sharing, collaborating, and monetizing of valuable assets. In the context of AI and technology-driven ecosystems, these assets often include code libraries, pre-trained models, and reusable workflows. The primary goal is to foster innovation while enabling contributors to profit from their efforts, thus driving a self-sustaining cycle of development and utilization.

Code Libraries

Code libraries form the backbone of modern software development, especially in AI. These libraries encapsulate reusable functionalities that developers can incorporate into their projects. A marketplace that allows contributors to share proprietary or open-source libraries encourages innovation and collaboration. For example, a contributor might create a library that simplifies a complex algorithm, such as natural language processing (NLP), and share it on the marketplace. Others can purchase, download, or integrate the library into their systems, saving time and resources.

It is critical to incentivize contributions to such marketplaces. This can be achieved through revenue-sharing models, subscription-based access, or a pay-per-download system. To ensure quality, marketplaces can employ peer reviews, ratings, and certifications, which provide confidence to potential buyers while recognizing high-quality contributors.

Pre-trained Models

Pre-trained AI models are another invaluable asset in a marketplace ecosystem. These models are trained on vast datasets and can be fine-tuned for specific applications. For instance, a pre-trained image recognition model could be adapted for medical imaging to detect abnormalities in X-rays. A marketplace that facilitates the sharing and monetizing of these models can dramatically accelerate innovation, especially for startups and researchers who lack the resources to train models from scratch.

Marketplaces can also enable collaboration between contributors by supporting transfer learning. This allows users to adapt existing models for their needs, creating a win-win scenario: contributors earn revenue while consumers save time and computational costs.

Reusable Workflows

Reusable workflows provide end-to-end solutions for specific tasks. For example, a workflow for deploying a machine learning model to the cloud might include steps for data preprocessing, model training, validation, and deployment. By sharing these workflows on a marketplace, contributors can help others bypass tedious development processes and focus on value-added activities.

Monetization models for workflows can include subscription plans, one-time purchases, or tiered pricing based on functionality. Marketplaces should offer documentation, tutorials, and community support to enhance usability and enable seamless adoption and adaptation.

Example: A Marketplace for AI-Generated Datasets in Healthcare

Healthcare presents a unique opportunity for AI-driven marketplaces due to its reliance on data for innovation and decision-making. Creating a marketplace for AI-generated datasets in healthcare can transform how the industry accesses, shares, and utilizes data. Below, we explore the concept in detail.

The Value of AI-Generated Datasets

AI-generated datasets are synthetic or derived datasets created using machine learning algorithms. These datasets are particularly useful in healthcare, where privacy and compliance concerns limit the availability of real-world data. By synthesizing anonymized datasets that retain statistical relevance, developers can work with high-quality data while adhering to privacy regulations like HIPAA or GDPR.

For instance, an AI algorithm could generate a dataset of synthetic patient profiles based on real-world hospital data. These profiles include information about symptoms, diagnoses, treatments, and outcomes, enabling researchers to test models without risking patient privacy.

MARKETPLACE FEATURES

A healthcare dataset marketplace could include the following features:

1. **Data Categories:** Organize datasets by categories such as radiology, oncology, cardiology, and public health, making it easier for users to find relevant datasets.

2. **Data Quality Metrics:** Provide completeness, accuracy, and bias assessment metrics to help users evaluate datasets.

3. **Search and Discovery:** Implement advanced search capabilities with filters for data type, size, and licensing options.

4. **Compliance and Certification:** Ensure all datasets meet privacy regulations and are certified by trusted organizations.

5. **Pricing and Access Models:** Offer flexible pricing models, including one-time purchases, subscriptions, and pay-per-query options.

6. **Community and Support:** Include forums, FAQs, and support channels to foster collaboration and address user queries.

STAKEHOLDER BENEFITS

A marketplace for AI-generated healthcare datasets offers distinct benefits for various stakeholders:

- **Hospitals and Research Institutions:** These organizations can monetize their data assets by providing de-identified datasets to the marketplace.

- **AI Developers and Startups:** Developers gain access to high-quality data at a fraction of the cost and effort required to collect it themselves.

- **Regulators and Policy Makers:** The marketplace can serve as a benchmark for ethical and compliant data sharing, setting standards for the industry.

- **Patients** Indirectly benefit from improved AI solutions, as access to diverse datasets enables the development of more accurate diagnostic and treatment tools.

MONETIZATION MODELS

Monetization is a critical aspect of sustaining such a marketplace. Several models can be employed:

1. **Subscription-Based Access:** Users pay a recurring fee to access a predefined set of datasets.

2. **Pay-Per-Use:** Users pay based on the volume of data accessed or downloaded.

3. **Revenue Sharing:** Contributors receive a percentage of the revenue generated from their datasets.

4. **Premium Datasets:** High-value datasets with additional features or annotations can be priced higher.

Use Case: Radiology Dataset Marketplace

Consider a marketplace specifically for radiology datasets. Radiologists and healthcare providers could upload de-identified imaging data annotated with relevant medical diagnoses, such as X-rays, CT scans, and MRIs. AI developers could then purchase these datasets to train or validate their models.

For example, a startup developing an AI tool to detect lung cancer in X-rays could purchase annotated datasets from the marketplace. By accessing diverse and high-quality datasets, the startup can improve its model's accuracy and reduce the time it takes to market. Meanwhile, contributors like hospitals earn revenue for their data assets, incentivizing further participation.

Challenges and Solutions

Building and sustaining a marketplace for healthcare datasets involves several challenges:

1. **Data Privacy and Compliance:** Ensure all datasets are de-identified and compliant with regulations through automated compliance checks and certifications.

2. **Data Quality and Standardization:** Implement quality control mechanisms and encourage standardization of data formats.

3. **Adoption and Trust:** Build trust by collaborating with reputable institutions and providing transparent policies.

4. **Technology Infrastructure:** Develop scalable and secure platforms for large datasets and user demands.

Partnerships between technology companies and regulatory bodies are essential to addressing these challenges. Additionally, robust security measures and user education can enhance adoption and trust.

Building a marketplace ecosystem, particularly for AI-driven assets, requires careful planning and execution. Marketplaces can drive innovation, reduce development costs, and foster collaboration by creating spaces for users to share and monetize contributions like code libraries, pre-trained models, and reusable workflows. The example of a healthcare dataset marketplace highlights the potential for AI-driven solutions to transform industries, improve accessibility, and unlock new revenue streams.

In the broader context of AI, marketplaces serve as catalysts for growth by democratizing access to resources and expertise. As the demand for AI solutions continues to grow, these ecosystems will play a pivotal role in shaping the future of technology and its impact on society.

9.2.2 FOSTERING TEAM COLLABORATION

Collaboration within teams is the cornerstone of successful projects, particularly in the fast-paced, technologically advanced world of AI and software development. Effective collaboration fosters creativity, reduces errors, and accelerates the delivery of quality solutions. Below, we explore two critical components of fostering team collaboration—leveraging version control and real-time collaboration tools—alongside strategies to ensure project reproducibility.

VERSION CONTROL AND REAL-TIME COLLABORATION TOOLS

In modern team-based environments, version control systems (VCS) and real-time collaboration tools are indispensable. They facilitate seamless coordination among team members, streamline project management, and minimize conflicts during development. By integrating AI into these tools, teams can enhance their workflows, improve code quality, and achieve greater efficiency.

The Importance of VCS and Real-Time Collaboration Tools in Teams

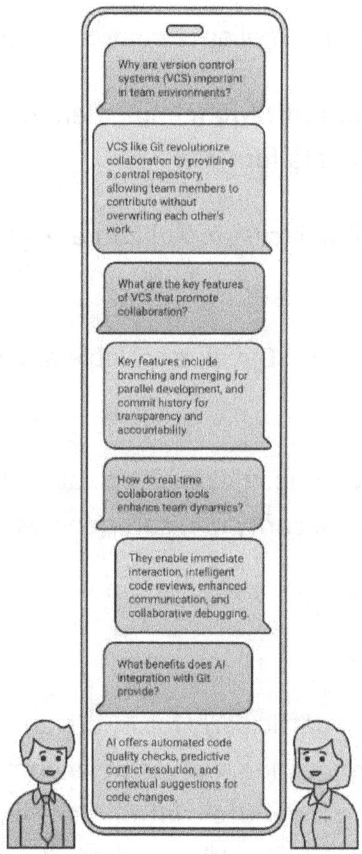

1. Version Control Systems (VCS)

Version control systems like Git have revolutionized the way developers collaborate on projects. By providing a central repository for code, Git ensures that every team member can contribute without overwriting others' work. Key features of VCS that promote collaboration include:

- **Branching and Merging:** Team members can work on separate branches, allowing parallel development of features or bug fixes. AI-powered tools integrated with Git can analyze potential merge conflicts and suggest resolutions, saving time and preventing errors.

- **Commit History and Audit Trails:** VCS maintains a comprehensive log of changes, providing transparency and accountability. AI-driven insights from commit histories can identify patterns, such as frequent errors by specific contributors, enabling proactive training or process improvements.

2. Real-Time Collaboration Tools

While VCS is ideal for asynchronous collaboration, real-time tools enable immediate interaction and collective problem-solving. Examples include Google Docs for documentation, Slack for communication, and Visual Studio Code Live Share for coding sessions. Integrating AI into these tools can transform team dynamics:

- **Intelligent Code Reviews:** AI models can review code in real time, flagging potential issues or recommending best practices during collaborative coding sessions.

- **Enhanced Communication:** Natural language processing (NLP) models embedded in chat tools can summarize lengthy discussions, suggest solutions based on historical conversations, and ensure clarity.

- **Collaborative Debugging:** AI-powered debugging tools can more rapidly identify the root causes of issues when multiple developers collaborate, making real-time problem resolution more efficient.

Example: AI Tools Integrated with Git

AI integration with Git can provide several benefits:

- **Automated Code Quality Checks:** AI models can analyze commits for adherence to coding standards, ensuring that all contributions meet the project's quality benchmarks.

- **Predictive Conflict Resolution:** AI can leverage historical data to predict merge conflicts and propose resolution strategies before disputes occur.

- **Contextual Suggestions:** AI can offer contextualized recommendations for code changes or documentation improvements directly within the Git environment, reducing the need for external consultations.

By combining VCS capabilities with real-time collaboration tools, teams can foster an environment of trust, transparency, and efficiency. Such systems enable diverse teams to work harmoniously on complex projects, even across geographical and temporal barriers.

9.2.3 ENSURING REPRODUCIBILITY

Reproducibility is fundamental in software development, particularly in AI and data science. It ensures that results can be consistently replicated, providing confidence in the reliability and accuracy of outcomes. Achieving reproducibility involves standardizing processes, documenting workflows, and leveraging tools that guarantee consistency across environments and team members.

The Importance of Reproducibility

Reproducibility is vital for several reasons:

1. **Trust and Reliability:** Stakeholders need assurance that models and systems behave predictably. Reproducibility guarantees this by demonstrating consistent results across different runs and environments.

2. **Regulatory Compliance:** Many industries, such as healthcare and finance, require reproducibility to meet regulatory standards.

3. **Collaboration and Knowledge Transfer:** When results are reproducible, new team members can seamlessly integrate into projects, accelerating knowledge transfer and reducing onboarding time.

STRATEGIES FOR ENSURING REPRODUCIBILITY

1. Environment Management

Differences in development environments can lead to inconsistent results. Tools like Docker and Conda address this challenge by creating isolated, consistent environments for projects:

- **Docker:** Docker containers encapsulate applications and their dependencies, ensuring the same environment is used across development, testing, and production. This eliminates discrepancies caused by differences in operating systems or library versions.

- **Conda:** Conda provides environment management for Python and R projects. It allows developers to specify exact package versions, guaranteeing consistency.

2. Automated Testing

Testing ensures that code changes do not introduce unexpected behavior. Automated testing frameworks like PyTest for Python or JUnit for Java allow teams to define test cases that are executed automatically during development. Key components of automated testing include:

- **Unit Tests:** Validate individual components of a system.

- **Integration Tests:** Verify that combined components function as expected.

- **Regression Tests:** Ensure that new changes do not disrupt existing functionality.

3. Data Versioning

The data used for training and testing models in AI projects is as critical as the code. Data versioning tools like DVC (Data Version Control) enable teams to:

- Track changes to datasets over time.
- Associate specific datasets with corresponding code versions.
- Revert to earlier versions of data if needed.

4. Workflow Documentation

Clear and comprehensive documentation is essential for reproducibility. Tools like Jupyter Notebooks allow developers to document workflows alongside executable code, providing a narrative explaining each step's rationale. Best practices include:

- Including detailed comments and annotations.
- Using Markdown cells to explain key concepts.
- Providing instructions for replicating results.

5. CI/CD Pipelines

Continuous Integration and Continuous Deployment (CI/CD) pipelines automate the process of building, testing, and deploying code. They ensure that every change is rigorously tested before integration, reducing the likelihood of errors. Tools like Jenkins, GitHub Actions, and GitLab CI/CD support:

- Automated environment setup.
- Execution of predefined test suites.
- Deployment of verified builds to production environments.

6. Model and Experiment Tracking

For AI projects, tracking model versions and experimental setups is critical. Tools like MLflow and Weights & Biases provide:

- Logging of hyperparameters, metrics, and model versions.
- Visualization of performance trends over time.
- Comparison of different experiment runs.

Challenges and Mitigation Strategies

While ensuring reproducibility is essential, it is not without challenges. Common obstacles include:

1. **Resource Constraints:** Reproducing results may require significant computational resources. Mitigation involves leveraging cloud platforms that provide scalable resources.

2. **Complex Dependencies:** Replicating projects with extensive dependencies can be challenging. Dependency management tools like Poetry or Pipenv simplify this process.

3. **Human Error:** Inconsistent manual processes can undermine reproducibility. Automating repetitive tasks and enforcing standard operating procedures minimize errors.

Benefits of Ensuring Reproducibility

- **Enhanced Collaboration:** Reproducible workflows allow team members to build on each other's work without ambiguity.

- **Improved Debugging:** When results are consistent, identifying and resolving issues becomes more straightforward.

- **Faster Innovation:** Teams can confidently iterate on reproducible workflows, accelerating innovation.

Conclusion

Fostering team collaboration and ensuring reproducibility are interdependent pillars of successful project execution. By leveraging advanced tools, standardizing workflows, and embracing automation, teams can unlock their full potential and deliver high-quality solutions efficiently and reliably. These practices enhance internal processes and build stakeholder trust, setting the foundation for long-term success.

9.3: MONETIZING USER CONTRIBUTIONS

9.3.1 REVENUE MODELS FOR USER CONTRIBUTIONS

User contributions are pivotal in creating value for platforms, particularly those fostering user-generated content or tools. These contributions are not limited to content but to software, tools, designs, and other creative assets. Effective monetization of such contributions can unlock significant revenue streams for platforms while incentivizing creators. Below, we explore various revenue models, with a case study of AppExchange, to illustrate these principles in practice.

EXAMPLES OF REVENUE MODELS FOR USER CONTRIBUTIONS

Platforms have adopted diverse revenue models to capitalize on user contributions, ranging from direct monetization to shared revenue mechanisms. Here are some examples:

Subscription Fees

Subscription-based models offer users access to content, tools, or services for a recurring fee. These models are particularly effective when the platform aggregates a large volume of high-quality user contributions. For instance:

- **Content Platforms**: Sites like Patreon or Substack enable creators to monetize their contributions by charging subscribers directly. The platform retains a percentage of the subscription fee as revenue.

- **Software Ecosystems**: Platforms like Atlassian Marketplace allow users to access plugins and tools developed by contributors through a subscription model. Contributors often set pricing, and the platform takes a cut from each transaction.

Subscription models ensure predictable revenue streams while allowing users to scale their earnings based on the value they provide.

PAY-PER-DOWNLOAD

This model charges users for each content or tool they download. While less predictable than subscriptions, it can be highly lucrative for creators whose contributions are in high demand. Examples include:

- **Creative Platforms**: Envato Market allows contributors to upload digital assets like website templates, graphics, and music. Users pay for individual downloads, and contributors receive some of the revenue.

- **Educational Platforms**: Sites like Udemy and Gumroad allow creators to sell courses or digital resources directly to learners.

Pay-per-download models work best when contributions are one-time-use products or services with clear standalone value.

AD REVENUE SHARING

Ad revenue sharing enables contributors to earn a portion of the ad income generated by their content. This model is prevalent in platforms with massive traffic and high ad revenue potential, such as:

- **Video Platforms**: YouTube's Partner Program shares ad revenue with creators based on views and engagement.

- **Content Platforms**: Medium shares revenue from memberships and advertising with writers based on the engagement their articles receive.

Ad revenue sharing is particularly effective when platforms can scale traffic and ad impressions, benefiting creators and the platform.

LICENSING AND ROYALTIES

Some platforms monetize user contributions by licensing them to third parties and sharing the royalties with creators. For instance:

- **Music Platforms**: Sites like Epidemic Sound allow musicians to license their tracks commercially. Contributors receive royalties based on usage.
- **Stock Photography**: Platforms like Shutterstock pay contributors royalties for each download of their images.

Licensing models provide recurring revenue opportunities, especially for evergreen content or assets with broad market appeal.

REVENUE FROM MARKETPLACE FEES

Marketplaces that host user-generated tools or services often charge fees for listing, transactions, or premium placements. Examples include:

- **E-commerce Platforms**: Etsy charges listing and transaction fees for handmade and unique items.
- **Software Marketplaces**: Salesforce's AppExchange charges fees to developers who list and sell apps.

This model ensures the platform earns consistently while providing contributors with tools to scale their offerings.

CASE STUDY: APPEXCHANGE AND THE MONETIZATION OF USER-CREATED TOOLS

AppExchange, Salesforce's marketplace for business applications, is a prime example of how platforms can monetize user contributions effectively. AppExchange has created a thriving marketplace that benefits all stakeholders by fostering a collaborative ecosystem of developers and businesses.

Background

Launched in 2005, AppExchange was designed to extend Salesforce's core functionality by allowing third-party developers to create and distribute custom applications. Over time, it has become a cornerstone of the Salesforce ecosystem, hosting thousands of applications and tools that cater to a wide range of business needs.

Monetization Strategies

1. **Listing and Transaction Fees**:

    - AppExchange charges developers a percentage of the revenue earned through app sales. This model incentivizes both high-quality app development and active marketing by contributors.

    - The platform also offers premium listing options, allowing developers to gain greater visibility in exchange for additional fees.

2. **Subscription Revenue**:

    - Many applications on AppExchange are available through subscription plans. Salesforce earns a share of these recurring revenues, ensuring consistent income.

3. **Ad Revenue and Promotions**:

    - AppExchange generates revenue by offering promotional slots and advertisements to app developers, helping them reach more users.

4. **Revenue Sharing for Packaged Services**:

    - For enterprise-focused apps or integrations, Salesforce collaborates with developers to bundle services and share revenue from sales.

Value Proposition

app exchange success lies in its ability to create a win-win scenario for all participants:

- **For Developers**: The platform provides access to Salesforce's massive customer base, reducing the need for independent marketing efforts. Developers can focus on innovation while leveraging Salesforce's ecosystem for distribution.

- **For Customers**: Businesses benefit from a curated selection of tools that seamlessly integrate with Salesforce, saving time and enhancing productivity.

- **For Salesforce**: The platform drives additional revenue streams while bolstering the core product's value proposition.

Results and Impact

AppExchange has significantly contributed to Salesforce's revenue growth and ecosystem expansion. By enabling third-party innovation, Salesforce has:

- Attracted a broader customer base, including niche industries.
- Enhanced customer retention by offering tailored solutions.
- Created a community-driven ecosystem that sustains itself through ongoing contributions.

The success of AppExchange highlights several best practices for monetizing user contributions:

1. **Build an Ecosystem**: A vibrant community of contributors ensures a steady stream of innovative solutions.
2. **Offer Flexible Revenue Models**: Combining subscriptions, transaction fees, and advertising allows platforms to maximize revenue.
3. **Prioritize Quality and Trust**: Curated marketplaces ensure user satisfaction and reduce churn.
4. **Leverage Data and Insights**: Platforms like AppExchange use analytics to identify high-performing apps and promote them effectively.

Monetizing user contributions is a multifaceted endeavor that requires a deep understanding of user behavior, contributor needs, and market dynamics. Revenue models like subscription fees, pay-per-download, ad revenue sharing, and marketplace fees offer platforms the flexibility to adapt to various contexts and industries. As demonstrated by AppExchange, fostering a thriving ecosystem of user contributions drives direct revenue and enhances the platform's overall value and customer loyalty. By aligning incentives and creating shared value, platforms can unlock the full potential of user contributions while ensuring sustainable growth.

9.3.2 INCENTIVIZING QUALITY CONTRIBUTIONS

In any collaborative ecosystem, incentivizing quality contributions is pivotal to ensuring the platform's growth and sustainability. Encouraging participants to engage with content, share insights, and provide valuable input can be achieved through a combination of financial and reputational incentives. These approaches foster healthy competition and motivate individuals to contribute consistently.

REWARDING TOP CONTRIBUTORS WITH FINANCIAL AND REPUTATIONAL INCENTIVES

FINANCIAL INCENTIVES

Financial rewards are among the most direct methods to recognize and incentivize quality contributions. Monetary compensation, bonuses, or vouchers can provide tangible benefits, encouraging participants to remain active and committed to the platform. For instance, platforms like YouTube or Twitch reward creators through ad revenue sharing and sponsorships, which motivates contributors to improve the quality and frequency of their content. Similarly, freelance platforms like Upwork or Fiverr often offer financial incentives for top-rated professionals, reinforcing the importance of delivering high-quality services.

In professional networks, financial rewards could be tied to performance metrics such as the number of meaningful contributions, the impact of shared content, or the engagement generated. For example, contributors who create popular resources, tutorials, or solutions that help others might receive monetary bonuses. Additionally, introducing a tiered rewards system can motivate participants by offering incremental financial gains as they reach higher levels of contribution or influence.

REPUTATIONAL INCENTIVES

While financial rewards are compelling, reputational incentives can have a longer-lasting impact on contributors' motivation and engagement. Publicly acknowledging top contributors enhances their visibility within the community and bolsters their professional credibility. Recognition mechanisms such as leaderboards, badges, and exclusive opportunities create an environment where contributors feel valued and appreciated.

LEADERBOARDS

Leaderboards are a simple yet powerful tool for fostering healthy competition. By ranking contributors based on metrics like activity level, quality of input, or overall engagement, leaderboards incentivize members to strive for excellence. For instance, platforms like Stack Overflow rank contributors based on the quality and frequency of their answers. Users who rank high on the leaderboard gain recognition and increased trust within the community.

Leaderboards also help identify subject-matter experts within specific domains. Highlighting these experts can encourage others to aspire toward similar recognition, thereby elevating the overall quality of contributions. To prevent the competitive environment from becoming overly aggressive or demotivating, it is essential to ensure that leaderboards reward positive and constructive behaviors rather than just volume.

BADGES AND CERTIFICATIONS

Badges and certifications are visual indicators of an individual's achievements and expertise. Platforms like GitHub, LinkedIn, and Coursera leverage badges to recognize skill acquisition, course completions, and professional milestones. These tokens of recognition encourage contributors to remain engaged and help them build their brand.

Organizations can create a culture of celebration and achievement by offering badges for specific accomplishments—such as "Top Problem Solver," "Innovator of the Month," or "Community Mentor." Contributors who earn these badges feel pride and accomplishment, motivating them to continue contributing at a high level. Furthermore, these badges can be integrated into professional profiles, resumes, or social media, amplifying their value beyond the immediate community.

EXCLUSIVE OPPORTUNITIES

Another effective way to incentivize quality contributions is to provide top contributors with exclusive opportunities. These opportunities can range from invitations to special events, such as conferences or webinars, to access to advanced tools, resources, or training sessions. For instance, companies like Google and Microsoft have programs inviting top contributors to join exclusive beta testing groups or advisory panels, allowing them to influence the development of new products and services directly.

Offering exclusive perks demonstrates appreciation for contributors and reinforces their sense of belonging and importance within the community. By engaging with high-performing members meaningfully, organizations can strengthen loyalty and foster a more profound commitment to the platform.

While financial and reputational incentives can be effective individually, their combined use can yield even more excellent results. For instance, a platform might reward top contributors with monetary bonuses while featuring them on leaderboards or awarding them exclusive badges. This dual approach ensures that contributors receive immediate, tangible rewards while gaining long-term professional benefits.

Moreover, combining these incentives can help cater to diverse motivations within a community. While some contributors may be driven primarily by financial gain, others may value recognition and the opportunity to enhance their professional reputation. By offering a variety of rewards, organizations can appeal to a broader audience and sustain engagement across different segments of their community.

Implementation Considerations

To successfully implement an incentive program, organizations must consider the following:

1. **Transparency:** Clearly define the criteria for earning rewards and recognition to ensure fairness and avoid potential disputes. Transparent guidelines help build trust within the community.

2. **Scalability:** Design an incentive program that can grow with the platform's growth. As the community expands, it's essential to maintain the integrity and value of rewards.

3. **Inclusivity:** Ensure that the incentive program accommodates a diverse range of contributors, from beginners to experts. Providing opportunities for all skill levels encourages widespread participation.

4. **Feedback Mechanisms:** The incentive program should be refined by regularly soliciting feedback from the community. Understanding contributors' preferences and motivations can help improve the effectiveness of rewards.

5. **Ethical Considerations:** Avoid creating an overly competitive or exploitative environment. Incentive programs should promote collaboration and mutual support rather than cutthroat competition.

Incentivizing quality contributions through financial and reputational rewards is essential for building and sustaining vibrant communities. Organizations can create a culture of recognition and achievement by leveraging tools like leaderboards, badges, and exclusive opportunities. Combining these incentives ensures that contributors remain motivated, engaged, and committed to delivering high-quality input. A well-designed incentive program ultimately benefits contributors and the community, fostering growth, innovation, and long-term success.

Monetization is a crucial component for the sustainability and growth of any platform or product. However, achieving profitability while maintaining user satisfaction can be challenging. Missteps in monetization strategies can erode trust, alienate users, and even jeopardize the long-term viability of the business. This section explores key considerations and best practices for avoiding common pitfalls in monetization, focusing on balancing monetization efforts with user satisfaction.

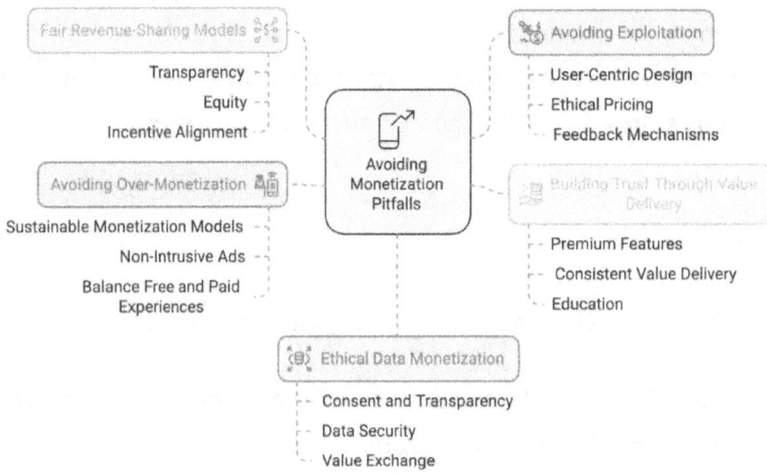

BALANCING MONETIZATION WITH USER SATISFACTION

Achieving a harmonious balance between monetization and user satisfaction requires a user-first approach to strategy. Effective monetization models generate revenue and enhance the overall user experience. Misaligned strategy, on the other hand, can lead to dissatisfaction and churn. Here are critical aspects to consider:

1. Ensuring Fair Revenue-Sharing Models

A revenue-sharing model often forms the foundation of monetization strategies in platforms involving creators, service providers, or contributors. Ensuring fairness in these models is paramount to fostering trust and sustained engagement. Fair revenue-sharing entails distributing earnings in a way that reflects the value contributed by each stakeholder. Platforms that unfairly skew revenue towards themselves risk alienating creators and damaging their ecosystem.

Best Practices:

- **Transparency:** Communicate the breakdown of revenue-sharing percentages and provide detailed reporting mechanisms. Transparency helps establish trust and minimizes potential disputes.
- **Equity:** The revenue-sharing framework should be regularly assessed to remain competitive and equitable. Benchmarking against peer platforms can provide valuable insights.

- **Incentive Alignment:** Design models that align incentives between the platform and its contributors. Reward high-performing creators with better revenue splits or bonus incentives to foster loyalty.

Case Study: Consider the success of platforms like YouTube, which share ad revenue with content creators. By offering a clear and relatively generous revenue-sharing policy, YouTube has cultivated a massive creator base that continually adds value to the platform. Conversely, platforms with opaque or exploitative practices often struggle to retain contributors and face public backlash.

2. Avoiding Exploitation

Exploitative monetization strategies can severely damage user relationships and brand reputation. Practices such as excessive fees, hidden charges, or overreliance on intrusive advertising often result in user dissatisfaction and attrition. Today's users are highly discerning and can quickly recognize when they are being taken advantage of.

Best Practices:

- **User-Centric Design:** When implementing monetization features, prioritize user experience. For instance, limit the frequency of ads to avoid disrupting the user journey or opt for non-intrusive formats like native ads.

- **Ethical Pricing:** Avoid predatory pricing practices such as exorbitant fees or exploiting users' lack of alternatives. Instead, adopt transparent user models that reflect the value offered.

- **Feedback Mechanisms:** Regularly collect user feedback to identify pain points related to monetization. Addressing these concerns proactively can prevent dissatisfaction from escalating.

Case Study: Gaming companies are often criticized for exploitative practices such as loot boxes or pay-to-win mechanics. Titles that overuse these tactics usually see short-term financial gains but long-term user attrition. In contrast, games like Fortnite have successfully balanced monetization through optional in-game purchases that enhance the user experience without disrupting gameplay.

3. Building Trust Through Value Delivery

Users are more likely to accept monetization when they perceive value in exchange for their investment, whether it's time, money, or data. Platforms must foit'son delivering tangible benefits that justify the costs imposed on users.

Best Practices:

- **Premium Features:** Offer high-quality premium features that significantly enhance the user experience. Ensure that free users are not alienated by gating essential functionalities.

- **Consistent Value Delivery:** Maintain a consistent service and user experience standard to ensure users feel their investment is worthwhile.

- **Education:** Educate users about the benefits of paid features or subscriptions to foster an appreciation for their value.

Case Study: Platforms like Spotify and Netflix have excelled in building trust by delivering exceptional value through their subscription models. They offer compelling free tiers to attract users and provide clear, consistent value for paid subscribers, leading to high retention rates.

4. Avoiding Over-Monetization

Overmonetization occurs when platforms attempt to extract too much value from their users quickly. This approach often leads to declining user satisfaction, with long-term consequences far outweighing short-term gains.

Best Practices:

- **Sustainable Monetization Models:** These models focus on long-term sustainability rather than short-term revenue maximization. For example, introducing gradual price increases instead of sudden hikes can help maintain user trust.

- **Non-Intrusive Ads:** If ad-based revenue is a key component, ensure ads are relevant and non-disruptive. Platforms like Instagram and Pinterest seamlessly integrate ads into the user feed.

- **Balance Free and Paid Experiences:** Avoid excessively limiting the free experience, as this can deter user acquisition and lead to negative word-of-mouth.

Case Study: LinkedIn's approach to monetization—offerings and premium accounts—is a textbook example of balance. The free tier provides sufficient functionality for casual users, while premium options cater to professionals seeking advanced features, ensuring user satisfaction across segments.

5. Ethical Data Monetization

With the rise of data-driven monetization models, ethical considerations around user data have become more critical than ever. Exploiting user data without consent can lead to significant backlash and legal challenges.

Best Practices:

- **Consent and Transparency:** Inform users how their data will be used and obtain explicit consent. Avoid burying this information in lengthy terms and conditions.

- **Data Security:** Invest in robust data protection measures to safeguard user information against breaches.

- **Value Exchange:** Highlight the benefits users receive in exchange for their data, such as personalized experiences or free access to services.

Case Study: Apple's emphasis on user privacy and transparency, as well as Apple's policies, has positioned it as a leader in ethical data practices. This approach contrasts sharply with companies that have faced criticism and regulatory scrutiny for data misuse, such as Cambridge Analytica's controversial practices.

9.4: SUPPORTING INNOVATION WITH TOOLS AND FEATURES

9.4.1 INTRODUCING INNOVATION-FRIENDLY FEATURES

Fostering an environment where innovation thrives requires tools and strategies to enhance creativity and streamline problem-solving processes. Introducing innovation-friendly features into workflows accelerates development and empowers individuals and teams to think outside the box and deliver transformative solutions. Below, we explore examples of tools for boosting creativity and dive into a case study showcasing a platform that revolutionized AI workflows with automated debugging tools.

TOOLS FOR BOOSTING CREATIVITY

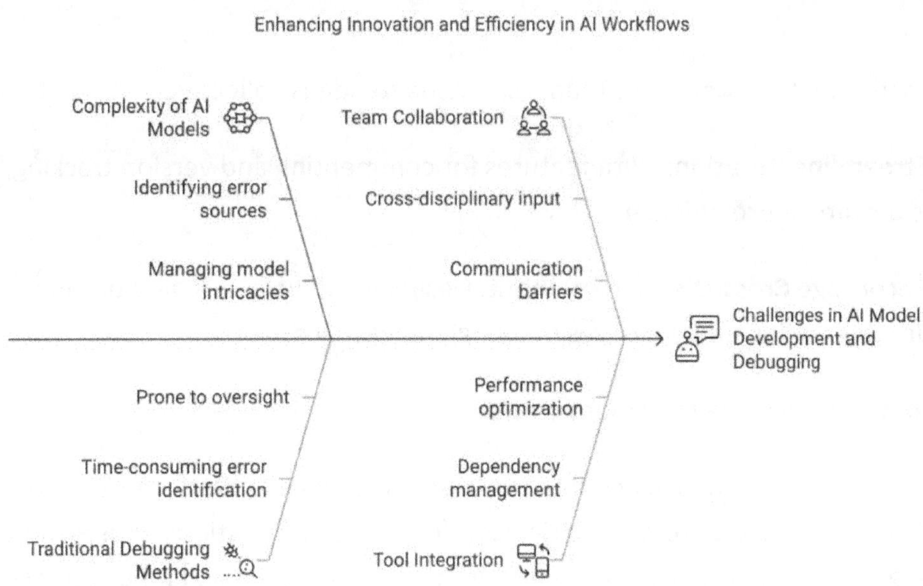

1. Generative AI APIs for Rapid Prototyping

Generative AI has emerged as a cornerstone of creativity in the modern era. By leveraging APIs powered by generative AI, developers and innovators can quickly build prototypes, test ideas, and iterate on concepts without requiring extensive manual effort. These APIs utilize deep learning models, such as GPT-4 and DALL-E, to create text, images, and other media, enabling users to:

- **Brainstorm Ideas**: Generative AI can produce a range of creative suggestions based on user inputs. For instance, an entrepreneur looking to design a new app can generate multiple user interface mockups or feature suggestions in minutes.
- **Generate Content**: Businesses can use AI-generated content for marketing campaigns, blog posts, or social media strategies. This eliminates the need for extended brainstorming sessions and provides instant, high-quality output.
- **Simulate Scenarios**: Innovators can test hypotheses by simulating user interactions or outcomes in controlled environments. For example, a game developer might use generative AI to create diverse characters or plotlines.

Practical Example: Imagine a startup developing an AI-driven music composition app. Using a generative AI API, the team could prototype features that create personalized music based on user preferences. They might generate multiple melody patterns, instrument arrangements, and lyrics within hours, significantly reducing the time required for development.

2. Collaborative Design Platforms

Collaboration is often the bedrock of innovation. Miro, Figma, and Notion enable teams to collaborate seamlessly, regardless of geographic location. By incorporating features like shared whiteboards, interactive design templates, and integrated feedback mechanisms, these platforms help:

- **Facilitate Brainstorming**: Teams can visualize ideas collectively in real-time.
- **Streamline Iteration**: With features for commenting and version tracking, design revisions become more efficient.
- **Encourage Cross-Disciplinary Input**: Designers, developers, and business strategists can contribute their unique perspectives in a single workspace.

3. No-Code and Low-Code Development Tools

Innovation often demands rapid execution. No-code and low-code platforms such as Bubble, Webflow, and OutSystems allow creators to develop functional applications with minimal coding knowledge. These tools lower the barrier to entry for non-technical users and enable technical users to focus on high-level problem-solving instead of foundational coding. Key benefits include:

- **Faster Time to Market**: Prototypes and MVPs can be built in days instead of weeks.
- **Ease of Experimentation**: Users can test various designs and functionalities without investing significant resources.

- **Broader Participation**: Non-developers can actively contribute to building solutions, fostering a more inclusive innovation process.

Case Study: A Platform Offering Automated Debugging Tools for AI Workflows

Integrating automated debugging tools into AI workflows represents a significant step forward in enhancing productivity and minimizing errors. One such platform that has successfully introduced these features is DebugAI, a pioneering solution designed to optimize the development and deployment of AI systems.

Challenge: As AI models grow more complex, debugging them becomes increasingly challenging. Developers often face issues such as:

- Identifying the root cause of errors in model training.
- Ensuring the reproducibility of experiments.
- Managing dependencies and conflicts within AI pipelines.

Traditional debugging methods rely heavily on manual inspection and trial and error. They are time-consuming and prone to oversight. This inefficiency hinders innovation and delays project timelines.

Solution: DebugAI introduced an automated debugging platform tailored to AI workflows. Its core features include:

1. **Error Localization**: DebugAI uses advanced algorithms to pinpoint the exact source of errors within a model's code or data pipeline. For instance, if a training dataset contains corrupted entries, the platform highlights these entries and provides suggestions for remediation.

2. **Dependency Management**: The platform automatically tracks dependencies within AI workflows, alerting developers to potential conflicts or outdated components. This ensures smoother integration and reduces the risk of runtime errors.

3. **Reproducibility Insights**: DebugAI logs every step of the AI development process, enabling teams to replicate experiments effortlessly. This feature is handy for research-intensive projects where reproducibility is critical.

4. **Performance Optimization**: DebugAI identifies bottlenecks and recommends optimizations by analyzing model performance metrics, such as adjusting hyperparameters or restructuring neural network layers.

Impact: The introduction of DebugAI's automated debugging tools transformed how developers approached AI model development:

- **Time Savings**: Debugging time was reduced by up to 60%, allowing teams to allocate more resources to innovation.
- **Error Reduction**: The platform's precision in identifying errors minimized the risk of deploying faulty models.
- **Enhanced Collaboration**: With shared logs and insights, team members could collaborate more effectively, regardless of their technical expertise.

Real-World Application: A leading healthcare AI company adopted DebugAI to streamline its model development process. Previously, the company's data scientists spent weeks debugging models designed to predict patient outcomes. With DebugAI, they not only reduced debugging time but also improved model accuracy by addressing hidden data quality issues. This accelerated the deployment of their solution, enabling faster delivery of life-saving insights to healthcare providers.

9.4.2 ENCOURAGING OPEN INNOVATION

Hosting hackathons, competitions, or collaborative sprints

In today's fast-paced digital era, innovation is no longer confined to the traditional boundaries of in-house research and development teams. Open innovation emphasizes harnessing the collective intelligence of a broader ecosystem—be it customers, developers, or independent researchers. By tapping into this diverse talent pool, organizations can accelerate problem-solving, foster creativity, and unlock groundbreaking solutions. Hosting hackathons, competitions, or collaborative sprints is a powerful way to enable open innovation. These events create dynamic environments where individuals with varied expertise come together to address complex challenges.

The Role of Hackathons in Open Innovation

Hackathons are time-bound events where participants collaborate intensively to build, design, or improve solutions to specific problems. These events are highly effective in fostering innovation due to their structured focus, collaborative nature, and competitive spirit. Hackathons encourage participants to step out of their comfort zones, explore unconventional ideas, and deliver functional prototypes within a limited timeframe.

From the perspective of organizations, hackathons serve as a conduit for sourcing fresh ideas, testing out new technologies, and even identifying talented individuals. For instance, tech giants like Google and Microsoft have successfully used hackathons to address internal challenges, identify high-potential employees, and prototype innovative products. Beyond large corporations, startups and nonprofits have also leveraged hackathons to engage their communities and co-create solutions tailored to specific needs.

An example is the NASA International Space Apps Challenge, an annual global hackathon that invites technologists, scientists, designers, and entrepreneurs to develop innovative solutions for

Earth—and space-related problems. Participants gain access to NASA's datasets and tools, fostering creativity and a shared sense of purpose and collaboration.

Competitions as Catalysts for Community-Driven Problem-Solving

Another effective means of driving open innovation is competitions designed around real-world challenges. These contests incentivize participants with monetary prizes, recognition, and career opportunities. Platforms like Kaggle, a Google subsidiary, have revolutionized how competitions contribute to innovation. Kaggle provides a platform for hosting data science competitions, where individuals or teams work on datasets to solve problems in healthcare and finance.

For example, in a Kaggle competition, pharmaceutical companies might provide anonymized patient datasets and task participants with building machine learning models to predict disease outcomes. Thanks to participants' sheer diversity and ingenuity, the insights generated through these competitions often surpass internal benchmarks. Companies benefit by acquiring cutting-edge solutions without long-term commitments or extensive in-house R&D investments.

Competitions also democratize innovation by enabling individuals from all over the world to contribute their expertise. This global inclusivity enhances the quality of solutions, as diverse perspectives often lead to unique and practical approaches. Additionally, competitions encourage skill development and knowledge sharing, benefiting the hosting organization and the broader community.

Collaborative Sprints for Rapid Prototyping

Collaborative sprints are highly focused events designed to bring cross-functional teams together for rapid prototyping and iteration. Unlike hackathons, which are often open to external participants, collaborative sprints typically involve internal teams or close partnerships with external collaborators. These sprints are invaluable for tackling complex problems that require deep domain expertise and coordination among multiple stakeholders.

A prime example of the effectiveness of collaborative sprints can be found in the tech industry's adoption of the Google Design Sprint framework. This methodology compresses months of development work into a five-day process, enabling teams to prototype and test ideas quickly. Organizations like Slack, Uber, and Airbnb have used design sprints to refine their product offerings and address user pain points efficiently. By incorporating external collaborators—such as users, partners, or industry experts—these sprints also integrate diverse viewpoints into the innovation process, ensuring practical and user-centric solutions.

Key Benefits of Hosting Open Innovation Events

1. **Diverse Perspectives:** Hackathons, competitions, and sprints unite participants with varied backgrounds, skill sets, and experiences. This diversity enhances creativity and helps uncover solutions that might not emerge in homogeneous teams.

2. **Accelerated Problem-Solving:** Time-bound events encourage rapid ideation, decision-making, and execution. This is particularly valuable in industries where speed to market is a critical success factor.

3. **Community Building:** By engaging external participants, organizations can foster a sense of community and loyalty. Participants often connect more with the organization's mission, leading to long-term advocacy and collaboration.

4. **Talent Identification:** These events provide a platform for organizations to identify high-potential individuals and teams. Many companies use hackathons and competitions as recruitment tools, offering winners opportunities to join their teams.

5. **Cost-Effective Innovation:** Open innovation events allow organizations to access high-quality solutions without incurring the overhead costs associated with in-house development. This model is particularly advantageous for startups and nonprofits with limited resources.

Best Practices for Hosting Open Innovation Events

To maximize the impact of hackathons, competitions, and collaborative sprints, organizations should adopt the following best practices:

1. **Define Clear Objectives:** Ensure the problem statement is well-defined and aligned with organizational goals. Ambiguous objectives can lead to unfocused solutions and participant frustration.

2. **Provide Resources and Support:** Equip participants with the tools, datasets, and mentorship they need to succeed. This will enhance the quality of solutions and ensure a positive participant experience.

3. **Foster Collaboration:** Encourage participants to form diverse teams and share knowledge. Platforms like Slack or Discord can facilitate communication and collaboration during virtual events.

4. **Recognize and Reward Contributions:** Acknowledge the efforts of all participants, not just the winners. Providing certificates, showcasing projects, or offering internships can create a lasting impression.

5. **Sustain Engagement Post-Event:** Follow up with participants to explore opportunities for further collaboration. Maintaining a community of innovators ensures continued value beyond the event itself.

Hosting hackathons, competitions, and collaborative sprints is a powerful way to encourage innovation. Organizations can unlock unparalleled creativity and drive meaningful impact by creating platforms for diverse participants to collaborate on real-world challenges. Events like Kaggle competitions exemplify how community-driven problem-solving can lead to breakthrough solutions, while collaborative sprints demonstrate the value of rapid, user-centric innovation. As industries increasingly embrace open innovation, these initiatives will play a pivotal role in shaping the future of problem-solving and technological advancement.

9.4.3 BUILDING FEEDBACK LOOPS

Building effective feedback loops is essential for continuously improving products, especially in the dynamic field of artificial intelligence and digital platforms. A feedback loop ensures that user inputs are actively collected, analyzed, and incorporated into feature development, allowing the product to evolve in alignment with user needs and expectations. This process fosters user trust, enhances engagement, and creates a competitive advantage by delivering highly relevant and functional features.

The Importance of Feedback Loops

User feedback is a goldmine of insights that clearly explains how features are perceived, utilized, and valued. By systematically collecting feedback, organizations can identify areas for improvement, detect unmet user needs, and uncover opportunities for innovation. Feedback loops close the gap between product developers and end-users, creating a symbiotic relationship where users feel heard and developers gain actionable insights.

In the context of AI platforms, where technology evolves rapidly, and user needs are diverse, feedback loops become even more critical. For example, an AI-powered analytics tool might receive feedback about the lack of intuitive visualization options. Such insights may go unnoticed without a structured feedback loop, leading to user dissatisfaction or churn. On the other hand, a robust feedback mechanism enables the product team to act quickly and effectively, iteratively enhancing the tool to serve its users better.

Example of Feedback-Driven Improvement

Consider a hypothetical case of a SaaS-based project management platform that integrates AI-powered task automation. The product team notices a common complaint: users find the automation rules challenging to configure. To address this, they implement a feedback loop that involves:

1. **Feedback Collection:** Using an in-app feedback widget and periodic surveys to ask users about their experience with task automation.

2. **Data Analysis:** Analyzing feedback to identify recurring themes and users' specific pain points.

3. **Solution Design:** Proposing a user-friendly interface with pre-built templates for standard automation rules.

4. **User Testing:** Sharing the prototype with select users and incorporating their feedback before finalizing the feature.

5. **Deployment:** Rolling out the improved automation rules and communicating the changes to users.

The result is a feature that directly addresses user needs, significantly improving adoption and satisfaction.

Leveraging Community Votes to Prioritize Feature Development

An innovative approach to collecting and acting on feedback is leveraging community votes to prioritize feature development. This technique involves creating a transparent system where users can suggest, upvote, or comment on feature requests. Platforms like Trello, GitHub, and even bespoke community forums provide excellent models for this.

For instance, a company developing an AI-based content recommendation system could use community voting to determine the next prominent feature. Users might vote for "personalized notification settings" over "dark mode" as a priority. This data informs the product roadmap, ensuring resources are allocated to the most impactful features.

The benefits of this approach include:

- **User Empowerment:** Users feel valued and directly involved in shaping the product.
- **Market-Driven Development:** Features are developed based on actual demand, reducing the risk of investing in low-priority projects.
- **Transparency and Trust:** A visible voting process builds trust as users see their voices influencing product decisions.

Continuous Improvement as a Competitive Advantage

By building effective feedback loops, organizations improve their products and nurture a loyal user base. Over time, this iterative process fosters a culture of continuous learning and adaptation, enabling companies to stay ahead in competitive markets. Feedback loops are a cornerstone of sustainable growth and innovation when properly implemented.

CHAPTER 10: PRODUCT VS. PLATFORM AND COMPETITIVE STRATEGY

INTRODUCTION

The strategic implications of building a product (niche, targeted solution) vs. a platform (scalable ecosystem).

The decision to build a product or a platform is one of the most consequential choices entrepreneurs and organizations face. It influences how the offering evolves and its scalability, competitive edge, and long-term relevance in the market. Both approaches have their own merits, risks, and strategic implications. While products often serve as targeted solutions to specific problems, platforms enable ecosystems where multiple stakeholders, solutions, and innovations converge.

This chapter delves into the core differences between products and platforms, emphasizing why understanding this distinction is critical for anyone entering the AI or technology-driven markets. Through examples such as Grammarly—a successful product—and TensorFlow—a thriving platform—readers will grasp the significance of each approach and the strategic thinking necessary to navigate this decision-making process.

WHY PRODUCT VS. PLATFORM MATTERS

The choice between building a product or a platform is not just technical—it is inherently strategic. Each route defines how businesses create, deliver, and capture value. Below, we explore the key considerations for both approaches.

Product: A Targeted, Niche Solution

A product typically solves a specific problem for a defined audience. For instance, Grammarly is an AI-driven writing assistant focusing solely on enhancing written communication. Its value lies in its simplicity, ease of use, and ability to cater to a targeted audience of students, professionals, and casual writers. Products focusing on a specific use case often deliver polished, high-quality solutions.

Advantages of Products:

1. **Faster Time-to-Market:** A product can be developed and launched relatively quickly with a narrower scope.

2. **Focused Expertise:** Businesses can channel resources into excelling at one thing, achieving depth rather than breadth.

3. **Targeted Marketing:** It is easier to identify and address the needs of a specific demographic.

However, the product-focused approach also presents challenges. Limited scalability is a primary concern, as products often have a finite market size. Furthermore, maintaining long-term relevance requires continuous innovation and feature expansion.

Platform: A Scalable Ecosystem

In contrast, a platform is designed as an ecosystem facilitating participant interaction. TensorFlow, for example, is not just a tool—it is an ecosystem that empowers developers, researchers, and businesses to build machine-learning models. TensorFlow has become a foundational platform in the AI industry by providing APIs, integrations, and community-driven support.

Advantages of Platforms:

1. **Scalability:** Platforms grow exponentially through network effects. More users attract more contributors, which, in turn, creates more value.

2. **User-Driven Innovation:** BCompanies benefit from external innovation by enabling others to build on the platform,

3. **Revenue Opportunities:** Platforms can monetize through multiple channels, such as freemium models, developer tools, and premium features.

However, platforms are not without their complexities. Building and maintaining a successful platform requires substantial upfront investment, sophisticated ecosystem management, and attracting and retaining a critical mass of users and developers.

Examples: Grammarly vs. TensorFlow

Two examples—Grammarly and TensorFlow—illustrate the product vs. platform debate.

Grammarly: A Case Study in Product Success

Grammarly began as a simple yet powerful solution to enhance writing quality. Its focus on spelling, grammar, and style enabled it to capture a loyal customer base. By positioning itself as a product rather than a platform, Grammarly could concentrate on refining its algorithms, user interface, and marketing strategy.

Key takeaways from Grammarly's product-focused approach:

- **Niche Expertise:** Grammarly excels because it solves a single problem exceptionally well.

- **Monetization Simplicity:** Its subscription-based revenue model aligns with user expectations for premium tools.
- **Agility:** By avoiding the complexities of platform management, Grammarly can quickly iterate and respond to user feedback.

TensorFlow: The Power of Platforms

TensorFlow, by contrast, represents the archetype of a platform. Developed by Google, it is a foundation for developers to create AI and machine learning models. Its ecosystem includes APIs, pre-built models, and an active community contributing tools and innovations.

Key takeaways from TensorFlow's platform-based approach:

- **Ecosystem Growth:** TensorFlow thrives on contributions from researchers, startups, and enterprises.
- **Scalability:** Unlike a product with a finite scope, TensorFlow's applications are virtually limitless, from natural language processing to computer vision.
- **Network Effects:** As more users adopt TensorFlow, its value increases for all participants.

WHAT THIS CHAPTER OFFERS

The debate between products and platforms is not merely academic—it is a decision with real-world implications for strategy, competition, and growth. This chapter provides actionable insights to guide readers through this critical choice.

Frameworks for Decision-Making

When should you choose a product over a platform? The answer depends on market size, resources, and long-term goals. This chapter introduces frameworks to help entrepreneurs and organizations evaluate these variables systematically. For instance, a decision matrix will help readers weigh considerations like initial investment, scalability potential, and competitive positioning.

Tools for Competitive Strategy

Standing out is imperative in both product and platform markets. This chapter offers tools and techniques for crafting a competitive strategy, such as identifying an underserved niche or leveraging network effects. Real-world examples illustrate how businesses have successfully differentiated themselves, providing readers with practical inspiration.

Choosing between a product and a platform is not just about what you build—it is about how you position yourself in the market, engage with users and scale. By understanding the nuances of these approaches and learning from successful examples like Grammarly and TensorFlow, entrepreneurs can make informed decisions that align with their goals. This chapter equips readers with the knowledge, frameworks, and tools to navigate this pivotal choice effectively.

10.1: UNDERSTANDING PRODUCT VS. PLATFORM

Although "product" and "platform" are often used interchangeably in business and technology, they represent fundamentally different approaches to creating and delivering value. Understanding these differences is crucial for entrepreneurs, business leaders, and innovators navigating the competitive landscape of today's digital economy. While products are standalone solutions that solve specific user problems, platforms are ecosystems that enable interactions and collaborations between multiple stakeholders.

This section explores each approach's key distinctions, advantages, and challenges. Businesses can align their efforts with their long-term objectives by defining what constitutes a product versus a platform and understanding its strategic implications. The choice between the two is not merely operational—it is deeply tied to scalability, innovation, and market positioning.

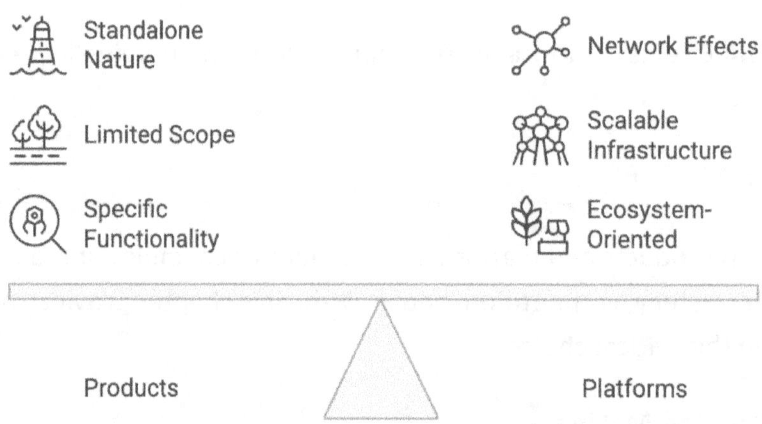

Comparing Product Specificity with Platform Scalability

10.1.1 DEFINING PRODUCTS AND PLATFORMS

WHAT IS A PRODUCT?

A product is a standalone solution designed to address a specific problem or fulfill a well-defined need for a particular audience. It is often developed with a focused approach, catering to a niche market segment, and designed to deliver immediate value. Products are straightforward in utility and usually work independently without needing external systems or integrations.

An excellent example of a product is an **AI-powered diagnostic tool for radiology**. This tool focuses exclusively on improving the accuracy and efficiency of medical imaging diagnoses. It uses machine learning algorithms to analyze radiological scans, assisting radiologists in identifying potential issues like tumors or fractures. The product provides precision, reliability, and a user-friendly interface tailored for medical professionals by addressing one specific use case.

Key Characteristics of Products:

- **Specific Functionality:** Products are designed to perform a defined task or solve a particular problem.
- **Limited Scope:** They serve a targeted audience and are built with a single use case in mind.
- **Ease of Use:** Products typically feature streamlined interfaces, making them intuitive for end-users.
- **Standalone Nature:** They do not require additional systems or external integrations to deliver value.

WHAT IS A PLATFORM?

Conversely, a platform is an ecosystem that enables multiple stakeholders to interact, create, and innovate. Platforms are not limited to a specific problem; they provide the infrastructure for other solutions to be developed and integrated. Platforms amplify their utility and scalability by fostering collaboration and enabling third-party contributions.

For example, **API-driven AI tools for medical imaging** serve as a platform for hospitals, developers, and researchers to build diagnostic solutions. This platform offers APIs and developer tools that integrate with various applications, enabling innovation in areas such as custom imaging software, AI-driven analytics, and patient care solutions. The platform's value increases as more developers contribute to its ecosystem, creating a cycle of growth and utility.

Key Characteristics of Platforms:

- **Ecosystem-Oriented:** Platforms facilitate the creation and integration of complementary solutions.
- **Scalable Infrastructure:** They provide tools, APIs, and frameworks for external developers and businesses.
- **Network Effects:** The value of a platform grows with the number of users and contributors.
- **Versatility:** Platforms cater to multiple use cases, industries, and demographics.

EXAMPLES IN CONTEXT

1. **Product Example: AI-Powered Diagnostic Tool for Radiology**

- Focuses on a single problem: improving radiology diagnostics.
- Offers immediate, measurable value to radiologists and medical institutions.
- Operates as a standalone application with minimal external dependencies.

2. **Platform Example: API-Driven AI Tools for Medical Imaging**
   - It acts as a foundation for developers and researchers to build.
   - Facilitates diverse applications, such as patient management systems or imaging software.
   - It relies on community contributions and integrations to grow its ecosystem.

By defining the core differences between products and platforms, businesses can align their strategies with their objectives, resources, and target audiences.

10.1.2 ADVANTAGES AND CHALLENGES

ADVANTAGES AND CHALLENGES OF PRODUCTS

ADVANTAGES OF PRODUCTS

1. **Faster Time-to-Market:**
Products have a defined scope and targeted functionality, allowing teams to develop and launch them quickly. For example, an AI-powered radiology diagnostic tool can be built and deployed within months, providing immediate benefits to its users.

2. **Easier Focus on a Niche:**
Products are designed to address specific problems for a particular audience. This focus allows businesses to excel in their chosen niche, providing high-quality solutions without the distractions of broader requirements.

3. **Lower Complexity:**
The development and management of a product are relatively straightforward compared to platforms. With fewer dependencies and external integrations, teams can focus solely on perfecting their solution.

CHALLENGES OF PRODUCTS

1. **Limited Scalability:**
Due to their specialized nature, products often have a finite market size. Expanding beyond their initial niche can be challenging and require significant reinvention or diversification.

2. **More challenging to Maintain Long-Term Relevance:**
Products risk becoming obsolete if competitors offer similar solutions or the market needs to evolve. Continuous innovation and feature updates are necessary to sustain user interest.

3. **Single Revenue Stream:**
Products typically rely on direct sales or subscriptions, limiting the potential for diverse income streams compared to platforms.

ADVANTAGES AND CHALLENGES OF PLATFORMS

ADVANTAGES OF PLATFORMS

1. **Scalability Through Network Effects:**
Platforms benefit from network effects, where each new user or contributor increases the platform's overall value. For example, an API-driven platform for medical imaging becomes more valuable as more developers create applications using its tools.

2. **User-Driven Innovation:**
Platforms enable external contributors to innovate and build upon the ecosystem, reducing the burden on the platform owner to generate all value internally.

3. **Diverse Revenue Opportunities:**
Platforms can monetize through various channels, such as licensing fees, premium features, marketplace commissions, and partnerships.

4. **Market Dominance Potential:**
Successful platforms often establish themselves as industry standards, creating high barriers to entry for competitors. Once a platform achieves critical mass, alternatives become increasingly challenging to gain traction.

CHALLENGES OF PLATFORMS

1. **Higher Initial Investment:**
Building a platform requires significant resources, both financial investment and technical expertise. Developing APIs, SDKs, and infrastructure is a time-consuming process.

2. **Ecosystem Management Complexity:**
Platforms must manage relationships with users, developers, and partners. Ensuring the quality and compatibility of third-party contributions can be challenging.

3. **Critical Mass Requirement:**
Platforms must reach a certain level of adoption to generate value. Achieving this critical mass often requires substantial marketing efforts, incentives, and community-building strategies.

4. **Risk of Fragmentation:**
As platforms grow, maintaining coherence within the ecosystem becomes difficult. Conflicts between stakeholders or inconsistent standards can undermine the platform's success.

Understanding the advantages and challenges of products and platforms is vital for making informed strategic decisions. While products excel in simplicity, focus, and speed, platforms offer scalability, innovation, and long-term growth potential. Businesses can determine the best path forward by weighing these factors against their goals and resources.

10.1.3 WHEN TO CHOOSE A PRODUCT VS. PLATFORM

The choice between building a product or a platform is pivotal for any organization, particularly in emerging technologies like artificial intelligence, blockchain, or software development. This decision influences a company's growth trajectory, resource allocation, and market positioning. While products offer quick solutions for specific problems, platforms provide ecosystems for innovation and scalability. However, the path to success is not a one-size-fits-all formula. This section explores the critical decision factors to help organizations determine whether to build a product or a platform.

KEY DECISION FACTORS

1. **Market Size** Market size is one of the most important considerations when choosing between a product and a platform. The scope and nature of the market directly influence which approach will yield the most value.

    - **For Products:**
    Products are best suited for niche markets with clearly defined problem-centered target audiences. If the market size is small but highly specific—such as a diagnostic tool for a rare disease or an AI solution for a specialized industry—building a standalone product allows businesses to penetrate the market quickly and establish dominance.

Example: An **AI-powered diagnostic tool for pediatric neurology** is a focused product that caters to a niche within the broader healthcare industry. Its potential market may be limited in size, but the problem it solves is urgent and well-defined, making a product approach ideal.

- **For Platforms:**
Platforms are more viable in larger, dynamic markets where diverse users and contributors can derive value. A platform requires a critical mass of participants to achieve network effects, so the market must be broad enough to sustain ongoing growth and attract innovation.

Example: An **API-driven AI platform** caters to hospitals, developers, and researchers. By targeting a larger and more varied audience, platforms can grow their user base and become indispensable in their ecosystem.

Key Insight:
Small, well-defined markets favor products, while significant, multi-faceted markets are better suited for platforms.

2. **Funding Availability** Building a platform is more resource-intensive than developing a product. Funding availability plays a significant role in determining which approach to pursue.

   - **For Products:**
     A product-oriented approach is more feasible for organizations with limited funding. Products can often be developed and launched with a relatively small budget, making them ideal for startups or businesses in their early stages. Furthermore, a successful product can serve as a stepping stone for generating revenue, which can later fund platform development.

Example: Grammarly started as a product focused on enhancing grammar and writing. Its success allowed the company to expand features and explore platform-like integrations over time.

   - **For Platforms:**
     Platforms require substantial investment in technology, infrastructure, and marketing. Companies must build tools like APIs, SDKs, and community engagement strategies to attract developers and users. Only organizations with significant funding—such as venture capital or substantial corporate backing—can afford to pursue a platform from the outset.

Example: TensorFlow was launched as a platform with robust support from Google, which had the resources to fund its development and ecosystem growth.

Key Insight:
Limited funding supports a product-focused strategy, while a platform approach requires substantial financial resources.

3. **Long-Term Goals** The business's long-term vision significantly impacts the choice between product and platform.

   - **For Products:**
     Building a product aligns well with the company's objectives of generating immediate revenue, establishing a strong foothold in a niche market, or providing a specialized solution. Products are suitable for businesses that aim to solve problems efficiently and establish a reputation for expertise in a particular domain.

Example: A company specializing in **AI-powered legal document analysis** may aim to dominate the legal tech by offering a top-tier product tailored to law firms and corporate legal teams.

   - **For Platforms:**
     If the vision includes scalability, long-term growth, and the creation of a collaborative

ecosystem, platforms are the better choice. Platforms are ideal for companies looking to establish themselves as industry leaders by enabling other businesses and users to build on their foundation.

Example: Salesforce began as a CRM product but evolved into a platform, enabling third-party developers to build applications and integrations. This platform-centric approach aligned with Salesforce's goal of becoming a dominant force in business technology.

Key Insight:
Products are suited for short-term goals and niche dominance, while platforms align with long-term scalability and ecosystem leadership.

Decision Matrix: Choosing Between Product and Platform

The following decision matrix provides a structured approach based on the key factors discussed above to assist businesses in making this critical decision. Organizations can use this tool to evaluate their circumstances and identify the optimal path.

Factor	Product	Platform
Market Size	Small, well-defined, niche markets	Large, dynamic, multi-stakeholder markets
Funding Availability	Limited funding or early-stage investment	Significant funding and long-term resources
Long-Term Goals	Short-term revenue and niche dominance	Long-term scalability and ecosystem creation
Scalability Needs	Low to moderate	High, with network effects driving growth
User Complexity	Direct end-user interaction	Multiple users (e.g., developers, businesses, end-users)
Time-to-Market	Rapid deployment	Longer due to ecosystem development

Applying the Decision Matrix

To illustrate the application of the decision matrix, consider the following scenarios:

1. **Scenario 1: AI Startup with Limited Funding**
A startup wants to use AI to optimize supply chain logistics. With limited funding, the company decides to develop a **product** that predicts inventory demand for small retailers. This niche approach allows the startup to launch quickly, generate revenue, and build a reputation in the logistics sector.

2. **Scenario 2: Tech Giant Expanding into AI**
A well-funded technology company plans to enter the AI healthcare market. Given its resources and long-term vision, it chooses to build a **platform** that integrates AI tools for diagnostics, patient management, and data analysis. The company aims to create a scalable ecosystem by attracting developers and healthcare providers.

3. **Scenario 3: Established Company Pivoting**
A mid-sized software company has a successful product: a project management tool. It evolved into a platform to achieve scalability and differentiation by enabling third-party integrations, APIs, and marketplaces for extensions. This shift aligns with its goal of fostering a collaborative ecosystem.

Balancing Risks and Rewards

The decision to build a product or platform involves weighing the risks and rewards of each approach. Products provide a clear path to market but can limit long-term growth. While offering greater scalability, platforms require significant investment and face challenges in reaching critical mass.

Choosing between a product and a platform is not a binary decision—it is a strategic choice that depends on factors such as market size, funding availability, and long-term goals. Businesses can align their strategy with their resources and vision by carefully analyzing these factors and leveraging tools like the decision matrix. Ultimately, understanding when to pursue a product or platform approach ensures a foundation for sustainable growth and success in a competitive market.

10.2: BUILDING A PLATFORM ECOSYSTEM

10.2.1 KEY COMPONENTS OF A PLATFORM ECOSYSTEM

A flourishing platform ecosystem relies on several key components that enable seamless interactions among users, developers, and other stakeholders. Platforms thrive not as standalone solutions but as interconnected systems where value is co-created and continuously amplified. This section explores the core components of a platform ecosystem—APIs, SDKs, and user-generated content—and illustrates their importance through the case study of TensorFlow. This widely recognized platform has grown exponentially through adequate community support and tools.

CORE COMPONENTS OF A PLATFORM ECOSYSTEM

1. **Application Programming Interfaces (APIs): The Foundation of Connectivity**
   APIs are the backbone of any platform ecosystem. They enable seamless communication and integration between the platform and external applications or services. APIs define how developers interact with the platform's resources, ensuring a standardized and consistent method for accessing features and data.

   - **Role of APIs in Platforms:**
     APIs provide developers with the tools to build platform applications, services, or extensions. They enable platforms to extend their functionality without directly involving every new feature or use case. For instance, an e-commerce platform can offer APIs for payment processing, inventory management, or order tracking, allowing third-party developers to build custom solutions for their clients.

   - **Benefits of APIs:**

     - **Scalability:** APIs allow platforms to grow by enabling third-party integrations.

     - **Flexibility:** Developers can create tailored solutions to meet specific needs.

     - **Ecosystem Growth:** APIs foster a vibrant ecosystem of applications and tools that enhance the platform's value.

Example: **Stripe's APIs** have revolutionized online payment processing, allowing businesses of all sizes to effortlessly integrate secure payment gateways.

2. **Software Development Kits (SDKs): Empowering Developers**
   SDKs are comprehensive toolkits that simplify building applications on a platform. They typically include libraries, documentation, code samples, and debugging tools, making it easier for developers to work with the platform's APIs and features.

   - **Role of SDKs in Platforms:**
     SDKs lower the barrier to entry for developers, enabling faster and more efficient application development. By providing pre-built components and templates, SDKs eliminate the need for developers to build everything from scratch. For example, an AI platform may offer SDKs for popular programming languages, allowing developers to implement machine learning algorithms quickly.

- **Benefits of SDKs:**
  - **Speed:** SDKs accelerate the development process by providing ready-to-use components.
  - **Ease of Adoption:** Developers can start using the platform with minimal learning curves.
  - **Standardization:** SDKs ensure consistency across applications built on the platform.

Example: **Unity's SDKs** empower game developers to create immersive experiences with minimal effort, contributing to Unity's dominance in the gaming industry.

3. **User-Generated Content (UGC): Driving Value Creation**
User-generated content is a hallmark of successful platforms. It encompasses any content, applications, or tools users or developers create within the ecosystem. UGC not only enriches the platform but also drives user engagement and innovation.

- **Role of UGC in Platforms:**
Platforms like YouTube, GitHub, and TensorFlow thrive because of their users' contributions. UGC transforms passive users into active participants, creating a self-sustaining cycle of growth and value generation. For example, on an AI platform, UGC might include pre-trained models, datasets, or tutorials shared by the community.

- **Benefits of UGC:**
  - **Scalability:** UGC allows the platform to grow without direct intervention from its creators.
  - **Engagement:** Users feel a sense of ownership and community involvement.
  - **Innovation:** UGC introduces diverse ideas and solutions that the platform owners might not have considered.

Example: **GitHub's open-source contributions** have driven innovation in software development, turning it into the go-to platform for collaborative coding.

CASE STUDY: TENSORFLOW'S GROWTH THROUGH APIS AND COMMUNITY SUPPORT

TensorFlow, Google's open-source machine learning platform, exemplifies how platforms can leverage APIs, SDKs, and user-generated content to build a thriving ecosystem.

1. APIs as the Foundation

TensorFlow provides robust APIs that allow developers to build machine learning models across various domains, from natural language processing to computer vision. These APIs simplify complex tasks such as defining neural network architectures and training models and deploying them in production environments. TensorFlow's APIs are well-documented, ensuring that developers—beginners or experts—can quickly understand and use them.

- **Impact of APIs on TensorFlow:**
  TensorFlow's APIs enable developers to integrate machine learning capabilities into their applications, driving widespread adoption across healthcare, finance, and autonomous systems.

2. SDKs for Developer Enablement

To complement its APIs, TensorFlow offers SDKs that simplify model development. TensorFlow Lite SDK, for instance, is designed explicitly to deploy machine learning models on mobile and embedded devices. This toolkit includes pre-trained models, conversion tools, and optimization libraries that allow developers to integrate AI into resource-constrained environments.

- **Impact of SDKs on TensorFlow:**
  By providing SDKs tailored to specific use cases, TensorFlow has lowered the barriers for developers, enabling them to bring AI applications to edge devices such as smartphones, IoT sensors, and autonomous drones.

3. User-Generated Content Driving Innovation

TensorFlow's community of developers and researchers is one of its greatest assets. Through platforms like TensorFlow Hub and GitHub, users contribute pre-trained models, datasets, and custom tools that extend TensorFlow's capabilities. The community also shares best practices, tutorials, and code samples, fostering a collaborative learning environment.

- **Impact of UGC on TensorFlow:**
  The contributions from TensorFlow's community have enriched the platform, making it a go-to resource for anyone working in machine learning. For example, TensorFlow Hub hosts reusable modules that save developers significant time and effort when building their projects.

WHY THESE COMPONENTS MATTER

The success of TensorFlow highlights the importance of APIs, SDKs, and user-generated content in building a robust platform ecosystem. Together, these components create a self-reinforcing cycle:

- **APIs** attract developers by providing a foundation for building solutions.
- **SDKs** empower developers to work efficiently, lowering the barrier to entry.

- **UGC** drives innovation and growth, ensuring the platform remains dynamic and relevant.

APIs, SDKs, and user-generated content are the pillars of any flourishing platform ecosystem. These components create scalable, sustainable platforms that can adapt to evolving market needs by enabling seamless integration, empowering developers, and fostering community-driven innovation. TensorFlow's success demonstrates how combining these elements can transform a platform into an indispensable resource for users and developers.

As we move into an increasingly interconnected digital world, the ability to leverage these core components will determine the success of future platforms. Organizations can build ecosystems that thrive in a competitive landscape by understanding and implementing these principles.

10.2.2 CREATING NETWORK EFFECTS

A platform is only as successful as the community of developers and users it attracts and engages. Developers extend the platform's utility by creating applications, integrations, or services while users drive adoption and provide valuable feedback. Building a strong developer and user base is crucial for achieving scalability, fostering innovation, and ensuring long-term growth. This section explores platforms' strategies to attract and retain developers and users, focusing on incentives and tools. It provides a case study on GitHub's success in fostering a developer community through open-source collaboration.

STRATEGIES FOR ATTRACTING DEVELOPERS AND USERS

1. **Offering Incentives**
Incentives are crucial in encouraging developers and users to engage with a platform. These can take various forms, including financial rewards, recognition, and resource access. Below are some ways incentives can be effectively deployed:

    - **Grants and Funding Programs:**
    Financial incentives such as grants and funding programs can motivate developers to create innovative solutions. Platforms like Google Cloud and AWS often run grant programs that provide free or discounted access to their tools and financial support for promising projects. These programs lower the barrier to entry for developers and startups, allowing them to experiment and innovate without worrying about upfront costs.

Example: TensorFlow runs research grants and sponsorships for developers who contribute significant improvements to the platform, such as creating new libraries or advancing machine learning techniques.

    - **Competitions and Hackathons:**
    Competitions such as hackathons encourage creativity and problem-solving. They allow

developers to showcase their skills and build solutions on the platform within a limited timeframe. Competitions also create buzz around the platform and generate a library of innovative use cases. Participants often receive prizes, recognition, or career opportunities.

Example: Microsoft Azure regularly hosts hackathons where participants solve real-world problems using Azure tools. Winners receive cash prizes, mentorship, and job opportunities.

- **Recognition and Rewards:**
  Platforms can incentivize developers by publicly recognizing their contributions. Leaderboards, badges, and public profiles showcasing accomplishments are great ways to reward contributors. Recognition creates a sense of community and encourages developers to remain active on the platform.

Example: GitHub recognizes contributors through stars, forks, and public contributions visible on user profiles. This incentivizes developers to contribute quality work and maintain a reputation within the community.

2. **Providing Easy-to-Use Tools**
   While incentives attract developers, providing intuitive and easy-to-use tools ensures they stay and actively contribute. A platform's success is directly tied to how well it supports its developers and users in achieving their goals.

- **Comprehensive Documentation:**
  Clear and detailed documentation is essential for helping developers understand and use a platform effectively. It should cover everything from getting started to troubleshooting advanced issues. Platforms with substantial documentation reduce developers' learning curves and encourage faster adoption.

Example: Stripe's payment APIs are famous for their detailed, easy-to-follow documentation, enabling developers to integrate payment solutions quickly.

- **Developer-Friendly Interfaces:**
  Platforms should prioritize creating APIs and SDKs that are intuitive and developer-friendly. Well-designed tools minimize complexity, allowing developers to focus on innovation rather than debugging.

Example: Twilio's communication APIs simplify integrating SMS, voice, and video into applications, making them a favorite among developers.

- **Tutorials and Learning Resources:**
  Platforms that provide step-by-step tutorials, code samples, and learning modules make it easier for new developers to start. These resources empower developers to experiment and build confidence in using the platform.

For example, Google's Firebase platform offers interactive tutorials and sample projects, allowing developers to learn to build scalable apps quickly.

- **Robust Developer Support:**
  Support through forums, live chat, or dedicated technical assistance ensures developers can resolve issues quickly. Active support systems create a sense of reliability and trust in the platform.

Example: AWS provides an extensive support network, including forums, FAQs, and 24/7 customer support, ensuring developers have help when needed.

CASE STUDY: GITHUB'S SUCCESS IN FOSTERING A DEVELOPER COMMUNITY

GitHub is one of the most successful platforms for attracting and engaging a massive developer community through open-source collaboration. By combining incentives with easy-to-use tools, GitHub has transformed how developers build and share software.

1. GitHub's Approach to Incentives

GitHub motivates developers to contribute to its platform by emphasizing collaboration and recognition. The platform provides several forms of incentives:

- **Open-Source Visibility:**
  GitHub allows developers to host and share their open-source projects for free, giving them a platform to showcase their work to millions of users. This visibility can lead to job offers, collaborations, and recognition within the tech community.

- **Community Recognition:**
  Developers gain stars, forks, and followers on their repositories, which serve as public endorsements of their work. These metrics act as badges of honor, motivating developers to create high-quality contributions.

- **Job Opportunities:**
  Companies frequently review GitHub's public repositories to find talented developers. Thus, GitHub is a coding platform and a career-building tool.

- **Hackathons and Events:**
  GitHub sponsors and participates in coding competitions, hackathons, and open-source summits, further incentivizing developer participation.

2. GitHub's Easy-to-Use Tools

GitHub's success is also attributed to its developer-friendly tools and ecosystem:

- **Version Control Made Easy:**

GitHub's integration with Git, a version control system, simplifies managing code repositories. Developers can easily track changes, collaborate on projects, and revert to previous versions.

- **Collaboration Features:**

GitHub's pull request and issue tracking features enable seamless collaboration between developers. Teams can review code, suggest changes, and manage projects efficiently.

- **GitHub Actions:**

The platform allows developers to automate workflows by introducing GitHub Actions, such as testing code or deploying applications. These tools save time and improve productivity.

- **Extensive Documentation and Tutorials:**

GitHub provides comprehensive guides for everything from basic Git commands to advanced repository management. Thus, new users can quickly learn the platform, while experienced developers can explore its advanced features.

- **Marketplace for Integrations:**

GitHub's marketplace offers plugins and integrations for various tools, such as CI/CD pipelines, analytics, and code scanning. This extensibility enhances the platform's utility for developers.

3. Community Engagement

GitHub has built a thriving community by fostering a sense of collaboration and ownership. Developers feel empowered to contribute to open-source projects, share ideas, and learn from one another. This community-driven approach has made GitHub the largest code repository in the world, hosting over 200 million repositories as of today.

The Importance of Attracting Developers and Users

A platform's ability to attract developers and users is directly linked to its long-term success. Developers extend the platform's functionality by creating applications and integrations while users provide the adoption and feedback necessary for growth. BPlatformscan creates a virtuous cycle of innovation, adoption, and engagement. by offering incentives and easy-to-use tools.

- **Incentives:** Encourage participation and innovation by rewarding contributions.
- **Developer Tools:** Simplify the development process to ensure retention and productivity.
- **Community Engagement:** Foster collaboration and ownership to build a loyal user base.

When implemented effectively, GitHub's success demonstrates how these strategies can transform a platform into a cornerstone of its industry.

A successful platform is built on attracting developers and users. By offering incentives such as grants, competitions, and recognition, platforms can motivate developers to engage with their ecosystem. At the same time, intuitive tools like APIs, SDKs, and robust support ensure developers can build applications efficiently. GitHub exemplifies how a platform can thrive by balancing these strategies, creating a community where developers feel empowered to innovate and collaborate.

Following these principles, platforms can become indispensable resources in their respective industries, driving growth and long-term success.

10.3: COMPETITIVE DIFFERENTIATION

10.3.1 IDENTIFYING UNIQUE VALUE PROPOSITIONS

In today's competitive business landscape, a Unique Value Proposition (UVP) is the cornerstone of differentiation. A UVP defines what distinguishes a product or platform from competitors and why customers should choose it. It captures a business's core value and resonates with its target audience. This section delves into the steps for defining a UVP and the importance of addressing underserved needs or outperforming competitors. It also illustrates these concepts through the example of a platform offering faster model deployment for AI developers.

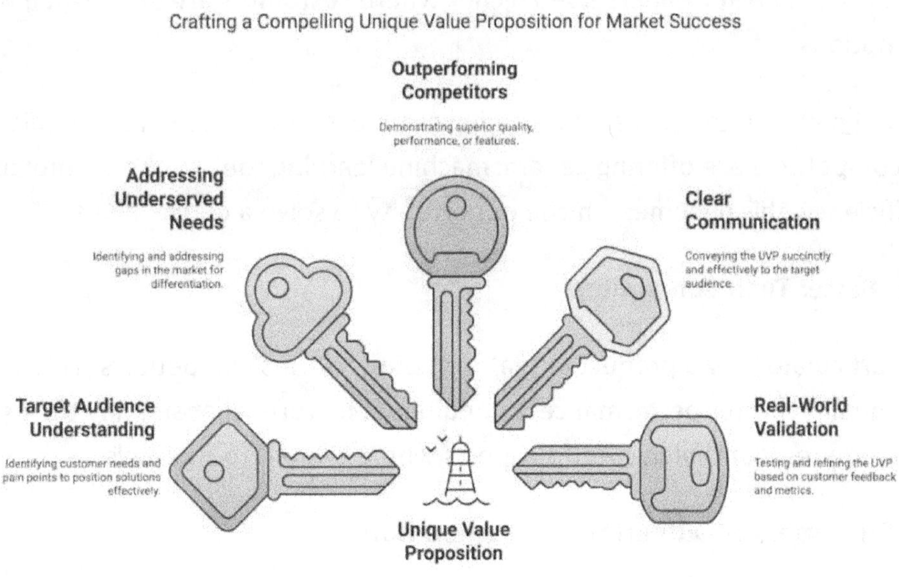

STEPS TO DEFINE A UNIQUE VALUE PROPOSITION (UVP)

1. Understand the Target Audience and Their Needs

The first step in defining a UVP is understanding the target audience. Businesses must identify their potential customers' needs, pain points, and aspirations. A comprehensive understanding of the audience enables a platform or product to position itself as a solution to its challenges.

- **How to Identify Needs:**
  - Conduct customer interviews and surveys to gather direct insights.
  - Analyze market trends and data to identify gaps in existing solutions.
  - Study competitors to understand areas where they fall short.

For example, AI developers may struggle with deploying machine learning models efficiently. Traditional deployment workflows could involve extensive manual configuration and debugging, leading to delays in bringing models to production. Understanding this pain point sets the foundation for crafting a UVP that addresses these inefficiencies.

2. Focus on Solving Underserved Needs

Underserved needs represent opportunities for differentiation. They are areas where existing products or platforms fail to meet customer expectations or do not offer a solution.

- **Approach:**
  - Identify gaps in the market or unmet demands through competitor analysis.
  - Look for underserved niches where customers are dissatisfied with existing options.

Example: An AI platform can focus on providing seamless, automated model deployment for developers. If competitors are offering generic machine learning tools without emphasizing deployment efficiency, this becomes a niche opportunity to solve a critical need.

3. Do Things Better Than Competitors

A UVP must articulate how a product or platform outperforms competitors. This could involve offering higher quality, better performance, or additional features that simplify the user experience. Differentiation requires identifying specific aspects where the platform excels.

- **Strategies for Outperforming Competitors:**
  - Leverage cutting-edge technology to enhance performance.
  - Simplify complex processes through intuitive design and automation.
  - Provide faster, more reliable solutions that reduce time-to-value for customers.

Example: A platform that automates 90% of the deployment workflow for machine learning models could advertise significantly reduced deployment times compared to manual processes. This efficiency becomes a clear differentiator.

4. Communicate Value Clearly and Concisely

Even the most compelling UVP is ineffective if not communicated clearly. Businesses must ensure that their UVP resonates with their audience through straightforward messaging and marketing.

- **Best Practices for Communication:**
  - Use simple, jargon-free language that highlights benefits over features.
  - Tailor messaging to specific customer segments for greater relevance.
  - Demonstrate value through case studies, testimonials, or data-driven results.

Example: The UVP for a faster model deployment platform could be communicated as: *"Accelerate your AI projects with automated deployment workflows—deploy models in hours, not weeks."*

5. Validate the UVP with Real-World Testing

Once a UVP is defined, it must be validated through real-world testing. This ensures that the value proposition resonates with the target audience and delivers on its promises.

- **Validation Steps:**
  - Pilot the product or platform with a small group of customers.
  - Gather feedback to refine the value proposition further.
  - Monitor key metrics such as adoption rates, customer satisfaction, and retention.

Example: The deployment platform could launch a beta program, inviting AI developers to test its features. Feedback from these users would help identify areas for improvement and validate the UVP.

Example: A Platform Offering Faster Model Deployment for AI Developers

AI and machine learning have led to a surge in tools and platforms designed to support model development, training, and deployment. However, deployment remains a bottleneck for many organizations, with challenges ranging from infrastructure setup to managing dependencies. This example illustrates how a UVP can address these challenges and differentiate a platform in a crowded market.

Identifying the Problem

AI developers often face significant delays when transitioning machine learning models from development to production. These delays can result from:

- Complex configuration processes.
- Dependency management issues.
- Lack of automation in deployment pipelines.

Competitors in the market may focus on model development and training but overlook the deployment phase. This creates an opportunity for a platform specializing in streamlined, efficient deployment.

Crafting the UVP

The platform positions itself with the following UVP:
"Revolutionize AI model deployment with our platform—seamless integration, automated workflows, and production-ready results in hours."

Key Features Supporting the UVP

1. **Automated Pipelines:** The platform automates the deployment process, eliminating manual configuration.
2. **Scalability:** Supports deployment across cloud, edge, and on-premises environments.
3. **One-Click Deployment:** Enables developers to deploy models with minimal effort.
4. **Real-Time Monitoring:** Provides insights into model performance post-deployment.

WHY THE UVP STANDS OUT

---

1. **Addressing Underserved Needs:**
   - Competitors may offer general AI tools without focusing on deployment. This platform solves a critical, overlooked challenge.
2. **Outperforming Competitors:**
   - By automating deployment workflows, the platform significantly reduces deployment times compared to manual processes.
3. **Clear Value Communication:**
   - The UVP is communicated through messaging such as:
     "Focus on building models, not deploying them. Save weeks of effort with automated, reliable deployment solutions."
4. **Real-World Validation:**

- The platform gains traction through beta testing and partnerships with early adopters, showcasing successful case studies and testimonials.

WHY DEFINING A UVP MATTERS

A well-defined UVP is essential for competitive differentiation. It ensures that a product or platform:

- **Addresses Real Needs:** Solves problems that matter to the target audience.
- **Stands Out:** Offers clear, compelling reasons for customers to choose it over competitors.
- **Drives Adoption:** Resonates with potential users, leading to higher adoption rates.
- **Ensures Longevity:** Continues to deliver value as market conditions evolve.

The AI deployment platform's UVP attracts AI developers and establishes it as a leader in solving deployment challenges. By addressing an underserved need and delivering better results than competitors, the platform secures its position in the market.

Defining a UVP is a strategic process that involves understanding customer needs, identifying gaps in the market, and outperforming competitors. Businesses can differentiate themselves and create lasting value by solving underserved problems and delivering superior results. The example of a platform offering faster model deployment for AI developers illustrates how a compelling UVP can attract users, drive adoption, and establish market leadership. For any business looking to thrive in today's competitive environment, a well-crafted UVP is not just a differentiator— but a necessity.

10.3.2 COMPETING IN NICHE VS. BROAD MARKET

Choosing whether to compete in a niche or a broad market is one of the most critical strategic decisions businesses face. Both approaches have unique advantages and challenges, and the right choice often depends on an organization's resources, goals, and long-term vision. Niche markets allow for a concentrated focus on a specific audience, usually leading to faster adoption and loyalty. On the other hand, broad markets offer the allure of scale and mass-market penetration but come with increased competition and resource demands. This section explores the advantages of niches and the risks of broad markets. We also provide an example of how an AI platform for precision agriculture has thrived by dominating a niche market.

ADVANTAGES OF NICHES

1. Strong Focus

Niche markets allow businesses to concentrate on solving specific problems for a well-defined audience. This focused approach enables organizations to fine-tune their offerings and tailor them to the unique needs of their target customers. By profoundly understanding a niche market, businesses can develop solutions that resonate more strongly with users than broader, generalized offerings.

For example, consider an AI platform designed for precision agriculture. By targeting farmers who need AI-powered tools for soil analysis, crop monitoring, and yield optimization, the platform can build highly specialized features that address the specific pain points of its audience. This focus allows the platform to deliver a superior user experience compared to a generalized AI platform that caters to multiple industries.

Strong focus also leads to operational efficiency. Companies with a narrower target market can allocate resources more effectively, ensuring that their research, development, and marketing investments yield maximum impact.

2. Faster Adoption

Niche markets often enable faster adoption of products and services. The smaller size and specificity of the target audience make reaching and engaging potential customers easier. In addition, niche audiences are typically more receptive to tailored solutions that address their unique challenges.

Faster adoption is particularly evident in industries with significant unmet needs. For instance, in agriculture, farmers may struggle to manually monitor crop health across large fields. An AI platform offering drone-based monitoring and real-time analytics would directly address this challenge, encouraging rapid uptake by farmers eager for efficiency and precision.

Moreover, businesses operating in niche markets can often rely on word-of-mouth marketing, as satisfied customers share their experiences within tightly knit communities. This organic growth strategy can accelerate adoption without requiring extensive marketing budgets.

3. Building Customer Loyalty

Niche markets foster closer relationships with customers. By focusing on a smaller audience, businesses can engage with their users more personally, creating a sense of trust and loyalty. This connection is often difficult to achieve in broad markets where customers may feel like just another number.

When an organization consistently meets or exceeds the expectations of its niche audience, it establishes itself as an expert in the field. This reputation strengthens customer loyalty and serves as a barrier to entry for competitors, who may struggle to replicate the same level of expertise and trust.

RISKS OF BROAD MARKETS

1. Higher Competition

Broad markets are attractive because of their scale, but this appeal also leads to intense competition. Large markets often attract multiple players, ranging from established corporations to well-funded startups. To stand out in such an environment, businesses must differentiate themselves, which requires significant investment in innovation, branding, and customer acquisition.

For example, consider an AI platform targeting the general business sector. Such a platform would face stiff competition from giants like Google, Microsoft, and Amazon, which have the resources and brand recognition to dominate the market. Competing against such players demands continuous innovation and aggressive marketing, which require substantial resources.

The presence of multiple competitors in broad markets also leads to price wars. Companies may feel compelled to lower their prices to remain competitive, which can erode profit margins and make it difficult to sustain long-term growth.

2. Resource Demands

Operating in a broad market requires considerable resources. From research and development to marketing and distribution, businesses must invest heavily to reach a diverse and dispersed audience. These resource demands can strain smaller companies or startups that lack the capital and infrastructure to compete at scale.

Broad markets also require companies to develop products or services that cater to a wide range of customer needs. This generalization can dilute the effectiveness of the offering, as it may fail to address specific pain points for individual user segments. The need to balance competing priorities often increases the complexity of product development and delivery.

Furthermore, scaling operations in a broad market can be challenging. Businesses must manage larger supply chains, handle more complex logistics, and maintain consistent quality across a broader customer base. These operational challenges can divert attention and resources from innovation and customer engagement.

3. Difficulty in Establishing a Unique Identity

Standing out in a broad market can be exceptionally difficult. With numerous players offering similar solutions, customers may struggle to differentiate between products or platforms. This lack of distinction can lead to commoditization, where price becomes the primary factor driving purchase decisions.

For example, a cloud-based AI platform targeting businesses may struggle to establish a unique identity in a market dominated by major players. Without a clear value proposition, the platform risks being overshadowed by competitors with more substantial brand recognition and larger marketing budgets.

EXAMPLE: AI PLATFORM FOR PRECISION AGRICULTURE

The success of an AI platform for precision agriculture illustrates how dominating a niche market can lead to significant competitive advantages. Precision agriculture is a specialized field that uses advanced technologies like AI, IoT, and drones to optimize farming practices. By focusing exclusively on the agricultural sector, this platform has addressed the specific needs of farmers and established itself as a leader in the industry.

Addressing Specific Needs

Farmers face numerous challenges, including unpredictable weather, pest infestations, and fluctuating market prices. Traditional farming methods often rely on manual monitoring and decision-making, which can be time-consuming and prone to errors. The AI platform solves these problems by offering tools for:

- **Soil Analysis:** Providing detailed insights into soil health and nutrient levels.
- **Crop Monitoring:** Using drones and satellite imagery to track crop growth and identify issues like disease or water stress.
- **Yield Optimization:** Offering data-driven recommendations for planting, irrigation, and fertilization.

The platform delivers tangible value to its users by addressing these pain points, ensuring high adoption rates and customer satisfaction.

Faster Adoption and Growth

The niche focus of the AI platform has enabled it to grow rapidly within the agricultural community. Farmers appreciate its tailored solutions, which are more effective and user-friendly than generic AI tools. The platform has also leveraged word-of-mouth marketing, with satisfied farmers recommending it to their peers.

The platform offers flexible pricing models to accelerate adoption, including subscription plans for small-scale farmers and enterprise solutions for large agricultural operations. This adaptability ensures that the platform appeals to a wide range of users within the niche market.

Building a Competitive Moat

The platform has built a strong competitive moat by dominating the precision agriculture niche. Its specialized features and deep understanding of the industry make it difficult for new entrants to replicate its success. Additionally, the platform invests in continuous innovation, regularly updating its tools to stay ahead of emerging challenges and trends in agriculture.

The platform has partnered with agricultural equipment manufacturers, government agencies, and research institutions. These collaborations enhance its credibility and create additional barriers for competitors attempting to enter the market.

Competing in niche versus broad markets presents unique opportunities and challenges. Niche markets offer the advantages of intense focus, faster adoption, and customer loyalty, making them ideal for businesses with limited resources or specialized expertise. While providing the potential for mass-market penetration and scalability, broad markets come with higher competition and resource demands, requiring significant investment and strategic planning.

The example of an AI platform for precision agriculture demonstrates the benefits of focusing on a niche market. By addressing specific needs, achieving faster adoption, and building a competitive moat, the platform has established itself as a leader in its industry. Businesses must carefully evaluate their goals, resources, and market conditions to determine whether a niche or broad market strategy aligns best with their vision for success.

10.3.3 ADAPTING TO CHANGING MARKET CONDITIONS

Adapting to changing market conditions is essential for any business aiming to achieve long-term success. Market demands, technology, and customer preferences constantly evolve in today's fast-paced and competitive environment. Businesses that fail to adapt risk losing relevance, while those that proactively respond to change often find opportunities for growth and innovation. This section explores strategies for staying relevant, including continuous innovation, user feedback, and market research. It also highlights the example of pivoting from a single-use AI product to a subscription-based platform, illustrating how adaptation can lead to sustained success.

STRATEGIES FOR STAYING RELEVANT

1. Continuous Innovation

Continuous innovation is one of the most effective ways to remain competitive in a rapidly changing market. Innovation ensures that businesses stay ahead of industry trends, meet evolving customer needs, and differentiate themselves from competitors. It involves creating new products or services and improving existing ones.

- **Product Innovation:**
  Companies must constantly refine and enhance their offerings to provide more value. This could involve adding new features, improving usability, or leveraging emerging technologies to create new capabilities.

Example: In the AI space, platforms that started with basic predictive models have evolved to include real-time analytics, natural language processing, and advanced automation tools. These innovations keep users engaged and attract new customers.

- **Process Innovation:**
  Beyond products, businesses can innovate their internal processes to improve efficiency and reduce costs. Automation, agile development methodologies, and advanced data analytics are process innovations that drive operational excellence.

- **Business Model Innovation:**
  Adapting how value is delivered to customers can also be a powerful form of innovation. For instance, shifting from a one-time purchase model to a subscription-based approach can create recurring revenue streams and increase customer lifetime value.

2. Leveraging User Feedback

User feedback is a valuable resource for staying relevant. By listening to customers, businesses can identify pain points, uncover unmet needs, and gain insights into how their products or services are used. Feedback-driven development ensures that offerings align closely with customer expectations.

- **Methods of Gathering Feedback:**
  - Surveys and questionnaires provide quantitative insights into customer satisfaction and preferences.
  - User interviews and focus groups offer qualitative feedback, revealing deeper motivations and challenges.
  - Monitoring customer reviews, social media, and online forums can highlight recurring issues and opportunities.
- **Acting on Feedback:**
  Gathering feedback is only the first step. Businesses must have processes in place to analyze and act on this information. Prioritizing feedback that aligns with strategic goals and implementing changes quickly demonstrates a commitment to customer-centricity.

Example: User feedback may indicate a SaaS company's onboarding process is too complex. By simplifying the workflow and providing better documentation, the company can improve retention and reduce churn b

3. Market Research

Ongoing market research helps businesses stay informed about industry trends, competitive dynamics, and emerging opportunities. It enables companies to anticipate changes in market conditions and adjust their strategies accordingly.

- **Analyzing Industry Trends:**
  Businesses should monitor technological advancements, regulatory changes, and shifts in consumer behavior. Staying informed about these trends helps companies anticipate and capitalize on opportunities.

Example: The rise of generative AI in recent years has spurred many companies to incorporate these capabilities into their platforms, ensuring they remain relevant in a rapidly evolving market.

- **Competitor Analysis:**
Understanding competitors' strategies, strengths, and weaknesses allows businesses to identify gaps and differentiate themselves. Competitive intelligence can also inform pricing strategies, product positioning, and marketing efforts.

- **Customer Segmentation:**
Market research can reveal new customer segments to target or highlight changes in existing segments. For example, a product initially aimed at small businesses might find demand among larger enterprises, prompting adjustments to the marketing strategy.

Example: Pivoting from a Single-Use AI Product to a Subscription-Based Platform

One of the most impactful ways a business can adapt to changing market conditions is by pivoting its business model. Pivoting allows companies to align their offerings with current demands, improve scalability, and capture additional value. A notable example is the transition from a single-use AI product to a subscription-based platform.

Initial Scenario: Single-Use AI Product

Imagine a company that developed an AI tool for automating customer support in e-commerce businesses. This product uses natural language processing to answer frequently asked questions, handle returns, and resolve simple issues. While the product solves an apparent problem, it is sold as a one-time license with optional updates.

Challenges faced by the company in this model:

- **Limited Revenue Streams:** Revenue depends on new sales, with minimal recurring income.
- **Market Saturation:** Growth decreases once most target customers have purchased the product.
- **Customer Retention Issues:** Customers may switch to competitors offering newer solutions without continuous engagement.

THE PIVOT: TRANSITION TO A SUBSCRIPTION-BASED PLATFORM

To address these challenges, the company has decided to transition from a single-use product to a subscription-based platform. The new platform offers additional features, continuous updates, and broader AI tools for e-commerce businesses.

Key changes implemented during the pivot:

1. **Expanded Functionality:**
The platform includes tools for advanced analytics, personalized customer recommendations,

and integration with other e-commerce software. These features provide ongoing value, encouraging customers to subscribe.

2. **Recurring Revenue Model:**

Customers pay a monthly or annual subscription fee, creating predictable and sustainable revenue streams. Premium tiers offer advanced features and dedicated support.

3. **Focus on Scalability:**

The platform is designed to handle a growing user base, with cloud-based infrastructure enabling seamless scaling.

4. **Community and Support:**

The platform fosters a community where users can share best practices, access tutorials, and collaborate. Regular webinars and dedicated support ensure high customer satisfaction.

BENEFITS OF THE PIVOT

1. **Increased Revenue Predictability:**

The subscription model provides steady income, reducing dependence on new customer acquisition. This stability allows the company to invest in innovation and growth.

2. **Enhanced Customer Retention:**

Continuous updates and expanded functionality keep users engaged, improving retention rates. Customers who perceive ongoing value from the platform are less likely to switch to competitors.

3. **Improved Market Positioning:**

By transitioning to a platform, the company differentiates itself from competitors offering standalone products. The platform's comprehensive suite of tools positions it as a one-stop solution for e-commerce AI.

4. **Alignment with Market Trends:**

The pivot aligns with the growing preference for SaaS and subscription-based services, ensuring the company remains relevant in an evolving market.

CHALLENGES OF THE PIVOT

While the transition offers numerous benefits, it is not without challenges:

- **Customer Transition:** Convincing existing customers to switch to the subscription model may require careful communication and incentives.

- **Upfront Investment:** Developing a platform and supporting infrastructure demands significant upfront investment.

- **Operational Complexity:** Managing subscriptions, ensuring uptime, and maintaining continuous updates add complexity to operations.

Despite these challenges, the benefits of pivoting to a subscription-based platform often outweigh the costs, particularly in markets where recurring revenue and scalability are key drivers of success.

Adapting to changing market conditions is essential for business survival and growth. Strategies such as continuous innovation, leveraging user feedback, and conducting market research enable companies to stay relevant and competitive. The example of pivoting from a single-use AI product to a subscription-based platform demonstrates how businesses can align their offerings with evolving customer demands, improve scalability, and create sustainable revenue streams.

10.4: PRICING MODELS AND REVENUE STRATEGIES

10.4.1 PRICING STRATEGIES FOR PRODUCTS VS. PLATFORMS

Pricing strategies are critical for the success of products and platforms, as they directly impact revenue generation, user adoption, and competitive positioning. The choice of pricing model depends on factors such as the target market, value proposition, scalability, and cost structure. This section explores key pricing strategies for products and platforms and provides examples to illustrate their application.

PRICING STRATEGIES FOR PRODUCTS

Products are typically standalone offerings that provide value to customers without requiring an ecosystem or network of contributors. The pricing models for products are straightforward and cater to various customer preferences. Common pricing strategies include:

1. **Pay-Per-Use Model**:
   - **Overview**: Customers pay based on the amount of usage, making this model ideal for variable demand or occasional use.
   - **Benefits**: Encourages adoption by reducing upfront costs and aligns pricing with actual value derived by the user.
   - **Challenges**: Revenue predictability can be low, and heavy users might perceive the cost as prohibitive.For example, Cloud computing services like Amazon Web Services (AWS) charge based on the computing power, storage, or bandwidth consumed.
2. **One-Time Purchase Model**:
   - **Overview**: Customers pay a single upfront fee for perpetual access to the product.

- **Benefits**: Provides immediate cash flow and simplifies the purchase process for customers.
- **Challenges**: Limited opportunities for ongoing revenue unless supplemented with paid upgrades or maintenance fees.
- **Example**: Traditional software licenses, such as Microsoft Office, before its subscription-based Office 365 model.

3. **Subscription Model**:
    - **Overview**: Customers pay a recurring fee (monthly or annually) for access to the product.
    - **Benefits**: Creates a steady revenue stream, improves customer retention, and provides opportunities for upselling.
    - **Challenges**: Requires consistent delivery of value to prevent churn.
    - **Example**: Adobe Creative Cloud offers a subscription-based model for its suite of creative tools.

PRICING STRATEGIES FOR PLATFORMS

Platforms are multi-sided ecosystems that connect users and contributors, creating value through network effects. Platform pricing strategies must balance all stakeholders' needs while driving growth and engagement. Common strategies include:

1. **Freemium Model**:
    - **Overview**: Offers basic functionality for free while charging for advanced features or premium access.
    - **Benefits**: Attracts a large user base quickly, creating network effects and opportunities to convert free users into paying customers.
    - **Challenges**: Requires careful planning to ensure free users do not overwhelm resources or cannibalize premium sales.
    - **Example**: Slack provides free access to essential team collaboration tools, premium plans for larger organizations, and advanced features.
2. **Tiered Pricing Model**:
    - **Overview**: Offers multiple pricing tiers based on feature sets, usage levels, or user types.

- **Benefits**: Provides flexibility for different customer segments and maximizes revenue potential by catering to diverse needs.
- **Challenges**: Clear differentiation between tiers is required to avoid confusion or dissatisfaction.
- **Example**: Netflix offers basic, standard, and premium plans with varying levels of video quality and simultaneous streaming options.

3. **Revenue-Sharing Model**:
   - **Overview**: Generates revenue by taking a percentage of transactions or earnings within the platform ecosystem.
   - **Benefits**: Aligns the platform's success with its contributors and incentivizes ecosystem growth.
   - **Challenges**: A robust marketplace with active contributors and users must be sustainable.
   - **Example**: App marketplaces like Apple's App Store and Google Play take a percentage of revenue from app sales and in-app purchases.

Example: Freemium AI Platform

A practical example of these strategies is a freemium AI platform for enterprise users. The platform could offer:

- **Free Tier**: Basic AI tools for individuals and small teams.
- **Premium Tier**: Advanced features like custom integrations, enterprise-grade security, and priority support.
- **Revenue Potential**: The platform attracts a broad user base by providing free access, while the premium tier drives revenue from businesses seeking enhanced capabilities.

Key Considerations for Choosing a Pricing Strategy

- **Value Proposition**: Align the pricing model with the perceived value delivered to users.
- **Target Audience**: Consider the target market's purchasing power, preferences, and behavior.
- **Competitive Landscape**: Evaluate pricing models used by competitors and identify opportunities for differentiation.

- **Cost Structure**: Ensure the pricing strategy covers costs while remaining competitive and attractive to users.
- **Scalability**: Choose a model that supports growth without significantly increasing operational complexity.

By tailoring pricing strategies to the unique characteristics of products and platforms, businesses can optimize revenue, drive adoption, and maintain a competitive edge in the market.

10.4.2 MAXIMIZING REVENUE POTENTIAL

Maximizing revenue potential is critical for businesses looking to enhance their profitability and sustain growth in competitive markets. Practical upselling and cross-selling strategies in AI products and platforms can significantly contribute to revenue growth by deepening customer relationships, increasing customer lifetime value (CLV), and expanding the product or platform's footprint within existing accounts. This section explores how businesses can leverage these strategies and highlights a case study on Salesforce's AppExchange marketplace to illustrate their practical application.

UPSELLING AND CROSS-SELLING OPPORTUNITIES

Upselling and **cross-selling** are complementary strategies that encourage customers to purchase additional products or features beyond their initial purchase. These strategies rely on a deep understanding of customer needs, behavior, and preferences, making them especially effective in the AI-driven digital economy.

1. Upselling

Upselling involves persuading customers to purchase a more advanced or higher-value version of a product or service. This strategy is effective when customers see clear added value and a strong return on investment (ROI) when upgrading their current solution. In the context of AI products and platforms, upselling opportunities include:

- **Advanced Features**: Access to premium AI models, enhanced processing power, or additional data storage.
- **Custom Integrations**: We offer tailored solutions that seamlessly integrate with the customer's existing systems.
- **Enterprise Solutions**: Delivering enterprise-grade security, scalability, and customer support for larger organizations.

Example: An AI-powered analytics tool might upsell customers from an introductory subscription to a premium plan with additional machine learning algorithms, real-time data visualization, and predictive analytics.

Benefits of Upselling:

- Increases average revenue per user (ARPU).
- Enhances customer satisfaction by meeting evolving needs.
- Reduces customer churn by offering solutions aligned with business growth.

2. Cross-Selling

Cross-selling involves encouraging customers to purchase complementary products or services. This approach capitalizes on the existing relationship and trust established with the customer. For AI platforms, cross-selling opportunities include:

- **Add-On Tools**: Suggest tools like chatbot development kits, speech recognition modules, or AI-driven marketing platforms.
- **Third-Party Integrations**: Promoting ecosystem offerings like plugins or APIs developed by external contributors.
- **Analytics and Reporting**: Providing access to advanced analytics tools for deeper insights into user behavior or system performance.

Example: A cloud-based AI platform might cross-sell an AI-driven CRM tool to customers using its data processing services, highlighting the synergy between the two products.

Benefits of Cross-Selling:

- Encourages customers to invest further in the ecosystem.
- Builds stronger relationships by offering a one-stop solution.
- Opens additional revenue streams without acquiring new customers.

Best Practices for Upselling and Cross-Selling

1. **Customer Segmentation**: Identify high-potential customers based on usage patterns, industry, and business size.
2. **Personalization**: Tailor offers to individual customer needs and preferences, leveraging AI-driven insights for accuracy.
3. **Value Communication**: Clearly articulate the additional value the customer will gain from the upsell or cross-sell.
4. **Seamless Integration**: Ensure new products or features integrate smoothly with the customer's setup.

5. **Timing and Relevance**: Offer upsells or cross-sells at the right time, such as during renewals, after achieving key milestones, or when addressing a specific pain point.

CASE STUDY: SALESFORCE AND APPEXCHANGE

Salesforce provides an exemplary case study in maximizing revenue potential through its AppExchange marketplace. Launched in 2005, AppExchange is an ecosystem of third-party applications and integrations that complement Salesforce's core customer relationship management (CRM) platform. It has become a cornerstone of Salesforce's revenue strategy, demonstrating the power of upselling, cross-selling, and ecosystem monetization.

1. AppExchange as a Cross-Selling Engine

Salesforce has positioned AppExchange as a one-stop marketplace for businesses to find solutions tailored to their needs. By offering a wide range of third-party apps, Salesforce encourages customers to expand their use of its platform. Examples of cross-selling opportunities include:

- **Vertical-Specific Solutions**: Apps designed for healthcare, finance, and retail industries.
- **Productivity Tools**: Add-ons like document automation, data visualization, and task management.
- **AI Enhancements**: Einstein AI-powered apps for predictive analytics and advanced data insights.

The revenue-sharing model incentivizes developers to create high-quality apps, while Salesforce benefits from a percentage of every sale, making AppExchange a win-win for all stakeholders.

2. Upselling Through Advanced Features

Salesforce uses AppExchange to upsell its premium features and services. For example:

- **Advanced Analytics**: Encouraging customers to adopt Tableau, Salesforce's data visualization platform, for deeper insights.
- **Scalable Solutions**: Promoting enterprise plans with higher user limits, enhanced security, and dedicated account management.
- **Custom Development**: Offering tools for businesses to build their apps on Salesforce's platform.

This strategy boosts revenue and strengthens customer loyalty by enabling businesses to tailor the platform to their unique requirements.

3. Building an Ecosystem

AppExchange has transformed Salesforce from a CRM provider into a platform ecosystem. By fostering a thriving developer community, Salesforce has ensured a continuous flow of innovative solutions that drive customer adoption and retention. The ecosystem's success is evident in its numbers: millions of installs and apps, ranging from simple utilities to complex enterprise-grade solutions.

4. Revenue Impact

Salesforce's AppExchange has significantly contributed to its bottom line by:

- **Driving Subscription Growth**: Customers who adopt third-party apps are more likely to upgrade their Salesforce plans.
- **Generating Partner Revenue**: Revenue-sharing agreements with app developers create an additional income stream.
- **Enhancing Customer Retention**: The ecosystem's value makes it difficult for customers to switch to competitors, leading to higher retention rates.

Key Takeaways from Salesforce's Strategy

- **Customer-Centric Approach**: By addressing specific business needs, Salesforce ensures its platform remains indispensable.
- **Value Co-Creation**: Partnering with third-party developers enables the creation of solutions that add value for all stakeholders.
- **Focus on Scalability**: Salesforce's AppExchange model is scalable, allowing It to serve various industries and business sizes.

Challenges and Considerations

While upselling and cross-selling present significant revenue opportunities, businesses must navigate specific challenges to maximize their effectiveness:

1. **Balancing Complexity**: Offering too many options can overwhelm customers and dilute the value proposition.
2. **Managing Customer Expectations**: Overpromising on the benefits of upsells or cross-sells can lead to dissatisfaction and churn.
3. **Ensuring Ecosystem Quality**: Maintaining a high standard of third-party offerings is critical to sustaining platform trust and engagement.

Maximizing revenue potential through upselling and cross-selling is a powerful strategy for businesses operating in the AI-driven digital landscape. Companies can unlock significant growth opportunities by understanding customer needs, delivering personalized offers, and leveraging ecosystem dynamics. The case study of Salesforce's AppExchange highlights how a well-executed strategy can transform a platform into a revenue-generating powerhouse, providing valuable lessons for companies seeking to emulate its success. Businesses can drive revenue and build long-term relationships and market leadership by focusing on customer-centric innovation and scalable solutions.

CHAPTER 11: ETHICAL CONSIDERATIONS AND THE FUTURE OF AI

INTRODUCTION

Artificial Intelligence (AI) is a transformative force shaping the modern world. Its potential is vast and profound, from revolutionizing industries to augmenting human capabilities. However, with great power comes great responsibility. As AI continues to permeate our lives, the ethical considerations surrounding its development and deployment have become a pressing concern. Ethics in AI is no longer just an academic debate; it is a real-world imperative that influences trust, fairness, and societal well-being.

WHY ETHICS IS CRITICAL IN AI DEVELOPMENT

AI's transformative power brings with it a spectrum of ethical risks. While the technology promises unprecedented innovation, it poses challenges that, if left unaddressed, could lead to significant societal harm. These challenges include bias, misuse, privacy violations, and job displacement.

Bias and Its Implications

Bias in AI systems often stems from the data they are trained on or the algorithms used. For example, underrepresentation in datasets can result in skewed outcomes, particularly in critical areas such as hiring, lending, and healthcare. Algorithmic bias, where systems unintentionally harm certain groups by optimizing for specific objectives, further exacerbates these issues. These biases can erode trust in AI and amplify societal inequalities, highlighting the need for rigorous ethical oversight.

Misuse and Privacy Violations

AI's capabilities can be misused in ways that infringe on privacy and autonomy. Facial recognition technology, for instance, has sparked significant controversy. Its use in surveillance raises concerns about mass monitoring, wrongful identifications, and potential misuse by authoritarian regimes. This underscores the importance of ethical frameworks to govern AI applications, ensuring they prioritize human rights and freedoms.

Job Displacement and Economic Inequality

AI-driven automation can potentially displace millions of jobs, disproportionately affecting low-skilled workers. While technological advancements have historically created new opportunities, the pace and scale of AI's impact necessitate proactive strategies to mitigate economic disruption and promote workforce reskilling.

Real-World Example: The Facial Recognition Debate

The debate around facial recognition technology exemplifies AI's ethical challenges. In recent years, companies like Amazon, Microsoft, and IBM have faced backlash over the societal implications of their facial recognition tools. Critics argue that these systems often exhibit racial and gender biases, leading to wrongful arrests and privacy violations. In response, several organizations have halted the sale of such technologies to law enforcement, emphasizing the need for ethical guidelines and regulatory oversight.

WHAT THIS CHAPTER OFFERS

To address these challenges, this chapter provides readers with practical tools and insights for building ethical AI solutions. It explores frameworks prioritizing fairness, transparency, and accountability, equipping organizations to navigate the complex landscape of AI ethics. Additionally, it examines emerging AI trends and their ethical implications, offering a forward-looking perspective on the future of responsible innovation.

11.1: BIAS IN AI SYSTEMS

Artificial Intelligence (AI) holds immense promise for transforming industries and solving complex problems. However, as with any powerful tool, it comes with challenges, one of the most critical being bias. AI systems can manifest in numerous ways, resulting from flaws in data collection, algorithm design, and deployment practices. Understanding and addressing these biases is essential for ensuring fairness, trust, and ethical outcomes in AI applications.

11.1.1 SOURCES OF BIAS IN AI

AI systems' bias arises primarily from data bias and algorithmic bias. Both have profound implications for the effectiveness and fairness of AI systems.

Data Bias

Data is the foundation of AI systems, and the data's quality, representation, and diversity directly influence the outputs. Data bias occurs when the datasets used to train AI models do not represent the target population or contain inherent prejudices. This can lead to biased outcomes that disproportionately favor or disadvantage certain groups.

Example: Underrepresentation in Datasets Leading to Biased Hiring Decisions

Consider AI systems designed to assist in hiring decisions. If the training data primarily consists of resumes from a specific demographic—say, male candidates—the AI model might develop a preference for male applicants. This was notably the case in a hiring tool developed by a major tech company, which exhibited bias against women because the training data reflected historical hiring patterns favoring men. Such biases can perpetuate systemic discrimination, undermining efforts to promote diversity and inclusion in the workplace.

To mitigate data bias, it is crucial to ensure datasets are diverse, representative, and regularly audited for potential biases. This includes collecting data from various demographics, geographies, and contexts to capture human experiences.

Algorithmic Bias

Algorithmic bias arises when AI systems optimize for objectives that inadvertently harm specific groups. This can occur due to flawed design choices, incomplete problem framing, or unintentional prioritization of specific metrics over others.

Example: Optimizing for Objectives That Harm Certain Groups

In credit scoring systems, algorithms often optimize for predictive accuracy without considering fairness. This can lead to outcomes where individuals from historically marginalized communities are disproportionately denied loans, even when they have similar financial qualifications as others. The root cause often lies in the algorithms' reliance on proxies that correlate with socioeconomic factors, such as zip codes, which can reflect systemic inequalities.

To address algorithmic bias, developers must carefully evaluate the objectives and metrics used during the design phase. Techniques like fairness-aware algorithms and adversarial debiasing can help reduce the likelihood of biased outcomes.

11.1.2 IMPACT OF BIAS

Bias in AI systems can have far-reaching societal consequences. These impacts extend beyond the technical domain and affect trust, equity, and social cohesion.

Societal Consequences

Bias in AI can exacerbate existing inequalities and erode public trust in technology. When AI systems perpetuate or amplify discrimination, they can reinforce societal divides and hinder progress toward equity.

Exacerbating Inequalities

AI hiring, lending, and law enforcement systems can disproportionately disadvantage marginalized communities. For instance, predictive policing algorithms trained on biased crime data may unfairly target specific neighborhoods, leading to over-policing and stigmatization. This creates a feedback loop where systemic biases are reinforced, making it even harder for affected communities to escape cycles of discrimination.

Eroding Trust in AI

Public trust in AI is crucial for its widespread adoption and success. Biased outcomes can undermine this trust, leading to skepticism and resistance. For example, if facial recognition systems frequently misidentify individuals from particular racial or ethnic groups, it raises questions about the reliability and fairness of AI technologies. This erosion of trust can stall innovation and adoption, depriving society of AI's potential benefits.

Example: Bias in Credit-Scoring Systems

A well-documented example of AI bias is in credit-scoring systems. Studies have shown that specific demographics, particularly minorities, are disproportionately affected by lower credit scores, even when their financial behaviors are comparable to those of other groups. This bias often stems from historical data that reflects systemic inequalities, such as discriminatory lending practices. The consequences are severe, as biased credit scores can limit access to housing, education, and employment opportunities, perpetuating cycles of disadvantage.

11.1.3 MITIGATION STRATEGIES

Addressing bias in AI systems requires a multi-faceted approach that combines technical solutions, organizational practices, and regulatory frameworks. The following strategies can help mitigate bias and promote fairness in AI.

Techniques

1. **Regular Audits** Conducting regular audits of AI systems can help identify and address biases in data, algorithms, and outcomes. To ensure a comprehensive evaluation, these audits should involve diverse teams of experts.

2. **Diverse Datasets** Building and maintaining diverse datasets is crucial for reducing data bias. This involves collecting data from varied sources and demographics to ensure representation.

3. **Fairness-Aware Algorithms** Incorporating fairness-aware algorithms into the development process can help minimize bias. These algorithms are designed to balance accuracy with fairness, ensuring equitable outcomes for all groups.

Tools

Several tools have been developed to mitigate bias and promote fairness in AI systems. These tools provide frameworks and methodologies for identifying, measuring, and addressing bias.

1. **IBM AI Fairness 360** is an open-source toolkit that provides metrics to test for bias and algorithms to mitigate it. The toolkit includes fairness metrics for various stages of the AI lifecycle, from data preprocessing to model evaluation.

2. **Microsoft Responsible AI Dashboard** Microsoft's Responsible AI Dashboard offers tools for assessing AI models' fairness, transparency, and accountability. It enables developers to identify and address potential biases during the development process.

11.2: FAIRNESS AND EXPLAINABILITY

Artificial Intelligence (AI) has become a cornerstone of decision-making in numerous domains, from healthcare to finance. While the benefits of AI are immense, concerns around fairness and explainability remain critical. These attributes are pivotal in ensuring trust, ethical application, and compliance with legal frameworks. This section explores the need for transparent AI, the balance between accuracy and fairness, and the importance of regulatory compliance.

11.2.1 THE NEED FOR TRANSPARENT AI

Transparent AI ensures that users understand and trust how AI systems make decisions. This is especially vital in high-stakes applications like healthcare, finance, and law enforcement, where opaque algorithms can lead to mistrust, harm, or unintended consequences.

ENSURING USERS UNDERSTAND HOW DECISIONS ARE MADE

AI systems often operate as black boxes, making it difficult for users to comprehend the logic behind their decisions. Explainable AI (XAI) addresses this challenge by providing insights into the decision-making process. For instance, in medical diagnostics, explainability is crucial. Consider an AI system used to diagnose diseases such as cancer. If a system predicts a malignant tumor, doctors and patients need to know why that conclusion was reached. By leveraging explainable models, healthcare providers can:

- Build trust with patients.
- Validate predictions with clinical knowledge.
- Enhance accountability in case of errors.

Example: A medical imaging AI might highlight areas where abnormalities are detected in an X-ray and correlate them to specific features indicative of disease. Such transparency fosters confidence in the technology and facilitates its integration into clinical workflows.

TECHNIQUES FOR EXPLAINABILITY

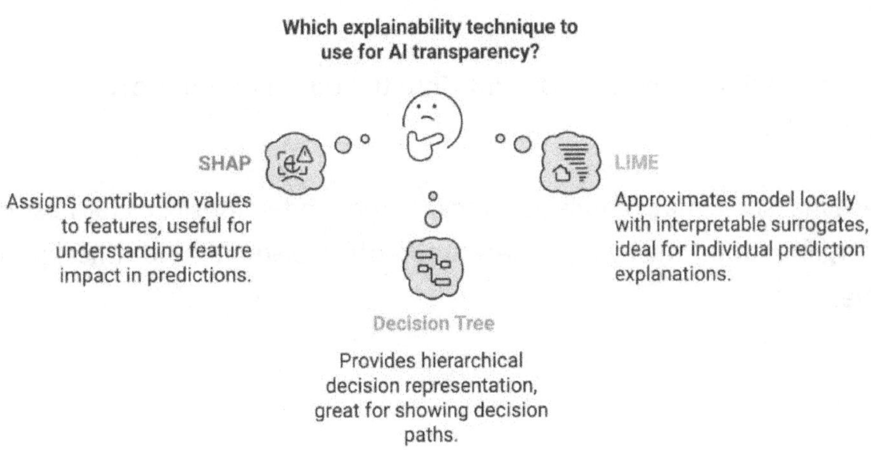

Several techniques and tools have been developed to enhance the transparency of AI systems:

1. **SHAP (SHapley Additive exPlanations):** This method assigns a contribution value to each feature in a prediction. For example, in a loan approval system, SHAP can illustrate how income, credit score, and existing debt influenced the decision.

2. **LIME (Local Interpretable Model-agnostic Explanations):** LIME explains individual predictions by approximating the model locally with interpretable surrogates. For instance, it can reveal why a specific patient's health outcome was predicted as "at risk."

3. **Decision Tree Visualizations:** Decision trees provide a hierarchical representation of decisions, making them inherently interpretable. A decision tree might show how customer demographics and purchase history lead to product recommendations in a retail setting.

These techniques enable stakeholders to understand and trust AI systems better, ultimately improving their adoption and effectiveness.

11.2.2 BALANCING ACCURACY WITH FAIRNESS

AI systems often have to choose between optimizing for performance (e.g., accuracy) and ensuring fairness. While accuracy is a key metric, prioritizing it without considering fairness can perpetuate biases and lead to discriminatory outcomes.

TRADE-OFFS BETWEEN OPTIMIZING PERFORMANCE AND ENSURING FAIRNESS

AI models trained on historical data often inherit and amplify biases present in the data. For example, a hiring algorithm trained on data from a predominantly male workforce might favor male candidates, thereby perpetuating gender inequality. Balancing accuracy with fairness requires conscious design choices, such as:

- **Reweighting data samples** to give underrepresented groups equal importance.
- **Adopting fairness metrics,** such as demographic parity or equalized odds, during model evaluation.
- **Incorporating fairness constraints** into the optimization process to mitigate bias while preserving performance.

However, these measures may reduce accuracy, as the model prioritizes fairness over perfectly fitting the data. Organizations must weigh these trade-offs based on their ethical priorities and business objectives.

CASE STUDY: REDESIGNING LOAN APPROVAL ALGORITHMS

A financial institution faced criticism for bias in its loan approval process, as minority applicants were disproportionately denied loans. An internal audit revealed that the algorithm relied heavily on zip codes, which correlated with socioeconomic disparities.

To address this, the institution:

1. Removed biased features such as zip codes from the model.
2. Incorporated fairness-aware techniques, including reweighting data and enforcing demographic parity constraints.
3. Conducted fairness audits to monitor outcomes for different demographic groups.

The redesigned algorithm balanced fairness and accuracy, ensuring equitable treatment of all applicants while maintaining reliable credit risk predictions. This case highlights the importance of aligning AI design with ethical and social responsibilities.

11.2.3 REGULATORY COMPLIANCE

As AI continues influencing society, governments and regulatory bodies have introduced laws to ensure its ethical and transparent use. Compliance with these regulations is crucial for organizations deploying AI systems.

OVERVIEW OF RELEVANT LAWS

1. **General Data Protection Regulation (GDPR):** Enforced in the European Union, GDPR includes automated decision-making and profiling provisions. Article 22 grants individuals the right to an explanation of decisions made by AI systems, ensuring accountability and transparency.

2. **California Consumer Privacy Act (CCPA):** CCPA emphasizes data privacy and grants consumers the right to know how their data is used. AI systems must provide clear disclosures about data usage and decision-making.

3. **Upcoming AI Regulations in the EU:** The European Union is drafting comprehensive AI regulations to address ethical concerns, promote fairness, and ensure safety. These regulations will likely mandate risk assessments, transparency documentation, and human oversight for high-risk AI applications.

ENSURING COMPLIANCE THROUGH TRANSPARENCY AND DOCUMENTATION

Organizations can meet regulatory requirements by:

1. **Maintaining detailed documentation** of AI models, including data sources, training processes, and evaluation metrics.

2. **Implementing explainability techniques** to provide users with clear insights into decision-making.

3. **Conducting regular audits** to ensure fairness, accuracy, and compliance with ethical guidelines.

Adhere to these practices, and organizations can mitigate legal risks, build trust with stakeholders, and contribute to the responsible advancement of AI technologies.

Fairness and explainability are fundamental to AI systems' ethical and effective deployment. Transparent AI fosters trust and accountability, while fairness ensures equitable outcomes across diverse populations. Although balancing these attributes with accuracy presents challenges, organizations can achieve meaningful progress through thoughtful design, fairness-aware techniques, and compliance with regulatory frameworks. By prioritizing these principles, AI can become a force for good, responsibly driving innovation and social progress.

11.3: AI SAFETY AND GOVERNANCE

Artificial Intelligence (AI) holds transformative potential across various domains, but its rapid development poses significant challenges and risks. To mitigate these risks and enable AI's benefits to society, it is crucial to ensure its safe deployment and governance. This section explores the dangers of unregulated AI, the need for governance frameworks, and strategies for long-term safety.

11.3.1 RISKS OF UNREGULATED AI

Artificial Intelligence (AI) holds transformative potential across various domains, but its rapid development poses significant challenges and risks. To mitigate these risks and enable AI's benefits to society, it is crucial to ensure its safe deployment and governance. This section explores the dangers of unregulated AI, the need for governance frameworks, and strategies for long-term safety.

11.3.1.1 RISKS OF UNREGULATED AI

The absence of robust regulations for AI systems can lead to significant societal, ethical, and security risks. These risks span multiple dimensions, from autonomous weaponry to misinformation campaigns and the loss of control over AI systems.

Potential Dangers

1. **Autonomous Weaponry**: Unregulated AI development could result in the proliferation of autonomous weapons capable of making life-and-death decisions without human

intervention. Such weapons could escalate conflicts and make war less predictable and controllable.

2. **Misinformation**: AI-powered tools, such as deepfake technology, can create highly realistic but false content, posing threats to democracies and public trust. These tools can spread disinformation on social media, manipulate elections, or tarnish reputations.

3. **Loss of Control**: As AI systems become more complex, developers and operators risk losing control over their behavior. Unanticipated outcomes from AI systems could lead to catastrophic consequences in high-stakes applications like healthcare or finance.

Example: Deepfake Technology

Deepfake technology exemplifies the dangers of unregulated AI. It uses machine learning models to generate realistic audio, video, and images, often indistinguishable from genuine content. For instance, deepfakes have been used in disinformation campaigns to impersonate political leaders, spread fake news, and incite societal unrest. In 2020, a deepfake video of a political figure caused public confusion and highlighted the urgent need for AI governance to address these challenges.

11.3.2 BUILDING GOVERNANCE FRAMEWORKS

Establishing robust governance frameworks is essential to address the risks posed by unregulated AI. These frameworks should promote accountability, oversight, and stakeholder collaboration to ensure responsible AI development and deployment.

Key Principles

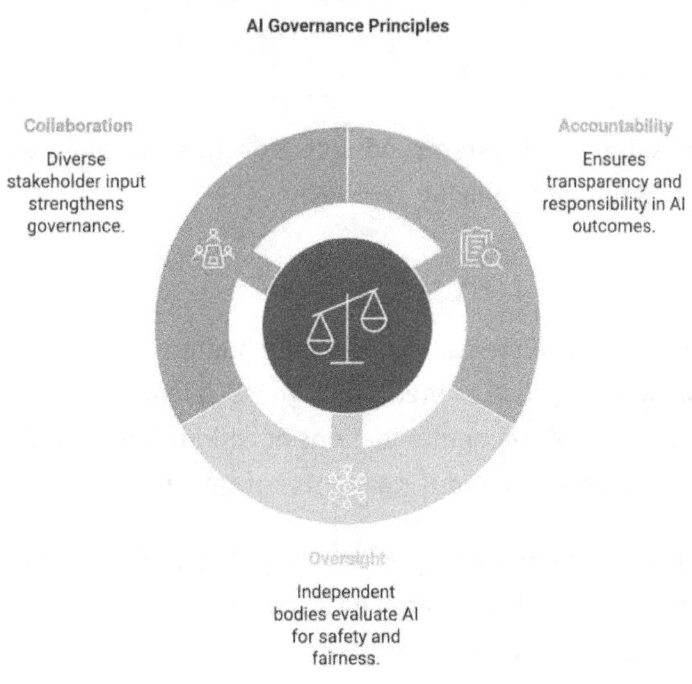

1. **Accountability**: Organizations developing AI systems must be accountable for their technologies' outcomes. This includes transparency about the AI's design, data sources, and decision-making processes. Regular audits and impact assessments can help maintain accountability.

2. **Oversight**: Independent oversight bodies should monitor AI development and deployment. This could include regulatory agencies or third-party auditors tasked with evaluating AI systems' safety, fairness, and ethical implications.

3. **Collaboration with Stakeholders**: Effective governance requires input from a broad range of stakeholders, including policymakers, technologists, ethicists, and civil society. Collaborative efforts ensure diverse perspectives are considered and improve the robustness of governance frameworks.

EXAMPLE: ESTABLISHING AN AI ETHICS BOARD

An AI ethics board within a startup provides a practical example of governance. The board would consist of diverse members, including technologists, ethicists, and external advisors. Its role would include:

- Reviewing AI projects for ethical implications.
- Setting guidelines for data usage and algorithmic transparency.
- Monitoring compliance with industry standards and regulations.

By embedding ethical considerations into the organization's core processes, the board ensures that AI technologies align with societal values and reduce potential harm.

11.3.3 ENSURING LONG-TERM SAFETY

Ensuring the long-term safety of AI systems requires proactive strategies that prioritize human oversight, collaboration, and forward-thinking approaches.

Strategies

1. **Human-in-the-Loop Systems**: Incorporating human oversight into AI systems is critical for high-stakes applications, such as medical diagnostics or autonomous driving. Human-in-the-loop systems ensure that AI's recommendations or actions are reviewed and approved by humans before implementation, reducing the risk of catastrophic errors.

2. **Partnerships with Industry Organizations**: Collaborating with organizations like OpenAI and the Partnership on AI can help share best practices, develop safety standards, and address global AI challenges collectively. These partnerships promote transparency and encourage responsible innovation.

Long-term safety also involves fostering a culture of responsibility within AI development communities. This includes ongoing research into AI alignment, where systems are designed to act in ways that align with human values and maintain open communication channels to address emerging risks.

Society can harness AI's potential while minimizing its harms by addressing the risks of unregulated AI, building comprehensive governance frameworks, and adopting strategies for long-term safety. The journey toward safe and ethical AI requires collaboration, vigilance, and a commitment to responsible innovation.

11.4: THE FUTURE OF AI

Artificial intelligence (AI) continues to revolutionize industries, reshape societal norms, and push the boundaries of technological capabilities. As we look ahead, the trajectory of AI innovation is expected to accelerate, bringing both opportunities and challenges. This section explores the future of AI through emerging trends, societal impacts, and strategies to prepare for an AI-driven future.

11.4.1 EMERGING AI TRENDS

AI is evolving rapidly, with advancements across various domains. Among the most promising trends are Quantum AI and Multimodal AI, which offer groundbreaking opportunities in optimization, cryptography, and integrated applications.

QUANTUM AI

Quantum computing has the potential to redefine AI by enabling unparalleled computational power. Quantum AI combines the principles of quantum mechanics with machine learning, unlocking solutions to problems intractable for classical systems. Key opportunities include:

1. **Optimization Problems**: Quantum AI is poised to revolutionize optimization, a cornerstone of many industries. From supply chain logistics to financial portfolio management, quantum algorithms can solve complex optimization challenges exponentially faster than traditional methods. For instance, airlines could optimize real-time flight routes to reduce fuel consumption and costs.

2. **Cryptography**: Quantum AI will seismically shift the security landscape. While quantum computing threatens traditional cryptographic methods, it also enables the development of quantum-safe encryption techniques. This dual impact is critical for securing sensitive data in a digital-first world.

MULTIMODAL AI

Multimodal AI represents another frontier, integrating data from multiple sources such as text, images, and videos. By synthesizing diverse inputs, multimodal AI facilitates richer and more nuanced applications. Its key attributes include:

1. **Contextual Understanding**: Multimodal systems can interpret and analyze information in ways that mimic human cognition. For example, integrating camera feeds, LIDAR data, and real-time traffic updates enhances decision-making accuracy in autonomous vehicles.

2. **Rich User Experiences**: Applications like augmented reality (AR) and virtual reality (VR) stand to benefit immensely from multimodal AI. Multimodal AI combines visual, textual, and audio data to enable immersive experiences for gaming, training simulations, and remote collaboration.

Example: Breakthroughs in Personalized Medicine

A practical illustration of these trends is the use of AI in personalized medicine. Multimodal AI can create tailored treatment plans by combining genomic data (text), diagnostic imaging (images), and patient histories (structured data). Quantum AI can further expedite drug discovery processes by optimizing molecular simulations, significantly reducing the time to market for critical therapies.

11.4.2 AI FOR GOOD

AI's potential extends beyond commercial applications to address humanity's most pressing challenges. From mitigating climate change to revolutionizing healthcare and education, AI can be a force for societal good.

LEVERAGING AI FOR SOCIETAL IMPACT

1. **Climate Change**: AI offers tools for monitoring and combating climate change. Predictive models can analyze satellite imagery to detect deforestation, monitor greenhouse gas emissions, and optimize renewable energy grids. For example, AI-driven weather prediction models can improve the efficiency of solar and wind energy utilization.

2. **Healthcare**: AI can bridge gaps in access and quality of care. Remote diagnostic tools powered by machine learning enable underserved communities to receive accurate medical assessments. Moreover, AI algorithms can identify patterns in patient data to predict disease outbreaks or recommend preventive measures.

3. **Education**: Personalized learning platforms use AI to adapt educational content to individual student needs. AI can suggest customized lesson plans by analyzing learning behaviors, helping students grasp concepts more effectively. This democratizes access to quality education, particularly in regions with teacher shortages.

CASE STUDY: PREDICTING AND MITIGATING NATURAL DISASTERS

AI's ability to predict and mitigate natural disasters exemplifies its societal impact. Machine learning models analyze historical data and real-time signals from sensors to forecast disasters such as hurricanes, earthquakes, and floods. AI-powered early warning systems enable timely evacuations, saving lives and reducing economic damage. For instance, IBM's Watson has been employed in projects to predict flooding patterns, helping governments allocate resources more efficiently.

11.4.3 PREPARING FOR AN AI-DRIVEN FUTURE

As AI transforms industries and societies, adaptability and continuous learning will be critical for entrepreneurs and teams to thrive.

IMPORTANCE OF ADAPTABILITY

In an AI-driven future, staying ahead requires embracing change and fostering a growth mindset. Organizations must:

1. **Invest in Training**: Regular upskilling initiatives ensure that employees remain relevant in an evolving job market. Machine learning, data analytics, and ethical AI should be integral to training programs.

2. **Promote Cross-Disciplinary Collaboration**: AI's multidisciplinary nature necessitates collaboration across engineering, business, and design. Encouraging diverse perspectives fosters innovative solutions to complex challenges.

CONTINUOUS LEARNING FOR ENTREPRENEURS AND TEAMS

Entrepreneurs must prioritize continuous learning to navigate the AI landscape effectively. This involves:

1. **Monitoring Trends**: Staying informed about AI advancements helps identify opportunities for innovation. Subscribing to industry reports and participating in conferences can provide valuable insights.

2. **Building Resilient Strategies**: Flexibility is key to adapting business models to emerging AI capabilities. Scenario planning and iterative development ensure organizations remain agile amid rapid technological shifts.

In summary, the future of AI is marked by transformative trends and unparalleled opportunities for societal advancement. By leveraging emerging technologies, fostering a commitment to societal good, and cultivating adaptability, stakeholders can harness AI to shape a better tomorrow.

CHAPTER 12: CONCLUSION AND CALL TO ACTION

INTRODUCTION

The journey from an abstract idea to a fully operational AI platform involves creativity, resilience, and transformation. This book, *AI - Idea to Platform: Don't Just Dream It, Build It*, is a practical guide for navigating this journey, bridging the gap between aspirations and impactful solutions. Through its pages, we have explored how to cultivate an innovative mindset, tackle foundational challenges, and build AI solutions that are ethical, scalable, and sustainable.

REFLECTING ON THE JOURNEY

Key Themes of the Book

This book is rooted in two overarching themes:

1. **Transitioning from Idea to Platform:**
Bringing an AI concept to life requires more than technological know-how. It demands clarity in defining the problem, a structured approach to solution design, and a commitment to iterative development. Each chapter delves into strategies for transforming raw ideas into platforms that effectively solve real-world problems.

2. **Building Sustainable, Ethical, and Scalable AI Solutions:**
Every successful AI initiative is founded on a commitment to ethics, scalability, and long-term sustainability. This book emphasizes designing user-centric solutions that respect privacy, uphold fairness, and adapt to changing demands without compromising quality.

A Standout Case Study: The Journey of AI in Education
A recurring example throughout the book is the case study of an AI-powered education platform that reshaped how students access knowledge. By leveraging adaptive learning algorithms, the platform catered to diverse learning styles, enabling students from underserved communities to achieve higher academic outcomes. This case encapsulates ethical design principles, user-centricity, and scalability, demonstrating how the methodologies outlined in this book translate into real-world success.

THE IMPORTANCE OF TAKING ACTION

The purpose of this book extends beyond theory and into actionable outcomes. The lessons shared are not just to inspire but to ignite action. The AI landscape is evolving rapidly, and those who hesitate risk being left behind. Here are three actionable steps to kickstart your journey today:

1. **Start Building:** Identify a pressing problem in your community, industry, or personal sphere. Begin with a simple prototype, validate your assumptions, and iterate continuously.

2. **Prototyping with Purpose:** Use the frameworks and templates in the book to build your Minimum Viable Product (MVP). Remember, the goal is not perfection but progress.

3. **Collaborate:** Join forces with others who share your vision. Participate in hackathons, contribute to open-source projects, or seek mentorship from industry leaders.

Taking the first step can be daunting but is also the most rewarding. Each small action builds momentum, bringing you closer to realizing your AI aspirations. This book aims to arm you with the tools, confidence, and clarity to take that step and transform your ideas into platforms that create a meaningful impact.

THE IMPORTANCE OF TAKING ACTION

The purpose of this book extends beyond theory and into actionable outcomes. The lessons shared are not just to inspire but to ignite action. The AI landscape is evolving rapidly, and those who hesitate risk being left behind. Here are three actionable steps to kickstart your journey today:

1. **Start Building:** Identify a pressing problem in your community, industry, or personal sphere. Begin with a simple prototype, validate your assumptions, and iterate continuously.

2. **Prototyping with Purpose:** Use the frameworks and templates in the book to build your Minimum Viable Product (MVP). Remember, the goal is not perfection but progress.

3. **Collaborate:** Join forces with others who share your vision. Participate in hackathons, contribute to open-source projects, or seek mentorship from industry leaders.

Taking the first step can be daunting but is also the most rewarding. Each small action builds momentum, bringing you closer to realizing your AI aspirations. This book aims to arm you with the tools, confidence, and clarity to take that step and transform your ideas into platforms that create a meaningful impact.

12.1: KEY TAKEAWAYS AND INSIGHTS

In this section, we distill the most critical insights and actionable points from the book, emphasizing lessons that resonate across chapters and equip readers with practical knowledge to implement in the real world of AI. These takeaways serve as a concise roadmap for navigating the challenges and opportunities in AI development, platform building, and ethical innovation.

12.1.1 CORE LESSONS FROM EACH CHAPTER

Defining AI Problems and Solutions

1. **Clarity in Problem Definition**: Begin every AI initiative with a well-defined problem statement. Use frameworks like SMART goals to ensure the problem is specific, measurable, achievable, relevant, and time-bound.

2. **A User-Centric Perspective**: Conduct in-depth user research and iterative testing to align AI solutions with end-user needs. Empathy maps and user personas can guide the design process.

3. **Data as a Foundation**: Prioritize high-quality, relevant data over sheer volume. Establish robust data governance practices to maintain accuracy, security, and ethical standards.

4. **Cross-functional collaboration**: Engage stakeholders from diverse disciplines—data scientists, domain experts, and business leaders—to ensure comprehensive solutions.

5. **Early Validation**: Develop proofs of concept (POCs) or minimum viable products (MVPs) to test assumptions and refine ideas before large-scale implementation.

Building and Scaling Platforms

1. **Architecture Matters**: Design platforms with scalability, flexibility, and resilience. Leverage modular architectures and cloud-native technologies.

2. **Agile Methodologies**: Adopt iterative development practices to ensure continuous improvement and rapid response to changing requirements.

3. **Integration Capabilities**: Prioritize APIs and interoperability to enable seamless integration with existing systems and future technologies.

4. **Monitoring and Feedback Loops**: Implement robust monitoring systems to track performance metrics and user feedback, enabling continuous refinement.

5. **Talent and Culture**: Foster a culture of innovation and upskilling within teams to maintain a competitive edge.

Fostering Innovation and Addressing Ethical Considerations

1. **Cultivate a Culture of Curiosity**: Encourage experimentation and reward innovative ideas. Set up innovation labs or 'hackathons' to inspire creative problem-solving.

2. **Ethical by Design**: Embed ethical considerations into every stage of AI development. Use ethical AI checklists and guidelines to avoid unintended biases and harm.

3. **Transparency and Accountability**: Communicate AI systems' purpose, limitations, and implications to all stakeholders and implement mechanisms for accountability.

4. **Inclusive Innovation**: Ensure diverse perspectives are included in the design and development processes, fostering solutions that cater to a broader audience.

5. **Regulatory Readiness**: Stay informed about evolving AI regulations and standards to ensure compliance and build trust.

Summary Table of Key Lessons by Chapter

Chapter	Key Lessons
Defining AI Problems	Problem clarity, user-centric design, data quality, collaboration, validation
Building and Scaling	Scalable architecture, agile practices, integration, feedback loops, culture
Fostering Innovation	Culture of curiosity, ethics, transparency, inclusivity, regulatory readiness

12.1.2 COMMON THREADS ACROSS THE BOOK

User-Centric Design

Across all chapters, user-centric design emerged as a cornerstone of successful AI initiatives. Understanding users' needs, behaviors, and pain points ensures that solutions are relevant and practical. This theme underscores the importance of empathy, iterative testing, and continuous end-user engagement to drive meaningful innovation.

Scalability

Scalability is another recurring theme, emphasizing the need for systems and platforms that can grow and adapt to changing demands. Whether it's scaling infrastructure, processes, or teams, the ability to anticipate and manage growth effectively determines long-term success.

Ethics as a Driver of Success

Ethical considerations are not merely a compliance requirement but a strategic advantage. Transparent, accountable, and fair AI systems build trust and foster long-term relationships with users and stakeholders. Addressing ethical concerns proactively ensures sustainability and mitigates risks.

In conclusion, these common threads highlight the interconnected nature of user-centricity, scalability, and ethics in building impactful AI solutions. By keeping these principles at the forefront, readers can confidently navigate the complexities of AI development.

12.2: INSPIRING CASE STUDIES

12.2.1 SUCCESS STORIES

In the evolving landscape of artificial intelligence, one platform stands as a testament to the transformative power of technology: EdWise AI. This AI-driven education platform has redefined how students around the globe access and engage with learning resources. Founded in 2018, EdWise AI seamlessly integrates cutting-edge machine learning algorithms with a personalized approach to education, delivering tailored learning experiences to students from diverse backgrounds.

The core principle behind EdWise AI aligns perfectly with the themes of this book: innovation, accessibility, and user-centric design. The platform employs adaptive learning algorithms to identify individual student strengths and weaknesses. EdWise AI creates custom learning paths that optimize comprehension and retention by analyzing student performance patterns. For instance, students struggling with algebra concepts receive targeted practice problems, video tutorials, and real-time feedback designed to bridge specific knowledge gaps.

Beyond personalized learning, EdWise AI also addresses the global education divide. The platform leverages natural language processing to translate content into over 50 languages, making quality education accessible to students in remote or underserved regions. Additionally, its low-bandwidth mode ensures that even students with limited internet connectivity can benefit from the platform's resources.

The impact of EdWise AI has been profound. A study conducted in 2022 revealed that students using the platform demonstrated a 30% improvement in test scores compared to traditional methods. Furthermore, teachers reported that the AI tools saved an average of 10 hours per week, which they could reinvest in personalized interactions with their students.

The journey of EdWise AI exemplifies the principles outlined in this book: a clear vision, a focus on user needs, and the ability to leverage AI to solve real-world problems. By putting students first and addressing global disparities, EdWise AI has proven that technology can be a force for good, inspiring innovation across the educational sector.

12.2.2 OVERCOMING CHALLENGES

The story of MedAI Solutions is one of resilience and ingenuity. Founded in 2017, this healthcare startup set out to revolutionize patient care through AI-powered diagnostics. However, the path to success was fraught with significant challenges, particularly data privacy and regulatory compliance.

MedAI's flagship product, a diagnostic AI tool for early detection of cardiovascular diseases, required access to vast amounts of patient data to train its machine learning models. This presented a dual challenge: securing patient data while adhering to stringent regulations like the Health Insurance Portability and Accountability Act (HIPAA) in the United States and the General Data Protection Regulation (GDPR) in Europe.

The company's initial attempts to collaborate with hospitals were resisted due to data breaches and patient privacy concerns. MedAI implemented advanced encryption techniques to address these concerns and developed a federated learning model. This innovative approach allowed the AI to train on decentralized data, ensuring that sensitive patient information never left the hospital's secure servers.

Regulatory compliance posed another significant hurdle. The media team worked closely with legal experts and healthcare authorities to navigate the complex landscape of medical device regulations. They adopted a proactive strategy by conducting thorough risk assessments and documenting every aspect of their technology's development and implementation. By engaging regulators early in the process, MedAI not only ensured compliance but also gained valuable insights that enhanced the reliability and safety of their product.

Despite these challenges, MedAI achieved a breakthrough in 2021 when its diagnostic tool received FDA approval. This milestone validated their efforts and opened the doors to partnerships with primary healthcare providers. By 2023, MedAI's technology was deployed in over 200 hospitals worldwide, helping physicians diagnose cardiovascular diseases with 95% accuracy and reducing diagnostic time by 40%.

MedAI's journey underscores the importance of perseverance, adaptability, and a commitment to ethical practices. Their success demonstrates that even in highly regulated industries, startups can overcome significant challenges and create impactful solutions that benefit society. MedAI has set a powerful example for other AI-driven ventures by embracing innovation and prioritizing trust.

12.3: CALL TO ACTION

Artificial intelligence (AI) transforms how we live, work, and interact with the world. As you turn the final pages of this book, consider this your call to action—a chance to take the insights, tools, and strategies you've gained and translate them into meaningful progress. This chapter outlines three distinct yet interconnected paths to guide your journey: starting your AI journey, building an ethical and sustainable future, and exploring opportunities to engage with the AI community.

12.3.1STARTING YOUR AI JOURNEY

The first step in any transformative endeavor is action. The AI revolution offers countless opportunities to innovate, solve real-world problems, and contribute to a rapidly growing field. But how do you begin?

Identify a Problem

AI's power lies in its ability to solve complex challenges efficiently and effectively. Start by identifying a problem that genuinely resonates with you. This could be a bottleneck in a process at work, an unmet need in your community, or a global issue you're passionate about. Whatever the problem, ensure it's specific, measurable, and relevant.

Build a Minimum Viable Product (MVP)

Once you pinpoint your problem, translate your vision into action by developing a Minimum Viable Product (MVP). Focus on creating a functional prototype that demonstrates the potential of your AI solution. This might involve designing a predictive model, developing a chatbot, or implementing a recommendation engine. Please keep it simple and iterate based on feedback. The goal is to create a proof of concept that you can refine over time.

Engage Your Target Audience

The success of any AI initiative hinges on its alignment with user needs. Engage your target audience early and often. Conduct surveys, host focus groups, or participate in user interviews to understand their pain points and priorities. This feedback will not only validate your MVP but also guide its development. Engagement fosters trust, ensures relevance, and lays the foundation for long-term adoption.

Starting your AI journey may seem daunting, but it can also be gratifying. You can take the first steps toward making a meaningful impact by identifying a problem, building an MVP, and engaging your audience.

12.3.2 BUILDING AN ETHICAL AND SUSTAINABLE FUTURE

The rapid growth of AI comes with immense responsibility. As creators, users, and advocates, we must ensure that AI serves immediate needs and contributes to a sustainable and equitable future. This section invites you to think beyond the present and focus on the long-term impact of your work.

Address Pressing Challenges

AI can potentially drive transformative change in critical areas such as climate change, global health, and accessibility. Imagine leveraging AI to optimize energy usage in smart grids, accelerate drug discovery, or design tools that empower individuals with disabilities. These are not distant possibilities; they are opportunities waiting to be seized. By aligning your AI initiatives with these global challenges, you contribute to a more just and sustainable world.

Prioritize Ethical Development

Ethics should be at the core of every AI project. This means ensuring transparency, fairness, and accountability in your algorithms. Biases in data and models can perpetuate inequality, while a lack of transparency can erode trust. Commit to ethical principles like data privacy, inclusivity, and environmental sustainability. Develop clear guidelines and frameworks to embed these values in your work.

Engage in Long-Term Thinking

Short-term results are essential, but they shouldn't come at the expense of long-term consequences. Consider the societal implications of your AI solutions. Will they create dependencies, displace jobs, or exacerbate inequalities? Proactively address these risks and explore ways to mitigate them. Building a sustainable future requires balancing innovation with responsibility, starting with planning.

Your role as an AI practitioner extends beyond technical implementation; it's about envisioning and contributing to a future where AI is a force for good. By focusing on ethical and sustainable practices, you can help shape a better tomorrow.

12.3.3 OPPORTUNITIES TO ENGAGE

AI thrives on collaboration, creativity, and shared knowledge. Whether you're a novice or a seasoned professional, there are countless ways to engage with the AI community. This section highlights practical opportunities to contribute, learn, and grow.

Join Forums and Communities
Online forums and communities like Reddit's r/MachineLearning, AI-focused LinkedIn groups, and specialized Slack channels are excellent starting points. These platforms offer a wealth of resources, from tutorials and papers to discussions on cutting-edge research. More importantly, they connect you with like-minded individuals who share your passion for AI. Participating in these communities allows you to exchange ideas, seek guidance, and build lasting relationships.

Participate in Hackathons
Hackathons are dynamic, hands-on events that challenge participants to solve real-world problems using AI. They are an opportunity to showcase your skills, collaborate with diverse teams, gain new perspectives, and learn from industry experts. Platforms like Kaggle and Devpost regularly host AI competitions and hackathons tailored to various skill levels.

Contribute to Open-Source Projects
The open-source community is a cornerstone of AI innovation. Contributing to projects on platforms like GitHub allows you to refine your technical skills, collaborate with experts, and make a tangible impact. Whether improving documentation, optimizing algorithms, or developing new features, your contributions help advance the field while building your reputation as an AI practitioner.

Mentor and Learn
Engagement isn't limited to technical contributions. Mentoring aspiring AI enthusiasts or volunteering for educational initiatives can be incredibly rewarding. Simultaneously, I continue to learn through online courses, webinars, and conferences. The AI landscape evolves rapidly, and staying updated ensures your knowledge remains relevant.

Immersing yourself in the AI community expands your horizons and amplifies your ability to drive change. Collaboration is the heart of innovation, and your active participation can inspire others to join the journey.

12.4: ADDITIONAL RESOURCES AND NEXT STEPS

The journey of understanding and implementing AI doesn't end with a single book or project. To ensure ongoing success, leveraging the right tools, frameworks, and learning resources is crucial. This section provides a curated list of recommended resources and the following steps to deepen your knowledge and practical expertise in AI.

12.4.1 RECOMMENDED TOOLS AND FRAMEWORKS

AI is supported by a wealth of platforms, frameworks, and guidelines that make it easier to develop, deploy, and govern AI systems responsibly. Below is a curated list of essential tools and resources:

AI Platforms and Frameworks:

- **TensorFlow**: An open-source framework widely used for machine learning and deep learning tasks. TensorFlow offers flexibility and scalability for building models ranging from small experiments to enterprise-grade applications.
- **PyTorch** is another popular open-source library for deep learning. It is favored for its dynamic computation graph and ease of use in research and production environments.
- **Hugging Face**: A platform that provides pre-trained models and libraries for natural language processing (NLP). It's a go-to resource for text generation, sentiment analysis, and translation tasks.
- **Scikit-learn**: A machine learning library in Python that is ideal for tasks like classification, regression, and clustering. It's user-friendly and well-suited for beginners and advanced users alike.

Datasets:

- **ImageNet**: A large-scale dataset used for visual recognition research. ImageNet is foundational for training and benchmarking computer vision models.
- **Kaggle Datasets**: Kaggle provides a platform for sharing and discovering datasets and tools for data analysis and collaboration.
- **Google Dataset Search**: A comprehensive tool for finding datasets across domains hosted by various publishers.
- **OpenAI's Gym**: A toolkit for developing and testing reinforcement learning algorithms using standardized environments.

Ethical Guidelines:

- **IBM AI Fairness 360**: A toolkit that includes metrics and algorithms to detect and mitigate bias in machine learning models.

- **The Partnership on AI's Principles**: A set of guidelines developed by leading organizations to ensure AI benefits society and is produced responsibly.
- **EU's Ethics Guidelines for Trustworthy AI**: A document outlining principles for ethical AI development, including transparency, accountability, and respect for human rights.
- **The Montreal Declaration**: A framework emphasizing ethical considerations in developing and deploying AI systems.

These tools and resources provide a solid foundation for anyone who wants to explore AI development further, ensure ethical compliance, and build robust applications.

12.4.2 CONTINUING THE LEARNING JOURNEY

AI is rapidly evolving, and continuous learning is key to staying current. Below are recommendations for books, courses, and communities to support ongoing growth in AI expertise:

Books:

- **"Deep Learning" by Ian Goodfellow, Yoshua Bengio, and Aaron Courville**: A comprehensive introduction to deep learning, covering theory, algorithms, and applications.
- **"Artificial Intelligence: A Modern Approach" by Stuart Russell and Peter Norvig**: A classic textbook that overviews AI, including search algorithms, machine learning, and robotics.
- **"Prediction Machines: The Simple Economics of Artificial Intelligence" by Ajay Agrawal, Joshua Gans, and Avi Goldfarb**: A book exploring the economic implications of AI and its impact on decision-making.
- **"The Ethical Algorithm" by Michael Kearns and Aaron Roth**: This book focuses on the ethics of algorithm design and provides insights into balancing fairness, privacy, and transparency.

nline Courses:

- **Coursera's AI for Everyone (Andrew Ng)**: A non-technical introduction to AI, suitable for beginners and business professionals.
- **Udemy's Python for Data Science and Machine Learning Bootcamp**: A practical course focusing on Python programming and its applications in data science and AI.
- **DeepLearning.AI's Specialization**: A series of courses on Coursera that delve into neural networks, sequence models, and more.
- **MIT's Introduction to Deep Learning**: A free course offering insights into the latest techniques and applications.

Influential AI Research Papers and Blogs:

- **"Attention Is All You Need" by Vaswani et al.**: The foundational paper introducing the Transformer model powers advancements in NLP and generative AI.
- **"Deep Residual Learning for Image Recognition" by He et al.**: This paper introduces ResNet, a groundbreaking architecture for deep learning in computer vision.
- **Blogs by OpenAI**: Insightful articles and research summaries on state-of-the-art AI developments.
- **The Gradient**: A blog featuring thought-provoking pieces on AI research, trends, and ethics.

Communities and Forums:

- **Kaggle**: In addition to datasets and competitions, Kaggle hosts a vibrant community where users can discuss machine learning topics and share insights.
- **Reddit (r/MachineLearning)**: A popular forum for AI enthusiasts to stay updated on research and trends.
- **AI Ethics Lab**: A platform for discussing and addressing ethical challenges in AI.
- **Meetup Groups**: Local AI and machine learning meetups provide opportunities to connect with like-minded individuals and professionals.

By leveraging these resources, you can continue to expand your understanding of AI, stay informed about the latest advancements, and build meaningful connections within the AI community. Whether you're a beginner or an experienced practitioner, ongoing education and engagement are essential for success in this dynamic field.

- Alan Turing's Turing Test: Turing, A. M. (1950). Computing Machinery and Intelligence. Mind, 59(236), 433–460. https://doi.org/10.1093/mind/LIX.236.433

- Newell, A., & Simon, H. A. (1956). The Logic Theory Machine—A Complex Information Processing System. IRE Transactions on Information Theory, 2(3), 61–79. https://doi.org/10.1109/TIT.1956.1056810

- IBM Deep Blue: Campbell, M., Hoane, A. J., & Hsu, F.-h. (2002). Deep Blue. Artificial Intelligence, 134(1–2), 57–83. https://doi.org/10.1016/S0004-3702(01)00129-1

- OpenAI GPT-3: Brown, T. B., Mann, B., Ryder, N., Subbiah, M., Kaplan, J., Dhariwal, P., ... & Amodei, D. (2020). Language Models are Few-Shot Learners. Advances in Neural Information Processing Systems, 33, 1877–1901. https://doi.org/10.48550/arXiv.2005.14165

- Google Cloud AI Platform: Google. (n.d.). Google Cloud AI Platform. Retrieved from https://cloud.google.com/ai-platform

- Amazon SageMaker: Amazon Web Services. (n.d.). Amazon SageMaker. Retrieved from https://aws.amazon.com/sagemaker

- Microsoft Azure Machine Learning: Microsoft. (n.d.). Azure Machine Learning. Retrieved from https://azure.microsoft.com/en-us/products/machine-learning/

- TensorFlow: Abadi, M., Barham, P., Chen, J., Chen, Z., Davis, A., Dean, J., ... & Zheng, X. (2016). TensorFlow: A System for Large-Scale Machine Learning. OSDI, 16, 265–283. Retrieved from https://www.tensorflow.org/

- PyTorch: Paszke, A., Gross, S., Massa, F., Lerer, A., Bradbury, J., Chanan, G., ... & Chintala, S. (2019). PyTorch: An Imperative Style, High-Performance Deep Learning Library. Advances in Neural Information Processing Systems, 32, 8024–8035. https://pytorch.org/

- Keras: Chollet, F. (2015). Keras. Retrieved from https://keras.io/

- Stability AI's Stable Diffusion: Stability AI. (n.d.). Stable Diffusion. Retrieved from https://stability.ai/

- Netflix Personalization Algorithms: Gomez-Uribe, C. A., & Hunt, N. (2016). The Netflix Recommender System: Algorithms, Business Value, and Innovation. ACM Transactions on Management Information Systems (TMIS), 6(4), 13. https://doi.org/10.1145/2843948

- Federated Learning: McMahan, H. B., Moore, E., Ramage, D., Hampson, S., & Arcas, B. A. Y. (2017). Communication-Efficient Learning of Deep Networks from Decentralized Data. Proceedings of the 20th International Conference on Artificial Intelligence and Statistics (AISTATS), 54, 1273–1282. Retrieved from https://arxiv.org/abs/1602.05629

- Tesla's Electric Vehicles: Tesla. (n.d.). Tesla Model S. Retrieved from https://www.tesla.com/models

- Slack's Market Validation: Butterfield, S. (2014). Slack: Be Less Busy. Retrieved from https://slack.com/

- Airbnb Validation Strategy: Chesky, B. (2015). The Airbnb Story. Retrieved from https://www.airbnb.com/

- Kaggle. (n.d.). DATASETS. Retrieved from https://www.kaggle.com/datasets

- UCI Machine Learning Repository. (n.d.). MACHINE LEARNING DATASETS. Retrieved from https://archive.ics.uci.edu/ml/index.php

- NOAA National Centers for Environmental Information (NCEI). (n.d.). CLIMATE DATA ONLINE. Retrieved from https://www.ncei.noaa.gov/

- GenBank. (n.d.). GENOMIC SEQUENCE DATABASE. Retrieved from https://www.ncbi.nlm.nih.gov/genbank/

- IBM. (n.d.). AI FAIRNESS 360: AN EXTENSIBLE TOOLKIT FOR DETECTING, UNDERSTANDING, AND MITIGATING UNWANTED BIAS IN MACHINE LEARNING MODELS. Retrieved from https://www.ibm.com/opensource/ai-fairness-360

- Microsoft. (n.d.). RESPONSIBLE AI PRINCIPLES. Retrieved from https://www.microsoft.com/en-us/ai/responsible-ai

- Google. (n.d.). EXPLAINABLE AI TOOLS. Retrieved from https://cloud.google.com/explainable-ai

- Data.gov. (n.d.). OPEN GOVERNMENT DATA. Retrieved from https://www.data.gov/
- Facebook. (2022). LITIGATION REGARDING DATA SCRAPING. Retrieved from https://about.fb.com/news/
- GDPR.eu. (n.d.). GENERAL DATA PROTECTION REGULATION (GDPR). Retrieved from https://gdpr.eu/
- California Consumer Privacy Act (CCPA). (n.d.). PRIVACY RIGHTS FOR CALIFORNIA RESIDENTS. Retrieved from https://oag.ca.gov/privacy/ccpa
- U.S. Department of Health and Human Services. (n.d.). HEALTH INSURANCE PORTABILITY AND ACCOUNTABILITY ACT (HIPAA). Retrieved from https://www.hhs.gov/hipaa/
- TensorFlow. (n.d.). TF.DATA: BUILD EFFICIENT INPUT PIPELINES. Retrieved from https://www.tensorflow.org/guide/data
- Apache Airflow. (n.d.). WORKFLOWS AS CODE. Retrieved from https://airflow.apache.org/
- Hugging Face. (n.d.). EVALUATE AND MODEL CARDS. Retrieved from https://huggingface.co/
- Google. (n.d.). TENSORFLOW. Retrieved from https://www.tensorflow.org
- Facebook. (n.d.). PYTORCH. Retrieved from https://pytorch.org
- OpenAI. (n.d.). GPT MODELS. Retrieved from https://openai.com
- Hugging Face. (n.d.). TRANSFORMERS LIBRARY. Retrieved from https://huggingface.co/transformers
- Nvidia. (n.d.). CLARA PLATFORM. Retrieved from https://developer.nvidia.com/clara
- Autodesk. (n.d.). FUSION 360. Retrieved from https://www.autodesk.com/products/fusion-360/overview
- Alphabet (Sidewalk Labs). (n.d.). URBAN PLANNING WITH GENERATIVE AI. Retrieved from https://www.sidewalklabs.com
- Semantic Scholar. (n.d.). RESEARCH SUMMARIZATION TOOLS. Retrieved from https://www.semanticscholar.org
- PubMed. (n.d.). BIOMEDICAL RESEARCH TOOLS. Retrieved from https://pubmed.ncbi.nlm.nih.gov
- Nvidia. (n.d.). TRITON INFERENCE SERVER. Retrieved from https://developer.nvidia.com/nvidia-triton-inference-server
- Google Cloud. (n.d.). VERTEX AI. Retrieved from https://cloud.google.com/vertex-ai
- Amazon Web Services (AWS). (n.d.). SAGEMAKER. Retrieved from https://aws.amazon.com/sagemaker/
- Microsoft Azure. (n.d.). AZURE MACHINE LEARNING. Retrieved from https://azure.microsoft.com/en-us/products/machine-learning/
- Tool Websites:
- TensorFlow: https://www.tensorflow.org/
- PyTorch: https://pytorch.org/
- Scikit-learn: https://scikit-learn.org/
- Keras: https://keras.io/
- ONNX: https://onnx.ai/
- Apache MXNet: https://mxnet.apache.org/
- OpenCV: https://opencv.org/

- AWS: https://aws.amazon.com/
- Google Cloud: https://cloud.google.com/
- Azure: https://azure.microsoft.com/
- AWS Lambda: https://aws.amazon.com/lambda/
- Google Cloud Functions: https://cloud.google.com/functions
- Azure Functions: https://azure.microsoft.com/en-us/services/functions/
- TensorFlow Lite: https://www.tensorflow.org/lite
- AWS IoT Greengrass: https://aws.amazon.com/greengrass/
- NVIDIA Jetson: https://www.nvidia.com/en-us/autonomous-machines/embedded-systems/jetson-platform/
- AWS Cost Explorer: https://aws.amazon.com/aws-cost-management/aws-cost-explorer/
- Google Cloud Billing: https://cloud.google.com/billing/
- Kubernetes Cost Analyzer: https://cloud.google.com/blog/products/containers-kubernetes/kubernetes-cost-analyzer-now-open-source
- Prometheus: https://prometheus.io/
- Spot.io: https://spot.io/
- CloudHealth: https://www.cloudhealth.vmware.com/
- Hugging Face Transformers: https://huggingface.co/transformers/
- Kubernetes: https://kubernetes.io/
- Jira: https://www.atlassian.com/software/jira
- Trello: https://trello.com/
- Asana: https://asana.com/
- Tableau: https://www.tableau.com/
- Power BI: https://powerbi.microsoft.com/en-us/
- Figma: https://www.figma.com/
- Slack: https://slack.com/
- Microsoft Teams: https://www.microsoft.com/en-us/microsoft-teams/
- Miro: https://miro.com/
- Clockify: https://clockify.me/
- RescueTime: https://www.rescuetime.com/
- TensorBoard: https://www.tensorflow.org/tensorboard
- TFX: https://www.tensorflow.org/tfx

- Pandas: https://pandas.pydata.org/

- DeepMind and University College London. (n.d.). COLLABORATIVE RESEARCH IN REINFORCEMENT LEARNING. Retrieved from https://www.ucl.ac.uk

- MIT's CSAIL. (n.d.). MIT STARTUP EXCHANGE AND COLLABORATIVE AI INITIATIVES. Retrieved from https://www.csail.mit.edu

- Stanford University. (n.d.). HUMAN-CENTERED ARTIFICIAL INTELLIGENCE INITIATIVES AND PARTNERSHIPS. Retrieved from https://hai.stanford.edu

- Indian Government & World Resources Institute. (n.d.). URBAN MOBILITY IMPROVEMENT THROUGH AI TOOLS. Retrieved from https://www.wri.org

- DeepMind & UK NHS. (n.d.). PREDICTIVE AI TOOLS FOR KIDNEY INJURY PREVENTION. Retrieved from https://www.deepmind.com

- Global Forest Watch & Norwegian Government. (n.d.). AI-DRIVEN DEFORESTATION MONITORING SYSTEMS. Retrieved from https://www.globalforestwatch.org

- PATH & African Governments. (n.d.). AI-DRIVEN INFECTIOUS DISEASE DIAGNOSIS COLLABORATIONS. Retrieved from https://www.path.org

- UNESCO Educational Platforms. (n.d.). AI FOR PERSONALIZED LEARNING IN MARGINALIZED COMMUNITIES. Retrieved from https://www.unesco.org

- Apple & Nike. (2006). NIKE IPOD SPORTS KIT AND PARTNERSHIP SUCCESS. Retrieved from https://www.apple.com

- DaimlerChrysler Merger. (1998). CASE STUDY ON FAILED MERGERS DUE TO CULTURAL AND STRATEGIC MISALIGNMENTS. Retrieved from https://www.businesscasestudies.com

- VisionAI & RetailMax. (n.d.). AI STARTUP SCALING STRATEGIES FOR INTERNATIONAL RETAIL. Hypothetical case study.

- Airbnb. (n.d.). TO CREATE A WORLD WHERE ANYONE CAN BELONG ANYWHERE. Retrieved from https://www.airbnb.com

- Dollar Shave Club. (n.d.). A GREAT SHAVE FOR A FEW BUCKS A MONTH. Retrieved from https://www.dollarshaveclub.com

- Microsoft. (n.d.). TO EMPOWER EVERY PERSON AND EVERY ORGANIZATION ON THE PLANET TO ACHIEVE MORE. Retrieved from https://www.microsoft.com

- Nike. (n.d.). TO BRING INSPIRATION AND INNOVATION TO EVERY ATHLETE IN THE WORLD. Retrieved from https://www.nike.com

- OpenAI. (n.d.). ENSURING THAT ARTIFICIAL GENERAL INTELLIGENCE (AGI) BENEFITS ALL OF HUMANITY. Retrieved from https://www.openai.com

- Slack. (n.d.). BE MORE PRODUCTIVE AT WORK WITH LESS EFFORT. Retrieved from https://www.slack.com

- Tesla. (n.d.). TO ACCELERATE THE WORLD'S TRANSITION TO SUSTAINABLE ENERGY. Retrieved from https://www.tesla.com

- Zoom. (n.d.). THE #1 VIDEO CONFERENCING SOLUTION THAT JUST WORKS. Retrieved from https://www.zoom.us

- Kaggle

Kaggle. (n.d.). KAGGLE: YOUR MACHINE LEARNING AND DATA SCIENCE COMMUNITY. Retrieved from https://www.kaggle.com

- GitHub

GitHub. (n.d.). GITHUB: WHERE THE WORLD BUILDS SOFTWARE. Retrieved from https://github.com

- ChatGPT by OpenAI

OpenAI. (n.d.). CHATGPT. Retrieved from https://openai.com/chatgpt

- Jasper

Jasper. (n.d.). JASPER AI: AI CONTENT GENERATOR. Retrieved from https://www.jasper.ai

- Mailchimp

Mailchimp. (n.d.). EMAIL MARKETING AND AUTOMATION. Retrieved from https://mailchimp.com

- HubSpot

HubSpot. (n.d.). HUBSPOT: MARKETING, SALES, AND SERVICE SOFTWARE. Retrieved from https://www.hubspot.com

- Buffer

Buffer. (n.d.). SOCIAL MEDIA MANAGEMENT. Retrieved from https://buffer.com

- Hootsuite

Hootsuite. (n.d.). SOCIAL MEDIA TOOLS AND SOLUTIONS. Retrieved from https://hootsuite.com

- Synthesia

Synthesia. (n.d.). AI VIDEO GENERATION PLATFORM. Retrieved from https://www.synthesia.io

- Pictory

Pictory. (n.d.). AI-POWERED VIDEO EDITING. Retrieved from https://pictory.ai

- Stack Overflow

Stack Overflow. (n.d.). STACK OVERFLOW: WHERE DEVELOPERS LEARN, SHARE, AND BUILD CAREERS. Retrieved from https://stackoverflow.com

- NASA. (n.d.). INTERNATIONAL SPACE APPS CHALLENGE. Retrieved from https://www.spaceappschallenge.org
- Spotify. (n.d.). MUSIC FOR EVERYONE. Retrieved from https://www.spotify.com
- DebugAI. (n.d.). AUTOMATED DEBUGGING FOR AI WORKFLOWS. Retrieved from https://debugai.com
- Salesforce. (n.d.). APPEXCHANGE: THE BUSINESS APP MARKETPLACE. Retrieved from https://appexchange.salesforce.com
- Ailman, R., Dykstra, P., & Nelson, J. (2024). UNDERSTANDING AI PLATFORMS AND ECOSYSTEMS. National Life Group.
- Google. (2024). TensorFlow. Retrieved from https://www.tensorflow.org
- Grammarly. (2024). ABOUT US. Retrieved from https://www.grammarly.com
- Microsoft Azure. (2024). Hackathons. Retrieved from https://azure.microsoft.com/en-us
- Salesforce. (2024). AppExchange. Retrieved from https://appexchange.salesforce.com
- Stripe. (2024). PAYMENT APIS. Retrieved from https://stripe.com
- Unity. (2024). SDKS AND DEVELOPER TOOLS. Retrieved from https://unity.com
- IBM. (n.d.). AI Fairness 360. Retrieved from https://aif360.mybluemix.net
- Microsoft. (n.d.). Responsible AI Dashboard. Retrieved from https://responsibleai.azure.com
- European Union. (2018). General Data Protection Regulation (GDPR). Retrieved from https://eur-lex.europa.eu/eli/reg/2016/679/oj
- State of California. (n.d.). California Consumer Privacy Act (CCPA). Retrieved from https://oag.ca.gov/privacy/ccpa
- Shapley, L. S. (n.d.). SHapley Additive exPlanations (SHAP). Retrieved from https://shap.readthedocs.io

- Ribeiro, M. T., Singh, S., & Guestrin, C. (2016). "Why Should I Trust You?" Explaining the Predictions of Any Classifier (LIME). Proceedings of the 22nd ACM SIGKDD International Conference on Knowledge Discovery and Data Mining. Retrieved from https://lime-ml.readthedocs.io

- OpenAI. (n.d.). AI alignment and safety research. Retrieved from https://openai.com/research

- Partnership on AI. (n.d.). Partnership on AI: Advancing AI for Humanity. Retrieved from https://www.partnershiponai.org

- Watson, I. (n.d.). Flooding prediction projects. IBM Watson for Natural Disasters. Retrieved from https://www.ibm.com/watson

- Goodfellow, I., Bengio, Y., & Courville, A. (2016). DEEP LEARNING. MIT Press. Retrieved from https://www.deeplearningbook.org

- Russell, S., & Norvig, P. (2020). ARTIFICIAL INTELLIGENCE: A MODERN APPROACH (4th ed.). Pearson. Retrieved from https://aima.cs.berkeley.edu

- Agrawal, A., Gans, J., & Goldfarb, A. (2018). PREDICTION MACHINES: THE SIMPLE ECONOMICS OF ARTIFICIAL INTELLIGENCE. Harvard Business Review Press. Retrieved from https://www.predictionmachines.ai

- Kearns, M., & Roth, A. (2019). THE ETHICAL ALGORITHM: THE SCIENCE OF SOCIALLY AWARE ALGORITHM DESIGN. Oxford University Press. Retrieved from https://global.oup.com/academic

- Vaswani, A., Shazeer, N., Parmar, N., Uszkoreit, J., Jones, L., Gomez, A. N., Kaiser, Ł., & Polosukhin, I. (2017). Attention Is All You Need. ADVANCES IN NEURAL INFORMATION PROCESSING SYSTEMS, 30, 5998-6008. Retrieved from https://arxiv.org/abs/1706.03762

- He, K., Zhang, X., Ren, S., & Sun, J. (2016). Deep Residual Learning for Image Recognition. PROCEEDINGS OF THE IEEE CONFERENCE ON COMPUTER VISION AND PATTERN RECOGNITION (CVPR), 770-778. Retrieved from https://arxiv.org/abs/1512.03385

- TensorFlow. (n.d.). Retrieved from https://www.tensorflow.org

- PyTorch. (n.d.). Retrieved from https://pytorch.org

- Hugging Face. (n.d.). Retrieved from https://huggingface.co

- Scikit-learn. (n.d.). Retrieved from https://scikit-learn.org

- ImageNet. (n.d.). Retrieved from https://www.image-net.org

- Kaggle. (n.d.). Retrieved from https://www.kaggle.com

- IBM AI Fairness 360. (n.d.). Retrieved from https://aif360.mybluemix.net

- Partnership on AI. (n.d.). TENETS OF PARTNERSHIP ON AI. Retrieved from https://www.partnershiponai.org

- European Commission. (2019). ETHICS GUIDELINES FOR TRUSTWORTHY AI. Retrieved from https://digital-strategy.ec.europa.eu/en/library/ethics-guidelines-trustworthy-ai

- Montreal Declaration. (2018). MONTREAL DECLARATION FOR A RESPONSIBLE DEVELOPMENT OF ARTIFICIAL INTELLIGENCE. Retrieved from https://www.montrealdeclaration-responsibleai.com

- Ng, A. (n.d.). AI for Everyone. Coursera. Retrieved from https://www.coursera.org/learn/ai-for-everyone

- Udemy. (n.d.). Python for Data Science and Machine Learning Bootcamp. Retrieved from https://www.udemy.com/course/python-for-data-science-and-machine-learning-bootcamp

- DeepLearning.AI. (n.d.). Retrieved from https://www.deeplearning.ai

- MIT. (n.d.). Introduction to Deep Learning. Retrieved from http://introtodeeplearning.com

www.ingramcontent.com/pod-product-compliance
Lightning Source LLC
LaVergne TN
LVHW060015210926
848481LV00013B/3713

* 9 7 9 8 3 4 8 5 3 1 9 9 7 *